Serials and Series

Serials and Series

A World Filmography, 1912–1956

BUCK RAINEY

McFarland & Company, Inc., Publishers
Jefferson, North Carolina, and London

ALSO BY BUCK RAINEY
AND FROM MCFARLAND

Serial Film Stars: A Biographical Dictionary, 1912–1956 (2005)

The Strong, Silent Type: Over 100 Screen Cowboys, 1903–1930 (2004)

Western Gunslingers in Fact and on Film: Hollywood's Famous Lawmen and Outlaws (1997)

The Reel Cowboy: Essays on the Myth in Movies and Literature (1996)

Sweethearts of the Sage: Biographies and Filmographies of 258 Actresses Appearing in Western Movies (1992)

Frontispiece: William Benedict, Kay Aldridge and Clayton Moore in *Perils of Nyoka* (15 chapters; Republic, 1942).

The present work is a reprint of the library bound edition of Serials and Series: A World Filmography, 1912–1956, *first published in 1999 by McFarland.*

LIBRARY OF CONGRESS CATALOGUING-IN-PUBLICATION DATA

Rainey, Buck.
Serials and series : a world filmography, 1912–1956
by Buck Rainey.
p. cm.
Includes bibliographical references and index.

ISBN 978-0-7864-4702-2
softcover : 50# alkaline paper ♾

1. Motion picture serials—Catalogs. I. Title.
PN1995.9.S3R33 2010 016.79143'3—dc21 98-25107

British Library cataloguing data are available

Front cover: *Zorro's Fighting Legion*, a 1939 serial (Photofest)

Manufactured in the United States of America

McFarland & Company, Inc., Publishers
Box 611, Jefferson, North Carolina 28640
www.mcfarlandpub.com

For my sons
REX, TIM and KEN
who have never learned to appreciate good movies—
"good" meaning westerns and serials

In memory of
BUCK JONES
all that an idol should be

ACKNOWLEDGMENTS

Special Thanks
to

Jim Stringham, Jose Simoes Filho, and William (Bill) McDowell
for significant research assistance

to

Kalton Lahue for his pioneering work on the silent serial;
Jack Mathis for his exhaustive study of Republic serials;
Alan Barbour for his many serial publications;
Jim Harmon, Donald Glut, Ken Weiss, Ed Goodgold, Roy Kinnard,
Raymond W. Stedman, William C. Cline, Gene Fernett, and Wayne Shultz
for their outstanding books on the motion picture serial

and

My warmest gratitude to the following men who, through their writings,
have kept the memory of the serials alive:

Edward Casali
Paul Dellinger
Norm Lynch
Gregg Jackson, Jr.
Elden K. Everett
Eric Hoffman
Charles McCleary
Robert Malcomson
Charles Ford
John Roberts
Gary Spencer
Anthony Slide
Jim Stringham
Jon Tuska
Edward Connor
Mario DeMarco
George Geltzer
George A. Katchmer

finally

A tip of the hat to the publications that have in the past or do now
frequently publish articles about serials:

Cliffhanger
Classic Images
Films in Review
Film Collector's Registry
Favorite Westerns
Motion Picture Classic
Motion Picture Magazine
Photoplay
Serial World
Serial Quarterly
Those Enduring Matinee Idols
Under Western Skies
Views and Reviews
Variety
Screen Thrills
Wranglers Roost
Screen Thrills Illustrated
Boys Cinema

CONTENTS

INTRODUCTION

A dispassionate analysis of most serials might reveal them to be enterprises of only incidental value to the advancement of motion pictures, but those who frequented the weekend offerings of neighborhood, back street, and small town theaters over four decades were not inclined to analyze them—merely to enjoy total absorption and exhilaration in the vicarious thrill of it all. The chapter play seemed to be the perfect vehicle for escaping the travail of one's own dull, callous life and capitalizing on one's emotional stirrings for adventure and capricious fantasies.

A word of explanation is in order for the benefit of those whose serial memories only extend back to the late thirties or the forties. The serials of the silent era were taken seriously by both fans and studios. Their production quality was often considerably better than those serials produced in the thirties and after. There was not the stigma attached to them that developed later, nor were serial performers looked down upon as "has-beens" or "never-weres." They were universally idolized, and serials played the best theaters as well as those in the boondocks.

Perhaps the high crest of the serial wave was reached when Billie Burke, a highly respected actress, signed her name to a contract calling for a salary of $4,000 a week to play the lead in a twenty-chapter serial titled *Gloria's Romance* (1916). Miss Burke drew a total of $140,000, and a like sum was spent in a well-directed advertising campaign that resulted in some theaters paying $1,000 a week to book the film. Its total production cost was around $600,000, making it the most expensive serial ever made. The cost of *Flash Gordon* (1936), the sound era's most expensive serial, was around $250,000.

In the silent era many serials were targeted at adult audiences and liberally flavored with love and romance, especially those made in Europe. In this country Pathé consistently made gilt-edged serials designed to entertain adults as well as children.

There was never any doubt that profit was the essential reason for serial production. This goal never wavered. In this respect the serial was analogous to the program western, with which it was quite often co-billed. Neither was meant to leave an indelible mark on filmdom, and the fact that both did is a tribute to all who worked so conscientiously in this subworld of Hollywood. The haunting charm that both the serial and the program western possessed—a charm that quickly enveloped the mind, heart, and spirit of boyhood—remains unsurpassed in Hollywood's glorious history.

Stupendously costly films with top-name stars, glorious color, and profound content might gradually be engulfed by the abyss of lost memories. But remembered always are such scenes as Flash Gordon, with beautiful Dale Arden in his arms, escaping from the clutches of Ming, the merciless; the Shadow's spine-tingling laughter; Ruth Roland's hair-raising stunts; the harrowing exploits of Elaine, The Lone Ranger, Captain Marvel, The Phantom, Superman, Batman, and curvaceous Jungle Girl; and the incredible thrill of the runaway boxcar hurtling down the tracks toward a bound and unconscious Helen Holmes. Such scenes are trapped in our minds forever.

The film industry began its exploitation of the continued story in 1912 and developed the form fully in the next twenty years, while successfully enmeshing audiences in the "heart-in-the-throat" fate of the serial performers.

The serial idea itself was conceived in 1912, although the basic principle no doubt dates back further than definite history. *What Happened to Mary* (1912) is credited with being the first of all screened "continued-next-week" stories. It was a series rather than a serial, as we think of the serial today. Edison produced it with the cooperation of *The Ladies' World*, in which the stories were published concurrently with their screening. This arrangement increased both circulation of the magazine and theater attendance. The series opened the floodgates to over five hundred American serials and series spanning forty-four years, although

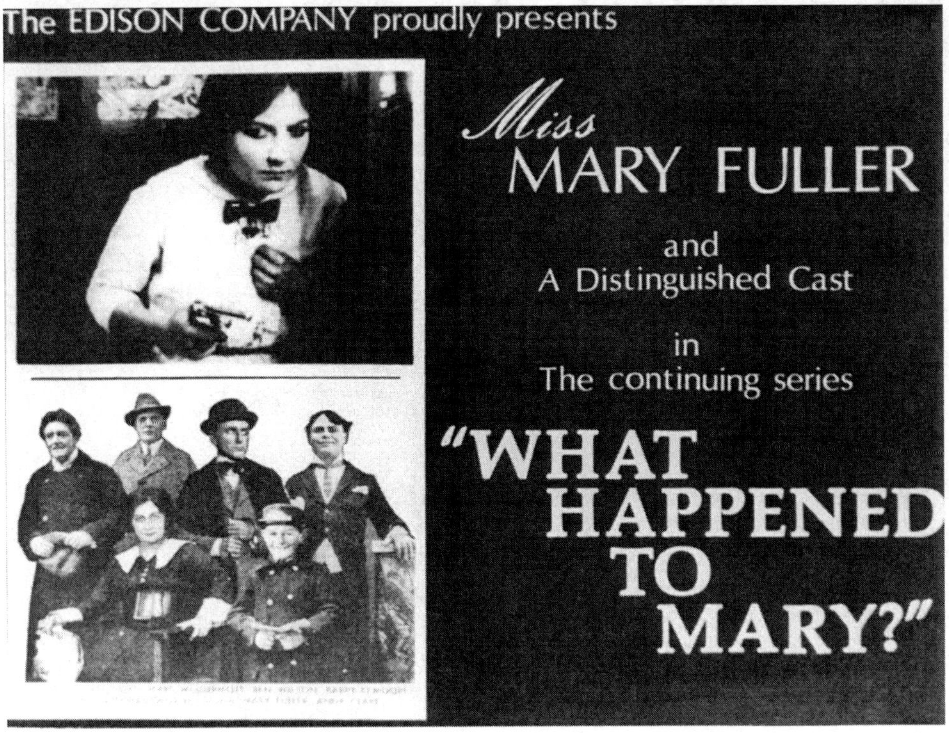

Mary Fuller in *What Happened to Mary?* (12 chapters, one reel each; Edison, 1912)

the chapter play was hardly an original idea, as a number of magazines and newspapers ran serialized fiction on a regular basis. Older newspaper readers may remember "Hairbreadth Harry," one of the first Sunday comics. Hairbreadth and his sweetheart, Beautiful Belinda, each week were beset by the scheming plots of that dastardly villain, Desperate Desmond. Weekly the couple would foil Desperate just in the nick of time. Like movie serial heroines, Belinda was never killed, never experienced the "fate worse than death," and never had the old homestead taken from her permanently.

The first "Mary" series was followed by *Who Will Marry Mary?* (1913) and *The Active Life of Dolly of the Dailies* (1914), both again starring Mary Fuller. The successful outcome of the Edison–*Ladies' World* affiliation was not long in attracting others. Kalem produced *The Hazards of Helen* (1914), the longest running and perhaps the most famous series ever filmed. It consisted of 119 one-reel episodes, each a complete story. These railroad tales featured Helen as the continued character in action-oriented stories told in ten to fifteen minutes. Helen Holmes and Helen Gibson each took a turn at portraying Helen.

The most extensive prolonged publicity campaign in the history of the theater and journalism combined was inaugurated in 1914 in Chicago by the Selig Polyscope Company, of which W. N. Selig was the head, and a group of big Sunday newspapers extending from coast to coast. They collaborated for the purpose of presenting a serial fiction story both on the screen and in the countless newspapers. The story was written by Harold MacGrath from a scenario by Gilson Willets and visualized in the Selig Studio in Los Angeles. It was called *The Adventures of Kathlyn* (1914), and it was the longest photoplay that had been released up to that time. Two reels constituted each of the twice-a-month releases save the first, which was three reels.

The Adventures of Kathlyn was the forerunner of the cliffhanger serial. Each chapter left the heroine, played by Kathlyn Williams, in some dangerous predicament designed to lure the audience back to see how she would extricate herself in the next chapter. *The Chicago Tribune* published the Kathlyn stories and also syndicated them to other newspapers in cities where the serial was being exhibited. These newspapers paid for the privilege of printing the stories. The *Tribune* gained some 60,000 new subscribers because of the Kathlyn stories.

The sensational vogue of MacGrath's *Adventures of Kathlyn* on screen and in the press alike attracted the attention of other film manufacturers to this author, who undoubtedly found his income vastly enlarged. The indefatigable Thanhouser Company came forth with the announcement that it would film MacGrath's *The Million Dollar Mystery*. The arrangements in this instance were on a prodigious scale. The number of publications to present the fiction story in weekly installments was in excess of two hundred, including *The Chicago Tribune*.

Few exhibitors of those days (the first release was December 29, 1913) forgot how *Adventures of Kathlyn* packed their houses. It was a gold mine for the theater owners, and it attracted many people who had previously scorned the movies.

Strangely enough, Colonel Selig never produced another serial. He thought that he had skimmed the cream off a new can of milk and that a repetition of the idea would be fruitless. But others liked the idea. Pathé started grinding out *The Perils of Pauline* (1914) at about the same time as Thanhouser was making *The Million Dollar Mystery*. Both were winners. *Mystery* stands as one of the biggest money-making serials of the silent era. The total bookings aggregated something like $2,000,000, and the syndicate that financed it divided profits of over half a million dollars.

The Perils of Pauline had the publicity backing of the Hearst newspapers, while the *Chicago Tribune* and a nationwide syndicate of newspapers published the *Mystery* stories. The latter series was in twenty-three chapters, whereas there were twenty "perils" from which Pearl White (as Pauline) escaped.

The Perils of Pauline turned out to be the best known serial ever made, although "series" is a better classification. It was merely an unfolding of loosely related adventures, with each episode complete in itself. They were primarily designed for adult audiences. And consequently, romance played a part in the stories.

It is said that Colonel William Selig's original motive in putting forth the *Kathlyn* serial was his desire to utilize a collection of wild animals he was bringing together in Los Angeles. He had also built a tropical zoo in that city. Of course he was also prompted by the showman's idea of having a hold on the exhibitors for an extended period, thus assuring a good income for the length of the serial and also permitting a concentrated campaign of publicity. These objectives are the basic foundation of the serials' right to live.

Kathlyn Williams in *The Adventures of Kathlyn* (13 chapters; Selig, 1914)

After *The Adventures of Kathlyn*, absurd complications, incredible villainy, ludicrous motives, and terrific escapes, with breath-stopping hangovers at the end of every episode, became the main meat of the serial. From that point, serial history is the record of a scramble to pile up golden shekels, a wild search for original ideas and stars who could draw dimes into the box office till. In one venture the harvest could be bins overflowing with gold, and in the next an empty sack and a barnful of regret.

By starring a heroine instead of a hero and putting her histrionics into the hands of lovely Pearl White (who was never seen on screen without her blonde wig), *The Perils of Pauline* uncovered a gold mine. Pearl took the movies by storm and leaped to stardom, going on to do a string of gooseflesh serials that crowded theaters to the aisles for each segment of her thrillers and brought her a $10,000 a week salary.

But Pearl was not alone in the thrill-a-minute world of ridiculous plots, weird disguises, hair-raising escapes, hidden treasures, diabolic scientific devices, wild animals, depraved men, runaway trains, claustrophobic horrors, and the endless procession of knock-down, drag-out fights. Also rising to prominence were Grace Cunard, Marie Walcamp, Neva Gerber, Louise Lorraine, Eileen Sedgwick, Ruth Roland, Juanita Hansen, Allene Ray, and others, all hapless heroines constantly plunged into perilous predicaments, from which they miraculously, and just barely, managed to disentangle themselves.

But while women were the glittering stars in a large number of the early serials, before long, eminence shifted to their male counterparts. William Duncan, for example, became so popular as a serial star that he could command a salary of $10,000 a week, with production on his serials taking several months. Also stirring a whirlwind of enthusiasm among serial devotees were William Desmond, Ben Wilson, Walter Miller, Francis Ford, Charles Hutchinson, Jack Daughtery, and Eddie Polo.

During the early years serials and series were exceedingly popular and were booked into the finest theaters. They were played straight, not for laughs. Nor were serial performers looked down upon by those in the movie industry. The movies could create a fantastic realism that left viewers gasping, and Hollywood gloried in its era of gooseflesh as the kings and queens of the serials escaped death again and again, the notes of a piano or pianola drowned out by the shrieks and clapping of an audience plunging with them into a spectacular abyss of fantasy and adventure.

When motion pictures became universally popular, the dime novel of the good old days fell into oblivion. In fact, the movie serial took the place of the nickel and dime novels that presented "Diamond Dick," "Nick Carter," "Old Sleuth," and so on to youngsters. Censors objected to serials on the ground that, while right was always finally triumphant, it took from twelve to twenty chapters to prove that fact, and the hero or heroine was always in imminent danger from the machinations of the criminal masterminds or the band of conspirators at the end of each chapter, until the wind-up of the story.

Crane Wilbur and Pearl White in *The Perils of Pauline* (20 chapters; Pathé, 1914)

In many states in 1921 censors ruled against certain aspects of the motion picture serial, prohibiting hold-ups, the liberal use of firearms, the torturing of the hero or heroine, and particularly the method of handling women characters of the story. Some censorship boards refused to permit even the laying of a hand upon a woman. Needless to day, such strict censorship made filming difficult for serial producers. However, censorship was soon relaxed and serial producers could again turn out action films without fear that their product would be banned in some states.

Near the end of the 1920s the serial had lost much of its lustrous appeal for adults, and only Pathé was seriously attempting to cater to older viewers. With the coming of sound, and Pathé's demise, the serial found a new niche, a comfortable and modestly profitable one, in the hearts of the young, who gladly shelled out ten cents a week to follow the adventures of their idols. Throughout the thirties and forties, in the less pretentious movie houses of the world, serials were staple ingredients for weekend showing, especially in the smaller towns of the south and southwest. The serials etched indelible impressions on the minds of millions of youngsters. These impressions would remain vivid even forty, fifty, or sixty years after having seen the films. *The Lone Ranger, Flash Gordon, The Wolf Dog, Ace Drummond, Gordon of Ghost City, Dick Tracy, Undersea Kingdoms, The Phantom Empire*—fans still get goosebumps at the recollection of the serials that contributed so much to childhood's pleasure.

The sound era had its own serial royalty, and reverence was heaped upon such continued-next-week idols as Buster Crabbe, Clayton Moore, Ralph Byrd, Herman Brix (Bruce Bennett), Buck Jones, Tom Tyler, Jean Rogers, Lucile Browne, Kane Richmond, and Linda Stirling. Outside the action arena their names might not have meant so much, but in their own fantasy world they reigned supreme as the kings and queens of thrills.

Few foreign serials were ever shown in the U.S., but there were exceptions—notably *Fantômas* (1913), *Les Vampires* (1916), *Judex* (1917), and *La Nouvelle Mission de Judex* (1918). Serials were popular throughout Europe until the era of sound films. Although the U.S. continued production with gusto, the European film companies practically stopped making serials after 1930, as their popularity waned.

France was foremost in serial production with a record of seventy or more films. Second in output was Italy, with Germany, England, Denmark, Norway, and Spain contributing to the genre as well.

Louis Feuillade, French director and principal supervisor of the Gaumont firm, was the promoter of the genre in France. *Fantômas* (1913), the story of a gentleman thief, had five episodes and was extremely popular. The incarnation of evil, Fantomas was pursued by police officer Juve and newspaper reporter Fandor. The film was based on the bestselling book of the same name by Piene Souvestre and Marcel Allein. With the success of this first effort, Feuillade, with the backing of studio owner Leon Gaumont, decided to make other serials. *Les Vampires* (1915) was also a big hit and was followed by *Judex* (1917) and *La Nouvelle Mission de Judex* (1918), which was released in the U.S. as *The New Mission of Judex*.

The French film producers of serials, namely Gaumont, Aubert, and Pathé, followed the American example of involving the newspapers in their publicity programs and were influenced by the success of *The Exploits of Elaine* (1914), the first American serial to be shown in France. In time the serials of Ruth Roland, Marie Walcamp, Louise Lorraine, Neva Gerber and other American serial heroines proved popular with the French audiences. Feuillade made serials until his death in 1925 on the set of *Le Stigmate*. By that time the French serial was waning badly. The last French serial was *Mephisto* (1931), a sound film starring René Navarre.

French serials varied in length, as did most European serials. There was emphasis on social or family situations, and children were sometimes the focus of attention. The film often told its story in a few chapters, whereas the American serial with one exception was at least ten chapters. American serials always emphasized "Bang, bang, you're dead!" adventure and action. French serials typically moved at a slower pace.

Emilio Ghione was the king of Italian serials. He both directed and starred in short serials comprised of three, four, or eight chapters. The most successful and popular period for these serials was 1915–20, although they continued to be made until the coming of sound.

Norway and Denmark produced a few serials with the most significant being *Dr. Gar-el-Hamma*, filmed in five chapters and released in the years 1911–16 (an unusual length of time between chapters), and *Japet Derboger Si Gen Pader* (1920).

Spain's chief contribution to the serial world was *Los Misteros de Barcelona* (1915), a remake of *The Exploits of Elaine* (1914).

Germany created *Homunculus* (1915), a character similar to Superman. Several other German serials were well made and received.

England contributed a number of serials to filmdom, many of them based on children's adventure novels. The most popular serials were probably *The Mysteries of Fu Manchu* (1923) and the trilogy of films revolving around Sherlock Holmes made in the early twenties.

The mountains have given up their gold and the desert has taken its toll, as the movies' surrender to expediency has done in the bold. But *Serials and Series: A World Filmography* should help satisfy the gluttonous appetite of enthusiasts with memories of chapter play action and settings that glossed over theatrical crudities. They are all here—the big ones, the small ones, the famous, the forgotten, the good, the bad, the classics, and the embarrassments. Most assuredly, these pages will conjure up many happy recollections for serial buffs, whose dreams of the serial as a perpetual genre came to a crushing end in 1956.

Within this book there is information on 471 American serials, 100 American series, 136 foreign serials, and 37 foreign series. Information on the foreign serials and series is limited. I apologize for the necessity of using Portuguese chapter/episode titles with some of the films. In these cases, English or French titles were unavailable, and the information came to me from Brazil, where Portuguese is spoken.

A distinction must now be made between serial and series. Sometimes a film is a borderline picture that could go either way. But we normally think of a serial having a continuing story, continuing characters, and cliffhanger endings that leave the hero or heroine in jeopardy. Viewers are drawn back the following week to see how the hero or heroine manages to emerge unscathed from some near-death experience. Series, on the other hand, although they may have one or more continuing characters, tell a story from beginning to resolution in one episode. Each episode is independent of all others in the series. There are no cliffhanger endings.

French serial hero René Cresté in *Judex* (Gaumont, 1917)

Historians do not always agree on the proper classification of a film. For example, many books classify *The Hazards of Helen* (1914) and *The Perils of Pauline* (1914) as serials when in reality they are series. But they have a superabundance of action, which is expected in a serial, and there was not a clear-cut distinction between the two in the early years. Europe presents yet another problem in classification, as cliffhanger endings and huge helpings of action were not necessary ingredients of serials. I have done my best to properly classify the foreign films presented in the following pages, given the pittance of information I had on many of the films.

My primary aim in choosing the series found in the following pages is, through this book, to preserve the memory of their having been made and shown. Film historians and students of the cinema may find some of the information valuable in their research and writing.

All films—silent, sound, American, foreign, serials, and series—are arranged alphabetically. Some long-forgotten comedy series are included, but emphasis is on the melodrama and action-oriented series. Since the coming of sound, few one- or two-reel series have been made except for comedies, cartoons, newsreels, travelogues, and miscellaneous productions. Major comedians of both the sound and silent era have been well covered in other books.

Among the miscellaneous productions of the sound era are *Crime Does Not Pay* (1935–1945) and *Ray Whitley and His Bar-6 Cowboys* (1937–1942). Also covered in other books are feature film series; therefore, they are not covered here.

Several books have been published on American sound serials. Only one author, to my knowledge, has seriously tackled the silent serial. However, this book presents more information on serials than do the previously published books; e.g., films, casts, character roles, and chapter titles. No book, again to my knowledge, has covered foreign serials.

The following abbreviations have been used throughout the book:

D:	Director
SP:	Screenplay*
Scen.	Scenario*
P:	Producer
S:	Story

(*Some studios used one term; others, the other term. Both refer to the same thing.)

Serial and series buffs, cinema students, and film historians will find in these pages answers to most of their "who," "what," "where," and "when" questions relative to American and foreign serials and series. As the most complete reference book on motion picture serials and series to date, it rates a place on that important reference shelf reserved for one's most frequently used books.

THE FILMS

1. Die Abenteuerin von Monte Carlo

(Germany—Ellen Richter Film GmbH, 1921) Series, 3 episodes. D: Adolf Gartner. SP: Willi Wolff and Arthur Somlay.

Ellen Richter, Anton Pointner, Albert Patry, Eduard Von Winterstein, Karl Huszar, Kurt Rottenburg, Carl Gunther, Karl Swoboda, Martha Hoffman, Tony Tetzlaff, Albert Paulig, Henry Bender, Magnus Stifter, Hamed Ben Melusi, Max Kronert, Paul Biensfeldt, Arthur Kraussneck, Adolf Klein, Rudolf Forster-Larrinaga, Karl Harbacher, Hugo Hummel.

1. Die Geliebte des Schah. 2. Marokkanische Nachte. 3. Der Mordprozess Stanley.

2. Ace Drummond

(Universal, October 19, 1936) Serial, 13 chapters, two reels each. D: Ford Beebe and Cliff Smith. SP: Wyndham Gitten, Norman S. Hall, and Ray Trampe. Assoc. P: Barney A. Sarecky and Ben Koenig. Based on Capt. Eddie Rickenbacker's King Features newspaper strip. Feature title: *Squadron of Doom*—MPTV release.

A mysterious criminal known as The Dragon is determined to stop the Mongolian link needed to complete a globe-circling airplane service. Ace Drummond, famed flyer, agrees to investigate. In Asia he not only seeks to learn the identity of The Dragon, but helps Peggy Trainor search for her lost father and a hidden mountain containing enormous quantities of jade.

John King (Ace Drummond), Jean Rogers (Peggy Trainor), Noah Beery, Jr. (Jerry), Guy Bates Post (Grand Lama), Arthur Loft (Chang-Ho/The Dragon), Chester Gan (Kai-Chek), Jackie Morrow (Billy Meredith), James B. Leong (Henry Kee), James Eagle (Johnny Wong), Selmer Jackson (Meredith, Sr.), Robert Warwick (Winston), Montague Shaw (Trainor), Frederick Vogedine (Bauer), Al Bridge (Wyckoff), Lon Chaney, Jr. (Ivan), Stanley Blystone (Sergei), Edmund Cobb (Nicolai), Richard Wessel (Boris), Louis Vinzinot (Lotan), Sam Ash (Le Page), Hooper Atchley (Caldoni), Ed Parker (Double for King and Beery), Diana Gibson, Russell Wade, House Peters, Jr., Lew Hicks, Ed Peil, Sr.

1. Where East Meets West. 2. Invisible Enemy. 3. Doorway of Doom. 4. The Radio Riddle. 5. Bullets of Sand. 6. Evil Spirits. 7. The Trackless Trail. 8. The Sign in the Sky. 9. Secret Service. 10. Mountain of Jade. 11. The Dragon Commands. 12. Squadron of Death. 13. The World Akin.

3. The Ace of Scotland Yard

(Universal, September 30, 1929) Serial, 10 chapters, two reels each. Released in both silent and sound versions; sequel to *Blake of Scotland Yard*. D: Ray Taylor. SP/S: Harold M. Atkinson.

These are the further adventures of Angus Blake, retired agent of Scotland Yard. This time he is opposed by the Queen of Diamonds, a female gangleader out to steal his fiancée Lady Diana's valuable ring.

The acquisition of the famous "Love Ring" by Lord Blanton, Lady Diana's father, brings fear to Blake because his analytical mind senses danger which the possession of the ring brings the owners. Lord Blanton entertains Prince Darius, who has taken the vow of his ancestors to recover the ring and the mummified image of an ancient princess of his race, which, now in Lord Blanton's house, were stolen from their resting place on the Gobi desert.

Crauford Kent (Angus Blake), Florence Allen (Lady Diana Blanton), Herbert Prior (Lord Blanton), Monte Montague (Jarvis), Grace Cunard (The Queen of Diamonds), Albert Prisco (Prince Darius).

1. The Fatal Circlet. 2. A Cry in the Night. 3. The Dungeon of Doom. 4. The Depths of Limehouse. 5. Menace of the Mummy. 6. Dead or Alive. 7. Shadows of Fear. 8. The Baited Trap. 9. A Battle of Wits. 10. The Final Judgment.

4. The Ace of Spades

(Universal, October 19, 1925) Serial, 15 chapters, two reels each. D: Henry MacRae. SP: Isadore Bernstein and William Lord Wright.

Villains try to steal a map showing rich mineral deposits. Victims of the gang receive the death card, the black ace of spades, as a warning. The Oklahoma landrush is the backdrop for all the action.

William Desmond (Dan Harvey), Mary McAllister (Olive

Top: **John King, Jean Rogers, Guy Bates Post and Chester Gan in *Ace Drummond* (1936); *bottom:* Florence Allen (reclining), Grace Cunard (standing) and Crawford Kent (talking to Cunard) in *The Ace of Scotland Yard* (1929)**

Heath), Albert J. Smith (Joe Deneen), William A. Steele (Jim Heath), Cathleen Calhoun ("Parker Dice" Ann), Jack Pratt (Gideon Trask), Clarke Comstock (Martin Heath), Frank Lanning (Francois), John Herdman (Thomas Jefferson), William P. De Vaul (Napoleon Bonaparte), John Shanks (Talleyrand), Aaron Edwards (Lucien Bonaparte), Bert Sprotts (James Monroe), Harry Lorraine (Barbe Barbois), Monte Montague, Alton Stone, Steven Carrie, Al Richmond (Henchmen).

1. The Fatal Card. 2. No Greater Love. 3. Whirling Waters. 4. Fires of Sacrifice. 5. Thundering Hoofs. 6. Flung from the Sky. 7. Trail of Terror. 8. Lariat of Death. 9. Fingers of Fate. 10. Road to Ruin. 11. Chasm of Peril. 12. The Avalanche. 13. The Fury of Fate. 14. The Chasm of Courage. 15. A Deal of Destiny.

5. The Active Life of Dolly of the Dailies

(Edison, January 31, 1914) Series, 12 episodes, 1 reel each. D: Walter Edwin. S: Acton Davies.

Dolly, refusing to apologize for a story on the local Ladies' Guild goes to the big city to pursue her career as a reporter. After a few setbacks she meets Rockwell Crosby, editor of the *Comet*, who not only hires her as a star reporter but falls in love with her. As a reporter out to prove herself to her fiancé-boss, Dolly finds herself in all kinds of predicaments.

Mary Fuller (Dolly), Gladys Hulette (Mrs. Yorke), Yale Boss, Charles Ogle, Harry Beaumont, William West, Edwin Clark, Richard Neill, Miriam Nesbitt.

1. The Perfect Truth. 2. The Ghost of Mother Eve. 3. An Affair of Dress. 4. Putting One Over. 5. The Chinese Fan. 6. On the Heights. 7. The End of the Umbrella. 8. A Tight Squeeze. 9. A Terror of the Night. 10. Dolly Plays Detective. 11. Dolly at the Helm. 12. The Last Assignment.

6. Adventures and Emotions of Edgar Pomeroy

(Goldwyn, April 1920–April 1921) Series, 12 episodes, two reels each. D: Paul Bern, E. Mason Hopper, and Mason N. Litson. Scen: Eleanor Flori and Barbara Kent. From the stories of Booth Tarkington. Presented by Samuel Goldwyn.

The adventures and experiences of a typical—or perhaps, not so typical—young boy.

Johnny Jones [Edward Peil, Jr.] (Edgar Pomeroy), Buddy Messinger, Lucille Rickson.

1. Edgar and Teacher's Pet. 2. Edgar's Hamlet. 3. Edgar's Jonah Day. 4. Edgar Takes the Cake. 5. Edgar's Sunday Courtship. 6. Edgar Camps Out. 7. Edgar's Little Saw. 8. Get-Rich-Quick Edgar. 9. Edgar the Explorer. 10. Edgar's Country Cousin. 11. Edgar's Feast Day. 12. Edgar the Detective.

7. Adventures of Bob and Bill

(Pathé, April 1921–February 1922) Series, 15 episodes, 1 reel each. P/D: Robert N. Bradbury.

These one-reel shorts are the first films in which Bob Steele played. His father, director Robert N. Bradbury, made these films of Bob and his twin brother William and sold them to Pathé.

Robert N. Bradbury, Jr. (Bob Steele), William Bradbury.

1. Trailing the Coyote (4-3-21). 2. Trapping the Bobcat (4-6-21). 3. Outwitting the Timber Wolf (5-29-21). 4. The Fox (6-26-21). 5. The American Badger (7-24-21). 6. The Mountain Lion (8-21-21). 7. Civit Cat (9-18-21). 8. The Skunk (10-16-21). 9. A Day in the Wilds (11-12-21). 10. Trapping the Weasel (12-11-21). 11. Capturing the Canadian Lynx (1-8-22). 12. Dangerous Trails (2-5-22). 13. Mysterious Tracks (3-4-22). 14. The Opossum (4-2-22). 15. Catching a Coon (5-1-22).

8. Adventures of Captain Africa

(Columbia, June 1955) Serial, 15 chapters, two reels each. D: Spencer G. Bennet. SP: George H. Plympton. P: Sam Katzman. Assist. D: Horace Hough. Photography: Ira H. Morgan. Music: Mischa Bakaleinikoff.

Captain Africa and friends help Caliph Hamid, whose prime minister has been kidnapped, regain his throne and vanquish the false caliph. Once again serial buffs were treated to a story of a lost civilization, crocodiles, slavers, and a gorilla, which seemed destined to try Captain Africa. Asian tigers even wound up in the African jungle. Much stock footage from *The Phantom* was used and in fact the serial was pretty much a remake of the earlier film starring Tom Tyler.

John Hart (Captain Africa), Rick Vallin (Ted Arnold), Ben Weldon (Omar), June Howard (Princess Rhoda), Bud Osborne (Nat Coleman), Paul Marion (Hamid), Lee Roberts (Boris), Terry Frost (Greg), Ed Coch (Balu), Michael Fox (Prime Minister).

1. Mystery Man of the Jungle. 2. Captain Africa to the Rescue. 3. Midnight Attack. 4. Into the Crocodile Pit. 5. Jungle War Drums. 6. Slave Traders. 7. Saved by Captain Africa. 8. The Bridge in the Sky. 9. Blasted by Captain Africa. 10. The Vanishing Princess. 11. The Tunnel of Terror. 12. Fangs of the Beast. 13. Renegades at Bay. 14. Captain Africa and the Wolf Dog. 15. Captain Africa's Final Move.

***Both:* William Desmond and Mary McAllister in *Ace of Spades* (1925)**

9. Adventures of Captain Marvel

(Republic, March 1941) Serial, 12 chapters, two reels each. D: William Witney and John English. SP: Ronald Davidson, Norman S. Hall, Arch B. Heath, Joseph Poland, and Sol Shor. Assoc. P: Hiram S. Brown, Jr. Photography: William Nobles. Music: Cy Feuer. Reissued as *Return of Captain Marvel*.

The Malcolm Expedition searches for the lost secret of the Scorpion, a powerful weapon controlled by focusing five highly polished lenses, in a remote section of Siam. Billy Batson is the only member of the group who does not enter a forbidden chamber inside an underground tomb. When a volcano eruption causes part of the tomb to collapse, Shazam, the tomb's guardian, appears because Billy had heeded the warning not to enter the tomb. Shazam endows him with the magic power to transform himself into Captain Marvel. The scientists discover the Scorpion, the lenses are divided among them, and they return home. However, a gang whose masked leader called himself The Scorpion finally succeeds in stealing the various lenses and activating the powerful Scorpion machine. But Captain Marvel thwarts The Scorpion's destructive plans, unmasks him, and destroys the deadly instrument.

Tom Tyler (Captain Marvel), Frank Coghlan, Jr. (Billy Batson), William Benedict (Whitey Murphy), Louise Currie (Betty Wallace), Robert Strange (John Malcolm), Harry Worth (Luther Bentley/The Scorpion), Gerald Mohr (Voice of the Scorpion), Bryant Washburn (Henry Carlyle), John Davidson (Tal Chotali), George Pembroke (Stephen Lang), Peter George Lynn (Dwight Fisher), Reed Hadley (Rahman Bar), Jack Mulhall (James Howell), Kenne Duncan (Barnett), Carleton Young

Rick Vallin (left) and John Hart in *Adventures of Captain Africa* (1955)

(Martin), Stanley Price (Owens), Eddie Dew (Cavalry Lieutenant), Ted Mapes (Seaman), Ken Terrell (Hawks), Major Sam Harris (Hudson), Bud Geary (Pete), Martin Lamont (Radio Sergeant), Nigel De Brulier (Shazam), John Bagni (Cowan), Leyland Hodgson (Rawley), Ernest Sarracino (Akbar), Loren Riebe, Duke Taylor, Earl Bunn, George Suzanne (Heavies), Tetsu Komai (Chan Lal), Paul Lopez (Ali), Wilson Benge (Benson), Jerry Jerome (Brandon), Dick Crochett (Bridge Heavy), Chick Morrison (Carlson), Francis Sayles (Carter), Edward Cassidy (Dodge), Frank Marlowe (Gus), Armand Cortes (Hamid), Lynton Brent (Lefty), Augie Gomez, Al Taylor, Curley Dresden, Henry Wills, Steve Clemente (Natives), Al Kikume (Native Chief), Carl Zwolsman (Sentry), Frank Wayne (Steve), Ray Hanson (Trucker), David Sharpe (Double), Joe Delacruz, Victor Cox.

1. Curse of the Scorpion. 2. The Guillotine. 3. Time Bomb. 4. Death Takes the Wheel. 5. The Scorpion Strikes. 6. Lens of Death. 7. Human Targets. 8. Boomerang. 9. Dead Man's Trap. 10. Doom Ship. 11. Valley of Death. 12. Captain Marvel's Secret.

10. The Adventures of Deadwood Dick

(Great Britain—Samuelson Films, 1915) Series, 6 episodes, two reels each.

It is in keeping with the premature sophistication of the early cinema that there was never a true film equivalent of either the penny dreadful or the later *Gem* or *Magnet* form of schoolboy serial literature, despite its very large circulation from the 1850s onwards. *The Adventures of Deadwood Dick*, made by arrangement with that famous source of boys' stories, the Aldine Publishing Company, seems to have been the only clear case of the adaptation of this type of story in Britain. Each episode tells a complete story, independent of all others.

Fred Paul (Deadwood Dick).

1. How Richard Harris Became Known as Deadwood Dick. 2. Deadwood Dick's Vengeance. 3. Deadwood Dick and the Mormons. 4. Deadwood Dick Spoils Brigham Young. 5. Deadwood Dick's Red Ally. 6. Deadwood Dick's Detective Pard.

11. The Adventures of Dick Turpin (First Series)

(British & Colonial Kinematograph Company, 1912–13) Series, 5 episodes. D: Charles Raymond. S/SP: Harold Brett.

Episode Titles and Casts • *The King of Highwaymen* (1912). Percy Moran (Dick Turpin), Frank Pollard (Tom King), Bert Murray (Blueskin), Madge Thorpe (Moonlight Nell), Ernest A. Trimingham (Beetles), Raymond Cox (O'Phelyn), Harry Missouri (Peters), Herbert Trumper (Ridgeway), Harold Houghton (Hitches). • *The Gunpowder Plot* (1912). Percy Moran (Dick Turpin), Douglas Payne (George II), George Foley (Sir Robert Walpole), Jack Houghton (Sir Hugh Melville), W. Gladstone Halley, Harold Brett, Herbert Trumper, Olympia Sumner. • *200 Guineas Reward, Dead or Alive* (1912). Percy Moran (Dick Turpin), Harry Paule (Constable Puffin), Tom Shelford (Sir Mortimer Biggott), Mabel Clarke (Lady Dennis), Dorothy Foster (Lady Dennis' Daughter), Frank Pollard (Tom King), Bert Murray (Blueskin), Raymond Cox (O'Phelyn), Ernest A. Trimingham (Beetles), Harry Missouri (Peters). • *A Deadly Foe, A Pack of Hounds, and Some Merry Monks* (1912). Percy Moran (Dick Turpin), Harry Missouri (Peters). • *Dick Turpin's Ride to York* (1913). Percy Moran (Dick Turpin).

12. Adventures of Frank and Jesse James

(Republic, June 24, 1948) Serial, 13 chapters, two reels each. D: Fred Brannon and Yakima Canutt. SP: Franklyn Adreon, Basil Dickey, and Sol Shor. Assoc. P: Franklyn Adreon. Photography: John MacBurnie. Music: Morton Scott. Special Effects: Howard and Theodore Lydecker.

Frank and Jesse plan to make amends for their past crimes and succeed in borrowing money to open an old silver mine. A gang of outlaws tries to prevent discovery of the mine's true value.

Clayton Moore (Jesse James/John Howard), Steve Darrell (Frank James/Bob Carroll), Noel Neill (Judy Powell), George J. Lewis (Rafe Henley), Stanley Andrews (Jim Powell), John Crawford (Amos Ramsey), Sam Flint (Paul Thatcher), House Peters, Jr. (Sheriff Towey), Dale Van Sickel (Thomas Dale/Art Carter/ Jones), Tom Steele (Mike Steele/ Gus), James Dale (J.B. Nichols), I. Stanford Jolley (Ward), Gene Stutenroth (Marshal), Lane Bradford (Bill), Jack Kirk (Casey), Steve Clark (Sheriff Barton), Duke Taylor (Bull), Carey Loftin (Carlson/Pete), Duke Green (Carver), Frank Ellis, Roy Bucko, Art Dillard (Citizens), Ralph Bucko (Davin), Augie Gomez (Hall), Joe Yrigoyen (Grady), Fred Graham (Dirk 1), Guy Teague (Dirk 2), Victor Cox (Dick), Joe Phillips (Zeb), Bob Reeves (Tim), Eddie Parker (Jergens/ Joe), Bud Osborne (Bat Kelsey), Bud Wolfe (Moody), David Sharpe (Seth), Rose Turich (Rosita).

Left: **Tom Tyler as Captain Marvel; *right:* Carleton Young and Tom Tyler in *Adventures of Captain Marvel* (1941)**

1. Agent of Treachery. 2. The Hidden Witness. 3. The Lost Tunnel. 4. Blades of Death. 5. Roaring Wheels. 6. Passage to Danger. 7. The Secret Code. 8. Doomed Cargo. 9. The Eyes of the Law. 10. The Stolen Body. 11. Suspicion. 12. Talk or Die. 13. Unmasked.

13. The Adventures of Frank Merriwell

(Universal, January 13, 1936) Serial, 12 chapters, two reels each. D: Cliff Smith. SP: George Plympton, Maurice Geraghty, Ella O'Neill, and Basil Dickey. Assoc. P: Henry McRae. Based on novels by Bert L. Standish (pseudonym of William Patton Gilbert).

When his dad disappears, Frank Merriwell is called home from college by his mother, who thinks a mysterious intruder she encountered was after a ring the senior Merriwell entrusted to her. Frank and his college chums manage to decipher an inscription on the ring, which leads them to $30,000 in gold nuggets and the imprisoned senior Merriwell. A stranger, later identified as a distant relative, and his gang attempt to steal the money through force and kidnapping but are thwarted and captured. Merriwell, a star athlete, arrives back at college to lead his team to victory in the school's big game.

Don Briggs (Frank Merriwell), Jean Rogers (Elsie Belwood), John King (Bruce Browning), Carla Laemmle (Carla Rogers), Summer Getchell (Harry Rotteltown), Bentley Hewlett (Daggett), Al Bridge (Flack), Dickie Jones (Jimmy McLaw), Monty Montague (Monte), Bud Osborne (Gorman), Dave O'Brien (George Baldwin), Edmund Cobb (Pete), Charles Whitaker (Lumberjack Dolan), William Desmond (Captain of the Viking), Bert Young (Judd), Dick Wessell (Joe), Dick Cramer (Road Engineer), Al Ferguson (Lumberjack), Wallace Reid, Jr., House Peters, Jr., Allan Hersholt, Bryant Washburn, Jr., Carlyle Blackwell, Jr., Peter Gowland (Themselves), Mike Frankovitch (Radio Announcer), Nick Lucats (2nd Mate of Viking), Walter Law (Murray Belwood), Ben Corbett (Butch), Hank Bell (Hank), Robert Walker (Lang, Lumberjack Foreman), Sam McDaniels (Jeff), Yancy (Bruce) Lane (Captain of Yacht), Philo McCullough (Lumberjack Berger), Ella Ethridge (Mrs. Merriwell), Isabelle LaMall (Mrs. Pelwood), Viola Callaghan (Mrs. McLaw), Fred Summer (Professor Baldwin), William Carleton (Charles Merriwell), King Baggott (Chemistry Professor), Joseph DeCrasse (Dr. Cummings), Jack Donovan (Fardale Coach), Carlos Montalban (Spanish Captain), Jack Hall (Theater Doorman), William Franey (Barbecue Cook), Chester Gann (Dixie, Lumber Camp Cook), Herschel, Jr. (Himself), Edward Arnold, Jr. (Himself), Vick Allen (Jerry), George Plues (Mack), William L. Thorne (Police Sergeant), John Irwin (Train Engineer), Morgan Brown (Baggage Agent), Rain-in-the-Face (Chief Tonaka), Charles Murphy (Bard), John Ince (Conductor), June Gittelsen (Fat Girl), Diana Gibson (Grace), Chief John Big Tree (Indian John), Frank Hagney (Swope), Max Wagner (Pug O'Leary), Lynton Brent (Merriwell Fan), James Pierce (Double for Briggs), Corky (A Dog), Walter Brennan.

1. College Hero. 2. The Death Plunge. 3. Death at the Cross Roads. 4. Wreck of the Viking. 5. Capsized in the Cataract. 6. Descending Doom. 7. Monster of the Deep. 8. The Tragic Victory. 9. Between Savage Foes. 10. Imprisoned in a Dungeon. 11. The Crash in the Chasm. 12. The Winning Play.

***Top:* Clayton Moore, Noel Neill and Steve Darrell star in *Adventures of Frank and Jesse James* (1948); *bottom:* John King and Don Briggs in *Adventures of Frank Merriwell* (1936)**

14. The Adventures of Kathlyn

(Selig, January, 1914) Serial, 13 chapters; Chapter One, three reels; others, two reels. D: F.J. Grandon. Scen: Gilson Willets. S: Harold McGrath. Reissued in 1916 as an eight-reel feature.

First film to introduce "hold-over" suspense which whetted the viewer's desire to see the next installment. This climax action interrupted at the close of all but the final episode developed into the cliffhanger ending familiar to later generations of serial lovers. It also introduced a powerful villain providing menace in every installment and getting his punishment at the end, a device used in most subsequent serials. This film was considered the first true serial.

The story centers upon Kathlyn Hare, daughter of an explorer and collector of wild animals, and has her in a mythical principality in India fighting off the advances of both the native Umballah and many wild animals (including lions, which are not native to India).

Colonel William Selig produced and released the serial in collaboration with the *Chicago Tribune*. The newspaper published each chapter's story concurrently with the release of that film chapter. This was at the time of the great circulation wars, and the *Tribune* was fighting for its life. Selig's idea was to pull even more fans to the theater (and subscribers to the paper) by making an adventure film filled with wild animals and thrills that would act as a magnet to draw the masses hungry for vicarious adventure. The *Tribune*'s circulation went up ten percent, Kathlyn's name became a household word, and Colonel Selig not only made a profit but proceeded to make a whole series of wild animal films using what became known as the Selig Zoo.

Kathlyn Williams (Kathlyn Hare), Charles Clary (Umballah), William Carpenter (Ramabai), Thomas Santschi (John Bruce), Goldie Colwell (Pundita), Lafayette McKee (Colonel Hare), Franklin Hall (Gunda Singh), C.J. Murphy (Chief of Boatmen), Charles Courtright (Member of Council), Harry Huckins (Member of Council), Edmund Cobb, Edwin L. Wallock, Hurri Tsingh, Raymond Cannon, Guy Oliver.

1. The Unwelcome Sign. 2. The Two Ordeals. 3. The Temple of the Lion. 4. The Royal Slave. 5. A Colonel in Chains. 6. Three Bags of Silver. 7. The Garden of Brides. 8. The Cruel Crown. 9. The Spellbound Multitude. 10. The Warrior Maid. 11. The Forged Parchment. 12. The King's Will. 13. The Court of Death.

15. Adventures of Mazie

(R.C./F.B.O., September 1925–February 1926) Series, 12 episodes, two reels each. D: Ralph Cedar and Jimmy Wilkinson. Scen: Doris Anderson. Based on stories by Nell Martin appearing in *Top Notch Magazine.* A comedy series.

Synopses 1. *Amazing Mazie:* Mazie has an invalid brother and is the breadwinner. She answers an advertisement for a typist from George Dorsey, a struggling barrister, in arrears with his rent. How Mazie gets the job and spoofs the landlord forms a very entertaining story. 2. *The Constant Simp:* Mazie, in her efforts to help her employer, endeavors to collect an overdue bill and runs, pell-mell, onto a nest of counterfeiters. But she is able to let her pals know of her predicament and emerges from the melee with several prisoners and the amount of the debt. 12. *Mazie's Married:* With this film the series reached its twelfth and final installment. As the title tells, Mazie gets married. The first reel is devoted to the ineffectual attempts made by Dorsey to propose, aided by Tripp and Fall. Then, a crook steals important papers, and, as usual, Mazie and her pals are on the job and finally get them back. There is plenty of action and excitement and the comedy situations are amusing.

Alberta Vaughn (Mazie), Albert Cooke, Kit Guard.

1. Amazing Mazie. 2. The Constant Simp. 3. Or What Have You. 4. Mazie Won't Tell. 5. So's Your Old Man. 6. Pike's Pique. 7. The Vanishing Armenian. 8. Tea for Toomey. 9. High But Not Handsome. 10. Little Andy Looney. 11. A Snitch in Time. 12. Marie's Wizard.

16. The Adventures of Peg o' the Ring

(Universal, May 1, 1916) Serial, 15 chapters, two reels each. D: Francis Ford and Jacques Jaccard. SP: Grace Cunard.

Peg's mother was clawed by a leopard while pregnant. Later Peg is affected by the incident. She goes mad each night at midnight and becomes a dangerous menace to anyone near her. Ruth Stonehouse and Eddie Polo replaced Cunard and Ford when they walked out in a dispute with Universal. After several weeks Cunard and Ford returned to work. A lot of completed footage was scrapped including that of Stonehouse and Polo. The screenplay was changed numerous times, which was par for the Ford–Cunard team.

Grace Cunard (Peg), Francis Ford, G. Raymond Nye, Peter Gerald, Charles Munn, Mark Fenton, Jean Hathaway, Irving Lippner, Jack Duffy, Jack [John] Ford, Lionel Bradshaw.

1. The Leopard's Mark. 2. A Strange Inheritance. 3. In the Lion's Den. 4. The Circus Mongrels. 5. The House of Mystery. 6. The Cry for Help. 7. The Wreck. 8. Outwitted. 9. The Leap. 10. In the Hands of the Enemy. 11. The Stampede. 12. On the High Seas. 13. The Clown Act. 14. The Will. 15. Retribution.

17. Adventures of Red Ryder

(Republic, June 28, 1940) Serial, 12 chapters, two reels each. D: William Witney and John English. Assoc. P: Hiram S. Brown, Jr. SP: Franklyn Adreon, Ronald Davidson, Norman S. Hall, Barney Sarecky, and Sol Shor. Photography: William Nobles. Music: Cy Feuer. Based on the newspaper strip by Fred Harmon.

Red Ryder's father is killed by a gang headed by Calvin Drake and Ace Hanlon, who wish to gain control of all the land in the territory through which they know a railroad is to be built. Red vows vengeance and with the help of Little Beaver and his other friends rids the territory of bad men.

Top: **William Farnum, Tommy Cook (center), and Donald Berry;** ***bottom:*** **Hal Taliaferro (Wally Wales), Donald Berry, and Carleton Young in** ***Adventures of Red Ryder*** **(1940)**

Donald Barry (Red Ryder), Noah Beery, Sr. (Ace Hanlon), Tommy Cook (Little Beaver), Maude Pierce Allen (The Duchess), Vivian Coe [Vivian Austin] (Beth Andrews), Harry Worth (Calvin Drake), Hal Taliaferro [Wally Wales] (Cherokee Sims), Robert Kortman (One-Eye Chapin), William Farnum (Colonel Tom Ryder), Ray Teal (Shark), Hooper Atchley (Treadway), Jack Rockwell (Wilson), Gene Alsace [Rocky Camron] (Lawson), Carleton Young (Sheriff Dade), Jack Kirk (Hank), Budd Buster (Johnson), Lloyd Ingraham (Sheriff Luke Andrews), Jack O'Shea (Lem), William Nestel (Bartender), Jimmy Fawcett (Bartender), Bob Burns (Jones), Edward Hearn (Lang), Reed Howes (Slade), William Benedict (Dan Withers), Edward Cassidy (Ira Withers), Post Parks (Seldeen), Charles Murphy (Driver), Roy Brent (Joe), Charles Thomas (Lon Walker), Joe Yrigoyen (Ambusher), John Dilson (Hale), Al Taylor (Slim), Ed Brady (Ed Madison), Chester Conklin (Judge), Duke Green (Janitor), Wheaton Chambers (Boswell), Gardner James (H. S. Barnett), Lynton Brent (Len Clark), Ernest Sarracino (Matt Grimes), Bob Jamison (Gus), Joe Delacruz (Apache Kid), Bud Geary (Pecos Bates), Matty Roubert (Pete), Ken Terrell (Bart Wade), Fred Burns (Jackson), Curley Dresden (Judd), Art Dillard (Stage Heavy), Gus Shindle (Bat Mallory), Ray James (Hall), Max Waizman (Cole), James Carlisle (Board Member), Walter Stiritz, Dan White, Art Mix, Chick Hannon, Barry Hays, Bill Wilkus, Frankie Marvin, Robert Wilkie (Heavies),

Merrill McCormick, Eddie Jauregui, David Sharpe, Charles Hutchison, Rose Plummer, Walter James, Bill Yrigoyen, Victor Cox.

1. Murder on the Sante Fe Trail. 2. Horsemen of Death. 3. Trail's End. 4. Water Rustlers. 5. Avalanche. 6. Hangman's Noose. 7. Framed. 8. Blazing Wells. 9. Records of Doom. 10. One Second to Live. 11. The Devil's Marksman. 12. Frontier Justice.

18. The Adventures of Rex and Rinty

(Mascot, August 25, 1935) Serial, 12 chapters, two reels each. D: B. Reeves Eason and Ford Beebe. Scen: John Rathmell and Barney Sarecky. S: B. Reeves Eason, Ray Trampe, and Maurice Geraghty. P: Nat Levine. Supervision: Barney Sarecky. Photography: William Nobles.

Rex, a "God Horse" to the natives of Sujan, a primitive island, is stolen by three American crooks and sold to Crawford, a wealthy ranch owner in the U.S., who attempts to train him as a polo pony. Escaping, Rex teams up with Rin-Tin-Tin, Jr. They roam the range and together outwit their tormentors, with the help of Frank Bradley, a rival of Crawford. Bradley ultimately corrals Rex and returns him to Sujan where further attempts to steal the horse are thwarted. In the end Rex and Rinty are free and happy as they roam the island together.

Rex (Himself), Rin-Tin-Tin, Jr. (Himself), Kane Richmond (Frank Bradley), Norma Taylor (Dorothy Bruce), Mischa Auer (Tanega), Harry Woods (Crawford), George Regas (Pasha), Smiley Burnette (Jensen), Wheeler Oakman (Weber), Al Bridge (Mitchell), Edmund Cobb (Johnny), Ralph Byrd (Jerry Morton), John Webb Dillon (Hammond), Hooper Atchley, Victor Potel, Alan Cavan, Jack Rockwell.

Kane Richmond in *The Adventures of Rex and Rinty* (1935)

1. The God Horse of Sujan. 2. Sport of Kings. 3. Fangs of Flame. 4. Homeward Bound. 5. Babes in the Woods. 6. Dead Man's Tale. 7. End of the Road. 8. A Dog's Devotion. 9. The Stranger's Recall. 10. The Siren of Death. 11. New Gods for Old. 12. Primitive Justice.

19. The Adventures of Robinson Crusoe

(Universal, March 29, 1922) Serial, 18 chapters, two reels each. D: Robert F. Hill. Scen: Emma Bell Clifton. S: Daniel Defoe.

Straight from the pages of Defoe's classic. Crusoe's plight is followed from the time he is captured by the Moors and returns to England to discover his parents dead and his sweetheart betrayed by a false friend. He sets forth in a pirate ship, is marooned on a desert island, and there befriends the native, Friday. The faithful servant arrives in the third chapter, when the navigator is marooned on his island with no company except the native animals.

Harry Myers (Robinson Crusoe), Noble Johnson (Friday), Gertrude Olmstead, Percy Pembroke, Aaron Edwards, Joseph Swickard, Gertrude Claire, Emmet King.

1. The Sea Raiders. 2. Shipwrecked. 3. The Cannibals' Captives. 4. Hidden Gold. 5. Ship of Despair. 6. Friday's Faith. 7. Swamp of Terror. 8. Marooned. 9. The Jaguar Trap. 10. A Prisoner of the Sun. 11. No Greater Love. 12. Island of Happiness. 13. Sword of Courage. 14. The Buccaneers. 15. Jolly Roger. 16. The Idol's Bride. 17. When the Heart Calls. 18. Back to the Primitive.

20. The Adventures of Ruth

(Ruth Roland Serials/Pathé, December 28, 1919) Serial, 15 chapters, two reels each. D: George Marshall and Ruth Roland. SP: Gilson Willets. Song: "Romantic Ruth."

As instructed by her father on his deathbed, Ruth Robin attempts to recover a peacock fan which hides a secret affecting her. She must also carry out the instructions she received on each of 13 keys handed her by an unknown person. Screenwriter Willets had an energetic imagination.

Ruth Roland (Ruth Robin), Herbert Heyes (Bob Wright), Thomas G. Lingham (LaFarge, the Hound), William Human (Paul Brighton), Charles Bennett (Wayman), Helen Case (Countess Zirka), Helen De Liane (Melody Morne), Charles Belcher, George Larkin, Al Hoxie (Double for Miss Roland).

1. The Wrong Countess. 2. The Celestial Maiden. 3. The Bewitching Spy. 4. The Stolen Picture. 5. The Bank Robbery. 6. The Border Fury. 7. The Substitute Messenger. 8. The Harem Model. 9. The Cellar Gangsters. 10. The Forged Check. 11. The Trap 12. The Vault of Terror. 13. Within Hollow Walls. 14. The Fighting Chance. 15. The Key to Victory.

21. The Adventures of Sherlock Holmes

(Stoll Picture Productions, 1921) Series, 15 episodes, two reels each. P/D: Maurice Elvey. S: Sir Arthur Conan Doyle. SP: William J. Elliott.

Episode Titles and Casts • *The Dying Detective* (38 min.) Eille Norwood (Sherlock Holmes), Hubert Willis (Doctor Watson), Madame d'Esterre (Holmes's housekeeper), Cecil Humphreys, J.R. Tozer. • *The Devil's Foot* (42 min.) Eille Norwood (Sherlock Holmes), Hubert Willis (Doctor Watson), Harvey Brabbam, Hugh Buckler. • *A Case of Identity* (43 min.) Eille Norwood (Sherlock Holmes), Hubert Willis (Doctor Watson), Edna Flugrath, Nelson Ramsey Nessie Blackford. • *The Yellow Face* (33 min.) Eille Norwood (Sherlock Holmes), Hubert Willis (Doctor Watson), Clifford Heatherley, Norma Whalley, L. Allen, Master Robey. • *The Red-Headed League* (35 min.) Eille Norwood (Sherlock Holmes), Hubert Willis (Doctor Watson), Arthur Bell (Inspector Lestrade), H. Townsend, Teddy Arundel. • *The Resident Patient* (40 min.) Eille Norwood (Sherlock Holmes), Hubert Willis (Doctor Watson), Arthur Bell (Inspector Lestrade), Madame d'Esterre (Holmes's housekeeper), Beatrice Templeton, Judd Green. • *A Scandal in Bohemia* (35 min.) Eille Norwood (Sherlock Holmes), Hubert Willis (Doctor Watson), Madame d'Esterre (Holmes's housekeeper), Alfred Drayton, Joan Beverley, Miles Mander, Annie Esmond. • *The Man with the Twisted Lip* (40 min.) Eille Norwood (Sherlock Holmes), Hubert Willis (Doctor Watson), Madame d'Esterre (Holmes's Housekeeper), Robert Vallis, Paulette del Baye. • *The Beryl Coronet* (39 min.) Eille Norwood (Sherlock Holmes), Hubert Willis (Doctor Watson), Madame d'Esterre (Holmes's Housekeeper), Jack Selfridge, Lawrence Anderson, Henry Bart, Mollie Adair (Charles Barnett wrote the scenario for this one). • *The Noble Bachelor* (35 min.) Eille Norwood (Sherlock Holmes), Hubert Willis (Doctor Watson), Madame d'Esterre (Holmes's Housekeeper), Temple Bell, Frederick Earle, Cyril Percival, Mr. Arlton, Miss Middleton. • *The Coffee Beeches* (36 min.) Eille Norwood (Sherlock Holmes), Hubert Willis (Doctor Watson), Lyell Johnston, Madge White, Lottie Blackford, Fred Raynham, Eve McCarthy, William J. Elliott, Jr., Bobbie Harwood, Arthur Bell (Inspector Lestrade), C. Nicholls.• *The Empty House* (30 min.) Eille Norwood (Sherlock Holmes), Hubert Willis (Doctor Watson), Arthur Bell (Inspector Lestrade), Sidney Seaward, Austin Fairman, J. Gelardi, Cecil Kerr. • *The Tiger of San Pedro* (34 min.) [from story "Wisteria Lodge"] Eille Norwood (Sherlock Holmes), Hubert Willis (Doctor Watson), Arthur Bell (Inspector Lestrade), George Harrington, Lewis Gilbert, Arthur Walcott, Valia Veritskeya. • *The Priory School* (35 min.) Eille Norwood (Sherlock Holmes), Hubert Willis (Doctor Watson), Madame d'Esterre (Holmes's Housekeeper), Leslie English, C.H. Croker-King, Charles Barnett [credit for scenario], Patrick Kay, Cecil Kerr, Tom Donald, Allen Leamy. • *The Solitary Cyclist* (35 min.) Eille Norwood (Sherlock Holmes), Hubert Willis (Doctor Watson), Madame d'Esterre (Holmes's Housekeeper), Violet Hewitt, R.D. Silvester, Alan Jeayes.

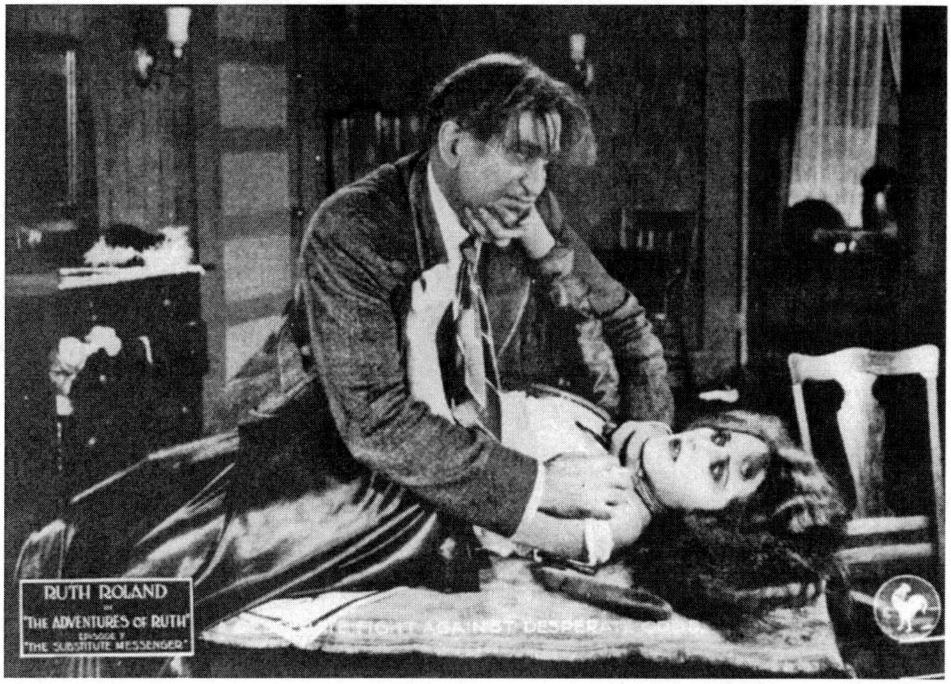

Ruth Roland in *The Adventures of Ruth* (1919)

22. The Adventures of Shorty Hamilton

(Monogram, January 20–April 28, 1917) Series, 17 episodes, two reels each. D: Bob Gray.

Comedy and action in unrelated episodes. Exterior shots at Inceville and interior scenes at the Monogram studio in Boyle Heights. The series premiered at Clune's Comedy Theater in Los Angeles in March 1917 with Shorty riding his horse, "Beauty," down the aisles of the theater to the roar of the audience. There were possibly other titles in this series.

John (Shorty) Hamilton.

1. Shorty and the Yellow Ring. 2. Shorty and the Tiger's Den. 3. Shorty Goes to College. 4. Shorty Joins the Secret Service. 5. Shorty Turns Wild Man. 6. Shorty Promotes His Love Affair. 7. Shorty Hooks a Loan Shark. 8. Shorty Traps a Lottery King. 9. Shorty Trails the Moonshiners. 10. Shorty Bags the Bullion Thieves. 11. Shorty Lands a Master Crook. 12. Shorty Solves a Wireless Mystery. 13. Shorty Reduces the High Cost of Living. 14. Shorty Lays a Jungle Ghost. 15. Shorty Unearths a Tartar. 16. Shorty Goes Insane. 17. Shorty Turns Wildman.

23. Adventures of Sir Galahad

(Columbia, January 1949) Serial, 15 chapters, two reels each. D: Spencer G. Bennet. SP: George H. Plympton, Lewis Clay, and David Mathews. P: Sam Katzman. Assist. D: R.M. Andrews. Photography: Ira H. Morgan. Music: Mischa Bakaleinikoff.

Marjorie Stapp and George Reeves in *Adventures of Sir Galahad* (1949)

Sir Galahad seeks the missing magic sword Excalibur, which makes its possessor invincible, so that he can be admitted to King Arthur's Round Table. Galahad must obtain it from the Saxons, who have invaded England, and is harassed at every turn by Merlin, the magician. The Black Knight, a traitor, is in league with the Saxons and hopes to overthrow King Arthur. Galahad finally obtains the sword of Excalibur from The Lady in the Lake, unmasks the Black Knight, and is seated as a full-fledged knight of the Round Table.

George Reeves (Sir Galahad), Charles King (Bors), William Fawcett (Merlin), Pat Barton (Morgan Le Fay), Hugh Prosser (Sir Lancelot), Lois Hall (The Lady of the Lake), Nelson Leigh (King Arthur), Jim Diehl (Sir Kay), Don Harvey (Bartog), Marjorie Stapp (Queen Guinevere), John Merton (Ulric), Pierce Lyden (Cawker), Rick Vallin (Gawain), Leonard Penn (The Black Knight), Ray Corrigan (One-Eye), Al Ferguson, Rusty Wescoatt.

1. Stolen Sword. 2. Galahad's Daring. 3. Prisoners of Ulric. 4. Attack on Camelot. 5. Galahad to the Rescue. 6. Passage of Peril. 7. Unknown Betrayer. 8. Perilous Adventure. 9. Treacherous Magic. 10. The Sorcerer's Spell. 11. Valley of No Return. 12. Castle Perilous. 13. The Wizard's Vengeance. 14. Quest for the Queen. 15. Galahad's Triumph.

24. Adventures of Smilin' Jack

(Universal, 1943) Serial, 13 chapters, two reels each. D: Ray Taylor and Lew Collins. SP: Morgan B. Cox. Based on newspaper feature by Zach Mosley. Photography: William Sickner.

The island of Mandon before World War II is the scene of a life-and-death espionage struggle. The Chinese and Americans, having secured the friendship of the local natives, confront the evil designs of the Japanese and Germans to dominate the island.

Smilin' Jack is spearheading the Sino-American effort to prevent the Axis takeover of the island. His opponents are formidable. They happily and hastily dispose of fellow agents who are on the verge of divulging more than they should. Fortunately, the Germans and the Japanese soon lose patience with one another and start to bicker. This breakdown in relations allows Jack a little room to maneuver.

With his friends Janet and Tommy, Jack is able to escape rope traps and avoid poison darts thrown by the enemy. He puts an end to German-Japanese machinations on Mandon and brings the local villains to justice.

Tom Brown (Smilin' Jack), Marjorie Lord (Janet), Sidney Toler (General Kai Ling), Edgar Barrier (Tommy), Rose Hobart (Frauline Von Teufel), Turhan Bey (Kageyama), Keye Luke (Captain Wing), Philip Ahn (Wu Tan), David Hoffman (Blinker), Cyril Delevanti (Mah Ling), Jay Novello (Kushimi), Jack Gardner (Yoshudo), Rico de Montez (Rito), Alex Havier (Samson/Samone), Nigel de Brulier (Lo San), Herbert Heyes (Sir Cedric), William Forrest (Secretary), Edward Keane (Hill), Paul Dubov (Native), James Khan (Ran Lal), Louis Vinzinot (Submarine Captain), Wheeler Oakman (First Mate), Edward Peil, Sr. (Freighter Captain), Grace Cunard (German Woman), George Eldredge (Detective), Paul Bryar (Bauer), Norma Drury (Mrs. Bauer), Victor Zimmerman (Markheim), Harry Strang (Sergeant), James Craven (Commissioner), Fred Giermann (Schlesser), Angelo Cruz (Jao), Jack Gardner (Yosnudo), Hans Fuerberg (German Sailor), Ralph Sancuya (Japanese Radio Operator), Jack Smart (Japanese Colonel), Frank Mitchell (Japanese Soldier), don Grusso (Japanese Soldier), Eleanor Soohoo (Woman Servant), Edward Colebrook (Submarine Captain), Tom Ung (Native), Terry Ray (Shuma), Bruce Wong (Oriental), Bert Freeman (Radio Operator/Jap Recorder), Eddie Blumfield (2nd Officer), Victor Wong (Japanese Operator), Charles Sherlock (Detective), Phil Warren (Cop #2), Kernan Cripps (Policeman), Emilio Alegetta (Captain Wu), Jack Santos (Japanese Stooge), Eddie Coke (Naval Pilot/Japanese 1st Officer), Charles Regan (Cop #4), Luke Chan (Farmer), Lee Murray (Native Court Guard/Radio Operator), Tony Javier (Chinese), Mike Gaddis (Native Guard), Tommy Lee (Japanese Guard), David Wengren (Helsman), Frank Marlowe (Driver of Car #5), Spencer Chan (Wireless Operator), Jerry Frank (Native Policeman).

1. The High Road to Doom. 2. The Rising Sun Strikes. 3. Attacked by Bombers. 4. Knives of Vengeance. 5. A Watery Grave. 6. Escape by Clipper. 7. 15 Fathoms Below. 8. Traveling at Sea. 9. The Bridge of Peril. 10. Blackout in the Island. 11. Held for Treason. 12. The Torture Test. 13. Sinking the Rising Sun.

25. The Adventures of Tarzan

(Great Western Producing Co./Numa, 1921) Serial, 15 chapters; Chapter One, three reels; others, two reels. D: Robert F. Hill. Scen: Lillian Valentine, Robert F. Hill. Based on Edgar Rice Burroughs' *Return of Tarzan* and *Tarzan and the Jewels of Opar*. Recut and re-released in 1928 by Weiss Brothers Artclass with sound effects.

Tarzan returns from civilization to his beloved jungle. There are enough wild animals introduced in each chapter to keep audiences on the edge of their seats. Much of the action centered on Tarzan's feud with Queen La of Opar, whose love he spurned, and his efforts to keep the bolshevik Rokoff and Clayton, pretender to Tarzan's title as Lord Greystoke, from reaching Opar.

Gabe Essoe in his book *Tarzan of the Movies* (1968) says *The Adventures of Tarzan* was one of the four most popular films of the year, equal to Rudolph Valentino's *The Four Horsemen of the Apocalypse*, Charlie Chaplin's *The Kid*, and Pola Negri's *Passion*. Hill's crisp direction, as much as Lincoln's fame as "the original Tarzan," was responsible for the serial's unprecedented success.

Elmo Lincoln (Tarzan), Louise Lorraine (Jane), Frank Whitson (Rokoff), George Momberg (Monsieur Gernot), Percy Pembroke (William Clayton), Lillian Worth (La, Queen of Opar), Charles Gay (Sheik Ben Ali), Charles Inslee (Professor Porter), Macer Bruce Sheffield (Chief of Wazini), Byrd Wheeler (The Governor), Frank Merrill (Arab Guard/Double for Lincoln), Joe Martin (An Ape), Regent (a leopard, Himself), Tantor (an elephant, Himself), Numa (a lion, Himself).

1. Jungle Romance. 2. City of Gold. 3. Sun Death. 4. Stalking Death. 5. Flames of Hate. 6. The Ivory Tomb. 7. The Jungle Trap. 8. The Tornado. 9. Fangs of the Lion. 10. The Simoon. 11. The Hidden Foe. 12. Dynamite Trail. 13. The Jungle's Prey. 14. Flaming Arrows. 15. The Last Adventure.

26. Adventures of Texas Jack

(Victor Adamson Productions, 1925) Series, 6 Episodes, two reels each. D: Denver Dixon (?).

These shorts were the only films in which McGaugh appeared billed as Bill Mack. As McGaugh, he was a character actor, usually the heavy, in many silent westerns. He later turned to production as an assistant director, most notably, on the early Tim McCoy Columbia westerns.

Bill Mack (Wilbur McGaugh).

1. The Buckskin Texan. 2. The Battle at Lone Star. 3. The Desert Scout. 4. Wheels of the Pioneers. 5. Frontier Love. 6. Broken Trails.

27. Adventures of the Flying Cadets

(Universal, September 7, 1943) Serial, 13 chapters, two reels each. D: Ray Taylor and Lewis D. Collins. SP: Morgan B. Cox, George H. Plympton, Paul Huston. Assoc. P: Henry MacRae. Photography: William Sickner. Music: H.J. Salter. Song: "Here Come the Air Cadets," by Everett Carter and Milton Rosen.

Danny Collins, Jinx Roberts, Scrapper MacKay, and Zombie Parker are air cadets suspected of a series of murders masterminded by The Black Hangman, a mysterious person pretending to be a Nazi agent. In reality he is Arthur Galt, an engineer who, as a member of an exploring expedition, locates lost helium deposits in Africa. To keep the location a secret, he kills all of the expedition members except Professor Mason and his daughter Andre, whom he imprisons. The cadets, believing Galt to be a friend, fly with him to Africa to try and clear their own names of murder charges. While there he leads them into a Nazi trap. Bombers are sent to bomb the base and Andre, professor Mason, Scrapper, and Zombie make their escape but Danny and Jinx are unable to get away and again become the prisoners of Galt. When Galt proposes that the cadets fly helium to Nazi bases or be killed, they agree. En route plane trouble develops and Danny is just barely able to make a forced landing. The boys overpower Galt and take him to Allied headquarters, but the authorities believe Galt and turn him loose. However, he does not remain free long, as the cadets catch him trying to contact Nazi agents. This time they are believed. The cadets are given their wings and prepare to fly with Allied forces.

Top and Bottom: **Elmo Lincoln in *Adventures of Tarzan* (1921)**

Johnny Downs (Danny Collins), Bobby Jordan (Jinx Roberts), Jennifer Holt (Andre Mason), Ward Wood (Scrapper MacKay), Eduardo Ciannelli (Karl Von Heiger), Billy Benedict (Zombie Parker), Robert Armstrong (Arthur Galt), Regis Toomey (Captain Ralph Carson), Selmer Jackson (Professor Mason), Joan Blair (Frau Klott), Phillip Van Zandt (Herman Klott), Pat Flaherty (Tanner), Charles Trowbridge (Colonel William Elliott), Joseph Crehan (Colonel George Bolton), Leyland Hodgson (Captain Hartley), Addison Richards (Jack Hill), Ian Keith (Colonel Lee), William Forrest (Major Charles Grey), Louis Varco (Ernest), John Merton (Wagner), Louis Adlon (Raum).

1. The Black Hangman Strikes. 2. Menaced by Murderers. 3. Into the Flames. 4. Door to Death. 5. Crashed in a Crater. 6. Rendezvous with Doom. 7. Gestapo Execution. 8. Masters of Treachery. 9. Wings of Destruction. 10. Caught in the Cavern of An-Kar-Ban. 11. Hostages for Treason. 12. The Black Hangman Strikes Again. 13. The Toll of Treason.

28. L'Affaire du Train 24

(France—Pathé, 1921) Serial, 8 chapters. D: Gaston Leprieur. Scen: Andre Bencey and M. Mandement.

Georges Mauloy, Adolphe Candé, Jeanne Brindeau, Gisèle Parcy, Suzanne Talba, Varoquet, Jane Reymond, Stephen Weber, Roux, Eugénie Nau, Mouraud, Norbert.

1. Fautes de jeunesse. 2. L'ombre du passe. 3. Beluchet opére lui-même. 4. A la recherche de l'inconnu. 5. Le rapide de Bordeaux. 6. Contre-enquête. 7. Une lueur dans les ténèbres. 8. Beluchet triomphe.

29. L'Aiglonne

(France, 1921) Serial, Chapters (?) D: Charles Keppens.

Andrew Brunnelle, Emile Drain, Suzy Prim, Andre Marnay, Poggi, Tomy Bourdelle.

30. The Airmail Mystery

(Universal, March 14, 1932) Serial, 12 chapters, two reels each. D: Ray Taylor. SP: Basil Dickey, George Plympton, George Morgan. S: Ella O'Neill. Dialogue: Ella O'Neill.

The Black Hawk plans to steal gold being shipped from a western mine by airmail plane. Pilot Bob Lee and Mary Ross and her brother Jimmy see that the gold gets through.

Lucille Browne (Mary Ross), James Flavin (Bob Lee), Wheeler Oakman (Judson Ward/The Black Hawk), Al Wilson (Jimmy Ross), Nelson McDowell ("Silent" Sims), Frank S. Hagney (Mason), Sidney Bracey (Driscoll), Walter Brennan (Holly), Bruce Mitchell (Captain Grant), Jack Holly (Andy), Cecil Kellogg, Bob Reeves, George Magrill, Al Ferguson.

1. Pirates of the Air. 2. Hovering Death. 3. A Leap for Life. 4. A Fatal Crash. 5. The Hawk Strikes. 6. The Bridge of Destruction. 7. The Hawk's Treachery. 8. Aerial Third Degree. 9. The Attack on the Mine. 10. The Hawk's Lair. 11. The Law Strikes. 12. The Mail Must Go Through.

31. Ali and the Camel

(England—Children's Film Foundation/World Safari Ltd., 1960) Serial, 8 chapters. P: Henry Geddes. D: Henry Geddes. SP: Henry Geddes.

Children's Serial—When Ali's father, a diver, has to go to the hospital, Ali is offered money by a professor involved in a jewel robbery. A camel, who talks only to Ali, persuades Ali to buy him to discover where the jewels are hidden.

Mohamed Rifai (Ali), Hal Mohamed (Father), Alan Rodman (Professor), Abdul Daabub (Inspector), Mohamed Cinema (Big Black), Mike Pirotta (Three-Finger), Maurice Denham (Voice of the Camel).

1. Talk of a Camel. 2. Into the Desert. 3. Sand Storm. 4. The Man with Three Fingers. 5. The Bomb. 6. Danger Ahead. 7. The Frog Man. 8. The Camel Takes a Hand.

James Flavin and Lucille Browne in *The Air Mail Mystery* (1932)

32. Alkali Ike

(Essanay, 1911–1913) Series, 18 episodes, 1 reel each. D: Roy Clements and others.

These short comedies were made at the height of Augustus Carney's career. He made the Universal Ike series in 1914 and retired from the screen in 1915.

Augustus Carney (Alkali Ike), William Todd (Mustang Pete), Fred Church (Coyote Simpson/Rawhide Bill), Victor Potel (Slippery Slim), David Kirkland (Doc Killem), Margaret Joslyn (Betty Brown [6 ep.])

And in 1 or more episodes: Broncho Billy Anderson, Harry Todd, Howard Missimer, Eleanor Blanchard, Lily Branscombe, John Steppling, Mrs. William Todd.

1. Alkali Ike's Auto (May 1911). 2. Alkali Bests Broncho Billy (March 1912). 3. Alkali Ike's Boarding House (April 1912). 4. Alkali Ike's Bride (May 1912). 5. Alkali Ike Plays the Devil (August 1912). 6. Alkali Ike's Pants (September 1912). 7. Alkali Ike Stung (October 1912). 8. Alkali Ike's Close Shave (November 1912). 9. Alkali Ike's Motorcycle (December 1912). 10. Alkali Ike in Jayville (January 1913). 11. Alkali Ike's Homecoming (April 1913). 12. Alkali Ike's Misfortunes (May 1913). 14. Alkali

Ike and the Hypnotist (June 1913). 15. Alkali Ike's Gal (August 1913). 16. Alkali Ike and the Wildman (October 1913). 17. Alkali Ike's Auto (November 1913) (different film to Number 1). 18. Alkali in a Western Kimona (February 1912).

33. The Amazing Quest of Mr. Ernest Bliss

(England—Hepworth Manufacturing Company, 1920) Serial, 5 chapters. D: Henry Edwards. S: E. Phillips Oppenheim.

Henry Edwards (Ernest Bliss), Chrissie White (Frances Clayton), Gerald Ames (Dorrington), Mary Dibley (Kate Brent), Reginald Bach (Jack Brent), Henry Vibart (Sir James Alroyd), Douglas Munro (John Masters), Mary Brough (Gloria Mott), Stanley Turnbull (Willie Mott), Gerald Hillier (Dick Honerton), James Annand (Crawley), Esme Hubbard (Mrs. Heath), James MacWilliams (Clowes), Ernest Milton (Mr. Montague), John R. Allan (Sam Brownley).

1. The Amazing Quest. 2. The Return of Ulysses. 3. A Racing Episode. 4. The Other Mr. Bliss. 5. Sir James Pays.

34. The American Girl

(Kalem, March–August, 1917) Series, 21 episodes minimum, two reels each. D: James W. Horne. S: Frederick R. Bechdolt.

Madge King, her father, her fiancé, and their followers combat western outlawry in unrelated stories. Though not a serial, it approaches the serial classification because of the serial-like thrills and situations making up each episode and the fact that it laid the foundation for later cliffhanger type serials.

Marin Sais (Madge King), Frank Jonasson (Roger King), Edward Hearn (Larry Kerwin), Edward Clisbee, Ronald Bradbury, Knute Ralman, Hart [Jack] Hoxie, Robert E. Bradbury, Grace Johnson (roles varied in each episode).

(Exact order of release is not certain) 1. The Golden Eagle Trail. 2. The Secret of the Lost Valley. 3. The Lost Legion of the Border. 4. The Black Rider of Tasajara. 5. The Phantom Mine. 6. The Fate of Juan Garcia. 7. The Vultures of Skull Mountain. 8. The Tyrant of Chiracahua. 9. The Trapping of Two-Bit Tuttle. 10. The Vanished Line Rider. 11. The Man Hunt at San Remo. 12. The Skeleton Canyon Raid. 13. The Door in the Mountain. 14. Sagebrush Law. 15. The Pot of Gold. 16. The Man from Tiajuana. 17. The Ghost of the Desert. 18. Treasure of Cibola. 19. Hole in the Mountain. 20. False Prophet. 21. The Fighting Heiress.

35. A Andorinha de Aço

(Brazil—Companhia Brazil Cinematográfica) Serial (?) 10 chapters.

Jorge Gauthier, Mlle. Pagliari.

1. A juventude de "Quebra-Ferro." 2. A morte de Rosita. 3. O homem primitivo. 4. O forte de Kerff. 5. O envelope lacrado. 6. O jazigo mysterioso. 7. O despertar do vulcão. 8. O baile das 4 estacãoes. 9. A torre de valdor. 10. Revelacão.

36. Los Arlequines de Seda y Oro

(Spain—Royal Films, 1919) Series, 3 episodes. D: Ricardo de Baños. SP: Amichatis. Photography: Ramón de Baños.

Raquel Meller (Ana, la gitana blanca), Ascensio Rodríguez (Juan de Diós), Luisa Oliván (Marta de Montemar), Asunción Casals (Marquésa de Rosicler), Juana Sanz (Gitana Siracusa), Carlos Beraza ("El Trianero"), Francisco Aguilló (Gitano Alifás), José Marti (Captitan Alvaro de Valdes), Myatis (Bailarina), Mercedes Bayona, Tina Meller, Visitación Lopez, Teresita Vinyals, Ramón Quadreny, Rafael Gomez, José Gomez, Juan Belmonte, Rodolfo Gaona.

1. El nido deshecho. 2. La semilla del fenomeno. 3. La voz de la sangre.

37. Around the World in Eighteen Days

(Universal, January 1, 1923) Serial, 12 chapters, two reels each. D: B. Reeves Eason and Robert F. Hill. SP: George Bronson Howard and Frank Howard Clark. S: Robert Dillon.

Phineas Fogg III is in love with the daughter of the president of an international corporation that manufactures fuel. The president is opposed by the vice-president in his plan to manufacture a cheap synthetic fuel to benefit the poor. A proxy fight results. Phineas, along with Madge, circles the globe in quest of proxies from the firm's scattered stockholders,

William Desmond in *Around the World in Eighteen Days* (1923)

experiencing a multitude of assorted adventures, but arriving back in time to swing the election.

William Desmond (Phineas Fogg III), Laura La Plante (Madge Harlow), William P. DuVall (Jiggs), Wade Boteler (Wallace J. Brenton), William J. Welsh (Matthew Harlow), Percy Challenger (Rand), Hamilton Morse (Smith), Tom S. Guise (Davis), Louis J. O'Connor (Detective), Arthur N. Millett (Detective), Gordon Sackville (White), Alfred Hollingsworth (Phineas' Father), Pat Calhoun (Butler), Spottswoode Aitken (Piggott), Harry T. DeVere (Book Maker), Boyd Irwin (Muriarc), Sydney De Gray (Hyppolyte Darcy), Jean de Briac (Desplayer), Antonio Rolando (Apache Dancer), Celeste Zimlich (Apache Dancer).

1. The Wager. 2. Wanted by the Police. 3. Apaches of Paris. 4. The Man Who Broke the Bank at Monte Carlo. 5. Sands of Doom. 6. The Living Sacrifice. 7. The Dragon's Claws. 8. A Nation's Peril. 9. Trapped in the Clouds. 10. The Brink of Eternity. 11. The Path of Peril. 12. The Last Race.

38. Arsene Lupin Contra Sherlock Holmes

(Germany—Vitascope GmbH, 1910–1911) Series D: Viggo Larsen

Adventures of the famed detective. No connection with the later series filmed in Great Britain.

Viggo Larsen (Sherlock Holmes), Paul Otto (Arsene Lupin).

1. Der Alte Sekretar (The Old Secretaire); in Great Britain: Arsene Lupin; 19 min., 9/20/1910. 2. Der Blaue Diamant (The Blue Diamond) 23 1/2 min., 9/10/1910. 3. Die Falschen Rembrandts (The Fake Rembrandts); in Great Britain: The Two Rembrandts; 16 min., 10/7/1910. 4. Die Flucht (The Escape) 19 min., 12/24/1910. 5. Arsene Lupins ende (The End of Arsene Lupin) 14 1/2 min., 3/4/1911.

39. Arsene Lupin, Utolso Kalandja

(Hungary—Studio Mobil, 1921) Serial, 6 chapters. D: Fejos Pal (Paul Fejos). Scen: Forro Pal. S: Maurice Leblank.

Gusztav Partos, Mara Jankovsfky, Aniko Urmosfy, Lajos Gellert, Odon Bardi, Lajos Gardonyi, Piroshka Szabados, Antal Matany, Pal Zilahy.

40. Atom Man vs. Superman

(Columbia, June 1950) Serial, 15 chapters, two reels each. D: Spencer G. Bennet. SP: George H. Plympton, Joseph F. Poland, David Mathews. Based on Superman adventure appearing in *Superman* and *Action* comics and the *Superman* radio program. P: Sam Katzman. Assis. D: R.M. Andrews. Second Unit D: Derwin Abrahams. Photography: Ira H. Morgan. Music: Mischa Bakaleinikoff.

Arch criminal Luthor invents a machine that can disintegrate people into their basic atoms and reassemble them again at any chosen spot. He also invents synthetic Kryptonite that keeps Superman at bay. Metropolis is threatened and Superman and his friends launch an offensive to bring Luthor to justice. From his secret hideout Luthor pits his scientific genius against the man of steel and for awhile seems to hold all the cards.

Luthor manages to subdue Superman with the synthetic Kryptonite at one point and to send him into outer space. But the man of steel returns with his powers diminished. Luthor plans to wreck Metropolis with his sonic vibrator and then to leave Earth in his spaceship taking Lois Lane along as his prisoner. Superman's strength finally comes back as the effects of the Kryptonite wear off. He flies after Luthor and Lois and crashes through the hull of the ship and returns to Earth with Luthor and Lois. Luthor is imprisoned and Lois fails in an attempt to prove that Clark Kent is Superman.

The film was far more gimmicky and gadget prone than the first serial, *Superman,* but the small budget showed in the cheapness of the production.

Kirk Alyn (Clark Kent/Superman), Noel Neill (Lois Lane), Lyle Talbot (Luthor/Atom Man), Tommy Bond (Jimmy Olsen), Pierre Watkin (Perry White), Jack Ingram (Foster), Don Harvey (Albert), Rusty Wescoatt (Carl), Terry Frost (Baer), Wally West (Dorr), Paul Stader (Killer Lawson), George Robotham (Earl), William Fawcett (Mayor), Stanley Blystone (Man in Street), Fred Kelsey (Police Chief).

1. Superman Flies Again. 2. Atom Man Appears. 3. A Blaze in the Sky. 4. Superman Meets Atom Man. 5. Atom Man Tricks Superman. 6. Atom Man's Challenge. 7. At the Mercy of Atom Man. 8. Into the Empty Room. 9. Superman Crashes Through. 10. Atom Man's Heat Ray. 11. Luthor's Strategy. 12. Atom Man Strikes. 13. Atom Man's Flying Saucer. 14. Rocket of Vengeance. 15. Superman Saves the Universe.

41. El Automóvil Gris (The Gray Automobile)

(Mexico—Azteca Films, 1919) Serial, number of chapters unknown. D: Enrique Rosas and Joaquín Coss. Scen: Miguel Necochea and Enrique Rosas. Based on materials supplied by Mexico City Assistant Chief of Police, Don Juan Manuel Cabrera. P: Enrique Rosas. Photography: Enrique Rosas.

Story concerns the adventures of a band of Mexico City delinquents who have a gray automobile that figures importantly in their escapades. Some of the gang's activities have political implications. The story unfolds during the revolutionary period preceding World War I and is based on actual police records with the scenarists building a story around them. The film was a magnificent testimony of its time.

The film premiered at twenty-eight Mexico City cinemas on December 12, 1919.

Years later a sound remake was done, but it did little to improve on the original film except to keep the remake to feature length and to accentuate the dramatic qualities.

Joaquín Coss, Juan Canaels De Homes, Manuel De Los Rios, Dora Vila, María Mercedes Ferriz, María Teresa Montoya, Don Juan Manuel Cabrera, Calentin Asperó, Miguel Ángel Ferriz, Ernesto Finance, Russo Conde.

42. The Avenging Arrow

(Pathé, January 23, 1921) Serial, 15 chapters, two reels each. D: W.S. Van Dyke and William Bowman. S: Arthur Preston Haskins—"The Honeymoon Quest." SP: Jack Cunningham.

Anita Delgado's female ancestors have all been killed on or shortly after their twenty-first birthday. When Anita reaches twenty-one a mysterious arrow is shot over the wall. Ralph Troy, a neighboring rancher, is attracted to Anita and joins with her to unravel the mystery behind the attempt on her life and the killing of her ancestors. The plot is rather complicated but there was no dearth of action and Roland fans seemed to like it.

Ruth Roland (Anita Delgado), Edward Hearn (Ralph Troy), Virginia Ainsworth (Luiza Traganza), S. E. Jennings (Don Jose Delgado), William Steele (Don Carlos Martinez), Chief Big Tree (Madoo), Frank Lackteen (Pablo), Robert Chandler (the Hermit), Vera Sisson (White Fawn[?]), Otto Lederer.

1. Vow of Mystery. 2. The Enemy Strikes. 3. The Hand of Treachery. 4. A Life in Jeopardy. 5. The Message Stone. 6. The Midnight Attack. 7. The Double Game. 8. The Strange Pact. 9. The Auction Block. 10. Outwitted. 11. Dangerous Waters. 12. House of Treachery. 13. On Perilous Grounds. 14. Shifting Sands. 15. The Toll of the Desert.

43. Les Aventures de Robert Macaire

(France—Société Albatros, 1925) Serial, 5 chapters. D: Jean Epstein. SP: Jean Epstein. S: Charles Vayre. Based on the drama "L'Auberge des Adrets" by Benjamin Antier, Saint-Amand, and Polyanthe.

Jean Angelo (Robert Macaire), Alex Allin (Bertrand), Suzanne Bianchetti (Louise de Sermèze), Lou Dovoyna (Victoire), Jean-Pierre Stock (Vicomte de La Ferté), Marquisette Bosky (Jeanne), Viguier, Bondireff, Mme. Niblia.

44. L'Aviateur Masque

(France—Pathé-Consortium, 1922) Serial, 8 chapters. D: Robert Péguy [Marcel Roberts]. Scen: Charles Vayre and R. Florigny.

Lucien Dalsace, Malou Raino, Victor Vina, Renee Carl, Gabriel Rosca, Georges Frère, Mme. Amazar, Morlas.

French: 1. L'enjeu. 2. Dans les airs. 3. Les ailes brisées. 4. La revanche de Hoffer. 5. Faute de jeunesse. 6. La journée des dupes. 7. Le réveil d'une intelligence. 8. Les ailes d'amour. *Portuguese:* 1. A aposta. 2. Nos ares. 3. As azas quebradas. 4. A desforra de Hoffer. 5. Os pecados da mocidade. 6. Dia dos logros. 7. O despertar da inteligencia. 8. Nas azas do amor.

45. La Baillonée

(France, 1921) Serial, chapters (?) D: Charles Burguet. S: Pierre Decourcelle. SP: Pierre Decourcelle.

Andrée Lionel, Paul Guidé, Louis Leubas, Irène Wells, Jules Mondos, Berthe Jalabert, Jean Dehelly, Camille Bardou.

46. Baluchet, Roi des Detectives

(France, 1920) Serial, chapters (?) D: Gaston Leprieur. Scen: Andre Bencey.

Georges Mauloy, Armand Numes, Suzanne Talba.

47. La Banda delle Cifre

(Italy—Tiber Films, 1915) Serial, 3 chapters. D: Emilio Ghione.

Emilio Ghione was the Italian originator of the serials. He did for Italy what Louis Feuillade did for France. But unlike Feuillade, Ghione was also a star. In this serial, he created and played the character Za La Mort, a French "Apache," who was violent and sentimental. He was a criminal "romantique" loving flowers and paupers alike. He fought against the villains as Grigione the thief. He also created a woman for Za La Mort named Za La Vie, played by Kally Sambucine. The two would play these roles in several more films.

Emilio Ghione (Za La Mort), Kally Sambucine (Za La Vie), Floriana [Diana D'Amore], Alberto Collo.

1. La banda delle cifre. 2. Za La Mort e Za La Vie. 3. L'imboscata.

48. The Bar-C Mystery

(Pathé, April 25, 1926) Serial, 10 chapters, two reels each. D: Robert F. Hill. SP: William Sherwood. S: Raymond Spears—*Janie of the Waning Glories* (Also released as a 5-reel feature).

A New York girl inherits a ranch in the West from a man she does not know. It seems that her benefactor, Nevada, has disappeared into the desert and is presumed dead. When she arrives, a crooked gambler and a dance hall owner try to get control of the ranch because they know there are gold deposits and other minerals on the land. A stranger comes to her rescue and the Bar-C mystery is solved.

Wallace McDonald (Nevada), Dorothy Phillips (Jane Cortelyou), Ethel Clayton (Mrs. Lane), Philo McCullough (Robbins), Johnny Fox (Tommy), Violet Schram (Wanda), Fred de Silva (Crisp), Jacqueline Wells [Julie Bishop], Victor Potel, Fred Kohler, Billie Bletcher, Francis McDonald.

1. A Heritage of Danger. 2. Perilous Paths. 3. The Midnight Raid. 4. Wheels of Doom. 5. Thundering Hoofs. 6. Against Desperate Odds. 7. Back from the Missing. 8. Fight for a Fortune. 9. The Wolf's Cunning. 10. A Six-Gun Wedding.

49. Le Baron Mystère

(France, 1920) Serial, 8 chapters. D: Maurice Chaillot. S: Henri Germain.

Albert Bras, Henri Rollan, Mlle. Margay, Remy, Rene Debray, Mlle. Joutel, Mlle. Delia Col, Pierre Alcover, Marthe Laroque, Scheur.

Portuguese: 1. Fascinacão. 2. Louco. 3. O casal das ruinas. 4. Ponte traiçoeira. 5. A casa misteriosa. 6. O esgrimista mascarado. 7. A gruta das fumaradas. 8. Expiacão.

50. Barrabas

(France, Gaumont, 1920) Serial, 12 chapters. D: Louis Feuillade. S/SP: Louis Feuillade. English Title: Barrabas, the Sinister.

Gaston Michel (Rudolph Strélitz), Fernand Hermann (Jacques Varese), Edouard Mathé (Raoul de Nerac), Georges Biscot (Biscotin), Violette Jyl (Noëlle Maupré), Blanche Montel (Francoise Varese), Jane Rollette (Biscotine), Albert Mayer (Rougler [Joseph d'Albane]), Bréon (Dr. Lucius), Mlle. Lugane (Simone Delpierre), Mlle. Lyne Stanka (Laure d'Herigny), Laurent Morlas (Laugier), Olinda Mano (Odette).

French: 1. La maîtresse du Juif errant. 2. La justice des hommes. 3. La villa des glycines. 4. Le stigmate. 5. Noëlle Maupré. 6. La fille du condamne. 7. Les ailes de Satan. 8. Le manoir mysterieux. 9. L'otage. 10. L'oubliette. 11. Le renevant. 12. Justice. *Portuguese:* 1. A amante do judeu errante. 2. A justiça dos homens. 3. A vila das glicinias. 4. O ferrete. 5. Noelle Maupre. 6. A filha do condenado. 7. As azas de Satanaz. 8. O solar misterioso. 9. O refem. 10. A masmorra. 11. O ressuscitado. 12. A justiça.

51. Batman

(Columbia, July 16, 1943) Serial, 15 chapters, two reels each. D: Lambert Hillyer. SP: Victor McLeod, Leslie Swabacker, and Harry Fraser. Based on the Batman feature in *Detective Comics* and *Batman* magazines. P: Rudolph C. Flothow. Assis. D: Gene Anderson. Music: Lee Zahler. Narration: Knox Manning.

Top: **Lewis Wilson and Douglas Croft;** ***bottom*: Lewis Wilson, Douglas Croft, and J. Carrol Naish in *Batman* (1943)**

Gotham City millionaire Bruce Wayne and his ward Dick Grayson, whose secret identities are Batman and Robin, battle the forces of Dr. Daka, a special agent for Hirohito, Emperor of Japan, here in America to help prepare our country for conquest by the New Order of the Axis. Daka has a ray-gun, kind of a miniature atom smasher. Requiring a small amount of radium to operate, however, the device's range is limited. With more radium, bigger and more powerful radium guns could be built. With such devices the Axis could defeat America and her allies with horrifying ease. With the help of Linda, Wayne's fiancée, Batman and Robin match wits and brawn with the agents of Japan.

Lewis Wilson (Bruce Wayne/Batman), Douglas Croft (Dick Grayson/Robin), J. Carrol Naish (D. Daka), Shirley Patterson (Linda Page), William C. Austin (Alfred), Charles Wilson (Captain Arnold), Charles Middleton (Ken Colton), Robert Fiske (Foster), Gus Glassmire (Martin Warren), Michael Vallon (Preston), John Maxwell (Sam Fletcher), Karl Hackett (Wallace), Ted Oliver (Marshall), George Chesebro (Barnard), Stanley Price (Chauffeur/Henchman), Sam Flint (Dr. Borden), Frank Shannon (Dr. Hayden), Earle Hodgins (Joe, the Barker), I. Stanford Jolley (Brett), Anthony Warde (Stone), George J. Lewis (Burke), Jack Ingram (Klein), Kenne Duncan (Fred, First Mechanic), Lynton Brent (Jim Bramble, Second Mechanic), Terry Frost (Intern), Tom London (Andrews), Dick Curtis (Croft), Lester Dorr (Lawson), Eddie Kane (Bail Bondsman), Bud Osborne (Brown/Zombie), Pat O'Malley (Policeman), Murdock MacQuarrie (Desk Clerk), Mauritz Hugo (Doctor), Jack Gardner.

1. The Electrical Brain. 2. The Bat's Cave. 3. Mark of the Zombies. 4. Slaves of the Rising Sun. 5. The Living Corpse. 6. Poison Peril. 7. The Phony Doctor. 8. Lured by Radium. 9. The Sign of the Sphinx. 10. Flying Spies. 11. A Nipponese Trap. 12. Embers of Evil. 13. 8 Steps Down. 14. The Executioner Strikes. 15. Doom of the Rising Sun.

52. Batman and Robin

(Columbia, June 1949) Serial, 15 chapters, two reels each. D: Spencer G. Bennet. SP: George H. Plympton, Joseph F. Poland, and Royal K. Cole. Based on the *Batman* comic feature appearing in *Detective* comics and *Barman* magazine and created by Bob Kane. P: Sam Katzman. Assis. D: R.M. Andrews. Photography: Ira H. Morgan. Music: Mischa Bakaleinikoff.

An important government project, a remote control machine, is stolen, and police commissioner Gordon calls on Batman and Robin to help him recover it. Vicki Vale, a commercial photographer, becomes involved in the dangerous pursuit. Batman and Robin clash with the hooded figure known as The Wizard, who desires to acquire a powerful explosive known as X-90.

Robert Lowery (Bruce Wayne/Batman), Johnny Duncan (Dick Grayson/Robin), Jane Adams (Vicki Vale), Lyle Talbot (Commissioner Gordon), Ralph Graves (Harrison), Don C. Harvey (Nolan), William Fawcett (Professor Hammil), Leonard Penn (Carter), Rick Vallin (Barry Brown), Michael Whalen (Dunne), Greg McClure (Evans), House Peters, Jr. (Earl), Eric Wilton (Alfred), Jim Diehl (Jason), Marshall Bradford (Roger Morton), Hal Landon (Jimmy Vale), Rusty Wescoatt (Ives).

1. Batman Takes Over. 2. Tunnel of Terror. 3. Robin's Wild Ride. 4. Batman Trapped. 5. Robin Rescues Batman. 6. Target—Robin. 7. The Fatal Blast. 8. Robin Meets the Wizard. 9. The Wizard Strikes Back. 10. Batman's Last Chance. 11. Robin Ruse. 12. Robin Rides the Wind. 13. The Wizard's Challenge. 14. Batman vs. Wizard. 15. Batman Victorious.

53. Battling Brewster

(Rayart, December 1, 1924) Serial, 15 chapters; Chapter One three reels; others, two reels. P/D: Dell Henderson. Supervisor: George Blaisdell. SP: Robert Dillon. Presented by: W. Ray Johnson.

Franklyn Farnum (Jack Brewster) [Farnum was a replacement for Bruce Gordon], Helen Holmes (Margaret Rand), Leon Holmes (Dempsey), Robert Walker (George Wendell), Jerome La Casse (Barbed Wire Ryan), Emily Barrye (Mara), Lafe McKee (Roland Rand).

1. Crashing to Eternity. [English titles unknown; Portuguese titles follow] 2. O alcapao da morte. 3. A emboscada. 4. Uma empreitada de vida e morte. 5. Enterrado vivo. 6. O homem do misterio. 7. A trilha da morte. 8. A fazenda do misterio. 9. A borda de desastre. 10. Acusado de morte. 11. Areias insidiosas. 12. Nas garras da morte. 13. Nas maos do destino. 14. Face a face. 15. Unknown.

54. Battling with Buffalo Bill

(Universal, November 23, 1931) Serial, 12 chapters, two reels each. D: Ray Taylor. SP: George Plympton and Ella O'Neill. P: Henry McRea. S: Henry McRae. Suggested by William F. Cody's *The West That Was.*

Buffalo Bill Cody and young Dave Archer oppose gambler Jim Rodney and his minions, who are out to seize the gold claims in Hard Rock. Rodney incites the Indians to attack the townspeople and also gets himself elected sheriff in a rigged election, but Cody and Archer are able to expose him, destroy his gang, and bring peace to the territory once again. (Tom Tyler replaced Tim McCoy, who was scheduled for this serial.)

Tom Tyler (Buffalo Bill Cody), Rex Bell (Dave Archer), Lucile Browne (Miss Archer), Francis Ford (Jim Rodney), William Desmond (John Mills), Jim Thorpe (Swift Arrow), Yakima Canutt (Jack Brady), Chief Thunder Cloud (Chief Thunderbird), Bud Osborne (Joe Tampas), John Beck (Hiram Podge), George Regas (Breed Johns), Joe Bonomo (Joe Bailey), Bobby Nelson (Ezrah Podge), Edmund Cobb, Fred Humes, Art Mix, Franklyn Farnum.

1. Captured by Redskins. 2. Circling Death. 3. Between Hostile Tribes. 4. The Savage Horde. 5. The Fatal Plunge. 6. Trapped. 7. The Unseen Killer. 8. Sentenced to Death. 9. The Death Trap. 10. A Shot from Ambush. 11. The Flaming Death. 12. Cheyenne Vengeance.

Top: **Robert Lowery and John Duncan in *Batman and Robin* (1949); *bottom:* Franklyn Farnum and Helen Holmes in *Battling Brewster* (1924)**

55. Beasts of Paradise

(Universal, October 1, 1923) Serial, 15 chapters, two reels each. D: William Craft. Scen/S: Val Cleveland.

The hero and heroine are opposed by murderous cutthroats in a treasure search that takes them on a wild sea adventure and into the jungles of Africa.

William Desmond, Eileen Sedwick, William H. Gould, Ruth Royce, Joe Bonomo (Double for Desmond)/Big Jack, Paul Malvern (Double for Sedgwick), Margaret Morris, Alfred

Top: **William Desmond, Rex Bell, and Tom Tyler in *Battling with Buffalo Bill* (1931); *bottom:* William Desmond in *Beasts of Paradise* (1923)**

Fisher, Gordon McGregor, Clark Comstock, Slim Cole, William J. Welsh.

1. The Mystery Ship. 2. The Unseen Peril. 3. The Typhoon. 4. The Sea Raider. 5. The Tidewater Trap. 6. The Alligator Attacks. 7. The Deluge. 8. The Mutiny. 9. Ship Aflame. 10. The Mad Elephant Charge. 11. Smothered in the Sand. 12. Millions in Gold. 13. Into the Bloodhound's Jaws. 14. Into the Whirlpool. 15. The Trail's End.

56. Beatrice Fairfax

(International Film Service, August 7, 1916) Series, 15 episodes, two reels each. D: Philip Van Loan. Scen: Basil Dickey.

At the beginning of each episode, Miss Fairfax, a journalist who conducts an "Advice to the Lovelorn" column for the *New York Journal*, receives a letter from some trusting reader. Behind each letter is an exciting story. In each episode, Jimmy Barton, a gifted reporter capable of assuming many disguises, unravels the story.

Grace Darling (Beatrice Fairfax), Harry Fox (Jimmy Barton), Betty Howe (Jane Hamlin), Nigel Barre (Clayton Boyd), Olive Thomas (Rita Malone), Mae Hopkins (Madeline Grey), Evelyn Fariss (Dorothy Dare), Mary Cranston (Mada Minturn), Robin Townley, Le Roy Baker, Elaine Hammerstein.

1. The Missing Watchman. 2. Adventures of the Jealous Wife. 3. Billie's Romance. 4. The Stone God. 5. Mimosa San. 6. The Forbidden Room. 7. A Name for the Baby. 8. At the Ainsley Ball. 9. Outside the Law. 10. Play Ball. 11. The Wages of Sin. 12. Curiosity. 13. The Ringer. 14. The Hidden Menace. 15. Wrist Watches.

57. The Beloved Adventurer

(Lubin, September 26, 1914) Series, 15 episodes, 1 reel each. D: Arthur V. Johnson. Scen: Emmett Campbell Hall.

A series of adventures, each complete in itself, in which Lord Cecil manipulates people and situations for the betterment of society, finding many a thrill along the way.

Arthur Johnson (Lord Cecil), Lottie Briscoe (Betty), Florence Hackett (Countess Lurovich), Jeanette Hackett (Rose Middlehurst), Howard M. Mitchell (Monte Carson), Ruth Bryan (Mary Harris), J. Robinson Hall (Luco), Ed McLaughlin (James), Josephine Longworth (Elsie Manning), D.E. Bentley (Lord Weston), Robert La Monte (Jimmy Hall), Earl Metcalfe.

1. Lord Cecil Intervenes. 2. An

Untarnished Shield. 3. An Affair of Honor. 4. An American Heiress. 5. The Girl from the West. 6. The Golden Hope. 7. The Hold Up. 8. A Partner to Providence. 9. Lord Cecil Plays a Part. 10. Lord Cecil Keeps His Word. 11. The Serpent Comes to Eden. 12. Fate's Tangled Threads. 13. Through Desperate Hazards. 14. A Perilous Passage. 15. In Port O'Dreams.

58. Belphegor

(France—Pathé–Cinéromans, 1927) Serial, 8 chapters. D: Henri Desfontaines. Scen: Arthur Bernede.

René Navarre (Chantecoq), Elmire Vautier (Simone Desrocnes), Lucien Dalsace (Jacques Bellegarde), Michèle Verly (Colette), Genica Missirio (Maurice de Thouars), Jeanne Brindeau (Elsa Bergen), Alice Tissot, Albert Mayer, Anna Lefeuvrier, Georges Paulais, Camille Bert, C.T. Terrore, Simone Montalet, Henri Volbert, Redelsperger, Emilien Richaud, Bérangère.

59. Bibi-la-Puree

(AKA "The Pedlar.") (France—G.M.G. Productions, 1925 or 1926) Serial. D: Maurice Champreux. SP: Andre Mouezy-Eon and Alex Fontanes.

Georges Biscot (Bibi-La-Puree), Bouboule, Derigal, Lise Jaux, Helene Fax, Henri Charpentier, Andre Morea, Emile Vervit, Louis Vonelly.

Believed to be six chapters.

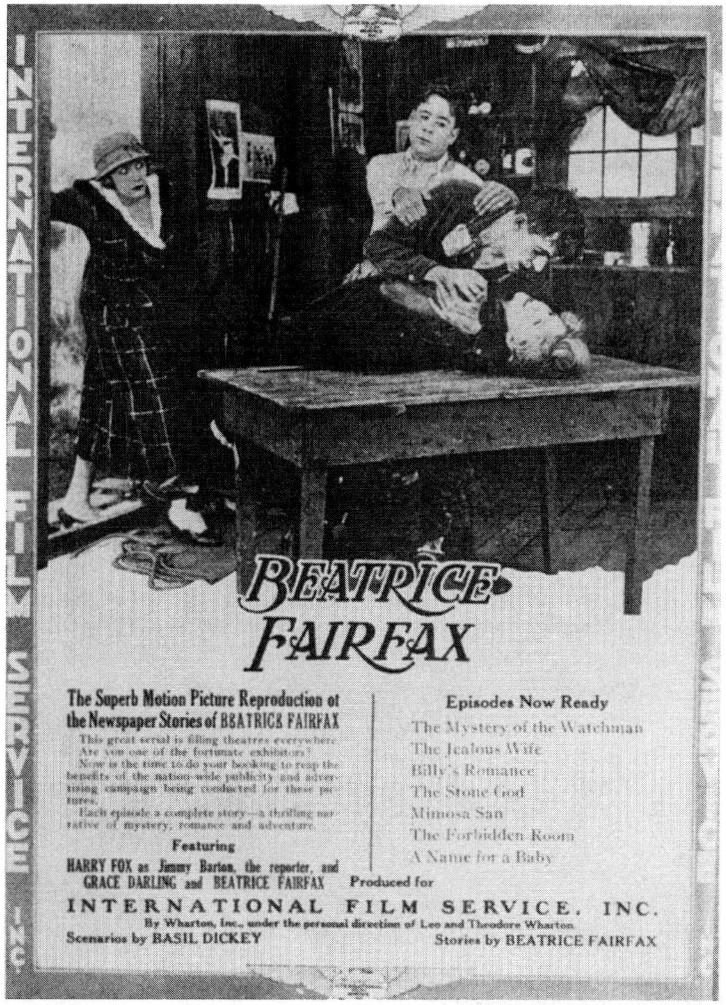

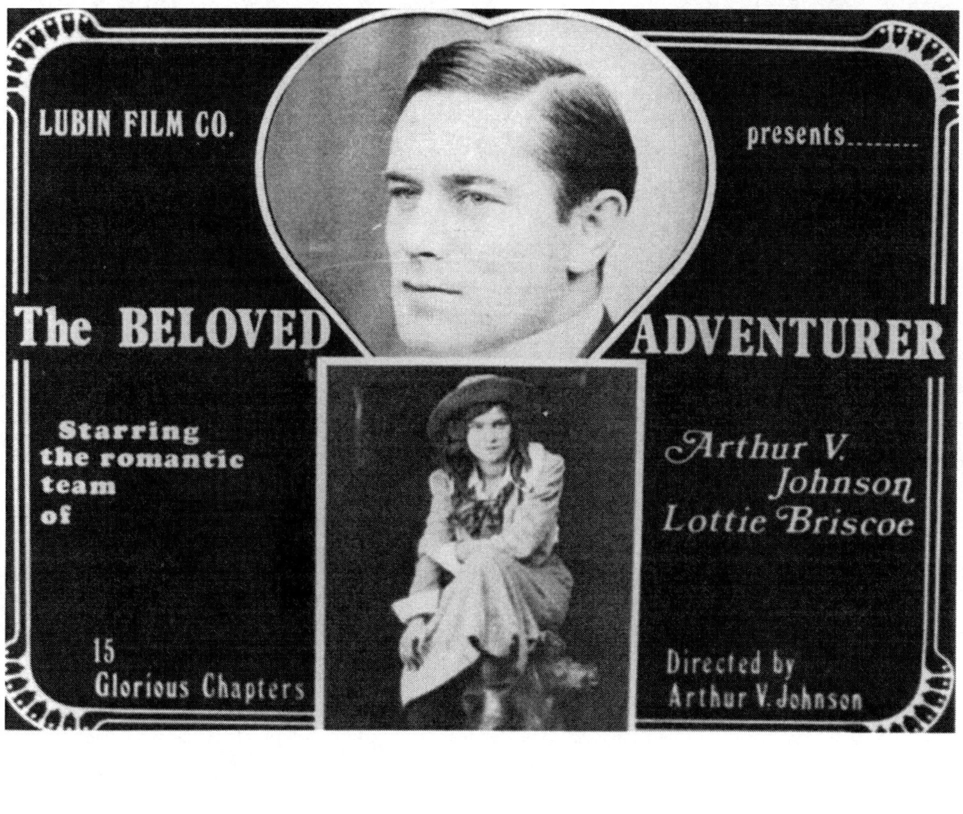

Right: **Harry Fox and Grace Darling in *Beatrice Fairfax* (1916); *below:* Arthur V. Johnson and Lottie Briscoe in *The Beloved Adventurer* (1914)**

60. Bill Grimm's Progress

(R-C/FBO, 1926) Series, 12 episodes, two reels each. D: Ralph Cedar and Arvid E. Gilstrom. S: H.C. Witwer. SP: Beatrice Van.

A series long forgotten, *Bill Grimm's Progress* had a taxi driver as the central figure. Perhaps best remembered of the cast is Jack Luden, who starred in a short series of westerns for Columbia in the thirties. Jack's career went bust and he died in prison for writing hot checks.

Kit Guard, Margaret Morris, Jack Luden.

1. The Lady of Lyons (8-15-26). 2. The Fight that Failed (8-29-26). 3. Where There's a Bill (9-12-26). 4. The Last of His Face (9-26-26). 5. When a Man's a Fan (10-10-26). 6. The Midnight Son (10-24-26). 7. Bruisers and Losers (11-7-26). 8. Little Miss Bluffit (11-21-26). 9. Ladies Prefer Brunettes (12-5-26). 10. Assorted Nuts (12-19-26). 11. Blisters Under the Skin (1-2-27). 12. The Knight Before Christmas (1-16-27).

61. Black Arrow

(Columbia, October 20, 1944) Serial, 15 chapters, two reels each. D: Lew Landers.

Top: **Robert Scott, Adele Jergens, Charles Middleton, and Martin Garralaga in** ***Black Arrow*** **(1944);** ***bottom:*** **Walter Miller** ***(center)*** **in** ***The Black Book*** **(1929)**

SP: Sherman Lowe, Jack Stanley, Leighton Brill, and Royal K. Cole. P: Rudolph C. Flothow. Assis. D: Maurie Suess. Photography: Richard Fryer. Music: Lee Zahler.

Two carpetbaggers in search of gold stir up trouble on the Navajo reservation when they secretly kill the chief. Black Arrow, son of the chief, driven off the reservation when he refuses to avenge the murder, is determined to find who actually killed the chief. In the end he is successful and also discovers that he is the long lost son of the Indian agent rather than the son of the chief.

Robert Scott [Mark Roberts] (Black Arrow), Adele Jergens (Mary), Kenneth MacDonald (Jack Jackson), Robert Williams (Buck Sherman), Charles Middleton (Tom Whitney), Martin Garralaga (Pancho), George J. Lewis (Snake-that-Walks), I. Stanford Jolley (Tobie West), Nick Thompson (Atalan), George Navarro (Running Water), Harry Harvey (Marshal Hayes), John Laurenz (Oso), Dan White (Brent), Eddie Parker (Hank), Stanley Price (Wade), Ted Mapes (Bill), Davison Clark (Thompson), Brooks Benedict (Bronson), Elmo Lincoln (Arano), Chief Thunder Cloud, John Elliott, Bud Osborne, Charles King, Kit Guard, Forrest Taylor, Iron Eyes Cody.

1. A City of Gold. 2. Signal of Fear. 3. The Seal of Doom. 4. Terror of the Badlands. 5. The Secret of the Vault. 6. Appointment with Death. 7. The Chamber of Horror. 8. The Vanishing Dagger. 9. Escape from Death. 10. The Gold Cache. 11. The Curse of the Killer. 12. Test by Torture. 13. The Sign of Evil. 14. An Indian's Revenge. 15. Black Arrow Triumphs.

62. The Black Book

(Pathé, July 21, 1929) Serial, 10 chapters, two reels each. D: Spencer G. Bennet. Co-D: Tom Storey. S: Joseph Anthony Roach. Assis. D: Ralph Hogue and Charles Stevens. Photography: Edward Snyder. Film Editor: Joe Kane.

A pretty young girl detective and a one time wastrel who becomes her adoring suitor pit their wits against a criminal coterie. The intrigue and mystery center around two black books containing information related to a rich platinum deposit.

This was Pathé's last serial and the last made by the Ray-Miller team.

Allene Ray (Dora Drake), Walter Miller (Ted Bradley), Frank Lackteen (Valdez), Edith London (Mrs. Valdez), Willie Fung (Tin Lung), Marie Mosquini (Sally), Edward Cecil (Limpy Lambert), John Webb Dillon (LeBec), Paul Panzer (The Hawk), Fred Malatesta (Sudro), Floyd Adams (Michael), Olga Vanna (The Maid), Jock Fraser (Crook), Clay de Roy (Crook), Evan Pearson (Crook).

1. The Secret of the Vault. 2. The Death Rail. 3. A Shot in the Night. 4. The Dagger Sign. 5. The Flaming Trap. 6. The Black Dam. 7. The Fatal Hour. 8. The Mystery Mill. 9. The Assassin Strikes. 10. Out of the Shadows.

63. The Black Box

(Universal, March 14, 1919) Serial, 15 chapters, two reels each. D/Scen: Otis Turner. S: E. Phillips Oppenheim.

Criminologist Sanford Quest dazzles his adversaries with all kinds of scientific wizardry, e.g. an elaborate electric mind-reading device, as he seeks to unravel the mystery of the black box. Actually a prototype for the James Bond films of half a century later, this Feuillade-type serial proved to be highly entertaining for 1915 audiences and a financial winner for the studio. The plot involves an ape-like creature and a suit that renders its wearer invisible.

Herbert Rawlinson (Sanford Quest), Anna Little (Lenora MacDougal), Laura Oakley (Laura, Quest's Assistant), William Worthington (Professor Ashleigh/Lord Ashleigh), Helen Wright (Lady Ashleigh), Beatrice Van (Lord Ashleigh's Daughter), Frank Lloyd (Ian MacDougal), Frank MacQuarrie (John Craig), Mark Fenton (Inspector French), Hylda Sloman (Mrs. Bruce Rheinholdt), J. Edwin Brown, Dorothy Brown, Duke Worne, Harry Tenbrook, Lionel Bradshaw, Osborne Chase.

1. An Apartment House Case. 2. The Hidden Hands. 3. The Pocket Wireless. 4. An Old Grudge. 5. On the Rack. 6. The Unseen Terror. 7. The House of Mystery. 8. The Inherited Sin. 9. Lost in London. 10. The Ship of Horror. 11. A Desert Vengeance. 12. 'Neath Iron Wheels. 13. Tongues of Flame. 14. A Bolt from the Blue. 15. The Black Box.

64. The Black Coin

(Stage and Screen, 1936) Serial, 15 chapters, two reels each. D: Albert Herman. S: George M. Marrick. SP: Eddy Graneman, Dallas M. Fitzgerald, Bob Lively, and Albert Herman. Supervision: Louis Weiss. Photography: James Diamond. Music: Lee Zahler. P: Weiss Productions.

The Caswell Shipping Company is being used by smugglers. Terry Navarro, an agent of the company, has papers which will unmask the actual criminals headed by The Clutching Hand. Quite aside from the smuggling operation is the matter of buried gold, the location of which is revealed by a map created by assembling twelve black coins. Secret Service agents Walter Prescott and Dorothy Dale enter the case and a complicated series of double-crosses and hair-raising thrills ensue before justice prevails.

Ralph Graves (Walter Prescott), Ruth

Top: **Herbert Rawlinson and Ann Little in *The Black Box* (1915); *right:* Dave O'Brien in *The Black Coin* (1936)**

Mix (Dorothy Dale), Dave O'Brien (Terry Navarro), Constance Bergen (Virginia Caswell), Mathew Betz (Jensen), Robert Frazer (Hacket), Snub Pollard (Vic Moran), Robert Walker (Shark Malone), Bryant Washburn (Caswell), Clara Kimball Young (Donna Louise), Josef Swickard (Don Pedro), Blackie Whiteford (McGuire), Yakima Canutt (Ed McMahon), Lane Chandler (Sir Philip), Jackie Miller (Bobbie), Pete de Grasse (Ali Ben Aba), Roger Williams (Gleason), Walter Taylor (Herb), Richard Cramer (Hank), Joe Garcia (Ozzie), Juan Duval (Juan), Lew Mehan (Ortego), Carter Wayne (Anderson), William Desmond (Bartender), Milburn Morante (Slim), Carl Mathews (Spotty).

1. Dangerous Men. 2. The Mystery Ship. 3. The Fatal Plunge. 4. Monster of the Deep. 5. Wolves of the Night. 6. Shark's Fang. 7. Midnight Menace. 8. Flames of Death. 9. Smuggler's Lair. 10. Flaming Guns. 11. Wheels of Death. 12. The Crash. 13. Danger Ahead. 14. Hidden Peril. 15. The Phantom Treasure.

65. The Black Secret

(Pathé, November 9, 1919) Serial, 15 chapters; Chapter one, three reels; others, two reels. D: George B. Seitz. Scen: Bertram Millhauser. S: Robert W. Chambers—*In Secret.*

Evelyn Ereth is an American girl attached to United States Secret Service and suspects her chief of being in sympathy with the enemy, a gang of organized and desperate adversaries determined to gain possession of a great secret. This secret is apparently in the keeping of a drunken young man whom Evelyn has to save from drinking himself to death.

Pearl White (Evelyn Ereth), Walter McGrail (Ray McKay), Wallace McCutcheon (Frederick), George B. Seitz, Henry Gsell, Marjorie Milton, Harry Semels.

1. The Great Secret. 2. Marked for Death. 3. The Gas Chamber. 4. Below the Water Line. 5. The Acid Bath. 6. The Unknown. 7. The Betrayal. 8. A Crippled Hand. 9. Webs of Deceit. 10. The Inn of Dread. 11. The Death Studio. 12. The Chance Trail. 13. Wings of Mystery. 14. The Hidden Way. 15. The Secret Host.

66. The Black Widow

(Republic, June 1947) Serial, 13 chapters, two reels each. D: Spencer Bennet and Fred C. Brannon. SP: Franklyn Adreon, Basil Dickey, Jesse Duffy, and Sol Shor. Asso. P: Mike Frankovich. Photography: John MacBurnie. Music: Mort Glickman. Special Effects: Howard and

Left: **Pearl White in *The Black Secret* (1919); *right:* Carol Forman in *The Black Widow* (1952)**

Theodore Lydecker. (Feature title: *Sombra, The Spider Woman*).

Steve Colt, author-criminologist, is hired by the *Daily Clarion* to solve a series of poison killings known as The Black Widow Murders. Masterminding the criminal element is Sombra, daughter of an Asian ruler who wants atomic secrets.

Carol Forman (Sombra), Bruce Edwards (Steve Colt), Virginia Lindley (Joyce Winters), Anthony Warde (Nick Ward), Ramsay Ames (Ruth Dayton), I. Stanford Jolley (Z.V. Jaffa), Virginia Carroll (Ann Curry), Theodore Gottlieh (Hitomu), Gene Stutenroth (John M. Walker), Sam Flint (Henry Weston), Tom Steele (Jack/Blair/Bard), Dale Van Sickel (Smith/Hodges/Bass/Bill), Peggy Wynne (Nurse MacIntyre), LeRoy Mason (Dr. Godfrey), Maxine Doyle (Fortune Teller), Frank Lackteen (A. Kabob), George Douglas (Harris), Gil Perkins (Burke), George Chesebro (J. Carter), Bob Reeves (Detective), Jack O'Shea (Finnegan), Ernie Adams (Blinky), Forrest Taylor (Bradley), Keith Richards (Michael Burns), Hal Landon (Andy Baldwin), Robert Wilkie (Jailer/Cab Driver), Bud Wolfe (Guard), Stanley Price (Fillmore Hagain), Larry Steers (Harcourt), Frank White (Lee), Laura Stevens (Trixie), Carey Loftin (Spike), Robert Barron (Link), John Phillips (Mark), Ken Terrell (Mendoza), Duke Green (Ted Mills), Bill Bailey (Morgue Attendant), Charles Sullivan (Officer), Dave Anderson (Porter), Jerry Jerome (Reporter), Richard Gordon (Reporter), Ted Mapes (Slade), Arvon Dale (Triangulator), John Alban (Triangulator).

1. Deadly Prophecy. 2. The Stolen Formula. 3. Hidden Death. 4. Peril in the Sky. 5. The Spider's Lair. 6. The Glass Guillotine. 7. Wheels of Death. 8. False Information. 9. The Spider's Venom. 10. The Stolen Corpse. 11. Death Dials a Number. 12. The Talking Mirror. 13. A Life for a Life.

Kirk Alyn, Carol Forman, Terry Frost, and John Crawford in *Blackhawk* (1952)

67. Blackhawk

(Columbia, July 1952) Serial, 15 chapters, two reels each. D: Spencer G. Bennet and Fred F. Sears. SP: George H. Plympton, Royal E. Cole and Sherman L. Lowe. Based on *Blackhawk* comic magazine created by Reed Crandell. P: Sam Katzman. Photography: William Whitley. Assis. D: Charles S. Gould. Music: Mischa Bakaleinikoff. Special Effects: Jack Erickson.

Blackhawk is the leader of an international brotherhood sworn to combat the forces of tyranny throughout the world. Foreign agent Laska, working for an unidentified boss known only as The Leader, plants one of her men in the organization and manages to steal a deadly electronic ray. Blackhawk battles spies and saboteurs until finally Laska is trapped in the secret office of The Leader. She is denouncing him for his efforts to destroy her as the Blackhawks enter the room. Laska kills The Leader, a double for Defense Council member Case, but is herself captured.

Kirk Alyn (Blackhawk), Carol Forman (Laska), John Crawford (Chuck), Michael Fox (William Case/The Leader), Don C. Harvey (Olaf), Rick Vallin (Stanislaus/Boris), Larry Stewart (Andre), Weaver Levy (Chop Chop), Zon Murray (Bork), Nick Stuart (Cress), Marshall Reed (Aller), Pierce Lyden (Dyke), William Fawcett (Dr. Ralph), Rory Mallinson (Hodge), Frank Ellis (Hendrickson), Terry Frost (The Leader's Aide), Jack Mulhall (Defense Council Member), Frank Gerstle (Defense Council Member), Dave Shape (Gunman).

1. Distress Call from Space. 2. Blackhawk Traps a Traitor. 3. In the Enemy's Hideout. 4. The Iron Monster. 5. Human Targets. 6. Blackhawk's Leap for Life. 7. Mystery Fuel. 8. Blasted from the Sky. 9. Blackhawk Tempts Fate. 10. Chase for Element X. 11. Forced Down. 12. Drums of Doom. 13. Blackhawk's Daring Plan. 14. Blackhawk's Wild Ride. 15. The Leader Unmasked.

68. Blake of Scotland Yard

(Universal, August 15, 1927) Serial, 12 chapters, two reels each. D: Robert F. Hill. S: Robert F. Hill and William Lord Wright. SP: William Lord Wright.

One of Universal's more profitable and popular serials. Made for $100,000, it grossed $3.5 million worldwide and led to a sequel in 1929.

The nefarious Spider is deadly serious about acquiring Lord Blanton's secret formula for manufacturing gold from common metals. Lady Diana persuades Angus Blake, formerly of Scotland yard, to capture the criminal. At the most opportune moments, a mysterious woman in white also lends a helping hand, then vanishes.

Hayden Stevenson (Angus Blake), Gloria Grey (Lady Diana Blanton), Herbert Prior (Lord Blanton), Monte Montague (Jarvis), Wilbur Mack (Albert Drexel), Albert Hart (The

Ralph Byrd in *Blake of Scotland Yard* (1937)

Spider), Grace Cunard (The Lady in White), Walter Brennan, Jack Kennedy, George Burton (Henchmen).

1. The Castle of Fear. 2. The Spider's Web. 3. The Vanishing Heiress. 4. The Room Without a Door. 5. Shots in the Dark. 6. Ambushed. 7. The Secret of the Coin. 8. Into the Web. 9. The Baited Trap. 10. The Lady in White. 11. The Closing Web. 12. The Final Reckoning.

69. Blake of Scotland Yard

(Victory, 1937) Serial, 15 chapters, two reels each. D: Bob Hill. SP: Basil Dickey and William Buchanan. S: Rock Hawkey. Supervision: Robert Stillman. Photography: Bill Hyer. P: Sam Katzman.

A foreign munitions maker offers a small fortune to a mysterious hooded criminal known as The Scorpion, who wears a claw-like apparatus on his right hand. In return, The Scorpion must steal a death-ray machine invented by Jerry Sheehan and Hope Mason, niece of Sir James Blake, formerly an inspector with Scotland Yard. Blake has invested heavily in the machine. A struggle for possession of the powerful weapon ensues. This serial was also released in feature form.

Ralph Byrd (Jerry Sheehan), Herbert Rawlinson (Sir James Blake), Joan Barclay (Hope Mason), Lloyd Hughes (Dr. Marshall), Dickie Jones (Bobby Mason), Nick Stuart (Julot), Lucille Lund (Duchess), Sam Flint (Henderson), Gail Newbury (Mimi), Jimmy Aubrey (Baron Polinka), Theodore Lorch (Daggett), George DeNormand (Pedro), Bob Terry (Peyton), William Farrell (Count Basil), Frank Wayne (Charles), Dick Curtis (Nicky), Herman Brix [Bruce Bennett] (Adolph), Herb Hollomb, John Elliott, Eric Mayne.

1. The Mystery of the Blooming Gardenia. 2. Death in the Laboratory. 3. Cleared Mysteries. 4. Mystery of the Silver Fox. 5. Death in the River. 6. The Criminal Shadow. 7. Face to Face. 8. The Fatal Trap. 9. Parisian House Tops. 10. Battle Royal. 11. The Burning Fuse. 12. The Roofs of Limehouse. 13. Sting of the Scorpion. 14. The Scorpion Unmasked. 5. The Trap is Sprung.

70. Blazing the Overland Trail

(Columbia, August 4, 1956) Serial, 15 chapters, two reels each. D: Spencer G. Bennet. Assis. D: Gene Anderson, Jr. SP: George H. Plympton. P: Sam Katzman. Photography: Ira H. Morgan. Music: Mischa Bakaleinikoff.

A greedy rancher turned outlaw organizes a gang which attacks and robs settlers coming into the territory. An army scout and an agent of the Pony Express, battling for law and order, emerge victorious. This was the last American Serial.

Lee Roberts (Tom Bridger), Dennis Moore (Ed Marr), Norma Brooks (Lola Martin), Gregg Barton (Captain Carter), Don C. Harvey (Rance Devlin), Lee Morgan (Alby), Pierce Lyden (Bragg), Ed Coch (Carl), Reed Howes (Dunn), Kermit Maynard (Al), Pete Kellett (Pete), Al Ferguson (Fergie), Frank Lackteen (Brave Eagle), Bud Osborne (Bart), Harry Tenbrook, Jack O'Shea, Ray Jones.

1. Gun Emperor of the West. 2. Riding the Danger Trail. 3. The Black Raiders. 4. Into the Flames. 5. Trapped in a Runaway Wagon. 6. Rifles for Redskins. 7. Midnight Attack. 8. Blast at Gunstock Pass. 9. War at the Wagon Camp. 10. Buffalo Stampede. 11. Into the Fiery Blast. 12. Cave-In. 13. Bugle Call. 14. Blazing Peril. 15. Raiders Unmasked.

71. The Blue Fox

(Arrow, May 1921) Serial, 15 chapters, two reels each. D: Duke Worne. SP: Hope Loring and Joe Brandt. S: Hope Loring.

When a white man marries an Eskimo Indian maiden, he is killed by her tribe and the wife dies of grief, leaving behind a baby girl that is taken to the States and raised. Reaching the age of eighteen, the girl returns to the north country intending to wreak vengeance on those who had mistreated her parents. She discovers a blue fox skin that gives the location of a valuable mine, but subsequently it becomes torn into separate pieces. Various forces struggle to obtain them.

Ann Little (Ann Calvin), J. Morris Foster (John Densmore), Joseph W. Girard (Hawk Baxter), Charles Mason (Robert Winslow), William La Rocke (Tarka), Long Seefeld, Fred L. Wilson, Hope Loring.

1. Message of Hate. 2. Menace from the Sky. 3. Mysterious Prisoner. 4. A Perilous Ride. 5. A Woman's Wit. 6. A Night of Terror. 7. Washed Ashore. 8. A Perilous Leap. 9. Lost Identity. 10. In Close Pursuit. 11. The Wilds of Alaska. 12. The Camp of the Charkas. 13. The Secret Skull.

14. The Desert Island. 15. Home and Happiness.

72. O Botão de Fogo

(France—Studio–Film De Franca) Serial, 10 chapters.

Jose Ardevol (campeão de Lucia Romana), Anita Stephenson (Valente Campina, a rival de Marie Valcamp), Marco Fox (o detetive de faro incansável).

1. Ordens secretas. 2. Charito a miserável. 3. Amor e fanatismo. 4. Condemnado a morte. 5. Em poder do inimigo. 6. O castello de Irving. 7. Poder de uma seita. 8. Ferido de morte. 9. A lucta pela liberdade. 10. A justiça.

Ann Little in *The Blue Fox* (1921)

73. Le Bouif Errant

(France—M. Vandal and Ch.Delac, 1926) Series, 3 episodes. D: Rene Hervil. S: G. De La Fouchardiere and F. Celval.

Tramel (Bicard dit "Le Bouif"), Albert Prejean (La Prince Ladislas), Malavier (Le Professeur Galigari), Jim Gerald (Le Comte Bossouzoff), Janine Merrey (La Princesse Mitzy), Frederique (Settel Kildy).

1. La momie récalcitrante. 2. Alfre Ier Plus que Bicard … et moins que Louis XIV. 3. Roi ne puis, prince ne daigne, le Bouif je suis.

74. Bound and Gagged

(Pathé, October 26, 1919) Serial, 10 chapters, two reels each. D: George B. Seitz. SP/S: Frank Leon Smith.

This is a comedy melodrama designed as a spoof on serials. It was also a light love story.

Marguerite Courtot (Princess Istra), George B. Sietz (Archibald A. Barlow), Nellie Burt (Margaret Hunter), Harry Semels (Don Esteban Carnero), Frank Redman (Roger Kipley [the villain]), John Reinhard (Oscar Ben Glade), Tom Goodwin (Willard Hunter), Joe Cuny (Barcelona Ben), Harry Stone, Bert Starke.

1. The Wager. 2. Overboard, 3. Help, Help. 4. An Unwilling Princess. 5. Held for Ransom. 6. Out Again, In Again. 7. The Fatal Error. 8. Arrested. 9. A Harmless Princess. 10. Hopley Takes the Liberty.

75. Boy Scouts! Be Prepared

(England—Translantic, 1917) Serial, 7 chapters, two reels each. Released in U.S.A. as *Boy Scouts to the Rescue* with number of chapters condensed to five and chapter titles changed. D: Percy Nash. SP: Bannister Merwin.

Eric Grey catches Jack Blake poaching a rabbit on his family estate. They become friends when Eric learns that Jack is hunting to feed his sick mother. Later the two trail Gypsy Don, a nomad who steals a horse from Eric's sister. They are captured and imprisoned in a deserted house. Sir Robert Baden-Powell, nearby with boy scouts, sees their signal and sends the scouts to release them. Eric and Jack join the troop.

Gypsy Don is captured and is sent to prison, from which he escapes. He seeks revenge on the boys. Later when war is declared, he is enlisted by a band of enemy spies. The scouts are assigned to patrol the coast, and while thus engaged manage to rescue survivors of a torpedoed ship. The scouts discover that Gypsy Don is supplying an enemy submarine with gasoline and aiding in the destruction of allied ships with explosives. They summon the police and close in on the spies' headquarters. Although Gypsy Don flees, he falls to his death from a roof when his enemies catch up to him.

Eric Stuart (Eric Grey), Derek Boddey (Jack Blake), Edward O'Neill (Gypsy Don), Madge Tree (Mother), Sir Robert Baden-Powell (Himself).

1. The Scout Instinct. 2. The Chief's Prophecy. 3. At Bay. 4. Friends in Need. 5. Their Enemy. 6. A Desperate Revenge. 7. The Admiralty's Call.

76. Boy Scouts to the Rescue

(Universal, 1918) Serial, 5 chapters, two reels each. This serial was edited from the seven chapter English serial *Boy Scouts Be Prepared*. D: Percy Nash. SP: Bannister Merwin.

A squire's son and a miner's son join scouts and foil a gypsy spy ring supplying petrol to German U-boats.

Eric Stuart (Buster Grey), Derek Boddey (Skinny Blake), Edward O'Neill (Gypsy), Madge Tree (Mother), Sir Robert Baden-Powell (Himself).

1. Aids of the Nation. 2. On the Trail. 3. The Great Mine Disaster. 4. The Spies' Nest. 5. Treachery at Sea.

77. The Branded Four

(Select, September 1920) Serial, 15 chapters, two reels each. D: Duke Worne. Scen: Hope Loring and George W. Pyper. S: Hope Loring and George W. Pyper. Supervision: Ben Wilson.

Four babies are branded at birth with mysterious marks which would appear visible when they had reached maturity. The marks, when decoded by use of Dr. Scragg's diary, would reveal the hiding place of gold which the four were to inherit. Scragg's lawyer covets the gold and attempts to secure the diary and Marion Leonard, one of the four who had just turned 21. Criminologist A.B.C. Drake steps in to uncover the secret behind the branding and to put his own brand on Marion.

Ben Wilson (A.B.C. Drake), Neva Gerber (Marion Leonard), Joseph Girard, William Dyer, Ashton Dearholt, William Carroll, Pansy Porter.

1. A Strange Legacy. 2. The Devil's Trap. 3. Flames of Revenge. 4. The Blade of Death. 5. Fate's Pawn. 6. The Hidden Cave. 7. Shanghaied. 8. Mutiny. 9. The House of Doom. 10. The Ray of Destruction. 11. Buried Alive. 12. Lost to the World. 13. The Valley of Death. 14. From the Sky. 15. Sands of Torment.

78. The Brass Bullet

(Universal, August 10, 1918) Serial, 18 chapters, two reels each. D: Ben Wilson. Scen: Walter Woods. S: Frank R. Adams—"Pleasure Island." P: Ben Wilson. Remade by Universal in 1928 as *Haunted Island*.

Rosalind Joy is the heiress to a hidden gold cache and is threatened by her uncle, Spring Gilbert, who would like to acquire the gold hidden on Pleasure Island for himself. Playwright Jack James becomes Rosalind's protector, while also trying to clear up the problem of his escape from a sanitarium to which he was mistakenly committed.

Juanita Hansen (Rosalind Joy), Jack Mulhall (Jack James), Joseph W. Girard (Spring Gilbert), Helen Wright (Mrs. Strong), Charles Hill Mailes (Homer Joy), Halam Cooley (The Mystery Man), Ashton Dearholt (Victor King), Charles Force (A Minister), Harry Dunkinson.

Wallace MacDonald and Carmel Myers in *Breaking Through* (1921)

1. A Flying Start. 2. The Muffled Man. 3. The Mysterious Murder. 4. Smoked Out. 5. The Mock Bride. 6. A Dangerous Honeymoon. 7. Pleasure Island. 8. The Magnetic Bug. 9. The Room of Flame. 10. A New Peril. 11. Evil Waters. 12. Caught by Wireless. 13. $500 Reward. 14. On Trail for His Life. 15. In the Shadow. 16. The Noose. 17. The Avenger. 18. The Amazing Confession.

79. Breaking Through

(Vitagraph, September 25, 1921) Serial, 15 chapters, two reels each. D: Robert Ensminger. Scen: C. Graham Baker. S: C. Graham Baker.

A young engineer helps a pretty young girl build a railroad track from a mine in the interior of Alaska to the coast, which she must do to retain title to her property. Members of a gang who wish her to lose the property oppose the track laying every way they can.

Carmel Myers (Bettina Lowden), Wallace MacDonald (Willard Ward), Vincent Howard (Bull Moakley), Walter Rodgers (Peter Martin), George Stanley (Harry Birkland), James Butler (Carter Birkland), Charles Dudley (Blevins), Martha Mattox, William McCall.

80. Brenda Starr, Reporter

(Columbia, February 1945) Serial, 13 chapters, two reels each. D: William W. Fox. SP: Ande Lamb and George H. Plympton. Based on the comic strip feature *Brenda Starr, Reporter* created by Dale Messick. P: Sam Katzman. Assis. D: Mel DeLay. Photography: Ira H. Morgan. Music: Edward Kay.

A gang of hoodlums believe that reporter Brenda Starr knows where a quarter of a million dollar payroll is hidden. She doesn't. A dying hoodlum has given her a coded message, which she is unable to decode. The gang makes repeated efforts to force Brenda to talk but with the aid of police lieutenant Larry Farrell she is able to resist until the gang is captured, the message decoded, and the money found.

Joan Woodbury (Brenda Starr), Kane Richmond (Lt. Larry Farrell), Syd Saylor (Chuck Allen), Joe Devlin (Tim), George Meeker (Frank Smith), Wheeler Oakman (Lew Heller/Joe Heller), Kay Forester (Vera Harvey), Marion Burns (Zelda), Lottie Harrison (Abretha), Ernie Adams (Charlie), Jack Ingram (Kruger), Anthony Warde (Muller), John Merton (Schultz), Billy Benedict (Pesky), Frank Jaquet (Mr. Walters).

1. Hot News. 2. The Blazing Trap. 3. Taken for a Ride. 4. A Ghost Walks. 5. The Big Boss Speaks. 6. Man Hunt. 7. Hideout of Terror. 8. Killer at Large. 9. Dark Magic. 10. A Double-Cross Backfire. 11. On the Spot. 12. Murder at Night. 13. The Mystery of the Payroll.

81. Brick Bradford

(Columbia, December 1947) Serial, 15 chapters, two reels each. D: Spencer G.

Bennet. SP: George H. Plympton, Arthur Hoerl, and Lewis Clay. Based on the comic strip *Brick Bradford*. P: Sam Katzman. Assis. D: R.M. Andrews. Second Unit D: Thomas Carr. Photography: Ira H. Morgan. Music: Mischa Bakaleinikoff.

Brick Bradford, on behalf of the United Nations, attempts to protect The Interceptor Ray, an antiguided missile weapon which Dr. Tymak is perfecting. Brick's efforts take him through the doctor's "crystal door" and to the moon, where he aids exiled forces in overthrowing the evil rulers there. He also goes back to eighteenth century Central America in a time capsule looking for a formula the doctor needs.

Kane Richmond (Brick Bradford), Rick Vallin (Sandy Sanderson), Linda Johnson (June Saunders), Pierre Watkin (Professor Salisbury), Charles Quigley (Laydron), Jack Ingram (Albers), Fred Graham (Black), John Merton (Dr. Tymak), Charles King (Creed), Leonard Penn (Byrus), Wheeler Oakman (Walthar), Carol Forman (Queen Khana), John Hart (Dent), Helene Stanley (Carol Preston), Nelson Leigh (Prescott), Robert Barron (Zuntar), George DeNormand (Meaker), Noel Neill (Lulah), Stanley Blystone (Stevens), Frank Ellis (Rork), Al Ferguson (Scoundrel).

1. Atomic Defense. 2. Flight to the Moon. 3. Prisoners of the Moon. 4. Into the Volcano. 5. Bradford at Bay. 6. Back to Earth. 7. Into Another Century. 8. Buried Treasure. 9. Trapped in the Time Top. 10. The Unseen Hand. 11. Poison Gas. 12. Door of Disaster. 13. Sinister Rendezvous. 14. River of Revenge. 15. For the Peace of the World.

82. Bride 13

(Fox, September 1920) Serial, 15 chapters, two reels each. D: Richard Stanton. SP: Edward Sedgwick and Thomas P. Fallen. S: Edward Sedgwick.

One might call the subject matter a variation on "Ali Baba and the Forty Thieves." It's a tale of brides who are snatched at the altar on their wedding day—a tale of intrigue, adventure, romance, thrills and stunts galore. Improbable? Decidedly. But what's the difference? One is looking at hokum in a serial and not at reality. The unlucky brides are held for ransom in a castle guarded by bestial blacks.

The action starts with the kidnapping of Bride 12 in spite of heavy security. The identity of the villain is not hidden from the onlooker. The Turk is not disclosed as some wild freak of automation. His motive is to collect a ransom and, if not successful, to keep them in a harem, in all likelihood. Bride 12 is safely secreted in his submarine. Bride 13 is kidnapped just as she had vowed to go through with the ceremony in order to clear up her sister's (Number 12) fate.

Marguerite Clayton (Bride 13), John O'Brien (Lt. Bob Norton), William Lawrence (Lt. James Morgan), Lynten Chambers (Stephen Winthrop), Justine Holland (Bride 2), Dorothy Langley (Bride 1), Mary Ellen Capers (Bride 8), Martha McKay (Bride 5), Helen Johnston (Bride 6), Leona Clayton (Bride 4), Florence Mills (Bride 9), Greta Hartman (Zara[?]), Mary Christensen, Arthur Earle, Frank Bennick (?).

1. Snatched from the Altar. 2. The Pirate's Fangs. 3. The Craft of Despair. 4. The Vulture's Prey. 5. The Torture Chamber. 6. The Tarantula's Trail. 7. Tongues of Flame. 8. Entombed. 9. Hurled from the Clouds. 10. The Cavern of Terror. 11. Greyhounds of the Sea. 12. The Creeping Peril. 13. Reefs of Treachery. 14. The Fiendish Tribesmen. 15. Thundering Vengeance.

Kane Richmond and Joan Woodbury in *Brenda Starr, Reporter* (1945)

83. The Broken Coin

(Universal, July 1915) Serial, 22 chapters, two reels each. D: F. Francis Ford. Scen: Grace Cunard. S: Emerson Hough. P: Francis Ford.

The map to a royal gold fortune is on two separate pieces of a coin, one of which Kitty Grey, a newspaperwoman, buys

in an old curio shop. Learning of its possible value and interested in the story, she goes to the small kingdom of Gretzhoffen to seek the other half, which is in the possession of the weakling King Michael. In Gretzhoffen she is opposed by the ruthless Count Frederick, bent on obtaining the fortune, as well as the king's throne, for himself.

Grace Cunard (Kitty Grey), Francis Ford (Count Frederick/Hugo LeBuque), Harry Schumm (King Michael II), Reese Gardiner (The Apache), Ernest Shields (Count Sacchio), W.C. Canfield (Gorgas), Doc Crane (The Pawnbroker), Harry Mann (servant), Victor Goss (Servant), E.A. Clarke (Henchman), O.J. Uttal (Henchman), Lewis Short (Prime Minister), Bert Wilson (Confidante to Frederick), Jack [John] Ford (Sacchio's Accomplice), Mina Cunard (The King's Sweetheart), Marc Fenton (King of Grahaffen), Eddie Polo (Rolleaux), Jack Holt (Captain Williams/Sacchio's Man), Carl Laemmle (Newspaper Publisher), Burton C. Law, William White, Neil Hardin.

1. The Broken Coin. 2. The Satan of the Sands. 3. When the Throne Rocked. 4. The Face at the Window. 5. The Underground Foe. 6. A Startling Discovery. 7. Between Two Fires. 8. The

Top: **Noel Neill, Stanley Blystone, Kane Richmond, Rick Vallin, George de Normand (?), and Al Ferguson; *bottom left:* Kane Richmond, Linda Johnson, Pierre Watkin, and Rick Vallin in *Brick Bradford* (1947); *bottom right:* Jack O' Brien and Marguerite Clayton in *Bride 13* (1920)**

Prison in the Palace. 9. Room 22. 10. Cornered. 11. The Clash of Arms. 12. A Cry in the Dark. 13. War. 14. On the Battle Field. 15. The Deluge. 16. Kitty in Danger. 17. The Castaways. 18. The Underground City. 19. The Sacred Fire. 20. Danger on the High Seas. 21. A Timely Rescue. 22. An American Queen.

84. Bruce Gentry

(Columbia, February 1949) Serial, 15 chapters, two reels each. D: Spencer G. Bennet and Thomas Carr. SP: George H. Plympton, Joseph F. Poland, and Lewis Clay. Based upon the comic strip *Bruce Gentry*. P: Sam Katzman. Assis. D: R.M. Andrews. Photography: Ira H. Morgan. Music: Mischa Bakaleinikoff.

Bruce Gentry, famed aviator, clashes with a gang headed by The Recorder who has control of a deadly flying disc that endangers the world. Unknown to Gentry, the Recorder is Dr. Benson, the scientist with whom he works. Bruce discovers Benson's double identity and apprehends the criminal's gang in time to stop a disc destined for destruction of the Panama Canal.

Tom Neal (Bruce Gentry), Judy Clark (Juanita Farrell), Ralph Hodges (Frank Farrell), Forrest Taylor (Dr. Alexander Benson), Hugh Prosser (Paul Radcliffe), Tristram Coffin (Krendon), Jack Ingram (Allen), Terry Frost (Chandler), Eddie Parker (Gregg), Charles King (Ivor), Stephen Carr (Hill), Dale Van Sickle (Gregory).

1. The Mystery Disc. 2. Fiery Furnace. 3. The Man of Menace. 4. Grade Crossing. 5. Danger Trail. 6. A Fight for Life. 7. The Flying Disc. 8. Fate Takes the Wheel. 9. Hazardous Heights. 10. Over the Falls. 11. Gentry at Bay. 12. Parachute of Peril. 13. Menace of the Mesa. 14. Bruce's Strategy. 15. The Final Disc.

85. Buck Rogers

(Universal, February 1939) Serial, 12 chapters, two reels each. D: Ford Beebe and Saul A. Goodkind. SP/S: Norman Hall and Ray Trampe. Asso. P: Barney Sarecky. Camera: Jerry Ash. Art D: Jack Otterson, Ralph DeLacy. Based on comic strip by Dick Calkins and Phil Nowlan. A later feature version was titled both *Planet Outlaws* and *Destination Saturn*, with Harry Revier given credit for new adaptation and direction.

Buck Rogers and Buddy Wade awaken after 500 years of suspended animation to discover that the world has been conquered by Killer Kane and a horde of supergangsters. They meet Wilma and Dr. Huer and agree to help them wipe out Kane. Their

Top: **Tom Neal and Forrest Taylor in *Bruce Gentry—Daredevil of the Skies* (1949); *bottom:* Henry Brandon, Philip Ahn, David Sharpe, Buster Crabbe, Constance Moore in *Buck Rogers* (1939)**

space adventures take them back and forth between Earth and Saturn as they battle Kane, his henchman Lasca, and the Zuggs of Saturn with 21st-century scientific wizardry.

Larry "Buster" Crabbe (Buck Rogers), Constance Moore (Wilma), Jackie Moran (Buddy Wade), Jack Mulhall (Captain Rankin), Anthony Warde (Killer Kane), C. Montague Shaw (Dr. Huer), Guy Usher (Aldar), William Gould (Marshall Kragg), Phillip Ahn (Prince Tallen), Henry Brandon (Captain Lasca), Wheeler Oakman (Patten), Kenneth Duncan (Lieutenant Lacy), Carleton Young (Scott), Reed Howes (Roberts), Edward Parker (Crabbe's Double), David Sharpe (Moran's Double).

1. Tomorrow's World. 2. Tragedy on Saturn. 3. The Enemy's Stronghold. 4. The Sky Patrol. 4. The Phantom Plane. 6. The Unknown Command. 7. Primitive Urge. 8. Revolt of the Zuggs. 9. Bodies Without Minds. 10. Broken Barriers. 11. A Prince in Bondage. 12. War of the Planets.

86. Bud 'n' Ben Featurettes

(Reliable, 1933–'34) Series, 7 episodes, two reels each. D: Bernard B. Ray. SP: Bennett Cohen (6), Carl Krusada and Rose Gordon (1). P: Bernard B. Ray.

These stories concerned the adventures of two cowboy pals. They were 20–30 minute featurettes and a welcome addition to any program where the booking was a single feature, a serial chapter, a cartoon or comedy, and Bud 'n' Ben. The viewer got a full two-hour program this way. Ben Corbett was in all seven of the films; Wally Wales in one, Fred Humes in one, Dennis Moore in one, and Jack Perrin in four.

Jack Perrin (Bud/Dick), Ben Corbett (Ben), Walt Williams [Wally Wales] (Bud), Denny Meadows [Dennis Moore] (Bud), Fred Humes (Bud), Starlight [Horse] (Himself), Jimmy Aubrey, Slim Whittaker, Bud Osborne, Al Ferguson, Charles K. French, Marie Quillan, Robert Walker, Lola Tate, Mary Draper, Josephine Hill, George Chesebro, Murdock McQuarrie, Lafe McKee, Frances Morris, Lew Meehan, Virginia Brown Faire, Ethan Laidlaw, Mack V. Wright, Grace Woods, Blackjack Ward, Jim Corey, Harry Maoris, Alex Franks, Jayne Regan, Franklyn Farnum, Fern Emmett, Philo McCullough, Merrill McCormick.

1. Girl Trouble (12-15-33). 2. Potluck (1-15-34). 3. Nevada Cyclone (3-15-34). 4. Arizona Nights (4-15-34). 5. Rainbow Riders (6-15-34). 6. Ridin' Gents (8-15-34). 7. West on Parade (10-15-34).

87. Buffalo E Bill

(Italy, 1919) Series, 3 episodes. SP: Carle Fangarini.

Adolfo Trouche, Maria Aloy, Lisette Paltrinieri, Emilio Graziani Walter.

Portuguese: 1. A aventureira. 2. A porfia mortal. 3. A fogueira do malvado.

88. Bull's Eye

(Universal, December 13, 1917) Serial, 18 chapters, two reels each. D: James W. Horne. S: Blaine Pearson, Harvey Gates, Henry McRae, and James W. Horne. Scen: Harvey Gates, Tom Gibson, and Frank H. Clark.

This is about sheepherders vs. cattlemen, with much of the story unfolding on a ranch named Bull's Eye. Cora Clayton is aided by ranch foreman Cody when her father is murdered by powerful business interests. Though Cora at first loves a secret service agent and is desired by an outlaw chieftain, Cody gets her in the end.

Eddie Polo (Cody), Vivian Reed (Cora Clayton), Frank Lanning (Nathan Loose), Ray Hanford (John Clayton), William Welsh (John North), Hal Cooley (Lee McGuire), Noble Johnson (Sweeney Bodin), Leo Willis, Wallace Coborn*.

*Wallace Coborn was known as "The Western Poet," and he later starred in a series of two-reel westerns for Clark-Cornelius.

1. First Blood. 2. The Fearless One. 3. Desperate Odds. 4. Still in the Ring. 5. The Swing of Death. 6. On the Brink. 7. Riding Wild. 8. Dynamite. 9. The Flaming Crisis. 10. Coyotes of the Desert. 11. Fired. 12. Burning Sands. 13. Sold at Auction. 14. The Firing Squad. 15. The Stained Face. 16. Running Wild. 17. In Irons. 18. The Runaway.

89. Burn 'Em Up Barnes

(Mascot, June 16, 1934) Serial, 12 chapters; Chapter 1, three reels; other, two reels. D: Colbert Clark and Armand Schaefer. SP: Al Martin, Armand Schaefer, Barney Sarecky, and Sherman Lowe. S: John Rothmell and Colbert Clark. P: Nat Levine.

Frankie Darro in *Burn 'Em Up Barnes* (1934)

Marjorie Temple, owner of a financially troubled bus line and a seemingly worthless piece of property is menaced by gangsters intent on getting the oil deposits they know to be on the property. Burn 'Em Up Barnes, a racing driver, comes to her rescue and also adopts a homeless boy who develops into a top flight newsreel cameraman. Because of film taken by his young ward, Barnes is cleared of any implication in a murder and the gangsters are brought to justice.

Jack Mulhall (Burn 'Em Up Barnes), Frankie Darro (Bobbie), Lola Lane (Marjorie Temple), Julian Rivero (Tony), Edwin Maxwell (Warren), Jason Robards (Drummond), Francis McDonald (Ray Ridpath), James Bush (George), Stanley Blystone (Joe Stevens), Al Bridge (Tucker), Robert Kortman (Frazer), Tom London (Parsons), Eddie Hearn (Parker), John Davidson (Chase), Lloyd Whitlock (District Attorney), Bruce Mitchell (Director Lambert), Jimmy Burtis (Assistant Director), Lew Meehan (Henchman), Gordon De Main (Henchman).

1. King of the Dirt Tracks. 2. The Newsreel Murder. 3. The Phantom Witness. 4. The Celluloid Clue. 5. The Decoy Drive. 6. The Crimson Alibi. 7. Roaring Rails. 8. The Death Crash. 9. The Man Higher Up. 10. The Missing Link. 11. Surrounded. 12. The Fatal Whisper.

90. Calamity Anne Series

(American Film Company, 1913–1914) Series, 12 episodes, two reels each. S/SP: Louise Lester was responsible for most of the entries.

Adventures of a Calamity Jane–type character.

Louise Lester.

1. Calamity Anne, Detective. 2. Calamity Anne, Heroine. 3. Calamity Anne, Parcel Post. 4. Calamity Anne Takes a Trip. 5. Calamity Anne's Beauty. 6. Calamity Anne's Dream. 7. Calamity Anne's Inheritance. 8. Calamity Anne's Sacrifice. 9. Calamity Anne's Trust. 10. Calamity Anne's Vanity. 11. Calamity Anne in Society. 12. Calamity Anne's Love Affair.

91. The Call of the Savage

(Universal, April 15, 1935) Serial, 12 chapters, two reels each. D: Lewis Friedlander (Lew Landers). S: Otis Adelbert Kline—*Jan of the Jungle*. SP: Nate Gazert, George Plympton, and Basil Dickey. An edited version was released as a feature, *Savage Fury*.

Deep in the jungles of Africa at a medical experiment station, Doctor Harry Trevor, father of Jan, discovers a formula for curing infantile paralysis. His colleagues attempt to steal it for the money it will bring them. Suspicious, Trevor writes half the formula on parchment and the other half on a band worn by young Jan. Subsequently, Jan's mother is killed, Trevor loses his memory, Jan is adopted by monkeys, and the scientists return to America empty-handed. Years later, the greedy scientists return to discover that Trevor is alive and that Jan, now a wild boy, has the key to the formula. Aided by Mona, the lost princess of Mu, Jan eventually defeats the evil doctors.

Noah Beery, Jr. (Jan Trevor), Dorothy Short (Mona Andrews), Harry Woods (Borno), Walter Miller (Doctor Frank Bracken), Frederic Mackaye (Doctor Charles Phillips), Bryant Washburn (Doctor Harry Trevor), Viva Tattersall (Georgie), Russ Powell (Thomas Andrews), Grace Cunard (Mrs. Andrews), King Baggot (Doctor Tangier), Nathan Curry (Kutu), Dickie Jones (Jan, as a child), William Desmond (Allen), J. Frank Glendon (Dean), J.P. McGowan (Captain of Freighter), Charles Murphy (Grubb), Gwendelyn Logan (Mrs. Torrence), John Davidson (Emperor Samu), Stanley Andrews (Emperor Mena), Albert Prisco (Draga), Wally Wales [Hal Taliaferro] (Captain of Lancers), Buddy Roosevelt (Samu's Aid), Don Brody, Eddie Kane, Al Ferguson, H. Burroughs.

1. Shipwrecked. 2. Captured by Cannibals. 3. Stampeding Death. 4. Terrors of the Jungle. 5. The Plunge of Peril. 6. Thundering Waters. 7. The Hidden Monster. 8. Jungle Treachery. 9. The Avenging Fire God. 10. Descending Doom. 11. The Dragon Strikes. 12. The Pit of Flame.

92. Canadian Mounties vs. Atomic Invaders

(Republic, July 1953) Serial, 12 chapters, two reels each. D/AP: Franklyn Adreon. SP: Ronald Davidson. Photography: John MacBurnie. Music: Stanley Wilson. Special Effects: Howard and Theodore Lydecker. Feature Title: *Missile Base at Taniak*.

Sergeant Don Roberts of the Canadian Mounted Police and Miss Kay Conway, undercover agent for the Canadian government, are assigned to track down a group of foreign agents who plan to launch guided atomic missiles aimed at key American cities.

Bill Henry (Don Roberts), Susan Morrow (Kay Conway), Arthur Space (Marlof/Smoky Joe), Dale Van Sickel (Beck), Pierre Watkin (Morrison), Mike Ragan (Reed), Stanley Andrews (Anderson), Harry Lauter (Clark), Edmund Cobb (Warner), Tom Steele (Mac), Hank Patterson (Jed Larson), Gayle Kellogg (Guy Sanders), Bob Reeves (Bartender), Fred Graham (Mason), George DeNormand (Ed Peters), William Fawcett (Murphy), Jean Wright (Betty Warner), Jeane Wood (Mrs. Anderson), Joe Yrigoyen, Carey Loftin (Heavies), Drew Cahill (Mills), Kenner Kemp (Officer), Duane Thorsen (Mailman), Gordon Armitage (Ed Olson), Paul Palmer (Turner), Duke Taylor, Bob Jamison, Earl Bunn, Jimmy Fawcett, Dave Sharpe.

1. Arctic Intrigue. 2. Murder or Accident? 3. Fangs of Death. 4. Underground Inferno. 5. Pursuit to Destruction. 6. The Boat Trap. 7. Flame Versus Gun. 8. Highway of Horror. 9. Doomed Cargo. 10. Human Quarry. 11. Mechanical Homicide. 12. Cavern of Revenge.

93. Captain America

(Republic, January 29, 1944) Serial, 15 chapters; Chapter 1, three reels; others, two reels. D: John English and Elmer Clifton. SP: Royal Cole, Ronald Davidson, Basil Dickey, Jesse Duffy, Harry Fraser, Grant Nelson, and Joseph Poland. Assoc. P: W.J. O'Sullivan. Photography: John MacBurnie. Music: Mort Glickman. Special Effects: Theodore Lydecker. Based on characters appearing in *Captain America* comics. Reissued in 1953 as *The Return of Captain America*.

Because he feels he was cheated out of fame and wealth that was rightfully his, Dr. Maldor, calling himself The Scarab, eliminates the former members of an archaeological expedition by means of a poison known as The Purple Death. He also steals plans for a dynamic vibrator that has great destructive power, a newly invented life-restoring machine, and the map to a Mayan treasure. Captain America, alias District Attorney Grant Gardner, intervenes, and with his assistant Gail Richards, brings Maldor and his hoodlums to justice.

Republic failed to do justice to a great comic character. Other than the title, any similarity between the serial and the comic hero was purely accidental.

Dick Purcell (Grant Gardner/Captain America), Lorna Gray (Gail Richards), Lionel Atwill (Cyrus Maldor/The Scarab), Charles Trowbridge (Commissioner Dryden), Russell Hicks (Mayor Randolph), George J. Lewis (Bart Matson), John Davidson (Gruber), LeRoy Mason (Bates), Norman Nesbitt (Newscaster), Jay Novello (Simms), Stanley Price (Carson), Al Ferguson (Detective), Ben Taggart (Donoval), Jack Kirk (Expressman), Post Parks (Detective), Dale Van Sickel (Rick), Fred Graham (Mead), Jack O'Shea (Expressman), Tom Steele (Kent), Bud Geary (Kane), Ken Terrell (Hunt), Edward Cassidy (Guard), George DeNormand (Pete), Roy Brent (Nick), Edward Van Sloan (Gregory), Keene Duncan (Ed Graham), Robert Wilkie (Garage Heavy), Brooks Benedict (Florist), Sam Ash (Florist), Frank Reicher (Professor Lyman), Hugh Sothern (Eldon Dodge), Tom Chatterton (J.C. Henley), John Bagni (Monk), Edward Keane (Agent 350), Terry Frost (Police Broadcaster), John Hamilton (Hillman), Crane Whitley (Dirk), Lynton Brent (Mechanic), Robert Strange (Hines), Charles Hutchison (Merritt), Allen Pomeroy (Walters), Joe Yrigoyen (Burns), Ralf Harolde (Tait), Robert Frazer, Helen Thurston, Wilson Benge, Paul Marion, George Magrill, John Daheim, Frank O'Connor.

1. The Purple Death. 2. Mechanical Executioner. 3. The Scarlet Scarab. 4. Preview of Murder. 5. Blade of Wrath. 6. Vault of Vengeance. 7. Wholesale Destruction. 8. Cremation in the Clouds. 9. Triple Tragedy. 10. The Avenging Corpse. 11. The Dead Man Returns. 12. Horror on the Highway. 13. Skyscraper Plunger. 14. The Scarab Strikes. 15. The Toll of Doom.

Dave O'Brien in *Captain Midnight* (1942)

94. Captain Kidd

(Star Serial Corp., June 1922) Serial, 15 chapters; Chapter one, three reels; others, two reels. D: J.P. McGowan and Burton King. SP: Anthony W. Coldeway and Philip Lonergan.

Edward Davis seeks a treasure buried long ago by Captain Kidd. An ancestor, also named Edward Davis, and his young fiancée, from whom the treasure was stolen, had escaped from Kidd with a map showing its location, but had never returned to recover the loot. In his quest Davis is opposed by his cousin, who is jealous of him and wants both the gold and Edward's girl friend, Louise.

Polo produced this serial and is reputed to have lost over $300,000 on this state-right film which flopped.

Eddie Polo (Edward Davis), Katherine Myers (Louise Bradley), Leslie J. Casey, Sam Polo, Malvina Polo, Bradley Barker, Carl Axalle.

1. Shanghaied. 2. The Pirate's Slave. 3. Hidden Treasure. 4. The Lost Fortune. 5. The Missing Plans. 6. Trapped. 7–9. [Unknown.] 10. Double Crossed. 11. [Unknown.] 12. A Fight for Fortune. 13. [Unknown.] 14. A Fight in Mid-Air. 15. Victory and Happiness.

95. Captain Midnight

(Columbia, February 15, 1942) Serial, 15 chapters, two reels each. D: James W. Horne. SP: Basil Dickey, George H. Plympton, Jack Stanley, and Wyndham Gittens. P: Larry Darmour. Assist. D: Carl Hiecke. Photography: James S. Brown, Jr. Music: Lee Zahler. Based on the Mutual Network radio serial.

The head of a vast enemy sabotage ring, Ivan Shark threatens the security of the U.S. by plotting to steal a vital range finder invented by John Edwards. Captain Albright, alias Captain Midnight, is called upon to find and stop the saboteurs. In carrying out his assignment he rescues the inventor, his daughter, and his own superior, all of whom have been made prisoners of Shark.

Dave O'Brien (Capt. Albright/Captain Midnight), Dorothy Short (Joyce), James Craven (Ivan Shark), Sam Edwards (Chuck), Guy Wilkerson (Ichabod Mudd), Bryant Washburn (John Edwards), Luana Walters (Fury Shark), Joseph Girard (Major Steel), Ray Teal (Borgman), George Pembroke (Doctor Jordan), Charles Hamilton (Martel), Al Ferguson (Gardo), Slim Whitaker (Policeman), Franklyn Farnum (Heavy).

1. Mysterious Pilot. 2. Stolen Range Finder. 3. The Captured Plane. 4. Mistaken Identity. 5. Ambushed Ambulance. 6. Weird Waters. 7. Menacing Fates. 8. Shells of Evil. 9. The Drop of Doom. 10. The Hidden Bomb. 11. Sky Terror. 12. Burning Bomber. 13. Death in the Cockpit. 14. Scourge of Revenge. 15. The Fatal Hour.

96. Captain Video

(Columbia, December 1951) Serial, 15 chapters, two reels each. D: Spencer G. Bennet and Wallace A. Grissell. SP: Royal K. Cole, Sherman L. Lowe, Joseph F. Poland, and George H. Plympton. P: Sam Katzman. Assist. D: Charles S. Gould. Photography: Fate Browne. Music: Mischa Bakaleinikoff. Special Effects: Jack Erickson. Based on characters from the TV series *Captain Video and His Video Rangers*.

The universe is threatened by Vultura, dictator of the planet Atoma, and it is up to Captain Video and Video Ranger to stop him. Captain Video traces unusual cosmic disturbances to Dr. Tabor, a mysterious scientist who denies responsibility. However, he later contacts Vultura who instructs him to leave for Atoma at once. Tabor develops various deadly weapons used by Vultura to carry out his solar conquests.

One unusual feature was the filming of whole sequences in Cinecolor to convey the feeling of alien atmospheres. But in spite of the use of limited color, the serial was a shoddy affair with appeal only to youngsters.

Judd Holdren (Captain Video), Larry Stewart (Ranger), George Eldredge (Dr. Tabor), Gene Roth (Vultura), Don C. Harvey (Gallagher), William Fawcett (Alpha), Jack Ingram (Aker), I. Stanford Jolley (Zarol), Skelton Knaggs (Retner), Jimmy Stark (Rogers), Rusty Wescoatt (Beal), Zon Murray (Elko), George Robotham (Drock), Oliver Cross (Professor Markham), Bill Bailey (Professor Dean).

1. Journey into Space. 2. Menace to Atoma. 3. Captain Video's Peril. 4. Entombed in Ice. 5. Flames of Atoma. 6. Astray in the Atmosphere. 7. Blasted by the Atomic Eye. 8. Invisible Menace. 9. Video Springs a Trap. 10. Menace of the Mystery Metal. 11. Weapon of Destruction. 12. Robot Rocket. 13. Mystery of Station X. 14. Vengeance of Vultura. 15. Video vs. Vultura.

97. The Carter Case (The Craig Kennedy Serial)

(Oliver Films, March 1919) Serial, 15 chapters; Chapter 1, three reels; others, two reels. D: Donald McKenzie and William F. Haddock. SP: Arthur B. Reeve and John W. Grey.

Shelby Carter, owner of big chemical works, whose secret formulas are being stolen and given to his competitors abroad, is driven by fear from his secret observation tower and killed by the mysterious Avion. His daughter, Anita, calls in Craig Kennedy to solve the mystery of the death of her father and of the missing formulas. Her life and fortune are imperiled by a band of mysterious evil-doers led by Avion.

Herbert Rawlinson (Craig Kennedy), Margaret Marsh (Anita Carver), Ethel Grey Terry (Cleo Clark), William Pike (Walter Jameson), Kempton Greene (Rance Dixon), Coit Albertson (Lester Mason), Joseph Marba (Hugo Geits/Avion), Donald Hall (Shelby Carter), Gene Baker (Alma), Louis R. Wolheim (Emanon), D.W. MacReynolds (Storpz), Leslie Stowe (Darky Joe), Franklyn Hanna (Colonel Culpepper), Frank Wunderlee (Bull Rudkin), John Reinhardt (Count Von Der Witz), Adrienne Richards (Julie), John V. De Lacy, George Dupree, Leroy L. Baker, Al Franklyn Thomas.

1. The Phosgene Bullet. 2. The Vacuum Room. 3. The Air Terror. 4. The Dungeon. 5. [Unknown.] 6. The Wireless Detective. 7. The Neragraph. 8. The Silent Shot. 9. The

Top: **Judd Holdren and Larry Stewart;** ***bottom:*** **Gene Roth in *Captain Video* (1951)**

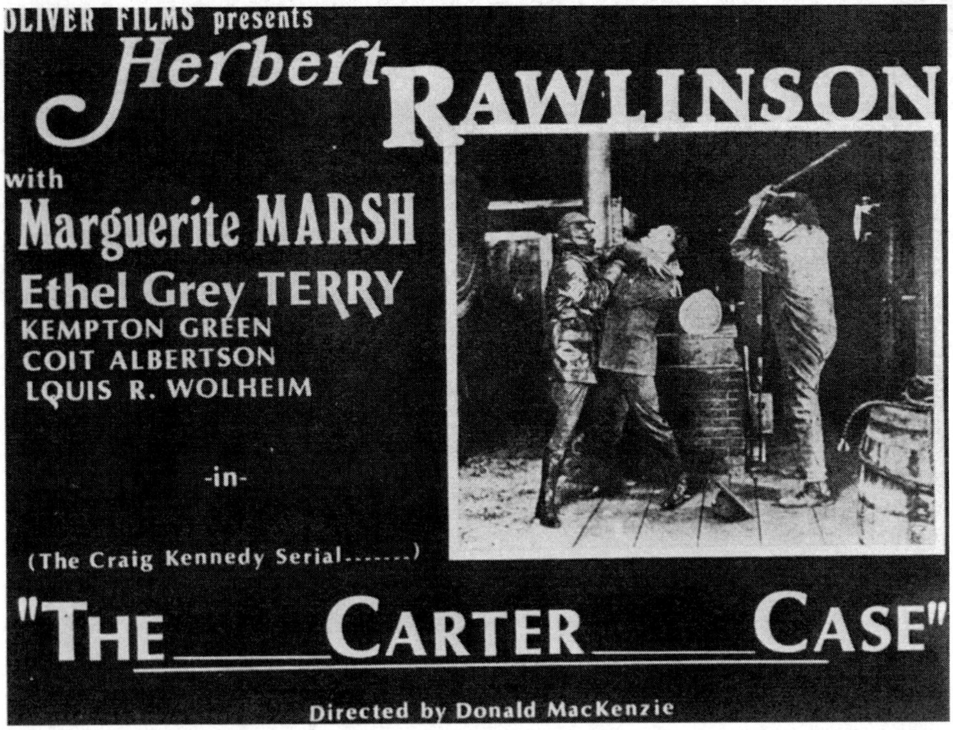

Herbert Rawlinson in *The Carter Case* (The Craig Kennedy Serial) (1919)

Camera Trap. 10. The Moonshiners. 11. The White Damp. 12. The X-Ray Detective. 13. The Ruse. 14. Unknown. 15. Unknown.

98. Casacche di Cuoio

(Italy—Tiber Films, 1918) Serial, 4 chapters. D: Emilio Ghione. SP: Emilio Ghione.

A number of the films made in Italy and Germany are borderline films. They can be classified as serial or series by the flip of a coin. The author is calling this one a serial on the basis of Emilio Ghione being the director and star. Kally Sambucini was also associated with serials, although not exclusively.

Emilio Ghione, Kally Sambucini.

99. Casey of the Coast Guard

(Pathé, April 14, 1926) Serial, 10 chapters, two reels each. D: Will Nigh. SP: Lewis Allen Browne. P: Schuyler E. Grey.

A gang of crooks, endeavoring to smuggle goods into the United States, plan to kill a young coastguard officer, Ensign George Casey, who has been too alert to make their business profitable. The plots of the gang to entrap him or to use his fiancée's father in their work make up the story.

George O'Hara (Ensign John Casey), Helen Ferguson (Doris Warren), J. Barney Sherry (John Warren), Jean Jarvis (Countess Zelina), Coit Albertson (Malverni), Robert Craig (James Corteau), James Mack (the Hunchback), Joseph Marba (Deep Water Kelly), Roland Flander (Jack Denton), William P. Burt.

1. The Smugglers' Ruse. 2. Shots in the Dark. 3. Watchful Waiting. 4. Under Suspicion. 5. The Gas Chamber. 6. Shot from the Depths. 7. Contraband Channels. 8. Smuggled Aliens. 9. Meshes of the Law. 10. Caught in the Net.

100. Il Castello di Bronzo

(Italy, 1919) Serial, 4 chapters. D: Emilio Ghione.

Although no information on this film is available to the author, it is a Ghione serial and needs to be made a part of this record of serials. Ghione was Italy's foremost serial director/star.

101. Champion Boy Rider

(Universal, 1927–28) Series, 13 episodes, two reels each.

Newton House.

Episode Titles, Releasing Dates, Directors (in italics), Supporting Actors

1. The Riding Whirlwind (10-1-27) *Lewis Collins*. 2. Red Warning (10-29-27) *Lew Collins*; Edmund Cobb, Gloria Gray. 3. Clearing the Trail (11-26-27) *Lew Collins*. 4. The Racing Wizard (12-24-27) *Lew Collins*. 5. Riding Cold (1-21-28) *Lew Collins*. 6. Buckskin Days (2-18-28) *Walter Fabian*; Edmund Cobb, Lillian Gilmore. 7. Winged Hoofs (3-17-28) *Lew Collins*; Gloria Gray. 8. A Son of the Frontier (4-14-28) *Walter Fabian*. 9. The Untamed (5-12-28) *Lew Collins*. 10. The Fighting Kid (6-9-28) *Josef Sevigard*. 11. The Ride for Help (7-7-28) *Walter Fabian*. 12. Ropin' Romance (8-4-28) *Walter Fabian*. 13. The Danger Trail (9-1-28) *Josef Sevigard*.

102. Chick Carter, Detective

(Columbia, July 11, 1946) Serial, 15 chapters, two reels each. D: Derwin Abrahams. SP: George H. Plympton and Harry Fraser. P: Sam Katzman. Assist. D: Mike Eason and Leonard Shapiro. Photography: Ira H. Morgan. Music: Lee Zahler.

Chick Carter is called into the case when the Blue Diamond disappears at a night club. Joe Carney had planned to have his own diamond stolen in order to collect $100,000 insurance with which to pay a debt to Nick Polio. Sherry Marvin double-crosses Joe and intends to pass off a fake to Joe "thief" and to pitch the real one to Nick in a cotton snowball carried in her tray. Things get fouled up and the real diamond disappears. Carter is aided by Ellen Dale, another private eye, and a newspaper reporter and photographer in ferreting out the crimes of the principals and recovering the diamond.

Lyle Talbot (Chick Carter), Douglas Fowley (Rusty Farrell), Julie Gibson (Sherry Marvin), Pamela Blake (Ellen Dale), Eddie Acuff (Spud), Robert Elliott (Dan Rankin), George Meeker (Nick Polio), Leonard Penn (Vasky), Charles King (Joe Carney), Jack Ingram (Mack), Joel Friedkin (Jules Hoyt), Eddie Parker (Frank Sharp), Frankie Darro (Creeper) Ernie Adams (Caretaker), Kermit Maynard (William).

1. Chick Carter Takes Over. 2. Jump to Eternity. 3. Grinding Wheels. 4. Chick Carter Trapped. 5. Out of

Control. 6. Chick Carter's Quest. 7. Chick Carter's Frame-Up. 8. Chick Carter Gives Chase. 9. Shadows in the Night. 10. Run to Earth. 11. Hurled into Space. 12. Chick Carter Faces Death. 13. Rendezvous with Murder. 14. Chick Carter Sets a Trap. 15. Chick Carter Wins Out.

103. The Chinatown Mystery

(Syndicate, September 1, 1928) Serial, 10 chapters, two reels each. D: J.P. McGowan. S: Francis Ford. P: Trem Carr.

Joe Master, Secret Service agent, battles evil forces led by The Sphinx as he attempts to protect Sally Warren and her formula for producing artificial diamonds.

Joe Bonomo (Joe Masters), Ruth Hiatt (Sally Warren), Paul Malvern, Francis Ford, Paul Panzer, Sheldon Lewis, Harry Myers, Rosemary Theby, Grace Cunard, George Chesebro, Helen Gibson, Jack Richardson, Billy Ford, William Clifford, Sybil Grove, Al Baffert, J.P. McGowan, Spencer Bell, Duke Green, Carl Sepulveda, Tom Curran, Rolf Sedan, Ernest Shields, Peggy O'Day, Frank Moran, Duke Worne, James Leong.

1. The Chinatown Mystery. 2. The Clutching Claw. 3. The Devil's Dice. 4. The Mysterious 13. 5. Galloping Fury. 6. The Depth of Danger. 7. The Invisible Hand. 8. The Wreck. 9. Broken Jade. 10. The Thirteenth Hour.

104. The Chronicles of Bloom Center

(Selig, 1915–1916) Series, 10 episodes, one, two or three reels each. D: Sidney Smith, Burton King, Edward LeSaint, Marshall Neilan.

Comedies revolving around a typical rural community, not unlike Essanay's Snakeville comedies or the later Universal Piperock comedies with Pee Wee Holmes and Ben Corbett.

Irene Wallace, Ralph McCormas, Harold Howard.

1915: 1. The Comeback of Percy (2R). 2. Landing the Hose Reel (3R). 3. The Manicure Girl (1R). 4. No Sir-ee Bob (1R). 5. Perkin's Pep Producer (2R). 6. The Run on Percy (2R). 7. Spooks (1R). 8. Thing or Two in Movies (?). *1916:* 9. Apple Butter (1R). 10. Come to Town (1R).

105. The Chronicles of Cleek

(Edison, 1913–1914) Series, 13 episodes, one reel each. D: George A. Lessey, Benjamin F. Wilson. P: Thomas W. Hanshew.

***Top:* Jack Ingram, Charles King, and Julie Gibson; *bottom:* Eddie Acuff, Lyle Talbot, and Douglas Fowley in *Chick Carter, Detective* (1946)**

Top: **Joe Bonomo in *The Chinatown Mystery* (1928);** ***bottom:*** **Tom Tyler in *Clancy of the Mounted* (1933)**

As "Hamilton Cleek," Ben Wilson solves a series of unrelated crimes in episodes constructed along the lines of the "Mary" films. The serial had not yet developed the characteristics (e.g., cliffhanger endings and a continuing story) that distinguished it after 1915.

Benjamin F. Wilson (Hamilton Cleek).

1. The Vanishing Cracksman. 2. The Mystery of the Dover Express. 3. The Mystery of the Talking Wire. 4. The Mystery of the Ladder of Light. 5. The Mystery of the Laughing Death. 6. The Mystery of the Silver Snare. 7. The Mystery of the Amsterdam. 8. The Mystery of the Fadeless Tints. 9. The Mystery of the Lost Stradivarius. 10. The Mystery of the Octagonal Room. 11. The Mystery of the Glass Tubes. 12. The Mystery of the Sealed Art Gallery. 13. The Heritage of Hamilton Cleek.

106. Les Cinq Sous de Lavarede

(France—Pathé, 1926) Serial, 12 chapters. D: Maurice Champreux. S: de Paul D'Ivoi and Henri Chabrilliate. Scen: Arthur Bernede.

Georges Biscot, Janine Liezer, Paulette Berger, Carlos Avril, Anna Lefeuvrier, J. David Evremond.

107. Clancy of the Mounted

(Universal, February 27, 1933) Serial, 12 chapters, two reels each. D: Ray Taylor. SP: Basil Dickey, Harry O. Hoyt, and Ella O'Neill. S: Based on the poem by Robert W. Service. P: Henry McRae.

Sergeant Tom Clancy has to go after his brother who is framed for a murder. Outlaws Pierce LaRue and "Black" MacDougal, responsible for the frame, are the murderers of Ann Louise's father, discoverer of a gold mine. Tom saves Ann from the badmen and is eventually able to clear his brother, kill the villain, and claim the girl for his own.

Tom Tyler (Sergeant Tom Clancy), Jacqueline Wells (Ann Louise), William Desmond (Dave Moran), Rosalie Roy (Maureen Clancy), Francis Ford (Inspector Cabot), Earl McCarthy (Steve Clancy), William L. Thorne ("Black" MacDougal), Leon Duval (Pierre LaRue), Tom London (Constable MacGregor), Edmund Cobb (Constable McIntosh), William Thorne, Al Ferguson, Frank Lanning, Fred Humes, Monte Motague, Frank Lackteen, Steve Clemente.

1. Toll of the Rapids. 2. Brother Against Brother. 3. Ambuscade. 4. The

Storm. 5. A Desperate Chance. 6. The Wolf's Fangs. 7. The Night Attack. 8. Crashing Timbers. 9. Fingerprints. 10. The Breed Strikes. 11. The Crimson Jacket. 12. Journey's End.

108 La Closerie des Genets

(France, 1922) Serial, chapters (?). D: Andre Liabel. Scen: Frederic Soulie.

Henry Krauss, Marcya Capri, Jean Dax, Andre Calmettes, Henry Bosc, Maillard, Viguier, Nina Vanna, Helene Darly, Yvonne Sergyl.

109. The Clutching Hand

(Stage and Screen, 1936) Serial, 15 chapters, two reels each. D: Albert Herman. Supervision: Louis Weiss. Adaptation: George M. Merrick and Eddy Graneman. SP: Louis D'Usseau and Dallas Fitzgerald. Photography: James Diamond. Music: Lee Zahler. Presented by George M. Merrick.

Doctor Paul Gironda discovers a formula for the manufacture of synthetic gold. Just before the board of directors of the International Research Foundation arrive at his laboratory to witness his achievement, he is heard screaming in his lab and disappears before help arrives. Walter Jameson, a newspaper reporter engaged to Gironda's daughter, calls in Craig Kennedy to find the abducted scientist. Directing criminal efforts is The Clutching Hand.

Jack Mulhall (Craig Kennedy), Ruth Mix (Shirley McMillan), Marion Shilling (Verna Gironda), Rex Lease (Walter Jameson), William Farnum (Gordon Gaunt), Yakima Canutt (Number 8), Reed Howes (Sullivan), Mae Busch (Mrs. Gironda), Bryant Washburn (Denton), Franklyn Farnum (Nicky), Olin Francis (Guard), Robert Frazer (Dr. Gironda), Robert Russell (Trusty), Gaston Glass (Louis Bouchard), William Desmond (Steve), Mahlon Hamilton (Montgomery), John Cowell (Policeman), John Ince (Policeman), Robert Walker (Mitchell), Joseph W. Girard (Cromwell), Artemus Nigolian (Servant), Frank Leigh (Wickham), Ethel Grove (Margaret), Charles Locher [Jon Hall] (Hobart), Gordon S. Griffith (Hamid), Roger Williams (Ali), Knute Erickson (Captain Hansen), Richard Alexander (Olaf), Milburn Morante (Marty), George Morrell (Jenkins), John Elliott (White), Vera Steadman (Secretary), Snub Pollard (Snub), Henry Hall (Warden), Art Howard, Eugene Burr, Bert Howard, Gil Patrick, Willard Kent (Members of Board of Directors), Bull Montana, Slim Whitaker, Tom London, Art Felix, George Allen (Sailors), Robert Kortman (Henchman), Roy Cardona (Henchman).

Top: **Bryant Washburn, Charles Locher [Jon Hall] (*center*), and Mae Busch;** ***bottom:*** **Jack Mulhall, Rex Lease, and Yakima Canutt in *The Clutching Hand* (1936)**

1. Who Is the Clutching Hand? 2. Shadow. 3. House of Mystery. 4. The Phantom Car. 5. The Double Trap. 6. Steps of Doom. 7. The Invisible Enemy. 8. A Cry in the Night. 9. Evil Eyes. 10. A Desperate Chance. 11. The Ship of Peril. 12. The Mystic Menace. 14. The Silent Spectre. 15. The Lone Hand.

110. Codicia

(Spain—Studio Films, 1917) Serial, 14 chapters. D: Jose Maria Codina. Photography: Sola Mestres and Alfredo Fontanals.

Lola Paris, Blanca Valoris, Ramon Quadreny.

111. Cody of the Pony Express

(Columbia, April 6, 1950) Serial, 15 chapters, two reels each. D: Spencer G. Bennet. SP: David Mathews, Lewis Clay, and Charles R. Condon. S: George H. Plympton and Joseph F. Poland. P: Sam Katzman. Assist. D: R.M. Andrews. Photography: Ira H. Morgan. Music: Mischa Bakaleinikoff.

Lieutenant John Archer is assigned as an undercover investigator to bring to justice a band of outlaws secretly headed by attorney Mort Black. Archer is aided by young Bill Cody. The outlaws are the minions of an Eastern syndicate that wants to control the territory by acquiring all of its transportation facilities.

Jock O'Mahoney (Lt. Jim Archer), Dickie Moore (Young Bill Cody), Peggy Stewart (Linda), William Fawcett (Ezra), Tom London (Doc Laramie), Helena Dare (Emma), George J. Lewis (Mort Black), Pierce Lyden (Slim), Jack Ingram (Pecos), Rick Vallin (Denver), Frank Ellis (Durk), Ross Elliott (Irv), Ben Corbett (Eric), Rusty Wescoatt (Chet), Michael Whalen, Hugh Prosser, Frank Yaconelli.

1. Cody Carries the Mail. 2. Captured by Indians. 3. Cody Saves a Life. 4. Cody Follows a Trail. 5. Cody to the Rescue. 6. The Fatal Arrow. 7. Cody Gets His Man. 8. Renegade Raiders. 9. Frontier Law. 10. Cody Tempts Fate. 11. Trouble at Silver Gap. 12. Cody Comes Through. 13. Marshal of Nugget City. 14. Unseen Danger. 15. Cody's Last Ride.

112. The Collegians

(Universal, Sept. 1926–Sept. 1929) Series, 46 episodes, two reels each. P: Carl Laemmle Jr. D: Wesley Ruggles, Harry Edwards, and Robert F. Hill.

The central figure (George J. Lewis) is an engaging young athlete who is working his way through Calford College. He falls boyishly in love with the pretty daughter (Dorothy Gulliver) of the Dean, and the girl's obvious reciprocation inspires the hatred of a rival, who is ever seeking the discomfiture of the favored lover. That, in a nutshell, is the theme which permeates each of the stories, a theme which offers many opportunities, duly seized upon, for a clever combination of youthful ebullience and truly diverting comedy. It is the comedy aspect, perhaps, which is most predominant, although the pace and brightness of the action rank a very good second. Each segment is a clean, wholesome story of American college life in more innocent days, and the series was probably the most popular two-reel series made in the 1920s.

George J. Lewis, Dorothy Gulliver, Eddie Phillips, Hayden Stevenson, Churchill Ross.

1. Benson at Calford. 2. Fighting to Win. 3. Making Good. 4. The Last Lap. 5. Around the Bases. 6. The Fighting Spirit. 7. The Relay. 8. The Cinder Path. 9. Flashing Oars. 10. Breaking Records. 11. Crimson Colors. 12. Winning Five. 13. The Dazzling Coeds. 14. A Fighting Finish. 15. Samson at Calford. 16. The Winning Punch. 17. Running Wild. 18. Splashing Through. 19. The Winning Goal. 20. Sliding Home. 21. The Junior Years. 22. Calford V. Redskins. 24. Calford in the Movies. 25. Paddling Co-Eds. 26. Fighting for Victory. 27. Dear Old Calford. 28. Calford on Horseback. 29. The Bookworm Hero. 30. Speeding Youth. 31. The Winning Point. 32. Farewell. 33. King of the Campus. 34. The Rivals. 35. On Guard. 36. Honeymoon Flats. 37. Junior Luck. 38. The Cross Country Run. 39. Sporting Courage. 40. The Varsity Drag. 41. Flying High. 42. College Love. 43. On the Side Lines. 44. Use Your Feet. 45. Splash Mates. 46. Graduation Daze.

Leon Mathot in *Le Comte de Monte-Christo* (1917)

113. Le Comte de Monte-Christo

(France—Les Films D'Art, 1917) Serial, 8 chapters. D: Henri Pouctal. S: Alexandre Dumas. SP: Henri Pouctal.

Léon Mathot (Edmond Dantés), Nelly Cormon (Mercedes), Garat (Fernand Mondego), Colas (Danglars), Albert Mayer (Villefort), Gilbert Dalleu (Caderousse), Marc Gerard (Abade Faria), Duparc (Morel), Madeleine Lyrisse (Aimée), Gaston Modot, Jacques Robert, Simone Damaury, Doubleau, Boulle, Charlier, Monti, Vaslin, Esquier, Mme. Dellanoy.

1. Edmundo Dantes. 2. O abade Faria. 3. O filantropo. 4. Simbad, o

marítimo. 5. A conquista de Paris. 6. As três vinganças. 7. As ultimas investigaçãoes de Caderousse. 8. A punição.

114. Congo Bill

(Columbia, October 1948) Serial, 15 chapters, two reels each. D: Spencer G. Bennet and Thomas Carr. SP: George H. Plympton, Arthur Hoerl, and Lewis Clay. Based upon the comic strip *Congo Bill* appearing in *Action Comics* and created by Whitney Ellsworth. P: Sam Katzman. Assist. D: R.M. Andrews. Photography: Ira H. Morgan. Music: Mischa Bakaleinikoff.

A circus manager who administers a $500,000 trust fund tries to keep Congo Bill from finding Ruth Culver, who disappeared as a baby in the African jungles. If she returns within a year he must relinquish the money and the circus. He causes the death of his honest brother, but not before a letter is given to Congo Bill with instructions to find Ruth and inform her of her inheritance. Rumors persist of a young white queen, Lureena, in the heart of Africa, and Bill leads an expedition to find out if it might be Ruth.

Don McGuire (Congo Bill), Cleo Moore (Ruth Culver/Lureena), Jack Ingram (Cameron), I. Stanford Jolley (Bernie MacGraw), Leonard Penn (Andre Bocar), Nelson Leigh (Dr. Greenway), Charles King (Kleeg), Armida (Zalea), Hugh Prosser (Moreli), Neyle Morrow (Kahia), Fred Graham (Villabo), Rusty Wescoatt (Ivan), Anthony Warde (Rogen), Stephen Carr (Tom MacGraw).

1. The Untamed Beast. 2. Jungle Gold. 3. A Hot Reception. 4. Congo Bill Springs a Trap. 5. White Shadows in the Jungle. 6. The White Queen. 7. The Black Panther. 8. Sinister Schemes. 9. The Witch Doctor. 10. Trail of Treachery. 11. A Desperate Chance. 12. The Lair of the Beast. 13. Menace of the Jungle. 14. Treasure Trap. 15. The Missing Letter.

Don McGuire in *Congo Bill* (1948)

115. Crime Does Not Pay

(Metro-Goldwyn-Mayer, 1935–1945) Series, 48 episodes, two reels each. P: Jack Chertok. D: George B. Seitz (3), Edward Cahn (4), Harold S. Bucquet (6), Leslie Fenton (2), Fred Zinnemann (3), Joe Newman (7), Gustav Machaty (1), Jacques Tourneur (1), Roy Rowland (5), Felix Feist (2), Allan Kenward (1), Basil Wrangell (1), Paul Burnford (4), Walter Hart (2), Harold Young (1), Joseph Losey (1), Sammy Lee (2), David Miller (1), Harold Kress (1).

The 48 shorts, produced over a period of twelve years, were obviously popular with theater patrons. Each episode concentrated on a particular crime that faced society and the average "Joe Doe." The series was a training ground for some yet to be stars.

Some of the better known actors who appeared in one or more of these shorts are Robert Taylor, Jo Ann Sayers, Leon Ames, Raymond Hatton, Irene Hervey, Robert Livingston, George Cleveland, Laraine Day, Marc Lawrence, Neil Hamilton, Lynn Carver, John Miljan, Claire DuBrey, Barbara Bedford, Alan Dinehart, Douglas Fowley, Dorothy Vaughn, Dennis Moore, Donald Barry, Reed Hadley, Joseph Crehan, Marsha Hunt, Ralph Morgan, Harry Woods, Darryl Hickman, John Archer, Van Johnson, Morris Ankrum, Rex Lease, David Durand, Tom Kennedy, Stanley Ridges, Jim Davis, Anthony Caruso, Henry O'Neill, Cameron Mitchell, Dick Curtis, Milton Kibbee, Tom Neal, Richard Lane, Dick Purcell, Harry Cheshire, William Tannen, Cy Kendall, Anna Q. Nilsson, William Pawley, Joseph Sawyer, Philip Terry, Louis Jean Heydt, Byron Foulger, Lloyd Corrigan.

1. Buried Loot (1-19-35). 2. Alibi Racket (9-14-35). 3. Desert Death (10-19-35). 4. A Thrill for Thelma (11-23-35). 5. Hit and Run Driver (12-28-35). 6. Perfect Set-up (2-1-36). 7. Foolproof (3-7-36). 8. The Public Pays (10-10-36). 9. Torture Money (1-2-37). 10. It May Happen to You (6-5-37). 11. Soak the Poor (8-32-37). 12. Give Till it Hurts (9-18-37). 13. Behind the Camera (10-30-37). 14. What Price

Safety (2-5-38). 15. Miracle Money (3-26-38). 16. Come Across (5-14-38). 17. A Criminal is Born (6-5-38). 18. They're Always Caught (7-3-38). 19. Think it Over (7-24-38). 20. The Wrong Way Out (12-24-38). 21. Money to Loan (3-11-39). 22. While America Sleeps (4-15-39). 23. Help Wanted (6-11-39). 24. Think First (9-9-39). 25. Drunk Driving (10-28-39). 26. Pound Foolish (1-27-40). 27. Know Your Money (1-27-40). 28. Jack Pot (3-9-40). 29. Woman in Hiding (6-22-40). 30. Buyer Beware (8-17-40). 31. Soak the Old (8-24-40). 32. You the People (11-9[?]-40). 33. Respect the Law (1-4-41). 34. Forbidden Passage (2-8-41). 35. Coffins on Wheels (6-7-41). 36. Sucker List (9-27-41). 37. For the Common Defense (6-20-42). 38. Keep 'Em Sailing (11-28-42). 39. Plan for Destruction (4-22-43). 40. Patrolling the Ether (4-22-44). 41. Easy Life (5-20-44). 42. Dark Shadows (12-16-44). 43. Fall Guy (4-14-45). 44. The Last Installment (5-5-45). 45. Phantoms, Inc. (6-9-45). 46. A Gun in His Hand (9-15-45). 47. Purity Squad (11-3-45). 48. Luckiest Guy in the World (1-25-47).

116. The Crimson Flash

(Pathé, June 19, 1927) Serial, 10 chapters, two reels each. D: Arch B. Heath. Scen: Paul Fairfax Fuller. S: George Arthur Gray.

The Ghost, a mysterious master criminal, is the leader of a gang of smugglers and thieves sought by Secret Service agent Jimmy Langwell. His task proves to be no picnic.

Linda Stirling and Clayton Moore in *The Crimson Ghost* (1946)

Cullen Landis (Jimmy Langwell), Eugenia Gilbert (Janet Keene), Tom Holding (Dr. Carson Banks), J. Barney Sherry (Andrew Keene), Walter P. Lewis (Simeon Acres), Ivan Linow (Shell), Tony Hughes (Dale), Mary Gardner, Gus De Well, Ed Roseman, Howard Carey.

1. A Shot in the Night. 2. The Ghost Takes a Hand. 3. When Thieves Fall Out. 4. Decoyed. 5. Held in Bondage. 6. Checkmate. 7. The Shadow of the Menace. 8. Into the Trap. 9. The Flaming Menace. 10. The End of the Trail.

117. The Crimson Ghost

(Republic, May 1946) Serial, 12 chapters, two reels each. D: William Witney and Fred Brannon. SP: Albert DeMond, Basil Dickey, Jesse Duffy, Sol Shor. Assoc. P: Ronald Davidson. Photography: Bud Thackery. Music: Mort Glickman. Special Effects: Howard and Theodore Lydecker. Feature Title: *Cyclotrode*.

A counteratomic device called the Cyclotrode is invented by Professor Chambers, whose assistant is Duncan Richards, a well-known criminologist. Secretly, one of Chambers' associates is The Crimson Ghost, who goes all out to acquire the device, with which he plans to destroy lighting and power systems and paralyze the activities of the police. At times Richards is assisted by secretary Diana Farnsworth.

Charles Quigley (Duncan Richards), Linda Stirling (Diana Farnsworth), Clayton Moore (Louis Ashe), I. Stanford Jolley (Blackton/Ghost's Voice), Kenne Duncan (Chambers), Forrest Taylor (Van Wyck), Emmett Vogan (Anderson), Sam Flint (Maxwell), Joseph Forte (Parker/The Crimson Ghost), Stanley Price (Fator), Virginia Carroll (Nurse), Rex Lease (Bain), Wheaton Chambers (Wilson), Tom Steele (Stricker/Chauffeur/Karl), Dale Van Sickel (Harte/Carson), Bud Wolfe (Cross/Smith), Bill Wilkus (Cole), Eddie Rocco (Kell), George Magrill (Fiske), Duke Taylor (Erickson), Ken Terrell (Dikes), John Daheim (Kelly), Loren Riebe (Logan), Rose Plummer (Mrs. Malloy), Carey Loftin (Palmer), Bill Yrigoyen (Milt), Dick Rush (Police Inspector), Eddie Parker (Sherman), Rod Bacon (Rosso), Robert Wilkie (Scott), Joe Yrigoyen (Slim), Fred Graham (Pete Snyder/Zane), Polly Burson (Stuntwoman).

1. Atomic Peril. 2. Thunderbolt. 3. The Fatal Sacrifice. 4. The Laughing Skull. 5. Flaming Death. 6. Mystery of the Mountain. 7. Electrocution. 8. The Slave Collar. 9. Blazing Fury. 10. The Trap That Failed. 11. Double Murder. 12. The Invisible Trail.

118. The Crimson Stain Mystery

(Consolidated Film Company/Metro, August 21, 1916) Serial, 16 chapters, two reels each. D: T. Hayes Hunter. S: Albert Payson Terhune.

Harold Stanley is a reporter on his father's paper. He witnesses a murder being committed and leaps into the room through a window, but is too late to save the victim; he sees the glint of the murderer's eye, and knows him for the Crimson Stain. The Crimson Stain is head of a band of desperate criminals, made so by a drug discovered by Dr. Montrose; the doctor expected this drug would elevate the mental and moral plane of the human race, but instead, to the doctor's great remorse, it has only bred a band of dangerous criminals.

Stanley's father begins an attack on the police for their failure to run down the criminals, and is murdered while a guest of Dr. Montrose.

Maurice Costello (Harold Stanley), Ethel Grandin (Florence Montrose), Thomas J. McGrane (Dr. Burton Montrose), Olga Olonova (Vanya Tosca), William Cavanaugh (Felix Driscoll), John Milton (Layton Parrish), N.W. Thompson (Jim Tanner), Eugene Strong (Robert Clayton).

1. The Brand of Satan. 2. In the Demon's Spell. 3. The Broken Spell. 4. The Mysterious Disappearance. 5. The Figure in Black. 6. The Phantom Image. 7. The Devil's Symphony. 8. In the Shadow of Death. 9. The Haunting Specter. 10. The Infernal Fiend. 11. The Tortured Soul. 12. The Restless Spirit. 13. Despoiling Brutes. 14. The Bloodhound. 15. The Human Tiger. 16. The Unmasking.

119. Custer's Last Stand

(Stage and Screen, 1936) Serial, 15 chapters, two reels each. D: Elmer Clifton. SP: George A Durlam, Eddy Graneman, and William Lively. P: George M. Merrick. Supervision: Louis Weiss. Camera: Bert Longenecker. Assist. D: Adrian Weiss. Music: Hal Chasnoff. Film Editors: Halbrook Todd and George M. Merrick. Prod. Mgrs.: George M. Merrick and William Solzman. A theatrical feature was also made from this serial.

A sacred medicine arrow is lost during one of the skirmishes between red men and whites and is recovered by Major Trent, who is unaware that it carries the secret of the location of an Indian cavern of gold. Knowing about the arrow, renegade Tom Blade seeks to steal it. To achieve this purpose, he finds it necessary to keep hostilities going. Scout Kit Cardigan suspects Blade and fights to prevent all-out war, but the stage is set for Custer's Last Stand.

Although an independent, cheaply made serial, this one probably boasted more "name" players than the serials of Universal, Mascot, or Columbia at that time.

Rex Lease (Kit Cardigan), William Farnum (Fitzpatrick), Reed Howes (Tom "Keen" Blade), Jack Mulhall (Lieutenant Cook), Lona Andre (Belle Meade), Dorothy Gulliver (Red Fawn), Helen Gibson (Calamity Jane), Ruth Mix (Mrs. George Custer), Frank McGlynn, Jr. (General Custer), George Chesebro (Lieutenant Roberts), Franklyn Farnum (Major Reno), Lafe McKee (Captain Benteen), Mabel Strictland (Mabel), Josef Swickard (Major Trent), Creighton Hale (Hank), Milburn Moranti (Buckskin), Bobby Nelson (Bobby), William Desmond (Wagon Boss), Nancy Caswell (Barbara Trent), Chief Thunder Cloud (Young Wolf), Marty Joyce (Buzz), Ted Adams (Buffalo Bill/Barney), George Morrell (Sgt. Flannigan), Howling Wolf (Sitting Bull), Robert Walker (Pete), Walter James (Judge Hooker), Cactus Mack (Lieutenant Weir), Budd Buster (Major Ware), Carl Mathews (Curly/True Eagle), Art Ortego (Quirt), Allen Greer (Wild Bill Hickok), Barney Fury (Sgt. Peters), James Sheridan (Jim), Chick Davis (Rain-in-the-Face), Ken Cooper (Spike), Chief Big Tree (Medicine Man), Iron Eyes Cody (Brown Fox), Patter Poe (Crow Scout), High Eagle (Crazy

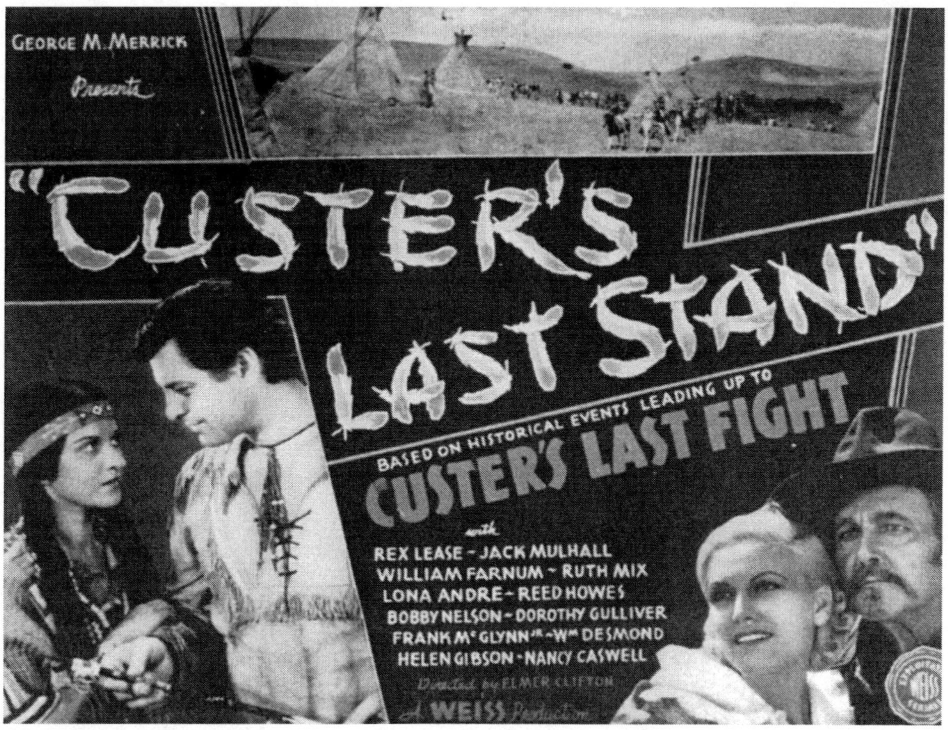

***Top:* Maurice Costello in *The Crimson Stain Mystery* (1916); *bottom: Custer's Last Stand* (1936)**

Horse), Carter Wayne (Striker Martin), Ed Withrow (Blue Crow), White Feather (Indian), Red Star Cody (Indian), Renegades: Whiten Sovern, Humming Bird, Buddy Fisher, Swift Eagle, Charles Hunter, Tall Tree, William Hunt, Little Eagle, Walter Gabel, Lone Pine, Bill Thompson, Herb Jackson, William Bartlett, J. Spencer.

1. Perils of the Plains. 2. Thundering Hoofs. 3. Fires of Vengeance. 4. The Ghost Dancers. 5. Trapped. 6. Human Wolves. 7. Demons of Disaster. 8. White Treachery. 9. Circle of Death. 10. Flaming Arrow. 11. Warpath. 12. Firing Squad. 13. Red Panthers. 14. Custer's Last Ride. 15. The Last Stand.

120. Cyclone Smith

(Universal, May–June 1919) Series, 10 (possibly more) episodes, two reels each. D: Jacques Jaccard, John P. McGowan, Karl Coolidge, George Holt, Jack Dillon. Scen: George Hively, Karl Coolidge, and others. S: Jacques Jaccard, Marie Walcamp, Milton Moore, J.A. Alexander, Tom Geraghty, Alvin J. Neitz, and George Hively.

Action was the key word in these shorts, and Eddie Polo, Universal serial star, was more than adequate for the rugged role he took on. A number of familiar players supported him.

Eddie Polo (Cyclone Smith), Eileen Sedgwick, Kate Meyers, Charles Brinley, Jack Perrin, Leo Maloney, Peggy O'Dare, Joe de la Cruz, Harry De More, Harry Todd, Pat Moore, Bob Anderson, Helen Gibson, Ruby Lafayette, Leonard Clapham [Tom London], Charles Downs, Charles Miller, Chick Morrison, J. Edwin Brown, Alfred Allen, Kathleen Myers, Joseph Hazelton, Dorothy Wood, Duke Lee, Jim Gibson, Jay Morley.

Episode Titles, Releasing Dates, Directors (in italics), Supporting Actors 1. A Prisoner for Life (5-12-19), *Jack Dillon*; Eileen Sedgwick, Harry De More, Harry Todd, Pat Moore. 2. The Phantom Fugitive (5-19-19), *Jacques Jaccard*; Eileen Sedgwick, Joe de la Cruz, Robert Anderson. 3. The Wild Rider (5-26-19), *Jacques Jaccard*; Eileen Sedgwick, Jack Perrin, Charles Hill Mailes, Chick Morrison, J. Edwin Brown. 4. Cyclone Smith's Comeback (6-2-19), *Jacques Jaccard*; Eileen Sedgwick. 5. A Pistol Point Proposal (6-9-19), *George Holt*; Eileen Sedgwick, Leo Maloney, Alfred Allen. 6. Cyclone Smith Plays Trumps (6-16-19), *Jacques Jaccard*; Eileen Sedgwick, Ruby Lafayette, Charles Dorian, Leonard Clapham, Robert Anderson. 7. The Missing Bullet (6-25-19), *J.P. McGowan*. 8. Down But Not Out (6-30-19), *Jacques Jaccard*; Helen Gibson, Charles Brimley. 9. Cyclone Smith's Partner (7-17-19), *Jacques Jaccard*; Beatrice Bruham, Jim Corey, Leonard Trainer, Carl Silvera. 10. For Life (7-14-19), director unknown; Peggy O'Dare.

121. La Dame de Monsoreau

(France—L. Aubert, 1923) Series, 6 episodes. D: René Le Somptier. S: Alexandre Dumas.

Genevieve Felix (Diana de Meridor), Gina Manes (Mme. de Saint-Luc), Madeleine Erickson (Gertrude), Rolla Norman (Bussy), Jean D'yd (Chicot), Cayol (Gorenflot), Victor Vina (Montsoreau), Georges Dnenbourg (Gonite de Meridor), Pierre Almette (M. de Saint-Luc), Raoul Praxy (Henriq III), Philippe Richard (Duc d' Anjou), Guilbert (Nicolas David), Lagrange (Duc de Guise), Pierre Finally (Duc de Mayenne), A. Thirard (Reny Le Harduin), Deneyren (Schomberg), Ralph Royce (Maugiron), San Juana (Quelus), Jean Merclay (D'Epernon), Jarcol, Henry Bosc.

122. Dämon der Welt

(Germany—William Kahn Film GmbH, 1919) Serial, 3 chapters. D: Rudolf del Zopp and Siegfried Dersaux. SP: William Kahn and Rudolf del Zopp.

Charles Willy Kayser, Dora Schluter, Marga Kohler, M. Hochstaetter, Toni Ebärg, Heinrich Peer, Fritz Feld, Preben Rist, E. Rennspiess, Ethel Scharo, Anna Von Palen, Karl Falkenberg, Bernhard Goetzke, Heinz Salfner, Mabel May-Yong, Kurt Middendorf, Georg John, Josef Reithofer.

1. Das Schicksal des Edgar Morton. 2. Wirbel des Verderbens. 3. Das goldene Gift.

123. Danger Island

(Universal, August 24, 1931) Serial, 12 chapters, two reels each. D: Ray Taylor. SP: Basil Dickey. S: Henry McRae. Dialogue: Ella O'Neill.

Bonnie Adams' father dies after telling her of a rich radium deposit on an African island. Ben Arnold and Aileen Chandos, pretending friendship for Bonnie, accompany her to the island planning to steal the riches for themselves. Captain Harry Drake falls in love with Bonnie and protects her, even when she believes him to be a scoundrel.

Kenneth Harlan (Captain Harry Drake), Lucile Browne (Bonnie Adams), Tom Rickells (Professor Adams), Walter Miller (Ben Arnold), W.L. Thorne (Bull Black), Beulah Hutton (Aileen Chandos), Andy Devine (Briney), George Regan (Lascara), Everett Brown (Cebu).

1. The Coast of Peril. 2. Death Rides the Storm. 3. Demons of the Pool. 4. Devil Worshipers. 5. Mutiny. 6. The Cat Creeps. 7. The Drums of Doom. 8. Human Sacrifice. 9. The Devil Bird. 10. Captured for Sacrifice. 11. The Lion's Lair. 12. For God's Vengeance.

124. A Dangerous Adventure

(Warner Bros., February 25, 1922) Serial, 15 chapters; Chapter One, three reels; others, two reels. D: Sam Warner and J.L. Warner. SP: Sam Warner. S: Frances Guihan. Camera: John W. Boyle, Andre Barlatier, Floyd Jackson, and W.R. Griffin. P: William N. Selig. Film also released in 1922 as a seven-reel feature.

Marjorie and Edith Stanton accompany their uncle to Africa in quest of a treasure chest he has hidden there. The evil uncle tries to sell Marjorie to a chieftain in exchange for a caravan. MacDonald Hayden, in love with Marjorie, goes to her rescue, aided by his buddy.

Grace Darmond (Marjorie Stanton), Philo McCullough (MacDonald Hayden), Jack Richardson (Herbert Brandon), Robert Agnew (Jimmy Morrison), Derelys Perdue (Edith Stanton), Rex De Roselli (Ubanga, High Priest), Omar Whitehead (Native), Mabel Stark, Captain J.R. Riccarde, Josephine Hill.

1. The Jungle Storm. 2. The Sacrifice. 3. The Lion Pit. 4. Brandon's Revenge. 5. At the Leopard's Mercy. 6. The Traitor. 7. The Volcano. 8. The Escape. 9. The Leopard's Cave. 10. The Jungle Water Hole. 11. The Hippopotamus.

12. The Lion's Prey. 13. In the Tiger's Lair. 14. The Treasure Cave. 15. The Rescue.

125. The Dangers of Doris

(Broadway Star, December 1916) Series, 10 episodes, two reels each. D: David Smith. Scen: A. Van Buren Powell, C. Graham Baker, Garfield Thompson, Will Courtney, Edward J. Montague, and Stanley Olmstead.

Doris is a continuing character in these unrelated episodes portraying her ups and downs.

Mary Anderson (Doris).

1. The Bit of Bent Wire. 2. The Luck Charm. 3. The Twin Fedoras. 4. One Good Turn. 5. The Suitor from Siam. 6. The Footlight Lure. 7. The Gang. 8. Up and Down. 9. The Old Fourth Ward. 10. The Road to Eternity.

Jim Bannon and Virginia Belmont in *Dangers of the Canadian Mounted* (1948)

126. Dangers of the Canadian Mounted

(Republic, April 24, 1948) Serial, 12 chapters, two reels each. Feature Version: *R.C.M.P. and the Treasure of Genghis Khan.* D: Fred Brannon and Yakima Canutt. SP: Franklyn Adreon, Basil Dickey, Sol Shor, and Robert C. Walker. Photography: John MacBurnie. Music: Mort Glickman. Special Effects: Howard and Theodore Lydecker.

A gang, ostensibly headed by Mort, but masterminded by a mystery figure called The Chief, is searching for riches left by Genghis Khan's treasure-hunting ships in the 13th century. The gang tries to stop the territory from being opened up to homesteaders, with the result that Captain Chris Royal of the Mounties is called in to apprehend those guilty of attacks on road builders. The search for the suspected fortune leads to the Cave of a Thousand Tunnels, then back to a Chinese junk and a chest. In the final confrontation in Skagway Kate's boarding house, it is discovered that two bottles of liquid are actually diamonds, the Mongols having discovered the secret of liquefying diamonds. Skagway Kate turns out to be The Chief and is arrested.

Jim Bannon (Christopher Royal), Virginia Belmont (Roberta Page), Anthony Warde (Mort Fowler), Dorothy Granger (Skagway Kate/The Chief), Bill Van Sickel (Dan Page), I. Stanford Jolley (J.P. Belanco), Dale Van Sickel (Boyd/Bart/Pete/Steele/Scott), Ken Terrell (Art/Curry/Fenton/Tom/Grady/Masters), Tom Steele (Carter/Fagan/Lou/Sloan/Spike), Phil Warren (George Hale), Holly Bane (Carson), Robert Wilkie (Baxter), Lee Morgan (Dale), James Dale (Andrew Knight), Ted Adams (Meggs), John Crawford (Danton), Jack Clifford (Marshal), Eddie Parker (Lowry), Frank O'Connor (Barton), James Carlisle (Martin Addison), Eddie Phillips (Baker), House Peters, Jr. (Ford), Marshall Reed (Dave/Williams/Jim), Tom McDonough (Frank), Paul Gustine (Ken), Ted Mapes (Mac), Carey Loftin (Clerk/Porter), Charles Regan (Ralph), Al Taylor, Harry Cording (Heavies), Arvon Dale (Roy Watson), Jack Kirk (A.L. Thomas), Roy Bucko, David Sharpe, Al Taylor, Bud Wolfe.

1. Legend of Genghis Khan. 2. Key to the Legend. 3. Ghost Town. 4. Terror in the Sky. 5. Pursuit. 6. Stolen Cargo. 7. The Fatal Shot. 8. Fatal Testimony. 9. The Prisoner Spy. 10. The Secret Meeting. 11. Secret of the Altar. 12. Liquid Jewels.

127. Daredevil Jack

(Pathé, February 15, 1920) Serial, 15 chapters, two reels each. D: W.S. Van Dyke. SP: Jack Cunningham. S: Frederic Chapin, Harry Hoyt. P: Robert Brunton.

College athlete Jack Derry saves Glory Billings from thugs who seek a bracelet given to her by her dying father. Leonard Billings, her foster father, and his son Edgar believe that when it is joined to a second bracelet it will give the location of a "lake of oil" discovered by the old man. Later, Jack learns that Leonard Billings is the man responsible for the imprisonment of his own father, Robert Derry, on false charges. James Meeney, gang leader, has obtained the other bracelet.

The Billings head west with Glory in search of the oil. Meeney pursues them, hoping to obtain Glory's bracelet. Desert outlaw Royce Rivers also learns of the secret and adds his gang to the conflict. Jack fights to protect Glory, while seeking Jordan, a miner in the area who can prove his father's innocence. The Billings' butler repeatedly aids the girl. He eventually reveals himself to be Kent, once her father's partner. In the end the criminals are killed or captured, and Kent reveals the secret of the lake of oil, making Glory a wealthy woman. Jack is able to clear his father's name with a confession forced from Jordan.

Jack Dempsey (Jack Derry), Josie Sedgwick (Glory Billings), Herschel Mayall (Leonard Billings), Albert Cody (Edgar Billings), Ruth Langston (Ninette), Edward Hearn (Cyril Dennison), Frederick Starr (James Meeney), Clyde Benson (the Butler), Frank Lanning (MacManus, the Indian), Aggie Herring (Mrs. Corcoran), Spike Robinson, Al Kaufman,

***Top:* Jack Dempsey in *Daredevil Jack* (1920); *bottom:* Herman Brix [Bruce Bennett], Carole Landis, Charles Quigley, and David Sharpe in *Daredevils of the Red Circle* (1939)**

S.E. Jennings (Members of the Gang), Carl Stockdale, Edgar Kennedy, Lon Chaney, Bull Montana.

1. The Mysterious Bracelets. 2. The Ball of Death. 3. Wheels of Fate. 4. Shanghaied. 5. The Race for Glory. 6. A Skirmish of Wits. 7. A Blow in the Dark. 8. Blinding Hate. 9. Phantoms of Treachery. 10. Paths of Destruction. 11. Flames of Wrath. 12. The Unseen Menace. 13. Baiting the Trap. 14. A Terrible Vengeance. 15. The Triple Chase.

128. Daredevils of the Red Circle

(Republic, July 1939) Serial, 12 chapters, two reels each. D: William Witney and John English. SP: Barry Shipman, Franklyn Adreon, Rex Taylor, Ronald Davidson, and Sol Shor. Assoc. P: Robert Beche. Photography: William Nobles. Music: William Lava. Special Effects: Howard and Theodore Lydecker.

Convict 39013 escapes from a penitentiary after 15 years imprisonment and engages in a campaign of vengeance against his former partner, Granville, who was responsible for his conviction as an embezzler. Kidnapping Granville, he assumes Granville's identity and sets about wrecking his enterprises. The Daredevils of the Red Circle, employed at a Granville amusement pier, become involved when the small brother of one of them is killed and the pier destroyed. They league themselves with Granville's granddaughter in a fight against 39013, receiving help from The Red Circle, a mysterious personage.

Charles Quigley (Gene Townley), Herman Brix [Bruce Bennett] (Tiny Dawson), David Sharpe (Burt Knowles), Carole Landis (Blanche Granville), Miles Mander (Horace Granville), Charles Middleton (Harry Crowel/39013), C. Montague Shaw (Malcolm), George Chesebro (Sheffield), Ben Taggart (Dixon), William Pagan (Landon), Corbet Morris (Klein), Raymond Bailey (Stanley), Fred Toones (Snowflake), Ray Miller (Jeff), Robert Winkler (Sammy Townley), Al Taylor (Al), Roy Brent (Bill), Truda Marson (Nurse Benson), Bernard Suss (Black), Bert LeBaron (Bob), Eddie Cherkose (Burton), John Merton (Davis), Edmund Cobb (Foreman), Earle Hodgins (Hinkle), Roy Barcroft (Superintendent), Stanley Price (Selden), Harry Strang (Peck), Bud Geary (Rex), Frank Wayne (Dan), Howard Mitchell (Dispatcher), Joe McGuinn (Ed), Earl Bunn (Frank), Broderick O'Farrell (Graves), Jack Chapin (Joe), Bud Wolfe (John), Forrest Dillon (Kid), Buel Bryant (Lab Heavy), Earl Askam (Lutens), Forest Burns (Mac), Jerry Jerome (Marco), Dave Wengren, Sailor Vincent, Jerry Frank (Miners), Norman Nesbitt (Newscaster), Bill Wilkus (Office Heavy), Reginald Barlow (Doctor), Lloyd Whitlock (Doctor), Yakima Canutt, Duke Taylor, Mike Jeffers, George DeNormand, Robert Wilke (G-Men), Charles Thomas (Sam), Ray Largay (Police Commissioner), Ken Terrell, George Turner, Fred Schaefer, William Nestel, Joe Yrigoyen, Cy Slocum, Wally West, Dick Scott, Bob Thom, Curley Dresden, Max Marx, Oscar

Hendrian, Jerry Frank (Heavies), Edward Foster (Zeke), Harry Anderson (Ward), Jack Kenney (Steve), Arthur Fowler (Sloan), Jimmy Fawcett, Ted Mapes, Millard McGowan.

1. The Monstrous Plot. 2. The Mysterious Friend. 3. The Executioner. 4. Sabotage. 5. The Ray of Death. 6. Thirty Seconds to Live. 7. The Flooded Mine. 8. S.O.S. 9. Ladder of Peril. 10. The Infernal Machine. 11. The Red Circle Speaks. 12. Flight to Doom.

129. Daredevils of the West

(Republic, April 17, 1943) Serial, 12 chapters, two reels each. D: John English. SP: Ronald Davidson, Basil Dickey, William Lively, Joseph O'Donnell, and Joseph Poland. Assoc. P: W.J. O'Sullivan. Photography: Bud Thackery. Music: Mort Glickman. Special Effects: Howard Lydecker.

Duke Cameron and June Foster fight shoulder to shoulder to complete a stageline road through the Comanche Strip. The villains wish to stop the project so that they can take over the Strip for their own purposes.

Allan Lane (Duke Cameron), Kay Aldridge (June Foster), Eddie Acuff (Red Kelly), William Haade (Barton Ward), Robert Frazer (Martin Dexter), Ted Adams (Silas Higby), George J. Lewis (Turner), Stanley Andrews (Andrews), Jack Rockwell (Watson), Charles Miller (Foster), John Hamilton (Garfield), Budd Bester (Jim Brady), Kenneth Harlan (Commissioner), Kenne Duncan (George Hooker), Rex Lease (Jack/Heavy), Chief Thunder Cloud (Indian Chief), Ken Terrell (Bartender), Joe Yrigoyen (Bill/Heavy, Guard, Indian Rustler), Tom Steele (Marker/Heavy/Double for Lane), Duke Green (Dave/Indian/Heavy/Henry), Bill Yrigoyen (Indian/Heavy/Blackie), Eddie Parker (Monk Mason/Heavy/Jim), Tom London (Miller), Crane Whitley (Maxwell), Babe Defreest (Double for Aldridge), Ray Jones, Frank McCarroll, Ralph Bucko (Heavies), Many Treaties (Blue Eagle), Jack O'Shea, George Magrill, Earl Bunn, Pierce Lyden, George Plues, Tex Cooper (Citizens), Herbert Rawlinson (T.M. Sawyer), Edward Cassidy (Russell), Allen Pomeroy (Roustbout), Edmund Cobb (Ed), Al Taylor (Indian/Citizen), Augie Gomez, Rodd Redwing, Charles Bruner, Art Dillard, Warren Fiske, Bryan Topetchy, George Sowards, Charles Soldani, George Sky Eagle (Indians), George Pembroke (Powers), Harry Smith (Kaiga).

1. Valley of Death. 2. Flaming Prison. 3. The Killer Strikes. 4. Tunnel of Terror. 5. Fiery Tomb. 6. Redskin Raiders. 7. Perilous Pursuit. 8. Dance of Doom. 9. Terror Trail. 10. Suicide Showdown. 11. Cavern of Cremation. 12. Frontier Justice.

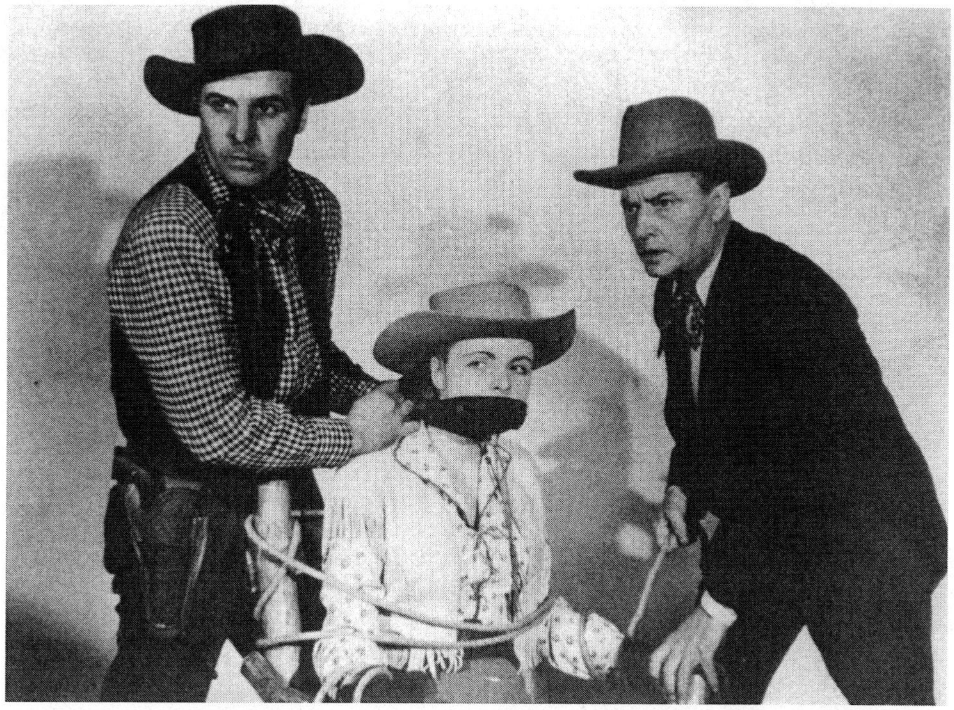

Top: **George J. Lewis, Kay Aldridge, and Robert Frazer in** ***Daredevils of the West*** **(1943);** ***bottom:*** **Clyde Beatty in** ***Darkest Africa*** **(1936)**

130. Darkest Africa

(Republic, March 1936) Serial, 15 chapters; Chapter 1, three reels; others, two reels. D: B. Reeves Eason and Joseph Kane. SP: John Rathmell, Barney Sarecky, Ted Parsons. S: John Rathmell, Tracy Knight. Supervisor: Barney Sarecky. Photography: William Nobles, Edgar Lyons. P: Nat Levine.

Both: **Adrian Booth and Kirk Alyn in *Daughter of Don Q* (1946)**

Feature Title: Batmen of Africa; reissued in 1949 as serial under the title King of the Jungleland.

Beatty meets Baru, a jungle boy, who has come to the outland for assistance in rescuing his sister, Valerie, the Goddess of Joba, a city in an unexplored part of Africa. Beatty and Baru start for Joba through the jungle. Enduring attacks by wild animals, they find Joba, only to encounter Dagna, the high priest, two crooked animal traders, and a force of bat men. Dagna relies on Valerie's influence with the natives to retain his power. The traders are after diamonds that are mined within the city by Dagna's slave labor. Alternately captured by and escaping from Dagna and his minions, Beatty, Baru, and Valerie escape the city just before it is swallowed up by an earthquake.

Clyde Beatty (Himself), Manuel King (Baru Tremaine), Elaine Sheppard (Valerie Tremaine), Lucien Prival (Dagna), Ray Benard [Ray Corrigan] (Bonga/Samabi), Wheeler Oakman (Durkin), Edward McWade (Gorn), Edmund Cobb (Craddock), Ray Taylor (Hambone), Donald Reed (Negus), Harrison Greene (Driscoll), Joe Delacruz (Mine Slave), Joseph Boyd (Nagga), Eddie Parker (Terrace Sentry), Henry Sylvester (Tomlin).

1. Baru, Son of the Jungle. 2. The Tiger-Men's God. 3. Bat-Men of Joba. 4. The Hunter Lions of Joba. 5. Bonga's Courage. 6. Prisoners of the High Priest. 7. Swing for Life. 8. Jaws of the Tiger. 9. When Birdmen Strike. 10. Trial by Thunder-Rods. 11. Jaws of Death. 12. Revolt of the Slaves. 13. Gauntlet of Destruction. 14. The Divine Sacrifice. 15. The Prophecy of Gorn.

131. A Daughter of Daring

(Kalem, March–November, 1917) Series, 11 episodes, one reel each. D: Walter Morton, Scott Sidney, James Davis. Scen: Edward W. Matlack, Herman A. Blackman, et al.

A series of railroad adventures, each story complete in itself.

Helen Gibson, G.A. Williams, George Routh, L.T. Whitlock, Tom Walsh, R. Ryan, Hal Clements, G. Pulliam, Lillian Clarke, Marion Emmonds.

1. In the Path of Peril. 2. The Registered Pouch. 3. The Borrowed Engine. 4. The College Boys' Special. 5. The Mystery of the Burning Freight. 6. The Lone Point Feud. 7. The Munitions Plot. 8. The Railroad Smugglers. 9. A Race to the Drawbridge. 10. The Detective's Danger. 11. The Deserted Engine.

132. Daughter of Don Q

(Republic, February 1946) Serial, 12 chapters, two reels each. D: Spencer Bennet and Fred Brannon. SP: Albert DeMond, Basil Dickey, Jesse Duffy, Lynn Perkins. Assoc. P: Ronald Davidson. Photography: Bud Thackery. Music: Raoul Kraushaar. Special Effects: Howard and Theodore Lydecker.

Carlos Manning sets out to kill the descendants of an

early-day Spanish land grant settler so that he can inherit a large fortune. However, Dolores Quantaro, also a descendant, and reporter Cliff Roberts uncover the plot and proceed to warn the descendants of Don Quantaro. Manning is finally exposed as the culprit.

Adrian Booth (Dolores Quantaro), Kirk Alyn (Cliff Roberts), LeRoy Mason (Carlos Manning), Roy Barcroft (Mel Donovan), Claire Meade (Maria Montenez), Kernan Cripps (Grogan), Jimmy Ames (Romero), Eddie Parker (George Tomkins), I. Stanford Jolley (Lippy Monroe), Buddy Roosevelt (Moody/Zarco/Edldie), Tom Steele (Norton/Blake/Dow/Lyons), Dale Van Sickel (Pete/Angus/Martin Murphy), Fred Graham (Rollins), Tom Quinn (R.J. Riggs), John Daheim (Morris Kelso), Ted Mapes (Ned Gray), Joe Yrigoyen (Jake Simmons), Arvon Dale (MacDuff), Bud Wolfe (Stone), D'Arcy Miller (Walters), Ken Terrell (Sam Sloan), Michael Gaddis (G-Man), Robert Wilkie (Smith), Charles Sullivan (Grogarty), Maxine Doyle (Knockout Nellie), Virginia Carroll (Rosa Peralta), George Magrill (Policeman), Eddie Rocco (Emelio Raymond), George Chesebro (Clay), Jack O'Shea (Juan Perez), Matty Roubert (Shipping Clerk), Frederick Howard (Philip Castilio), Betty Danko.

1. Multiple Murder. 2. Vendetta. 3. Under the Knives. 4. Race to Destruction. 5. Blackout. 6. Forged Evidence. 7. Execution by Error. 8. Window to Death. 9. The Juggernaut. 10. Cremation. 11. Glass Guillotine. 12. Dead Man's Vengeance.

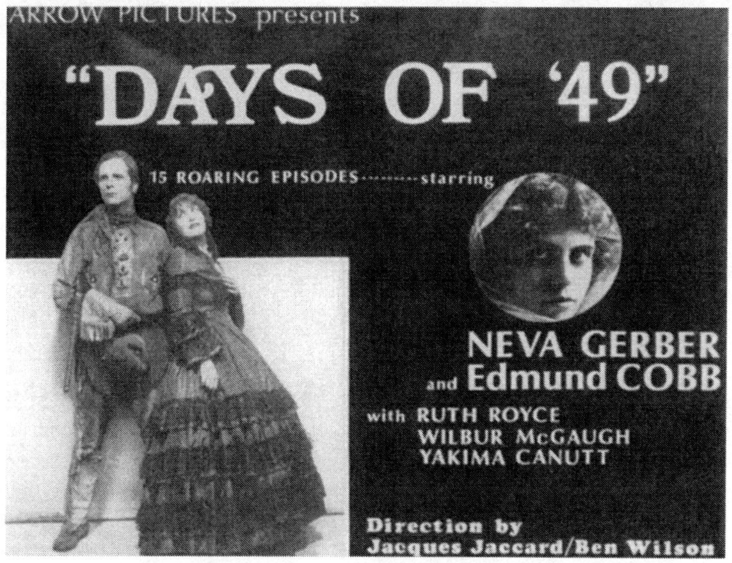

Top: Jane Vance, William Sorelle, Henry Carleton, and Lewis Dayton in *A Daughter of Uncle Sam* (1918); bottom: Edmund Cobb and Neva Gerber in *Days of '49* (1924)

133. A Daughter of Uncle Sam

(Jaxon Film Company, January 19, 1916) Serial, all chapters one reel. D: James Morton.

A story of spies and the secret service in World War I. Von Prague, a foreign spy, steals a government code from Jessie Emerson, a young American society belle who has taken up wireless telegraphy as a hobby and accidentally has intercepted the coded message. Von Prague suggests that she turn the message over to Lieutenant Blake, an inventor who has been working on an invention which promises to overthrow the traditional methods of warfare.

Securing the confidence of Jessie, Von Prague copies the message and then directs one of his agents to steal the secret code used by the government. That night Von Prague and a group of plotters meet at the Von Prague home to discuss spy and intrigue activities in the United States.

Captain Taylor meets Jessie, who offers her aid in tracking down the enemies of her country. He obtains for her a position in a private wireless station where she will be able to intercept suspicious messages.

Jane Vance (Jessie Emerson), William Sorelle (Captain Leonard Taylor), Henry Carleton (Henry Von Prague), Lewis Dayton (Lieutenant Blake).

134. Days of '49

(Arrow, March 15, 1924) Serial, 15 chapters, two reels each. D: Jacques Jaccard and Jay Marchant. S: Karl Coolidge.

(Released November 1924 as a six-reel feature titled *California in '49.*)

Scout Cal Coleman is nursed back to health by Sierra Sutter after he arrives at Fort Sutter suffering from winter exposure in an attempt to reach aid for a snowbound party at Donner Pass. Cal helps Miss Sutter when Robert Marsdon and Arabella Ryan try to deprive her of land she has inherited.

Neva Gerber (Sierra Sutter), Edmund Cobb (Cal Coleman), Charles Brinley (John Sutter), Wilbur McGaugh (Robert

Marsdon), Ruth Royce (Arabella Ryan), Clark Coffey (Judge Coleman), Yakima Canutt, Elias Bullock, Al Hoxie.

1. Soldiers of Fortune. 2. Red Men and White. 3. A Night of Terror. 4. The Empire Builders. 5. A Web of Lies. 6. Demetroff's Vow. 7. Facing Death. 8. Under the Bear Flag. 9. A Ride of Peril. 10. Yellow Metal and Blue Blood. 11. Gold Madness. 12. Crimson Nights. 13. Vigilantes Justice. 14. For Life and Love. 15. Trail's End.

Top: **Keene Duncan, Don Douglas, and Constantine Romanoff;** ***bottom:*** **Don Douglas and Edmund Cobb in** ***Deadwood Dick*** **(1940)**

135. Deadwood Dick

(Columbia, July 19, 1940) Serial, 15 chapters, two reels each. D: James W. Horne. SP: Wyndham Gittens, Morgan B. Cox, George Morgan, John Cutting. P: Larry Darmour.

As statehood seems imminent for the Dakota Territory, The Skull, a grotesquely masked criminal, seeks to create an outlaw empire and gain control of rich mineral lands. *Dakota Pioneer Press* publisher Dick Stanley adopts the disguise of Deadwood Dick, a masked figure, to battle the outlaws.

Don Douglas (Dick Stanley/Deadwood Dick), Lorna Gray [Adrian Booth] (Anne Butler), Lane Chandler (Wild Bill Hickok), Marin Sais (Calamity Jane), Harry Harvey (Dave), Jack Ingram (Buzz Ricketts), Charles King (Tex), Edward Cassidy (Drew/The Skull), Robert Fiske (Ashton), Lee Shumway (Bentley), Edmund Cobb (Steele), Edward Peil, Sr. (Sears), Edward Hearn (Sharp), Karl Hackett (Jack McCall), Roy Barcroft (Jim Bridges), Bud Osborne (Stagecoach Driver), Fred Kelsey (Bartender), Edward Cecil (McCall's Defense Lawyer), Joseph W. Girard (Judge), Tom London, Kit Guard, Al Ferguson (Skull's Henchmen), Constantine Romanoff, Yakima Canutt, Franklyn Farnum, Kenneth Duncan, Charles Hamilton, Eddie Featherstone, Jim Corey.

1. A Wild West Empire. 2. Who is the Skull? 3. Pirates of the Plains. 4. The Skull Baits a Trap. 5. Win, Lose, or Draw. 6. Buried Alive. 7. The Chariot of Doom. 8. The Secret of Number Ten. 9. The Fatal Warning. 10. Framed for Murder. 11. The Bucket of Death. 12. A Race Against Time. 13. The Arsenal of Revolt. 14. Holding the Fort. 15. The Deadwood Express.

136. The Demon Shadow

(Arrow, 1919) Serial, 10 chapters, two reels each. D: Howell Hansell. Scen: Lloyd Lonergan and F. W. Doughty. S: Daniel Carson Goodman.

This is a re-release of the 1914 Thanhouser serial entitled *Zudora* or *The Twenty Million Dollar Mystery*, re-edited and trimmed to 10 chapters in lieu of the original 20 chapters.

Zudora and her newspaper boyfriend try to unravel the mystery of a huge money cache and outwit those that would make off with the fortune.

James Cruze (Hassam Ali/Jim Baird), Marguerite Snow (Zudora), Harry Benham

(John Storm), Sidney Bracy (Tom Hunt), Frank Farrington (Captain Radcliffe), Mary Elizabeth Forbes (Mme. Du Val), Jane Fairbanks (Mrs. Ramsey), Morgan Niblack (Mr. Brine), Helen Badgley.

137. The Desert Hawk

(Columbia, May 12, 1944) Serial, 15 chapters, two reels each. D: B. Reeves Eason. SP: Sherman Lowe, Leslie Swabacher, Jack Stanley, Leighton Brill. P: Rudolph C. Flothow. Assist. D: Earl Bellamy. Photography: James S. Brown, Jr. Music: Lee Zahler.

Kasim, the caliph of Ahad, is kidnapped and almost murdered on instructions of his evil twin brother, who takes his place on the throne. Later, when Kasim denounces Hasson as an impostor, no one believes him. He assumes the identity of The Desert Hawk to regain his throne and to keep his brother from marrying Azala, whom the emir of a neighboring country has brought to Ahad to marry Kasim. As The Desert Hawk, Kasim wins Azala's confidence and she helps him expose his brother as a false caliph.

Gilbert Roland replaced James Ellison, who was injured during production.

Gilbert Roland (The Desert Hawk/ Kasim/Hasson), Mona Maris (Princess Azala), Ben Welden (Omar), Kenneth MacDonald (Akbar), Frank Lackteen (Faud), I. Stanford Jolley (Saladin), Charles Middleton (Koda Bey), Egan Brecher (Grey Wizard), Norman Willis (Andor), Georges Renavent (Emir of Telef), Kermit Maynard, Forrest Taylor, George J. Lewis, Reed Howes, Lloyd Ingraham, Eddie Parker.

1. The Twin Brothers. 2. The Evil Eye. 3. The Mask of the Scimitar. 4. A Caliph's Treachery. 5. The Secret of the Palace. 6. The Feast of the Beggars. 7. Double Jeopardy. 8. The Slave Traders. 9. The Underground River. 10. The Fateful Wheel. 11. The Mystery of the Mosque. 12. The Hand of Vengeance. 13. The Sword of Fate. 14. The Wizard's Story. 15. The Triumph of Kasim.

138. Desperadoes of the West

(Republic, December 1950) Serial, 12 chapters, two reels each. D: Fred C. Brannon. SP: Ronald Davidson. Assoc.

Top: **Gilbert Roland, I. Stanford Jolley, and Kermit Maynard in** ***The Desert Hawk*** **(1944);** ***bottom left:*** **Richard Powers (Tom Keene), I. Stanford Jolley, and John Carson;** ***bottom right:*** **Richard Powers, Judy Clark, Roy Barcroft, I. Stanford Jolley, and Lee Phelps in** ***Desperadoes of the West*** **(1950)**

P: Franklyn Adreon. Photography: John MacBurnie. Music: Stanley Wilson. Special Effects: Howard and Theodore Lydecker.

Representing an Eastern syndicate that wants the property for itself, Dude Dawson uses every foul means possible to stop oil well drilling by a cooperative before its lease expires. Colonel Arnold and Ward Gordon furnish the leadership for the cooperative. There are the expected amounts of flying fists and bullets as the serial grinds to a conclusion with a gusher brought in and the outlaws rounded up.

Richard Powers [Tom Keene] (Ward Gordon), Judy Clark (Sally Arnold), Roy Barcroft (Hacker), I. Stanford Jolley (Dude Dawson), Lee Phelps (Rusty Steele), Lee Roberts (Larson), Cliff Clark (Colonel Arnold), Edmund Cobb (Bowers), Bud Osborne (Joe), Dennis Moore (Ned Foster), George Chesebro (Becker), Bob Reeves (Jerry), Hank Patterson (Hardrock Haggerty), Dale Van Sickel (Reed), Tom Steele (Gregg/Blake), Sandy Sanders (Kern), John Cason (Casey), Guy Teague (Jack), Stanley Blystone (Storekeeper), Steve Clark (Freight Agent), Al Taylor (Jenson), Bert LeBaron (Bart), Mauritz Hugo (Hadley), Ace Hudkins (Horse Heavy), Jack Jarden (Ed Harper), Chick Hannon (Guard), Frank O'Connor (Bartender), Art Dillard (Ben), Holly Bane (Bryant), Duke Taylor (Cody), Cactus Mack (Drake), Eddie Parker (Martin), Tom McDonough (Larkin), John Daheim (Bill Murdock), Paul Gustine (Oil Worker), Harold Goodwin (Sheriff), Fred Kohler, Jr. (Plummer), Ray Morgan, Billy Dix, Ralph Bucko, Merrill McCormick, Joe Phillips, Augie Gomez, Wayne Burson, Jim Rinehart.

1. Tower of Jeopardy. 2. Perilous Barrier. 3. Flaming Cargo. 4. Trail of Terror. 5. Plunder Cave. 6. Six-Gun Hijacker. 7. The Powder Keg. 8. Desperate Venture. 9. Stagecoach to Eternity. 10. Hidden Desperado. 11. Open Warfare. 12. Desperate Gamble.

139. Desperate Desmond

(Nestor, November 1911–February 1912) Series, 6 episodes, one reel each. D: Thomas Rickets. S/SP: Harry Hersfield.

Short series based on the old comic strip.

Betsy Keller.

1. Desperate Desmond Pursued by Claude Eclaire (November 1911). 2. Desperate Desmond Almost Succeeds (November 1911). 3. Desperate Desmond Abducts Rosamond (December 1911). 4. Desperate Desmond Foiled by Claude Eclaire (December 1911). 5. Desperate Desmond on the Trail Again (January 1912). 6. Desperate Desmond Fails (January 1912). 7. Desperate Desmond at the Cannons' Mouth.

140. Detective Lloyd

(Mutual Pictures, Ltd./Universal, March 8, 1932) Serial, 12 chapters, two reels each. D: Henry McRae. Dialogue: Ella O'Neill. S: Henry McRae. Filmed in England and released there as *Lloyd of the C.I.D.*; also known as *In the Hands of the Hindu*; a feature-length version under the title *The Green Spot Mystery* was released in August 1932.

Inspector Jack Lloyd of Scotland Yard is assigned to find a missing jewel and unravel a mysterious murder connected with it. England's foremost criminal, Giles Wade, known as The Panther, is his chief antagonist, although Egyptians, too, are after the gem to return it to its native land. Lloyd must constantly save Diana Brooks, niece of the jewel's owner, whom The Panther and his female accomplice, Sybil Craig, use to get at the fabled jewel. Both sides are endangered by the mysterious green spot poison.

Claude Saunders (Inspector Jack Lloyd), Janice Adair (Diana Brooks), Muriel Angelus (Sybil Craig), Wallace Geoffrey (Giles Wade/The Panther), Lewis Dayton (Randall Hale), Tracy Holmes (Chester Dunn), Emily Fitzroy (the Manor Ghost), John Turnbull (Superintendent Barclay), Shayle Gardner (Inspector Walters), Clifford Buckton (Sergeant Sherwood), Vic Kaley (Charwoman), Diana Wilson (Lady Darrington), Fewless Llewellyn (Curator), Ethel Ramsey (Housekeeper), Gibb McLaughlin (Abdul), Earle Stanley (Egyptian), Cecil Musk (Egyptian), Kenneth McLaughlin (Sam), Humberston Wright (Lodgekeeper), Fanny Wright.

1. The Green Spot Murder. 2. The Panther Strikes. 3. The Trap Springs. 4. Tracked by Wireless. 5. The Death Ray. 6. The Poison Dart. 7. The Race with Death. 8. The Panther's Lair. 9. Imprisoned in the North Tower. 10. The Panther's Cunning. 11. The Panther at Bay. 12. Heroes of the Law.

141. Les Deux Gamines

(France—Gaumont, 1921) Serial, 12 chapters. D: Louis Feuillade. S: Louis Feuillade. Scen: Louis Feuillade. Feature Title: *Two Little Urchins*.

Georges Biscot (Chambertin), Sandra Milowanoff (Ginette), Olinda Mano (Gaby), Violette Jyl (Lisette Fleury, leur mère), Alice Tissot (Flora Bènazer), Gaston Michel (Le grand–père Bertal), Fernand Hermann (Pierre Mannin, le père), Mlle. Lugane (Mlle. De Bersanges), Edouard Mathé (M. De Bersanges), Amedée Charpentier (Bénazer, le fripier), Martel (Maugars, son complice), Jane Rollette (Joséphine, la servante), Blanche Montel (Blanche), Bout-de-Zan (René), Laure Mouret (Sephora Bénazer), Mme. De Gordenko (Soeur Véronique).

1. Fleurs de Paris. 2. La nuit de printemps. 3. Le fugitive. 4. La morte vivante. 5. Le lis sous l'orage. 6. L'accalmie. 7. Celle qu'on n'attendait plus. 8. Parmi les loups. 9. Le serment de Ginette. 10. Le candidat à la mort. 11. La cité des chiffons. 12. Le retour.

142. Les Deux Gosses

(France—Cinématographes Phocea, 1924) Serial, 8 chapters (?). D: Louis Mercanton. S: Pierre Decourcelle. Scen: Pierre Decourcelle.

Gabriel Signoret (Bill Mullins), Edouard Mathé (Robert Carville), Carlyle Blackwell (George Thornton), Yvette Guilbert (Biddy Mullins), Albert Decoeur (Dido Bunce), Marjorie Hume (Marion Thornton), Gina Relly (Barbara Scarth), Jane Rollette (the Maid), Paul Guidé (John Scarth), Rene Koval Kerly (Joseph, the Butler), Andrée Rolane (Biddy Mullins' Nephew), Andrews Engelman (the Cough Drop), Jean Mercanton (Master Gerald Thornton), Leslie Shaw (Dick, a little vagabond), Jean Forest (Wally, a little vagabond).

143. The Devil Horse

(Mascot, November 1, 1932) Serial, 12 chapters, Chapter 1 three reels, others two reels. D: Otto Brower. Second Unit D: Yakima Canutt. SP: George Morgan, Barney Sarecky, George Plympton, and Wyndham Gittens. P: Nat Levine. Camera: Ernest Miller, Carl Webster, and Victor Schurich.

An outlaw and his gang stop at nothing to gain possession of the Devil Horse, leader of a wild horse pack in which a wild boy is reared. The villains' plot is to recapture the horse that had once been a great racehorse and present it as a new "discovery," but they are frustrated by the presence of the Wild Boy, who protects the Devil Horse and in turn is protected by him. When the gang kills a forest ranger, his brother vows vengeance and becomes a friend of the Wild Boy and the Devil Horse in tracking down outlaw leader Canfield and his gang. But it is the wild steed that has the final revenge.

Harry Carey (Norton Roberts), Noah Beery, Sr. (Canfield), Frankie Darro (Wild Boy), Greta Granstedt (Linda Weston), Apache (The Devil Horse/El Diablo), Al Bridge (Bates), Barrie O'Daniels (Lee Weston), Jack Mower (Adams), Jack Byron (Jake), Paul Jones (Boyd), Carli Russell (Wild Boy at age 5), Lou Kelley (Wild Boy's Father), Dick Dickinson (Martin), Lane Chandler (Elliott Norton), Henry Hall (Conductor), Yakima Canutt (Slim), Jack Goodrich, Rube Schaefer, Ken Cooper, Wes Warner, Al Taylor.

1. Untamed. 2. The Chasm of Death. 3. The Doom Riders. 4. Vigilante Law. 5. The Silent Call. 6. The Heart of the Mystery. 7. The Battle of the Strong. 8. The Missing Witness. 9. The Showdown. 10. The Death Trap. 11. Wild Loyalty. 12. The Double Decoy.

144. The Diamond from the Sky

(American, May 3, 1915) Serial, 30 chapters, two reels each. D: Jacques Jaccard and William Desmond Taylor. Scen: Roy L. McCardell and Jacques Jaccard. S: Roy L. McCardell.

A large diamond, handed down in a family for several generations, is sought by two cousins. Judge Stanley would inherit the diamond unless Arthur Stanley had a male heir. Arthur passes off a stolen gypsy baby boy as his own male heir in order to obtain the stone. Later the gypsy mother steals his daughter and the diamond, turning both over to Dr. Harding, who adopts the girl, Esther. Arthur Stanley dies. Years pass and the sons of Judge and Arthur Stanley both grow up to continue the fight for possession of the diamond and for the hand of Esther.

Top: **Harry Carey and Frankie Darro;** ***bottom:*** **Frankie Darro, Greta Granstedt, Barrie O' Daniels, Reed Howes, Harry Carey, and Noah Beery, Sr. (*on ground*) in *The Devil Horse* (1932)**

Lottie Pickford (Esther), Irving Cummings (Arthur Stanley II), William Russell (Blair Stanley), Charlotte Burton (Vivian Marston), Eugenie Ford (Hagar Harding), George Periolat (Luke Lovell), Orral Humphrey (Marmaduke Smythe), William Tedmarsh (Quabba, the Hunchback), Hartford [Jack] Hoxie (Matt Hardigan), Charles Watt, Lillian Buckingham, Roy Stewart.

1. A Heritage of Hate. 2. Eye for an Eye. 3. The Silent Witness. 4. The Prodigal's Progress. 5. For the Sake of a False Friend. 6. The Queen of Love and Beauty. 7. The Fox and the Pig. 8. A Mind in the Past. 9. A Runaway Match. 10. Old Foes with New Faces. 11. Over the Hills and Far Away. 12. To the Highest Bidder. 13. The Man in the Mask. 14. For Love and Money. 15. Desperate Chances. 16. The Path of Peril. 17. King of

Diamonds and Queen of Hearts. 18. Charm Against Harm. 19. Fire Fury of Confusion. 20. The Soul Stranglers. 21. The Lion's Bride. 22. A Rose in the Dust. 23. The Double Cross. 24. The Mad Millionaire. 25. A House of Cards. 26. The Garden of Gods. 27. Mine Own People. 28. The Falling Airplane. 29. A Deal with Destiny. 30. The American Earl.

145. The Diamond Master

(Universal, February 3, 1929) Serial, 10 chapters, two reels each. D: Jack Nelson. S: Jacques Futrelle—"The Diamond Master." A remake of *The Diamond Queen* of 1921.

Criminals wish to steal the secret of how to make diamonds from dust and attempt to steal a machine developed to do just that. The inventor's daughter is in constant jeopardy from a group of diamond merchants, but a detective comes to her aid and is eventually able to round up the guilty culprits and send them to their diamond-less reward.

Hayden Stevenson (Mark Van Cortland Wynne), Louise Lorraine (Doris Killner), Al Hart (Randolph Latham), Monte Montague (Van's Manservant), Louis Stern (John Killner), Walter Maly.

1. The Secret of the Night. 2. The Diamond of Death. 3. The Tunnel of Terror. 4. Trapped. 5. The Diamond Machine. 6. The Wolf Pack. 7. The Death Trap. 8. Into the Flames. 9. The Last Stand. 10. The Reckoning.

146. The Diamond Queen

(Universal, March 15, 1921) Serial, 18 chapters, two reels each. D: Ed Kull. Scen: George W. Pyper. Adaptation: Robert F. Roden and George W. Pyper. S: Jacques Futrelle. Remade by Universal in 1929 as *The Diamond Master*.

A machine that will produce pure diamonds from simple dust is coveted by criminals who are not above murder, kidnapping, and torture to accomplish their goal. The inventor's daughter and her detective friend suffer close calls with death but foil the gangster's plans to utilize the machine and bring them to justice. The action takes place in Africa, where Doris at one point becomes a cannibal queen in her fight to keep the diamond cartel from flooding the market with artificial diamonds.

Eileen Sedgwick (Doris Harvey), George Chesebro (Bruce Weston), Frank M.

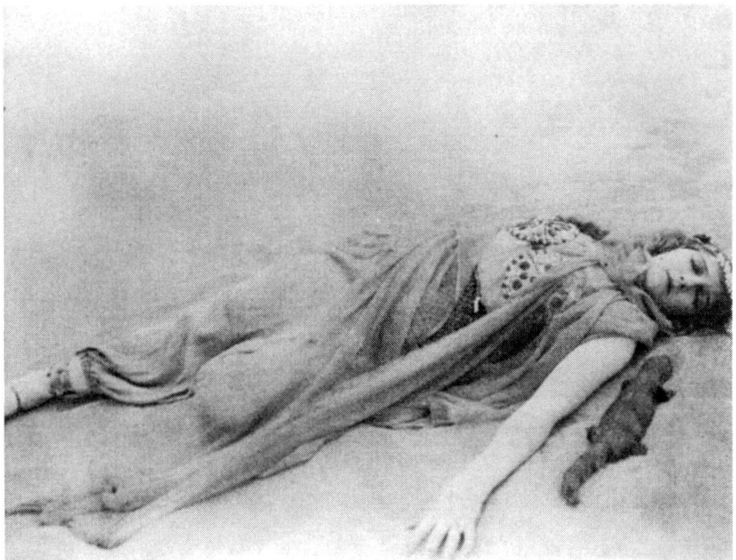

Top: **Lottie Pickford In *The Diamond from the Sky* (1921); *bottom left and right:* Eileen Sedgwick in *Diamond Queen* (1921)**

Clark (Julius Zeidt), Burton Wilson (John Harvey), Alfred Fisher (Professor Harvey), Josephine Scott (Aline Earl), Lew Short (Reitman), Albert J. Smith (Professor Ramsey[?]).

1. Vow of Vengeance. 2. Plunge of Doom. 3. Perils of the Jungle. 4. Fires of Hate. 5. Tide of Destiny. 6. The Colossal Game. 7. An Amazing Ultimatum. 8. In Merciless Clutches. 9. A Race with Rogues. 10. The Betrayal. 11. In Torture's Grip. 12. The Kidnapping. 13. Weird Walls. 14. The Plunge. 15. The Decoy. 16. The Dip of Death. 17. The Hand of Fate. 18. The Hour of Reckoning.

Kay Hughes and Ralph Byrd in *Dick Tracy* (1937)

147. Dick Tracy

(Republic, March 1937) Serial, 15 chapters; Chapter 1, three reels; others, two reels. D: Ray Taylor, Alan James. SP: Barry Shipman and Winston Miller. S: Morgan Cox, George Morgan. Based on characters created by Chester Gould. Assoc. P: J. Laurence Wickland. P: Nat Levine. Photography: William Nobles and Edgar Lyons. Music: Harry Grey.

Detective Dick Tracy tenaciously seeks to discover the identity of the "Lame One," bring an end to the terrorist activities of the Spider gang, and find his brother, Gordon, who has been kidnapped. Unknown to Tracy, his brother becomes a pawn to the Lame One through an operation performed by Moloch, the Lame One's lieutenant. Tracy must not only contend with ordinary hoodlums but also with scientific apparatus and a disintegrating machine located aboard "The Wing," the Lame One's super-modern aircraft.

Ralph Byrd (Dick Tracy), Kay Hughes (Gwen Andrews), Smiley Burnette (Mike McGurk), Lee Van Atta (Junior), John Picorri (Moloch), Carleton Young (Gordon Tracy), Fred Hamilton (Steve Lockwood), Francis X. Bushman (Clive Anderson), John Dilson (Ellery Brewster), Dick Beach (Gordon Tracy before operation), Wedgewood Nowell (H.T. Clayton), Theodore Lorch (Patorno), Edwin Stanley (Walter Odette/The Lame One), Harrison Greene (Cloggerstein), Herbert Weber (Tony Martino), Buddy Roosevelt (Burke/Whitney/Diner Heavy), George DeNormand (Flynn/Claude Destino/Max), Byron K. Foulger (Korvitch), Ed Platt (Oscar), Lou Fulton (Elmer), Sam Flint (Brock), Bruce Mitchell (Brandon), Nicholas Nelson (Andrea), Monte Montague (Clancy), John Holland (Carter), Al Taylor (Costain/Hank/Riveter/Taylor), Ann Ainslee (Betty Clayton), Mary Kelley (Georgetta Clarabelle), Robes Murray (Henry Coulter), Hal Price (Joe Crane), Henry Sylvester (Dirigible Commander), Milburn Morante (Death Valley Johnny), Loren Riche (Peters/Riveter/Diner Heavy), Leander de Cordova (Dock Official/Stevens), Kit Guard (Farley), William Stahl (Fox), Edward LeSaint (Governor), Wally West (Harry/Craft), Al Ferguson (John Henderson), Jane Keckley (Mrs. Henkin), Jack Stewart (Motor Cop), William Humphrey (James), Bob Reeves (Officer), Jack Gardner (Secretary/Miller), John Bradford (Joe), Harry Strang (Bill Moffett), Jack Ingram (Reporter), Don Kerr (Reporter), Charley Phillips (Reporter), John Butler (Noble), Roy Barcroft (Wing Heavy), Alice Fleming (Teacher), Brooks Benedict (Wing Pilot), Harry Anderson (Pete), Henry Hale (Radioman), Kernan Cripps (Police Announcer), Andre Cheron (Clare Renee), Walter Long (Whitey), Burr Caruth (Wickland).

1. The Spider Strikes. 2. The Bridge of Terror. 3. The Fur Pirates. 4. Death Rides the Sky. 5. Brother Against Brother. 6. Dangerous Waters. 7. The Ghost Town Mystery. 8. Battle in the Clouds. 9. The Stratosphere Adventure. 10. The Gold Ship. 11. Harbor Pursuit. 12. The Trail of the Spider. 13. The Fire Trap. 14. The Devil is White. 15. Brothers United.

148. Dick Tracy Returns

(Republic, December 1938) Serial, 15 chapters; Chapter 1, three reels; others, two reels. D: William Witney and John English. SP: Barry Shipman, Franklyn Adreon, Ronald Davidson, Rex Taylor, and Sol Shor. Based on *Dick Tracy* comic strip by Chester Gould. Assoc. P: Robert Beche. Photography: William Nobles.

Dick Tracy is assigned to apprehend the Stark gang, comprised of Pa Stark and his five sons, whose trail of crime is reminiscent of that of John Dillinger, Pretty Boy Floyd, and Ma Barker. One by one the Starks are killed in the act of committing crimes, with Pa the last to die as he attempts to escape in an airplane.

Ralph Byrd (Dick Tracy), Lynn Roberts (Gwen Andrews), Charles Middleton (Pa Stark), Jerry Tucker (Junior), David Sharpe (Ron Merton), Lee Ford (Mike McGuirk), Michael Kent (Steve Lockwood), Reed Howes (Rance), Tom Steele (G-Man), Eddie Parker (Burton), John Merton (Champ Stark), Raphael Bennett (Trigger Stark), Jack Roberts (Dude Stark), Ned Glass (Kid Stark), Edward Foster (Joe Hammer), James Blaine (Clive

Top: **Dave Sharpe and Ralph Byrd;** ***bottom:*** **Ralph Byrd, Lynn Roberts, and Dave Sharpe in** ***Dick Tracy Returns*** **(1938)**

Anderson), Lynton Brent (Attendant), Jack Ingram (Slasher Stark), Eddie Dew (Pilot), Archie Hall (Blackie), Maston Williams (Bill), Alan Gregg (Jimmy Madison), Robert Terry (Reynolds), Tom Seidel (Hunt), Duke Green, Bob Thom, Roy Darmour, Dick Bitgood (Dick Tracy's Men), Eddie Cherokee (Brand), Bill Hunter (Buck), Douglas Evans (Burke), Gordon Hart (Carston), William Stahl (Casey), Al Taylor (Karl), J.P. McGowan (Kurger), Ted Wells, Buddy Mason, Loren Riebe, Duke Green, Allen Pomeroy, Earl Bunn, Harry Tenbrook, George Magrill, Jerry Frank, Frank Wayne, Jack Montgomery, Walter Jones, Pat McKee (Heavies), Budd Buster (Gas Station Attendant), James Carlisle (Naval Commissioner), Jenifer Gray (Nurse), Bud Wolfe (Jake), Oscar Hendrian (Joe), Allan Cravan (Plover), William Mitchell (Proprietor), Monte Montague (Sam), Frank Hagney (Slim), Virginia Carroll (Stewardess), Frank LaRue (Strobach), John Wade (Worthing), Walter Low (Rex), Jack Egan (Radio Announcer), Gloria Rich (Irene), John Gustin (Pilot), Charles Sullivan (Pete), Ralph McCullough (Perlita Operator), Sid Troy (Harmon), Larry Steers (Duke), Ian Rayo (Clem), Ralph Bowman (Clark), Bruce Mitchell (Foreman), Douglas Meins (Newsboy), King Mojave (Sailor), Frank Hall Crane (Doctor), Wedgewood Nowell (Draper), Charles McMurphy (Driver), Henry Sylvester (Doctor Grant), Charles Martin (Jones), Willard Kent, Sherry Hall, Jerry Frank, Millard McGowan, Warren Jackson, Harrison Greene, Malcolm Graham, Forrest Taylor, Yakima Canutt, Art Dillard, Kernan Cripps.

1. The Sky Wreckers. 2. The Runway of Death. 3. Handcuffed to Doom. 4. Four Seconds to Live. 5. Death in the Air. 6. Stolen Secrets. 7. Tower of Death. 8. Cargo of Destruction. 9. The Clock of Doom. 10. High Voltage. 11. The Kidnapped Witness. 12. The Runaway Torpedo. 13. Passengers to Doom. 14. In the Hands of the Enemy. 15. G-Men's Dragnet.

149. Dick Tracy vs. Crime, Inc.

(Republic, December 1941) Serial, 15 chapters, two reels each. D: William Witney, John English. SP: Ronald Davidson, Norman S. Hall, William Lively, Joseph O'Donnell, and Joseph Poland. Assoc. P: W.J. O'Sullivan. Photography: Reggie Lanning. Music: Cy Feuer. Special Effects: Howard Lydecker. Based on characters created by Chester Gould. Reissued in 1952 as *Dick Tracy vs. Phantom Empire*.

Dick Tracy's genius and luck are taxed to the limit as he endeavors to capture and learn the identity of The Ghost, a master criminal determined to destroy the city in revenge for the death of his brother. The Ghost, so called because he can make himself invisible, is actually a member of an anti-crime council. Because Tracy suspects that a member of the council is The Ghost, he is ultimately able to bring about the downfall of the scoundrel.

Ralph Byrd (Dick Tracy), Jan Wiley (June Chandler), John Davidson (Lucifer), Ralph Morgan (J.P. Morton/The Ghost), Michael Owen (Bill Carr), Kenneth Harlan (Cosgrove), Jack Mulhall (Jim Wilson), Robert Frazier (Daniel Brewster), Robert Fiske (Walter Cabot), Hooper Atchley (Arthur Trent), Anthony Warde (John Corey), John Merton (Brent), Forrest Taylor (Butler), Edward Hearn (Cutter Captain), John James (Davis), Terry Frost (Drake), Walter Miller (Morgan), Selmer Jackson (Vincent), Nora Lane (Ella Gilbert), John Dilson (Henry Welden), Howard Hickman (Stephen Chandler), Chuck Morrison (Trask), Archie Twitchell (Announcer), Frank Meredith (Army Officer), Jack Kenny (Berke), Dick Lamarr (Canfield), Edmund Cobb (Kelly), Robert Wilke (Helmsman), John Webb Dillon (Inspector), Pat O'Shea (Car Heavy), Hugh Prosser (Patrol Captain), Sam Benard (Green), Charles Miller (Hawes), Stanley Price (Jackson), Buddy Roosevelt, George Allen, Dave Sharpe (Pier Heavies), Eddie Parker (Hideout Heavy), Fred Kohler, Jr. (House Heavy), William Hammer (Intern), Bud Wolfe (Grill Heavy), Carol Adams (Nurse), Raphael Bennett, Jacques Lory, Joseph Kirk (Brownstone Heavies), Marjorie Kane (Cigarette Girl), Bill Wilkus (Chuck/Plant Heavy), George Peabody (Driver), Frank Alten (Arno Draga), Walter McGrail (Junction Heavy/Marine Captain), Richard Kipling (Customs Inspector), Bert LeBaron (Pete Collins/Plant Heavy), William Hammer (Intern), Barry Hayes (Chester), Fred Schaefer (Dawson), Charles McAvoy (Clancy), Al Taylor (Boat Heavy), C. Montague Shaw (Jonathan Martin), Charley Phillips, Evan Thomas, Jimmy Fawcett, Ken Terrell, Bob Robinson, Al Seymour, Bud Geary, Duke Taylor (Plant Heavies), Douglas Evans (Police Broadcaster), John Bagni (Pete), Frances Morris (Operator), Benny Burt (Nick), Julian Madison (Ranger), Howard Mitchell (Riley), Wally Rose (Roof Heavy), Lynton Brent (Serviceman), Griff Banrette (Watchman), Dick Rush (Tom), Ray Hanson (Tim), Sid Troy (Slade), Alex Lockwood (Smith), Max Waizman (Telegrapher).

1. The Fatal Hour. 2. The Prisoner Vanishes. 3. Doom Patrol. 4. Dead Man's Trap. 5. Murder at Sea. 6. Besieged. 7. Sea Racketeers. 8. Train of Doom. 9. Beheaded. 10. Flaming Peril. 11. Seconds to Live. 12. Trial by Fire. 13. The Challenge. 14. Invisible Terror. 15. Retribution.

Top: **Robert Fiske in *Dick Tracy vs. Crime, Inc.* (1941); *bottom:* Ralph Byrd in *Dick Tracy's G-Men* (1939)**

150. Dick Tracy's G-Men

(Republic, October 1939) Serial, 15 chapters; Chapter 1, three reels; others, two reels. D: William Witney, John English. SP: Barry Shipman, Franklyn Adreon, Rex Taylor, Ronald Davidson, and Sol Shor. Based on the comic strip by Chester Gould. Assoc. P: Robert Beche. Photography: William Nobles. Music: William Lava.

Zarnoff, foremost international criminal, is executed in the lethal gas chamber of a California prison. But before execution a newspaper printed in ink to which a drug has been added is smuggled in to Zarnoff, who dissolves pieces of the paper in water and drinks the mixture. The drug keeps gas from entering his lungs, but makes him appear dead. His body is then stolen and revived by his minions. Swearing revenge on Dick Tracy, he resumes his diabolical spy and crime activities, with Tracy in hot pursuit.

Ralph Byrd (Dick Tracy), Irving Pichel (Nicholas Zarnoff), Phylis Isley (Gwen Andrews), Ted Pearson (Steve

Ralph Byrd in *Dick Tracy's G-Men* (1939)

Lockwood), Walter Miller (Robal), George Douglas (Sandoval), Kenneth Harlan (Clive Anderson), Ted Mapes (Ted Murchison), Jack Ingram (Al), Merrill McCormick (Assistant), Bud Geary (Ben), Monte Montague (Bourke), Edward Cassidy (Captain), Charles Hutchison (Brandon), Charles Sullivan (Brody), Lee Shumway (Burke), Budd Buster (Cappy), Joe Yrigoyen (Crewman), George Allen (Crewman), Edmund Cobb (Reynolds), Stanley Price (Shang), Reed Howes (Slim), Forrest Taylor (Stevens), Lloyd Ingraham (Stoddard), Sammy McKim (Sammy Williams), George Cleveland (Williams), Tristram Coffin (Zobar), William Stahl (Bruce), Ken Terrell (Ed Hardy), Joe McGuinn (Tom), Robert Wayne (Wilbur), Bud Wolfe (Bill), Curley Dresden (Boat Heavy), Charley Phillips (Boat Heavy), Jim Cassidy (Ralph Collins), Frank Meredith (Duffy), Jack Raymond (Gus Fleming), Bob Terry (Benton), Harrison Greene (Baron), Harry Humphrey (Stover), Julian Madison (Foster), Robert Carson (Scott), Bigelow Sayre (Davis), Russell Collier (Dispatcher), Peter Von Ziegler (Green), Bruce Mitchell (Guard), Robert Hartford (Gus), Reginald Barlow (Albert Guttenbach), Bill Yrigoyen (Howard), Frank O'Connor (Huxley), Bernard Suss (Lasen), Robert Brister (Kranz), Gilman Shelton (Joe), Barry Hays (Johnson), Ed Brady (Jonas), Walter Merrill (Junior Officer), Charles Sherlock (Trooper), Cary Loftin (Trooper), Allan Cavan (Warden), John Maloney (Tim), Joseph Forte (Stanton), Edward Hearn (Ranger), Jerry Frank (Jake), George DeNormand (Jack), Perry Ivins (Telef), Charles Murphy (Stopes), Jack Roberts (Lenny Robinson), Milton Frome (Officer), John Locke (Newscaster), Joseph Swickard (Huenemo Mendoza), Allan Davis (Link), Ray Harper (A.B. Martin), Louis Caits (Jerry), Jack Kenney (Ward), Harry Lang (Borossa), Al Taylor (Heavy), Bert LeBaron (Heavy), Eddie Cherkose (Heavy), Tom Steele (Heavy), Eddie Parker (Heavy), William Nestel (Heavy), Bill Wilkus (Heavy), Bill Lally (Heavy), Jimmy Fawcett (Heavy), Allen Pomeroy (Heavy), Fred Schaefer (Heavy), George Burton (Heavy), Charles Regan (Heavy).

1. The Master Spy. 2. Captured. 3. The False Signal. 4. The Enemy Strikes. 5. Crack-Up. 6. Sunken Peril. 7. Tracking the Enemy. 8. Chamber of Doom. 9. Flames of Jeopardy. 10. Crackling Fury. 11. Caverns of Peril. 12. Fight in the Sky. 13. The Fatal Ride. 14. Getaway. 15. The Last Stand.

151. Dick Turpin

(British Filmcraft, 1929) Series, 4 episodes. D: Reginald Fogwell (1 & 2); Leslie Eveleigh (3 & 4). S: Reginald Fogwell. P: George J. Banfield.

Outlawed: Kenneth McLaglen (Dick Turpin), Wally Patch (Jonathan Wild), Betty Siddons (Betty Leigh), J.R. Tozer (Sir Anthony Lethridge), Gabrielle Morton (Hon. Mary Carrouthers). *The Impostor:* Kenneth McLaglen (Dick Turpin/Sir Simon Kyle), Wally Patch (Jonathan Wild), Eve Terry (Dorothy), Wallace Bosco (Uncle), Holland Bennett (John Watkin). *The Snare:* Kenneth McLaglen (Dick Turpin), Wally Patch (Jonathan Wild), James Knight (Tom King), Betty Siddons (Betty Leigh), J.R. Tozer (Sir Anthony Lethridge), Gabrielle Morton (Hon. Mary Carrouthers). *Nemesis:* Kenneth McLaglen (Dick Turpin), Wally Patch (Jonathan Wild), Betty Siddons (Betty Leigh).

152. Do or Die

(Universal, May 30, 1921) Serial, 18 chapters, two reels each. D: J.P. McGowan. S: Anthony W. Coldeway.

The exact nature of the plot is not known, but once again hidden treasure is the catalyst for all the action which was partially filmed in Cuba and the West Indies.

Eddie Polo (Jack Merton), Inez McDonald (Dolores Nunez), Magda Lane (The Mystery Woman), J.P. McGowan (Captain Alvarez/Satan), Jay Marchant (Mendez), Jean Perkins (Rafael).

1. The Buccaneer's Bride. 2. The Hornet's Nest. 3. The Secret of the Sea. 4. The Hidden Danger. 5. The Bandit's Victim. 6. The Escape. 7. In Hiding. 8. The Trap. 9. Under Sentence. 10. The Secret Cavern. 11. Satan's Twin. 12. The Lost Ring. 13. The Cipher Key. 14. The Midnight Attack. 15. The Race for Life. 16. The Crystal Lake. 17. A Fight to the Finish. 18. Hidden Treasure.

153. Dr. Gar-El-Hama

(Norway—Nordisk Films, 1911–1916) Serial, 5 chapters. D: Eduard Schnedler-Serensen (Chapters 1 and 2), Robert

Dinesen (Chapters 3–4–5). SP: Ludvig Landmann (Chapters 1 and 2), Fritz Magnussen (Chapter 3), Peter Nielsen (Chapters 4 and 5). Camera: Axel Graatkjaer (Chapter 2), Sofus Wangoe (Chapters 3–4–5).

Aage Hertel (Dr. Gar-El-Hama), Einar Zangenberg (Newton), Henry Seemann (Baron von Sternberg), Edith Buemann (Edith Wolfhagen), Carl Johan Lundquist (Count Wolfhagen), Otto Lagoni (James Pendleton), Frederik Jocobsen (A Servant), Robert Schyberg (Dr. Watson), Ella Sprange (Dr. Watson's Wife), Robert Dinesen (Lieutenant Erskin), Ebba Thomsen (Katarina Johannidis), Johannes Ring (Counsel Johannidis), Svend Kornbeck (Tom Handie), Robert Dinesen (Sam Blinkton), Gerda Christoffersen (Countess Sinclair), Johannes Ring (Count Sinclair), Frantz Skondrup (Jeweler Lewenstein), Moritz Bielawski (Jeweler Hase), Gerhard Jessen (Mr. Gee), Svend Melsing (Andor Tremonie), Ingeborg Bruun-Berthelsen (Ellinor Stevens), Anton de Verdier (E. Stevens), Elith Pio, Carl Lauritzen, Christian Schroder, Amanda Lund, Lauritz Olsen, Gerda Christoffersen, Frantz Skondrup, Charles Willumsen, Dagmar Kofoed, Nita Blichfeldt, Birger von Gotta Schonberg, Peter Jorgensen, Ingeborg Olsen, Holger Syndergaard, H. Clausen, Goerge Berthelsen, Carl Schenstrom, Oscar Nielsen, Carl Petersen.

1. Bedraget i Doden (Eng. Title: A Dead Man's Child), 11-16-11, 800 meters. 2. Dr. Gar-El-Hama's Flugt (Eng. Title: Dr. Gar-El-Hama, Sequel to A Dead Man's Child), 9-16-12, 800 meters. 3. Slangeoen (Eng. Title: The Abduction), 10-26-14, three reels. 4. Den orientalske Giftblander (Eng. Title: The Great Jewel Robbery), 2-21-16, 995 meters. 5. Sfinxens Son (Eng. Title: The Three Thousand Pounds Checque), 3-11-18, three reels.

Aage Hertel, Ebba Thomsen, and Robert Dinesen in *Dr. Gar-El-Hama* (1916)

154. Dr. Mabuse, der Spieler

(Germany—Decla–Bishop AF, 1922) Serial, 15 chapters, two reels each. D: Fritz Lang. S: Norbert Jacques. SP: Thea Von Harbou.

Dr. Mabuse, der Spieler is perhaps Lang's best German film. He was at his best when aided by his script-writing wife, Thea von Harbou. The film was actually four hours in length but, in Brazil at least, it was cut up into fifteen chapters. The four-hour epic has, formally, much of the serial about it.

Odd for the serial form, though, is its lack of action. After a brilliantly conceived robbery at the start the film settles down comfortably to a series of dialogues and arias, only now and then interspersed by some burst of activity. Mabuse is a gambler in the grip of vice. His professions are psychiatry and banking. Through hypnotism he is able to make puppets of others, and with this power insinuates himself into a Count's mansion and swiftly makes his way into the Countess's bed.

In the story, detective von Wenk is a mastermind, alone capable of stopping Mabuse's rise to total power. The forces of good as embodied in him are feeble, yet he is the only good in the film. In the end we find Count Todd playing cards with phantoms and Mabuse, driven insane, wildly hatching plots.

Rudolf Klein-Rogge (Dr. Mabuse), Bernhard Goetzke (von Wenk, o Promotor), Alfred Abel (Conde Told), Gertrude Welcker (Condessa Dusy Told), Aud Egede-Nissen (Cara Carozza), Paul Richter (Edgar Hull), Robert Forster-Larrinaga (Spoerri), Hans Adalbert Von Schlettow (Georg), Georg John (Pesch, o "maître d'hotel"), Karl Huszar (Hawasch), Grete Berger (Fine, a criada), Julius Falkenstein (Karsten), Lydia Potechina (A Russa), Julius E. Herrmann (Schramm), Karl Platen (o criado de Told), Anita Berber (a dansarina), Edgar Pauly (o espectador gordo), Julie Brandt, Auguste Prasch-Grevenberg, Adele Sandrock, Max Adalbert, Paul Biensfeldt, Gustav Botz, Heinrich Gotto, Leonhard Haskel, Erner Hübsch, Gottfried Huppertz, Hans Junkermann, Alfred Klein, Erich Pabst, Hans Sternberg, Olaf Storm, Erich Walter.

Portuguese: 1. Jogando Milhies na Belsa. 2. Visionario contra milionário. 3. A força do hipnotismo. 4. Um colar de 50 mil dólares. 5. A força desconhecida. 6. Vence a polícia. 7. Amor de bandido cruel. 8. Um assassinato misterioso. 9. Luxúria de um demônio. 10. O aparelho infernal. 11. Espectros noturnos. 12. Leão contra leão. 13. Tsin-Nam-Fu!!! 14. Remorso pavoroso. 15. Nas garras da Loucura.

155. Dog Detective Series (aka *Fearless* Series)

(Van Pelt Prod./Chesterfield, 1926) Series, 12 episodes, two reels each. D: Ernest Van Pelt

Fearless was an Alaskan Wolfhound. Action devised to show off the cleverness of Fearless in his jumping, fighting, and trailing specialties. An intelligent animal even if a little unpolished in his screen technique.

Fearless. Appearing in the series at times are Jack Mower, Bruce Gordon, and Grace Cunard.

1. A String of Diamonds. 2. The Love Fighter. 3. The Wolf. 4. Detective K-9. 5. A Dumb Romeo. 6. Fangs of Vengeance. 7. The Silent Trailer. 8. Dog Scents. 9. Dog of Dogs. 10. The Thief of ____(?) 11. His Pal. 12. Almost Human.

156. Dollari e Fraks

(Itály—Tiber Films, 1919) Serial, 4 chapters. D: Emilio Ghione. SP: Emilio Ghione.

Emilio Ghione was the foremost producer of Italian serials. He often wrote, directed, and starred in the productions.

Emilio Ghione, Kally Sambucine, Amilcare Taglienti, Léonie Laporte.

1. La X di un delitto. 2. La mano guantata. 3. Il quaranta pugnali. 4. La sedia elettrica.

157. Don Daredevil Rides Again

(Republic, September 1951) Serial, 12 chapters. D: Fred C. Brannon. SP: Ronald Davidson. Assoc. P:. Franklyn Adreon. Photography: Ellis W. Carter. Music: Stanley Wilson. Special Effects: Howard and Theodore Lydecker.

Lee Hadley dons the mask of Don Daredevil to battle Douglas Stratton who, under a forged Spanish land grant, is trying to claim title to valuable ranch lands owned in part by Lee's cousin, Patricia. Supposedly a tenderfoot Easterner, Lee homesteads the Doyle Ranch and encourages ranchers to stand pat against Stratton's night riders and his crooked sheriff co-conspirator.

Ken Curtis (Lee Hadley/Don Daredevil), Aline Towne (Patricia Doyle), Roy Barcroft (Douglas Stratton), Lane Bradford (Weber), Robert Einer (Gary Taylor), John Cason (Hagen), I. Stanford Jolley (Sheriff), Hank Patterson (Buck Bender), Lee Phelps (Michael Doyle), Sandy Sanders (Dirk), Guy Teague (Deputy), Tom Steele (Black), Mike Ragan (Miller), Cactus Mack (Turner), Dale Van Sickel (Dan Farley), Jack Ingram (Jack), Bud Osborne (Bartender), Art Dillard (Raider), Forrest Taylor (Taylor), Joe Phillips (Attacker), Roy Bucko (Barnett), Saul Gorss (Briggs), David Sharpe (Clark), Carey Loftin (Owens), Jack Harden (Jake Miller), Charles Horvath (Davis), George Lloyd (Martin), Frank McCarroll (Deputy), Carlie Taylor (Sloan), Bert LeBaron (Tex), James Linn (Thompson), Townsmen: Herman Hack, Frank Meredith, Tex Terry, Bob Reeves, Chick Hannon, Gene Christopher, Tony DeMario, Don Harvey.

1. Return of the Don. 2. Double Death. 3. Hidden Danger. 4. Retreat to Destruction. 5. Cold Steel. 6. The Flaming Juggernaut. 7. Claim Jumper. 8. Perilous Combat. 9. Hostage of Destiny. 10. Marked for Murder. 11. The Captive Witness. 12. Flames of Vengeance.

158. Don Winslow of the Coast Guard

(Universal, July 1943) Serial, 13 chapters, two reels each. D: Ford Beebe and Ray Taylor. SP: George H. Plympton, Paul Huston, and Griffin Jay. Music: H.J. Salter. Assoc. P: Henry MacRae. Based on the newspaper feature *Don Winslow of the Navy* by Frank V. Martinek.

Don Winslow and his pal, Red, on loan to the Coast Guard, continue their struggle against The Scorpion and his Nazi and Japanese aides.

Don Terry (Don Winslow), Walter Sande (Red Pennington), Elyse Knox (Mercedes Colby), Nestor Paiva (The Scorpion), Lionel Royce (Reichter), Henry Victor (Heilrich), Charles Wagenheim (Mussanti), Philip Ahn (Hirota), Paul Bryar (Anders), Stanley Blystone (Collins), Rex Lease (Captain Tyler), Cyril Delevanti (Officer), Richard Crane (Pilot), Paul Dubov (Sailor).

1. Trapped in the Blazing Sun. 2. Battling a U-Boat. 3. The Crack in the Clouds. 4. The Scorpion Strikes. 5. A Flaming Target. 6. Ramming the Submarine. 7. Bombed in the Ocean Depths. 8. Blackout Treachery. 9. The Torpedo Strikes. 10. Blasted from the Skies. 11. A Fight to the Death. 12. The Death Trap. 13. Capturing the Scorpion.

159. Don Winslow of the Navy

(Universal, December 1941) Serial, 12 chapters, two reels each. D: Ford Beebe and Ray Taylor. SP: Paul Huston and Griffin Jay. Adaptation: Morgan B. Cox. Based on comic strip *Don Winslow of the Navy* by Frank V. Martinek. Photography: William Sickner.

Don Winslow and his friends clash with a master saboteur called The Scorpion, whose agents are attempting to stop construction of a naval base on an island in the Pacific.

Don Terry (Don Winslow), Walter Sande (Lt. Red Pennington), Wade Boteler (Mike Splendor), John Litel (Merlin), Clare Dodd (Mercedes Colby), Anne Nagel (Melissa Gay), Samuel S. Hinds (The Admiral), Kurt Hatch (The Scorpion), Robert Barron (Prindle), Peter Leeds (Chapman), Herbert Rawlinson (Admiral Warburton), Lane Chandler (Corby), Ben Taggart (Blake), John Holland (Barsac), Ethan Laidlaw (Spike), Arthur Loft (Tranker), Dirk Thane (Commander Grady), Paul Scott (Captain Fairfield), Frank Lackteen (Koloki).

1. The Human Torpedo. 2. Flaming Death. 3. Weapon of Horror. 4. Towering Doom. 5. Trapped in the Dungeon. 6. Menaced by Man Eaters. 7. Bombed by the Enemy. 8. The Chamber of Doom. 9. Wings of Destruction. 10. Fighting Fathoms Deep. 11. Caught in the Caverns. 12. The Scorpion Strangled.

160. Double Adventure

(Pathé, January 23, 1921) Serial, 15 chapters, two reels each. D: W.S. Van Dyke. S: Jack Cunningham. P: Robert Brunton.

Financier Benton Biddle discovers that his associate, Jules Fernol, has embezzled money from the fortune of Martha Steadman, Biddle's ward. Fernol kills Biddle and the murder is blamed on Bob Cross, a double for Biddle's son Dick, who has gone to South America after quarreling with his father. Bob proves his identity and is released.

Fernol plots to kill Dick, heir to his father's fortune, and gain it by marrying Martha. They sail to Central America, trailed by Bob. There, Dick Biddle is leading a rebellion against the government. Dick and Bob are often mistaken for one another in a series of battles. Dick, as Bob, returns to America with Vincente Garcia, daughter of the Central American president. Bob is able to stop Fernol from killing Dick and exposes the man as the murderer of Benton Biddle. Dick has married Vincente, and Bob and Martha are about to wed.

Charles Hutchison (Bob Cross/Dick Biddle), Josie Sedgwick (Martha Steadman), Carl Stockdale (Jules Fernol), S.E. Jennings (Rebel Chief), Ruth Langston (Vincente Garcia), Louis D'Or (President Garcia).

1. On the Trail of Fate. 2. The Harbor Bandits. 3. Hearts of Stone. 4. The Gun Runner. 5. The Rebel's Nest. 6. Troubled Trail. 7. War in the Oil Fields. 8. The Grill of Fate. 9. The Black Whirlpool. 10. A Devil's Bargain. 11. The Danger Ledge. 12. Hazardous Heights. 13. By Air and Sea. 14. The House in the Canyon. 15. The Wages of Crime.

161. The Dragon's Net

(Universal, August 23, 1920) Serial, 12 chapters, two reels each. D: Henry McRae. SP: George Hively, Henry McRae. S: J. Allen Dunn—"The Pearls of Loa-Tze." P: Henry McRae.

The story centers about a set of eight lotus leaves made of gold. A formula to perpetual life may be gleamed from an inscription which can be determined only by having the entire set.

A crooked old fellow feigns friendship and swindles one of the leaves from the heroine to add to what he has. The heroine endeavors to square accounts by getting the lotus leaves back. The search leads the heroine, hero, and villain across the Pacific. Portions of the serial were actually filmed in China, Japan, and the Philippines. Marie Walcamp married Harlan Tucker following completion of the serial.

Marie Walcamp (Marie Carlton), Harlan Tucker (Harlan Keeler), Otto Lederer (King Carson), Wadsworth Harris (Doctor Redding).

1. The Mysterious Murder. 2. Thrown Overboard. 3. A Watery Grave. 4. Into the Chasm. 5. A Jump for Life. 6. Captured in China. 7. The Unseen Foe. 8. Trailed in Peking. 9. On the Great Wall of China. 10. The Train of Death. 11. The Shanghai Peril. 12. The Unmasking.

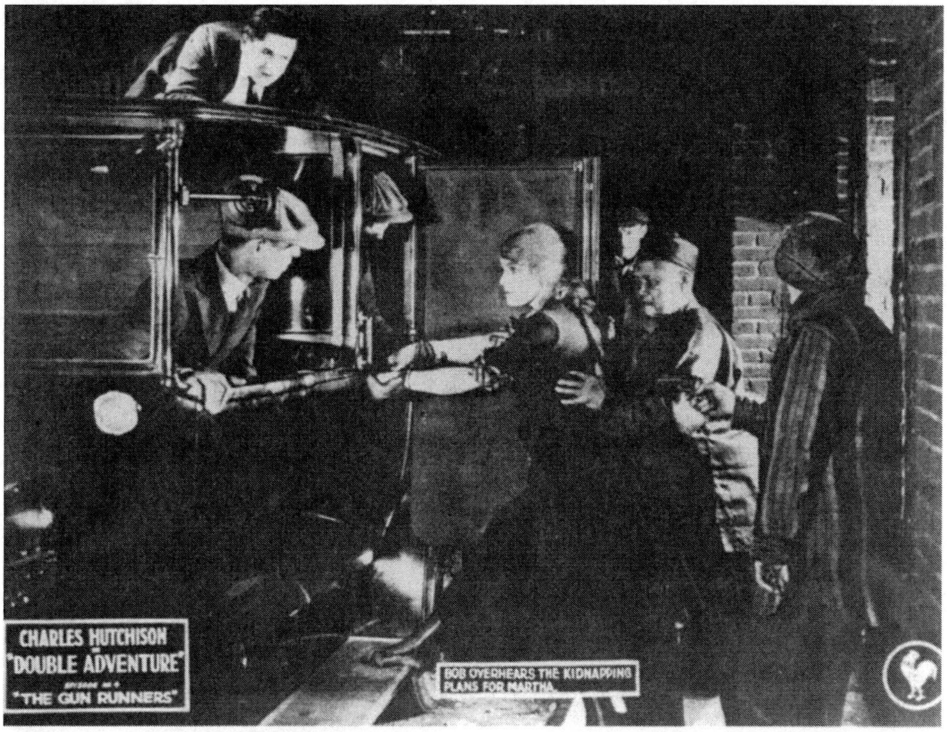

Top: **Charles Hutchison and Josi Sedgwick in *Double Adventure* (1921);** ***bottom:*** **Marie Walcamp in *The Dragon's Net* (1920)**

162. Drums of Fu Manchu

(Republic, 1940) Serial, 15 chapters, two reels each. D: William Witney and John English. SP: Franklyn Adreon, Morgan Cox, Ronald Davidson, Norman Hall, Barney Sarecky, Sol Shor. Suggested by Sax Rohmer. Assoc. P: Hiram S. Brown, Jr. Photography: William Nobles. Music: Cy Feuer.

Fu Manchu is bent on the conquest of Asia and the annihilation of everyone who does not bow to his will. He has promised the hill tribes of Asia that during the Holy year the Sacred Scepter will appear. It reposes in the tomb of Genghis Khan. Fu Manchu needs to acquire three scrolls that will lead him to the tomb. With his sinister crew of gruesome, mind-enslaved henchmen—the decoits—he sets about obtaining the scrolls, only to run up against his old nemesis, Sir Dennis Nayland Smith of Scotland Yard.

Henry Brandon (Fu Manchu), William Royle (Sir Dennis

Top: **Henry Brandon; *bottom:* Henry Brandon and John Merton in *Drums of Fu Manchu* (1940)**

Nayland Smith), Gloria Franklin (Fah Lo Suee), Robert Kellard (Allan Parker), Luana Walters (Mary Randolph), Tom Chatterton (Edward Randolph), Olaf Hytten (Flinders Pstrie), George Cleveland (James Parker), John Dilson (Ezra Howard), Lal Chend Mehra (Sirdar Prahni), John Merton (Loki), Dwight Frye (Anderson), George Pembroke (C.W. Crawford), Philip Ahn (Chang), Lee Shumway (Corrigan), Ann Baldwin (Miss Frisbie), John Picorri (Krantz), Jenifer Gray (Stewardess), Joe de Stefani (High Lhama), Wheaton Chambers (Humphrey), Guy D'Ennery (Ranah Sang), Charley Phillips (Baggage Clerk), Lowden Adams (Blake), John Lester Johnson (Cardo), Evan Thomas (Carlton), Jamiel Hasson (Chieftain), Eric Lansdale (Richards), Robert Blair (Sergeant), Frank Ellis, Henry Wills, Victor Cox (Tarters), Carl Sepulveda, Jack Montgomery, Bob Woodward (Tribesmen), John Ward (Wilson), Norman Nesbitt (Wally Winchester), Michael Vallon (Temple Guard), Tony Paton (Temple Guard), George Bruggerman (Telegrapher), Robert Stevenson (Russian), Merrill McCormick (Attendant), Walter Stiritz (Attendant), Bert LeBaron (Fireman), John Meredith (Gate Sentry), Budd Buster, Decoits: Eddie Kaye, Bob Jamison, Joe Yrigoyen, Duke Taylor, Bill Wilkus, Frank Wayne, Ken Terrell, George Suzanne, Duke Green, Augie Gomez, Tommy Coats, Vinegar Roan, Jack Roper, Ernie Sarracino, Al Taylor, David Sharpe (Double), Bill Yrigoyen (Hillman), Tofik Mickey (Hindu), Paul Renay (Khandar), Kam Tong (Houseboy), Francis Walker (Koomerow), Paul Marion (Messenger), James B.Leong (Chinese), Ted Wells (Decoit).

1. Fu Manchu Strikes. 2. The Monster. 3. Ransom in the Sky. 4. The Pendulum of Doom. 5. The House of Terror. 6. Death Dials a Number. 7. Vengeance of the Si Fan. 8. Danger Trail. 9. The Crystal of Death. 10. Drums of Death. 11. The Tomb of the Genghis Khan. 12. Fire of Vengeance. 13. The Devil's Tattoo. 14. Satan's Surgeon. 15. Revolt.

163. Eagle of the Night

(H.V. Productions/Pathé, October 14, 1928) Serial, 10 chapters, two reels each. D: Jimmie Fulton. S/SP: Paul Cruger.

An inventor is on the border perfecting a silencer which can be applied to any airplane and make its presence in the sky practically noiseless. Hero is the aviator ace of the Secret Service and is sent to the inventor's house to put the device through a final test. Then the smuggling gang get busy and try to steal the appliance for their own purposes. Some good airplane thrills are worked in and as one of the first serials of this type it will attract the youngsters. The serial is based on airplane stunts. Frank Clarke, well known aviator, plays the part of the hero, so that any stunts he pulls appear to be authentic and not the work of a double.

Frank Clarke, Shirley Palmer, Earle Metcalfe, Joseph Swickard, Maurice Costello, Max Hawley, Roy Wilson, Jack Richardson.

1. The Death Plunge. 2. Snatched into Space. 3. Trapped in the Flames. 4. Dead Wings. 5. The Brink of Eternity. 6. The Fangs of the Wolf. 7. The Sky Hitcher. 8. The March of Death. 9. Headlong to Earth. 10. No Man's Land.

164. The Eagle's Eye

(Wharton/American, March 27, 1918) Serial, 20 chapters, two reels each. D: George A. Lessey and Wellington Playter. S: William J. Flynn. SP: Courtney Ryley Cooper. Last serial produced by the Whartons.

William J. Flynn, who in 1918 was the recently retired Chief of the United States Secret Service, is the Eagle's Eye referred to by the title of the serial in which the efforts of Von Bernstorff, Von Papen, Boy-Ed, Dr. Albert and other German spies to spread terror and ruin through this country are disclosed. Courtney Ryley Cooper wrote the scenario from information furnished by the ex-chief of the Secret Service, and wove in the fictitious characters and incidents required to give the story form and the proper dramatic interest for the screen.

Frank Clarke in *Eagle of the Night* (1928)

Harrison Grant, president of the Criminology Club, and secret service agent Dixie Mason combat the furtive, un-uniformed armies whose weapons are spying, sabotage, bomb-planting, murder, incendiarism, and a hundred forms of insidious and demoralizing propaganda as they take on the Kaiser's spies in the U.S. during World War I.

King Baggot (Harrison Grant), Marguerite Snow (Dixie Mason), Bertram Marburgh (Count Van Bernatoff), William N. Bailey (Heinrich von Lertz), Paul Everton (Captain Franz von Papen), John P. Wade (Captain Earl Boy-Ed), Fred Jones (Doctor Heinrich Albert), Florence Short (Madame Augusta Stephan), William Cavanaugh, George A. Lessey, Le Roy L. Baker, Louise Hotelling, Wellington Playter.

1. Hidden Death. 2. The Naval Ball Conspiracy. 3. The Plot Against the Fleet. 4. Von Rintelen, the Destroyer. 5. The Strike Breeders. 6. The Plot Against Organized Labor. 7. Brown Portfolio. 8. The Kaiser's Death Messenger. 9. The Munitions Campaign. 10. The Invasion of Canada. 11. The Burning of Hopewell. 12. The Canal Conspirators. 13. The Reign of Terror. 14. The Infantile Paralysis Epidemic. 15. The Campaign Against Cotton. 16. The Raid of the U-53. 17. German's U-Base in America. 18. The Great Hindu Conspiracy. 19. The Menace of the I.W.W. 20. The Great Decision.

165. The Eagle's Talons

(Universal, April 30, 1923) Serial, 15 chapters, two reels each. Presented by Carl Laemmle. D: Duke Worne. Scen: Anthony Coldeway, Jefferson Moffitt, and Bertram Millhauser. S: Theodore Wharton and Bertram Millhauser.

A group of Wall Street investors seek to manipulate the wheat market, but a businessman possesses an incriminating document that holds them back. Fearing what the group might do, the man goes into hiding. By capturing his daughter, the crooked investors hope to bring him out into the open and to their terms. But the daughter, Enid, has the help of Jack Alden and together they outmaneuver the enemy until justice prevails.

The story is full of mystery, with menacing eyes peering through slits in the wall, mysterious passages, subterranean bypaths, and a scrawny hand ready to grab hero or heroine. And then there are a series of death-defying aerial raids and stunts by Al Wilson, holder of all records for stunt flying.

Ann Little (Enid Markham), Fred Thomson (Jack Alden), Al Wilson (Charles Dean), Herbert Fortier (Gregory Markham), Joseph Girard (Burton Thorne), Edith Stayart (Helen Thorne), Edward Cecil (Judson Steele), Toy Tompkins (Cinders), Joe Bonomo, Albert J. Smith, George Magrill (Thorne's Henchmen), Cliff Bergere, Jack Fowler (Thomson's Double).

1. House of Mystery. 2. Edge of Eternity. 3. Hulk of Horror. 4. Daring Hearts. 5. A Deal in Diplomacy. 6. The Flood of Fury. 7. The Road to Doom. 8. Against Odds. 9. A Fighting Chance. 10. Into the Chasm. 11. The Betrayal. 12. The Sacrifice. 13. Dodging the Conspirators. 14. The Inferno. 15. The Eagle Foiled.

166. Elmo, the Fearless

(Universal, February 1, 1920) Serial, 18 chapters, two reels each. D: J.P. McGowan. S: Arthur H. Gooden.

The hero is a husky young fellow looking for adventures. He picks up a stray dog in a rainstorm and drops into a tough dive on the Barbary Coast. The canine has won his sympathy and Elmo orders a glass of milk to feed it. The men in the dive give him a laugh and Elmo proves his ready courage by cleaning the place up in short order.

Eventually he arrives with his dog at the boarding house

of Checko the Crimp. Here his great physical prowess attracts attention and Checko determines to shanghai him along with some other men. The unsuspecting individuals are all given a doped drink and are soon on board a steamer headed for the Big Bear lumber country.

On the same vessel are Robert Stillwell and his daughter, Edith. Stillwell is going to claim a certain mine on his property, discovered by his own prospectors. There has been a shooting and a murder on the property and Stillwell has a photograph and plate which provides valuable evidence. Unknown to Stillwell, his own attorney is conspiring with a gang that is seeking to jump the claim. A mutiny is incited on board the vessel, which is wrecked by an explosion.

The story is one of intense action and big melodramatic moments. Louise Lorraine makes a pleasing impression in the part of the heroine.

Elmo Lincoln (the Stranger), Louise Lorraine (Edith Stillwell), William Chapman (Robert Stillwell), Roy Watson (Paul Horton), Frank Ellis (Dan Bulger), V.L. Barnes (Checko), Gordon McGregor (Guy Hatherton), J.P. McGowan, Monte Motague.

1. Wreck of the Santiam. 2. The Racing Death. 3. The Life Line. 4. The Flames of Death. 5. The Smugglers' Cave. 6. The Battle Under the Sea. 7. The House of Mystery. 8. The Fatal Crossing. 9. The Assassin's Knife. 10. The Fatal Bullet. 11. The Temple of the Dragon. 12. Crashing Through. 13. The Hand on the Latch. 14. The Avalanche. 15. The Burning Fuse. 16. The House of Intrigue. 17. The Trap. 18. The Fateful Letter.

167. Elmo the Mighty

(Great Western Producing Co./Universal, June 1919) Serial, 18 chapters, two reels each. D: Henry McRae. S: Joe Brandt and William E. Wing.

A syndicate attempts to steal valuable timber land, but forest ranger Howard Armstrong and his girl friend Lucille Gray intervene, sometimes with the assistance of the Phantom Menace of Mad Mountain, a cloaked motorcycle rider.

Elmo Lincoln (Captain Howard Armstrong), Grace Cunard (Lucille Gray), Fred Starr, Virginia Craft, Ivor McFadden, James Cole, Rex De Rosselli, William A. Orlamond, Bob Reeves, Madge Hunt, Grace McClean, William Chapman, Chai Hong.

1. The Mystery of Mad Mountain. 2. Buried Alive. 3. Flames of Hate. 4. A Fiendish Revenge. 5. The Phantom Rescue. 6. The Puma's Paws. 7. The Masked Pursuer. 8. The Flaming Pit. 9. The House of a Thousand Tortures. 10. Victims of the Sea. 11. The Burning Den. 12. Lashed to the Rocks. 13. Into the Chasm. 14. The Human Bridge. 15. Crashing to Earth. 16. Parachute Perils. 17. The Plunge. 18. Unmasked.

168. L'Empereur des Pauvres

(France—Société des Cinéromans, 1921) Serial, 6 chapters. D: René Leprince. S: Felicien de Champsaur. Scen: René Leprince.

Léon Mathot (Marcos Anavan), Gina Relly (Silvetta), Henry Krauss (Sarrias), Gilbert Dalleu (Maire de S. Saturnino), Andrée Pascal (Clemencia Sarrias), Lily Deslys [Damita] (Riquette), Maupain (Sílvio, pai de Silvetta), Charles Lamy (Bonafede), Lucy Mareil (Josette), Albert Bras, André Luguet, Maurice Schutz, Charles Mosnier, Charles De Rochefort, Rene Hiéronimus, Andrew F. Brunelle, Jeanne Brindeau, Charlotte Barbier-Krauss, Madeleine Erickson, Suzy Pierson, René Lorrain, Halma, Jean Lorette, Madeleine Sené, Champdor.

1. Le pauvre. 2. Les millions. 3. Les flambeaux. 4. Les crassiers. 5. L'orage. 6. Floréal.

169. L'Enfant des Halles

(France—Société des Cinéromans, 1924) Serial, 5 chapters (?). D: René Leprince. S: H.J. Bagog.

Jean-Paul De Baëre, Gabriel Signoret, Suzanne Bianchetti, Monique Chrysés, Lucien Dalsace, Francine Mussey, Camille Bert, Pierre Labry, Thomy Bourdelle, Louis Blanche, Simone Vaudry.

170. L'Enfant Roi

(France—Société des Cinéromans, 1924) Serial, 6 chapters. D: Jean Kemm and Henriette Kemm. Scen: Henriette Kemm. S: Pierre Gilles Veber.

Andrée Lionel, Joë Hamman, Georges Vaultier, Marguerite Madys, Louis Sance, Christian Argentin, Jean-Paul De Baëre, Antonin Artaud, Georgette Sorelle, Mlle. Dumont, J. Munier, De Savoye.

1. L' éveil des géantes. 2. Louis XVI et Marie Antoinette. 3. L' armoire de fer. 4. Le drame de Varennes. 5. Les deux Orpheline. 6. Thermidor.

171. Enfants de Paris

(France, 1924) Serial, chapters (?). D: André Francis Bertoni. S: Leon Sazie.

Tramel, Lucien Dalsace, Margueritte Madys, Charley Sov, Alexis Ghasne, Martial Verdellet, Gilbert Dalleu, Sabine Sandré, Therese Kolb.

172. La España Trágica

(Spain—Rafael Salvador Films, 1918) Serial, 4 chapters. D: Rafael Salvador. Photography: José María Maristany and Fructuoso Gelabert. SP: Pedro de Répide.

Carmen Villasán (María Luz), José Portes (Pepe Luis), Antonio Calvache (Antonio Romero), José Durany ("El Alijaor"), Angelita Ribas (Bailarina Sara Fiore), José Argelague [Argelagues] ("El Lechuzo"), Manoel Viola, Fernando Viola (Los amigos del torero).

1. Flor de serranía. 2. Flor de espino. 3. Entre España y Africa. 4. El laurel y el olvido.

173. L'Espionne aux Yeux Noirs

(France—Société des Cinéromans, 1926) Serial, chapters (?). D: Henri Desfontaines. Scen: Paul Dambry.

Maria Dalbarcin, Suzanne Delmas, Paulette Berger, Roger Karl, Genica Missirio, Fernand Herrman, Andre Marnay, Pierre Hot, C.T. Terrore, Volbert.

174. Essanay Fables

(Essanay, 1914–1915) Series, 56 episodes, one reel each. S: George Aide.

Each story complete. No continuing characters.

[Numbers in parentheses indicate what film the actor/actress was in.] Eugene Acker (26, 53), Sidney Ainsworth (28,

29), Wallace Beery (1, 3, 5, 9, 11, 13, 46), Beverly Bayne (5, 11), Willie Belmont (53), Lester Cuneo (6), Sidney Carlyle (54), Thomas Commerford (23), Leota Chrider (41), Camille D'Arcy (35, 44), Lillian Drew (16, 19), Helen Dunbar (15), Mabel Eaton (16), Alice Edwards (49), Mayme Gehrue (37), Hope Gordon (37),Gerda Holmes (15, 33), Lloyd Holton (55), Rapley Holmes (24, 32), Adele McLelland (15), Albert Martin (25, 42), Ernest Maupain (37, 44), Anzinette Moore (53), Charlotte Mineau (56), Frankie Raymond (42, 50), Eddie Redway (16), Ruth Stonehouse (10, 26, 34, 38, 41, 55), Earl Stanhope (40), Peggy Sweeney (40, 42, 54), Richard C. Travers (15, 33), Frank Wade (49), Anna May Walthall (53), Frank Owens (4), Charles Stine (23, 25, 26, 28, 35, 40, 42, 44, 46), De Wess Seowir (49), Gloria Swanson (24), Louise Willis (16), Bryant Washburn (41), Harry Dunkinson (6, 19, 23, 47, 50), Leo White (3, 36).

1914: 1. Fable of the Busy Business Boy and the Droppers-In. 2. Fable of Aggie and the Aggravated Attacks. 3. Fable of the Higher Education That Was Too High for the Old Man. 4. Fable of How Uncle Brewster Was Too Shifty for the Tempter. 5. Fable of the Brash Drummer and the Nectarine. 6. Fable of the Author and the Dear Public and the Plate of Mush. 7. Fable of the Adult Girl Who Got Busy. 8. Fable of One Samaritan Who Got Paralysis of the Helping Hand. 9. Fable of Napoleon and the Bumps. 10. Fable of Lutie, the False Alarm. 11. Fable of the Bush League Lover Who Failed to Qualify. 12. Fable of the Club Girls and the Four Times Veteran. 13. Fable of the Coming Champion Who Was Delayed. 14. Fable of the Difference Between Learning and Learning How. 15. Fable of the Family That Did Too Much for Nellie. 16. Fable of the "Good Fairy". 17. Fable of the Honeymoon That Tried to Come Back. 18. Fable of the Husband Who Showed Up and Did His Duty. 19. Fable of the Long Range Lover and the Lallypalooze. 20. Fable of the Maneuvers of Joel and Father's Second Time on Earth. 21. Fable of the Two Mandolin Players and the Willing Performer. 22. Fable Proving That Spongers Are Found in a Drugstore. *1915:* 23. Fable of a Night Given Over to Revelry. 24. Fable of Elvira and Farina and the Meal Ticket. 25. Fable of Handsome Jethro, Who Was Simply Cut Out to be a Merchant. 26. Fable of Hazel's Two Husbands and What Became of Them. 27. Fable of High Faluting Tillie and Her Plain Parents. 28 Fable of Sister Mae, Who Did as Well as Could be Expected. 29. Fable of the Bachelor and the Back-Pedal. 30. Fable of the Busy Man and the Idle Woman. 31. Fable of the City Grafter and the Unprotected Rubes. 32. Fable of the Cold Gray Dawn and the Morning After. 33. Fable of Demand That Must Be Supplied. 34. Fable of the Divine Spark That Had a Short Circuit. 35. Fable of the Escape of Arthur and the Salvation of Herbert. 36. Fable of the Fellow Who Had a Friend Who Knew a Girl Who Had a Friend. 37. Fable of the Galloping Pilgrim Who Kept on Galloping. 38. Fable of the Galumptious Girl. 39. Fable of Good People Who Rallied to the Support of the Church. 40. Fable of the Heir and the Heiress. 41. Fable of the Highroller and the Buzzing Blondine. 42. Fable of the Home Treatment and the Sure Cure. 43. Fable of the Intermittent Fusser. 44. Fable of the Low Down Expert on the Subject of Babies. 45. Fable of Men at the Women's Club. 46. Fable of Roistering Blades. 47. Fable of the Scoffer Who Fell Hard. 48. Fable of the Search for Climate. 49. Fable of Sorrows of the Unemployed and the Danger of Changing from Bill to Herald. 50. Fable of the Statesman Who Didn't Make Good. 51. Fable of the Struggle Between Personal Liberty and the Wave of Reform. 52. Fable of the Syndicate Lover. 53. Fable of the Through Train. 54. Fable of the Tip and the Treasure. 55. Fable of Two Sensational Failures. 56. Fable of Two Unfettered Birds.

175. Essanay Fables

(Essanay, 1916–1917) Series, 27 episodes, one or two reels each. D: Richard Foster Baker (16); Fred E. Wright (1); Lee Metford (1); Charles McGuirk (?). S: George Aide. SP: Charles J. McGuirk (6); H. Tipton Steck (3); Charles Mortimer Peck (2).

Each of the fables was complete in itself. By far the most famous actor to appear in these shorts was Rod La Rocque, who graced nine of them.

Rod La Rocque, Marguerite Clayton, Virginia Valli, Edmund F. Cobb, Charles J. Stine, Harry Dunkinson, Beatrice Fairfax, Marion Skinner, Hazel Coates, Julian Barton, Donald Clayton, Marian Murray, Robert Bolder, Magna Anderson, Jane Thomas, Thomas Commerford, William Burke, Burt Weston, Leona Ball, William Brotherhood, William Clifton, Fred Wagner, Ullrich Haupt, Alice McChesney, Harry B. Watson, Royal Douglas, R. Paul Harvey, Katherine Amos, John Cossar, Russell McDermott, Walter Schoeller, Tommy Carey, Bobby Bolder, Thelma Blossom, Margaret Wiggin, Warda Howard, Carroll C. James, George Bean, Frankie Raymond.

1916: 1. Fable of Flora and Adolph and a Home Gone Wrong (1R). 2. Fable of How Wisenstein Did Not Lose Out to Buttinsky (1R). 3. Fable of the Fearsome Feud Between the First Families (2R). 5. Fable of Books Made to Balance (1R). 6. Fable of the Kittenish Super-Anns and the World-Weary Snipes (2R). 7. Fable of the Preacher Who Flew His Kite but Not Because He Wished to Do So (1R). 8. Fable of the Good Fairy with the Lorgnette and Why She Got It So Good (1R). 9. Fable of the Grass Widow and the Mesmeree and the Six Dollars (1R). 10. Fable of the Kid Who Shifted His Ideal to Golf and Finally Became a Baseball Fan and Took the Only Known Cure (1R). 11. Fable of the Small Town Favorite Who Was Ruined by Too Much Competition (1R). 12. Fable of the Slim Girl Who Tried to Keep a Date That Was Never Made (1R). 13. Fable of the Throbbing Genius of a Tank Town Who Was Encouraged by Her Folks Who Were Prominent. 14. Fable of the Two Philanthropic Sons (1R). 15. Fable of the Undecided Brunette (1R). 16. Fable of the Willing Collegian Who Worked to Get a Foothold (1R). *1917:* (all titles two reels): 1. Fable of Prince Fortunatus, Who Moved Away from Easy Street, and Silas, the Saver, Who Moved In. 2. Fable of the Back Trackers from the Hot Sidewalks. 3. Fable of the Film Fed Families. 4. Fable of the Girl Who Took Notes and Got Wise and Then Fell Down. 5. Fable of the Speedy Sprite. 6. Fable of the Toilsome Ascent and the Shiny Table Lamp. 7. Fable of the Twelve-Cylinder Speed of the Leisure Class. 8. Fable of the Uplifter and His Dandy Little Opus. 9. Fable of the Wandering Boy and the Wayward Parents. 10. Fable of What the Best People Are Not Doing. 11. Fable of What Transpires After the Wind-Up.

176. L' Essor

(France—Cinématographes Phocea, 1921) Serial, chapters (?). D: Charles Burguet.

Suzanne Grandais, Berthe Jalabert, Aimée Tessandier, Yvonne Garat, Jacques Robert, Maurice Escande, Henry Bosc, Camiller Bardou, Pierre Fresnay.

177. The Evil Eye

(Hallmark, May 1920) Serial, 15 chapters, two reels each. D: J. Gordon Cooper. S/SP: Roy L. McCardall.

The serial starred Benny Leonard, the Lightweight Champion of the World. It was not a step forward in serial making. Leonard ought to have been satisfied with being a good fighter and let it go at that. Not that the plot gives him much acting to do. It is a story of a relentless, powerful gang of crooks who are pursuing a million dollars in bonds, the heroine, and the family jewels. The star is shown in few close-ups. One thing, however, he does do—he supplies good action in every episode. His fist fights are truly realistic and display the cleverness and speed that brought him fame in the prize ring.

Of course there is a "mastermind" of the underworld, who plans the daring Wall Street bond robberies. This time he is a combination of Shylock, the witches of Macbeth and the notorious Mr. Hyde. He is wheeled about in an invalid chair, burning his "evil eye" into everyone he meets, and blinding those who fall under his disfavor.

Benny Leonard (Frank Armstrong), Ruth Dwyer (Dora Bruce), Stuart Hansen (Berton Bruce), Maria Shotwell (Mrs. David Bruce), Madame Marie Marstini (Marcia Lamar), Leslie King (The Money Lender), Bernard Randall, Mary Jepp.

1. Below the Deadline. 2. In the House of the Blind Man. 3. The Golden Locket. 4. Vengeance of the Dead. 5. Trapped by Treachery. 6. On the Wings of Death. 7. The Double Cross. 8–10. [Unknown.] 11. A Monstrous Menace. 12–15. [Unknown.]

178. Excuse Makers

(Universal, 1926–'27) Series, 13 (or more) episodes, two reels each. D: Sam Neufield, Scott Pembroke, and Francis Corby.

This series is included in this book for the sole reason that it starred Charles King, one of the best known villains of both serials and westerns of the sound era. As a younger man his forte was comedy, and he was good at it. In 1927–28 he costarred with Charles Dorety in the "Mike and Ike" comedies for Stern Brothers, released through Universal.

Charles King.

1. Love's Hurdle. 2. Which Is Which. 3. Please Excuse Me. 4. Second-Hand Excuse. 5. What'll You Have? 6. Some More Excuses. 7. Be My Wife. 8. She's My Cousin. 9. Keeping His Word. 10. That's No Excuse. 11. My Mistake. 12. What an Excuse. 13. Please Don't.

179. Exploits of Elaine

(The Star Company/Pathé, December 28, 1914) Serial, 14 chapters, two reels each. D: Louis Gasnier and George B. Seitz. SP: C.W. Goddard and George B. Seitz. S: Arthur B. Reeve, Bertram Milhauser, and Charles L. Goddard. P: Leopold V. and Theodore W. Wharton. Camera: Joseph Dubray. Released in Europe as *The Mysterey of New York*. Also popularly remembered as *The Clutching Hand*, the title of the first chapter.

Elaine Dodge's father is killed by electrocution by The Clutching Hand in order for the ruthless master thief and killer to secure certain papers which reveal one of his hideouts. Elaine seeks to bring the malefactor to justice. Helping her is master detective Craig Kennedy, the most popular fictional American crimefighter of his day, who was called "the American Sherlock Holmes."

Like Holmes, Kennedy had a roommate, newspaperman Walter Jameson, a "Watson" who wrote first person accounts of the great detective's cases.

Among The Clutching Hand's minions are various low life people including an unscrupulous professor who invents a diabolical killing machine, a South American Indian who kills by shooting blow gun darts dipped in curari, and a gang called "The Brotherhood of the Falsers." Devious devices are used by The Clutching Hand to kill Elaine and Kennedy but he fails each time.

Kennedy himself is no slouch when it comes to knowledge of scientific gadgets and he comes up with his own weapons to fight the master criminal.

Not only must Elaine defend herself from The Clutching Hand but she is framed in a blackmail scheme by Long Sin, a sinister oriental who heads a cult of devil worshippers that try to sacrifice Elaine as the white consort to their evil god.

The mystery figure gambit proved popular and it became a standard serial ingredient. This serial grossed over $1 million and became the prototype of the scientific mystery.

Pearl White (Elaine Dodge), Arnold Daly (Craig Kennedy), Creighton Hale (Walter Jameson, first 3 chapters), Raymond Owens (Walter Jameson, chapters 4–14), Sheldon Lewis (Perry Bennett/The Clutching Hand), Edwin Arden (Wu Fang), Ramond Owens (Kennedy's assistant), Le Roy Baker (The Butler), Bessie Wharton (Aunt Josephine), William Riley Hatch (Taylor Dodge), Robin Towney (Limpy Red), Floyd Buckley, Lionel Barrymore, G.B. Seitz.

1. The Clutching Hand. 2. The Twilight Sleep. 3. The Vanishing Jewels. 4. The Frozen Safe. 5. The Poisoned Room. 6. The Vampire. 7. The Double Trap. 8. The Hidden Voice. 9. The Death Ray. 10. The Life Current. 11. The Hour of Three. 12. The Blood Crystals. 13. The Devil Worshippers. 14. The Reckoning.

180. Fanfan-la-Tulipe

(France—Société des Cinéromans, 1925) Serial, 5 chapters. D: René Leprince. Scen: Pierre Gilles Veber.

Aimé Simon-Girard, Simone Vaudry, Jacques Guilhene, Claude France, Pierre de Guingand, Renee Heribel, Paul Guidé, Alexandre Colas, Jean Peyriére, Ninon Gilles, Thomy Bourdelle.

1. Pour l'amour d'une belle. 2. Le peloton d' execution. 3. Le Marechal de Saxe. 4. Madame de Pompadour. 5. La Bataille de Fontenoy.

181. Fantômas

(France—Gaumont, 1913) Serial, 5 chapters. D: Louis Feuillade. S: Pierre Souvestre and Marcel Allain. SP: Louis Feuillade.

France's first serial and one of its all-time great serials with René Navarre portraying to the hilt the gentleman thief who, nevertheless, was evil. Theater goers were irresistibly drawn back the next week to see what unpredictable events would occur that would irrevocably link Fantômas with those who had fallen into harm's way, and whether L'inspecteur Juve would get his man.

René Navarre (Fantômas), Bréon (L'inspecteur Juve), Georges Melchoir (Fandor), Renée Carl (Lady Beltnam), Henri Volbert (L'acteur Valgrand), Naudier (Le gardien Nibet), Jane Faber (Princesse Danidoff), Yvette Andreyor (Joséphine la pierreuse), Luitz-Morat (Thomery), André Luguet (Jacques Dollon), Fabienne Fabreges (Elisabeth Dollon), Maury (Le chef de la Sureté), Marthe Vinot, Jean Morlas, J.F. Martial, Jean

Mesnery, Mlle. Alexianne, Priader, Fernand Hermann, Nelly Palmer, Paul Manson, Mlle. Pelisse, Suzanne Le Bret.

1. Fantômas. 2. Juve contre Fantômas. 3. Le mort qui tue. 4. Fantômas contre Fantômas. 5. Le faux magistrat.

182. Fantomas

(Fox Film Corp., December 1920) Serial, 20 chapters, two reels each. D: Edward Sedgwick. Scen: Edward Sedgwick and George Eshenfelder. Based upon characters created by Marcel Allain and Pierre Souvestre.

Fantomas is a super criminal who is a specialist in disguises. When his offer to the police to give up his criminal career for amnesty is rejected, he vows revenge and begins his new crime wave. He kidnaps Professor Harrington, much to the consternation of the professor's daughter, Ruth, her fiancée, Jack, and Fantomas's nemesis, detective Dixon.

Edward Roseman (Fantomas), Edna Murphy (Ruth Harrington), Johnie Walker (Jack Meredith), Lionel Adams (James D. Harrington), John Willard (Detective Fred Dixon), Eve Balfour (The Woman in Black), Rena Parker (The Countess), Irving Brooks (The Duke), Ben Walker (The Butler), Henry Armetta (The Wop), Rita Ragan.

1. On the Stroke of Nine. 2. The Million Dollar Reward. 3. The Triple Peril. 4. Blades of Terror. 5. Heights of Horror. 6. The Altar of Sacrifice. 7. Flames of Destruction. 8. At Death's Door. 9. The Haunted Hotel. 10. The Fatal Card. 11. The Phantom Sword. 12. The Danger Signal. 13. On the Count of Three. 14. The Blazing Train. 15. The Sacred Necklace. 16. The Phantom Shadow. 17. The Price of Fang Wu. 18. Double-Crossed. 19. The Hawk's Prey. 20. The Hell Ship.

183. The Fast Express

(Universal, March 10, 1924) Serial, 15 chapters, two reels each. D: William Duncan. Scen: Frank H. Clark and Paul Bryan. S: Courtney Ryley Cooper.

The story deals with the efforts of a band of thieves to delay the fast train on which depends the fate of the "road." All

***Left:* William Duncan; *right:* William Duncan and Edith Johnson in *The Fast Express* (1924)**

the surefire material is used—the haunted house, the fight in the underworld dive, blackmail, abduction—with the hero battling away in every scene.

William Duncan (Brent McAdams), Edith Johnson (Lucille Worth), Edward Cecil (Christopher Langley), Eva Gordon (Rita), Jim Welsh (Theobold Mason), Albert J. Smith (Edward Winston), Harry Woods (Tom Boyd), Jose Dominquez (Black Tony), John Cossar, Harry Carter.

1. Facing the Crisis. 2. Vanishing Diamonds. 3. Woman of Mystery. 4. Haunted House. 5. Perils of the City. 6. Cipher Message. 7. Bandit Raiders. 8. Impostor's Scheme. 9. Falsely Accused. 10. Path of Danger. 11. The Abduction. 12. The Trial Run. 13. The False Summons. 14. Black Treasure. 15. Retribution.

184. Fast Steppers

(Universal, 1924) Series, 6 episodes, two reels each. P/D: Edward Laemmle. Based on stories by Gerald Beaumont published in *Red Book.*

These stories all deal with horseracing and gambling. A brief synopsis of *The Fiddlin' Doll* exemplifies the stories.

Broke, the Information Kid finds some money, but almost immediately loses it at craps, while 50-50 Henry, his pal, who has just eaten a big meal on the Kid, has to wash dishes to pay for his repast. The Kid's girl, the Fiddlin' Doll, plays for Paladine Rabinsky, a noted violinist, but he tells her she will never amount to anything as a musician. The Doll, disappointed by his verdict, breaks down, and the Kid begs Rabinsky to drop her some encouragement, but he refuses.

Eager to find a good husband for the Doll, the Kid and Henry make the acquaintance of Larry, an Easterner, whose roll they increase by several thousand dollars. Ten days of lucky gambling follow, and the joint bankroll has grown to $40,000. Larry proposes to the Doll, but she puts him off.

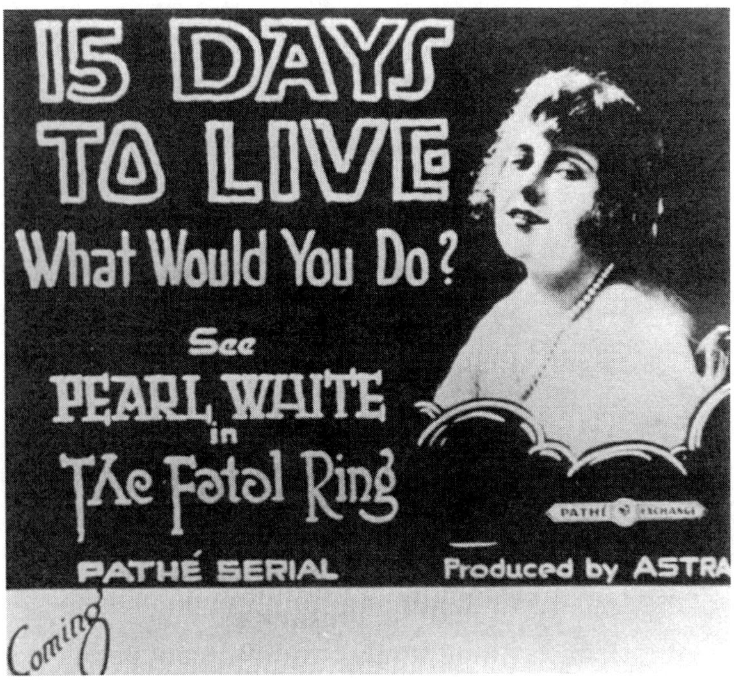

Pearl White in *The Fatal Ring* (1917)

The trio stake their wad on "Wedding Bell." The horse is left at the post and the Kid is down to a capital of thirty cents. The Doll refuses to marry Larry and he returns East. The Kid imagines another rival and leaves the Doll in anger. Henry, recognizing the Doll's love for the Kid, puts him wise and tells him to go and win.

Billy Sullivan ("The Information Kid"), Shannon Day ("The Fiddlin' Doll"), James Quinn ("50-50 Henry"), Bert Woodruff (Jimmy Whiskers), Duke R. Lee (Black Murdock), Frank Kingsley (Larry Beveridge), Cesare Gravina (Paladine Rabinsky), Wedding Bell (a horse), Polly Oliver (a horse), Shooting Star (a horse), Iron Duke (a horse), Tarcutta (a horse), Alabam' (a horse).

1. The Fiddlin' Doll. 2. The Empty Stall. 3. Shooting Star. 4. The Christmas Handicap. 5. The Hot Dog Special. 6. Getaway Day.

185. The Fatal Fortune

(SLK Serial Corp., December 15, 1919) Serial, 15 chapters, two reels each. D: Donald McKenzie. SP: Walter Richard Hall. P: Sherman S. Krellberg. Music: Hall and Sullivan—"Pretty Helen."

This is a South Seas adventure in which a newspaper woman leads a search for buried treasure on a desolate island, meeting many obstacles in the process.

Helen Holmes (Helen), Jack Levering, Leslie King, Bill Black, Frank Wunderlee, Floyd Buckley, Sidney Delbrook, Nellie Lindrith, Lillian Worth.

1. The Trader's Secret. 2. Men of Tigerish Mold. 3. Tortured by Flames. 4. A Climb for Life. 5. The Forced Marriage. 6. Desperate Chances. 7. A Plunge to Death. 8. A Struggle in Mid-Air. 9. The Deadly Peril. 10. Sure Death. 11. A Leap for Life. 12. A Fiendish Plot. 13. Set Adrift. 14. The Hidden Treasure. 15. Unmasked.

186. The Fatal Ring

(Astra/Pathé, July 8, 1917) Serial, 20 chapters, two reels each. D: George B. Seitz. Scen: Bertram Millhauser. S: Fred Jackson.

Pearl Standish, aided by Nicholas Knox, an adversary she has won over to her side, fights to retain the violet diamond supposedly stolen by her father from an underground lost city in Egypt. The ring gives the wearer the power of invisibility. Pearl is threatened at every turn by the High Priestess of the Sacred Order and her henchmen and one Richard Carlslake, a villain with his own plans for the diamond.

Pearl White (Violet Standish), Earle Fox (Nicholas Knox), Warner Oland (Richard Carlslake), Ruby Hoffman (The Priestess), Henry G. Sell (Tom Carlton), Floyd Buckley, Casare Gravaina, Mattie Ferguson, Richard La Marr, Burt Starkey, Louis J. O'Connor, Harriet Reller, Mrs. Spencer Bennet.

1. The Violet Diamond. 2. The Crushing Wall. 3. Borrowed Identity. 4. The Warning on the Ring. 5. Danger Underground. 6. Rays of Death. 7. The Signal Lantern. 8. The Switch in the Safe. 9. The Dice of Death. 10. The Perilous Plunge. 11. The Short Circuit. 12. A Desperate Chance. 13. A Dash for Arabia. 14. The Painted Safe. 15. The Dagger Duel. 16. The Double Disguise. 17. The Death Weight. 18. The Subterfuge. 19. The Cryptic Maze. 20. The End of the Trail.

187. The Fatal Sign

(Arrow Film Corp., February 1920) Serial, 15 chapters (?), two reels each. D: Stuart Paton. Scen: Bertram Millhauser.

Claire Anderson (Genevieve), Harry Carter (Indigo), Leo Maloney (Jerry), Boyd Irwin (Sydney), Joseph Girard, Frank Tokonaga, Fontaine Larue, Jack Richardson.

1. The Sign of the Rat. 2. The Lair of the Rat. 3. The Devil's Web. 4. Out of the Night. 5–15. [Unknown.]

188. The Fatal Warning

(Mascot, February 15, 1929) Serial, 10 chapters, two reels each. D: Richard Thorpe. P: Nat Levine.

In the middle of releasing a novel, entitled *The Fatal Warning*, William Rogers is surprised by an assailant. There is a terrific struggle, in the course of which the imprint of a man's scarred foot is left on the book. Rogers is whisked away, and his daughter, Dorothy, seeking to solve the mystery of his disappearance, meets with strange adventures at the hands of his enemies. She is, however, aided by Russell Thorne, an expert detective, and the pair encounter innumerable perils, which end in happiness and romance.

Helene Costello (Dorothy Rogers), Ralph Graves (Russell Thorne), George Periolat (William Rogers), Phillip Smalley (Leonard Taylor), Boris Karloff (Mullens), Lloyd Whitlock (Norman Brooks), Sid Crossley (Dawson), Thomas Lingham (John Harmon), Symoni Boniface (Marie Jordan), Martha Mattox (Mrs. Charles Peterson), Gertrude Astor.

1. The Fatal Warning. 2. The Phantom Flyer. 3. The Crash of Doom. 4. The Pit of Death. 5. Menacing Fingers. 6. Into Thin Air. 7. The House of Horror. 8. Fatal Fumes. 9. By Whose Hand. 10. Unmasked.

Clara Kimball Young in *The Fates and Flora Fourflush* (1915)

189. The Fates and Flora Fourflush

(Vitagraph, January 2, 1915) Serial, 3 chapters, one reel each. D: Wally Van Nostrand. Scen: James Young and Mark Swan. S: Charles Brown.

Also referred to as *The Ten Billion Dollar Vitagraph Mystery Serial*, it is tongue-in-cheek comedy parodying Thanhouser's *The Million Dollar Mystery* (1914) and *The Twenty Million Dollar Mystery* (1914).

After being run over by a ponderous four-horse-power 1892 combustible, belonging to millionairess Flora Fourflush, Frank Goodheart, a poor but true-hearted young street-cleaner, is carried home in her car. While Frank is recuperating, Sir Simon Blackheart, a ferocious villain and a persistent suitor for Flora's hand, calls and when his love is scorned, seizes Flora in his arms and attempts to kiss her. Frank hurls himself upon the rascal and throws him out the door, while Flora exclaims "My Hero!" but he refuses her hand in marriage until he has first made his fortune.

At the end of Chapter 1 Frank and Flora are hurling towards earth after their balloon's gas bag has been shot by the villain.

As Chapter 2 opens, the balloon basket containing Frank and Flora drops through the glass conservatory of Flora's house, arriving just in time for tea. The thrills continue in a Laurel and Hardy or Three Stooges manner.

Clara Kimball Young (Flora Fourflush), Charles Brown (Frank Goodheart), L. Rogers Lytton (Sir Simon Blackheart), Templer Saxe, George Stevens.

1. Treachery in the Clouds. 2. Treasure Temple of Bhosh. 3. A Race for Life.

190. Federal Agents vs. Underworld, Inc.

(Republic, January 1949) Serial, 12 chapters, two reels each. D: Fred C. Brannon. SP: Royal K. Cole, Basil Dickey, William Lively, Sol Shor. Assoc. P: Franklyn Adreon. Photography: John MacBurnie. Music: Stanley Wilson. Special Effects: Howard and Theodore Lydecker. Feature Title: *Golden Hands of Kurigal.*

Federal agent Dave Worth's assignment is to find Professor Clayton, who is missing after discovering the famous Golden Hands of Kurigal, key to a great fortune. Nila, an international thief and one of the founders of Underworld, Inc., is responsible for Clayton's disappearance and has one of the hands. With her minions, she is ruthlessly murdering anyone in her way as she seeks the second hand.

Kirk Alyn (David Worth), Rosemary LaPlanche (Laura Keith), Roy Barcroft (Spade Gordon), Carol Forman (Nila), James Dale (Steve Evans), Bruce Edwards (Paul Williams), James Craven (James Clayton), Tristram Coffin (Frank Chambers), Jack O'Shea (Ali), Dale Van Sickel (Mac/Guard), Tom Steele (Tim Grey/Haskell/Native), Marshall Reed (O'Hara),

Robert Wilkie (Zod), Dave Anderson (Porter), Carey Loftin (Black), Post Parks (Bleek), Joe Yrigoyen (Carson/Native), Bud Wolfe (Corby), Saul Gorss (Digger), Loren Riebe (Digger), James Carlisle (Elwood Graves), John Daheim (Guard), Bert LeBaron (Karnak), Duke Taylor (Matson), Ken Terrell (Murdock/Native), Robert St. Angelo, Art Dillard, Dave Sharpe (Natives).

1. The Golden Hands. 2. The Floating Coffin. 3. Death in the Skies. 4. Fatal Evidence. 5. The Trapped Conspirator. 6. Wheels of Disaster. 7. The Hidden Key. 8. The Enemy's Mouthpiece. 9. The Stolen Hand. 10. Unmasked. 11. Tombs of the Ancients. 12. The Curse of Kurigal.

191 Federal Operator 99

(Republic, June 1945) Serial, 12 chapters, two reels each. D: Spencer Bennet, Yakima Canutt, and Wallace A. Grissell. SP: Albert DeMond, Basil Dickey, Jesse Duffy, and Joseph Poland. Assoc. P: Ronald Davidson. Photography: Bud Thackery. Music: Richard Cherwin. Special Effects: Theodore and Howard Lydecker. Feature Title: *FBI 99*.

Jerry Blake, Operator 99, seeks Jim Belmont, a prisoner who escapes from a train en route to the West Coast. Free, Belmont and his confederates steal Princess Cornelia's crown jewels. Blake, with the aid of Joyce Kingston, a secretary, captures the criminals and Belmont plunges to his death during a fight with Blake on a high catwalk.

Marten Lamont (Jerry Blake), Helen Talbot (Joyce Kingston), George J. Lewis (Jim Belmont), Lorna Gray [Adrian Booth] (Rita Parker), Hal Taliaferro [Wally Wales] (Matt Farrell), Bill Stevens (Fred Morton), Maurice Case (Giuseppe Morello), Kernan Cripps (Tom Jeffries), Elaine Lange (Countess Delremy), Frank Jaquet (Warren Hunter), Forrest Taylor (Otto Wolfe), Jay Novello (Heinrick), Tom London (Crawford), Jack Ingram (Biggs), Tom Steele (Gorman/Snyder/Dorgan/Daniels/Driver), Jack Kirk (Duke/Hood), Rex Lease (Bower), Ernie Adams (Tony), Walter Shumway (Joe/Policeman), George Chesebro (Solko), Frederick Howard (Ed Atkins), Jack O'Shea (Baker), Duke Green (Clay), Ken Terrell (Norton Corby), Dale Van Sickel (Carlson/Sands/Sharon/Clark), Edmund Cobb (Corwin), Craig Lawrence (Austin), Harry Strang (Bank Manager), Michael Gaddis (Benson), Jack George (Roberto Carlotti), Nolan Leary (Cashier), Fred Graham (Hinds), Frank Marlowe (Mack), Stanley Price (Monte Mason), Jimmy Zaner (Messenger Boy), Curt Barrett (Photographer).

1. The Case of the Crown Jewels. 2. The Case of the Stolen Ransom. 3. The Case of the Lawful Counterfeit. 4. The Case of the Telephone Code. 5. The Case of the Missing Expert. 6. The Case of the Double Trap. 7. The Case of the Golden Car. 8. The Case of the Invulnerable Criminal. 9. The Case of the Torn Blueprint. 10. The Case of the Hidden Witness. 11. The Case of the Stradivarius. 12. The Case of the Musical Clue.

William Duncan and Edith Johnson in *A Fight for Millions* (1918)

192. Il Fiacre N. 13

(Italy—Ambrosio Films, 1916) Serial, 4 chapters. D: Gero Zambuto and Alberto Capozzi. S: Xavier de Montepin. SP: Arrigo Frusta.

Alberto Capozzi, Helena Makowska, Gigetta Morano, Fernanda Negri-Pouget, Maria Bayma Riva.

Portuguese: 1. O crime de Ponte de Neully. 2. João Quinta-feira. 3. A filha do guilhotinado. 4. Justiça.

193. Fight and Win

(Universal, 1924) Series, 10 episodes, two reels each. D: Erle C. Kenton, Jesse Robbins. Based on stories by Gerald Beaumont.

Tiger Jack O'Day comes out of retirement to win the heavyweight championship in spite of his trainer's attempts to train him the wrong way. Later Jack inherits an orphanage. Many mishaps befall Jack as he engages in several more bouts to raise money for his orphanage. Jack discovers that he is in love with Holly Malloy and she with him. Holly and Jack are married and have two children of their own to add to the bunch at the orphanage.

Jack Dempsey (Tiger Jack O'Day), Esther Ralston (Holly Malloy), Hayden Stevenson, Edgar Kennedy, Chuck Reisner, George Ovey, Carmelita Geraghty, Kate Price, Beatrice Burnham, Virginia Corbin, Gertrude Astor, James O. Barrows, Ethel Shannon, Malvina Polo, Frank Hagney, Otto Lederer, Florence Lee, Gladys Varden, Pat Harmon, Margaret Quimby, Louise Carver, Teddy Hayes.

1. Winning His Way. 2. A Society Knockout. 3. West of the Water Bucket. 4. So This Is Paris. 5. All's Swell on the Ocean. 6. Bring Him In. 7. The Title Holder. 8. The Town Hall Tonight. 9. The Health Farm Wallop. 10. Kayo for Cupid.

194. A Fight for Millions

(Vitagraph, July 15, 1918) Serial, 15 chapters, two reels each. D: William Duncan. SP: Graham Baker. S: Albert E. Smith and Cyrus Townsend Brady.

The will of Jean Benton's father specifies that she is to

marry either of two distant relatives in order to inherit the fortune he is leaving her. Neither man is acceptable to her and both are unscrupulous in their efforts to force her into marriage so that they can acquire the money. Bob Hardy comes to her rescue, defeats the would-be husbands, and finds the loophole freeing her from the provisions of the will.

Beginning with this film Edith Johnson became Duncan's screen heroine and co-starred with him in eight serials, working with him until the two retired from serial production in 1924. She also became Mrs. Duncan in real life.

The Duncan-Johnson team proved a winning combination for Vitagraph and their serials and features were the principal assets of the firm, not only keeping the wolf from the door but allowing the studio the luxury of other film productions financed by the huge profits on the Duncan-Johnson films. Four more serials were made before they sought greener pastures at Universal.

William Duncan (Bob Hardy), Edith Johnson (Jean Benton), Joe Ryan (Jacob Lawless), Willie Calles (Iron Star), Walter Rodgers, S.E. Jennings, Leo Maloney, Hartford [Jack] Hoxie, Vincent Howard, William McCall.

1. The Snare. 2. Flames of Peril. 3. The Secret Stockade. 4. The Precipice of Horror. 5. The Path of Thrills. 6. The Spell of Evil. 7. The Gorge of Destruction. 8. In the Clutches. 9. The Escape. 10. The Secret Tunnel. 11. The Noose of Death. 12. The Tide of Disaster. 13. The Engine of Terror. 14. The Decoy. 15. The Sealed Envelope.

195. The Fighting Devil Dogs

(Republic, June 1938) Serial, 12 chapters; Chapter 1, three reels; others, two reels. D: William Witney and John English. SP: Barry Shipman, Franklyn Adreon, Ronald Davidson, and Sol Shor. Assoc. P: Robert Beche. Photography: William Nobles. Music: Alberto Colombo. Feature Title: *The Torpedo of Doom.*

A mysterious villain calling himself The Lightning invents an artificial thunderbolt weapon capable of discharging huge amounts of electricity from his superplane, The Wing. Two marine lieutenants are assigned to track down the criminal and put a stop to his terror. A group of scientists is organized to develop a countermeasure to The Lightning's device, but it becomes obvious that one of their number is The Lightning himself. But which one?

***Top:* Herman Brix [Bruce Bennett] and Lee Powell; *bottom:* "The Lightning," Eleanor Stewart, and John Picorri in *The Fighting Devil Dogs* (1938)**

Lee Powell (Tom Grayson), Herman Brix [Bruce Bennett] (Frank Corby), Eleanor Stewart (Janet Warfield), Montagu Love (General White), Hugh Sothern (Ben Warfield/The Lightning), Sam Flint (Colonel Grayson), Forrest Taylor (Benson), John Picorri (Gould), Lester Dorr (The Lightning in disguise), Perry Ivins (Crenshaw), Carleton Young (Johnson), Henry Otho (Sam Hedges), Edwin Stanley (Voice of The Lightning), Edmund Cobb (Ellis),Tom London (Wilson), John Davidson (Lin

Wing), Reed Howes (Parker), Thomas Carr (Clerk), Alan Gregg (Macro), Allan Mathews (Todd), Lee Baker (Dirigible Crewman), Lloyd Whitlock (Dirigible Captain), Jack Ingram (Dirigible Radioman), Buddy Roosevelt (Pawnee Lieutenant), Edward Cassidy (Pawnee Captain), Fred Schaefer (Ambulance Driver), Sherry Hall (Brown), Harry Strang (Bennet), Howard Chase (Cuttle), Robert Wilke (Soldier), Joe Yrigoyen (Soldier), George Magrill (Jamison), George DeNormand (Room Guard), Francis Sayles (Renault), Monte Montague (Jacobs), William Stahl (Lake), John Merton (Thompson), Eddie Dew, Earl Douglas, Jack Roberts, Frederick Freeman (Radiomen), Buel Bryant, Lee Frederick, Tom Steele (Marine Guards), Jack Daley (Inspector), James Carlisle (Officer), Bruce Lane (Marine Corporal), Victor Wong (Mikichan), Larry Steers (King), John Hiestand (Newscaster), Joe Delacruz (Native), Ray Hanson (Smith), Edward Argyle (Watchman), Frank Baker (Snell), Duke York (Sam), Harry Anderson, Ken Cooper, Jerry Frank, Jack O'Shea, Robert Kortman, Bud Osborne, F. Herrick Herrick. Millard McGowan, Dirk Thane, Theodore Lorch, Al Taylor, Robert Wilbur, Eddie Parker (Heavies).

1. The Lightning Strikes. 2. The Mill of Disaster. 3. The Silent Witness. 4. Cargo of Mystery. 5. Undersea Bandits. 6. The Torpedo of Doom. 7. The Phantom Killer. 8. Tides of Trickery. 9. Attack from the Skies. 10. In the Camp of the Enemy. 11. The Baited Trap. 12. Killer at Bay.

196. Fighting Fate

(Vitagraph, January, 1921) Serial, 15 chapters, two reels each. D: William Duncan. Scen: C. Graham Baker and William B. Courtney. S: Albert E. Smith and Arthur F. Hankins.

A man, working under the shadow of a false accusation of crime, is forced to associate with the bloodiest and craftiest of gangsters, yet never forgets that love and fortune lie outside of that life. Kern Lambert, a miner wrongly suspected of murdering his pal, is a passenger on a steamship with a man remarkably like him in appearance. The man commits suicide in the cabin they share and Ken decides to throw off pursuit until he can prove his innocence. He changes to the suicide victim's clothes, takes his baggage, and steps into a new life fraught with unsuspected danger.

Both Duncan and Johnson consistently risked their lives for the sake of screen realism, performing stunts that no star would be allowed to perform today. One such stunt was a double leap from a lofty cliff into a turbulent river, the stars actually risking their lives to get the utmost out of this thrill and with no doubles or safety nets used.

William Duncan (Kern Lambert/Judson Cross), Edith Johnson (Josie Mahoney), Ford West (Lew Muggins), George Stanley (Brand X. Mahoney), Larry Richardson (Van Orion), Frank Weed (Snag Flippen), William McCall (Detective Lassiter), Will Badger, Charles Dudley, C.L. Davidson, Burwell Hamrick, Laddie Earle, Jean Carpenter.

1. A Borrowed Life. 2. Playing the Game. 3. A Modern Daniel. 4. A Desperate Dilemma. 5. Double Crossed. 6. The Crown Jewel Clue. 7. A Demon's Bluff. 8. The Treasure Hunt. 9. The Air Avenger. 10. The Stolen Bride. 11. A Choice of Death. 12. Indian Vengeance. 13. Mystery Mountain. 14. When Thieves Fall Out. 15. Cleaning the Bolt.

William Duncan and Edith Johnson in *Fighting Fate* (1921)

197. Fighting for Fame

(Rayart, January 1, 1927) Serial, 10 chapters, two reels each. D: Duke Worne. SP: George Pyper.

Frank Manning, a newspaper reporter, exposes a harbor ring and obtains further information that will criminally implicate Gordon Burr, the controller of the waterfront interests. Burr plants a spy in the newspaper office and learns that Manning is close to the facts and plots to get him out of the way. Mary Aynsworth, Burr's secretary, resolves to assist Manning, who is also aided by Danny Ryan, a printer's devil. Eventually the criminals are brought to justice.

Ben Alexander (Danny Ryan), Hazel Dean (Mary Aynsworth), Eddie Featherstone (Frank Manning).

198. Fighting Hearts

(R-C/F.B.O., March–July, 1926) Series, 12 episodes, two reels each. D: Ralph Oder. Scen: Paul Gangelin, Doris Anderson. S: Sam Mellman, Doris Anderson.

A comedy series.

Alberta Vaughn, Larry Kent.

1. Roll Your Own. 2. It's a Buoy. 3. Plane Jane. 4. Sock Me to Sleep. 5. Smoldering Tires. 6. Whiskering Chorus. 7. The Lightning Slider. 8. The Big Charade. 9. Up and Wooing. 10. When Sally's Irish Rose. 11. Twelve Smiles Out. 12. All's Swell that Ends Swell.

199. The Fighting Marine

(Pathé, 1926) Serial, 10 chapters, two reels each. D: Spencer G. Bennet. SP: Frank Leon Smith. S: Frank Leon Smith.

A reporter seeks to protect an heiress who, under the terms of a will, must reside in a western mining town for six months. Naturally there are those who are determined that the conditions of the will not be met in order that they might gain the inheritance.

Gene Tunney (Dick Farrington), Marjorie Day (Lady Chatfield), Walter Miller (Larry Stuart), Virginia Vance (ruby), Sherman Ross (Charles Vellard), Anna May Walthall (Mazzie), Wally Oettel (Roger Poole), Jack Anthony (Matt), Mike Donlin, David Dunbar, Joe North, W.J. Allen, Ben Walker, Bert Gardner.

1. The Successful Candidate. 2. The Second Attack. 3. In the Enemy's Trap. 4. The Desperate Foe. 5. Entombed. 6. The Falling Tower, 7. Waylaid. 8. Challenged. 9. The Signal Shot. 10. Fired and Hired.

200. The Fighting Marines

(Mascot, November 13, 1935) Serial, 12 chapters, two reels each. D: B. Reeves Eason and Joseph Kane. SP: Barney Sarecky and Sherman Lowe. Supervisor: Barney Sarecky. S: Wallace MacDonald, Maurice Geraghty, and Ray Trampe. P: Nat Levine. Music: Arthur Kay.

Corporal Lawrence and Sergeant McGowan endeavor to discover the identity of The Tiger Shark, a mysterious scientific wizard who is sabotaging attempts by marines to establish a landing field on Halfway Island. Joining them in their harrowing adventures is Frances Schiller, whose father, a Sergeant Schiller, has invented a new type of gyro-compass and is held captive by The Tiger Shark. The master criminal is defeated during a battle in a cave on the island.

Grant Withers (Corporal Lawrence), Adrian Morris (Sergeant McGowan), Ann Rutherford (Frances Schiller), Robert Warwick (Colonel Bennet), George J. Lewis (Sergeant Schiller), Pat O'Malley (Captain Grayson), Robert Frazer (Douglas), Frank Reicher (Steinbeck), J. Frank Glendon (Buchanan), Victor Potel (Native Chief), Warner Richmond (Metcalf), Richard Alexander (Ivan), Donald Reed (Pedro), Max Wagner (Gibson), Jason Robards (Kota), Tom London (Miller), Ted Adams (Peter), Jim Corey (Karlsson), Milburn Stone (Red), Franklyn Adreon (Captain

Top: **Gene Tunney in** ***The Fighting Marine*** **(1926);** ***bottom:*** **Grant Withers in** ***The Fighting Marines*** **(1935)**

Holmes), Billy Arnold (Captain Henderson), Lee Shumway (Captain Drake), Grace Durkin (Mrs. Martin, Secretary), Edwin Parker (Olson), Stanley Blystone, Robert Walker.

1. Human Targets. 2. Isle of Missing Men. 3. Savage Horde. 4. Mark of the Tiger Shark. 5. Gauntlet of Grief. 6. Robber's Roost. 7. Jungle Terrors. 8. Siege of Halfway Island. 9. Death from the Sky. 10. Wheels of Destruction. 11. Behind the Mask. 12. Two Against the Horde.

201. The Fighting Ranger

(Universal, May 11, 1925) Serial, 18 chapters, two reels each. D: Jay Marchant. S: F.J. McConnell and George W. Pyper.

Forest Ranger Terrence O'Rourke is nursed back to health by Mary Marshall and her father after being injured upon landing in a parachute when his plane developed engine trouble and crashed. The Marshalls have been hiding in the mountains for years following a self-defense killing by John Marshall. His ranch foreman is stealing him blind. O'Rourke sets about righting matters, spurred on by his love of Mary.

Jack Dougherty (Terrence O'Rourke), Eileen Sedgwick (Mary Marshall), Al Wilson (Bud Hughes), Bud Osborne ("Topaz" Taggart), William Welsh (John Marshall), Charles Avery (Miguel Cordero), Frank Lanning (Komi), Sam Polo (Ramon), Slim Cole (Buck), Gladys Roy (Stella Montrose).

1. The Intruder. 2. The Frame-Up. 3. The Secret Trail. 4. Falsely Accused. 5. The Betrayal. 6. The Lost Fortune. 7. Cattle Wolves. 8. Under Fire. 9. Man to Man. 10. The Fatal Message. 11. Hidden Fangs. 12. False Friends. 13. Stolen Secrets. 14. Steeds of the Sky. 15. Yaqui Gold. 16. Left for Dead. 17. Yaqui Gold (copyrighted title same as Chapter 15). 18. [Unknown.]

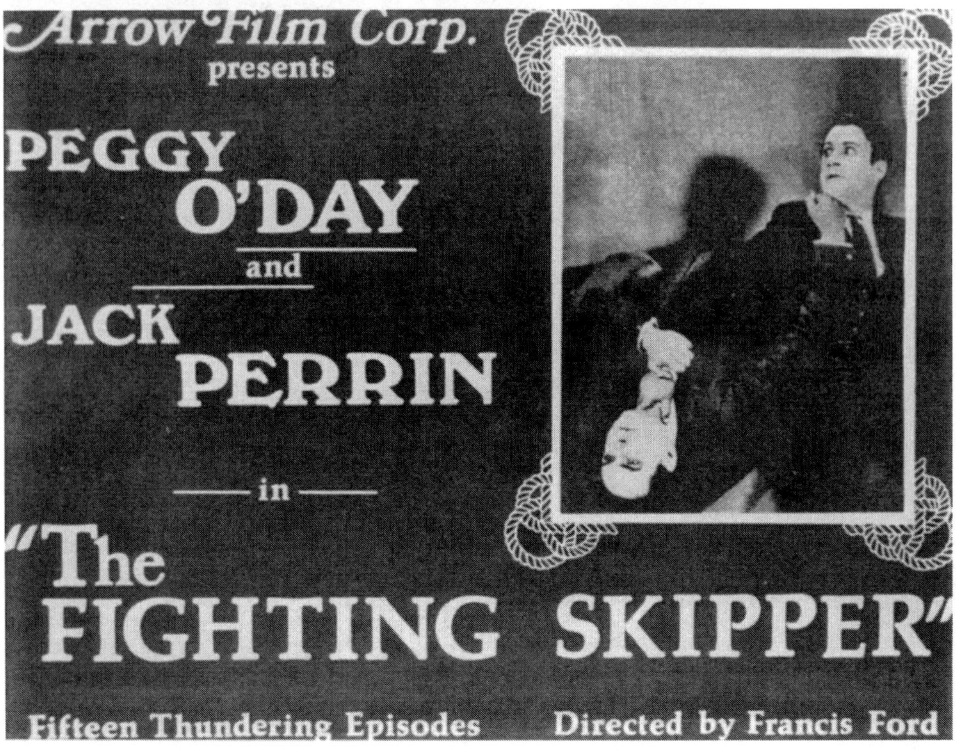

Top: **Jack Daugherty and Eileen Sedgwick in *The Fighting Ranger* (1925); *bottom: The Fighting Skipper* (1923)**

202. The Fighting Skipper

(Arrow Film Corp., March 1923) Serial, 15 chapters, two reels each. D: Francis Ford.

Skipper is the rightful heir to a buried fortune on Thunder Island. However, her father's map and deed to the island disappear after his death, and Skipper struggles to obtain her inheritance. She is hampered by a half-sister who is identical to her in appearance, but aided by a forthright young chap who loves her.

Peggy O'Day (Skipper), Jack Perrin, Bill White, Francis Ford, Steve Murphy.

1. Pirates of Pedro. 2. Harbor of Hate. 3. Pirates' Playground. 4. In the Fog. 5. Isle of Intrigue. 6. Trapped. 7. Silent Valley. 8. House of Mystery. 9. Snowbound. 10. The Mystery Car. 11. Across the Border. 12. Secret of Buoy # 3. 13. Human Plunder. 14. Lost Island. 15. Love and Law.

203. The Fighting Trail

(Vitagraph, September 10, 1917) Serial, 15 chapters; Chapter 1, three reels; others, two reels. D: William Duncan. SP: J. Stuart Blackton and Cyrus Townsend Brady.

John Gwyn, a mining engineer, knows the location of a mine which contains valuable minerals used in the preparation of a powerful explosive needed to carry on the war in Europe. Agents of the Central powers try to locate the mine, which is on the property of Ybarra, whose Foster daughter, Nan, is loved by Gwyn.

Duncan became so popular as a serial star that Vitagraph tore up his contract in 1919 and rewrote it to call for six serials budgeted at $1,500,000 and with Duncan to receive an average salary of $10,000 per week for directing and starring in two serials a year.

William Duncan (John Gwyn), Carol Holloway (Nan), George Holt, Joe Ryan, Walter Rodgers, Fred Burns.

1. The Priceless Ingredient. 2. The Story of Ybarra. 3. Will Yaqui Joe Tell? 4. The Other Half. 5. The Torrent Rush. 6. The Ledge of Despair. 7. The Lion's Prey. 8. Strands of Doom. 9. The Bridge of Death. 10. The Sheriff. 11. Parched Trails. 12. The Desert of Torture. 13. The Water Trap. 14. The Trestle of Horrors. 15. Out of the Flame.

204. Fighting with Buffalo Bill

(Universal, August 30, 1926) Serial, 10 chapters, two reels each. D: Ray Taylor. S: William F. Cody—*The Great West That Was*.

A crooked lawyer is on the way west with his son and his ward, Doris. He intends to confiscate a gold mine belonging to the girl's father, whom she believes to be dead. On the same wagon train is Ned Wheeler, who competes with Bart Crosby, the lawyer's son, for Doris's affections. Doris loves Ned and, with the occasional help of Buffalo Bill, the two manage to uncover the lawyer's plot, thwart it, and bring about a reunion with Doris's father.

Wallace MacDonald (Ned Wheeler), Elsa Benham (Doris Carberry), Edmund Cobb (Buffalo Bill Cody), Robert E. Homans (Caleb Crosby), Cuyler Supplee (Bart Crosby), Grace Cunard (Lola), Howard Truesdell (Carberry), Nelson McDowell (Lem Brady), Harry Blake (The Boy).

1. Westward. 2. The Red Menace. 3. The Blazing Arrow. 4. The Death Trap. 5. The Renegade. 6. The Race for Life. 7. Buried Alive. 8. Desperate Chances. 9. The Shadow of Evil. 10. End of the Trail.

205. Fighting with Kit Carson

(Mascot, July 15, 1933) Serial, 12 chapters, two reels each. D: Armand Schaefer and Colbert Clark. SP: J.F. Natteford, Barney Sarecky, Colbert Clark, Wyndham Gittens. P: Nat Levine. (Reissued in 1947 as feature film titled *The Return of Kit Carson*).

Top: **William Duncan and Carol Holloway in *The Fighting Trail* (1917); *bottom left:* Wallace MacDonald; *bottom right:* Wallace MacDonald, Elsa Benham, and Edmund Cobb in *Fighting with Buffalo Bill* (1926)**

Left: **Noah Beery, Sr., and Al Bridges;** *right:* **Johnny Mack Brown and Edward Hearn in** ***Fighting with Kit Carson*** **(1933)**

Kit Carson is employed to escort a caravan carrying a large quantity of gold destined for army posts in California. Unscrupulous men attempt to steal the gold by causing the murder of Chief Dark Eagle and placing the blame on Carson and his party, thus setting the Indians on the warpath. However, Carson, with the help of his young friends Nakomas and Joan triumphs in the end by rounding up the outlaw band known as the Mystery Riders, exposing Kraft as the leader, and saving the gold.

Johnny Mack Brown (Kit Carson), Betsy King Ross (Joan Fargo), Noah Beery, Sr. (Cyrus Draft), Noah Beery, Jr. (Nakomas), Tully Marshall (Jim Bridger), Edmund Breese (Matt Fargo), Robert Warwick (Dark Eagle), Edward Hearn (Morgan), Lafe McKee (Foster), Ernie Adams (Wade), Al Bridge (Reynolds), Lane Chandler (Sergeant), Reed Howes (Duke), Jack Mower (Carter), Frank Ellis (Guard), Slim Whittaker (Guard), Lew Meehan (Outlaw), Mason Williams, William Farnum, Iron Eyes Cody, DeWitt Jennings, Yakima Canutt.

1. The Mystery Riders. 2. The White Chief. 3. Hidden Gold. 4. The Silent Doom. 5. Murder Will Out. 6. The Secret of Iron Mountain. 7. The Law of the Lawless. 8. Red Phantoms. 9. The Invisible Enemy. 10. Midnight Magic. 11. Unmasked. 12. Trail to Glory.

206. Le Fille Sauvage

(France—Pathé–Consortium–Cinema, 1922) Serial, 12 chapters. D: Henri Etievant. S: Jules Mary. Scen: Jules Mary. P: Ermolieff–Cinema.

Nathalie Lissenko (Jacqueline Gervoise), Romuald Joubé (Renaud Raigice), Irene Wells (Liliane), Nicolas Rimsky (Gervoise), Gaston Rieffler (Villedieu), Victor Tourjansky (Robertson), Milo (Jérémit), Lily Deslys [Damita] (Henriette Villedieu), Janvier (M. Jodry-Thuret), Maupain (Cobs), Angely (Papa Damloup), P. Delmonde (Dorritt), Mlle. Wrangel (Marie Jérémit), Mlle. Volkonskaia (Mme. Villedieu), Angele Decory (Maman Damloup), M. Dubuisson (Maman Raigice).

1–3. [Unknown.] 4. L'ange du foyer. 5. Un cri dans la nuit. 6. Dans l'engrenage. 7. Un baiser aux enchères. 8. Liliane contre tous. 9. Entre deux devoirs. 10. La jolie fugitive. 11. Les vautours. 12. L'absolution.

207. Le Fils de la Nuit

(France—Eclair, 1919) Serial, 12 chapters. D: Gerard Bourgeois. S: Jules De Gastyne and Gerard Bourgeois.

Alfred Zorilla, Elmire Vautier, L. Courtois, Jacques Robert, Jacqueline Farnese, Fernand Mailly, Volbert, Georges Wague, Gildes, Mme. Joffre, Dartagnan, Teddy, Ginette Darson, Yvonne Desvignes, Varnes, Jeanne Roulet.

208. Le Fils du Flibustier

(France—Gaumont, 1922) Serial, 12 chapters. English Feature Title: *Son of a Buccaneer*. D/Scen: Louis Feuillade.

Aime Simon-Girard (Yves le Paimpolais/Jacques Lafont), Georges Biscot (Miraut le Borgne/Sergent Pacoulin), Sandra Milowanoff (Josette Bertrand/Bertrande), Derigal (Le flibustier Mathias/Le financier Malestan), Lise Jaux (La Renarde/La mère de Jacques Lafont), Fernand Hermann (Le capitaine/Montbrun le fou), Amedée Charpentier (Le cabaretier Binic/Le docteur Perdonnel), Pierre de Canolle (Laurent le basque), Morlay (Un officier du gouverneur), Arnaud (Corentin), Laurent Morlas.

French: 1. La flibuste. 2. Le pavillon noir. 3. Le vaisseau maudit. 4. Maman. 5. La noce d'Anais. 6. La mission d'un fils. 7. Le justicier. 8. La drogue blanche. 9. Le passe. 10. Le revenant de Saint-Fons. 11. Le maître chanteur. 12. Le testament. *Portuguese:* 1. O navio fantasma. 2. Ivo, o bretão. 3. O castigo. 4. O morto vivo. 5. A boda interrompida. 6. A missão de Jacques. 7. Os justiceiros. 8. O mercador de veneno. 9. O passado. 10. O ressuscitado de Saint-Fons. 11. O burlão. 12. O testamento.

209. Les Fils du Soleil

(France—Société des Cinéromans, 1924) Serial, 8 chapters. D: René Le Somptier. Scen: René Le Somptier.

Marquisette Bosky, Georges Charlia, Marcel Vibert, Joë Hamman, Mario Nasthasio, Leclerc, Leilah Djali, Georges Bernier, C.T. Terrore.

Portuguese: 1. Desonross intriga. 2. O capitão Yossuf. 3. Cristãoe muçulmana. 4. A justiça do emir. 5. A evasão. 6. A guerra santa. 7. A derrota. 8. A honra triunfa.

210. A Final Reckoning

(Universal, April 15, 1928) Serial, 12 chapters, two reels each. D: Ray Taylor. SP: Basil Dickey and George Morgan. S: G.A. Henry. Camera: Frank Redman.

In the Australian bush a prospector finds gold. He sends a map of the location to his young son and daughter in England with instructions to join him. Black John and his gang kill him before the youngsters arrive. Vowing vengeance on the outlaws, a friend of the prospector helps the kids attain what is rightfully theirs.

Newton House (Ruben Whitney), Louise Lorraine (Miss Whitney, Ruben's Sister), Jay Wilsey [Buffalo Bill, Jr.] (Captain Wilson), Edmund Cobb (Black Jack), Frank Clark (Jim Whitney).

1. A Treacherous Friend. 2. The Man Trap. 3. Trapped. 4. Face to Face. 5. Ambushed. 6. Unmasked. 7. In Wolf's Clothing. 8. An Attack in the Dark. 9. A Ride for Life. 10. The Blast of Death. 11. The Living Dead. 12. The Reward.

Top: **Jay Wilsey (Buffalo Bill, Jr.) and Newton House in *A Final Reckoning* (1929); *bottom:* Kenneth Harlan and Edna Murphy in *Finger Prints* (1931)**

211. Finger Prints

(Universal, March 23, 1931) Serial, 10 chapters, two reels each. D: Ray Taylor. S: Arthur B. Reeve. SP: George Morgan, George H. Plympton, and Basil Dickey.

A Secret Service agent apprehends a gang of smugglers, saves his girlfriend from a lustful suitor, and clears the girl's father of murder charges.

Kenneth Harlan (Gary Gordon), Edna Murphy (Lola Mackey), Gayne Whitman (Kent Martin), Gertrude Astor (Jane Madden), William Worthington (John Mackey), William Thorne (Joe Burke), Monte Montague (Officer Rooney).

1. The Dance of Death. 2. A Fugitive of Fear! 3. Toll of the Sea! 4. The Sinister Shadow. 5. The Plunge of Peril. 6. The Finger of Fate. 7. The Depths of Doom. 8. The

Top: **Jack Daugherty in *The Fire Fighters* (1927);** ***bottom*: Herbert Rawlinson in *The Flame Fighter* (1925)**

Thundering Terror! 9. Flames of Fury. 10. The Final Reckoning.

212. The Fire Detective

(Pathé, March 3, 1929) Serial, 10 chapters, two reels each. D: Spencer Gordon Bennet and Thomas L. Storey. SP: George Anthony Gray. S: Frank Leon Smith.

The hero is a special investigator for the fire department endeavoring to uncover the perpetrators of a series of disastrous incendiary fires. Evidence shows that a band of criminals are setting the fires. A U.S. senator and a criminal attorney are drawn into the proceedings, along with a convict and a chemist.

Gladys McConnell, Hugh Allan, Leo Maloney, John Cossar, Frank Lackteen, Larry Steers, Bruce Gordon, Carlton King.

1. The Arson Trail. 2. The Pit of Darkness. 3. The Hidden Hand. 4. The Convict Strikes. 5. On Flaming Waters. 6. The Man of Mystery. 7. The Ape Man. 8. Back from Death. 9. Menace of the Past. 10. The Flame of Love.

213. The Fire Fighters

(Universal, January 17, 1927) Serial, 10 chapters, two reels each. D: Jacques Jaccard. S: John A. Moroso—"Cap Fallon, Firefighter."

Two generations of fire-fighting Powers, Fred and Jimmie, fight against the efforts of Grant Stewart to gain control of Fred's homestead, where valuable water power potentialities are located. Fred is framed for a murder and has to flee town, leaving his son Jimmie in the care of Captain Fallon and giving up his fiancee, Mary, forever.

Years later Jimmie himself is a fire fighter, Mary is dead, and her daughter, also named Mary, is editor of *The Daily Clarion* and making it hot for Stewart politically. When Stewart attempts to have Fred declared legally dead, so as to get at the property, Fred returns in disguise to do battle against Stewart. On another front Jimmie and Mary Kent fight his corruption. In the long run Stewart is exposed as a crook, Fred is freed of murder charges, and Jim and Mary are married.

Jack Daugherty (Jimmie Powers), Helen Ferguson (Mary Kent), Florence Allen, Robert Irwin, Milt Brown, George German.

1. For Life and Liberty. 2. Paths of Peril. 3. The Crimson Terror. 4. Out of the Past. 5. The False Alarm. 6. Fighting Fate. 7. Plunge of Peril. 8. Face to Face. 9. Wanted for Murder. 10. The Reckoning.

214. The Flame Fighter

(Beacon Films/Rayart, September 10, 1925) Serial, 10 chapters, two reels each. D/S: Robert Dillon.

Fireman Jack sparks squares off against corruption and crooked contractors in the process of proving his innocence of malfeasance.

Herbert Rawlinson (Jack Sparks), Brenda Lane (Alice Baker), Jerome La Gasse

(Darcy Johns), Edward Fetherstone (Ned Carney), Dorothy Donald (Mary Carney), Florence Lee (Mrs. Sparks), Purnell Pratt (Mike Turney), Steve Murphy (Smokey Joe Gallagher), Richard Gordon (Kendall Vance), Leigh Willard (John Baker).

1. Smoke Eaters. 2. Scarlet Patrol. 3. The Silent Alarm. 4. Blazing Paths. 5. Scalding Seas. 6. Death's Battalion. 7. Daring Deeds. 8. Danger Ahead. 9. A Desperate Chance. 10. Heroic Hearts.

215. The Flaming Disc

(Universal, November 21, 1920) Serial, 18 chapters, two reels each. D: Robert F. Hill. Scen: Jerry Ash and Arthur H. Gooden. S: Arthur Henry Gooden. Working Title: Disc of Flames.

Elmo Gray, Secret Service agent, must apprehend criminal Rodney Stanton before Stanton can make use of what he has stolen—a powerful lens that can reduce steel to ashes in a matter of moments. Stanton has also kidnapped the inventor, Professor Wade, and his daughter, Helen. Elmo is opposed by his own twin brother, who is a member of Stanton's gang, having been put under a hypnotic spell by the criminal.

Elmo Lincoln (Elmo Gray/Jim Gray), Louise Lorraine (Helen Wade), Fay Holderness (Stella Dean), Roy Watson (Rodney Stanton), George Williams (Stanley Barrows), Lee Kohlmar (Professor Robert Wade), Fred Hamer (Briggs), Monte Montague ("Bat" Hogan), Jenks Harris (Dawson), Bob Reeves (Henchman), Lillian Lorraine.

1. Rails of Death. 2. Span of Life. 3. Perilous Leap. 4. Fires of Hate. 5. Vanishing Floor. 6. Pool of Mystery. 7. Circle of Fire. 8. Through Walls of Steel. 9. The Floating Mine. 10. Spiked Death. 11. The Dynamite Trail. 12. The Tunnel of Flames. 13. Caged In. 14. The Purple Rays. 15. Poisoned Waters. 16. Running Wild. 17. Rails of Destruction. 18. End of the Trail.

Top: Louise Lorraine and unidentified players in *The Flaming Disc* (1920)

216. Flaming Frontiers

(Universal, May 1938) Serial, 15 chapters, two reels each. D: Ray Taylor and Alan James. S: Peter B. Kyne, *The Tie that Binds*. SP: Wyndham Gittens, George Plympton, Basil Dickey, and Paul Perez. P: Henry McRae. A remake of *Heroes of the West* with Brown, Hansen, and Bowman in roles originally played by Onslow Stevens, Diane Duval, and Noah Beery, Jr. Bowman later was known as John Archer; Duval became Jaqueline Wells/Julie Bishop.

Indian scout Tex Houston aids Tom Grant and his sister Mary against outlaws who wish to steal their gold mine.

Johnny Mack Brown (Tex Houston), Eleanor Hansen (Mary Grant), Ralph Bowman (Tom Grant), Charles Middleton (Ace Daggett), Charles Stevens (Breed), Chief Thunder Cloud (Himself), James Blaine (Bart Eaton), William Royle (Tom Crosby), Horace Murphy (Sheriff), Michael Slade (Postmaster), John Rutherford (Buffalo Bill), Edward Cassidy, Charles King, Eddy C. Waller, Roy Barcroft, Karl Hackett, Jim Farley, Jim Corey, Bob Woodward, Frank Straubringer, Tom Steele, Iron Eyes Cody, Helen Gibson, Suni Chorre, Pat O'Brien, George Plues, Jack Saunders, Jack Roper, Ferris Taylor, Frank Ellis, Blackjack Ward, Earle Hodgins, Alan Bridge, Hank Bell, Horace Carpenter, J.P. McGowan, Charles Murphy, Charles Whitaker, Frank LaRue, Jim Toney.

1. The River Runs Red. 2. Death Rides the Wind. 3. Treachery at Eagle Pass. 4. A Night of Terror. 5. Blood and Gold. 6. Trapped by Fire. 7. The Human Target. 8. The Savage Horde. 9. Toll of the Torrent. 10. In the Claws of Cougar. 11. The Half Breed's Vengeance. 12. The Indians are Coming. 13. The Fatal Plunge. 14. Dynamite. 15. A Duel to the Death.

217. Flash Gordon

(Universal, April 6, 1936) Serial, 13 chapters, two reels each. D: Frederick Stephani. SP: George Plympton, Frederick Stephani, Basil Dickey, and Ella O'Neill. Based on Alex Raymond's comic strip. P: Henry McRae. Camera: Jerry Ash and Richard Fryer. Several features were constructed from this serial: *Rocketship*, *Spaceship to the Unknown*, *Perils from the Planet Mongo*, *Space Soldiers*, and *Atomic Rocketship*.

The planet Mongo is hurtling through space on a collision course with Earth. Flash Gordon, Dale Arden, and Professor Zarkov fly to the planet in Zarkov's rocket ship, there to clash with Emperor Ming and to experience unusual adventures in a strange land. This serial—one of the most expensive and most successful ever made—has today taken on the aura of a classic and is still being shown on television and at film festivals. The Flash Gordon strip was extremely popular and the serial equaled the comic strip in popularity.

Larry "Buster" Crabbe (Flash Gordon), Jean Rogers (Dale

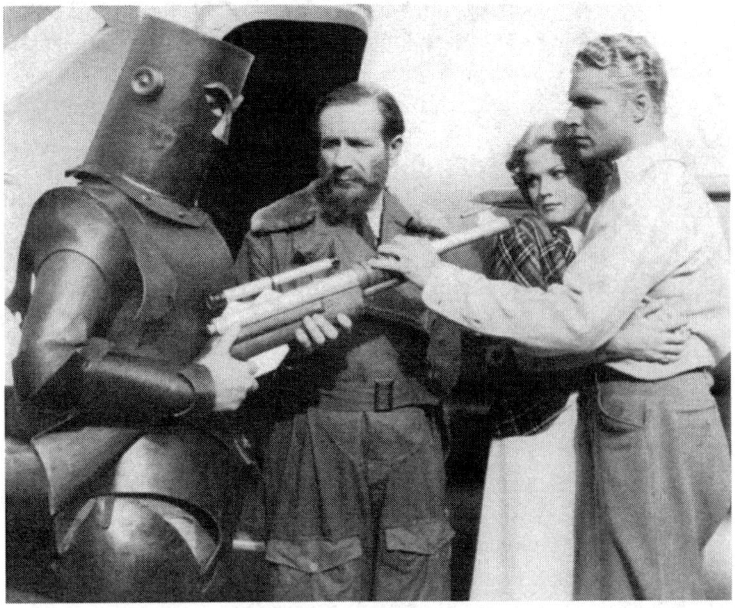

Above: **Buster Crabbe, Jean Rogers, and Frank Shannon;** ***right:*** **Buster Crabbe and Jean Rogers in** ***Flash Gordon*** **(1936)**

Arden), Charles Middleton (Emperor Ming), Priscilla Lawson (Princess Aura), Richard Alexander (Prince Barin), Frank Shannon (Dr. Zarkov), John Lipson (King Vultan), Duke York, Jr. (King Kala), Earl Askam (Officer Torch), George Cleveland (Professor Hensley), Theodore Lorch (High Priest), House Peters, Jr. (Shark Man), James Pierce (King Thun), Muriel Goodspeed (Zona), Richard Tucker (Professor Gordon), Fred Kohler, Jr., Lane Chandler, Al Ferguson (Soldiers), Constantine Romanoff (Ape-Man), Bull Montana (Ape-Man), Glenn Strange (Fire Monster), William Desmond (Guard), Reed Howes, Roy Barcroft.

1. The Planet of Peril. 2. The Tunnel of Terror. 3. Captured by Shark Men. 4. Battling the Sea Beast. 5. The Destroying Ray. 6. Flaming Torture. 7. Shattering Doom. 8. Tournament of Death. 9. Fighting the Fire Dragon. 10. The Unseen Peril. 11. In the Claws of the Tigron. 12. Trapped in the Turret. 13. Rocketing to Earth.

218. Flash Gordon Conquers the Universe

(Universal, February 1940) Serial, 12 chapters, two reels each. D: Ford Beebe and Ray Taylor. SP: George H. Plympton, Basil Dickey, Barry Shipman. Based on Alex Raymond's comic strip. P: Henry MacRae. Camera: Jerry Ash. Feature titles: *Perils from the Planet Mongo*; *Purple Death from Outer Space*; *Space Soldiers Conquer the Universe*.

The valiant trio of Flash Gordon, Dr. Zarkov, and Dale Arden is off again on another adventure against old foe, Ming the Merciless. Ming's scientists have perfected a Purple Dust that kills those intelligent enough to pose a threat to Ming, while only making slaves out of the less intelligent. His rocket ships are depositing the Purple Dust in the Earth's atmosphere and the fate of the planet depends on Dr. Zarkov's finding an antidote or in stopping Ming directly.

Larry "Buster" Crabbe (Flash Gordon), Carol Hughes (Dale Arden), Charles Middleton (Ming, the Merciless), Anne Gwynne (Sonja), Frank Shannon (Dr. Zarkov), Roland Drew (Prince Barin), Shirley Deane (Princess Aura), Victor Zimmerman (Thong), Don Rowan (Torch), Michael Mark (Karm), Sigmund Nilssen (Korro), Lee Powell (Roka), Edgar Edwards (Turan), Ben Taggart (Lupi), Harry C. Bradley (Keedish), Luli Deste (Fria), Donald Curtis (Ronal), Ray Mala (King's Son), Lane Chandler (Guard), Roy Barcroft (Guard), John Hamilton (Professor Gordon), Herbert Rawlinson (Professor Froman), Clarice Sherry (Brenda), Carmen D'Antonio (Dancer), Jeanne Kelly (Olga), Mimi Taylor (Verna), Byron Foulger (Druk), Tom Chatterton (Professor Arden), Earl Dwyer (Janda), Allan Cavan (Nobleman).

1. The Purple Death. 2. Freezing Torture. 3. Walking Bombs. 4. The Destroying Ray. 5. The Palace of Horror. 6. Flaming Death. 7. The Land of the Dead. 8. The Fiery Abyss. 9. The Pool of Peril. 10. The Death Mist. 11. Stark Treachery. 12. Doom of the Dictator.

219. Flash Gordon's Trip to Mars

(Universal, May 1938) Serial, 15 chapters, two reels each. D: Ford Beebe and Robert Hill. S/SP: Wyndham Gittens, Norman S. Hall, Ray Trampe, and Herbert Dalmas. Based on the newspaper feature *Flash Gordon* by Alex Raymond. Feature titles: *Mars Attacks the World* and *The Deadly Ray from Mars*.

Flash Gordon, Dale Arden, Prince Baron, and Dr. Zarkov again do mortal combat with Ming the Merciless, who has allied himself with Queen Azura of Mars. Ming has developed a great lamp that saps nitrogen from the Earth's atmosphere and Queen Azura uses her magic powers to enslave the clay people and others who balk at doing her bidding. Flash is finally able to destroy the lamp and Ming is thrown into a disintegration chamber.

Buster Crabbe (Flash Gordon), Jean Rogers (Dale Arden), Charles Middleton (Emperor Ming), Frank Shannon (Dr. Zarkov), Beatrice Roberts (Queen Azura), Donald Kerr (Happy Hapgood), Richard Alexander (Prince Baron), C. Montague Shaw (King of the Clay People), Wheeler Oakman (Tarnak), Kane Richmond (Pilot Captain), Kenneth Duncan (Airdrome Captain), Warner Richmond (Toran), Anthony Warde (King Fir of the Forest People), James Eagels (High Priest of Kalu), Lane Chandler, Ben Lewis, Jack Mulhall, Thomas Carr, Reed Howes, Stanley Price, Hooper Atchley, Jerry Frank.

1. New Worlds to Conquer. 2. The Living Dead. 3. Queen of Magic. 4. Ancient Enemies. 5. The Boomerang. 6. Tree Men of Mars. 7. The Prisoner of Mongo. 8. The Black Sapphire of Kalu. 9. Symbol of Death. 10. Incense of Forgetfulness. 11. Human Bait. 12. Ming the Merciless. 13. The Miracle of Magic. 14. A Beast at Bay. 15. An Eye for an Eye.

Top: **Buster Crabbe, Frank Shannon, Donald Kerr, Kane Richmond, and Wheeler Oakman;** ***bottom:*** **Charles Middelton in** ***Flash Gordon's Trip to Mars*** **(1938)**

220. Der Fluch der Menschheit

(Germany—Eichberg-Film, 1920) Series, 2 episodes. D: Richard Eichberg. Scen: William Merkel and Arthur Teuber.

This two-episode series is included for the purpose of presenting one of Bela Lugosi's earliest screen efforts. Star status was yet far in the future.

Les Parry, Violette Napierska, Robert Scholz, Gustav Birkholz, Willi Kaiser-Heyl, Reinhold Pasch, Herr Dorr, Herr Schmasow, Marga Kohler, Felix Hecht, Bela Lugosi, Frau Funk, Paul Ludwig.

1. Die Tochter der Arbeit. 2. Im Rausche der Milliarden.

221. Flying Disc Man from Mars

(Republic, January 1951) Serial, 12 chapters, two reels each. D: Fred C. Brannon. SP: Ronald Davidson. Assoc. P: Franklyn Adreon. Photography: Walter Strenge. Music: Stanley Wilson. Special Effects: Howard and Theodore Lydecker. Feature Title: *Missile Monsters* (1958). Film is virtually a remake of *The Purple Monster Strikes* (1945).

A Martian, Mota, lands on Earth and coerces Dr. Bryant, atomic research scientist, into helping him set up the conquest of Earth by Martians. Opposing Mota are Kent Fowler and Helen Hall, owner and secretary respectively of the Fowler Air Patrol. Mota establishes a secret base within a volcano crater from which he begins to accumulate refined uranium and other materials to power his weapons of war. He embarks on a campaign of terror and extortion to secure the things he needs. Ultimately Kent learns that Bryant is in league with Mota and is thus able to overcome them. The two would-be world conquerors are killed by erupting lava caused by one of their own atomic bombs.

Walter Reed (Kent Fowler), Lois Collier (Helen Hall), Gregory Gay (Mota), James Craven (Bryant), Harry Lauter (Drake), Richard Irving (Ryan), Sandy Sanders (Steve), Dale Van Sickel (Watchman), Tom Steele (Taylor), Clayton Moore (Louis Ashe), Ken Terrell (Graves), Carey Loftin (Hagen), Michael Carr (Trent), George Sherwood (Gate Guard), Jimmy O'Gatty (Gradey), Chuck Hamilton (Driver), Bill Wilkus (Cole), John Daheim (Boyd), Dick Crockett (Bill), Paul Gustine (Technician 1), David Sharpe (Technician 2), Guy Teague (Workman), Saul Gorss (Ed), Barry Brooks (Garrett), Dick Cogan (Kirk), Lester Dorr (Crane), John DeSimone (Curtis).

1. Menace from Mars. 2. The Volcano's Secret. 3. Death Rides the Stratosphere. 4. Execution by Fire. 5. The Living Projectile. 6. Perilous Mission. 7. Descending Doom. 8. Suicidal Sacrifice. 9. The Funeral Pyre. 10. Weapons of Hate. 11. Disaster on the Highway. 12. Volcanic Vengeance.

222. Flying Fists

(Henry Ginsberg and Jacob Wilk, 1924) Series, 6 episodes, two reels each. S: Sam Hellman.

Lorna Gray (Adrian Booth) and Robert Paige in *Flying G-Men* (1939)

Benny Leonard, former light-weight champion, is featured in six boxing dramas, each containing a set fight.

Benny Leonard (Benny Lane), Diana Allen (Helen), Frank Evans (Helen's Father), Billy Mitchell ("Cream-Cheese").

1. Breaking In. 2. Hitting Hard. 3. Soft Muscles. 4. The Comeback. 5. The Surprise Fight. 6. The Jazz Fight.

Synopses of First Three Episodes 1. *Breaking In:* Benny Lane, a hardworking clerk, is helping his crippled brother through college, and badly wants money. On his way home one evening he saves his brother from attack by ruffians, and the way he lays them out strikes a boxing manager as being full of promise. Benny is induced to enter the ring, and wins the bout and the money. 2. *Hitting Hard:* Benny's new manager is so satisfied with the prospects that he induces Benny's employer to fire him, in order that he can begin a ring career. Benny secretly loves the boss's daughter, Helen, and is unaware that the boss himself is secretly a wild-eyed fight fan. Benny signs on against a tough opponent, managed by a crooked promoter. He wins the fight, but only after a lot of trouble with the crooks. 3. *Soft Muscles:* Benny is out for the world light-weight title, but success has rather spoiled him, and he patronizes night clubs and permits himself to be "vamped." In his contest he is decidedly on the soft side, and only wins when his trainer plays on the affection he has for Helen. Then he scores and wins a tough fight.

223. Flying G-Men

(Columbia, February 1939) Serial, 15 chapters, two reels each. D: Ray Taylor and James W. Horne. SP: Robert E. Kent, Basil Dickey, and Sherman Lowe. P: Jack Fier. Assist D: Norman Deming. Executive P: Irving Briskin. Photography: Ben Kline, John Stumar. Music: Lee Zahler.

Four flying G-Men, one of whom is The Black Falcon, are charged with the responsibility of running down a gang of saboteurs striking at American defenses. Secretly headed by Brewster, an airport owner, the spies kill one of the four G-Men before The Falcon and his two buddies discover the leader's identity and put the miscreants out of commission for good.

Robert Paige (Hal Andrews/The Black Falcon), Robert Fiske (Bart Davis), James Craig (John Cummings), Lorna Gray [Adrian Booth] (Babe McKay), Don Beddoe (Hamilton), Forbes Murray (Brewster), Dick Curtis (Korman), Ann Doran (Secretary), Nestor Paiva (Everett), George Chesebro (Red), Bud Geary (Radioman), Tom Steele (Williams), George Turner (Crawford), Hugh Prosser (Stokes).

1. Challenge in the Sky. 2. Flight of the Condemned. 3. The Vulture's Nest. 4. The Falcon Strikes. 5. Flight from Death. 6. Phantom of the Sky. 7. Trapped by Radio. 8. The Midnight Watch. 9. Wings of Terror. 10. Flaming Wreckage. 11. While a Nation Sleeps. 12. Sealed Orders. 13. Flame Island. 14. Jaws of Death. 15. The Falcon's Reward.

224. Den Flyvende Hollender

(Denmark—Nordisk Films Kompagni, 1919) Serial, 4 chapters. (English Title: *The Phantom Ship.*) D: Emanuel Gregers. SP: Valdemar Andersen. S: Captain Marryat. Camera: S. Kruse.

Carlo Wieth (Filip Vanderdecken), Inger Nybo (Amiene Poots), Jutta Lund (Mrs. Vanderdecken), Charles Wilken (Doctor

Poots), Hans Dynesen (Father Seysen), Peter S. Andersen (Schriften), Bertel Krause (Mynheer Kloots), Carl Lauritzen (Supercargo), Svend Kornbeck (Father Mathias), Gerhard Jessen (Krantz), Fritz Lamprecht (The Viceking), Peter Nielsen (The Inquisitor).

1. Levende Fordømt (11-1-20). 2. Den enøjede Lods (11-15-20). 3. Den døde Ø (11-22-20). 4. Døden paa Baalet (11-29-20).

225. The Forest Ranger

(Universal, 1928–29) Series, 12 episodes, two reels each.

Edmund Cobb.

Episode Titles, Releasing Dates, Directors (in italics), Supporting Actors 1. Riders of the Woods (9-15-28) *Josef Levigard*. 2. The Fighting Forester (10-20-28) *Walter Favian*; Voceil Viking, Bud Osborne, Merrill McCormick. 3. The Boundary Battle (11-17-28) *Josef Levigard*; Lillian Gilmore, Clark Comstock, David Dunbar. 4. The Scrappin' Ranger (12-22-28) *Josef Levigard*. 5. The Claim Jumpers (1-19-29) *Josef Levigard*. 6. In Line of Duty (2-23-29) *Bruce Mitchell*; Lotus Thompson, Bill Patton. 7. Beyond the Smoke (3-23-29) *Bruce Mitchell*; Regina Doyle, Walter Shumway, William Clifford. 8. A Rider of the Sierras (4-27-29) *Ray Taylor*; Marjorie Bonner, Robert Kortman. 9. Dodging Danger (5-25-29) *Doran Cox*; Gloria Gray, Claude Payton. 10. Perilous Paths (6-29-29) *Ray Taylor*; Regina Doyle, Buck Connors, Robert Kortman. 11. The Danger Line (7-27-29) *Bruce Mitchell*; Regina Doyle. 12. Just in Time (8-17-29) *Doran Cox*; Regina Doyle, Wilbur Mack.

Robert Paige, James Craig, and Richard Fiske in *Flying G-Men* (1939)

226. The Fortieth Door

(Pathé, May 25, 1924) Serial, 10 chapters, two reels each. D: George B. Seitz. SP: Frank Leon Smith. S: Mary Hastings Bradley. Photography: Vernon Walker. P: C.W. Patton. Also released in a six-reel feature version.

Aimee grows up as the daughter of a Mohammedan desert merchant, but she is actually French. She is betrothed to a rascal named Hamid Bey but falls in love with Jack Ryder, an American archeologist, who helps her escape the clutches of Hamid Bey when Jack and Aimee discover she is French.

With George Seitz directing and Frank Leon Smith writing the scenario, the film's success was almost assured. Again a feature version was prepared. Allene possessed a rare girlish charm that made her immensely popular with all those with whom she worked, and that same charm was projected on screen. Pathé had hit the mother lode when they discovered this actress.

Allene Ray (Aimee), Bruce Gordon (Jack Ryder), Frank Lackteen (Hamid Bey), Anna May Wong (Zina), Frankie Mann (Jimmy Jeffries), Lillian Gale (Mariam), Bernard Siegel (Tefick Pasha), White Horse (Sheik Hassan), Scott McKee (Commissioner of Police), David Dunbar (Andy McLean), Omar Whitehead (Paul Delcarte), Eli Stanton (Ali).

1. The Secret Portal. 2. Two Lockets. 3. The Wedding. 4. Buried Alive. 5. Desert Trails. 6. The Tomb of a King. 7. Claws of the Vulture. 8. Held for Hostage. 9. The Rack. 10. The Temple of the Forty Doors.

227. Fortune Hunter Series

(Produced and distributed by Sun Pictures, 1926) Series, 8 episodes, two reels each.

Kenneth McDonald, Clara Horton, Milburn Morante.

1. Over There. 2. Up in the Air. 3. Steppin' on the Gas. 4. Three Faces West. 5. Test Night. 6. Sherlock's Rival. [Possibly other titles in this series.]

228. Fuerza y Nobleza

(Spain—Royal Film, 1918) Series, 4 episodes. D: Ricardo de Baños.

Jack Johnson, Lucielle (Esposa de Jack Johnson), Fernando Delgado, Bailarino Max Besancon, Nicolas Diaz Perchicot, Miguel Del Llano, Ticiano Lombia, Duque E. Gaby (Bailarinos Brasil).

1. El testamento de un principe. 2. Entre fieras. 3. El film revelador. 4. Jack Johnson, justiciero.

229. The Further Adventures of Sherlock Holmes

(England—Stoll Pictures Productions, 1922) Series, 15 episodes, two reels each. D: George Ridgewell. S: Sir Arthur Conan Doyle. SP: Patrick L. Mannock, Geoffrey H. Malins.

Regular cast: Eille Norwood (Sherlock Holmes), Hubert Willis (Doctor Watson), Madame d' Esterre (Mrs. Hudson), Teddy Arundel (Inspector Stanley Hopkins).

1. Charles Augustus Milberton (1900 ft., 32 min.; *with* George Foley, Tony Edgar-Bruce, Edith Bishop, Annie Hughes, Harry J. Worth). 2. The Abbey Grange (2193 ft., 36 1/2 min.; *with* Madeleine Seymour, Lawford Davidson, Leslie Stiles, Madge Tree). 3. The Norwood Builder (2067 ft., 34 1/2 min.; *with* Fred Wright, Cyril Raymond, Laura Walker). 4. The Reigate Squires (1885 ft., 31 1/2 min.; *with* Arthur Lumley, Teddy O'Neill, Richard Atwood, C. Seguin). 5. The Naval Treaty (1536 ft., 25 1/2 min.; *with* Jack Hobbs, Francis Duguid, Nancy May). 6. The Second Strain (2179 ft., 36 1/2 min.; *with* A. Scott-Gatty, Dorothy Fane, Wallace Bosco, Maria Minetti, Cecil Ward). 7. The Red Circle (1770 ft., 29 1/2 min.; *with* Sybil Archdale, Maresco Marescini, Bertram Burleigh, Tom Beaumont, Esme Hubbard). 8. The Six Napoleons (1753 ft., 29 1/2 min.; *with* George Bellamy, Jack Raymond, Alice Moffatt). 9. Black Peter (1776 ft., 29 1/2 min.; *with* Fred Paul, Hugh Buckler, Jack Jarman, Fred Rains, Mrs. Hubert Wallis, Miss Wallis). 10. The Bruce-Partington Plans (2130 ft., 36 min.; *with* Ronald Power, Edward Sorley, Malcolm Gilbert, Leslie Brittain). 11. The Stockholder's Clerk (1841 ft., 30 1/2 min.; *with* Olaf Hytten, Aubrey Fitzgerald, George Ridgewell. 12. The Bascombe Valley Mystery (2410 ft., 40 min.; *with* Ray Raymond, Hal Martin, Fred Raynham, Themma Murray). 13. The Musgrave Ritual (1698ft., 29 min.; *with* Geoffrey Wilmer, Clifton Boyne, Betty Chester). 14. The Golden Pince-Nez (1638 ft., 28 min.; *with* Cecil Morton York, Norma Whalley). 15. The Greek Interpreter (1796 ft., 30 min.; *with* H. Wheeler (Inspector Stanley Hopkins), Cecil Dane, J.E. Tozer, Edith Saville, Robert Vallis, L. Andre).

230. The Further Adventures of Stingaree

(Kalem, June 1917) Series, 15 episodes. D: Paul C. Hurst. SP: Joseph F. Poland. S: E.W. Hornung.

Irving Randolph, the respected master of Randolph Towers, London, whom the world once knew as Stingaree, the Australian Bushranger, receives notice from his attorneys that an appraisal of his family estate shows that his entire fortune has been squandered by his deceased brother while he (Irving) was absent in Australia. He realizes that as a penniless man he cannot marry his fiancée, Ethel Porter.

He is surprised by a visit from Howie, his old partner of the bushranger days, who has crossed the seas to warn Stingaree that government officers are on his trail with a warrant for his arrest. He persuades Stingaree to return to Australia with him, thus setting off a whole new series of adventures in the Australian back country. Naturally, Ethel follows him down under.

True Boardman (Irving Randolph/Stingaree), Marin Sais (Ethel Porter), Paul C. Hurst (Howie), Frank Jonasson (The Governor), Ollie Kirby (The Governor's Wife), Thomas Lingham (Lucius Brady), Edward Clisbee (Kent), Edythe Sterling (Mildred Summerfield), Barney Furey (Harry Summerfield), G.A. Williams (Black Hill), Frank M. Clark (Gypsy Prince), Jack Lott (Tom Blanks), Hal Clements (Howie [in some episodes]), Jack Waltemeyer.

1. The Fugitive Passenger. 2. A Model Marauder 3. A Double Deception. 4. An Eye for an Eye. 5. Mark of Stingaree. 6. Through Fire and Water. 7. An Order of the Court. 8. Tracking of Stingaree. 9. A Bushranger's Strategy. 10. Poisoned Cup. 11. Arrayed with the Enemy. 12. The Jackaroo. 13. At the Sign of the Kangaroo. 14. The Stranger at Dumcriff. 15. A Champion of the Law.

231. The Further Mysteries of Fu Manchu

(England—Stoll Film Company, 1924) Series, 8 episodes, two reels each. D/Scen: Fred Paul. Based on characters created by Sax Rolmer (Arthur Ward).

Harry Agar Lyons (Fu Manchu), Fred Paul (Sir Neyland Smith), Humbertson Wright (Inspector Weymouth), Dorinea Shirley (Karamaneh), Fred Morgan, John Butt, Harry Gignold, George Foley, Frank Wilson, Julie Suedo.

1. The Café L'Egypte. 2. The Coughing Horror. 3. The Craigmire Tower. 4. The Golden Pomegranates. 5. The Green Mist. 6. Greywater Park. 7. Karamaneh. 8. The Midnight Summons.

232. G-Men Never Forget

(Republic, October 1947) Serial, 12 chapters, two reels each. D: Fred Brannon and Yakima Canutt. Assoc. P: Mike Frankovich. SP: Franklyn Adreon, Basil Dickey, Jesse Duffy, and Sol Shor. Photography: John MacBurnie. Music: Mort Glickman. Special Effects: Howard and Theodore Lydecker. Feature Version: (*Code 645*)

A notorious gangster escapes from prison, kidnaps the police commissioner and with plastic surgery assumes his identity. He then tries to create an impregnable protection racket in the city. Government operatives Ted O'Hara and Frances Blake finally penetrate the gang and discover the true identity of the man they believed to be the commissioner.

Clayton Moore (Ted O'Hara), Ramsey Ames (Frances Blake), Roy Barcroft (Angus Cameron/Victor Murkland), Drew Allen (Duke Graham), Edmund Cobb (R.J. Cook), Tom Steele (Parker/Gifford/Jack), Dale Van Sickel (Fred Brent/Bud/Gill/Pete), Ken Terrell (John Kelsey/Bert/Joe), Stanley Price (Robert Benson), Jack O'Shea (Slater), Barry Brooks (George), Doug Aylesworth (Hayden), John Crawford (Dale), Bud Wolfe (Foy), Robert Barron (Garson), Carey Loftin (Hodge), Frank O'Connor (McLain), Dian Fauntelle (Miss Stewart), Eddie Acuff (Fidler), George Magrill (Saley), Russ Whiteman (Baxter), James Linn (Bailey), Tom McDonough (Al), Glenn Turner (Dorsey), Gil Perkins (Finch), Robert Wilkie (Steele), Duke Green (Nichols), John Daheim (Kramer), Charles Sullivan (Morgan), Charles Regan (Hinkey), Tom Monroe (Joe), David Sharpe (Vance/Trent), Phil Warren (Roberts), Arvon Dale (Moore), Matty Roubert (Foreman)

1. Death Rides the Torrent. 2. The Flaming Doll House. 3. Code Six–Four–Five. 4. Shipyard Saboteurs. 5. The Dead Man Speaks. 6. Marked Money. 7. Hot Cargo. 8. The Fatal Letter. 9. The Death Wind. 10. The Innocent Victim. 11. Counter-Plot. 12. Exposed.

233. G-Men vs. The Black Dragon

(Republic, February 1943) Serial, 15 chapters, two reels each. D: William Witney. SP: Ronald Davidson, William Lively, Joseph O'Donnell, Joseph Poland. Photography: Bud Thackery. Music: Mort Glickman. Special Effects:

Howard Lydecker. Film Editors: Edward Todd and Tony Martinelli. Unit Manager: Mack D'Agostino.

The time is World War II. Rex Bennett, Special Investigator, Vivian Marsh, British secret service, and Chang of the Chinese secret service join forces to search out and destroy the deadly and ruthless Black Dragon Society led by Haruchi. Once he has been smuggled into the U.S., Haruchi leads his agents in a campaign of terrorism and sabotage against the American war effort. In the final chapter Haruchi and most of his agents are blown up when Rex runs an explosive-loaded boat into the side of a submarine that has just surfaced to take on Haruchi. Rex goes overboard just in time to avoid being blown up himself. Haruchi, with whom Rex has been fighting in the speedboat, was not so lucky.

Rod Cameron (Rex Bennett), Roland Got (Chang Sing), Constance Worth (Vivian Marsh), Nino Pipitone (Oyama Haruchi), George J. Lewis (Lugo), Noel Cravat (Ranga), Maxine Doyle (Marie), Donald Kirke (Muller), Ivan Miller (Custom Inspector), Walter Fenner (Williams), C. Montague Shaw (Professor Nicholson), Harry Burns (Tony Mills), Forbes Murray (James Kennedy), Hooper Atchley (Harrison J. Caldwell), Robert Homans (Captain Gorman), Allen Jung (Fuji), Norman Nesbitt (Newscaster), John Daheim (Balcony Heavy), Tom Steele (Garage Heavy/Intern), Lawrence Grant (Sir John Brookfield), Crane Whitley (Dale Burnell), Eddie Parker (Butler), Ken Terrell (Galt/Farm Heavy), Kenneth Harlan (Casey), Harry Tauvera (Crewman), Peter George Lynn (Garr), Stanley Price (Gibbs), Pat O'Malley (Gibson), Edward Keane (Gordon), Walter Low (Graham), George DeNormand (Interceptor Pilot), Gil Perkins (Intern/Mansion Heavy), William Forrest (Jackson), Paul Fung (Japanese Commander), Kay Parsons (Jones), Sam Bernard (Karl), Robert Strange (Kettler), Baron Licher (Kettler's Voice), Kenneth Harlan (Lance), Eddie Phillips (Laundry Heavy 1), Bill Cody (Laundry Heavy 2), Duke Taylor (Mansion Heavy/Truck Heavy), John Hamilton (Raymond Martin), Mary Bayless (Matron), Virginia Carroll (Nurse), Edmund Cobb (Stewart), Martin Faust (Mill Heavy), Bud Geary (Morse), John Wallace (News Dealer), Charles LaTorre (Nick), Dick French (Norris), Dale Van Sickel (Pier Heavy), Arvon Dale (Pilot), John James (Power Clerk), Harry Tauvera (Seaman), Tom Seidel (Spencer), Norman Willis (Tarner), Walter Thiel (Tarner's Voice), Buddy Roosevelt (Truck Heavy's Voice), Bud Wolfe (Warehouse Heavy), Eddie Dew (Z–24), Otto Metzetti.

1. The Yellow Peril. 2. Japanese Inquisition. 3. Arsenal of Doom. 4. Deadly Sorcery. 5. Celestial Murder. 6. Death and Destruction. 7. The Iron Monster. 8. Beast of Tokyo. 9. Watery Grave. 10. The Dragon Strikes. 11. Suicide Mission. 12. Dead on Arrival. 13. Condemned Cargo. 14. Flaming Coffin. 15. Democracy in Action.

234. The Galloping Ghost

(Mascot, September 1, 1931) Serial, 12 chapters, two reels each. D: Reeves Eason. Assist. D: Armand Schaefer. P: Nat Levine.

Red Grange is wrongfully accused of accepting a bribe from a gambling ring and dismissed from Clay College. He maintains his silence to protect his friend and teammate Buddy Courtland. Red fails to convince Buddy's Sister, Barbara, of his innocence and is accused of killing another teammate by the police. Following up various clues, Red finally ferrets out the leader of the gambling ring and clears himself of all charges.

Clayton Moore and Ramsay Ames in *G-Men Never Forget* (1948)

Harold [Red] Grange (Red Grange), Dorothy Gulliver (Barbara), Walter Millet (Elton), Gwen Lee (Irene), Francis X. Bushman, Jr. (Buddy), Tom Dugan (Jerry), Theodore Lorch (Mystery Man/Dr. Julian), Tom London (Mullins), Edward Hearn (Harlow), Ernie Adams (Brady), Frank Brownlee (Tom), Stepin Fetchit (Snowball), Dick Dickinson, Wilfred Lucas, Joe Mack, Edward Peil, Sr., Creighton Chaney [Lon Chaney, Jr.], Jack Cookson.

1. The Idol of Clay. 2. Port of Peril. 3. The Master Mind. 4. The House of Secrets. 5. Man Without a Face. 6. The Torn $500 Bill. 7. When the Lights Went Out. 8. The Third Degree. 9. The Sign in the Sky. 10. The Vulture's Lair. 11. The Radio Patrol. 12. The Ghost Comes Back.

235. Galloping Hoofs

(Pathé, December 21, 1924) Serial, 10 chapters, two reels each. D: George B. Seitz. S: Frank Leon Smith.

Carole Page has a box that her deceased father directed her

Top: **Harold (Red) Grange (*being choked*), George [last name unknown] (*choking Grange*), Tom London (*at top of ladder*), and Dorothy Gulliver; *bottom:* Harold (Red) Grange and Dorothy Gulliver in *The Galloping Ghost* (1931)**

to open at a specified time. Before she can open it, crooks steal it. Carole enlists the help of David Kirby and together they undertake to recover the box and its contents. Carole is about to lose her horse farm because of debts, but in the end the box is recovered. The oil deed it contains solves her financial problems.

Allene Ray (Carole Page), Johnnie Walker (David Kirby), J. Barney Sherry (Richard Shaw), Ernest Hilliard (Stephen Carrington), Armand Cortez (Perry Gerard), William Nally (Bob Monson), George Nardelli (Emir of Smyrniston), Albert Roccardi (Aby Y' Souf).

1. The Sealed Box. 2. The Mountain Raid. 3. Neck and Neck. 4. The Duplicate Box. 5. The Fateful Jump. 6. Raging Waters. 7. Out of the Depths. 8. Ambushed. 9. Tricked. 10. Flying Colors.

236. Gang Busters

(Universal, March 31, 1942) Serial, 13 chapters, two reels each. D: Ray Taylor and Noel Smith. SP: Morgan B. Cox, Al Martin, Vin Martin, and George H. Plympton. AP: Ford Beebe. Photography: William Sickner and John Boyle. Based on radio series by Phillips H. Lord.

Detectives find that a gang of terrorists is made up of criminals officially listed as dead in police files. Lieutenant Bill Bannister and detective Tim Nolan are assigned to run down the League of Murdered Men. Professor Mortis, the ringleader, has a death-stimulating drug and an anti-death treatment that he uses to recruit gang members. The detectives, aided by Vicki Logan, a news photographer girl friend of Bannister, are able to crush the gang.

Kent Taylor (Bill Bannister), Irene Hervey (Vicki Logan), Ralph Morgan (Professor Mortis), Robert Armstrong (Tim Nolan), Richard Davies (Happy Haskins), Joseph Crehan (Chief O'Brien), George J. Lewis (Mason), George Watts (Mayor Hansen), Ralf Harolde (Halliger), John Gallaudet (Wilkinson), Victor Zimmerman (Barnard), Johnnie Berkes (Mr. Grubb), Pat O'Malley (Police Chemist Randall), Robert Barron (Cop Pushing Car), Stanley Blystone (Doctor), Riley Hill (Lucky Bannister), Beatrice Roberts (Secretary to Chief O'Brien), Grace Cunard (Mrs. Megg), Lynton Brent (Police Broadcaster), Jack C. Smith (Desk Sergeant), Eddie Fetherstone (Airport Radioman), Edward Peil, Sr. (Police Guard), Frank Marlowe (Mechanic), Eddie Foster (Jerry Rogan), William Desmond (Bystander), Stanley Price (Corky Watts), Eddie Dew (Matty Simms), Edward Emerson (Frenchy Ludoc), Mickey Simpson (Bouncer), Ethan Laidlaw (Bartender), George Eldredge (Policeman), Karl Hackett (Henry), Phil Warren (Henchman), Carleton Young (Motorcycle Policeman), Jack Mulhall (Police Lab Technician), Milton Kibbee (Station Master), Paul McVey (H.B. Malloy), Dale Van Sickel (Stunt Double), Carey Loftin (Stunt Double), David Sharpe (Stunt Double), Eddie Polo.

1. The League of Murdered Men. 2. The Death Plunge. 3. Murder Blockade. 4. Hangman's Noose. 5. Man Undercover. 6. Under Crumbling Walls. 7. The Water Trap. 8. Murder by Proxy. 9. Gang Bait. 10. Mob Vengeance. 11. Wanted at Headquarters. 12. The Long Chance.

237. Das Geheimnis der sechs Spielkarten

(Germany—William Kahn–Film GmbH, 1921) Serial, 6 chapters. D: William Kahn and Rolf Brunner. SP: William Kahn and Robert Heymann.

Carl Auen, Tony Ebärg, Paul Rehkopf, Robert Forster-Larrinaga, Hedi Sven, Hans Tillo, Edith Posca, Max Wogritsch, Preben Rist, Hugo Doblin, Hardy V. Francois, Georg John, Alfred Scherzer, Max Laurence, Fritz Bading, M. Stanior, O. Henckels, Emil Wittig, Paul Meyer, Karl Falkenberg, Bodo Serp.

1. Karo 10. 2. Pique Bube. 3. Treff As. 4. Pique Sieben. 5. Herz Köning. 6. Herz Dame.

238. Die Geheimnisse von Berlin

(Germany Esha–Film GmbH–Berlin, 1921) Series, 4 episodes. D: Arthur Teubel. SP: Edmund Edel.

Evi Eva.

1. Berlin N. Die Dunkle Grossstadt. 2. Berlin W. Die Grossstad in Glanz und Licht. 3. Berlin-Moabit. Hinter Gitterfenstern. 4. Berlin Frobelstrasse. Im Asyl für Obdachlose.

239. El Genio del Mal

(Cuba production, November 1920) Serial, 10 chapters. D/Photography: Enrique Diaz Quesada. P: Esteban Ramirez. English translation: "The Genius of Evil." No information of plot.

Maria Luisa Santos, José Ughetti, Leo de Córdoba, Pepito Fuentes Duany, Marina Ughetti, Bernabé Boza.

240. Die Geschichte des Grauen Hauses

(Germany—Delta Films GmbH, 1921) Series, 4 episodes. D: Erik Lund. SP: Hans Hyan and Arthur Schetter.

Alfred Abel, Edith Meller, Albert Steinruck, Hanni Weisse, Leopold Von Ledebur, Robert Leffler, Frieda Wald, Ernst Rotmund, Georg John, Georg Baselt, Hermann Leffler, Paul Biensfeldt, Gertrud Von Hoschek.

1. Der Mord aus verschmahter Liebe. 2. Der Mord aus Verworfenheit. 3. Der Mord aus Verzweiflung. 4. Der Mord aus Habsucht.

241. Ghost City

(Universal, December 3, 1923) Serial, 15 chapters, two reels each. D: Jay Marchant. Scen: Karl Coolidge and George W. Pyper.

In Sunshine Valley there is trouble brewing. Laughing Larry Lewton and his pal, Sagebrush Hilton, are informed that unless the ranch owners place $10,000 in a designated spot on a certain day the reservoir supplying the valley will be drained. At the same time, Austin Sinclair, a wealthy New Orleans man, recently bought Ghost City Ranch in Sunshine Valley. He receives word that a conspiracy is in progress to take the ranch away from him. Unable to leave his home in New Orleans, he allows his daughter Alice to go to Sunshine Valley to see what she can do. There she is saved from a stampede by Larry and the two immediately take a liking to one another.

Kent Taylor, Irene Hervey, Robert Armstrong, and Ralph Morgan in *Gang Busters* (1942)

Together they survive to defeat the Harwell gang and find a secret gold mine.

Pete Morrison (Laughing Larry Lewton), Margaret Morris (Alice Sinclair), Frank Rice (Sagebrush Hilton), Al Wilson (Raymond Moreton), Bud Osborne (Jasper Harwell), Lola Todd (Ginger Harwell), Slim Cole, Alfred Allen, Princess Neela, Valeria Olivo, William Quinn, Frank Tommick.

1. The Thundering Herd. 2. The Bulldogger. 3. The Maelstrom. 4. The Water Trap. 5. Following the Rustler. 6. Death's Spectre. 7. Stolen Gold. 8. Midnight Intruder. 9. Talons of the Night. 10. The Frame-Up. 11. Ambushed. 12. The Betrayal. 13. Man to Man. 14. Flames of Vengeance. 15. Face to Face.

242. Ghost of Zorro

(Republic, August 6, 1949) Serial, 12 chapters, two reels each. D: Fred C. Brannon. SP: Royal Cole, William Lively, Sol Shor. Assoc. P: Franklyn Adreon. Photography: John MacBurnie. Music: Stanley Wilson. Special Effects: Howard and Theodore Lydecker.

Top: **Margaret Morris and Pete Morrison; *bottom:* Bud Osborne, Margaret Morris, and Pete Morrison in *Ghost City* (1923)**

In fear that his outlaw empire will be jeopardized, an outlaw leader, ostensibly the town's blacksmith, plots to stop the Pioneer Telegraph Company from extending its lines to Twin Bluffs. The owner of the telegraph company is killed and his daughter vows to carry on. Ken Mason, in charge of the company's work crew, learns that he is a grandson of the original Zorro and decides to continue the tradition. As the Ghost of Zorro, he wins the battle against the outlaws and exposes the leader.

Clayton Moore (Ken Mason/Zorro), Pamela Blake (Rita White), Roy Barcroft (Hank Kilgore), George J. Lewis (Moccasin), Gene Stutenroth (George Crane), I. Stanford Jolley (Paul Hobson), John Crawson (Mulvaney), Steve Clark (Jonathan White), Steve Darrell (Ben Simpson), Dale Van Sickel (Mike Hodge/Mead), Tom Steele (Brace/Spike), Alex Montoya (Yellow Hawk), Post Parks (Zeke), Charles King (Joe), George Chesebro (Jason), Eddie Parker (Jim Cleaver), Robert Wilke, Roy Bucko, Art Dillard, Frank Ellis (Townsmen), Bob Robinson (Winch Operator), Bob Reeves (Andy), Marshall Reed (Fowler), Frank O'Connor (Doctor), Jack O'Shea (Freight Agent), Holly Bane (Larkin), John Daheim (Black), Stanley Blystone (Dan Foster), Joe Yrigoyen (Indian), Roger Creed (Mike), Ken Terrell (Morley).

1. Bandit Territory. 2. Forged Orders. 3. Robber's Agent. 4. Victims of Vengeance. 5. Gun Trap. 6. Deadline at Midnight. 7. Tower of Disaster. 8. Mob Justice. 9. Money Lure. 10. Message of Death. 11. Runaway Stagecoach. 12. Trail of Blood.

243. Gigolette

(France—Pathé Consortium, 1921) Serial, chapters (?). D: Henri Pouctal. S: Pierre Decourcelle.

Sephora Mosse (Zelie Vauquelin), Charles De Rochefort (Georges de Margemont), Andree Lionel (Blanche de Margemont), Camille Bert (Jean Vauquelin), Elaine Vernon (Genevieve/Marie), Maud Gipsy (Lina), Georges Colin (Charles Arnaud), Paul Olivier (Dr. Bernay), Berthe Jalabert, Paul Guide, Pierre Stephen, Philipe Garnier, Louise Danville, Christiane Delval, Jeanne Brindeau, Fabien Haziza, Isabelle Sandry, Paul Labry.

244. The Girl and the Game

(Signal Film Corp./Mutual, December 27, 1915) Serial, 15 chapters, two reels each. D: J.P. McGowan. SP: J.P. McGowan and Helen Homes. S: Frank Hamilton Spearman. P: Samuel S. Hutchinson.

The adventures of Helen, the daughter of a railroad president, and Storm, the fireman and later engineer, who met in their childhood days when Storm saved Helen from a miniature locomotive. Segrue also loves Helen but is the enemy of her father, as Segrue wants the plans of a contemplated railroad cut for his own company.

Helen Holmes (Helen), Leo D. Maloney (Paul Storm), J.P. McGowan (Spike), George McDaniel (Robert Segrue), J.H. Farley (Amos Rhinelander), William Brunton, Edward Sutherland.

1. Helen's Race with Death. 2. The Winning Jump. 3. A

Life in Peril. 4. Helen's Perilous Escape. 5. The Fight at the Signal Station. 6. Helen's Wild Ride. 7. Spike's Awakening. 8. A Race for the Right of Way. 9. A Close Call. 10. A Dash Through Flames. 11. The Salting of Superstition Mine. 12. Buried Alive. 13. A Fight for a Fortune. 14. Helen's Race Against Time. 15. Driving the Last Spike.

245. The Girl Detective

(Kalem, January 1915) Series, 14 or more episodes, two reels each. D: James W. Horne. Scen: Hamilton Smith; possibly others.

A society girl has a position as a special investigator for the police and works on various cases where her unique talents can help to solve crimes. Each episode is complete in itself. Miss Roland was star of the first seven episodes, then dropped out to be replaced by Miss Ridgely, who had played a supporting role up to that point.

Ruth Roland, Cleo Ridgely, Thomas Lingham, William H. West, Edward Clisbee, Frank Jonasson, Paul Hurst, James Horne, Robert Gray, Knute Rahman, Anna Lingham, Arthur Shirley.

(Order of release is uncertain. Known titles are listed.) Affair of the Deserted House. The Apartment House Mystery. The Disappearance of Harry Worthington. The Mystery of the Tea Dansant. Following a Clue. Old Isaacson's Diamonds. Jared Fairfax's Millions. The Trap Door. The Diamond Broker. The Writing on the Wall. The Thumb Prints on the Safe. Mike Donegal's Escape. The Tattooed Hand. Scotty Weed's Alibi.

***Top*: Clayton Moore and Pamela Blake in *Ghost of Zorro* (1949); bottom: *The Girl and the Game* (1915)**

246. The Girl from Frisco

(Kalem, 1916) Series, 25 episodes, two reels each. D: James W. Horne. S: Robert Welles Ritchie.

A western cowgirl, Barbara Brent, aids the cause of justice and humanity in the Old West, often aided by her rancher father, Ace Brent, and her fiancé, Congressman John Wallace. Each episode tells a complete story, but with the three continuing principal characters. It was shown by a number of theaters in lieu of the traditional serial—though it is doubtful that in 1916 any serial could be termed a "traditional" one. The episodes are similar to serial chapters in that there is action—action—and more action.

Marin Sais (Barbara Brent), True Boardman (Congressman John Wallace), Frank Jonasson (Ace Brent), Ronald Bradbury (Jim Bliss/Ace Miller/The Hawk/Daniel/Dick Dingle/Anson Dukes/Sing Lee/and a number of other characters), Edward Clisbee (Lanny/Jose/John Tisbury/Saint Sam Doolittle/Pedro/an old prospector and a number of other characters), Josephine West (Fanny), Steve Murphy (Siwash), Hart [Jack] Hoxie (Santone/The Sheriff), Karl Formes, Jr. (Black Feather), Barney Fury (Lobez), Jack Hutchison (Andy), E. Forrest Taylor (Terry), Jack MacDonald (Sidewinder Steve). [Most of these actors also played other characters in the various stories.]

1. The Fighting Heiress. 2. The Turquoise Conspiracy. 3. The Oil Field Plot. 4. Tiger Unchained. 5. The Ore Plunderers. 6. The Treasure of Cibola. 7. The Gun Runners. 8. A Battle in the Dark. 9. The Web of Guilt. 10. The Reformation of Dog Hole. 11. The Yellow Hand. 12. Harvest of Gold. 13. The Son of Cain. 14. The Witch of the Dark House. 15. The Mystery of the Brass Bound Chest. 16. Fight for Paradise Valley. 17. Border Wolves. 18. The Poisoned Dart. 19. The Stain of Chuckawalla. 20. On the Brink of War. 21. False Prophet. 22. The Resurrection of Gold Bar. 23. The Homesteaders' Feud. 24. The Wolf of Los Alamos. 25. The Dominion of Fernandez.

***The Girl Detective* (1915)**

247. Gloria's Romance

(Kleine, May 22, 1916) Serial, 20 chapters, two reels each. D: Walter Edwin. S: Mr. and Mrs. Rupert Hughes. P: Randolph Film Co.

This 20-chaptered endeavor which started out to be a novel in the magazine style ended as a disastrous enterprise. The extremely popular Miss Burke was paid $140,000, and total production costs ran to $640,000. The public rejected its "high-browism," having grown accustomed to Pearl White thrillers.

Gloria, a sweet girl of 16, leads a sheltered life without a mother's love but protected by a very watchful governess. On a prank she takes her dad's highpowered auto out into the night, only to wind up in the surf of the Everglades—the beginning of her romantic and adventurous interlude.

Billie Burke (Gloria Stafford), David Powell (Richard Freneau), William Roselle (David Stafford), Frank Belcher (Frank Mulry), William T. Carleton (Pierpoint Staffford), Jule Power (Lois Freeman), Henry Weaver (Judge Freeman), Frank McGlynn (Gideon Trask), Helen Hart (Nell Trask), Henry Kolker (Dr. Stephen Royce), Maurice Gasimur (Stass Casimur), Ralph Holmes ("Chooey" McFadden), Harriette Sterling (Gloria's Governess), Lillian Beck, Ralph Bunker, Henry Hallam, Richard Barthelmess.

1. Lost in the Everglades. 2. Caught by the Seminoles. 3. A Perilous Love. 4. The Social Vortex. 5. The Gathering Storm. 6. Hidden Fires. 7. The Harvest of Sin. 8. The Mesh of Mystery. 9. The Shadow of Scandal. 10. Tangled Threads. 11. The Fugitive Witness. 12. Her Fighting Spirit. 13. The Midnight Riot. 14. The Floating Trap. 15. The Murderer at Bay. 16. A Modern Pirate. 17. The Tell-Tale Envelope. 18. The Bitter Truth. 19. Her Vow Fulfilled. 20. Love's Reward.

248. Go Get 'Em Hutch

(Pathé, April 9, 1922) Serial, 15 chapters; Chapter 1, three reels; others, two reels. D: George B. Seitz. S: Frank Leon Smith. P: George B. Seitz.

The plot swings into its element with a crooked lawyer as the god of the crime syndicate. He has placed his hirelings about to discourage Hutch and to prevent the operation of the ships owned by the heroine. For good contrast a scheming adventuress is employed.

These are the big moments of the first chapter. The company's boat is set adrift and the hero and his sweetheart are the only people on board. The anchor is loosened and her foot is caught in one of the links and she is dragged to the bottom of the harbor. Then comes some undersea photography. There is a life-size thrill gained when the hero finds himself overcome with deadly fumes. And another pops up immediately when he gives chase on his motorcycle to the adventuress's car. Her machine has reached the ferryboat and it has left its moorings. He leaps the chasm and makes the deck safely. Similar thrills are found in each chapter. There was no let-up in the stunts performed by Hutchison.

Charles Hutchison (Hutch), Marguerite Clayton, Richard R. Neill, Frank Hagney, Pearl Shepard, Joe Cuny, Cecile Bonnell.

1. Chained to the Anchor. 2. The Falling Wall. 3. The Runaway Car. 4. The Crushing Menace. 5. Shot into Space. 6. Under the Avalanche. 7. On Danger's Highway. 8. The Broken Life Line. 9. Under the Cauldron. 10. The Edge of the Roof. 11. The Air Line Route. 12. Between the Rails. 13. Under the Ice. 14. In the Doorway of Death. 15. Ten Minutes to Live.

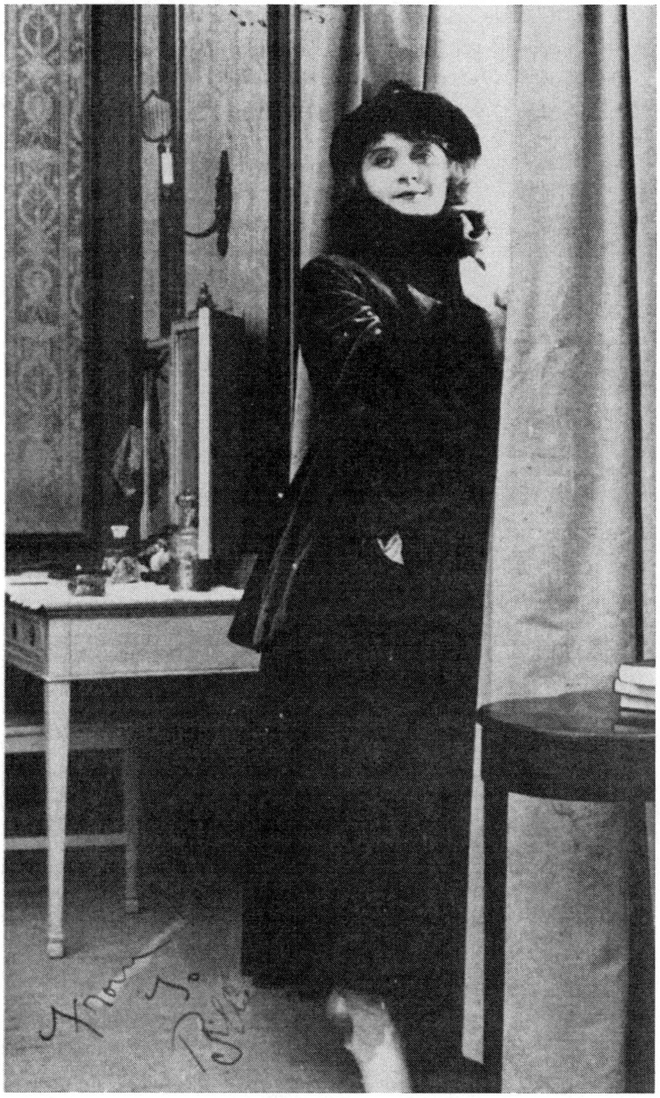

***Top left and right*: Billie Burke in *Gloria's Romance* (1916); *bottom:* Charles Hutchison in *Go Get 'Em Hutch* (1922)**

249. The Go-Getters

(R-C/F.O.B., 1924–'25) Series, 12 Episodes, two reels each. D: Del Andrews. Assist. D: Church Hamm. S/Scen: George Marion, Jr., and Beatrice Van.

A series of railroad thrillers which had a love interest, comedy, and pathos woven into them. Peggy Davis is a lone girl telegraph operator (shades of Helen Holmes and Helen Gibson in *Hazards of Helen*). A young man from a humble background becomes a railroad fireman and falls in love with Peggy. One need not examine stories very closely, for there is an element of comedy, well handled, that disarms the critic and makes him/her a willing acquiescent in the amusing adventures.

Getting Going, the first of the 12 episodes, introduces a young stoker who rescues a telegraph operator from a band of kidnapping crooks. *In the Knicker Time* has as its subject a train accident in a tunnel. *Never the Trains Shall Meet* has as a prominent incident the abduction of a heroine by crooks, who use a stolen engine. *A Kick for Cinderella* is notable for a boxing tournament and a burlesque tennis match.

Alberta Vaughn (Peggy Davis), George O'Hara (Railroad Fireman), Al Cooke (Station Master), Kit Guard (Expressman).

1. Getting Going. 2. In the Knicker Time. 3. Never the Trains Shall Meet. 4. A Kick for Cinderella. 5. Fire When Ready. 6. A Miss in the Dark. 7. The Going of Cumming. 8. Who's Hooligan. 9. Playing with Fire. 10. The Sleeping Cutie. 11. Ain't Love Grand. 12. The Ways of a Maid.

250. The Goddess

(Vitagraph, May 1915) Serial, 15 chapters, two reels each. D: Ralph W. Ince. Scen: Gouverneur Morris and Charles W. Goddard.

This is Vitagraph's first true serial. Story concerns a modern Joan of Arc, reared on a desert island in the belief she is a goddess. Upon her escape from the island, Celestia meets Tommy Barclay and goes about spreading her gospel of love and kindness. A hypnotist, Stilleter, uses her for his own advantage for a while but in the end his spell is broken and Celestia is free to marry Tommy and return to a happy life on Gull Island. The story is superior but somewhat lacking in familiar serial action.

Anita Stewart (Celestia), Earle Williams (Tommy Barclay), Paul Scardon (Prof. Stilleter), William Dangman (Freddie, the Ferret), Ned Finley (Gunsdorf), Louise Beaudet (Kidnapper), Frank Currier (Barclay), Thomas Brooks (Blackstone), Charles Wellesley (Semmes), [The 3 Millionaires], Lilian Burns (Mary, Blackstone's Daughter), Mary Anderson (Nellie), Edward Elkas (Silas Kehr), Enlalie Jensen (Gunsdorf's wife), Robert Gaillard (Carson), Anders Randolf (Sweetzer), Mary Maurice (Dear Old Lady), Baby Wiley (Celestia, as a Child), Katherine Frank, Mae Halpin, James Dent, Ethel Corcoran, Harold Foshay, Billie Billings, Julia Swane Gordon, Nellie Anderson.

251. The Golden Stallion

(Mascot, January 15, 1927) Serial, 10 chapters, two reels each. D: Harry Webb. S/SP: Karl Krusada and William Lester.

In a novel twist to an old plot, the map of a hidden treasure is branded partially on the neck of a wild horse and partially on an old Indian belt.

Maurice "Lefty" Flynn (Wynne Randall), Joe Bonomo (Ewart Garth), Molly Malone (Joan Forsythe), Tom London (Jules La Roux), Burr McIntosh (Elmer Kendall), Joseph Swickard (John Forsythe), Jay J. Bryan (Black Eagle), Ann Small (Watona), White Fury [a horse] (The Golden Stallion), Billy Franey, Burt Demarco.

1. The Golden Stallion. 2. The Flaming Forest. 3. The Stallion's Fury. 4. The Path of Peril. 5. Fighting Fury. 6. The Killer. 7. The Death Pace. 8. The Lake of Hate. 9. The Trap. 10. The Lost Treasure.

252. Gordon of Ghost City

(Universal, August 14, 1933) Serial, 12 chapters, two reels each. D: Ray Taylor. SP: Ella O'Neill, Basil Dickey, George Plympton, Harry O. Hoyt, Het Mannheim. S: Peter B. Kyne—"Oh, Promise Me!" P: Henry McRae.

Buck Gordon is hired to stop cattle rustling on the ranch of John Mulford, but soon finds himself spook hunting in Ghost City. There he meets Mary Gray, who enlists his help in protecting her grandfather's secret gold strike underneath one of the stores in the town. Rance Radigan, foreman of the Mulford Ranch and leader of the outlaws, uses Ghost City as a gang hideout. A mystery man with a gun makes it rough for both Buck and the outlaws, but Gordon is able to defeat the outlaws, capture the leader, unravel the mystery of the grizzly old gunman, and win himself a bride.

Buck Jones (Buck Gordon), Madge Bellamy (Mary Gray), Walter Miller (Rance Radigan), Hugh Enfield (Ed), William Desmond (John Mulford), Tom Rickett (Amos Gray), Francis Ford (Jim Carmody), Dick Rush (Sheriff), Edmund Cobb (Scotty), William Steele (Bob), Bob Kerrick (Tom), Ethan

Top: **Earle Williams and Anita Stewart in *The Goddess* (1915); *bottom: The Golden Stallion* (1927)**

Laidlaw (Pete), Jim Corey (Jeff), Bud Osborne (Hank), Silver [a horse] (Himself), Cliff Lyons (Double for Jones), Cecil Kellogg, Artie Ortego, Tom London.

1. A Lone Hand. 2. The Stampede. 3. Trapped. 4. The Man of Mystery. 5. Riding for Life. 6. Blazing Prairies. 7. Entombed in the Tunnel. 8. Stampede. 9. Flames of Fury. 10. Swimming in the Torrent. 11. A Wild Ride. 12. Mystery of Ghost City.

Buck Jones, Madge Bellamy, and Bud Osborne in *Gordon of Ghost City* (1933)

253. Government Agents vs. Phantom Legion

(Republic, August 1951) Serial, 12 chapters, two reels each. D: Fred C. Brannon. SP: Ronald Davidson. Assoc. P: Franklyn Adreon. Photography: John L. Russell, Jr. Music: Stanley Wilson. Special Effects: Howard and Theodore Lydecker.

A wave of hijacking sweeps the Interstate Truck Owners' Association. Hal Duncan, a government agent, is assigned to tracking down the culprits stealing critical materials the government is stockpiling. Heading the hijackers is a man called The Voice. Duncan comes to believe that The Voice is one of four members of the Association, and he is finally able to expose The Voice and to squelch his nefarious activities.

Walter Reed (Hal Duncan), Mary Ellen Kay (Kay Roberts), Dick Curtis (Regan), John Pickard (Sam Bradley), Fred Coby (Cady), Pierce Lyden (Armstrong/The Voice), George Meeker (Willard), John Phillips (J.J. Patterson), Mauritz Hugo (Thompson), Edmund Cobb (Turner), Eddie Dew (Barnett), George Lloyd (Coroner), Dale Van Sickel (Brice/Kern), Tom Steele (Brandt), Roy Barcroft (Dispatcher), Ben Taggart (Donovan), Eddie Parker (Payne), Duke Taylor (Kirk), Terry Frost (Car Heavy), Dick Crockett (Crane), Frank Alten (Casey), Gene Christopher (Bystander), Arthur Space (Crandall), Norval Mitchell (District Attorney), Frank Meredith (Motorcycle Officer), George Volk (Daly), Richard Grant (Station Attendant), Dean Henson (Gray), Jay Merrick (Hospital Attendant), Frank O'Connor (Policeman), David Sharpe (Double), Ralph Dunn (McGee), Joe Phillips (Miller), Buddy Thorpe (Larson).

1. River of Fire. 2. The Stolen Corpse. 3. The Death Drop. 4. Doorway to Doom. 5. Deadline for Disaster. 6. Mechanical Homicide. 7. The Flaming Highway. 8. Sea Saboteurs. 9. Peril Underground. 10. Execution by Accident. 11. Perilous Plunge. 12. Blazing Retribution.

254. Graft

(Universal, December 11, 1915) Series, 20 episodes, two reels each. D: Richard Stanton and George A. Lessey. Scen: Walter Woods, Hugh Weir, and Joe Brandt. S: *The Crack O'Doom*, a selection of short stories by Zane Grey, Irwin Cobb, Frederick Isham, Nina Wilcox Putnam, James Oppenheim, Louis Joseph Vance, A.M. Williamson, Joe Mitchell Chappie, Leroy Scott, George Bronson Howard, Wallace Irwin, Rupert Hughes, Mrs. Woodrow Wilson, Reginald Wright Kauffman, James Francis Dwyer, and Anna Katharine Green.

Each episode is complete in itself and based on a chapter of the book from which the scenario is taken. Stories revolve about the efforts of first Bruce Larnigan, then his brother Tom, to uncover graft and corruption in the textile, grain, railroad, and other trusts.

Hobert Henley starred in the first three episodes and then dropped out of the series in the fourth episode, due to an accident. Harry Carey starred in Chapters 4 through 20.

Harry Carey (Tom Larnigan), Jane Novak (Dorothy Maxwell), Hobert Henley (Bruce Larnigan), Richard Stanton (Robert Harding), Glen White (Stanford Stone), Nanine Wright (Mrs. Larnigan), Mark Fenton (Roger Maxwell), Mina Cunard (Kitty Rockford), Jack F. Connolly (Ben Travers), Jack Abbott (Jim Stevens), Wadsworth Harris (Mark Gramble), William Harris (H.S. Blanchford), Margaret Mayburn, Eddie Polo, Edward Brown, W. Horne, Hayward Mack, Bert Law, L.M. Wells, Fred Hearn, Yona Landowaka, Rex De Rosselli, Malcolm Blevins, Violet Schram, Rosita Marstini, Frederick Montague, E.P. Evers, Andrew Arbuckle, Gypsy Sartoris, Hector V. Sarno, Mary Ruby, William Shearer, Jack Curtis, Helen Orr, Burton S. Wilson, Mr. Spooner, Charles Bachman, Elmer Wilson, E. Clark, Frank MacQuarrie, George Bonn, Mary Haines, Mr. McDaniels.

1. Liquor and the Law. 2. The Tenement House Evil. 3. The Traction Grab. 4. The Power of the People. 5. Grinding Life Down. 6. The Railroad Monopoly. 7. America Saved from War. 8. Old King Coal. 9. The Insurance Swindlers. 10. The Harbor Transportation Trust. 11. The Illegal Bucket Shops. 12. The Milk Battle. 13. The Power Trust. 14. The Iron Ring. 15. The Patent Medicine Danger. 16. The Pirates of

Finance. 17. Queen of the Prophets. 18. The Hidden City of Crime. 19. The Photo Badger Game. 20. The Final Conquest.

255. Grand Guignol

(England—Screen Plays, 1921) Series, 28 episodes, one reel each. D: Fred Paul.

Episode Titles and Casts 1. *The Oath*. Lewis Gilbert, Margot Drake. 2. *The Flat*. Jack Raymond, George Foley. 3. *The Last Appeal*. Jack Raymond, Jeanne de Ramo, Henry

***Left: Government Agents vs. Phantom Legion* (1951); *above:* Harry Carey reading a letter to two players in *Graft* (1915)**

Doughty. 4. *The Woman Upstairs*. Joan Beverly, Frank Hill. 5. *The Gentle Doctor*. 6. *Delilah*. 7. *A Voice from the Dead*. 8. *The Guardian of Honour*. 9. *The Happy Pair*. 10. *The Return*. George Foley, Ethel Oliver. 11. *The Sting of Death*. Fred Paul, Lionel d'Aragon. 12. *The Nurse*. Fred Morgan, Reginald Fox. 13. *Polly*. 14. *The Secret of the Safe*. 15. *The Jest*. 16. *A Bit of Black Stuff*. 17 *Six and Half a Dozen*. 18. *Her Romance*. 19. *That Love Might Last*. 20. *Letters of Credit*. 21. *The Upper Hand*. Frank Stanmore, Muriel Minty. 22. *A Game for Two*. Charles Tilson-Chowne, Enid Sass. 23. *The Flirtation of Phyllis*. 24. *Mary's Work*. 25. *The Curse of Westacott*. Annette Benson, Bertram Burleigh. 26. *A Woman Misunderstood*. 27. *The Joke That Failed*. Leo Carelli, Margaret Denniston. 28. *Barbara Elopes*. Vivian Gibson, Harry Paulo.

"Grand Guignol" is an expression applied loosely to any short play (or the like) concerned with horror. It comes from the name of a small Paris theater which specialized in them. The theater in turn was named after "Guignol"—originally the principal character in a popular 18th century puppet show comprising macabre and gruesome incidents.

256. Grant, Police Reporter

(Kalem, November 4, 1916–October 20, 1917) Series, 29 episodes, one reel each. D: George Larkin, Robert Ellis, and others. SP: Robert Welles Ritchie and others.

This was one of early filmdom's most popular series. Like *The Hazards of Helen* the episodes were only one reel in length, but each was action all the way. Larkin had been a circus acrobat before entering films and his acrobatic talents were used in practically every episode of this series. Known as Daredevil George, he did stunts that Douglas Fairbanks, Yakima Canutt, Richard Talmadge, or Dave Sharpe backed away from. Each episode told a complete story. Synopses of Episodes 8 and 23 are given here to show the serial-like characteristics of this all but forgotten series turned out by Kalem shortly after *The Hazards of Helen* was completed.

The Trunk Mystery: Once again a murder furnishes the idea for the plot. The murder is solved by Grant and a detective, and it is in pursuit of the murderer that Grant furnishes a thrill. The girl (Ollie Kirkby) is beaten unconscious by her father (the murderer) and is placed on a belt that carries waste lumber to the top of a burning heap of waste. Larkin jumps to a belt of the machine, is carried on the belt for about a hundred feet, jumps to a suspended rope, and leaps to the spot where the other belt discharges its cargo. He catches the unconscious form of the girl just as she is about to be dashed on to the burning wood pile.

The Missing Financier: This time Larkin obtains entrance to a room by climbing up between the walls forming a narrow alleyway. He does this by bracing his hands against one wall and his feet against the other. This is a difficult stunt and registers well. In this manner he rescues the daughter of a financier who has been kidnapped and brought aboard a yacht. After he rescues the girl Larkin forms a bridge over the alley with his body. The girl walks over him to an adjoining roof. The financier is finally rescued by the crew of a U.S. Monitor.

No double was ever used to replace Larkin in a dangerous stunt. He did them all himself.

George Larkin, Ollie Kirkby, Robert Ellis, William McKey, Harry Gordon, Cyril Courtney, Mary Taylor-Ross, A.B. Foreman, M. Cohen, Bert Tracy, T. Justin Down, Mrs. Welsh, Bettie Dial, G. Chira, Arthur Albertson.

1. The Code Letter. 2. The Missing Heiress. 3. The Pencil Clue. 4. The Man from Yukon. 5. The Rogue's Pawn. 6. The House of Three Deuces. 7. The Wizard's Plot. 8. The Trunk Mystery. 9. The Menace. 10. The Tiger's Claw. 11. A Mission of State. 12. The House of Secrets. 13. The Trail of Graft. 14. The Black Circle. 15. The Violet Ray. 16. The Net of Intrigue. 17. The Trap. 18. Winged Diamonds. 19. The Screened Vault. 20. The Mirror of Fear. 21. The Veiled Thunderbolt. 22. In the Web of the Spider. 23. The Missing Financier. 24. The Secret of the Borgias. 25. The Vanishing Bishop. 26. Mystery of Room 422. 27. A Deal in Bonds. 28. The Man with the Limp. 29. Sign of the Scarf.

257. The Gray Ghost

(Universal, July 1, 1917) Serial, 16 chapters; Chapter 1, three reels; others, two reels each. D/Scen: Stuart Paton. S: Arthur Somers Roche.

The Gray Ghost and his gang loot a jewelry store in broad daylight, taking a necklace worth $2,000,000 that was intended as a wedding present for Lady Gwendolyn. A series of thriller cops-and-robbers chases ensues, as The Gray Ghost also steals money intended to pay for the necklace from the bank and frames the banker's son for murder.

Harry Carter (The Gray Ghost), Priscilla Dean (Morn Light), Emory Johnson (Wade Hildreth), Eddie Polo (Marco), Gypsy Hart (Cecilia), Wilton Taylor (Ashby), Gertrude Astor (Lady Gwendolyn), Lewis [Lew] Short (Jerry Tyron), Richard La Reno (Mr. Olmstead), John Cook (John Reis), T.D. Crittenden (Mr. Carlow), J. Morris Foster (Fred Olmstead), Howard Crampton, Sidney Dean, Francis McDonald, Charles Dorian.

1. The Bank Mystery. 2. The Mysterious Message. 3. The Warning. 4. The Fight. 5. Plunder. 6. The House of Mystery. 7. Caught in the Web. 8. The Double Floor. 9. The Pearl Necklace. 10. Shadows. 11. The Flaming Meteor. 12. The Poisoned Ring. 13. The Tightening Snare. 14. At Bay. 15. The Duel. 16. From Out of the Past.

258. The Great Adventures of Captain Kidd

(Columbia, September 1953) Serial, 15 chapters. D: Derwin Abbe and Charles S. Gould. SP: George H. Plympton and Arthur Hoerl. P: Sam Katzman. Assist. D: Leonard Katzman. Photography: William Whitley. Music: Mischa Bakaleinikoff.

Captain Kidd is not the villain he is made out to be, but is the victim of false propaganda put out by one of his crew, who teams up with pirate captain Culliford to pin their crimes on Kidd. Although two British naval officers believe in him and plead his case, Kidd goes to the gallows after helping the British fleet destroy the pirates' stronghold. The two officers, Richard Dale and Alan Duncan, leave England bound for America firmly believing that Kidd was the greatest man who ever sailed the sea.

Richard Crane (Richard Dale), David Bruce (Alan Duncan), John Crawford (Captain Kidd), George Wallace (Buller), Lee Roberts (Devry), Paul Newlan (Long Ben Avery), Nick Stuart (Doctor Brandt), Terry Frost (Moore), John Hart (Jenkins), Marshall Reed (Captain Culliford), Eduardo Cansino, Jr. (Native), Willetta Smith (Princess Fatima), Lou Merrill (Lord Bellmore), Ray Corrigan (Docklin), Charles King (Andrews), Bud Osborne (Hannibal), Gene Roth (Nardo Thompson), Lyle Talbot, Myron Healey, Edmund Cobb, William Fawcett, George Eldredge.

1. Pirates vs. Man of War. 2. The Fatal Shot. 3. Attacked by Captain Kidd. 4. Captured by Captain Kidd. 5. Mutiny on the Adventure Galley. 6. Murder on the Main Deck. 7. Prisoners of War. 8. Mutiny Unmasked. 9. Pirate Against Pirate. 10. Shot from the Parapet. 11. The Flaming Fortress. 12. Before the Firing Squad. 13. In the Hands of the Mohawks. 14. Pirate Gold. 15. Captain Kidd's Last Chance.

259. The Great Adventures of Wild Bill Hickok

(Columbia, June 30, 1938) Serial, 15 chapters, two reels each. D: Mack V. Wright and Sam Nelson. SP: George Rosenor, Charles A. Powell, G. A. Durlan, Dallas Fitzgerald, and Tom Gibson. Assoc. P: Harry Webb. P: Jack Fier. Photography: George Meehan and Ben Kline. Music: Abe Meyer.

The Phantom Raiders, organized by Morrell, a sinister and powerful character in the territory, attempt to keep Southern cattle from the Chisholm Trail and the railroad from reaching Abilene. Morrell realizes that these events could destroy his hold over the territory. Wild Bill Hickok is appointed as U.S. Marshal to see that both the cattle and the railroad reach their destination.

This serial is considered by most serial buffs as probably the best of Columbia's chapterplays. Both the budget and production values were above par at Columbia. Its popularity led to Elliott becoming a major western star and gave him a name change to "Bill." He was usually called "Wild Bill." A series of feature films followed in which Elliott played "Wild Bill."

Gordon Elliott (Wild Bill Hickok), Carole Wayne (Ruth Cameron), Frankie Darro (Jerry), Monte Blue (Cameron),

Dickie Jones (Bud), Sammy McKim (Boots), Kermit Maynard (Kit Lawson), Roscoe Ates (Snake Eyes), Monty Collins (Danny), Reed Hadley (Blakely), Chief Thunder Cloud (Gray Eagle), Mala (Little Elk), Walter Wills (Bruce), J.P. McGowan (Scudder), Eddy Waller (Stone), George Chesebro (Metaxa), Alan Bridge (Blackie), Lee Phelps (Catty), Robert Fiske (Morrell), Earle Hodgins (Kimball), Ed Brady (Wilson), Earl Dwyer (Jenkins), Ray Jones, Edmund Cobb, Hal Taliaferro, Art Mix, Blackie Whiteford, Slim Whitaker, Bill Patton, Charles Brinley, Blackjack Ward, Richard Cramer, Bud McClure, Jack Montgomery, Frank Ellis, Steve Clark, Artie Ortego, Curley Dresden, Budd Buster, Jack Rockwell, Tom London, Ernie Adams, Hank Bell, Carl Matthews, Ray Henderson, Francis Walker, Al Haskill, Iron Eyes Cody, Herman Hack, William Gould, Jack Evans, Ethan Laidlaw, Gene Alsace, Ted Mapes, Bob Burns, Lew Meehan, Al Thompson, Chuck Hamilton, Dick Botiller, Horace B. Carpenter, A.R. Haysee, Bruce Lane, Buck Connors, Jesse Graves, Allan Cavan, David McKim, George Morrell, Edward Hearn, Jack Perrin, Robert Walker.

1. The Law of the Gun. 2. Stampede. 3. Blazing Terror. 4. Mystery Canyon. 5. Flaming Brands. 6. The Apache Killer. 7. Prowling Wolves. 8. The Pit. 9. Ambush. 10. Savage Vengeance. 11. Burning Waters. 12. Desperation. 13. Phantom Bullets. 14. The Lure. 15. Trail's End.

Top: **Kermit Maynard, Wild Bill Elliott, Charles Whitaker, and Carol Wayne in *The Great Adventures of Wild Bill Hickok* (1938); *bottom:* Milburn Stone and Margorie Weaver in *The Great Alaskan Mystery* (1944)**

260. The Great Alaskan Mystery

(Universal, April 1944) Serial, 13 chapters, two reels each. D: Ray Taylor and Lewis D. Collins. SP: Maurice Tombragel and George H. Plympton. S: Jack Foley.

Doctor Miller, an American scientist, invents a machine that promises to be successful as a defense weapon. Dr. Miller, his daughter Ruth, Jim Hudson, and Bosun go to Alaska to examine a mine discovered by Jim's dad in the hope that the element necessary to develop the Paratron will be found. Doctor Hauss accompanies the party. He is in league with a ring of fascists headed by Captain Greeder and Herman Brock, seemingly an honest businessman. Many attempts are made to steal the Paratron. In one skirmish Grit, an aid to Dr. Miller, kills Greeder with the Paratron. On another day Brock orders Brandon to attack the mine. In so doing he is killed by Bill Hudson. However, Hauss strikes down Doctor Miller and escapes with the Paratron. When he is trailed to Brock's office and when Brock tries to place all blame on him, Hauss kills him and in turn is arrested.

Milburn Stone (Jim Hudson), Marjorie Weaver (Ruth Miller), Edgar Kennedy (Bosun), Samuel S. Hinds (Herman Brock), Martin Kosleck (Dr. Hauss), Ralph Morgan (Dr. Miller), Joseph Crehan (Bill Hudson), Fuzzy Knight ("Grit" Hartman), Harry Cording (Captain Greeder), Anthony Warde (Brandon), Ken Terrell (Double for Kosleck).

1. Shipwrecked Among Icebergs. 2. Thundering Doom. 3. Battle in the Clouds. 4. Masked Murder. 5. The Bridge of

Disaster. 6. Shattering Doom. 7. Crashing Timbers. 8. In a Flaming Plane. 9. Hurtling Through Space. 10. Tricked by a Booby Trap. 11. The Tunnel of Terror. 12. Electrocuted. 13. The Boomerang.

261. The Great Circus Mystery

(Universal, March 9, 1925) Serial, 15 chapters, two reels each. D: Jay Marchant. Scen: Leigh Jacobson. Continuity: George Morgan. S: Isadore Bernstein and William Lord Wright.

"Red" Landow and Trixie Tremaine, circus performers, become involved in a plot by Hindu agents to regain a stolen sacred ruby.

Joe Bonomo (Welles "Red" Landow), Louise Lorraine (Trixie Tremaine), Robert J. Graves (Adams), Robert Seiter (Darrell), Carmen Phillips (Natchi), Slim Cole (The Mystery Man), Sam Polo, Albert Prisco, Monte Montague, Jackie Goodrich, Floyd Criswell, Eduardo Martini, Carlo Bernardi, Cecil Woodworth, Tui Loraine, Charles Magetti, Tony Brock, The Sieberling Four.

1. Pact of Peril. 2. A Cry for Help. 3. A Race with Death. 4. The Plunge of Peril. 5. The Ladder of Life. 6. A Leap for Liberty. 7. Harvest of Hate. 8. Fires of Fate. 9. Cycle of Fear. 10. The Leopard Strikes. 11. The Sacred Ruby. 12. Dive of Destiny. 13. The Leap for Liberty. 14. Buried Treasure. 15. The Leopard Strikes.

262. Great Events Series

(Technicolor Corp./MGM—Filmed in Technicolor) two reels each.

The Flag (10-1-27) P: Samuel Bischoff. D/S: Arthur Maude. SP: L. V. Jefferson. Francis X. Bushman. *Buffalo Bill's Last Fight* (11-26-27) P: Samuel Bischoff. D: John W. Nobel. S: Russell Hickson. Duke Lee. *The Lady of Victories* (1-21-28) P: Samuel Bischoff. D: Roy William Neill. S: Leon Abrams. Agnes Ayres. *The Czarina's Secret* (3-17-28) P: Herbert T. Kalmus. D: Roy William Neill. S: Aubrey Scotto. SP: Leon Abrams. Olga Baclanova. *The Virgin Queen* (5-12-28) P: Herbert T. Kalmus. D: Roy William Neill. SP: Leon Abrams. Dorothy Dawn, Forrest Stanley, Aileen Manning. *Cleopatra* (7-7-28) P: Herbert T. Kalmus. D: Roy William Neill. S: Natalie Kalmus. SP: Leon Abrams. Dorothy Revier, Robert Ellis.

263. The Great Gamble

(Western Photoplays/Pathé, August 3, 1919) Serial, 15 chapters, Chapter 1, three reels; others, two reels. D/SP: Joseph A. Golden.

Twin sisters have been reared apart—one wealthy, one poor. An attempt is made to substitute the poor sister for the wealthy sister by the villains of the piece, but the hero is Johnny-on-the-spot to thwart their plans.

Charles Hutchison (Ralph Darrell), Anne Luther (Aline Moreton/Nell Moreton), Richard Neill (Richard Blake), Billy Moran (Shorty), William Cavanaugh (Cooley), Warren Cook (Roger Morton), Edith Thornton (Mrs. Morton).

1. The Great Gamble. 2. The Clock of Doom. 3. Into the Chasm. 4. In the Law's Grip. 5. Draught of Death. 6. Out of the Clouds. 7. The Crawling Menace. 8. The Ring of Fire. 9. Through Iron Doors. 10. Written in Blood. 11. The Stolen Identity. 12. The Wolf Pack. 13. Barriers of Flame. 14. Under Arrest. 15. Out of the Shadows.

264. The Great London Mystery

(England, 1920) Serial, 12 chapters. D: Charles Raymond.

This story line concerns a magician's efforts to outwit villainous chinamen.

David Derant, Lady Doris Stapleton, Charles Raymond.

265. The Great Radium Mystery

(Universal, November 1919) Serial, 18 chapters, two reels each. D: Robert Broadwell and Robert F. Hill. SP: Frederick Bennett.

The heir to one of the greatest fortunes on earth disappears and the heroine has to contend with a tank-type vehicle that can vanish and reappear at will.

Cleo Madison (Countess Nada), Eileen Sedgwick (Gloria Marston), Bob Reeves (Jack Turner), Edwin J. Brady (Frank Bird), Robert Kortman (The Buzzard), Jeff Osborne (John Marston), Robert Gray (The Hawk), Gordon McGregor (The Rat), Fred Hammer.

1. The Mystic Stone. 2. The Death Trap. 3. The Fatal Ride. 4. The Swing for Life. 5. The Torture Chamber. 6. The Tunnel of Doom. 7. A Flash in the Dark. 8. In the Clutches of the Mad Man. 9. The Roaring Volcano. 10. Creeping Flames.

Eileen Sedgwick in *The Great Radium Mystery* (1919)

Top: **Francis X. Bushman and Beverly Bayne in *The Great Secret* (1917)**

11. Perils of Doom. 12. Shackled. 13. The Scalding Pit. 14. Hemmed In. 15. The Flaming Arrow. 16. Over the Cataract. 17. The Wheels of Death. 18. Liquid Flames.

266. The Great Reward

(Burston Films/National Exchanges, May 1921) Serial, 15 chapters, two reels each. D: Francis Ford. SP: Elsie Van Name. Producer: Francis Ford. Photography: Jerome Ash.

This serial is of the "Graustark" type of story. The action is located in the mythical kingdom of Lyria and centers around the adventures of two young Americans who get mixed up in a plot to get rid of the rightful king who at times loses his reason. One of the Americans is the living image of the king and finds himself forced by the real king's friends to masquerade in his stead. There is, of course, a beautiful princess who is continually in trouble and whose predicaments cause numerous exciting adventures.

Trick photography and double exposure work wherein little figures climb out of glasses, crawl over books, dance upon tables, etc. form an important part of the serial and proved a big attraction to patrons who were unfamiliar with this kind of work.

Francis Ford (The American Adventurer), Ella Hall (The Princess), Carl Gerard, Phil Ford, Mark Fenton, Valeria Olivo.

1. His Living Image. 2. The Life Current. 3. In Bondage. 4. The Duel. 5. The Madman. 6. Caves of Doom. 7. Burning Sands. 8. The Thunderbolt. 9. Cross Fires. 10. Forgotten Halls. 11. On the Brink. 12. At Bay. 13. The Silent Hour. 14. High Treason. 15. The Reward.

267. The Great Secret

(Metro, January 8, 1917) Serial, 18 chapters; Chapter one, three reels; others, two reels. D/P/SP: William Christy Cabanne. S: Fred de Gresac.

A beautiful girl inherits a fortune and is threatened by villains who want to steal it. Hardly a novel plot, and the casting of Bushman and Bayne was a mistake. Although popular idols, serial patrons were not willing to accept the couple whose fame was built on romantic society dramas. The serial proved an artistic fiasco and barely broke even financially.

Francis X. Bushman (William Montgomery Strong), Beverly Bayne (Beverly Clarke), Fred R. Stanton (The Great Master), Ed Connelly (Dr. Eulph), Tom Blake ("Bull" Whalen), Helen Dunbar (Jane Warren), Sue Belfour (Mrs. Clarke), Belle Bruce (Sava Laring), Dorothy Haydel (Eunice Manton), William J. Butler (Tom Clarke), Charles Ripley (The Spider), Art Ortego (The Rat), Charles Fang, Tammany Young, John Clark, Lillian Sullivan, Kid Broad, Bert Keyes, Jim Quinn, William J. Calhoun, Matilda Brundage, Jack Goodman, Spike Robinson, Ed Kelly, Paddy Sullivan, Baby Ivyward, John Leach, Neva Gerber, El Laurence, Monte Attel, Robert Carson, Eugene Beandino, Fred Roberts, Marie De Chett.

1. The Whirlpool of Destiny. 2. The Casket of Tainted Treasure. 3. The Hidden Hand. 4. From Sunshine to Shadow. 5. The Trap. 6. The Dragon's Den. 7. The Yellow Claw. 8. A Clue from the Klondike. 9. Cupid's Puzzle. 10. The Woman and the Game. 11. A Shot in the Dark. 2. Caught in the Web. 13. The Struggle. 14. The Escape. 15. The Test of Death. 16. The Crafty Hand. 17. The Missing Finger. 18. The Great Secret.

268. The Green Archer

(Pathé, December 6, 1925) Serial, 10 chapters, two reels each. D: Spencer G. Bennet. Scen: Frank Leon Smith. S: Edgar Wallace.

A heartless, criminal millionaire erects a castle on the Hudson brought over from England stone by stone. Shortly afterwards a mysterious green archer begins to haunt its corridors, always appearing at critical moments. His actions seem neither wholly evil nor wholly good. The owner of the castle keeps a mysterious prisoner confined in a dungeon. Curiosity overcomes Valerie Howett, a neighbor girl who is loved by Jim Featherstone, captain of the State Police.

Allene Ray (Valerie Howett), Walter Miller (Jim Featherstone), Burr McIntosh (Abel Bellamy), Frank Lackteen (Julius Savini), Dorothy King (Gay Savini), Steven Grattan (Walter Howett), William R. Randall (John Wood), Walter P. Lewis ("Cold Harbor" Smith), Wally Oetrell ("Spike" Holland), Tom Cameron (Butler), Rae Allan (Elaine Holding), Jack Tanner (Creager).

1. The Ghost of Bellamy Castle. 2. The Midnight Warning. 3. In the Enemy's Stronghold. 4. On the Storm King Road. 5. The Affair at the River. 6. The Mystery Ship. 7. Bellamy Baits a Trap. 8. The Cottage in the Woods. 9. The Battle Starts. 10. The Smoke Clears Away.

269. The Green Archer

(Columbia, November 1940) Serial, 15 chapters, two reels each. D: James W. Horne. SP: Morgan B. Cox, John Cutting, Jesse A. Duffy, James W. Horne. S: Edgar Wallace, *The Green Archer*. P: Larry Darmour. Photography: James S. Brown, Jr. Music: Lee Zahler.

After having him imprisoned unjustly, Abel Bellamy moves into a castle inherited by his brother Michael. When other members of Michael's family become inquisitive and hire a detective, Spike Holland, to inquire into the matter, Abel tries to kill them all. He wants to keep his association with a gang of jewel thieves a secret. His attempts at murder are thwarted by The Green Archer, a masked man who rejects modern weaponry in favor of bow and arrow.

Victor Jory (Spike Holland/The Green Archer), Iris Meredith (Valarie Howett), James Craven (Abel Bellamy), Robert Fiske (Savini), Dorothy Fay (Elaine Bellamy), Forrest Taylor (Howett), Jack Ingram (Brad), Joseph Girard (Inspector Ross), Fred Kelsey (Captain Thomspon), Kit Guard (Dinky), Kenne Duncan, Charles King, Franklyn Farnum, Eddie Polo.

1. The Ghost of Bellamy Castle. 2. The Midnight Warning. 3. In the Enemy's Stronghold. 4. On the Storm King Road. 5. The Affair at the River. 6. The Mystery Ship. 7. Bellamy Baits a Trap. 8. The Cottage in the Woods. 9. The Battle Starts. 10. The Smoke Clears Away. 11. The Flaming Arrow. 12. The Devil Dogs. 13. The Deceiving Microphone. 14. End of Hope. 15. The Green Archer Exposed.

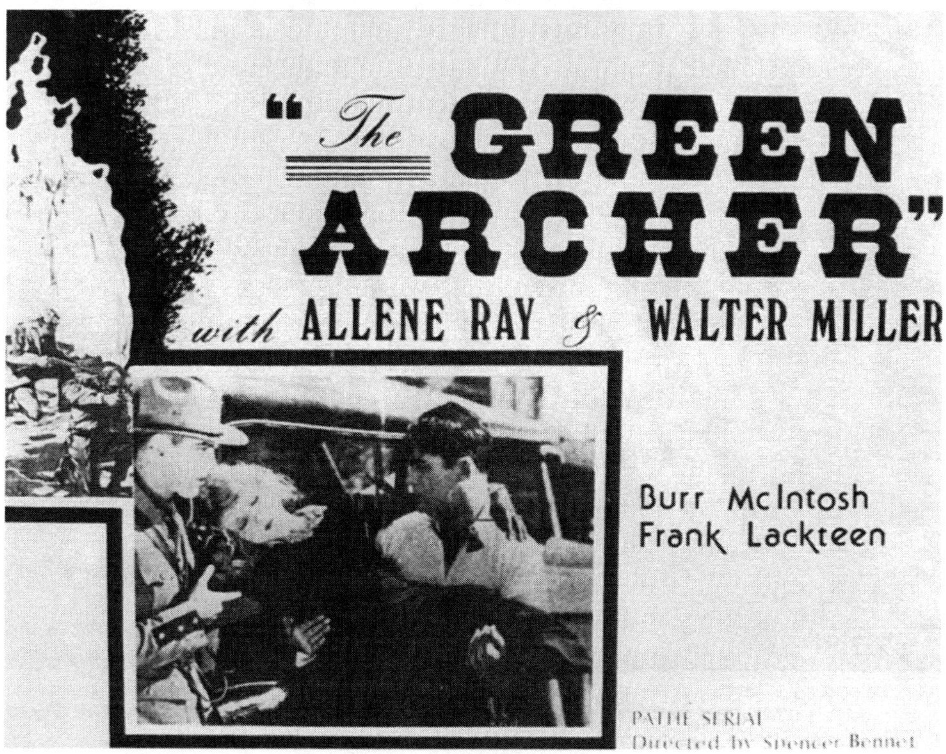

Top: **Burr McIntosh;** ***bottom:*** ***The Green Archer*** **(1925)**

270. The Green Hornet

(Universal, November 1939) Serial, 13 chapters, two reels each. D: Ford Beebe and Ray Taylor. Based on the radio serial "The Green Hornet." SP: George Plympton, Basil Dickey, Morrison C. Wood, and Lyonel Margolies. Assoc. P: Henry MacRae. Camera: William Sickner, Jerry Ash.

Unknown to publisher Britt Reid, alias The Green Hornet, the rackets operating in the city are controlled by a crime syndicate headed by an unknown "chief," whose messages to his henchmen are broadcast through an intercommunications system. When Britt learns that subgrade materials are being used in various public projects around town, he tries to investigate but is stopped from inspecting construction projects. The Green Hornet then swings into action, aided by his faithful valet Kato.

Gordon Jones (Britt Reid/The Green Hornet), Anne Nagel (Lenore Case), Keye Luke (Kato), Wade Boteler (Mike Axford), Philip Trent (Jasper Jenks), Walter McGrail (Dean), Gene Rizzi (Corey), John Kelly (Pete Hawks), Ralph Dunn (Andy), Douglas Evans (Martin Mortinson), Jerry Marlowe (Bob Stafford), Anne Gwynne (Josephine Weaver), Cy Kendall (Monroe), Joseph Crehan (Judge Stanton), Selmer Jackson (District Attorney), Arthur Loft (Ogden), Stanley Andrews (Commissioner), Fred Vogeding (Gegory), Clyde Dilson (Meadows), Eddie Dunn (Sligby), Eddie Keane (Williams), Ben Taggart (Bart), Georg Lloyd (Rockford), Ann Doran (Josephine Allen), Joe Whitehead (Gunnigan), Edward Earle (Grant), Ray Bailey (West), John Harmon (Bates), James Blaine (Cooper), Kenneth Harlan (Charles Roberts), Don Rowan (Markheim), Robert

***Top:* Victor Jory and Iris Meredith in *The Green Archer* (1940); *bottom: The Green Hornet* (1940)**

Brister (Lavenson), Guy Usher (Lynch), Monte Montague (Traffic Cop), Alan Ladd (Gilpin), Wallace Gregory (Acme Driver), Lane Chandler (Charlie), Reed Howes (Bill), Edward LeSaint (Captain Ridge), Paul Seardon (Bryan), Robert Long (Lew), James Farley (Police Captain), Bill Pagan (Slim), Edward Cassidy (Election Judge), Karl Hackett (Gorman), Wilson Benge (Butler), Myrtis Crinley (Clicker Binnie), Bill Hunter (Peebles), Tom Mizer (Joe), Charles Sherlock (Bus Driver #16), Jack Donovan (Bus Driver #57), Colin Kenny (Dispatcher), Heinie Conklin (Watchman), Michael O'Hara (Armored Car Driver), Kernan Cripps (Radio Cop), Edgar Edwards (Tim), Jack Carr (Policeman), Charles McMurphy (Radio Officer), Sigfrid Tor (Farrell), Chuck Morrison (Radio Cop), Charles Sullivan (Jake), Robert Kortman (Henchman), John Pine (Radio Cop).

1. The Tunnel of Terror. 2. The Thundering Terror. 3. Flying Coffins. 4. Pillar of Flames. 5. The Time Bomb. 6. Highways of Peril. 7. Bridge of Disaster. 8. Dead or Alive. 9. The Hornet Trapped. 10. Bullets and Ballots. 11. Disaster Rides the Rails. 12. Panic in the Zoo. 13. Doom of the Underworld.

271. The Green Hornet Strikes Again

(Universal, October 1940) Serial, 15 chapters, two reels each. D: Ford Beebe and John Rawlins. Assoc. P: Henry MacRae. Based on the radio serial *The Green Hornet* created by Fran Striker.

Britt Reid, crusading newspaper publisher, again dons his disguise as The Green Hornet to bring to justice a sinister criminal named Grogan and the syndicate he controls. Warren Hull's replacement of Gordon Jones in the key role made this a better serial than the first, if one is to believe the critics.

Warren Hull (Britt Reid/The Green Hornet), Keye Luke (Kato), Wade Boteler (Michael Axford), Anne Nagel (Lenore Case), Eddie Acuff (Lowery), Pierre Watkin (Grogan), Joe A. Devlin (Dolan), William Hall (Don DeLuca), Dorothy Lovett (Frances Grayson), Jay Michael (Foranti), Montague Shaw (Weaver), Roy Barcroft, Arthur Loft, James Seay, Charles Miller, Alan Bridge, Lane Chandler.

1. Flaming Havoc. 2. The Plunge of Peril. 3. The Avenging Heavies. 4. A Night of Terror. 5. Shattering Doom. 6. The Fatal Flash. 7. Death in the Clouds. 8. Human Targets. 9. The Tragic Crash. 10. Blazing Fury. 11. Thieves of the Night. 12. Crashing Barriers. 13. The Flaming Inferno. 14. Racketeering Vultures. 15. Smashing the Crime Ring.

272. The Green Room

(February-March 1920) Series, 13 episodes, two reels each. Propaganda films for the stage women's war relief fund. D: George W. Terwilliger directed 8 of the films. Other directors were Constance Binney, Otis Skinner, Henry Miller, Blanche Bates, Henry Hull, John W. Cope, and Florenz Ziegfeld. SP: Colder Johnstone wrote 8 of the screenplays. Other authors were Jack Larrie, Rachel Crothers, Frederick A. Kummer, Calder Johnston, Ethelynn Brewer DeFoe, Wallace Clifton, Howard El Miller, Jesse Bonstelle, Katherine Kavanaugh, Otis Skinner, Ann Irish.

Enid Markey, Blanche Yurka, Montagu Love, Harry Davenport, Adele Rolland, Fred Nichols, Mabel Taliaferro, Robert Edeson, Margaret Leslie, Julia Arthur, Frank Sheridan, DeWitt Jennings, Forest Winant, Helen Duggan, Ben Grauer, George T. Meech, William Courtenay, John Morris, Jessie Ralph, Victor Sutherland, Elizabeth Risdon, Hamilton Revelle, Gladys Morris, Jane Grey, Alphonse Ethier, Lorraine Frost, Charles Wells, Richard Turner, Nance O'Neil, Alfred Hickman, Tyrone Power, Sr., Mathilde Cottrelly, Paul Gilmore, Ben Grower, Mildred Holland, Thomas Swirskaya, Amelita Galli-Curci, Holbrook Blinn, Jeanne Eagles, Helen MacKellar, Ethel Intropidi, Luis Alberni, Maude Van Turk, Conrad Nagel, Helen Lowell, Jack Cagwin, Cyril Maude, Violet Heming, Fred Lloyd, Mrs. Sam Harris, David Bispham, Mrs. Charles King, Louise Closser Hale, Yvette Guilbert, Edmund Breese, Shelly Hull, Ethelbert Hales, Julia Dean, Phoebe Foster, Mrs. William Farnum, Mrs. John M. Pierce, Robert Edeson, Margaret Leslie, Ralph Morgan, Lucia Moore, Forest Robinson, Robert Lowell, David Belasco, Russian Quarteete.

1. The Mite of Love. 2. She's Everywhere. 3. The Mad Woman. 4. The Madonna of the Slums. 5. His Woman. 6. An Honorable Cad. 7. A Star Over Night. 8. Winning His Wife. 9. A Bit of Love. 10. The Inner Ring. 11. The Littlest Reason. 12. Tom's Little Star. 13. Romeo's Dad.

273. The Grip of Evil

(Pathé, July 17, 1916) Serial, 14 chapters, two reels each. D: Sherwood MacDonald. S: Lewis Tracy. SP: Douglas Bronston.

A poor man inherits a large sum of money, which allows him to indulge his concerns for society. Naturally, certain others do not share his social concerns but do have an interest in his money. Ingratitude, jealousy, treachery, murder, and criminal carelessness—all are confronted in the hero's search for the answer to the question: "Is humanity in the grip of evil?"

Jackie Saunders (Jessie), Roland Bottomely (John Burton), Charles Dudley, Gordon Sackville, Philo McCullough, Gloria Payton, Myrtle Reeves.

1. Fate. 2. The Underworld. 3. The Upper Ten. 4. The Looters. 5. The Way of a Woman. 6. The Hypocrites. 7. The Butterflies. 8. In Bohemia. 9. The Dollar Kings. 10. Down to the Sea. 11. Mammon and Moloch. 12. Into the Pits. 13. Circumstantial Evidence. 14. Humanity Triumph.

274. The Gumps

(Universal, 1923–1928) Series, 48 episodes, two reels each. P: Sam Van Ronkel (Episodes 1–12). D: Eric C. Kenton, Ray Gray, William Watson, Norman Taurog, David Kirkland, Craig Hutchison, Francis, Corby, Del Andrews, Norman Dawn, Robert Kerr, Vin Moore. S: Phil Dunham, Melville Brown, Dick Smith, Norman Taurog, Marks and Pagano, Vin Moore, Robert Kerr, William Weber. SP: Victor Potbel and Kerry Clark. Based on the cartoon strip by Sidney Smith.

Obviously the series was a popular one to have lasted five years and 48 films. "The Gumps" was a long-running comic strip that Universal was successful in adapting to the screen. Audiences found the two-reel comedies a welcome respite from the daily grind.

Joe Murphy (Andy Gump), Fay Tincher (Min), Jackie Morgan (Chester).

1923–1925: 1. Uncle Bim's Gift. 2. Watch Papa. 3. Oh, What a Day. 4. Aggravatin' Mama. 5. Oh, Min. 6. What's the Use? 7. Andy's Temptation. 8. A Day of Rest. 9. Westbound. 10. Andy's Hat in the Ring. 11. Andy's Stump Speech. 12. Andy in Hollywood. *1925–1926:* 1. Andy's Lion Tale. 2. Chester's Donkey Party. 3. Dynamited. 4. Andy Takes a Flier. 5. The Smash-Up. 6. Min's Home on the Cliff. 7. Min Walks in Her Sleep. 8. California, Here we Come. 9. Shady Rest. 10. Min's Away. 11. Dumb Luck. 12. Tow Service. *1926–1927:* 1. Never Again. 2. Lots of Grief. 3. Better Luck. 4. The Big Surprise. 5. A Close Call. 6. I told You So. 7. Rooms for Rent. 8. Up Against It. 9. Youth and Beauty. 10. Broke Again. 11. I'm the Sheriff. 12. Circus Daze. *1927–1928:* 1. Too Much Sleep. 2. A Battle Scared Hero. 3. When Greek Meets Greek. 4. And How. 5. Ocean Bruises. 6. Total Loss. 7. Andy Nose His Onions. 8. The Mild West. 9. A Case of Scotch. 10. Any Old Count. 11. The Cloud Buster. 12. Out in the Rain.

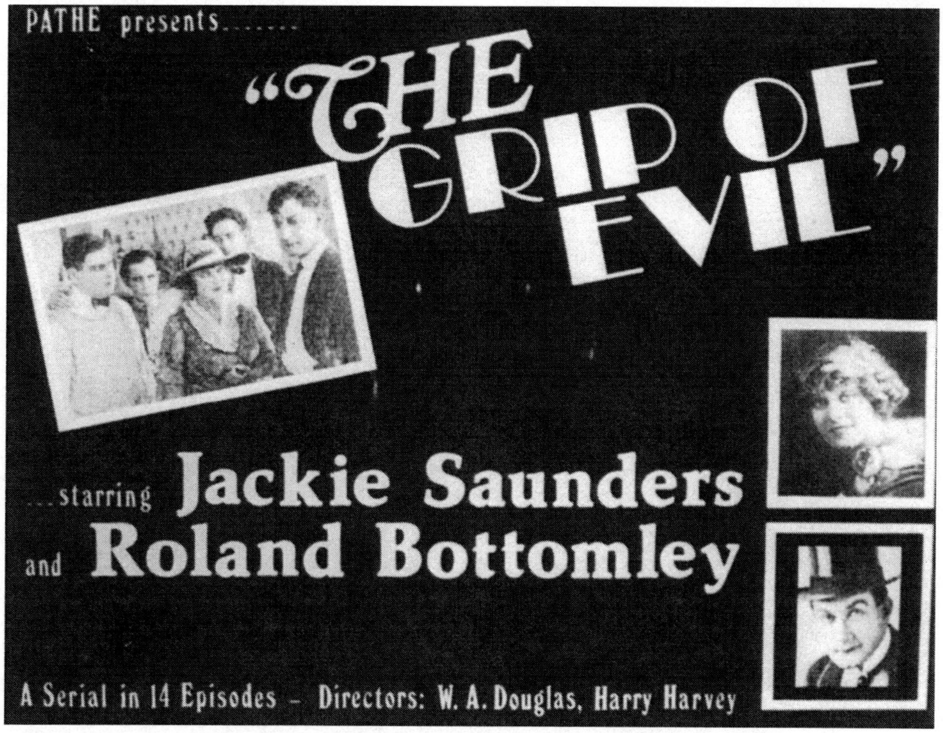

Jackie Saunders and Roland Bottomley in *The Grip of Evil* (1916)

275. Gunfighters of the Northwest

(Columbia, April 15, 1953) Serial, 15 chapters. D: Spencer G. Bennet and Charles S. Gould. SP: George H. Plympton, Royal Cole, Arthur Hoel. P: Sam Katzman. Photography: William Whitley. Music: Mischa Bakaleinikoff. Special Effects: Jack Erickson.

A mysterious villain called The Leader is trying to locate a lost gold mine in Indian Territory. He pits the Indians against the Mounties by creating trouble for the Indians and blaming the Mounties. A white horse symbol is used by the white renegades to place blame for their crimes on the Blackfoot.

Jock Mahoney [O'Mahoney] (Joe Ward), Clayton Moore (Bram Nevin), Phyllis Coates (Rita), Don Harvey (Otis Green), Marshall Reed (Lynch), Rodd Redwing (Bear Tooth), Lyle Talbot (Inspector Wheeler), Tom Farrell (Arch Perry), Terry Frost (Wildfoot), Lee Roberts (Arnold Reed), Joe Allen, Jr. (Fletcher Stone), Gregg Barton (Hank Bridger), Chief Yowlachie (Running Elk), Pierce Lyden (Dakota), Gene Roth [Stutenroth] (Superintendent Drake), John Hart (Recruit), Bud Osborne, Kermit Maynard, Zon Murray, William Fawcett.

1. A Trap for the Mounties. 2. Indian War Drums. 3. Between Two Fires. 4. Midnight Raiders. 5. Running the Gauntlet. 6. Mounties at Bay. 7. Plunge of Peril. 8. Killer at Large. 9. The Fighting Mounties. 10. The Sergeant Gets His Man. 11. The Fugitive Escapes. 12. Stolen Gold. 13. Perils of the Mounted Police. 14. Surprise Attack. 15. Trail's End.

Clayton Moore and Jock Mahoney in *Gunfighters of the Northwest* (1954)

276. Ham Series

(Kalem, 1914–1915) Series, 15 episodes, one reel each. D: Marshall Neilan, Chance E. Ward, Rube Miller, and Harry Edwards.

These one-reel comedies, although slap-dash affairs filmed in a few days, were quite popular and therefore profitable for Kalem. It is said that the two comedians made close to 200 one-reelers. But apparently these 15 films officially constituted the Ham series.

Lloyd V. Hamilton (Ham), Dub Duncan (Bud), Ruth Roland (Episodes 1, 2, 7, 10), Marin Sais (Episodes 13, 15), Marshall Neilan, Norma Nicholls, Charles Inslee.

1. Ham, the Lineman. 2. Ham, the Piano Mover. 3. Ham the Iceman. 4. Ham, the Detective. 5. Ham and the Jitney Bus. 6. Ham and the Sausage Factory. 7. Ham and the Villain Factory. 8. Ham at the Beach. 9. Ham at the Fair. 10. Ham at the Garbage Gentlemen's Ball. 11. Ham and the Haram. 12. Ham in the Nut Factory. 13. Ham Among the Redskins. 14. Ham and the Experiment. 15. Ham's Harrowing Duel.

277. The Hand of Vengeance

(Gaumont, 1918) Serial, 10 chapters, two reels each. D: George Pearson. S: George Pearson and Thomas Welsh.

After discovering the biggest diamond field in Australia, Morgan and Townsend start across the great desert for home and England. Yielding to the promptings of avarice, Townsend attacks Morgan and leaves him wounded and dying in the desert.

In London, years later, Sir Gilbert Townsend, diamond magnate, is feted when he presents a gunboat to the nation. That night, in a mysterious house in London, Ultus, the "man from the dead," tells his confederates he is ready to strike. Late that night he appears, ghost-like, before Townsend and tells him he intends to take away, bit by bit, his fraudulent wealth.

The ten chapters were in part edited out of several short English features from 1915, 1916 and 1917. They were an attempt to match the popularity of the French *Fantômas*.

Aurele Sydney (Dick Morgan/Ultus), J.L.V. Leigh (Conway Bass), Marjorie Dunbar (Lady Townsend), A. Caton Woodville (Sir Gilbert Townsend), M. Gouget (Eugene Lester), Mary Dibley (Mary Ferris), Frank Dane (Dick), Lionel d'Aragon (Banks), Mary Forbes (Lady Fleet), Leonard Shepherd (Sir Miles Fleet), Manora Thew (Elsie Meredith), Charles Rock (Derwent), Alice DeWinton, Fred Morgan.

1. The Sign of the Scar. 2. Scheming for Millions. 3. The Ambassador's Diamond. 4. The Grey Lady. 5. The League of Silence. 6. The Mysterious Manor. 7. The Secret of the Night. 8. The Kidnapped Statesman. 9. The Girl in the Hotel. 10. A Woman's Aid.

278. Hands Up

(Astra Film Corp./Pathé, August 18, 1918) Serial, 15 chapters; Chapter 1, three reels; others, two reels. D: James W. Horne. SP: Jack Cunningham. S: Gilson Willets.

Remnants of an Incan tribe living in California believe that Echo Delane, a magazine writer, is their missing princess, who they call Princess of Prophecy. She is also believed to be the lost heiress of Strange Ranch—a belief not to the liking of her cousin, Judith, who wants the ranch. A mystery figure, The Phantom Rider, aids Echo when she is in peril (much as did the garbed Buck Jones and Robert Kent in serials titled *The Phantom Rider* in 1936 and 1945 respectively).

During production leading man George Chesebro entered the U.S. Army; he was replaced by George Larkin for the remainder of the production.

Ruth Roland (Echo Delane), George Chesebro ("Hands Up"), George Larkin ("Two Gun" Carter), Easter Walters (Judith Strange), William A. Carroll (Sam Killman/Omar, the High Priest), George Gebhardt (The Grand Envoy), William E. Lawrence (Prince Pampas), Monte Blue, Thomas Jefferson.

1. Bride of the Sun. 2. The Missing Prince. 3. The Phantom and the Girl. 4. The Phantom Trail. 5. The Runaway Bride. 6. Flames of Vengeance. 7. Tossed into the Torrent. 8. The Fatal Jewels. 9. A Leap Through Space. 10. The Sun Message. 11. Stranger from the Sea. 12. The Silver Book. 13. The Last Warning. 14. The Oracle's Decree. 15. The Celestial Messenger.

279. Haunted Harbor

(Republic, August 26, 1944) Serial, 15 chapters, two reels each. D: Spencer Bennet and Wallace Grissell. SP: Royal Cole, Basil Dickey, Jesse Duffy, Grant Nelson, and Joseph Poland. S: Dayle Douglas. Assoc. P: Ronald Davidson. Photography: Bud Thackery. Music: Joseph Dubin. Special Effects: Theodore Lydecker. Reissued in 1951 as *Pirate's Harbor*.

Jim Marsden is a schooner owner falsely convicted of murder. He escapes from prison and attempts to clear himself. A million dollars reportedly went down with his schooner but in reality was stolen by murderer Kane. Working undercover, Marsden investigates native stories of sea monsters in Haunted Harbor and rescues Dr. Harding and his daughter Patricia. When Kane kills the doctor, who has recognized him, Patricia vows revenge and joins Marsden in solving the mystery of Haunted Island and tracking down Kane.

Kane Richmond (Jim Marsden), Kay Aldridge (Patricia Harding), Roy Barcroft (Kane/Carter), Clancy Cooper (Yank), Marshall Reed (Tommy), Oscar O'Shea (John Galbraith), Forrest Taylor (Oliver Harding), Hal Taliaferro (Lawson), Edward Keane (Frederick Vorhees), George J. Lewis (Dranga), Kenne Duncan (Gregg), Bud Geary (Snell), Robert Homans (Port Captain), Duke Green (Neville/Dunning/Gort), Tom Steele (Ronson), Dale Van Sickel (Sailor/Guard), Nick Thompson (Native Chief), Dick Boteler (Policeman), Pietro Sosso (Priest), Kit Guard (Roustabout), Fred Cordova (Policeman), Ken Terrell (Taola), Fred Graham (Stokes), Charles Hayes (Citizen), Bud Wolfe, Eddie Parker, Carey Loftin, Jack O'Shea (Heavies).

1. Wanted for Murder. 2. Flight to Danger. 3. Ladder of Death. 4. The Unknown Assassin. 5. Harbor of Horror. 6. Return of the Fugitive. 7. Journey into Peril. 8. Wings of Doom. 9. Death's Door. 10. Crimson Sacrifice. 11. Jungle Jeopardy. 12. Fire Trap. 13. Monsters of the Deep. 14. High Voltage. 15. Crucible of Justice.

280. Haunted Island

(Universal, March 27, 1928) Serial, 10 chapters, two reels each. D: Robert F. Hill. S: Frank R. Adams—*Pleasure Island*. SP: George Morgan and Karl Krusada. Remake of *The Brass Bullet*, Universal, 1918.

Pirate gold is buried on Pleasure Island. The heroine, who stands to inherit the gold when it is found, is opposed by her uncle and aided by a young man who becomes enamored of her after he, too, becomes marooned on the island after escaping false imprisonment in a sanitarium. But she also has another protector—a mystery figure called "The Phantom Rider."

Jack Daugherty (Jerry Fitzjames), Helen Foster (Rosalind Joy), Carl Miller (Yetor King), Al Ferguson (Spring Gilbert), John T. Prince (Mark Joy), Grace Cunard (Mary Strong), Wilbur Mack, Myrtis Grinley, Jon Wallace, Scotty Mattraw.

1. A Night of Fear. 2. The Phantom Rider. 3. A Trail of Terror. 4. The Haunted Room. 5. Buried Alive. 6. A Race with Death. 7. Fires of Fury. 8. The Treasure Trap. 9. Unmasked. 10. Uncut Diamonds.

281. Haunted Valley

(Pathé, May 6, 1923) Serial, 15 chapters, two reels each. D: George Marshall. SP: Frank Leon Smith.

Ruth Roland in *Haunted Valley* (1923)

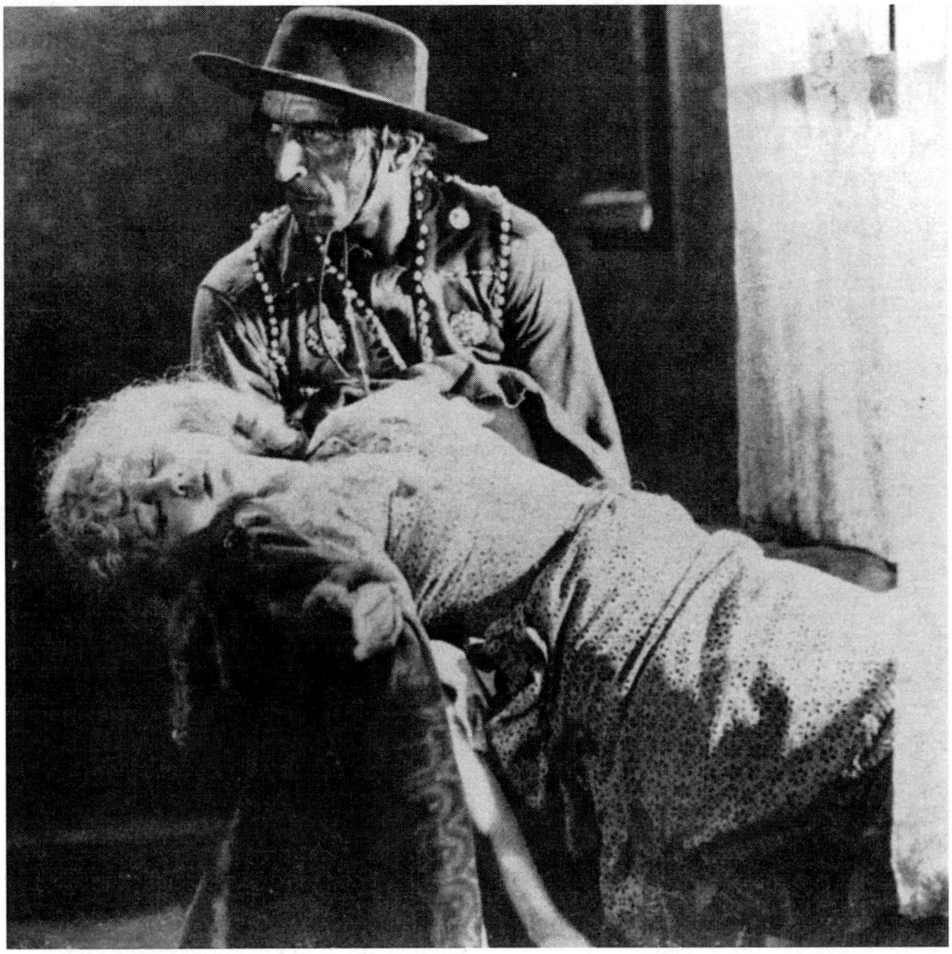

Allene Ray and Frank Lackteen in *The Hawk of the Hills* (1927)

Ruth Ranger, owner of Haunted Valley, borrows $1 million from the villain in order to finish construction of a dam. The terms of the loan specify that if she cannot pay the money back in three months, he gets Ruth, Haunted Valley, and Lost River Dam. Naturally he wants her to fail. To complicate matters, he has a television device that can project a 3-dimensional view of him anywhere, giving him a perfect alibi when he is out doing his dirty work. Apparently the script girl, film editor or someone was nodding when the film was edited because not only did the gadget transmit the guy's image but it also changed his clothes in the process.

Upon completion of this, her eleventh serial, Ruth retired to devote more time to her business affairs. She had made a fortune in real estate. She bought and sold more real estate, invested in various enterprises, made concert tours, and did a lot of vaudeville.

Ruth Roland (Ruth Ranger), Jack Daugherty (Eugene Craig), Larry Steers (Henry Mallinson), Eulalie Jensen (Vivian Delamar), Aaron Edwards (Denslow), William Rhyno (Weatherby), Francis Ford (Sharkey), Edouard Treboal (Dinny), Noble Johnson.

1. Bound to the Enemy. 2. Adventure in the Valley. 3. Imperiled at Sea. 4. Into the Earthquake Abyss. 5. The Fight at Lost River Dam. 6. Brink of Eternity. 7. Midnight Raid. 8. Radio Trap. 9. Ordeal of Fire. 10. The 100th Day. 11. Called to Account. 12. Double Peril. 13. To Hazardous Heights. 14. In Desperate Flight. 15. Disputed Treasure.

282. The Hawk of the Hills

(Pathé, August 28, 1927) Serial, 10 chapters, two reels each. D: Spencer G. Bennet. S: George Arthur Gray. Photography: Edward Snyder and Frank Redman. A five-reel feature version was released in 1929.

The Hawk, the half-breed leader of a band of Indians and renegade whites, captures Mary Selby, daughter of a miner who has a secret gold mine, hoping to trade her for the secret of the mine's location. Laramie, a government agent, poses as an outlaw and joins the Hawk's gang, quickly becoming Mary's friend and protector.

Allene Ray (Mary Selby), Walter Miller (Laramie), Frank Lackteen (The Hawk), Paul Panzer (Manson), Harry Semels (Sheckard), Jack Pratt (Colonel Jennings), John T. Prince (the Hermit), Robert Chandler (Clyde Selby), Frederick Dana (Larry), Wally Oettel (Shorty), Jack Ganzhorn (Henry Selby), Chief Yowlachie (Chief Long Hand), J. Parks Jones (Lieutenant MacCreedy), Evangeline Russell, George Magrill, Chief white Horse.

1. The Outlaws. 2. In the Talons of the Hawk. 3. Heroes in Blue. 4. The Attack. 5. The Danger Trail. 6. The Death Menace of Lost Canyon. 7. Demons of the Darkness. 8. Doomed to the Arrows. 9. The House of Horror. 10. The Triumph of Law and Order.

283. Hawk of the Wilderness

(Republic, December 1938) Serial, 12 chapters, two reels each. Feature title: *Lost Island of Kioga*. D: William Witney and John English. S: William L. Chester—*Hawk of the Wilderness*. S: Barry Shipman, Rex Taylor, and Norman Hall. Assoc. P: Robert Beche. Photography: William Nobles. Music: William Laya.

Kioga, infant survivor of a shipwreck, grows to manhood in Tarzan-like fashion on an unknown Pacific island populated by a lost tribe. When an expedition arrives looking for survivors it brings evil men as well as good, and when it is discovered that rare gems abound on the island, the crooks show their colors. Kioga must use all of his cunning and strength to save his friends, thwart the badmen, and appease the superstitious natives.

Herman Brix [Bruce Bennett] (Lincoln Rand, Jr./Kioga), Ray Mala (Kias), Monte Blue (Yellow Weasel), Jill Martin (Beth Monro), Noble Johnson (Mokuyi), William Royle (Manuel Solerno), Tom Chatterton (Edward Munro), George Eldredge (Allan Kendle), Patrick J. Kelly (William Williams), Dick Wessel (Dirk), Fred Toones [Snowflake] (George), Lane Chandler (Lincoln Rand, Sr.), George Letz [George Montgomery] (Tom), Iron Eyes Cody (Storm Cloud), Ann Evers (Helena Rand), Earl Askam (Red), Jerry Sheldon (Joe), Fred Miller (Jansen), William Stahl

(Bart), Harry Tenbrook (Pete), Lorne Riebe (Carl), Tuffie [dog] (Tawnee), John Big Tree (Medicine Doctor), Joe Garcia (Bright Star), Art Felix, Frank Hill, L.Y. Maxwell, Clarence Chorre, Art Miles, Jerry Frank, Henry Wills, John Roy, Moe Malulo, Jerome DeNuccio, Jack Minton, Jimmy Dime, Tony Urchel, Jim Spencer, Alex Montoya, Gertrude Chorre, Cy Shindell, Wally Rose, Sonny Chorre, Ted Mapes, Jack O'Shea (Natives).

1. Mysterious Island. 2. Flaming Death. 3. Tiger Trap. 4. Queen's Ransom. 5. Pendulum of Doom. 6. The Dead Fall. 7. White Man's Magic. 8. Ambushed. 9. Marooned. 10. Camp of Horror. 11. Valley of Skulls. 12. Trail's End.

284. The Hawk's Trail

(Burston/W.H. Productions, January 13, 1920) Serial, 15 chapters, two reels each. D: W.S. Van Dyke. SP: John B. Clymer, Louis and George Burston. S: Nan Blair. Supervision: Louis Burston.

King Baggot shows that he is able to play many different roles, as he is seen in a protean role of ten great characterizations. Stanton Steele, noted criminologist, is hired by Claire Drake to investigate a mysterious burglary. "Iron" Dugan, a master criminal, poses as the uncle of Jean and Claire Drake in an effort to obtain their fortunes. First, he arranges to have Claire abducted by a swami but Steele is on the job and foils the abduction. Dugan tries time after time to do away with Claire but Steele thwarts each attempt. Finally Dugan is exposed and Jean is freed.

King Baggot (Sheldon Steele/The Hawk), Rhea Mitchell (Claire Drake), Grace Darmond (Jean Drake), Harry Lorraine ("Iron" Dugan/Stephen Drake), Fred Windermere (Bob Dugan), Stanton Heck ("Bull" Cruze), George Siegmann (Quang Goo Hai), Carmen Phillips (Mimi), Edna Robirson (Tina Torelli), Carl Stockdale, Sylvia Jocelyn, Billy White, Art Belasco, Nigel De Brulier, Leo White.

1. False Faces. 2. The Superman. 3. Yellow Shadows. 4. Stained Hands. 5. House of Fear. 6. Room Above. 7. The Bargain. 8. The Phantom Melody. 9. The Lure. 10. The Swoop. 11. One Fatal Step. 12. Tides That Tell. 13. Face to Face. 14. The Substitute. 15. The Showdown.

Top: **Herman Brix [Bruce Bennett] and Mala in *Hawk of the Wilderness* (1938); *bottom:* Helen Holmes in *The Hazards of Helen* (1914)**

285. The Hazards of Helen

(Kalem, November 13, 1914) Series, 119 episodes, one reel each. D: J.P. McGowan and James Davis. S: W. Scott Darling. Based on John Russell Corvell's novelized version of the play by Denman Thompson.

Probably the best known of all series. Each episode a complete story. No cliffhanger endings. All the stories have railroad themes and the continuing character of Helen, who was placed in every conceivable railroad danger. Miss Holmes starred in the first 48 episodes and Miss Gibson in the remaining 71 episodes.

Helen Holmes (Helen), Helen Gibson (Helen). [The following players appeared in one or more episodes, playing an assortment of characters] Robyn Adair, Ethel Clisbee, Tom Trent, G.A. Williams, Pearl Anibus, Hoot Gibson, Leo Maloney, Jack Hoxie, P.S. Pembroke, Roy Watson, George Routh, Billy Boy, Franklin Hall, Clement Graw, Clarence Burton, M.Z. Woods, Anna Q. Nilsson, Harry Schumm, O. Fillipi, Hi Sing, Jack Messick, Richard Johnson, Thomas Means, Frank Henderson, Betty

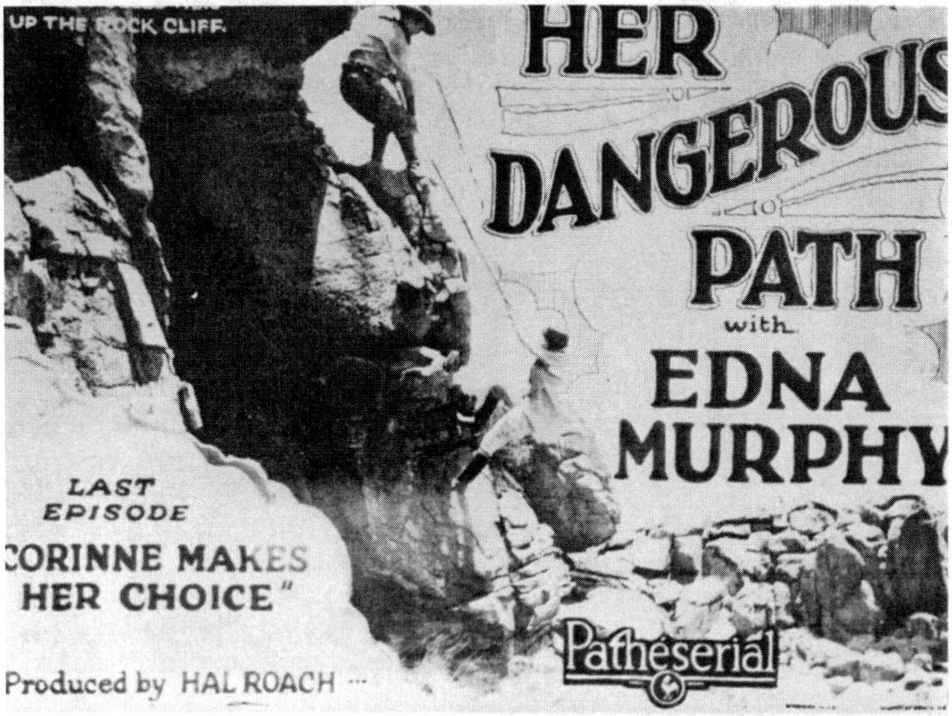

Edna Murphy in *Her Dangerous Path* (1923)

Hartigan, Hal Clements, True Boardman, E.Z. Roberts, M.J. Murchison, Charles Mulgro, Jennie Antibus, Norma Antibus, Bobbie Antibus, Elsie McLeod.

1. Helen's Sacrifice. 2. The Plot at the R.R. Cut. 3. The Girl at the Throttle. 4. The Stolen Engine. 5. The Flying Freight's Captive. 6. The Black Diamond Express. 7. The Escape on the Limited. 8. The Girl Telegrapher's Peril. 9. The Leap from the Water Tower. 10. The Broken Circuit. 11. The Fast Mail's Danger. 12. The Little Engineer. 13. Escape of the Fast Freight. 14. The Red Signal. 15. The Engineer's Peril. 16. The Open Drawbridge. 17. The Death Train. 18. Night Operator at Buxton. 19. Railroad Raiders of '62. 20. The Girl at Lone Point. 21. A Life in the Balance. 22. The Girl on the Trestle. 23. The Girl Engineer. 24. A Race for a Crossing. 25. The Box Car Trap. 26. The Wild Engine. 27. A Friend at the Throttle. 28. The Broken Train. 29. A Railroader's Bravery. 30. The Human Chain. 31. The Pay Train. 32. Near Eternity. 33. In Danger's Path. 34. The Midnight Limited. 5. A Wild Ride. 36. A Deed of Daring. 37. The Girl on the Engine. 38. The Fate of #1. 39. The Substitute Fireman. 40. The Limited's Peril. 41. A Perilous Chance. 42. Train Order #45. 43. The Broken Rail. 44. Nerves of Steel. 45. A Girl's Grit. 46. A Matter of Seconds. 47. The Runaway Boxcar. 48. The Water Tank. 49. A Test of Courage. 50. A Mile a Minute. 51. Rescue of the Brakeman's Children. 52. Danger Ahead. 53. The Girl and the Special. 54. The Girl on the Bridge. 55. The Dynamite Train. 56. The Tramp Telegrapher. 57. Crossed Wires. 58. The Wrong Train Order. 59. A Boy at the Throttle. 60. At the Risk of Her Life. 61. When Seconds Count. 62. The Haunted Station. 63. The Open Track. 64. Tapped Wires. 65. The Broken Wire. 66. Peril of the Rails. 67. A Perilous Swing. 68. The Switchman's Story. 69. A Girl Telegrapher's Nerve. 70. A Race for a Life. 71. The Girl Who Dared. 72. The Detective's Peril. 73. The Trapping of Peeler White. 74. The Record Run. 75. The Race for a Siding. 76. The Governor's Special. 77. The Trail of Danger. 78. The Human Telegraph. 79. The Bridge of Danger. 80. One Chance in a Hundred. 81. The Capture of Red Stanley. 82. Spiked Switch. 83. Treasure Train. 84. A Race Through the Air. 85. The Mysterious Cypher. 86. The Engineer's Honor. 87. To Save the Road. 88. The Broken Brake. 89. In Death's Pathway. 90. A Plunge from the Sky. 91. A Mystery of the Rails. 92. Hurled Through the Drawbridge. 93. With the Aid of the Wrecker. 94. At Danger's Call. 95. Secret of the Boxcar. 96. Ablaze on the Rails. 97. The Hoodoo of Division B. 98. Defying Death. 99. The Death Swing. 100. The Blocked Track. 101. To Save the Special. 102. A Daring Chance. 103. The Last Messenger. 104. The Gate of Death. 105. The Lone Point Mystery. 106. The Runaway Sleeper. 107. The Forgotten Train Order. 108. The Trial Run. 109. The Lineman's Peril. 110. The Midnight Express. 111. The Vanishing Boxcar. 112. A Race with Death. 113. The Morgul Mountain Mystery. 114. The Fireman's Nemesis. 115. The Wrecked Station. 116. Railroad Claim Intrigue. 117. The Death Siding. 118. The Prima Donna's Special. 119. The Side Tracked Sleeper.

286. Her Dangerous Path

(Pathé, August 12, 1923) Series, 10 episodes; No. 1, three reels; others, two reels. D: Roy Clements. SP: Frank Howard Clark. P: Hal Roach.

A rather disjointed but nevertheless good series in which Miss Murphy plays a different type of woman in each episode and pursues the different paths that fate might dictate for such a woman.

Edna Murphy (Corinne Grant), Charles Parrott [Charlie Chase] (Glen Harper), Hayford Hobbs (Donald Bartlett), William Moran (Dr. Philip Markham), Percy Pembroke (Dr. Harrison), William Gillespie (John Dryden), Glen Tryon (Reporter), Roy Myers (Clinton Hodge), Colin Kenny (Stanley Fleming), Ed Baker (Jack Reynolds), Fred McPherson (Prof. Pritchard), Frank Lackteen (Malay George), Sam Lufkin (Sam Comstock), Fong Wong (Oracle of the Sands).

1. What the Sands Told. 2. Fetters of Gold. 3. At the Brink. 4. If You Become a Society Reporter on a Newspaper. 5. If You Marry an Artist. 6. If You Marry a Rancher. 7. Should She Become a Society Reporter? 8. Should She Marry a Scientist? 9. Should She Become Assistant to a Detective? 10. [Unknown.]

287. Heroes of the Flames

(Universal, June 2, 1931) Serial, 12 chapters, two reels each. D: Robert F. Hill. SP: George Morgan, Basil Dickey, and George H. Plympton.

Bob Darrow, a firefighter, rescues Jane and Jackie Madison

from a fire. They are the daughter and son of John Madison. In gratitude Madison allows Darrow to use his laboratory for conducting experiments on a chemical fire extinguisher. Dan Mitchell, a crook, wants Darrow's formula and June, with whom Darrow is romantically involved. He and his henchmen do everything they can to steal the formula and discredit Bob in the eyes of his benefactors.

Tim McCoy (Bob Darrow), Marion Shockley (June Madison), William Gould (John Madison), Grace Cunard (Mrs. Madison), Bobby Nelson (Jackie Madison), Gayne Whitman (Dan Mitchell), Beulah Hutton (Trixie Farrell), Monte Montague (Pat), Joe Bonomo, Bud Osborne, Buck Moulton, Edmund Cobb (Henchman), Charles Lemoyne, Andy Devine, Marshall Ruth, Bruce Cabot, Walter Brennan.

1. The Red Peril. 2. Flaming Hate. 3. The Fire Trap. 4. Death's Chariot. 5. The Avalance. 6. The Jaws of Death. 7. Forests of Fire. 8. Blank Cartridges. 9. The House of Terror. 10. The Depths of Doom. 11. A Flaming Death. 12. The Last Alarm.

288. Heroes of the West

(Universal, June 20, 1932) Serial, 12 chapters, two reels each. D: Ray Taylor. S: Peter B. Kyne—*The Tie That Binds.* Continuity: George Plympton, Basil Dickey, and Joe Roach. Adaptation and Dialogue: Ella O'Neill. Photography: John Hickson. Remade in 1938 as *Flaming Frontiers*, with John Archer, Eleanor Hansen, and Johnny Mack Brown in roles played by Noah Beery, Jr., Miss Duval, and Charles Stevens.

Political intrigue and Indian raids take a heavy toll on the builders of a section of the transcontinental railroad, but Tom Blaine and his son and daughter, with the aid of engineer Tom Crosby, survive to fulfill Blaine's contract to complete a portion of the railroad in Wyoming.

Noah Beery, Jr. (Noah Blaine), Diane Duval [Jacqueline Wells and Julie Bishop] (Ann Blaine), Onslow Stevens (Tom Crosby), William Desmond (John Blaine), Martha Mattox (Martha Blaine), Philo McCullough (Rance Judd), Harry Tenbrook (Butch Cole), Frank Lackteen (Buckskin Joe), Edmund Cobb (Bart Eaton), Jules Cowles (Missouri), Francis Ford (Captain Donovan), Thunderbird (Thunderbird), Lafe McKee (Townsman), Grace Cunard.

1. Blazing the Trail. 2. The Red Peril. 3. The Avalanche. 4. A Shot from the Dark. 5. The Hold-Up. 6. Captured by the Indians. 7. Flaming Arrows. 8. Frontier Justice. 9. The Iron Master. 10. Thundering Death. 11. Thundering Hoofs. 12. End of the Trail.

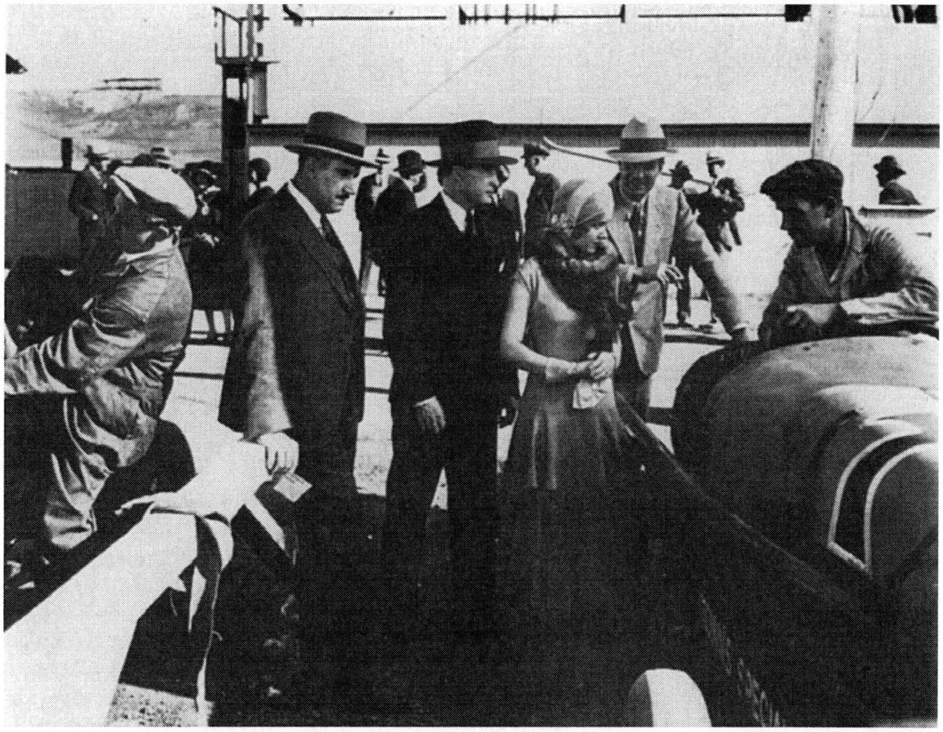

Top: **Tim McCoy, Marion Shockley, and William Gould in *Heroes of the Flames* (1931); *bottom:* Jack Hoxie and Josephine Hill in *Heroes of the Wild* (1927)**

289. Heroes of the Wild

(Mascot, November 1, 1927) Serial, 10 chapters, two reels each. D: Harry Webb. S/SP: Harry Webb and Karl Krusada. P: Nat Levine.

Good guys and bad guys struggle for supremacy in a story centering on finding the location of a secret mine, the clues to which are divided between a diary and a silver chain worn around the hoof of a wild white stallion.

Jack Hoxie, Josephine Hill, Joe Bonomo, Tornado [a dog], White Fury [a horse], Linda Loredo, Jay J. Bryan, Emily Gerder, Helen Gibson.

1. Heroes of the Wild. 2. Sword to Sword. 3. The Plunge of Peril. 4. The Slide of Life. 5. The Trap of Death. 6. The Flaming Fiend. 7. The Clutching Hand. 8. The Broken Cable. 9. The Fatal Arrow. 10. The Crown of the Incas.

290. Die Herrin der Welt

(Germany—May–Film GmbH, 1919) Serial, 8 chapters. D: Joe May, Uwe Jens Kraft, Karl Gerhardt. SP: Joe May, Richard Hutter, Ruth Goetz, Dr. Wilhelm Roellinghoff. S: Karl Figdor.

Mya May (Maud Gregaards), Michael Bohnen (Consul Madsen), Henry Sze (Dr. Kien Lung), Hans Mierrendorff (Baron Murphy/Dr. Frohner), Ernst Hofmann (Credo Menville), Eduard Rothauser, Paul Hansen, Paul Morgan, Hans Pagay, Hedwig Bleibtreu, Bruno Decarli, Henry Bender, Hedy Searle, Hermann Picha, Wilhelm Diegelmann, Victor Janson, Alexander Ekert, Nien-Sön-Ling, Louis Brody, Bernhard Goetzke.

1. Die Freudin des gelben Mannes. 2. Die Geschichte der Maud Gregaards. 3. Der Rabbi von Kuang-Fu. 4. Kônig Macombe. 5. Ophir, die Stadt der Vergangenheit. 6. Die Frau mit den Milliarden. 7. Die Wohltäterin der Menschheit. 8. Die Rache der Maud Fergusson.

291. Hidden Dangers

(Vitagraph, 1920) Serial, 15 chapters, two reels each. D: William Bertram. SP: Albert E. Smith and Cleveland Moffett. SP: C. Graham Baker and William C. Courtney.

Dr. De Brutel, inventor, scientist and investigator, is infected with a strange disease which in its irregularly intermittent and recurrent attacks, destroys the balance of his faculties and his nature. When under this "influence" his brain is exalted at the expense of his soul. His mental capacity is developed at the expense of his moral nature. He becomes a superman without any sense of right or wrong. Dr. Brutel has overcome certain powers of nature. He has developed a "double X-Ray" through which he is able to pass through solid objects, become invisible, overcome gravitation, etc.

In his "possessed" moments, he loses the identity entirely of his former self, even his face and other physical characteristics. In his normal state, he remembers nothing of what he does during his "possessed" condition. When "possessed" however, he recalls what happens in his normal state. Occasionally he can avert this attack by a potent draught. His change from normal to abnormal is generally dependent upon atmospheric conditions. As Dr. Brutel, he is a respected citizen. In his abnormal state, he is the leader of the Black Circle, a secret organization of men with no moral scruples who indulge in every sort of crime and vice.

One can see the possibilities of this science film which predated *Dr. Jekyll and Mr. Hyde* and *The Wolf Man*.

Joe Ryan (Dr. De Brutel), Jean Paige (Madeline Stanton), George Stanley (Robert Stanton), E.J. Denny (Hammer), Sam Polo (Pinchers), Bert Ensminger (Sheriff Macklin), Charles Dudley, William McCall, Camille Sheeley.

1. The Evil Spell. 2. The Murder Mood. 3. Plucked from Peril. 4. The Fatal Choice. 5. Hands of Horror. 6. Springing the Trap. 7. Hindoo Hate. 8. Hemmed In. 9. An Inch from Doom. 10. A Fanatic's Revenge. 11. The Tank's Secret. 12. Human Bait. 13. A Woman's Grit. 14. The Fatal Escape. 15. The Lifting Fog.

Doris Kenyon in *The Hidden Hand* (1917)

292. The Hidden Hand

(Pathé, November 23, 1917) Serial, 15 chapters, two reels each. D: James Vincent. Scen: Arthur B. Reeve and Charles W. Goddard.

Two men are murdered, a millionaire named Whitney and his visitor, the grand Duke of a foreign country. Before they die, the millionaire accuses Jack Ramsey, a secret service man, of having inflicted a mortal wound on him in some mysterious way. The grand duke's story, however, which he relates in his dying moments, opens up a series of events dating back to his own previous country years. These events have to do with the birth of a girl known as Doris Whitney, who believes herself to be Mr. Whitney's daughter. The villain, The Hidden Hand, a creature whose right hand is covered by a claw-like mitten, is a master of plastic surgery and a wizard with deadly chemicals and gases. He tries to pass off a confederate, Vera Orane, as the millionaire's daughter.

Doris Kenyon (Doris Whitney), Sheldon Lewis (Dr. Scarley), Mahlon Hamilton (Jack Ramsey), Arline Pretty (Vera Orane), Henry Sedley.

1. The Gauntlet of Death. 2. Counterfeit Faces. 3. The Island of Dread. 4. The False Locket. 5. The Air-Lock. 6. The Flower of Death. 7. The Fire Trap. 8. Slide for Life. 9. Jets of Flame. 10. Dogs of Death. 11. Trapped by Treachery. 12. Eyes in the Wall. 13. Jaws of the Tiger. 14. The Unmasking. 15. The Girl of the Prophecy.

293. L'Hirondelle d'Acier

(France—Parisienne Films, 1919) Serial, 10 chapters. D: Louis Palieri.

Georges Gauthier, Mlle. Pierson, Anton de Verdier, Rieffler, Mme. L. Paglieri, Dartagnan, Mlle. Follin, Soniem, Paul May, Mlle. Suterre, Mlle. Grandjean, Perrier.

Portuguese: 1. A juventude de "Quebra-Ferro" 2. A morte de rosita. 3. O homem primitivo. 4. O forte de Kerff. 5. O envelope lacrado. 6. O jazigo misterioso. 7. O despertar do vulcão. 8. O baile das quatro estacãoes. 9. A torre de valdor. 10. Revelacão.

Jack Holt and Tristram Coffin (*at desk*) in *Holt of the Secret Service* (1941)

294. Holt of the Secret Service

(Columbia, December, 1941) Serial, 15 chapters, two reels each. D: James W. Horne. SP: Basil Dickey, George H. Plympton, Wyndham Gittens. Assist. D: Carl Hiecke. Photography: James S. Brown, Jr. Music: Lee Zahler. P: Larry Darmour. Released in feature form in England.

When a gang of brilliantly fiendish counterfeiters force a kidnapped treasury agent into making priceless engravings, super agent Jack Holt and his tough female partner attempt to discover the criminal mastermind's identity and stop his insidious activities. Constantly risking exposure and death, they daringly infiltrate the enemy's secret mountainside headquarters and his treacherous gambling ship. Holt poses as Nick Farrel, a desperate criminal; thus, he is accepted by the gang after he breaks out of prison with Crimp Evans. Kay Drew pretends to be Farrel's wife.

Most authors rate this serial as a cheapie and one of Columbia's worst chapterplays. This author would agree that it is a low budget film but not that it is one of Columbia's embarrassments. If you like Jack Holt, you will enjoy this serial; if you don't, you won't.

Jack Holt (Jack Holt/Nick Farrel), Evelyn Brent (Kay Drew), Montague Shaw (Malloy), Tristram Coffin (Valden), John Ward (Lucky Arnold), Ted Adams (Quist), Joe McQuinn (Crimp Evans), Edward Hearn (Jim Latham), Ray Parsons (Severn), Jack Cheatham (Frank), Stanley Blystone (Geraghty), George Chesebro (Rankin), Franklyn Farnum.

1. Chaotic Creek. 2. Ramparts of Revenge. 3. Illicit Wealth. 4. Menaced by Fate. 5. Exits to Terror. 6. Deadly Doom. 7. Out of the Past. 8. Escape to Peril. 9. Sealed in Silence. 10. Named to Die. 11. Ominous Warnings. 12. The Stolen Signal. 13. Prisoner of Jeopardy. 14. Afire Afloat. 15. Yielded Hostage.

295. L'Homme aux Trois Masques

(France—Eclair–Cinéromans, 1921) Serial, 12 chapters. D: Emile Keppens. Scen: Arthur Bernede.

André Marnay, Elmire Vautier, Charles Casella, Jacqueline Arly, Mario Nasthasio, Gina Manés, Eveline Janney, Dutertre, Hélène Helia, Jane Doly, Rex Stocken, Malou Vasseur, Pierre Bordery.

1. Les briseus d' ailes. 2. Le calvaire de Pascaline. 3. L'innocent. 4. Les remords de Fergus. 5. Je me vengerai! 6. La fille du forcat. 7. Le marquis de Santa-Fiore. 8. Le mendiant mystérieux. 9. La lutte à mort. 10. L'horrible complot. 11. Jean Claude et Jeannine. 12. Le justicier.

296. Homunculus

(Germany—Deutsche Bioscop 1916) Serial, 6 chapters, each feature length. D: Otto Rippert. S: Robert Reinert. Camera: Carl Hoffman. SP: Robert Neuss and Otto Rippert.

Homunculus is a creature manufactured in a laboratory by a professor. When Homunculus discovers that he has no soul and that he is incapable of love he revenges himself on society in a Frankenstein monster fashion. In the end he is killed by a bolt of lightning.

Homunculus was the most popular serial in Germany during World War I and was also received favorably elsewhere.

In 1920 the serial was released in a condensed version of 275 minutes by Decla-Bioscop in three parts: Part I: Der Künstliche Mensch (97 min.). Part II: Die Vernichtung der Menschheit (93 min.). Part III: Ein Titanenkampf (85 min.).

Olaf Föenss (Homunculus), Friedrich Küehne (Professor Hansen), Ernst Ludwig, Albert Paul, Lore Rueckert, Max Ruhbeck, Lia Borré, Ernst Benzinger, Margarete Ferida, Ilse Lersen, Josef Bunzl, Mechthild Thëin.

1. Homunculus (70 min.). 2. Das Geheimnisvolle Buch (76 min.). 3. Die Liebestragödie des Holmunculus (65 min.). 4. Die Rache des Holmunculus (68 min.). 5. Die Vernichtung der Menschheit (62 min.). 6. Das Ende des Homunculus (60 min.).

297. Hop Harrigan

(Columbia, March 23, 1946) Serial, 15 chapters, two reels each. D: Derwin Abrahams. SP: George H. Plympton and Ande Lamb. Adapted from the "Hop Harrigan" adventure strip by Jon Blummer, appearing in *All American Comics Magazine* and the "Hop Harrigan" radio program over the Mutual Network. P: Sam Katzman. Assist. D: Mike Eason. Photography: Ira H. Morgan. Music: Lee Zahler.

Hop Harrigan and his associates Tank Tinker and Gail Nolan become involved in rescuing an eccentric inventor, Dr. Tabor, from a gang commanded by a mystery figure called The Chief Pilot. Tabor manages to escape but not with a sound mind. He plans to destroy the world with his super power unit, and it is up to Harrigan to stop him.

William Bakewell (Hop Harrigan), Jennifer Holt (Gail Nolan), Robert "Buzz" Henry (Jackie Nolan), Sumner Getchell (Tank Tinker), Emmett Vogan (Arnold), Claire James (Gwen Arnold), John Merton (Dr. Tabor), Wheeler Oakman (Ballard), Ernie Adams (Retner), Peter Michael (Craven), Terry Frost (Barry), Anthony Warde (Edwards), Jackie Moran (Fraser), Bobby Stone (Gray), Jack Buchanan (Deputy Sheriff), Jim Diehl (Carter).

1. A Mad Mission. 2. The Secret Ray. 3. The Mystery Plane. 4. Plunging Peril. 5. Betrayed by a Madman. 6. A Flaming Trap. 7. One Chance for Life. 8. White Fumes of Fate. 9. Dr. Tabor's Revenge. 10. Juggernaut of Fate. 11. Flying to Oblivion. 12. Lost in the Skies. 13. No Escape. 14. The Chute that Failed. 15. The Fate of the World.

Top: **Jennifer Holt, Robert "Buzz" Henry, Ernie Adams, and William Bakewell in *Hop Harrigan* (1946);** ***bottom:*** **Grace Darmond in *The Hope Diamond Mystery* (1921)**

298. The Hope Diamond Mystery

(Kosmik Films, March 1921) Serial, 15 chapters, two reels each. D: Stuart Paton. Scen: Charles Goddard, John B. Clymer. P: George Kleine. Photography: William Thornley. S: May Yoke.

Harry Carter (Shug/Sidney Atherton/Nang Fu), Grace Darmond (Bibi/Mary Hilton), George Chesebro (Tavanier/John Gregg), Boris Karloff (Dakor), Carmen Phillips (Mirza/Wanda, Nang Fu's wife), William Marian (James Marcon/Bagi), Frank Seka (Saki), Harry Archer (Johnson), Arthur Clayton (Lord Francis Hale), Ethel Shannon (Lady Hale), William Buckley (Putnam Bradley Stone).

1. The Hope Diamond Mystery. 2. The Vanishing Hand. 3. The Forged Note. 4. The Jewel of Sita. 5. A Virgin's Love. 6. The House of Terror. 7. Flames of Despair. 8. Yellow Whisperings. 9. The Evil Eye. 10. In the Spider's Web. 11. The Cup of Fear. 12. The Ring of Death. 13. The Lash of Hate. 14. Primitive Passions. 15. An Island of Destiny.

299. The House of Hate

(Astra/Pathé, March 10, 1918) Serial, 20 chapters; Chapter 1, three reels, others, two reels. D: George B. Seitz. S: Arthur B. Reeve and Charles A. Logue. Scen: Bertram Millhauser.

Pearl Grant is heir to the House of Walden munitions works. Pearl has been betrothed to a cousin that she does not love to insure that control over the firm remains in the Walden family. However, she loves scientist Harry Gresham, who is also loved by her cousin Zelda, a troublemaker. When The Hooded Terror and his gang set out to destroy the House of Walden, Pearl has her hands full in preserving it.

Pearl White (Pearl Grant), Antonio Moreno (Harry Gresham), Peggy Shanor (Naomi Walden), John Gilmour (Winthrop Walden), John Webb Dillon (Haynes Walden), Floyd Buckley, Paul Dillon, Joe Cuny, Paul Clerget, Ruby Hoffman, Helene Chadwick, Louis Wolheim, Paul Panzer.

1. The Hooded Terror. 2. The Tiger's Eye. 3. A Woman's Perfidy. 4. The Man from Java. 5. Spies Within. 6. A Living Target. 7. Germ Menace. 8. The Untold Secret. 9. Poisoned Darts. 10. Double Crossed. 11. Haunts of Evil. 12. Flashes in the Dark. 13. Enemy Aliens. 14. Underworld Allies. 15. The False Signal. 16. The Vial of Death. 17. The Death Switch. 18. At the Pistol's Point. 19. The Hooded Terror Unmasked. 20. Following Old Glory.

Pearl White and Antonio Moreno in *The House of Hate* (1918)

300. The House of Terror

(William M. Pizor, 1928) Serial, 10 chapters, two reels each. D: Roland Reed. SP: William M. Pizor.

Practically nothing is known about this serial. It was never copyrighted and was distributed on the States Right market with few takers. Only the cheapest theaters would book it. Pat O'Brien is not the better known star of the sound era, and it is doubtful that this Jack LaRue is the same actor who specialized in gangster roles in the Thirties and Forties.

Pat O'Brien, Dorothy Tallcot, Jack LaRue, Roy Watson, Gene Burr, Earle Gunn, Valerie Burr.

1–4. [Unknown.] 5. Perilous Trails. 6. Secret Passage.

301. The House Without a Key

(Pathé, November 21, 1926) Serial, 10 chapters; Chapter 1, three reels, others, two reels. D: Spencer Gordon Bennet. SP: Frank Leon Smith. S: Earl Derr Biggers—*House Without a Key*.

Though based on a Charlie Chan story by Earl Derr Biggers, the character of Chan is relegated to the sidelines in this story of a crime supposedly committed many years before and of the enmity existing between two brothers. Carry Egan, the daughter of the righteous brother's partner, and John Winterclip, a nephew of the wealthy brother, attempt to recover a stolen treasure chest and to solve the mystery of the ancient crime.

Allene Ray (Carry Egan), Walter Miller (John Quincy Winterclip), E.H. Calvert (Dan Winterclip), Betty Caldwell (Barbara Winterclip), Natalie Warfield (Minerva Winterclip), Jack Pratt (James Egan), William Norton Bailey (Harry Jennison), Frank Lackteen (Kaohla), George Kuwa (Charlie Chan), Harry Semels (Saladine), Charles H. West (Bowker), John Cossar (District Attorney), Scott Seaton (Detective), Clifford Saum (Kennedy).

1. The Spite Fence. 2. The Mystery Box. 3. The Missing Numeral. 4. Suspicion. 5. The Death Buoy. 6. Sinister Shadows. 7. The Mystery Man. 8. The Spotted Menace. 9. Sinister Shadows. 10. The Culprit.

302. Der Hund von Baskerville

(Germany—Greenbaum Film GmbH, 1920) Serial, 6 chapters. D: Willy Zeyn. SP: Robert Liebmann. S: Irene Daland.

Lu Jurgens, Erwin Fichtner, Ludwig Rex.

1–4. [Unknown.] 5. Dr. Macdonald's Sanatorium. 6. Das Haus ohne Fenster.

303. The Hurricane Express

(Mascot, August 1932) Serial, 12 chapters; Chapter 1, three reels, others, ? reels. D: Armand Schaefer and J.P. McGowan. SP: George Morgan and J.P. McGowan. S: Colbert Clark, Barney Sarecky, and Wyndham Gittens. Camera: Ernest Miller and Carl Wester. P: Nat Levine.

Larry Baker's father is killed in a mysterious train wreck occurring on the L & R Railroad and he sets out to track down

The Wrecker, a shadowy figure who effectively disguises himself with masks of various principals in the story. Gloria, daughter of one of the suspects, helps Larry, a transport pilot, as he fights to bring the master criminal to justice.

John Wayne (Larry Baker), Shirley Grey (Gloria), Conway Tearle (Stevens), Tully Marshall (Howard Edwards), J. Farrell MacDonald (Jim Baker), Matthew Betz (Jordan), Edmund Breese (Stratton), Joseph Girard (Matthews), Lloyd Whitlock (Walter Gray), James Burtis (Hemmingway), Alan Bridges (Carlson), Ernie Adams (Barney), Charles King (Mike), Glenn Strange (Jim), Al Ferguson (Sandy), Fred Toomes (Porter), Eddie Parker (Co-Pilot).

1. The Wrecker. 2. Flying Pirates. 3. The Masked Killer. 4. Buried Alive. 5. Danger Lights. 6. The Airport Mystery. 7. Sealed Lips 8. Outside the Law. 9. The Invisible Enemy. 10. The Wrecker's Secret. 11. Wings of Death 12. Unmasked.

304. Hurricane Hutch

(Pathé, September 25, 1921) Serial, 15 chapters, two reels each. D: George B. Seitz. S: Charles Hutchison.

In this story Hutch strives to obtain a lost formula for making paper from seaweed so that he might pay the mortgage and save a paper mill from financial foreclosure by the villain.

There is less violence here than in previous Pathé thrillers. Hutchison was still suffering from injuries received in the production of his two previous serials. Therefore, he had become cautious about performing dangerous or difficult stunts. Joe Cuny was his chief double, but in this film director Seitz, Spencer Bennet, and Joe Bonomo doubled Hutchison at times.

Charles had an inflated ego. It must have been hard on him when, in the Forties, he was relegated to the smallest bit parts in the serials of Republic.

Charles Hutchison (Larry Hutchdale), Lucy Fox (Nancy Kellogg), Warner Oland (Clifton Marlowe), Diana Deer (Belle Brinkley), Ann Hasting (Ann Haviland), Harry Semels (Jim Tiegerley), Frank Redman (John Brinkley), Thomas C. Goodwin (Silas Haviland), Charles Revada (Bill Hogan), Joe Cuny (Wilson Winslow), Spencer Bennet, George B. Seitz, Joe Bonomo (Doubles for Hutchison).

1. The Secret Cipher. 2. The Cycle Bullet. 3. The Millionth Chance. 4. Smashing Through. 5. One Against Many. 6. At the Risk of His Neck. 7. On a Dangerous Coast. 8. Double Crossed. 9. Overboard. 10. The Showdown. 11. Hare and Hounds. 12. Red Courage. 13. Neck and Neck. 14. The Secret of Flame. 15. The Last Duel.

Charles Hutchinson and Lucy Fox in *Hurricane Hutch* (1921)

305. Idaho

(Pathé, March 1, 1925) Serial, 10 chapters, two reels each. D: Robert F. Hill. SP: Frank Leon Smith. S: Theodore Burrell—"The Girl Vigilante." P: C.W. Patton.

David Cameron and his daughter Beth arrive in Carters Creek, a boisterous mining camp. Cameron is keeping it as a surprise that he is half-owner in a rich mine—a secret he holds too long, for an attack by bandits, covetous of the Kentucky thoroughbreds driven by the traveler, brings his death. The daughter escapes and swears vengeance. She is aided by a doctor of the town and Boston Graham, the pony express rider.

Vivian Rich (Beth Cameron), Mahlon Hamilton (Boston Graham), Frederick Vroom (David Cameron), Frank Lackteen (Tex Osborne), Omar Whitehead (Doctor Gibbs), William J. Quinn (Ike Rogers), Fred De Silva (Sam Kellerman), Charles Brinley (Yarrow), Nelson McDowell (Angus McPherson), William Dale (Alexander Jones), Lillian Gale (Mrs. Jones), Roy E. Bassett (The Mysterious Stranger), Gus Saville, Robert Irwin, George Burton.

1. Road Agents. 2. Hands Up. 3. The Stampede. 4. Forbidden Testimony. 5. Lawless Laws. 6. Aroused. 7. The Trap. 8. The White Streak. 9. Unmasked. 10. Vigilantes.

306. Imperia

(France—Pathé Consortium, 1920) Serial, 12 chapters. D: Jean Durand. Scen: Arthur Bernèdé.

Jacqueline Forzane (Imperia), Berthe Dagmar, Charles de Rochefort, Ch. Caselle, Louis Leubas, Arnaud Boisville, Frederic Mariotti, Gaston Modot, Melle Doudjam, Jacqueline Arly, Gilles.

1. Sworn Upon the Sword. 2. Diadem Dance. 3. An Unsolved Mystery. 4. Hearts in Distress. 5. Found Guilty, 6. Ligert in the Prison. 7. Exploits of Herzelius. 8. Gypsies' Revenge. 9. Squirrels Leap. 10. Miarkas Love. 11. Philtre of Hate. 12. Love's Crucible.

307. In the Days of Buffalo Bill

(Universal, September 11, 1922) Serial, 18 chapters; Chapter 1, three reels; others, two reels. D: Edward Laemmle. SP: Robert Dillon. S: Robert Dillon.

This serial deviates from the lost treasure theme to concentrate on the building of the transcontinental railway. Acord stays busy saving Dorothy Woods from both renegade whites and Sioux, and protecting the railroad crews as they seek to lay track. There is something doing every minute in the shape of vigorous action and the suspense keeps pace with it. Both history and fiction are given equal footage.

Art Acord (Art Taylor), Dorothy Woods (Alice Carter), Duke R. Lee (Buffalo Bill Cody), Ruth Royce (Aimee), George A. Williams (Calvert Carter), Jay Morley (Lambert Ashley), Otto Nelson (Alden Carter), Pat Harmon (Gaspard), Joe Hazelton (Gideon M. Wells), Burton C. Law (Allen Pinkerton), William Duvaull (Edward M. Stanton), Joel Day (Abraham Lincoln), Burt Frank (General Hancock), Clark Comstock (Thomas C. Durant), G.R. Phillips (Frank Blair), William Moran.

1. Bonds of Steel. 2. In the Enemy's Hands. 3. The Spy. 4. The Sword of Grant and Lee. 5. The Man of the Ages. 6. Prisoners of the Sioux. 7. Shackles of Fate. 8. The Last Shot. 9. From Tailor to President. 10. Empire Builders. 11. Perils of the Plains. 12. The Hand of Justice. 13. Trails of Peril. 14. The Scarlet Doom. 15. Men of Steel 16. The Brink of Eternity. 17. A Race to the Finish. 18. Driving the Golden Spike.

Top: **Art Acord in *In the Days of Buffalo Bill* (1922);** ***bottom:*** **Bud Osborne, Francis Ford (*arms around Allene*), Allene Ray, Edmond Cobb (*arms raised*), Tim McCoy, and Jim Corey in *The Indians Are Coming* (1930)**

308. In the Days of Daniel Boone

(Universal, June 25, 1923) Serial, 15 chapters; Chapter 1, three reels; others, two reels. D: William Craft, Jay Marchant, and Frank Messinger. Scen: Jefferson Moffitt. S: Paul Bryan and Jefferson Moffitt.

A story of pre-revolutionary America and the French and Indian War. Daniel Boone attempts to establish a frontier colony over opposition by Tories and Indians. A rather routine outing with, if you can believe it, Duke R. Lee playing both George Washington and Simon Girty.

Jack Mower (Jack Gordon), Eileen Sedgwick (Susan Boone), Charles Brinley (Daniel Boone), Duke R. Lee (George Washington/Simon Girty), Ruth Royce (Claire De Voe), Albert J. Smith (Captain Charles Redmond), Frank Farrington (Judge Henderson), Herschel Mayall (General Braddock), Jack Lewis (James Monroe).

1. His Country's Need. 2. At Sword's Point. 3. Liberty or Death. 4. Foiling the Regulators. 5. Perilous Paths. 6. Trapped. 7. In the Hands of the Enemy. 8. Over the Cliff. 9. The Flaming Forest. 10. Running the Gauntlet. 11. The Wilderness Trail. 12. The Fort in the Forest. 13. The Boiling Springs. 14. Chief Blackfish Attacks. 15. Boone's Triumph.

309. The Indians Are Coming

(Universal, October 20, 1930) Serial, 12 chapters, two reels each. D: Henry McRae. SP: Ford Beebe and George Plympton. S: William F. Cody—*The Great West That Was*. P: Henry McRae.

Jack Manning accompanies George Woods and his daughter Mary on a wagon train to join George's brother, Jack, who has struck it rich in Gold Creek. Rance Carter, who has staked George, first tries to force his attentions on Mary, then tries to steal everything he can. In battling the Carter gang and surviving an Indian uprising, Jack and Mary are aided by scout Bill Williams but Mary's father and many innocent people fall prey to the two disruptive forces before they are brought under control.

Tim McCoy (Jack Manning), Allene Ray (Mary Woods), Charles Roy (Uncle Amos), Edmund Cobb (Bill Williams), Francis Ford (Tom Woods/George Woods), Dynamite [a dog] (Ring), Wilbur McGough (Rance Carter), Bud Osborne (Bull McGee), Don Francis, Bob Reeves, Jim Corey, Dick Hatton, Lafe McKee.

1. Pals in Buckskin. 2. A Call to Arms 3. A Furnace of Fear. 4. The Red Terror. 5. The Circle of Death. 6. Hate's Harvest. 7. Hostages of Fear. 8. The Dagger Duel. 9. The Blast of Death. 10. Buckskin's Vengeance. 11. Frontiers Aflame. 12. The Trail's End.

310. Into the Net

(Pathé, August 3, 1924) Serial, 10 chapters, two reels each. D: George B. Seitz. S: Richard E. Enright. SP: Frank Leon Smith.

The story opens with the discovery of a murder committed by a famous criminal, identified by his fingerprints. Immediately upon the heels of this event a wealthy girl is kidnapped. The murderer accomplishes this crime before he is taken by the police. The girl is the nineteenth to disappear in this mysterious fashion.

Madge Clayton, the missing girl, was on her way to the home of a woman who was playing hostess at a card party. Among the guests there was Natalie Van Cleef, another wealthy girl. The brother of the missing girl joins the police in a hunt for Madge and he discovers that a Dr. Vining is connected with the kidnapping. Vining tries to kidnap Natalie but is thwarted by Bob Clayton.

The action thereafter is very brisk. The plot is quite complicated, but very clearly presented. The action swings from one melodramatic peak to another.

Edna Murphy (Natalie Van Cleef), Jack Mulhall (Bob Clayton), Constance Bennett (Madge Clayton), Bradley Barker (Bert Moore), Frank Lackteen (Dr. Vining), Frances Landau (Mrs. Fawcette), Harry Semels (Ivan Ivanovitch), Tom Goodwin (Inspector Cabot), Paul Porter (The Emperor), Tom Blake.

1. The Shadow of the Web. 2. The Clue. 3. Kidnapped. 4. Hidden Talons. 5. The Raid. 6. The House of the Missing. 7. Ambushed. 8. The Escape. 9. To the Rescue. 10. In the Toils.

311. The Invisible Hand

(Vitagraph, January 1920) Serial, 15 chapters, Chapter 1, three reels; others, two reels. D: William J. Bowman and Jack Pierce. S: Cyrus Townsend Brady and Albert E. Smith. SP: C. Graham Baker.

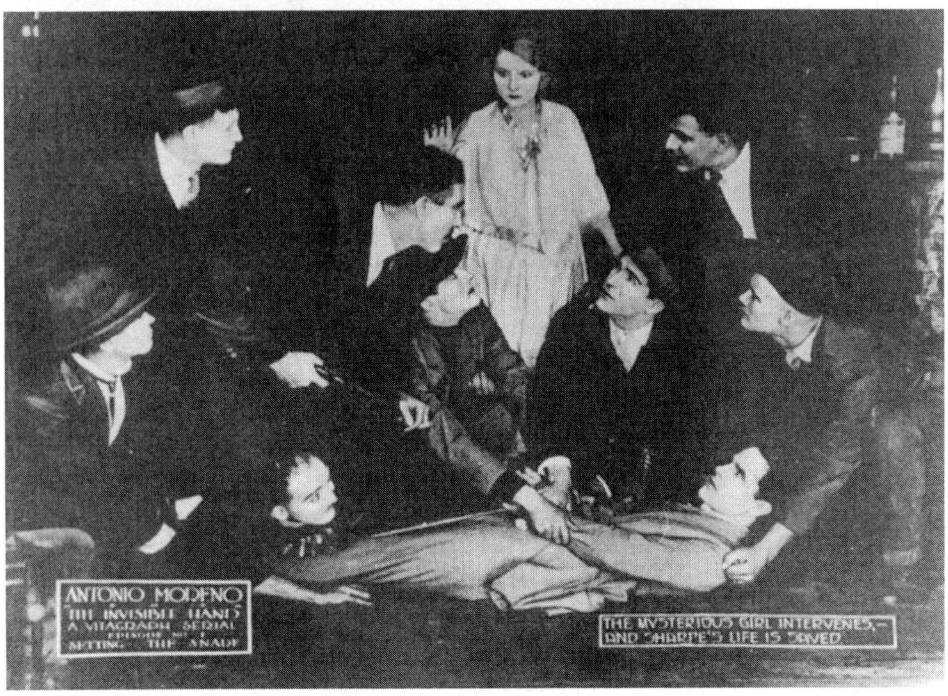

Top: **Tim McCoy and Allene Ray in** ***The Indians Are Coming*** **(1930);** ***bottom:*** **Antonio Moreno and Pauline Curley in** ***The Invisible Hand*** **(1920)**

With the country agog over the conspiracies and depredations of a band of organized crooks in the West, the Secret Service is called upon to bring them to justice. This organized clique of dangerous criminals is led by a cunning and cultured master crook, Iron Hand. Large gold shipments were systematically plundered, jewels stolen and wholesale raids made on commerce. The Secret Service have found themselves stumped and Assistant Chief Burnett, at Chicago, in desperation finally decides to call in John Sharpe, the most famous analytical detective in the country. Sharpe is hated and feared by every criminal of any consequence on two continents and is known to them in their parlance as "the needle."

Burnett summons Sharpe, explains the situation and appeals to him to take up the job of bringing Iron Hand and his criminal pests to justice. "No matter how you get them—dead or alive, nobody will care, just get them, that is all I ask," says Burnett. Sharpe is finally prevailed upon to take charge of the Government crusade against Iron Hand and his gang.

It is fifteen chapters of action, romance, and mystery, and the role of Iron Hand stands out as one of the finest "heavy part" delineations on the screen.

Antonio Moreno (John Sharpe), Pauline Curley (Ann Crawford/Violet "X" Ray), Jay Morley (Burnett, Secret Service Chief), Brinsley Shaw (Iron Hand), George Mellcrest (Potsdam), Sam Polo (Red Black), Gordon Sackville, Charles G. Rich.

1. Setting the Snare. 2. T-N-T. 3. Winged Death. 4. Gassed. 5. Dodging Disaster. 6. The Closing Jaws. 7. The Submarine Cave. 8. Outwitted. 9. Heathen Sacrifice. 10. The Fender of Flesh. 11. Flirting with Death. 12. The Dungeon of Despair. 13. The Plunging Peril. 14. The Modern Mazeppa. 15. The Closing Net.

312. The Invisible Monster

(Republic, May 1950) Serial, 12 chapters, two reels each. Feature Title: *Slaves of the Invisible Monster*. D: Fred C. Brannon. SP: Ronald Davidson. Assoc. P: Franklyn Adreon. Photography: Ellis W. Carter. Music: Stanley Wilson. Special Effects: Howard and Theodore Lydecker.

Lane Carson and his assistant, Carol Richards, investigate a bank robbery for their employer, an insurance company. They match wits and bullets with the Phantom Ruler, a criminal who has devised a way to make himself invisible.

Richard Webb (Lane Carson), Aline Towne (Carol Richards), Lane Bradford (Burton), Stanley Price (The Phantom Ruler), John Crawford (Harris), Tom Steele (Bill Haines/Mac), Dave Sharpe (Watchman/Guard), George Meeker (Harry Long), Keith Richards (Doctor), Dale Van Sickel (Otto Wagner), Marshall Reed (MacDuff), George Magrill (Sam), Duke Taylor (Officer), Carey Loftin (Kirk), Bud Wolfe (Harding), Guy Teague (Al), Forest Burns (Joe), Eddie Parker (Stoner), Frank O'Connor (Hogan), Douglas Evans (James Hunter), George Volk (Guard), Charles Sullivan (Grogarty), Howard Mitchell, Mark Strong, Bert LeBaron (Watchmen), Edward Keane (Warren Madison), John Hamilton (Henry Miller), Roy Gordon (Moore), Harold Goodwin (Kirk), Ken Terrell (Kern).

1. Slaves of the Phantom. 2. The Acid Clue. 3. The Death Car. 4. Highway Holocaust. 5. Bridge to Eternity. 6. Ordeal by Fire. 7. Murder Train. 8. Window of Peril. 9. Trail to Destruction. 10. High Voltage Danger. 11. Death's Highway. 12. The Phantom Meets Justice.

Richard Webb and Aline Towne in *The Invisible Monster (1950)*

313. The Invisible Ray

(Frohman Amusement Corp., 1920) Serial, 15 chapters, two reels each. D: Harry A. Pollard and Jack Sherrill. SP: Guy McConnell.

A young mineralogist is scouring the rocky countryside of Persia when he accidentally exposes a strange new substance which seems to possess an unusual ray power that can have a fatal effect on humans. He hurriedly secures enough samples of the rock and places them in a sealed lead box. Two keys are required to open the box. One is placed around the neck of his infant daughter and the other sent to Professor Stone, a famous mineralogist in his own right. Thinking himself dying, the explorer sends his infant daughter back to England to live with a relative. However, blunders are made and she winds up in a foundling home.

The years pass and she grows to womanhood still retaining the key around her neck. A chance meeting occurs with Professor Stone who informs her she is the lost daughter of his friend and he also relates the story behind the key she wears. She also meets Jack Stone, son of the professor, and the two fall in love. Mystery is kidnapped by a gang known as the Crime Creators, thus, the action begins.

For the 1920s this serial contains a lot of scientific information and data of the future, making it an excellent entry into the science fiction productions of the period.

This serial did not have chapter titles. In addition, individual chapters were not copyrighted, and, according to the Library of Congress, the serial itself was not even copyrighted.

Jack Sherrill (Jack Stone), Ruth Clifford (Mystery), Sidney Bracey (Jean Deaux), Ed Davis (John Haldane), Corrine Uzzell (Mariana, Crystal Gazer), W.H. Tooker (Gang Member), Edith Forrest.

314. The Iron Claw

(Feature Film Co./Pathé, February 22, 1916) Serial, 20 chapters, two reels each. D: Edward Jose and George B. Seitz. Scen: George B. Seitz. S: Arthur Stringer. P: Leopold and Theodore Wharton.

Margery is kidnapped as a baby by Legar, The Iron Claw, as revenge for Margery's father having cut off Legar's arm as punishment for making love to Margery's mother and blackmailing her to acquire the family jewels. Margery grows up among thieves and is about to start a life of crime herself when she is rescued by a mystery hero (a serial "first") called The Laughing Mask and returned safely to her father. As evil and good clashed and Margery is about to be done in, The Laughing Mask saves the day. Only in the last chapter is he divulged to be her fiancé. The gimmick of a masked hero unidentified to the viewer was again used successfully in *The Lone Ranger* (Republic, 1938).

Pearl White (Margery Golden), Creighton Hale (Davey), Sheldon Lewis (Legar, The Iron Claw), Harry Fraser (The Laughing Mask), J.E. Dunn (Enoch Golden), Carey Lee (Mrs. Golden), Clare Miller (Margery as a child), Henry G. Sell (Wrench), Edward Jose (Manley), E. Cooper Willis, Allan Walker, Bertrand Gudgeon.

1. The Vengeance of Legar. 2. The House of Unhappiness. 3. The Cognac Mask. 4. The Name and the Game. 5. The Incorrigible Captive. 6. The Spotted Warning. 7. The Hooded Helper. 8. The Stroke of 12. 9. Arrows of Hate. 10. The Living Dead. 11. The Saving of Dan O'Mara. 12. The Haunted Canvas. 13. The Hidden Face. 14. The Plunge for Life. 15. The Double Resurrection. 16. The Unmasking of Davey. 17. The Vanishing Fakir. 18. The Green-Eyed God. 19. The Cave of Despair. 20. The Triumph of the Laughing Mask.

***Top: The Invisible Ray* (1920); *bottom:* Pearl White in *The Iron Claw* (1916)**

315. The Iron Claw

(Columbia, 1941) Serial, 15 chapters, two reels each. D: James W. Horne. SP: Basil Dickey, George H. Plympton, Jesse A. Duffy, Charles R. Condon, and Jack Stanley. S: Arthur Stringer. P: Larry Darmour. Assist. D: Carl Hiecke. Photography: James S. Brown, Jr. Music: Lee Zahler.

A number of people are after a fortune in gold. Patricia Benson, like her uncle before her, becomes a target of the Iron Claw. Unknowingly, she is heiress to the money. The Iron Claw wears a glove-like device which gives him his name. Facial bandages and dark glasses further conceal his identity. Reporter Bob Lane finally unmasks The Iron Claw and he and his gangsters are jailed.

Charles Quigley (Bob Lane), Joyce Bryant (Patricia Benson), Forrest Taylor (Anton Benson), Walter Sande (Jack Strong), Norman Willis (Roy Benson), Alex Callam (James Benson), James Metcalfe (Culver Benson), Allen Doone (Simon Leach), Edythe Elliott (Milly Leach), John Beck (Gyves), Charles King (Silk), James Morton (Casey), Hal Price (O'Malley).

1. The Shaft of Doom. 2. The Murderous Mirror. 3. The Drop to

Destiny. 4. The Fatal Fuse. 5. The Fiery Fall. 6. The Ship Log Talks. 7. The Mystic Map. 8. The Perilous Pit. 9. The Cul-de-Sac. 10. The Curse of the Cave. 11. The Doctor's Bargain. 12. Vapors of Evil. 13. The Secret Door. 14. The Evil Eye. 15. The Claw's Collapse.

316. The Iron Man

(Universal, June 18, 1924) Serial, 15 chapters, two reels each. D: Jay Marchant. S/SP: Arthur Henry Gooden and William E. Wing.

Arlene Graham is kidnapped in Paris and a look-alike is substituted for her. Arlene's uncle, suspecting nothing, returns to America with Mini, the look-alike, to claim Arlene's inheritance. In Paris, Paul Breen, a reporter, rescues Arlene and they follow the impostor to the States and face many close calls before righting the injustice.

Lucien Albertini (Paul Breen), Margaret Morris (Arlene Graham), Joe Bonomo (Gaston La Rue), Jack Daugherty (Dick Clifford), Lola Todd (Mini), Jean DuBriac (Jules Despaed), William Welsh, Rose Dione, Harry Mann, W.T. Horne, Jack Pratt.

1. Into the Sewers of Paris. 2. The Impostor. 3. The Dynamite Truck. 4. Wings Aflame. 5. The False Trail. 6. The Stolen Passport. 7. False Faces. 8. Shadowed. 9. The Missing Heirloom. 10. Sinister Shadows. 11. The Betrayal. 12. Flames of Fate. 13. The Crisis. 14. Hidden Dangers. 15. The Confession.

317. The Iron Test

(Vitagraph, October 21, 1918) Serial, 15 chapters, two reels each. D: Robert N. Bradbury and Paul C. Hurst. Scen: Graham Baker. S: Albert E. Smith and Cyrus Townsend Brady.

A mysterious hooded figure known as The Red Mask seeks to kill two circus acrobats who stand between him and the fulfillment of his nefarious ambitions.

Antonio Moreno (Bert Ford), Carol Holloway (Edith Paige), Barney Furey (Lewis Craven), Chet Ryan (Pesky Flynn), Frank Jonasson Morgan Jenkins), Hart [Jack] Hoxie, Charles G. Rich, Jack Waltemeyer.

1. The Ring of Fire. 2. The Van of Disaster. 3. The Blade of Hate. 4. The Noose. 5. The Tide of Death. 6. Fiery Fate. 7. The Whirling Trap. 8. The Man Eater. 9. The Pit of Lost Hope. 10. In the Coils. 11. The Red Mask's Prey. 12. The Span of Terror. 13. Hanging Peril. 14. Desperate Odds. 15. Riding with Death.

Both: Joyce Bryant in *The Iron Claw* (1941)

318. Is Marriage Sacred?

(Essanay, December 23, 1916–April 7, 1917) Series, 16 Episodes, two reels each. D: E.H. Colvert. S: Charles Mortimer Peck.

The author has no information on this series; however, it is believed that each episode tells a complete story and that the continuing cast play different roles in each episode.

Marguerite Clayton, Sydney Ainsworth, Thomas Commerford, Edward Arnold, Lillian Drew, John Cossar, Ernest Maupain, Marion Lydston.

1. The Burning Band. 2. Dancing with Folly. 3. Wife in Sunshine. 4. When the Man Speaks. 5. The Wide, Wrong Way. 6. The Sinful Marriage. 7. The Magic Mirror. 8. Shifting Shadows. 9. Desertion and Non-Support. 10. Ashes on the Hearthstone. 11. The Extravagant Bride. 12. The Vanishing Woman. 13. The Pulse of Madness. 14. The Pallid Dawn. 15. The Wifeless Husband. 16. Meddling with Marriage.

319. The Isle of Sunken Gold

(Mascot, September 1, 1927) Serial, 10 chapters, two reels each. D: Harry Webb. P: Nat Levine.

A sea captain possesses part of a map showing the location of a treasure on a remote island. Traveling there he finds that the other half of the map is held by a white princess who is practically a prisoner of the natives. Together the captain and the princess battle hostile natives and white mutineers to recover the treasure and to free the princess from enslavement.

Anita Stewart, Bruce Gordon, Duke Kahanomoku, Evangeline Russell, Curtis McHenry, John Pierce, Vincent Howard, Ammett Wagner, Jay J. Bryan, Alfred Sabota, K. Nambu.

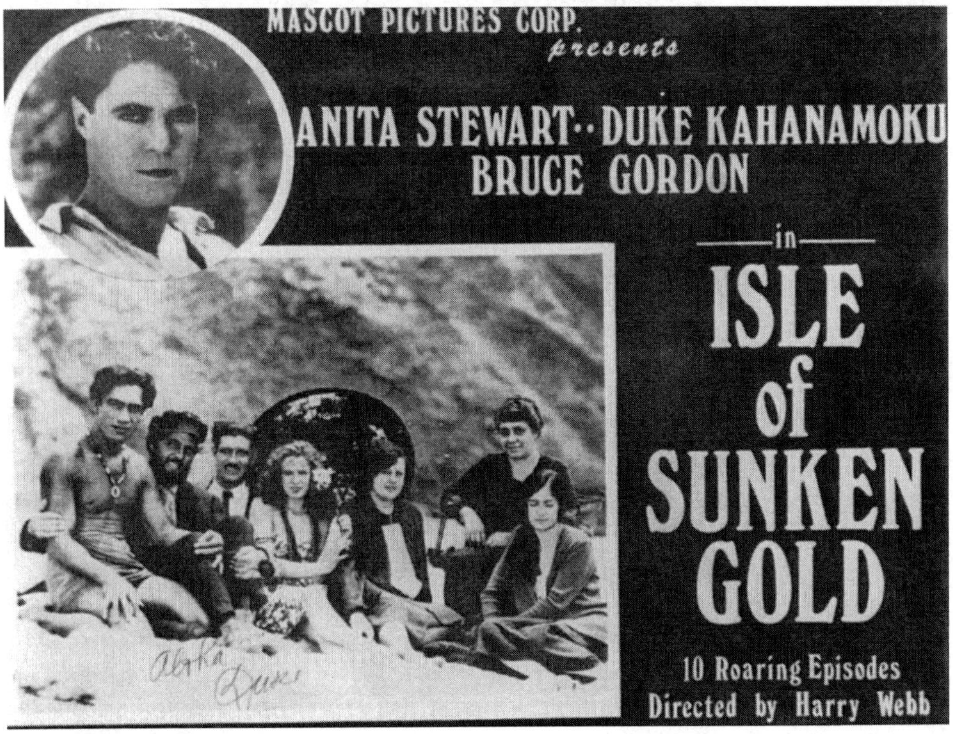

Top: **Anita Stewart, Duke Kahanamoku, and Bruce Gordon in *The Isle of Sunken Gold* (1927); *bottom:* Joe Brown, John Hart, and Rosemary La Planche in *Jack Armstrong* (1947)**

1. Isle of Sunken Gold. 2. Trapped in Mid-Air. 3. Engulfed by the Sea. 4. The Volcano's Pit. 5. The Hulk of Death. 6. The Prey of Sharks. 7. Fire of Revenge. 8. The Battle of Canoes. 9. Trapped by the Ape. 10. The Devil Ape's Secret.

320. Jack Armstrong

(Columbia, March 1947) Serial, 15 chapters, two reels each. D: Wallace Fox. SP: Arthur Hoerl, Lewis Clay, Royal Cole, and Leslie Swabacker. Adapted from the radio serial *Jack Armstrong, the All-American Boy*. P: Sam Katzman. Assist. D: Mike Eason and Leonard Shapiro. Assoc. P: Mel DeLay. Photography: Ira H. Morgan. Music: Lee Zahler.

Jack Armstrong is a friend of Jim Fairfield, head of an aviation company concerned with the development of atomic-powered motors. Jack is also a friend to Fairfield's nephew, Billy, and niece, Betty. Vic Hardy, an employee of Fairfield, makes the discovery that cosmic radiations are being used by human agencies. Hardy is subsequently kidnapped and taken to an island far out in the Pacific. Armstrong and friends follow to encounter J. Grood, the brains behind a scheme to develop a ray gun to be suspended in outer space, which will dominate the earth and destroy all opposition. After harrowing adventures on the sland, the trio rescue Hardy, kill Grood, and save the world from possible annihilation.

John Hart (Jack Armstrong), Rosemary La Planche (Betty), Joe Brown, Jr. (Billy), Claire James (Alura), Pierre Watkin (Uncle Jim Fairfield), Charles Middleton (J. Grood), Wheeler Oakman (Professor Zorn), Jack Ingram (Blair), Eddie Parker (Slade), Hugh Prosser (Vic Hardy), John Merton (Gregory Pierce), Frank Marlo (Naga), Russ Vincent (Umala), Gene Stutenroth (Dr. Albour).

1. Mystery of the Cosmic Ray. 2. The Far World. 3. Island of Deception. 4. Into the Chasm. 5. The Space Ship. 6. Tunnels of Treachery. 7. Cavern of Chance. 8. The Secret Room. 9. Human Targets. 10. Battle of the Warriors. 11. Cosmic Annihilator. 12. The Grotto of Greed. 13. Wheels of Fate. 14. Journey into Space. 15. Retribution.

321. Jack London's Tales of the Fish Patrol

(Universal, 1922–23) Series, 8 episodes, two reels each.

Jack Mulhall.

Episode Titles, Releasing Dates, Directors (in italics), Supporting Actors 1. White and Yellow (9-23-22) *Edward Kull*, Louise Lorraine, Albert Gronell, John Wallace, Robert Gray, Jim Wang. 2. The Channel Raiders (10-14-22) *Edward Kull*; 3. Pirates of the Deep (11-4-22) *Edward Kull*. 4. The Law of the Sea (11-28-22) *Edward Kull*. 5. The Siege of the Lancaster Queen (12-16-22) *Edward Kull*. 6. Dangerous Waters (1-6-23) *Edward Kull*; 7. Yellow Handkerchief (1-27-23)

Edward Kull; Louise Lorraine, Jim Wang. 8. Wolves of the Waterfront (2-17-23) *Edward Kull.*

322. The Jade Box

(Universal, February 25, 1930) Serial, 10 chapters, two reels each. D: Ray Taylor. S: Fred Jackson. Released in both silent and sound versions.

Jack Lamar's father is held by members of an Eastern cult, who threaten to kill him unless a jade box he purchased in the Orient is turned over to them. It seems that the box holds a vial that contains the secret of invisibility. Martin Morgan, father of Jack's fiancée, has stolen it and plans to use the secret for his own evil purposes. Jack and Helen Morgan's attempts to restore the box to its rightful resting place in the Far East are aided by a mysterious figure called The Shadow.

Jack Perrin (Jack Lamar), Louise Lorraine (Helen Morgan), Monroe Salisbury (John Lamar), Francis Ford (Martin Morgan), Wilbur S. Mack (Edward Haines), Leo White (Percy Winslow), Jay Novello.

1. The Jade of Jeopardy. 2. Buried Alive! 3. The Shadow Man. 4. The Fatal Prophecy. 5. The Unseen Death. 6. The Haunting Shadow. 7. The Guilty Man. 8. The Grip of Death. 9. Out of the Shadows. 10. The Atonement.

323. Jafet, der Søger sig en Fader (The Adventures of Japhet)

(Denmark—Nordisk Film Co., 1920) Serial, 15 chapters. D: Emanuel Gregers. S: Captain Frederick Marryat—"Midshipman Easy" and "Japhet in Search of His Father."

Carlo Wieth (Jafet Newland), Elisabeth Jacobsen (Fleta), Rasmus Christiansen (Tim), Harry Komdrup (Jan), Peter Nielsen (Melchoior), Carl Lauritzen (Lord Windemear), Karen Lund (Natte), Bertel Krause (Tom Robbins), Gerhard Jessen (The Stranger), Hans Egede Budtz (Major Carbonnell), Frederik Jacobsen, Ebba Buch, Knud Rassow, Ingeborg, Spangsdeldt, Aage Schmidt.

1. The Apothecary's Apprentice. 2. The Gypsy Encampment. 3. Matteo's Revenge. 4. The Mysterious Letter. 5. Japhet Finds an Uncle. 6. The Duel. 7. The Mount Castle Inn. 8. The Castle Dungeon. 9. On Board the "Diomedes." 10. The Pirate. 11. The Sea Fight. 12. Surprised by Indians. 13. The Shadow of Murder. 14. A Race with Death. 15. The Search is Ended.

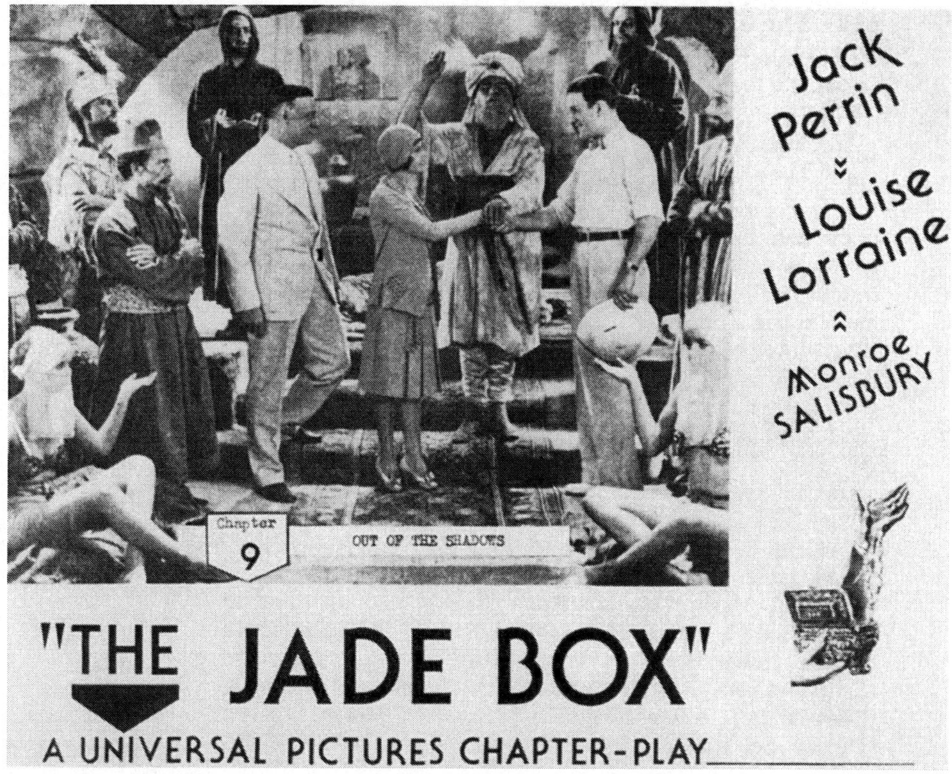

Top: **Jack Perrin, Louise Lorraine, and Monroe Salisbury;** ***bottom:*** **Jack Perrin (*behind Louise*), Louise Lorraine, and Francis Ford (*arm raised*) in *The Jade Box* (1930)**

324. The James Brothers of Missouri

(Republic, January 1950) Serial, 12 chapters, two reels each. D: Fred C. Brannon. SP: Royal Cole, William Lively, Sol Shor. Assoc. P: Franklyn Adreon. Photography: Ellis W. Carter. Music: Stanley Wilson. Special Effects: Howard and Theodore Lydecker.

Using the aliases John Howard and Bob Carroll, Jesse and Frank help Peggy Sawyer run a freight line after her brother, who was their friend, is killed by thugs employed by a rival freight line. Ace Marlin and Belle Calhoun are the leaders of the crooked element, but it is really Belle who is the brains. When Jesse and Frank survive attempts on their lives and defeat the outlaws at every turn, Marlin demands getaway money from Belle but Jesse arrives on the scene and in the process of subduing Marlin the outlaw's gun goes off and Belle is killed.

After finally bringing about the downfall of the outlaws, a grateful marshal allows Jesse and Frank to remain free, even though he knows their identity.

Keith Richards (Jesse James/John Howard), Robert Bice (Frank James/Bob Carroll), Noel Neill (Peg Royer), Roy Barcroft (Ace Marlin), Patricia Knox (Belle Calhoun), Edmund Cobb (sheriff), Lane Bradford (Monk Tucker), Gene Stutenroth (Rand), John Hamilton (Long Royer), Hank Patterson (Duffy/Waller), Dale Van Sickel (Harry Sharkey), Tom Steele (Slim/Drake), Nolan Leary (Pop Keever), Marshall Reed (Dutch), Lee Roberts (Brandy Jones), Frank O'Connor (Citizen), Wade Ray (Deputy Sheriff), Duke Green (Brad/Cowl), Ken Terrell (Stark/Trent), Tommy Coats, Robert Wilke, Ray Morgan (Townsmen), Post Parks (Wagoner), Cactus Mack (Outlaw), Al Ferguson (Outlaw), Duke Taylor (Pete/Flint), Ray Morgan (Driver), Jim Rinehart(Davis), John Crawford (Carson), Art Dillard (Blears/Townsman), Dave Sharpe (Bailey), Joe Phillips (Jackson), Bert LeBaron (Price), Ted Hubert (Ed Thorne), Ralph Bucko, Forest Burns, Helen Griffith, Rocky Shahan, Frosty Royce, Herman Hack, Chick Hannon, Chuck Roberson, Bud Wolfe.

1. Frontier Renegades. 2. Racing Peril. 3. Danger Ahead. 4. Murder at Midnight. 5. Road to Oblivion. 6. Missouri Manhunt. 7. Hangman's Noose. 8. Coffin on Wheels. 9. Dead Man's Return. 10. Galloping Gunslingers. 11. The Haunting Past. 12. Fugitive Code.

325. Jean Chouan

(France—Pathé–Cinéromans, 1925) Serial, chapters (?). D: Luitz-Morat. Scen: Arthur Bernede.

Maurice Schutz (Jean Chouan), René Navarre (Maxime Ardouin), Claude Mérelle (Marise Fleurys), Elmire Vautier (La Marquise), Marthe Chaumont (Maria Chiara), Maurice Lagrenée (Giacomo), Daniel Mendaille (Marceau), Thomy Bourdelle, Albert Decoeur, Anna Lefeuvrier, Jean-Paul de Baëre, Maurice Mariaud, Clery, Paul Amiot, Cesar Tullio Terrore, Angelo Nors.

326. "Jerry" Series

(Cub, 1916–1917) Series, 56 episodes, one reel each. D: Milton H. Fahrney (at least 38), Charles Bartlett (at least 5). SP: Milton H. Fahrney wrote most of the shorts.

Comedian George Ovey headlines these short comedies produced at the rate of 2.33 films per month.

[Numbers in parentheses indicates how many of the shorts the player was in] George Ovey (56) (Jerry), Claire Alexander (44), George George (35), Louis Fitzroy (20), Janet Sully (18), Jefferson Osborne (15), Gordon MacGregor (13), Harry Jackson (12), Arthur Mund (9), Goldie Colwell (8), C.E. Feehan (7), Tom Riley (7), Joseph Von Meter (6), Ray Lincoln (6), Helen Gilmore (6), Tom Riley (6), Louise Horner (6), Mike McCarthy (5), John Rand (5), V. Omer Whitehead (4), Harry DeRoy (4), Harry Archer (3), Abe Lincoln (3), Roy Watson (3), Arthur Jackson (3), Belle Bennett (3), Robert Kenyon (3), Bert Wilson (2), John J. Hays (2), Lincoln Stedman, Edgar Sherrod, Al Valentine, Dave Allen, Joe Hazelton, George Gebhart, H.M. Lindley, Norma Conterno, C. Eastwood, Charles Cummings, Edward Power, Margaret Cullington, Roy L. Saeger, Fernando Galvey, G.M. Morang, Al Blake, Sadie Gordon, Beulah Booker, John McCarthy, Bessie Clark, Tommy Hayes, Pearl Elmore, Harry Edmondson, J.J. Hayes, Sam Allen, Lester LeMay, Rosebud Hill, Ruby Hearst, Claire DeWitt, Joseph Hazelton, George Odell.

[Dates are release dates] 1. Jerry in the Movies (1-8-16). 2. Jerry in Mexico (1-15-16). 3. Jerry's Millions (2-19-16), 4. Jerry's Big Game (3-18-16). 5. Jerry and the Smugglers (4-1-16). 6. Jerry's Perfect Day (5-13-16). 7. Jerry's Big Lark (6-10-16). 8. Jerry and the Moonshiners (6-17-16). 9. Jerry's Elopement (6-24-16). 10. Jerry's Big Hand (7-1-16). 11. Jerry's Stratagem (7-22-16). 12. Jerry's Celebration (8-12-16). 13. Jerry and the Counterfeiters (8-19-16). 14. Jerry and the Bandits (9-2-16). 15. Jerry and the Blackhanders (9-16-16). 16. Jerry's Double Header (11-25-16). 17. Jerry's Winning Way (12-2-16). 18. Jerry' Big Doings (12-9-16). 19. Jerry and the Outlaws (1-27-17). 20. Jerry and His Pals (2-3-17). 21. Jerry's Big Raid (2-10-17). 22. Jerry's Big Mystery (2-17-17). 23. Jerry's Brilliant Scheme (2-24-17). 24. Jerry's Romance (3-3-17). 25. Jerry's Triple Alliance (3-17-17). 26. Jerry's Trial (5-5-17). 27. Jerry's Picnic (5-12-17). 28. Jerry's Finishing Touch (5-19-17). 29. Jerry Joins the Army (5-26-17). 30. Jerry's Master Stroke (6-2-17). 31. Jerry's Getaway (6-16-17). 32. Jerry's Red Hot Trail (6-23-17). 33. Jerry's Hopeless Tangle (6-30-17). 34. Jerry at the Waldorf (7-14-17). 35. Jerry's Gentle Nursing (7-17-17). 36. Jerry's Star Bout (7-21-17). 37. Jerry's Big Stunt (8-4-17). 38. Jerry on the Railroad (8-11-17). 39. Jerry on the Farm (8-25-17). 40. Jerry's Eugenic Marriage (9-1-17). 41. Jerry's Whirlwind Finish (9-8-17). 42. Jerry Tries Again (9-8-17). 43. Jerry's Big Deal (9-29-17). 44. Jerry in Yodel Land (10-6-17). 45. Jerry and the Bully (10-13-17). 46. Jerry's Jam (10-20-17). 47. Jerry's Soft Snap (10-27-17). 48. Jerry and the Vampire (11-10-17). 49. Jerry's Lucky Day (11-10-17). 50. Jerry's Running Fight (11-17-17). 51. Jerry's Victory (11-24-17). 52. Jerry and the Burglars (12-1-17). 53. Jerry Takes Gas (12-8-17). 54. Jerry's Boarding House (12-22-17). 55. Jerry's Double Cross (12-22-17). 56. Jerry's Best Friend (12-29-17).

327. Jesse James Rides Again

(Republic, March 21, 1947) Serial, 13 chapters, two reels each. D: Fred C. Brannon and Thomas Carr. SP: Franklyn Adreon, Basil Dickey, Jesse Duffy, and Sol Shor. Assoc. P: Mike Frankovich. Photography: John MacBurnie. Music: Mort Glickman. Special Effects: Howard and Theodore Lydecker.

Jesse James, trying to go straight, flees into Missouri where he helps the Bolton family fight off an attack by hooded raiders. Jesse and his friend Steve discover oil under Peaceful Valley and they stay around to rout the outlaws and expose the leaders.

Clayton Moore (Jesse James/John C. Howard), Linda Stirling (Ann Bolton), Roy Barcroft (Frank Lawton), John Compton (Steve), Tristram Coffin (James Clark), Tom London (Sam Bolton), Edmund Cobb (Wilkie), Holly Bane (Tim), Gene Stutenroth (Duffie), Fred Graham (Amos Hawks), LeRoy Mason (Finlay), Edward Cassidy (Grant), Dave Anderson (Sam), Eddie Parker (Flint), Tom Steele (Goff), Dale Van Sickel (Brock/Boyd/Gow/Raider), Robert Blair (Bartender), Ted Mapes (Bass), Tex Terry (Blair), Gil Perkins (Cody), Tex Palmer (Doty), Casey MacGregor (Jim Doyle), Emmett Lynn (Drunk), Duke Taylor (Gil), Monte Montague (Green), Lee Shumway (Hammond), Carey Loftin (Harlan), Loren Riebe (Haynes), Charles Morton (Farmer), Watson Downs (Farmer), Frank Marlowe (Joe), Herman Hack (Kaw), Chuck Roberson (Lafe), Carl Sepulveda (Mort), Ken Terrell (Price), Nellie Walker (Rose), Bert LeBaron, Pascale Perry (Raiders), Chester Conklin (Roy), Tommy Coats (Saloon Patron), George Chesebro (Gus Simmons), Charles King (Trent), Bud Wolfe (Stock), Tom Chatterton (Mark Tobin), Robert Riordan (Waldon), Howard Mitchell (Ward), Richard Alexander (Clem Williams), Keith Richards (Wynn), Victor Cox, Helen Griffith, Don Summers.

1. The Black Raiders. 2. Signal for Action. 3. The Stacked Deck. 4. Concealed Evidence. 5. The Corpse of Jesse James. 6. The Traitor. 7. Talk or Die. 8. Boomerang. 9. The Captured Raider. 10. The Revealing Torch. 11. The Spy. 12. Black Gold. 13. Deadline at Midnight.

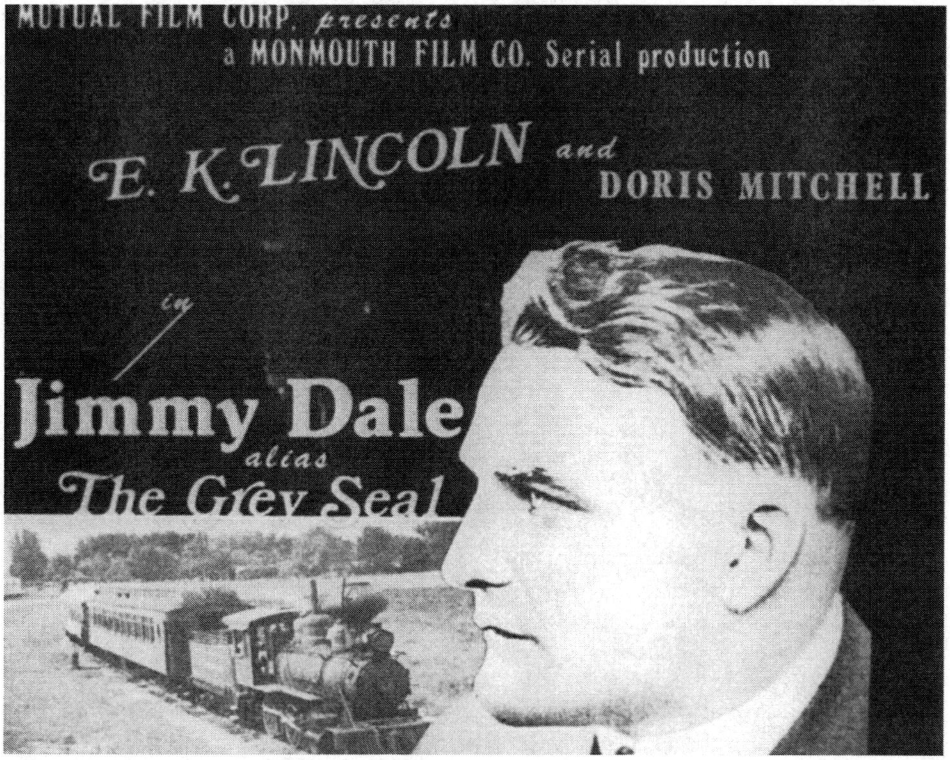

E.K. Lincoln in *Jimmy Dale Alias the Grey Seal* (1917)

328. Jimmy Dale Alias the Grey Seal

(Mutual, March 23, 1917) Serial, 16 chapters, two reels each. D: Harry Webster. S: Frank L. Packard. SP: Mildred Considine.

Socially prominent Jimmy Dale uses three aliases to fight crime: "The Grey Seal" (a safecracker), "Larry the Bat" (underworld figure), and "Smarlinghue" (a second-rate artist). Aided by a woman of mystery, Dale commits crimes to correct wrongs.

Elmo K. Lincoln (Jimmy Dale), Edna Hunter (Marie La Sale), Doris Mitchell (The Woman in Black), Paul Panzer (Henry La Sale), Leslie King, Louis Haine, George Pauncefort, Austin Webb, Jules Ferrer, William H. Turner.

1. The Grey Seal. 2. The Stolen Rubies. 3. The Counterfeit Five. 4. The Metzer Murder Mystery. 5. A Fight for Honor. 6. Below the Deadline. 7. The Devil's Work. 8. The Underdog. 9. The Alibi. 10. Two Crooks and a Knave. 11. A Rogue's Defeat. 12. The Man Higher Up. 13. Good for Evil. 14. A Sheep Among Wolves. 15. The Tapped Wires. 16. The Victory.

329. Judex

(France—Gaumont, 1916) Serial, 12 chapters. D: Louis Feuillade. SP: Arthur Bernede and Louis Feuillade. S: Arthur Bernede.

René Cresté (Henri de Tremeuse [Judex]), Mlle. Musidora (Diana Monti), Yvette Andreyor (Jacqueline Favraux), Marcel Levesque (Cocantin), Bout-de-Zan (Le Môme Réglisse), Louis Leubas (Le banquier Favraux), Edouard Mathe (Roger de Tremeuse), Georges Plateau (Vte. De la Rochefontaine), Gaston Michel (Le vieux Kerjean), Jean Devalde (Moralès), Yvonne Dario (Comtesse de Tremeuse), Olinda Mano (Le petit Jean), Juliette Clarens (Gisèle).

French: 1. L'ombre mystérieuse. 2. L'Expiation. 3. La meute fantastique. 4. Le secret de la tombe. 5. Le moulin tragique. 6. Le môme réglisse. 7. La femme en noir. 8. Les souterrains du chateau rouge. 9. Lorsque l'enfant paru. 10. Le coeur de Jacqueline. 11. L'ondine. 12. Le pardon d'amour. *Portuguese:* 1. A sombra misteriosa. 2. A expiacão. 3. A matilha fantástica. 4. O segredo do túmulo. 5. O moinho trágico. 6. O pequeno Réglisse. 7. A mulher de preto. 8. Os subterraneos do Chateau-Rouge. 9. Assim que o filho apareceu. 10. O segredo de Jacqueline. 11. Ondina e … sereia. 12. O perdão de amor. *English:* 1. The Mysterious Shadow. 2. Expiation. 3. The Fanciful Pack. 4. The Empty Coffin. 5. The Tragic Mill. 6. The Licorice Kid. 7. The Lady in Black. 8. The Cellars of the Red Castle. 9. When the Child Appeared. 10. Jacqueline's Love. 11. The Genius of Water. 12. Forgiveness.

330. Le Juif Errant

(France—Société des Cinéromans, 1926) Serial, 5 chapters. D: Luitz-Morat. S: Eugene Sue. SP: Prosper Dinaux. P: Les Films de France.

Gabriel Gabrio, Claude Merelle, Maurice Schutz, Andre Marnay, Jeanne Helbling, Antonin Artaud, Sylvio De Pedrelli, Suzanne Delmas, Jean Devalde, Louis Allibert, Adolphe Cande, Fernand Mailly, Georges Bernier, Suzanne Hiss, Fournez Goffart.

1. Les ardents. 2. Monsieur rodin. 3. Carnaval. 4. Le 13 février. 5. Le justicier.

Top: **Phyllis Coates in *Jungle Drums of Africa* (1953); *bottom:* Frances Gifford and Eddie Acuff in *Jungle Girl* (1941)**

331. Jungle Drums of Africa

(Republic, 1953) Serial, 12 chapters, two reels each. D: Fred C. Brannon. SP: Ronald Davidson. Assoc. P: Franklyn Adreon. Unit Manager: Roy Wade. Photography: John MacBurnie. Art Director: Fred A. Ritter. Film Editors: Cliff Bell and Joe Harrison. Assist. D: A.J. Vitarelli. Sound: T.A. Carman. Special Effects: Howard and Theodore Lydecker. Makeup: Bob Mark. TV Title: *U-238 and the Witch Doctor*. Music: Stanley Wilson.

Alan King and his assistant, Bert Hadley, arrive in Africa to develop uranium mining properties on the tribal lands of Chief Douanga. Alan meets Regas who offers to take the boys to the Chief's village. Regas sabotages their jeep. Menaced by animals and attacked by natives led by the Witch Doctor, acting under Regas' orders, Alan and Bert are rescued by Carol Bryant, whose late father was a missionary with Douanga's tribe.

Alan and Bert go to Kurgan's Trading Post to arrange for transportation. We learn that Kurgan is a foreign agent trying to prevent Alan's company from securing the uranium concessions, aided by his assistant, Gauss, Regas and the Witch Doctor. Alan, Bert, and Carol are endangered many times but always manage to escape death. In the end Kurgan and Gauss die in quicksand and the Witch Doctor and natives are defeated, and Regas is killed by dynamite.

Clayton Moore (Alan King), Phyllis Coates (Carol Bryant), Johnny Spencer (Bert), Roy Glenn (Naganto), John Cason (Regas), Henry Rowland (Kurgan), Steve Mitchell (Gauss), Bill Walker (Chief Douanga), Don Blackman (Ebola), Felix Nelson (Nodala), Joel Fluellen (Matambo), Bill Washington (Tembo), Tom Steele (Constable), Roy Engel (Constable), Robert Davis (Native), Bob Johnson (Native), DeForest Covan, Walter Smith, Maxie Thrower, Joe Yrigoyen.

1. Jungle Ambush. 2. Savage Strategy. 3. The Beast-Fiend. 4. Voodoo Vengeance. 5. The Lion Pit. 6. Underground Tornado. 7. Cavern of Doom. 8. The Water Trap. 9. Trail to Destruction. 10. The Flaming Ring. 11. Bridge of Death. 12. The Avenging River.

332. Jungle Girl

(Republic, June 1941) Serial, 15 chapters, two reels each. D: William Witney and John English. SP: Ronald Davidson, Norman S. Hall, William Lively, Joseph O'Donnell, Joseph F. Poland, and Alfred Batson. Based on Edgar Rice Burroughs' *Jungle Girl*. Assoc. P: Hiram S. Brown, Jr. Photography: Reggie Lanning. Music: Cy Feuer.

Dr. Meredith, friend of a savage tribe, brings up his daughter, Nyoka, in the jungles of Africa, a la Tarzan. His twin brother learns that he has access to a hoard of diamonds and is determined to acquire them. He has Dr. Meredith murdered and enters into an alliance with the village witch doctor. Jack Stanton and Curly Rogers, American pilots, come to the aid of Nyoka and a young native boy, Kimbu, and the four eventually defeat the jungle criminals, both whites and blacks.

Frances Gifford (Nyoka Meredith), Tom Neal (Jack Stanton), Trevor Bardette (John Meredith/Bradley Meredith), Gerald Mohr (Slick Latimer), Eddie Acuff (Curly Rogers), Frank Lackteen (Shamba), Tommy Cook (Kimbu), Robert Barron (Bombo), Bud Geary (Brock), Al Kikume (Lutembi), Al Taylor (Claggett), Joe McGuinn (Ted Bone), Jerry Frank (Lion Chief), Ken Terrell (Mananga), Yakima Canutt, David Sharpe, Duke Green, Harry Smith, Tom Steele, Duke Taylor, Helen Thurston (Doubles).

1. Death by Voodoo. 2. Queen of Beasts. 3. River of Fire. 4. Treachery. 5. Jungle Vengeance. 6. Tribal Fury. 7. The Poison Dart. 8. Man Trap. 9. Treasure Tomb. 10. Jungle Killer. 11. Dangerous Secret. 12. Trapped. 13. Ambush. 14. Diamond Trail. 15. Flight to Freedom.

Elinor Field in *The Jungle Goddess (1922)*

333. The Jungle Goddess

(Export-Import Film Co., May 15, 1922) Serial, 15 chapters; Chapter 1, three reels; others, two reels. D: James Conway. Scen: Frank Dazey and Agnes Johnston. P: William N. Selig. Reissued in 1929. Most of the action footage from this serial was used in the 1935 serial *Queen of the Jungle*. Lafe McKee repeated his original role for matching up purposes.

In a balloon disaster a little girl falls from the sky and is considered by the natives to be a goddess. She is actually Betty Castleton, the daughter of an English lord. Many years after the mishap, her childhood playmate, Ralph Deane, goes to Africa to look for her, and the two, once reunited, experience innumerable hair-raising adventures before reaching civilization. The serial was produced on a rather lavish scale and contained many elaborate sets and wild animals.

Elinor Field (Lady Betty Castleton), Truman Van Dyke (Ralph Deane), Marie Pavis (Betty's Mother), L.M. Wells (Dr. James Scranton), Lafe McKee (Chief Obar Sen), Vonda Phelps (The Girl), Olin Francis, William Platt, H.G. Wells, George Reed.

1. Sacrificed to the Lions. 2. The City of Blind Waters. 3. Saved by the Great Ape. 4. The Hell Ship. 5. Wild Beasts in Command. 6. Sky High with a Leopard. 7. The Rajah's Revenge. 8. The Alligator's Victim. 9. At Grips with Death. 10. The Leopard Woman. 11. Soul of Buddha. 12. Jaws of Death. 13. Cave of Beasts. 14. Jungle Terrors. 15. The Mad Lion.

334. Jungle Jim

(Universal, January 18, 1937) Serial, 12 chapters, two reels each. D: Ford Beebe and Cliff Smith. SP: Wyndham Gittens, Norman S. Hall, Ray Trampe. Based on the comic strip by Alex Raymond. Assoc. P: Henry McRae.

Two safaris travel into the African jungles in search of a white girl raised there who has inherited a fortune in America. One expedition is headed by Jungle Jim; the other, by Bruce Redmond, who wants the white girl killed so that the inheritance can become his. Acting independently of Redmond is The Cobra, an escaped convict who has found refuge with the natives and poses as a friend of Joan, the white girl. His safety depends on her power over the natives, and he is willing to do anything short of murder to keep her in the jungle.

Grant Withers (Jungle Jim Bradley), Betty Jane Rhodes (Joan), Raymond Hatton (Malay Mike), Henry Brandon (The Cobra), Evelyn Brent (Shanghai Lil), Bryant Washburn (Bruce Redmond), Selmer Jackson (Tyler), Al Bridge (Slade), Paul Sutton (La Bat), Al Duvall (Kolu), William Royle (Hawks).

1. Into the Lion's Den. 2. The Cobra Strikes. 3. The Menacing Herd. 4. The Killer's Trail. 5. The Bridge of Terror. 6. Drums of Doom. 7. The Earth Trembles. 8. The Killer Lion. 9. The Devil Bird. 10. Descending Doom. 11. In the Cobra's Coils. 12. The Last Safari.

335. Jungle Menace

(Columbia, August 1937) Serial, 15 chapters; Chapter 1, three reels; others, two reels. D: George Melford and Harry Fraser. S: George M. Merrick, Arthur Hoerl, Dallas Fitzgerald and Gordon Griffith. SP: George Rosener, Sherman L. Lowe, Harry Hoyt [Harry Frase], and George

Top: **Frank Buck and Charlotte Henry in *Jungle Menace* (1937);** ***bottom:*** **Tom Tyler, Cecilia Parker, William Desmond, Frank Lackteen, and Noah Beery, Jr., in *The Jungle Mystery* (1932)**

Melford. P: Jack Fier and Louis Weiss. Photography: Edward Linden and Herman Schopp. Music: Abe Meyer. Also released in feature format.

A murderous gang attempts to acquire a rubber plantation in Asia through murder and sabotage. Adventurer Frank Hardy vows to find out who is behind the plot and why, and is especially determined when his plantation owner friend is killed and the man's daughter endangered. Adding to the mysterious events is a powerful stalking Tiger Man.

Frank Buck (Frank Hardy), Esther Ralston (Valerie Shields), John St. Polis (Edward Elliott), Reginald Denny (Tom Marshall), Charlotte Henry (Dorothy Elliott), Sash Siemel (Tiger Man), William Bakewell (Tom Banning), Clarence Muse (Lightning), Willie Fung (Chiang), LeRoy Mason (Jim Murphy), Matthew Betz (Starrett), Richard Tucker (Robert Banning), Duncan Renaldo (Rogers), Fred Kohler, Jr. (Quinn), Sherwood Bailey (Paul Marshall), Gertrude Sutton (Mrs. Maitland), George Rosener (Professor), John Davidson (Dr. Coleman), Milburn Moranti (Singapore Joe), Dirk Thane (Nolan), Robert Warwick (McLeod), Snub Pollard (Campbell), Merrill McCormick (Peters), Roger Williams (Williams), Robert Walker (Captain Lee), Lightning [a dog] (Himself), Willy Castello, Harry Harvey, Earle Douglas, Tom London, Henry Hale, Richard Alexander, Blackie Whiteford, Jack Ingram, Jim Corey, Richard Goddard.

1. River Pirates. 2. Deadly Enemies. 3. Flames of Hate. 4. One-Way Ride. 5. Man of Mystery. 6. Shanghaied. 7. Tiger Eyes. 8. The Frame-Up. 9. The Cave of Mystery. 10. Flirting with Death. 11. Ship of Doom. 12. Mystery Island. 13. The Typhoon. 14. Murder at Sea. 15. Give 'Em Rope.

336. The Jungle Mystery

(Universal, September 12, 1932) Serial, 12 chapters, two reels each. D: Ray Taylor. SP: George Plympton, Basil Dickey, and George Mason. S: Talbot Mundy—"The Ivory Trail." Assoc. P: Henry McRae. Adaptation: Ella O'Neill. Camera: John Hickson.

Competing expeditions vie for 1,000,000 tusks of buried ivory hidden in Africa by a slave trader, long dead. The ivory is not the main concern of the Morgan party. The young Morgan boy is somewhere in the jungle and his sister and father are joined by two American hunters in an attempt to find him. Fearing that the Morgans will find the ivory first, the Shillow expedition tries to discourage the Morgans, even attempting murder. A strange jungle-creature, an ape-like man, comes to the aid of the Morgan party.

Tom Tyler (Kirk Montgomery), Cecilia Parker (Barbara Morgan), William Desmond (Mr. Morgan), Philo McCullough (Shillow), Noah Beery, Jr. (Fred Oakes), Carmelita Geraghty (Belle Waldron), Sam Baker (Zungu), James Marcus (Boris Shillow), Frank Lackteen (Kazimoto), Peggy Watts (Azu), Anders Van Haden (Comrade Krotsky), Beulah Hutton.

1. Into the Dark Continent. 2. The Ivory Trail. 3. The Death Scream. 4. Poisoned Fangs. 5. The Mystery Cavern. 6. Daylight Doom. 7. The Jaws of Death. 8. Trapped by the Enemy. 9. The Jungle Terror. 10. Ambushed. 11. The Lion's Prey. 12. Buried Treasure.

337. Jungle Pictures

(Chesterfield, 1926) Series, 6 episodes, two reels each. P: William Selig. D: Paul Hurst.

Hedda Nova adequately sustains the part of the woman lead in all these pictures, and she is ably supported; however, it is the highly trained animals from the Selig Zoo that provide the thrills in each film.

For example, *The Lion's Mate* depicts a missionary and his daughter captured by slave traders in the Malayan jungle and rescued eventually through the instrumentality of an ape whom the girl has befriended.

The Were Tiger is a tale of unscrupulous employees of a gold mine, who attempt to decamp with the precious burden they are carrying to the coast, only to be foiled eventually by a girl with whom they have been traveling. She, making her way to a native village, is believed by superstitious tribesmen to be a woman who is at times transformed into a man-eating tiger (disregarding the fact that tigers live in Asia, not Africa). She takes refuge in a cave, not knowing it to be the home of the tiger in question. The beast is frightened by the storm, but by soothing words she reassures it, and they remain together in the cave, where the renegade employees find them. She is rescued, however, in the nick of time by a rubber planter from a neighboring village.

A Jungle Heroine shows the vicissitudes of the wife of a planter on an Eastern compound, who excites the desire of her husband's foreman. By a ruse he gets the husband out of his way, but finding himself rebuffed by the wife, plans his revenge by leaving the wife and child to the mercy of the jungle beasts. Fortunately, both are rescued by an intelligent elephant, while the foreman makes a meal for a jungle tiger.

Hedda Nova, Philo McCullough, Mitchell Lewis.

1. The Lion's Mate. 2. The Were Tiger. 3. A Jungle Heroine. 4. The Last Man. 5. A Jungle Tragedy. 6. Beasts of the Veldt.

338. The Jungle Queen

(Universal, January 1945) Serial, 13 chapters, two reels each. D: Ray Taylor and Lewis D. Collins. SP: George H. Plympton, Ande Lamb, and Morgan B. Cox. Exec. P: Ben Pivar. Assoc. P: Morgan B. Cox and Ray Taylor. Assist. D: Ralph Slosser. Photography: William Sickner.

The Nazi High Command sends agents into the African jungle to stir up the Tongghill tribes against the Allies, but they must reckon with Lothel, the mysterious Queen of the Jungle, who can walk through walls of fire. In times of peril she comes to the aid of three Americans who also oppose the Nazis and their leader, a doctor posing as a friendly scientist.

Edward Norris (Bob Elliott), Lois Collier (Pamela Courtney), Eddie Quillan (Chuck Kelly), Douglas Dumbrille (Lang), Ruth Roman (Lothel), Tala Birell (Dr. Elise Bork), Clarence Muse (Kyba), Napolean Simpson (Maati), Cy Kendall (Tambosa Tim), Clinton Rosemond (Godac), Lumsden Hare (Mr. X), Lester Mathews (Branam Chatterton), Budd Buster (Jungle Jack), Emmett Smith (Noma), Jim Basquette (Orbon), Crane Whitley (Henchman), George Eldredge (Muller), Edmund Cobb (Johann), Cyril Delevanti (Rogers), John Merton (Scholank).

Douglas Dumbrille in *The Jungle Queen* (1948)

1. Invitation to Danger. 2. Jungle Sacrifice. 3. The Flaming Mountain. 4. Wildcat Stampede. 5. The Burning Jungle. 6. Danger Ship. 7. Tri-Wire Murder. 8. The Mortar Bomb. 9. Death Watch. 10. Execution Chamber. 11. The Trail to Doom. 12. Dragged Under. 13. The Secret of the Sword.

339. Jungle Raiders

(Columbia, September 1945) Serial, 15 chapters, two reels each. D: Lesley Selander. SP: Ande Lamb and George H. Plympton. P: Sam Katzman. Photography: Ira H. Morgan. Music: Lee Zahler.

The hero and heroine search for their fathers in the African jungles. Jake Regan, owner of a trading post, following up on rumors of a gigantic Arzec treasure, kidnaps Dr. Reed, one of the parents, hoping to extract information about the treasure from him. When Bob Moore and Ann Reed show up, the villain tries to liquidate them. Meanwhile Dr. Moore, Bob's father, has aroused the enmity of Zara, Priestess of the hidden village, after curing the chief of a malady. Zara aligns herself with Regan. After surviving a number of attempts on their lives Bob and Ann find their fathers and the bad guys fall victims to one of their own traps.

Kane Richmond (Bob Moore), Eddie Quillan (Joe), Veda Ann Borg (Cora), Carol Hughes (Zara), Janet Shaw (Ann Reed), John Elliott (Dr. Moore), Jack Ingram (Tom), Charles King (Jake), Ernie Adams (Charlie), I. Stanford Jolley (Brent), Kermit Maynard (Cragg), Budd Buster (Dr. Reed), George Turner (Carter), Nick Thompson (The Chief), Jimmy Aubrey (Mark), Ted Adams, P.J. Kelly, Alfredo Dess, Jack Gordon.

1. Mystery of the Lost Tribe. 2. Primitive Sacrifice. 3. Prisoners of Fate. 4. Valley of Destruction. 5. Perilous Mission. 6. Into the Valley of Fire. 7. Devil's Brew. 8. The Dagger Pit. 9. Jungle Jeopardy. 10. Prisoners of Peril.

Top: **Kane Richmond and Eddie Quillan in** ***Jungle Raiders*** **(1947);** ***bottom:*** **Kenneth Howell and Billy Halop (*center*) in** ***Junior G-Men*** **(940)**

11. Vengeance of Zara. 12. The Key to Arzac. 13. Witch Doctor's Treachery. 14. The Judgment of Rama. 15. The Jewels of Arzac.

340. Junior G-Men

(Universal, 1940) Serial, 12 chapters, two reels each. D: Ford Beebe and John Rawlins. SP: George H. Plympton, Basil Dickey, and Rex Taylor. Assoc. P: Henry MacRae. Photography: Jerome Ash. Dialogue Director: Jacques Jaccard.

A group of youngsters must cope with a subversive gang known as The Order of the Flaming Torch when the father of one of the boys is kidnapped.

Billy Halop (Billy Barton), Huntz Hall (Gyp), Gabriel Dell (Terry), Bernard Punsley (Lug), Philip Terry (Jim Bradford), Roger Daniels (Midge), Kenneth Lundy (Buck), Harris Berger (Boy), Russell Hicks (Colonel Barton), Cy Kendall (Brand), Kenneth Howell (Harry Trent), Tom London, William Desmond, Lane Chandler, Dick Rush (Policemen), Ethan Laidlaw (Watchman), Kenneth Harlan (Airport Guard), William Hall (Federal Agent), Dave Sharpe (Halop's Double), Ben Taggart (Heavy), Victor Zimmerman, Florence Halop, Gene Rizzi, Edgar Edwards, Ralph Peters, Al K. Hall.

1. Enemies Within. 2. The Blast of Doom. 3. Human Dynamite. 4. Blazing Danger. 5. Trapped by Traitors. 6. Traitor's Treachery. 7. Flaming Death. 8. Hurled Through Space. 9. The Plunge of Peril. 10. The Toll of Treason. 11. Descending Doom. 12. The Power of Patriotism.

341. Junior G-Men of the Air

(Universal, May 1942) Serial, 12 chapters, two reels each. D: Ray Taylor and Lewis D. Collins. SP: Paul Huston, George H. Plympton, and Griffin Jay. Assoc. P: Henry MacRae. Additional Dialogue: Brenda Weisberg.

Assisting Jerry Markham of the FBI, Ace Holden and his buddies "Bolts" Larson, "Stick" Munsey, and "Greaseball" Plunkett oppose a Japanese spy ring known as The Black Dragonflies when the ring attempts to steal the plans for a new airplane muffler invented by Ace's brother Eddie. Heading the Japanese organization is The Baron, who has his headquarters in a camouflaged place a few miles from the city. His instructions are to destroy anything vital to the Allied war effort. After a number of harrowing experiences the sabotage ring is brought to justice. Ace and Jerry personally capture The Baron.

Billy Halop ("Ace" Holden), Gene Reynolds (Eddie Holden), Lionel Atwill (The Baron), Frank Albertson (Jerry Markham), Richard Lane (Don Ames), Huntz Hall ("Bolts" Larson), Gabriel Dell ("Stick" Munsey), Bernard Punsley ("Greaseball" Plunkett), Frankie Darro (Jack), Turhan Bey (Araka), John Bleifer (Beal), Noel Cravat (Monk), Edward Foster (Comora), John Bagni (Augar), Billy Benedict (Blackie), Paul Phillips (Dick Parson), David Gorcey (Double Face Barker), Eddy Waller (Jed), Paul Bryar (Oriental Chemist), Fred Burton (Colonel), Jack Arnold (Flyer), Mel Ruick (Official), Jay Novello (Dogara), Angelo Cruz (Ito), Lynton Brent (Sergeant), Pat O'Malley (Conductor), Guy Kingsford (Soldier), Win Wright (Soldier), Jimmy O'Gatty (Alien Jap American), Hugh Prosser (Lieutenant, State Guard), William Desmond (Customer), Rolland Morris (Customer), Guy Usher (Senator), George Sherwood (Instructor), Ken Lundy (Newsboy), Ben Wright (Corporal), Heenan Elliott (Watchman), Bert Freeman (Scientist), Dick Thomas (Patrolman), Rico de Montez (Jap Clerk), Bill Hunter (Policeman), Bill Moss (Policeman).

1. Wings Aflame. 2. The Plunge of Peril. 3. Hidden Danger. 4. The Tunnel of Terror. 5. The Black Dragon Strikes. 6. Flaming Havoc. 7. The Death Mist. 8. Satan Fires the Fuse. 9. Satanic Sabotage. 10. Trapped in a Blazing Chute. 11. Undeclared War. 12. Civilian Courage.

342. La Justicière

(France, 1925) Serial, chapters (?). D: Maurice de Marsan and Maurice Gleize. Scen: Jean Cassagne.

René Navarre, Elmire Vautier, Albert Prejean, Viguier, Albert Combes, Colette Darfeuil, Max Berty, Marianne Lauf.

343. Katzenjammer Kids

(Selig, May–June, 1912) Series, 8 episodes, one-half reel each. Based on the long-running comic strip.

Guy Mohler (Hans) [Midget], Emil Nuchberg (Fritz) [Midget], Other players appearing in one or more episodes: Chauncey B. Herbert (The Captain), Lillian Leighton (Mrs. Katzenjammer), John Lancaster (Uncle Heine).

1. The Katzenjammer Kids. 2. The Katzenjammer Kids: They Go Tobogganing. 3. The Katzenjammer Kids: They Plan a Trip to Germany. 4. The Katzenjammer Kids: They Entertain Company. 5. The Katzenjammer Kids: They Go to School. 6. The Katzenjammer Kids: The School Days. 7. The Katzenjammer Kids: Unwilling Scholars. 8. The Katzenjammer Kids: The Arrival of Cousin Otto.

344. The Katzenjammer Kids

(International Film Service, 1917) Series, 15 episodes [length unknown].

This series was made five years later than the first series and by a different studio. Names of actors or technical credits unknown. Titles are listed alphabetically; films not necessarily released in this order.

1. By the Sad Sea Waves. 2. Der Captain Discovers the North Pole. 3. Der Captain Goes A-Flivvering. 4. Der Captain is Examined for Insurance. 5. Der Captain's Valet. 6. Der End of Der Limit. 7. Der Great Bear Hunt. 8. Der Last Straw. 9. Down Where the Limburger Blows. 10. Fat and Furious. 11. Mysterious Yarn. 12. Robbers and Thieves. 13. Sharks Is Sharks. 14. Tempest in a Paint Pot. 15. 20,000 Legs Under the Sea.

345. King of the Carnival

(Republic, June 1955) Serial, 12 chapters, two reels each. D: Franklyn Adreon. SP: Ronald Davidson. Assoc. P: Franklyn Adreon. Photography: Bud Thackery. Music: R. Dale Butts. Special Effects: Howard and Theodore Lydecker. This was the last Republic Serial.

A counterfeit ring operates a printing press set up in the watertight cabin of a submerged wreck. In the same vicinity Bert King and June Edwards work as high wire acrobats in a carnival. Suspecting that carnival personnel may be involved in the counterfeiting operation, the Treasury Department enlists the help of Bert and June in breaking up the ring, which is secretly led by circus ringmaster Carter.

Harry Lauter (Bert King), Fran Bennett (June Edwards),

Harry Lauter in *King of the Carnival* (1955)

Keith Richards (Daley), Robert Shayne (Jess Carter), Rick Vallin (Art Kerr), Gregory Gay (Zorn), Robert Clarke (Jim Hayes), Terry Frost (Travis), Mauritz Hugo (Sam), Lee Roberts (Hank), Chris Mitchell (Bill), Stuart Whitman (Mac), Tom Steele (Matt Winston), George DeNormand (Garth), Richard Alexander, Brick Sullivan, Ray Spiker (Tent Workers), Guy Teague (Watchman), Jean Harvey (Screaming Woman), Bill Scully (Burton), Tom McDonough (Hal), Harry Hollins (Mike), Bert LeBaron (Tent Rigger), Eddie Parker (Tent Rigger), Dorothy Andre, Godfrey Wainwright, Duke Taylor, John Cason.

1. Daredevils of the Air. 2. Death Takes the Wheel. 3. The Trap that Failed. 4. Operation Murder. 5. The Mechanical Bloodhound. 6. Undersea Peril. 7. High Hazard. 8. Death Alley. 9. Cave of Doom. 10. The Masked Executioner. 11. Undersea Warfare. 12. Vengeance Under the Big Top.

346. King of the Circus

(Universal, 1920) Serial, 18 chapters, two reels each. D: J.P. McGowan. SP: Anthony W. Goldeway.

Eddie King is a circus performer in a tent show owned by James Gray. The latter is a cold-hearted individual, who has an instinctive fear of apes. Mary Warren, who works with Eddie in the feature attraction was adopted by Gray from an orphanage, but the girl seems to distrust him. An old half-witted fellow named John Winters receives an injury which suddenly restores his lost memory. He informs Eddie King, whose father had originally owned the circus that James Gray had tricked his sire out of the ownership and was responsible for the elder King's death.

Eddie, determined to bring about a solution to the mystery soon finds himself in a series of clashes with Gray and his hirelings. Early in the story Eddie has an automobile accident while conveying John Winters to a hospital. This accident brings about his acquaintance with Helen Howard, the daughter of a noted physician and philanthropist, who plays an important part in the story from that point on.

The film has the fine lure of the big tops, with elephants, camels, horses and all the glitter of a real circus in evidence. The glimpses of circus life had a special appeal for children.

Eddie Polo (Eddie King), Corrine Porter (Helen Howard), Kittoria Beveridge (Mary Warren), Henry Madison (James Gray), Charles Fortune (John Winters), J.P. McGowan. J.J. Bryson, Dorothy Hagan, Viola Tasma, Tom London, Jay Marchant, Frank Shaw, Bruce Randall, Jack Lewton.

1. Blood Money. 2. The Mushroom Bullet. 3. Stolen Evidence. 4. Facing Death. 5. The Black Wallet. 6. The Lion's Claws. 7. Over the City. 8. Treachery. 9. Dynamite. 10. The Mystic Power. 11. Man and Beast. 12. Deep Waters. 13. A Fight for Life. 14. Out of the Clouds. 15. The Woman in Black. 16. The Cradle of Death. 17. The Final Reckoning. 18. The Lost Heritage.

347. King of the Congo

(Columbia, January 1952) Serial, 15 chapters, two reels each. D: Spencer G. Bennet and Wallace A. Grissell. SP: George H. Plympton, Royal K. Cole, and Arthur Hoerl. P: Sam Katzman. Assis. D: Charles S. Gould. Photography: William Whitley. Music: Mischa Bakaleinikoff. Film Editor: Earl Turner. Based on *Thunda* comic magazine, drawn by Frank Frazetta.

Larry "Buster" Crabbe in *King of the Congo* (1952)

Thunda, King of the Congo, alias Captain Roger Drum of the U.S. Air Force, plays a dangerous game of double agent in the African jungles. A subversive group headed by Boris is attempting to locate a mineral deposit that is more radioactive than uranium. For a time Boris believes Drum to be one of his own men, while the Rock People, under Queen Pha, consider him a traitor to their cause. But when his true identity is discovered, he teams up again with Pha to defeat the subversives and to establish a friendship between the Rock People and the Cave Men, who had been fighting against both sides. *King of the Congo* was the last serial to be made featuring an imitation Tarzan. It was also Crabbe's last serial.

Buster Crabbe (Thunda/Roger Drum), Gloria Dea (Pha), Leonard Penn (Boris), Jack Ingram (Clark), Rusty Wescoatt (Kor), Nick Stuart (Degar), Rick Vallin (Andreov), Neyle Morrow (Nahee), Bart Davidson (Alexis), Alex Montoya (Lipah), Bernie Gozier (Zahila), William Fawcett (High Priest), Lee Roberts (Blake), Frank Ellis (Ivan).

1. Mission of Menace. 2. Red Shadows in the Jungle. 3. Into the Valley of Mist. 4. Thunda Meets His Match. 5. Thunda Turns the Tables. 6. Thunda's

Desperate Chance. 7. Thunda Trapped. 8. Mission of Evil. 9. Menace of the Magnetic Rocks. 10. Lair of the Leopard. 11. An Ally from the Sky. 12. Riding Wild. 13. Red Raiders. 14. Savage Vengeance. 15. Judgment of the Jungle.

348. King of the Forest Rangers

(Republic, April 27, 1946) Serial, 12 chapters, two reels each. D: Spencer G. Bennet and Fred Brannon. SP: Albert DeMond, Basil Dickey, Jesse Duffy, Lynn Perkins. Assoc. P: Ronald Davidson. Photography: Bud Thackery. Music: Raoul Kraushaar. Special Effects: Howard and Theodore Lydecker.

A professor and his hired thugs learn where valuable radium deposits are located after murdering a man to obtain a rug on which picture writing pinpoints the location. They secretly start a campaign to secure the sights by trickery and force. Steve King of the Forest Rangers investigates the murder and is soon in a full-fledged confrontation with the thugs of Carver, who maintains his front of respectability. One of the sites Carver desires is owned by Marion Brennan, whose life thus becomes endangered. However, she and King persevere to learn the secret of the ancient prehistoric towers and save the properties for the owners.

Larry Thompson (Steve King), Helen Talbot (Marion Brennan), Stuart Hamblen (Professor Carver), Anthony Warde (Burt Spear), LeRoy Mason (Flush Haliday), Tom London (Tom Judson), Scott Elliott (Andrews/Merkle/Bryan/Sands), Walter Soderling (Miner), Robert Wilkie (Carleton), Marin Sais (Mrs. Barton), Dale Van Sickel (Hughes/Smith/Blaine), Tom Steele (Al/Wade/-Baker/Martin), Eddie Parker (Stover), Ernie Adams (Hiram Bailey), Bud Geary (Rance Barton), Harry Strang (Hank), Rex Lease (Toler), Buddy Roosevelt (Brooks), Jay Kirby (Hale), Carey Loftin (Forbes), Stanley Blystone (Harry Lynch), Ken Terrell (Naylor), Bud Wolfe (Pilot), Wheaton Chambers (Ronald Spencer), Joe Yrigoyen (Harbin), Charles Sullivan (Turner), Sailor Vincent (Graham), Sam Ash (Citizen), James Martin (Todd), David Sharpe (Stuntman).

1. The Mystery of the Towers. 2. Shattered Evidence. 3. Terror by Night. 4. Deluge of Destruction. 5. Pursuit into Peril. 6. Brink of Doom. 7. Design for Murder. 8. The Flying Coffin. 9. S.O.S. Ranger. 10. The Death Detector. 11. The Flaming Pit. 12. Tower of Vengeance.

349. King of the Jungle

(Hercules Films/Rayart, July 1927) Serial, 10 chapters, two reels each. D: Webster Cullison.

By this time Elmo Lincoln had been typecast as the apeman. This was his final serial. In it he plays a white hunter. Actor Gordon Standing was attacked and killed by a lion during production. Lincoln thought the accident could have been prevented. With his screen career on a downhill slide, Elmo retired after making this cheap serial. Years later he returned to Hollywood and became a bit player in scores of films.

Elmo Lincoln, Sally Long, Gordon Standing, George Kotsonaros, Arthur Morrison, Cliff Bowes, Virginia True Boardman.

1. A Great Tragedy. 2. The Elephant Avenger. 3. Battling for Her Life. 4. Into the Lion's Jaws. 5. The Stripped Terror. 6. Gripped by the Death Vice. 7. The Slinking Demons. 8. The Giant Ape Strikes. 9. No Escape. 10. The Death Trap.

350. King of the Kongo

(Mascot, August 9, 1929) Serial, 10 chapters, two reels each. D: Richard Thorpe. SP: Harry Sinclair Drago. P: Nat Levine. Released in two versions, silent and sound; synchronized musical score, sound effects, and some dialogue.

Secret Service agent Larry Trent and Diana Martin meet while both are searching for missing relatives in the African jungle. Larry has found a golden trinket near an old temple, and Diana's father had given her one evidently found in the same area. Returning to the temple they clash with a band of ivory thieves who are searching for hidden treasure they believe to be there.

Jacqueline Logan (Diana Martin), Walter Miller (Larry Trent), Richard Tucker (Chief of Secret Service), Larry Steers (Jack Drake), Boris Karloff (Scarface Macklin), Harry Todd (Commodore), Richard Neill (A Prisoner), Lafe McKee (Trader John), J.P. Lockney (Priest), William Bert (Mooney), Gordon Russell (Derelict), Robert Frazer (Native Chief), Ruth Davis (Poppy), Joe Bonomo (Gorilla).

1. Into the Unknown. 2. Terrors of the Jungle. 3. The Temple of Beasts. 4. Gorilla Warfare. 5. Danger in the Dark. 6. The Fight at the Lion's Pit. 7. The Fatal Moment. 8. Sentenced to Death. 9. Desperate Chances. 10. Jungle Justice.

351. King of the Mounties

(Republic, October 10, 1942) Serial, 12 chapters, two reels each. D: William Witney. SP: Taylor Caven, Ronald Davidson, William Lively, Joseph O'Donnell, and Joseph Poland.

William Bakewell in *King of the Mounties* (1942)

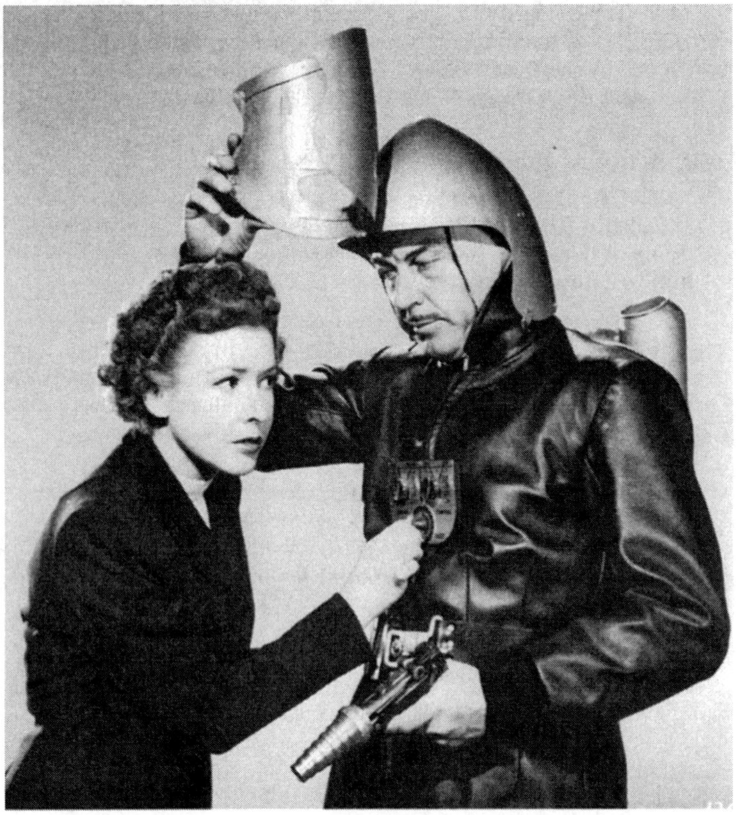

Mae Clarke and Tris Coffin in *King of the Rocket Men* (1949)

Based on Zane Grey's *King of the Royal Mounted*. Assoc. P: W.J. O'Sullivan. Photography: Bud Thackery. Music: Mort Glickman. Special Effects: Howard Lydecker.

Nazi agents in Canada are bombing key targets mercilessly with a mystery plane called The Phantom. When they are threatened with identification of the plane by a new type of plane detector invented by Professor Brent, they kidnap the professor. When Sergeant King tries to rescue him, the professor is killed. His daughter, Carol, carries on her father's work. With King's aid she keeps the Nazi agents from getting the detector, and King rescues Carol after she is captured, also managing to blow up volcano headquarters of the enemy.

Allan Lane (Dave King), Peggy Drake (Carol Brent), Gilbert Emery (Commissioner Morrison), Russell Hicks (Marshal Carleton), George Irving (Professor Brent), Abner Biberman (Admiral Yamata), William Vaughn (Marshal Von Horst), Nestor Paiva (Count Baroni), Bradley Page (Charles Blake), Douglas Dumbrille (Gil Harper), William Bakewell (Hal Ross), Duncan Renaldo (Pierre), Francis Ford (Zeke Collins), Jay Novello (Lewis), Anthony Warde (Stark), Tom Steele (Jack/Spike), Duke Taylor (Becker/Mountie/Heavy), Arvon Dale (Craig), Hal Taliaferro (Ed Johnson), Kam Tong, Sam Serrano, King Kong (Japanese Heavies), Forrest Taylor (Telegrapher), Earl Bunn (Joe), Stanley Price (McGee), Duke Green (Lookout/Ord/Spike), Tommy Coates (Mike), Bob Jamison (Pete), Jack Kenney (Plant Guard), Jimmy Fawcett, John Roy, Bud Weiser (Heavies), Carleton Young (Gus), Harry Cording (Wade Garson), Pete Katchenara (Falcon Pilot), Frank Wayne (Brant), Ken Terrell (Al), Paul Fung (Bombardier), Allen Jung (Sato), John Hiestand (Lane), Norman Nesbitt (Newscaster), David Sharpe (Double).

1. Phantom Invaders. 2. Road to Death. 3. Human Target. 4. Railroad Saboteurs. 5. Suicide Dive. 6. Blazing Barrier. 7. Perilous Plunge. 8. Electrocuted. 9. Reign of Terror. 10. The Flying Coffin. 11. Deliberate Murder. 12. On to Victory.

352. King of the Rocket Men

(Republic, June 1949) Serial, 12 chapters, two reels each. D: Fred C. Brannon. SP: Royal Cole, William Lively, Sol Shor. Assist. P: Franklyn Adreon. Photography: Ellis W. Carter. Music: Stanley Wilson. Special Effects: Howard and Theodore Lydecker. Feature Title: *Lost Planet Airmen*.

The mysterious Dr. Valcan is trying to seize control of Science Associates of which, as Professor Bryant, he is a member. The materials being developed by the organization are highly desirable to those who would make war. Jeff King, a project member, and Professor Mellard develop a rocket-propelled flying suit, which Jeff uses to thwart Valcan's attempts to seize control of various devices. Valcan is successful in stealing a decimotor and plans to use it to destroy New York unless a ransom of $1 billion is received; however, the Rocket Man, alias Jeff King, destroys the decimotor before it can penetrate a volcanic fault in the ocean's floor, and Valcan is killed as bombers drop their cargo on his island hideout.

Tristram Coffin (Jeffery King/Rocket Man), Mae Clarke (Glenda Thomas), Don Haggerty (Tony Dirken), House Peters, Jr. (Burt Winslow), James Craven (Millard), I. Stanford Jolley (Bryant/Valcan), Douglas Evans (Chairman), Ted Adams (Martin Conway), Stanley Price (Gunther Von Strum), Dale Van Sickel (Martin/Drake/Gates/Rand/Miller), David LeBaron (Morgan), Art Gilmore (Newscaster), Carey Loftin (Sparkes), Jack O'Shea (Walter), Buddy Roosevelt (Phillips), Michael Ferro (Turk), Frank O'Connor (Guard), Tom Steele (Cab Driver/Knox), Bud Wolfe (Clay), Arvon Dale (Aide).

1. Dr. Valcan Traitor. 2. Plunging Death. 3. Dangerous Evidence. 4. High Peril. 5. Fatal Dive. 6. Mystery of the Rocket Man. 7. Molten Menace. 8. Suicide Flight. 9. Ten Seconds to Live. 10. The Deadly Fog. 11. Secret of Dr. Valcan. 12. Wave of Disaster.

353. King of the Royal Mounted

(Republic, September 20, 1940) Serial, 12 chapters, two reels each. D: William Witney and John English. SP: Franklyn Adreon, Norman. S. Hall, Joseph Poland, Barney A. Sarecky, and Sol Shor. Assoc. P: Hiram S. Brown, Jr. Photography: William Nobles. Music: Cy Feuer. Released as a feature *Yukon Patrol* in 1942.

Sergeant King of the Royal Mounted is assigned to find and capture the murderer of Merritt, a Canadian who has invented a substance called Compound X, which has the power to cure infantile paralysis. A foreign power has learned that the substance has certain magnetic properties which would make their mines effective against the British fleet. Accordingly, agents are dispatched to insure a steady flow of the compound from the Caribou Mine.

Allan Lane (Sergeant Dave King), Robert Strange (John Kettler), Robert Kellard (Corporal Tom Merritt, Jr.), Lita Conway (Linda Merritt), Herbert Rawlinson (Inspector Ross King), Harry Cording (Wade Garson), Bryant Washburn (Matt Crandall), Budd Buster (Vinegar Smith), Stanley Andrews (Tom

Merritt, Sr.), John Davidson (Doctor Shelton), John Dilson (Doctor Wall), Paul McVey (Excellency Zarnoff), Lucien Prival (Admiral Johnson), Norman Willis (Tarner), Tony Paton (LeCouteau), Ken Terrell (Al), Ted Mapes (Blake), Richard Simmons (Carter), Curley Dresden (Kelly), Bud Geary (Klondike), Dale Van Sickel (Radioman), Al Taylor (Red), William Stahl (Bob Hastings), Wallace Reid, Jr. (Doyle), Loren Riebe (Dinwoodie), Charles Thomas (Bayliss), Bill Wilkus (Bill), Tommy Coats (Mike), Earl Bunn (Joe), George DeNormand (Kent), Dave Marks (Knife Heavy), John Bagni (Higgins), Major Sam Harris (Harold Bolton), George Plues (Brakeman), Frank Wayne (Brant), William Justice (Hallett), Robert Wayne (Lieutenant), William Kellogg (MacCloud), Alan Gregg (Mills), Denny Sullivan, Walter Low, George Ford, (Paralytics), Bob Jamison (Pete), Cy Slocum (Sanitarium Heavy), Douglas Evans (Sergeant), Duke Taylor, Jimmy Fawcett (Heavies), Duke Green, David Sharpe (Doubles).

1. Man Hunt. 2. Winged Death. 3. Boomerang. 4. Devil Doctor. 5. Sabotage. 6. False Ransom. 7. Death Tunes In. 8. Satan's Cauldron. 9. Espionage. 10. Blazing Guns. 11. Master Spy. 12. Code of the Mounted.

***King of the Royal Mounted* (1940)**

354. King of the Texas Rangers

(Republic, October 4, 1941) Serial, 12 chapters, two reels each. D: William Witney and John English. SP: Ronald Davidson, Norman S. Hall, William Lively, Joseph Poland, and Joseph O'Donnell. Assoc. P: Hiram S. Brown, Jr. Photography: Reggie Lanning. Music: Cy Feuer.

Saboteurs try to destroy Texas oil fields to disrupt the war effort. Sergeant Tom King, out to avenge his father's murder, combines forces with Pedro Garcia of the Mexican Rurales to hunt down the foreign agents and their American cohorts, receiving ample help and encouragement from Sally Crane, not only his sweetheart but a first-rate newspaper woman as well. The serial was marred by Baugh's poor acting but proved a popular serial anyway.

Slingin' Sammy Baugh (Tom King, Jr.), Neil Hamilton (John Barton), Pauline Moore (Sally Crane), Duncan Renaldo (Pedro Garcia), Charles Trowbridge (Robert Crawford), Herbert Rawlinson (Lee Avery), Frank Darien (Pop Evans), Robert O. Davis (His Excellency), Monte Blue (Tom King, Sr.), Stanley Blystone (A.J. Lynch), Kermit Maynard (Wichita Bates), Roy Barcroft (Ross), Kenne Duncan (Nick), Jack Ingram (Shorty), Robert Barron (Blake), Frank Bruno (Cole), Monte Montague (Dade), Joseph Forte (Nelson), Lucien Prival (Captain), Paul Gustine (Army Observer), Henry Hall (L.H. Bowen), William Kellogg (Hank Breen), Richard Simmons (Red Cameron), Alan Gregg (Carl), Iron Eyes Cody (Carlos), Forrest Taylor (Clerk), Lee Shumway (Coach), Ernest Sarracino (Cowan), Bud Geary (Cramer), Bob Jamison (Dam Guard), John James (Dave), Dick Scott (Derrick Heavy 1), Bud Wolfe (Derrick Heavy 2), Barry Hays (Dirigible Heavy 1), Earl Bunn (Dirigible Heavy 2), George Burrows (Dirigible Lieutenant 1), Pat O'Shea (Dirigible Lieutenant 2), Bert LeBaron (Dock Heavy), Jerry Jerome (Ed), Bobby Barber (Eduardo), Forest Burns (Gate Guard), Max Waizman (Gus), Charles [Slim] Whitaker (Jake), Jack Chapin (Stub Latner), Howard Hughes (Johnny Logen), Michael Owen (Ronnie Nelson), Ken Terrell (Oil Field Heavy), Hooper Atchley (Porter), Otto Reichow (Radioman), Chick Hannon (Raider 1), Herman Hack (Raider 2), Tommy Coats, Charles Thomas, Bob Robinson, Carlie Taylor (Rancho Heavies), Edward Cassidy (Sedley), Buddy Roosevelt (Sherwood), John Bagni (Slater), Eddie Dew (Thomas), George Allen (Truck Heavy 1), Jimmy Fawcett (Truck Heavy 2), Al Taylor (Dude Ward), Dick Scott, Bud Wolfe, Barry Hays, Earl Bunn (Heavies).

1. The Fifth Column Strikes. 2. Dead End. 3. Man Hunt. 4. Trapped. 5. Test Flight. 6. Double Danger. 7. Death Takes the Witness. 8. Counterfeit Trail. 9. Ambush. 10. Sky Raiders. 11. Trail of Death. 12. Code of the Rangers.

355. King of the Wild

(Mascot, March 1, 1930) Serial, 12 chapters, Chapter 1, three reels; others, two reels. D: Richard Thorpe and B. Reeves Eason. P: Nat Levine. S: Wyndham Gittens and Ford Beebe. SP: Wyndham Gittens and Ford Beebe. Camera: Bob Kline and Edward Kull. Music: Lee Zahler. Also released as feature titled *Bimi*.

***King of the Texas Rangers* (1941)**

A soldier of fortune, blamed for a murder he did not commit, escapes from India on the same ship carrying the real murderers, one of whom has a letter written in invisible ink that will clear him. The steamer is wrecked on the coast of Africa. The villains find a young man delirious with fever who babbles about a diamond field he has found. They attempt to force the secret from him, while the hero aligns himself with the young man's sister and a secret service agent to rescue the young man and also to find the villain guilty of the murder for which the hero is blamed.

Walter Miller (Robert Grant), Nora Lane (Muriel Armitage), Dorothy Christy (Mrs. LaSalle), Tom Santschi (Harris), Boris Karloff (Mustapha), Cyril MacLaglen (Bimi), Mischa Auer (Dakka), Lafe McKee (Officer), Carroll Nye (Tom Armitage), Victor Potel (Peterson), Martha LaLande (Mrs. Colby), Otto Hoffman, Albert DeWinton, Fletcher Norton, Merrill McCormick, Earle Douglas, Larry Steers, Eileen Schofield, Walter Ferdna.

1. The Tiger of Destiny. 2. Man Eaters. 3. The Avenging Horde. 4. The Secret of the Volcano. 5. The Pit of Peril 6. The Creeping Doom. 7. Sealed Lips. 8. The Jaws of the Jungle. 9. The Door of Dread. 10. The Leopard's Lair. 11. The Fire of the Gods. 12. Jungle Justice.

356. Kotetsu no Kyojin (aka Supergiant)

(Shin Toho, Japan) Series, 12 episodes, varying lengths. D: Teruo Ishii (8 ep.), Akira Miwa (1 ep.), Chogi Akasaka (2 ep.), Tetsu Taguchi (1 ep.).

Japanese Superman series. Each episode a complete story independent of the other episodes. In the Superman role Ken Utsui saves the world from flying saucers, germ warfare, synthetic monsters, aliens from other planets, etc.

Ken Utsui was in all episodes. The following players appear in 1 or more episodes: Utako Motsuya, Minako Yamada, Junko Ikeuchi, Ken Hayashi, Chisako Tawara, Reiko Seto, Terumi Hoshi, Akemi Tsukushi, Teruhisha Ikeda, Minoru Takada, Ryo Iwashita.

1. Supah Jaianto (aka The Steel Man from Outer Space) 1956, 49 min. 2. Supah Jaianto (aka Rescue from Outer Space) 1956, 52 min. 3. Kotetsu No Kyojin—Kaiseijin No Mayo (aka Devils from the Planet, Invaders from the Planet) 1957, 49 min. 4. Kotetsu No Kyojin—Chikyu Metzubo Sunzen (aka The Earth in Danger) 1957, 40 min. 5. Jinko Eisen To Jinrui No Hametsu 1958, 40 min. 6. Uchutei To Jinko Eisen No Gekitotsu (aka The Destruction of the Space Fleet) 1958, 39 min. 7. Uchu Kaijin Shutsugen (aka Spacemen Appear) 1958, 44 min. 8. Akuma No Keshiin (aka The Devil Incarnate) 1959. 9 Dokuga Okoku (aka Kingdom of the Poison Moth) 1959. 10. Araumi No Oja. 11. Gonin No Hanzaisha. 12. Jotai Sambashi (aka Red Piers).

357. Los Ladrones del Gran Mundo

(Spain—Royal Films, 1916) Serial, 5 chapters. D: Alberto Marro.

Margarita Miró, Lucila Porres, Pablo Frou De Vendrell, Julián De La Cantera, Lucie Pomar, Jose Roges, Tressols, Suárez De Figueros, Bermudez, Irma Remini, Teresa Salome.

Portuguese: 1. O tesouro do marinheiro. 2. Sonâmbula e vidente. 3. Os alvores da justiça. 4. O que custa um desejo. 5. A vitória.

358. Lady Baffles and Detective Duck

(Powers, 1915) Series, 11 episodes, one reel each. P: Henry Gale. D: Allen Curtis. S: Clarence C. Badger.

Detective Duck manages to outwit Lady Baffles, a lovable lady crook. Duck, an inventor as well as a detective, manages to invent various contraptions that enable him to solve cases and to triumph at the last moment. Each episode is complete in itself. There are no cliff-hanger endings that lead into the next episode.

Max Asher (Detective Duck), Lillian Peacock (Lady Baffles), Henry Gale, William Henry, Milburn Morante, William Franey.

1. The Great Egg Robbery. 2. The Sign of the Safety Pin. 3. The 18 Carrot Mystery. 4. Baffles Aids Cupid. 5. At the Sign of Three Cocks. 6. Saved by a Scent. 7. The Dread Society of the Sacred Sausage. 8. The Ore Mystery. 9. When the Wets Went Dry. 10. The Lost Roll. 11. Kidnapping the King's Kids.

359. Lady Harrington

(France, 1927) Serial, chapters (?). D: Fred-Leroy Granville and H.C. Grantham-Hayes. Scen: Maurice Level.

Claude France, Maurice de Feraudy, Warwick Ward, Joë Hamman, Charley Sov, Francine Mussey, Andre Dubose, J.F. Martial.

Helen Holmes in *A Lass of the Lumberlands* (1916)

360. A Lass of the Lumberlands

(Signal Film Corp./Mutual, October 23, 1916) Serial, 15 chapters, two reels each. D: J.P. McGowan and Paul C. Hurst. SP: E. Alexander Powell, Ford Beebe, and others.

Newborn Helen Holmes is raised by foster parents after her mother dies following an injury sustained when she is running away from her husband, "Dollar" Holmes, who was angered when she bore a daughter instead of a son. He subsequently marries a wealthy woman who does bear him a son, Stephen. Eighteen years later, Helen, known as Helen Dawson, saves the youth's life and they become good friends. As a result, "Dollar" Holmes gives her a job on his railroad, neither of them knowing of their relationship.

The railroad became a virtual alter ego for Helen Holmes, who thought nothing of engaging in death defying feats without a double. She became known as "Queen of the Iron Horse Dramas." At this time in her career she was riding high in popularity and her railroad serials were packing in audiences to the tune of $2,000,000 or more. As for Leo Maloney, he would become one of the silent era's most popular western stars.

Helen Holmes (Helen Holmes/Helen Dawson), Leo D. Maloney (Tom Dawson), Thomas Lingham ("Dollar" Holmes), William M. Chapman, Paul C. Hurst, Katherine Goodrich, F.L Hemphill, William Behren.

1. The Lumber Pirate. 2. The Wreck in the Fog. 3. First Blood. 4. A Deed of Daring. 5. The Burned Record. 6. The Spiked Switch. 7. The Runaway Car. 8. The Fight in Camp 1. 9. The Double Fight. 10. The Gold Rush. 11. The Ace High Loses. 12. The Main Line Wreck. 13. Unknown. 14. The Indian's Hand. 15. Retribution.

361. The Last Adventures of Sherlock Holmes

(England—Stoll Pictures, 1923) Series, 15 episodes, two reels each. D: George Ridgewell. S: Sir Arthur Conan Doyle. SP: Geoffrey H. Malins, Patrick L. Mannock.

Eille Norwood (Sherlock Holmes), Hubert Willis (Doctor Watson), Madame d'Esterre (Mrs. Hudson), Tom Beaumont (Inspector Gregory). Each of these supporting players appeared in at least one episode. Knighton Small, Sam Marsh, Norma Whalley, Bert Barclay, Lewis Gilbert, Cynthia Murtagh, Jane Graham, H. Wilson, Celia Bird, Red Raynham, Reginald Fox, Laurie Lesley, Ernest Shannon, Charles Barratt, Douglas Payne, Sebastian Smith, Gordon Hopkins, Miss Hanbury, Archer Hunter, Mary Mackintosh, Bertram Burleigh, Henry Latimer, Mercy Hatton, Ward McAllister, Nelson Ramsey, R. Van Courtland, Kate Gurney, Alec Flood, Ralph Forster, Watts Phillip, John Butt, Hilda Anthony, Eric Lugg, Maud Wulff, David Hawthorne, Evelyn Cecil, Madge Tree, Dorothy Wilkins, Cecil Morton York, William Lugg, A. Harding Steerman, Sam Austin, L. Verne, Hal Martin, Cliff Davies, Albert R. Rayner, Leigh Gabell, Jack Raymond, A.B. Imeson, Violet Graham, Noel Grahame, Harry J. Worth, Lionel d'Aragon, Laurie Leslie, Frank Goldsmith, Wallace Bosco, Dezma du May, Jack Hobbs, Gladys Jennings, Dora de Winton, Richard Lindsay, Percy Standing, P. Francis, Ray Raymond.

The third and final series of 15 films released simultaneously in March 1923. Silver Blaze (34 ½ min.). The Speckled Band (30 min.). The Gloria Scott (34 ½ min.). The Blue Carbuncle (32 min.). The Engineer's Thumb (33 ½ min.). His Last Bow (26 min.). The Cardboard Box (30 min.). The Disappearance of Lady Frances Carfax (30 ½ min.). The Three Students (41 min.). The Missing Three-Quarter (37 min.). The Mystery of Thor Bridge (35 min.). The Mazarin Stone (31 min.). The Mystery of the Dancing Men (40 min.). The Crooked Man (37 min.). The Final Problem (28 min.).

362. The Last Frontier

(RKO, September 2, 1932) Serial, 12 chapters, two reels each. D: Spencer Gordon Bennet and Thomas L. Story. SP:

Leroy Mason, Creighton Chaney [Lon Jr.], Benny Corbett, and Francis X. Bushman, Jr., in *The Last Frontier* (1932)

George Plympton and Robert F. Hill. S: Courtney Riley Cooper. Supervision: Fred J. McConnell. Producer: Van Buren Productions. [This was a serial remake of the 1926 William Boyd film, *The Last Frontier*, Metropolitan-PDC].

Because he knows where to find a great deal of gold, outlaw Tiger Morris attempts to drive settlers off their property. Newspaper editor Tom Kirby, aided by several friends, fights to see that the outlaw does not achieve his goal. Although help comes from General Custer, Wild Bill Hickok, and Colonel Halliday, it is in the disguise of The Black Ghost that Tom turns the tide for law and order.

Creighton [Lon, Jr.] Chaney (Tom Kirby), Dorothy Gulliver (Betty Halliday), Mary Jo Desmond (Aggie Kirby), Francis X. Bushman, Jr. (Jeff Maitland), Joe Bonomo (Blackie), Slim Cole (Happy), Judith Barrie (Rose Maitland), Richard Neill (Tiger Morris), William Desmond (General Custer), Leroy Mason (Buck), Yakima Canutt (Wild Bill Hickok), Pete Morrison (Hank), Benny Corbett (Jake), Claude Peyton (Colonel Halliday), Fritzi Fern (Maria Morris), Bill Nestell (Tex), Walt Robbins, Leo Cooper, Ray Steel, Frank Lackteen, Fred Burns.

1. The Black Ghost Rides. 2. The Thundering Herd. 3. The Black Ghost Strikes. 4. A Single Shot. 5. Clutching Hands. 6. The Terror Trail. 7. Doomed. 8. Facing Death. 9. Thundering Doom. 10. The Life Line. 11. Driving Danger. 12. The Black Ghost's Last Ride.

363. The Last of the Mohicans

(Mascot, May 17, 1932) Serial, 12 chapters, Chapter 1, three reels; others. two reels. D: B. Reeves Eason and Ford Beebe. SP: Colbert Clark, John Francis Natteford, Ford Beebe, and Wyndham Gittens. S: Based on James Fenimore Cooper's novel. P: Nat Levine. Photography: Ernest Miller and Jack Young. [Also released as feature film: *The Return of the Mohicans*].

In this filmed version of the famed novel, Hawkeye, his friends, and the last two surviving Mohicans, fight their mortal enemy, the treacherous Huron chief Magua.

Harry Carey (Hawkeye), Hobart Bosworth (The Sagamore), Frank Coghlan, Jr. (Uncas), Edwina Booth (Cora Munro), Lucile Browne (Alice Munro), Walter Miller (Major Duncan Hayward), Robert Kortman (Magua), Walter McGrail (Dulac), *Nelson McDowell (David Gamut), Edward Hearn (Colonel Munro), Mischa Auer (General Montcalm), Yakima Canutt (Black Fox), Chief Big Tree (Indian), Joan Gale (Red Wing), Tully Marshall (Courier), Allan Cavan (General Stanwix), High Eagle (Indian), Little Pine (Indian), White Feather (Indian), Jewel Richford. *Nelson McDowell also played David Gamut in the 1920 *Last of the Mohicans*.

1. Wild Waters. 2. Flaming Arrows. 3. Rifles or Tomahawks. 4. Riding with Death. 5. Red Shadows. 6. The Lure of Gold. 7. The Crimson Trail. 8. The Tide of Battle. 9. A Redskin's Honor. 10. The Enemy's Stronghold. 11. Paleface Magic. 12. The End of the Trail.

364. The Law of the Wild

(Mascot, September 5, 1934) Serial, 12 chapters; Chapter 1, three reels; others, two reels. D: Armand Schaefer and B. Reeves Eason. S: Ford Beebe, John Rathmall, and Al Martin. P: Nat Levine. SP: Sherman Lowe and B. Reeves Eason.

Rex, a wild horse tamed by Sheldon, a young rancher, is stolen by an employee, Salter, who wounds Sheldon in the process. Later, while searching for Rex, Sheldon meets Alice Ingram and her father, who is a racehorse owner. At the track Sheldon's horse is entered in a race and wins. In a dispute over the winnings, Salter is killed by a co-conspirator and the blame is put on Sheldon. Rex, Rinty, Sheldon, and Alice survive numerous ordeals before justice is served and horse and master reunited, with Alice riding Rex in the sweepstakes in the final showdown.

Bob Custer (Sheldon), Rex (Himself), Rin-Tin-Tin, Jr. (Rinty), Ben Turpin (Henry), Lucile Browne (Alice Ingram), Richard Cramer (Frank Nolan), Ernie Adams (Raymond), Edmund Cobb (Jim Luger), Charles Whitaker (Mack), Dick Alexander (Lou Salter), Jack Rockwell (Sheriff), George Chesebro (Parks), Wally Wales, Charles King, Lafe McKee, Hank Bell, Art Mix, Bud Osborne, Glenn Strange, Silver Harr, Al Taylor, Jack Evans, Bud McClure, Herman Hack.

1. The Man Killer! 2. The Battle of the Strong. 3. The Cross-Eyed Goony. 4. Avenging Fangs. 5. A Dead Man's Hand. 6. Horse-Thief Justice. 7. The Death Stampede. 8. The Canyon of Calamity. 9. Robbers' Roost. 10. King of the Range. 11. Winner Take All! 12. The Grand Sweepstakes.

365. The Leather Pushers

(Knickerbocker Photoplays/Universal Jewel, 1922–1924) Series, 24 episodes, two reels each. D: Harry A. Pollard. Scen: Harry A. Pollard, Harvey Thew.

Billy Sullivan.

1. Let's Go. 2. Round Two. 3. Payment Through the Nose. 4. A Fool and His Money. 5. The Taming of the Shrewd. 6. Whipsawed. 7. Young King Cole. 8. He Raised Kane. 9. Chickasha Bone Crusher. 10. When Kane Met Able. 11. Strike Father, Strike Son. 12. Joan of Newark. 13. The Wandering Two. 14. The Widower's Mite. 15. Don Coyote. 16. Something for Nothing. 17. Columbia the Gem of the Ocean. 18. Barnaby's Grudge. 19. That Kid from Madrid. 20. He Loops to Conquer. 21. Girls will be Girls. 22. A Tough Tenderfoot. 23. Swing Bad the Sailor. 24. Big Boy Blue.

366. The Leather Pushers

(Universal, 1930–31) Series, 10 episodes, two reels each. Released in both silent and talking versions. D: Albert Kelley. SP: Douglas Doty, Ralph Cedar, Harry Fraser. Continuity and Dialogue: Ralph Cedar, Harry Fraser. Supervision: Sam Freedman. P: Stanley Bergman.

Kane Richmond (Kid Roberts), Sam Hardy (Jack Rooney), Sally Blane, Jack White, Nora Lane, Joan Marsh, Tom Muskie, Jerry the Greek.

1. Kid Roberts. 2. Hammer and Tongs. 3. The Knockout. 4. The Comeback. 5. The Mardi Gras. 6. All for a Lady. 7. Framed. 8. The Lady Killer. 9. Kane Meets Abel. 10. The Champion.

367. Leatherstocking

(Pathé, March 23, 1924) Serial, 10 chapters, two reels each. D: George B. Seitz. P: C.W. Patton. Based on novels by James Fenimore Cooper.

Leatherstocking is a white man who has lived ten years with the Delaware Indians and learned their language and customs. He becomes the protector of the heroine, her weak-minded sister, and their father, who has established his family on a picturesque houseboat of logs which is floating on a lake in the Indian country. While the Delawares are friendly, the Hurons, allies of the French, are enemies.

***Top*: Bob Custer, Ben Turpin, Ernie Adams, and Richard Cramer in *The Law of the Wild* (1934); *bottom:* Edna Murphy and Harold Miller in *Leatherstocking* (1924)**

Edna Murphy (Judith Hutter), Harold Miller (Leatherstocking), Whitehorse (Tom Hutter), Frank Lackteen (Briarthorn), Ray Myers (Rivenoak), James H. Pierce (Harry March), Lillian Hall (Hetty Hutter), Aline Goodwin (Wah-Ta-Wah), David Dunbar (Chingachgook), Tom Tyler (Indian), Emily Barrye.

1. The Warpath. 2. The Secret Trail. 3. The Hawk's Eyes. 4. The Paleface Law. 5. Ransom. 6. The Betrayal. 7. Rivenoak's Revenge. 8. Out of the Storm. 9. The Panther. 10. Mingo Torture.

368. Des Lebens Umgenisschte Freude

(Germany, 1915) Serial, chapters (?). Fern Andra, the German Pearl White.

369. Lederstrumpf

(Germany—Luna–Film GmbH, 1920) Series, 2 episodes. D: Arthur Wellin. SP: Robert Heymann. S: Based on *Last of the Mohicans* by James Fenimore Cooper.

Future serial star is elevated to second lead in this retelling of the Cooper novel.

Emil Mamelok, Bela Lugosi, Herta Heden, Gottfried Krause, Eduard Eysenck, Margot Skolowska.

1. Der Wildtoter. 2. Der Letzte der Mohikanner.

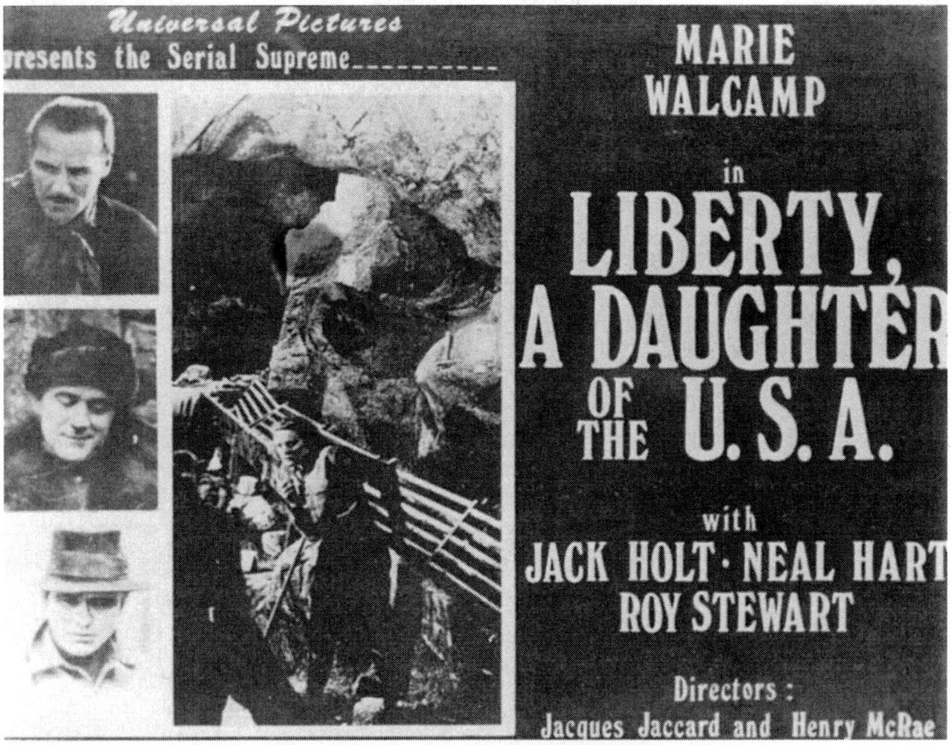

Top: **Marie Walcamp;** ***bottom:*** **Marie Walcamp, Jack Holt, Neal Hart, and Roy Stewart in** ***Liberty*** **(1916)**

370. Liberty

(Universal, August 14, 1916) Serial, 20 chapters; Chapter 1, three reels; others, two reels. D: Jacques Jaccard and Henry McRae. SP: Jacques Jaccard. S: W.B. Pearson. P: W.B. Pearson.

Liberty's father dies, leaving a vast estate in Mexico and appointing as her guardians Major Winston and Jose Leon. His will specifies that she is not to marry until she is 21, unless both guardians approve. A rebel leader kidnaps her hoping to use the ransom money to finance a revolution. Captain Rutledge of the Texas Rangers rescues and falls in love with her. Jose Leon blackmails Liberty into marrying his son, Manuel, to prevent exposure of Major Winston who has gambled and lost estate funds. Later Manuel, a member of the revolution, is killed, leaving Liberty free to marry Rutledge.

This was the first western serial, the first serial for Marie Walcamp, and Jack Holt's first starring role in a serial. He had a small bit role in *The Broken Coin* the previous year.

Marie Walcamp (Liberty Horton), Jack Holt (Captain Rutledge), Eddie Polo (Pedro), G. Raymond Nye (Pancho Lopez), Neal Hart (Major Winston), Bertram Grassby (Manuel Leon), Maude Emory (Theresa), L.M. Wells (Jose Leon), Charles Brinley (Alvarez), Leonard Clapham (Tom London), Roy Stewart, Hazel Buckham.

1. The Fangs of the Wolf. 2. Riding with Death. 3. American Blood. 4. Dead or Alive. 5. Love and War. 6. The Desert of Lost Souls. 7. Liberty's Sacrifice. 8. Clipped Wings. 9. A Daughter of Mars. 10. The Buzzard's Prey. 11. The Devil's Triumph. 12. For the Flag. 13. Strife and Sorrow. 14. A Modern Joan of Arc. 15. Flag of Truce. 16. Court-Martialled. 17. A Trail of Blood. 18. The Wolf's Nemesis. 19. An Avenging Angel. 20. A Daughter of the U.S.A.

371. Lieutenant Daring

(British & Colonial Kinematograph Company-1911–1914) Series, 18 episodes, (?). D: Dave Aylott (1–4), Charles Raymond (5–6; 8–11), Charles Weston (12), Ernest G. Batley (13–14). S/SP: Harold Brett (1–8), ? (9–13).

Episode Titles and Casts • *The Adventures of Lieutenant Daring RN in a South American Port.* (1911) Clifford Marle (Lieutenant Daring), Fred Paul (The Villain), Dorothy Foster (The Girl). • *Lieutenant Daring RN and the Secret Service Agents* (or) *Lieutenant Daring RN Saves HMS Medina.* (1911) Percy Moran (Lieutenant Daring), Edward Durrant

(Spy). • *Lieutenant Daring Avenges an Insult to the Union Jack* (1911) Percy Moran (Lieutenant Daring), Fred Paul (Paulo). • *Lieutenant Daring and the Ship's Mascot* (1912) Percy Moran (Lieutenant Daring), Dorothy Foster (Margherita), Fred Rains (Miguel), Sam Jones (Jumbo). • *Lieutenant Daring Defeats the Middleweight Champion* (1912) Percy Moran (Lieutenant Daring), Ivy Martinek (Ivy Mountford), Charles Calvert (Lt. Derrick), Jack Stokes (Jack Dent), Edward Durrant (Martin Glover), J.W. Bremner (Stumpy Dick), Harold Brett (The Gent), Frank Bradley (The Referee), Jack Mullins (The Second). • *Lieutenant Daring Quells a Rebellion* (1912) Percy Moran (Lieutenant Daring), Ivy Martinek (Carmencita), H.O. Martinek (Jose), A. Brian Plant (Bianca), Jack Houghton (Carlos). • *Lieutenant Daring Captures a Spy* (1912) Percy Moran (Lieutenant Daring). • *Lieutenant Daring, RN* (1912) Percy Moran (Lieutenant Daring). • *Lieutenant Daring and the International Spies* (?). • *Lieutenant Daring and the Plans of the Minefields* (or) *The International Spies* (1912) Percy Moran (Lieutenant Daring), Charles Raymond (Leon Scumwasser), Dickie Thorpe (Marcella), Lt. E.H. Hotchkiss (Himself), Charles Austin (Himself). • *Lieutenant Daring and the Photographic Pigeon* (1912) Percy Moran (Lieutenant Daring), Ivy Martinek (The Girl), W. Gladstone Haley (The Spy). • *Lieutenant Daring and the Labour Riots* (1913) Percy Moran (Lieutenant Daring), Dorothy Foster (Edith Carr), J.O. Neil Farrell (Oswald Carr), Charles Raymond (Agitator). • *Lieutenant Daring and the Dancing Girl* (1913) Percy Moran (Lieutenant Daring), Dorothy Foster (The Dancing Girl). • *Lieutenant Daring and the Mystery of Room 41* (1913) Harry Lorraine (Lieutenant Daring), George Foley (Thief). • *Lieutenant Daring, Aerial Scout* (1914) Harry Lorraine (Lieutenant Daring). • *Lieutenant Daring RN and the Stolen Invention* (1914) James Russell (Lieutenant Daring), George Foley (Officer). • *Lieutenant Daring, RN and the Water Rats* (1924). • *Lieutenant Daring, RN* (1936).

372. Lieutenant Rose

(England—Clarendon, 1910–1915) Series, 17 episodes. D: Percy Stow.

P.G. Norgate (Lieutenant Rose [all episodes except number 12]), Harry Lorraine (Lieutenant Rose [Episode 12 only]), Dorothy Bellew (The Girl [Episodes 4, 13, and probably others]).

1. Lieutenant Rose and the Robbers of Fingall's Creek (1910). 2 Lieutenant Rose and the Foreign Spy (1910). 3. Lieutenant Rose and the Gun Runners (1910). 4. Lieutenant Rose and the Stolen Submarine (1910). 5. Lieutenant Rose and the Chinese Pirates (1910). 6. Lieutenant Rose and the Stolen Code (1911). 7. Lieutenant Rose and the Boxers (1911). 8. Lieutenant Rose and the Royal Visit (1911). 9. Lieutenant Rose and the Stolen Ship (1911). 10. Lieutenant Rose and the Moorish Raiders (1912). 11. Lieutenant Rose and the Hidden Treasure (1912). 12. Lieutenant Rose and the Train Wreckers (1912). 13. Lieutenant Rose and the Patent Aeroplane (1912). 14. Lieutenant Rose in China Seas (1912). 15. Lieutenant Rose and the Stolen Bullion (1913). 16. Lieutenant Rose and the Sealed Orders (1914) [Norgate assumed to be the star]. 17. How Lieutenant Rose RN Spiked the Enemy's Guns (1915).

373. Lightning Bryce

(National Film Corp./Arrow, October 14, 1919) Serial, 15 chapters, two reels each. D: Paul C. Hurst. Scen: Harvey Gates. S: Joe Brandt.

The location of a large gold deposit is sought by Bryce and Kate, whose fathers had mined it originally. Outlaws led by Solvang also want it. To complicate matters, the map is not in one piece. The daughter of one of the partners is made the recipient of a string; the son of the other, a hunting knife.

The mine can only be located by winding the string over the blade—the string carrying the precious information. The knife and string are stolen by different parties. A mysterious figure helps keep up the suspense.

Jack Hoxie (Lightning Bryce), Anna Little (Kate Arnold), Paul C. Hurst (Powder Solvang), Jill Woodward (Mystery Woman), Noble Johnson, Steve Clemente, Ben Corbett, Walter Patterson, George Champion, Slim Lucas, George Hunter.

1. The Scarlet Moon. 2. Wolf Nights. 3. Perilous Trails, 4. The Noose. 5. The Dragon's Den. 6. Robes of Destruction. 7. Bared Fangs. 8. The Yawning Abyss. 9. The Voice of Conscience. 10. Poison Waters. 11. Walls of Flame. 12. A Voice from the Dead. 13. Battling Barriers. 14. Smothering Tides. 15. The End of the Trail.

374. The Lightning Express

(Universal, June 3, 1930) Serial, 10 chapters, two reels each. D: Henry McRae. S: Frank H. Spearman—"Whispering

Louise Lorraine in *The Lightning Express* (1930)

Pearl White in *The Lightning Raider* (1919)

Smith Rides." This was a remake of *Whispering Smith Rides*, Universal, 1927.

Frank Sanger, guardian of Bobbie Van Tyme, refuses to allow railroad construction across his ward's property. However, she sides with Jack Venable, son of the railroad builder, and Whispering Smith, railroad detective, and the three are able to defeat Sanger and to produce a valid will showing Whispering Smith to be Bobbie's guardian and proving the one held by Sanger to be a forgery.

Lane Chandler (Jack Venable), Louise Lorraine (Bobbie Van Tyme), Al Ferguson (Whispering Smith), Greta Grandstedt (Kate), J. Gordon Russell (Frank Sanger), John Oscar (Bill Lewellyn), Martin Clichy (Hank Pardelow), Jim Pierce (Henchman), Floyd Criswell (Henchman), Robert Kelly (Henchman), Bob Reeves (Henchman).

1. A Shot in the Dark. 2. A Scream of Terror. 3. Dangerous Rails. 4. The Death Trap. 5. Tower of Terror. 6. A Call for Help. 7. The Runaway Freight. 8. The Show Down. 9. The Secret Survey. 10. Cleared Tracks.

375. Lightning Hutch

(Arrow, April 19, 1926) Serial, 10 chapters, two reels each. D: Charles Hutchison. Scen: John Francis Natteford. Also released by Cosmos Pictures in 1930 as a six-reel feature with a music score and sound effects.

A Secret Service agent attempts to capture a group of blackmailers. This was Arrow's last serial and Hutchison's last serious attempt at a comeback.

Charles Hutchison (Larry Hutchdale), Edith Thornton (Diana Winters), Virginia Pearson (Janet Thornwall), Eddie Phillips (Clifford Price), Violet Schram (Maria Bruseff), LeRoy Mason (Thornwell), William St. James (Henry), Sheldon Lewis, Ben Walker.

1. The Conspiracy. 2. Life or Liberty. 3. The Deadly Discovery. 4. In the Trap. 5. The Impossible Escape. 6. The Thousandth Chance. 7. The Mysterious Island. 8. The Walls of Doom. 9. The Unexpected Happens. 10. A Woman's Wit.

376. The Lightning Raider

(Pathé, January 1919) Serial, 15 chapters, two reels each. D: George B. Seitz. SP: George B. Seitz and Bertram Milhauser.

Considered by many to be the best serial ever produced by Pathé. There is not a foot of wasted film. Each scene has its place. Interestingly, there is more mental conflict than is usually found in a serial, but as handled here it is just as thrilling as the physical action. The story concerns the struggle of two opposing factions seeking an ebony block of great value. The Lightning Raider, a girl who robs for the love of it, replaces her booty when the game is played out. However, in this case she endeavors to help Thomas Norton, whom she likes, recover the ebony block which has been stolen from him. The fight over the little piece of ebony is one of the most sustaining little wars ever put into a serial. Opposing she and Norton is Wu Fang, a wily Chinaman, leader of a notorious band of denizens of the underworld.

Pearl White (The Lightning Raider), Warner Oland (Wu Fang), Henry Gsell (Thomas Babbington North), Ruby Hoffman (Lottie), William Burt (The Wasp), Frank Redman (Hop Sing), Nellie Burt (Sunbeam), Sam Kim, Henrietta Simpson, Boris Karloff, William A. Sullivan, Anita Brown.

1. The Ebony Block. 2. The Counterplot. 3. Underworld Terrors. 4. Through Doors of Steel. 5. The Brass Key. 6. The Mystic Box. 7. Meshes of Evil. 8. Cave of Dread. 9. Falsely Accused. 10. The Baited Trap. 11. The Bars of Death. 12. Hurled Into Space. 13. The White Roses. 14. Cleared of Guilt. 15. Wu Fang Atones.

377. The Lightning Warrior

(Mascot, November 1, 1931) Serial, 12 chapters. D: Armand Schaefer and Ben Kline. SP: Wyndham Gittens, Ford Beebe, and Colbert Clark. P: Nat Levine. Supervising Editor: Wyndham Gittens. Photography: Ernest Miller, William Nobles, and Tom Galligan. Music: Lee Zahler.

"The Wolf Man," a mysterious outlaw, and his Indian followers attempt to drive the whites out of a mining district and to prevent young Jimmy Carter from taking possession of his murdered father's mine. Unknown to the settlers, there is a rich vein of gold beneath many of the claims in the district. Alan Scott, brother of a murdered lawman, aids Jimmy as does the dog Rinty and Dianne, adopted daughter of the sheriff.

Rin-Tin-Tin (Rinty), Frankie Darro (Jimmy Carter), Georgia Hale (Dianne), George Brent (Alan Scott), Pat O'Malley (Sheriff), Theodore Lorch (Pierre La Farge), Lafe McKee (John Hayden), Robert Kortman (Wells), George Magrill (Adams),

Frank Lanning (Indian George), Frank Brownlee (Augus McDonald), Hayden Stevenson (Carter), Yakima Canutt (Ken Davis/Double for Brent), Dick Dickinson(Adams), Helen Gibson (Pioneer Woman), Bertee Beaumont (Pioneer Woman), Kermit Maynard (Pioneer Man), Cliff Lyons (Stunt Man), Ted Lorch, Steve Clemente.

1. Drums of Doom. 2. The Wolf Man. 3. Empty Saddles. 4. Flaming Arrows. 5. The Invisible Enemy. 6. The Fatal Name. 7. The Ordeal of Fire. 8. The Man Who Knew. 9. Traitor's Hour. 10. The Secret of the Cave. 11. Red Shadows. 12. Painted Faces.

378. The Lion Man

(Universal, December 19, 1919) Serial, 18 chapters, two reels each. D: Albert Russell and Jack Wells. SP: Karl Coolidge. S: Randall Parrish—*The Strange Case of Cavendish.*

Cavendish draws up a new will which disinherits his nephew John, who plots with a crooked lawyer and an actress to murder Cavendish and destroy the will. Cavendish disappears during a fire in his home and Jim Westcott is accused of murdering him, having quarreled with Cavendish shortly before over a business matter. Stella, a reporter, who had overheard the earlier plot to kill Cavendish, also becomes involved, and she and Westcott team up to find the will. They are assisted in times of peril by The Lion Man, an unknown benefactor wearing a disguise.

Kathleen O'Connor (Stella Donovan), Jack Perrin (Jim Westcott), Mack Wright (The Lion Man), J. Barney Sherry (Frederick Cavendish), Gertrude Astor (Celeste La Rue), Henry Barrows (Enright), C. Norman Hammond (Ching), Robert Walker (John Cavendish), Leonard Clapham [Tom London], Slim Padgett, William Carroll.

1. Flames of Hate. 2. Rope of Death. 3. Kidnappers. 4. A Devilish Device. 5. In the Lion's Den. 6. House of Horrors. 7. Doomed. 8. Dungeon of Despair. 9. Sold into Slavery. 10. Perilous Plunge. 11. At the Mercy of Monsters. 12. Jaws of Destruction. 13. When Hell Broke Loose. 14. Desperate Deeds. 15. Furnace of Fury. 16. Relentless Renegades. 17. In Cruel Clutches. 18. In the Nick of Time.

***Top:* George Brent, Robert Kortman, and Rin-Tin-Tin; *bottom*: Frankie Darro, Georgia Hale, and George Brent in *The Lightning Warrior* (1931**

379. The Lion's Claws

(Universal, April 6, 1918) Serial, 18 chapters, two reels each. D: Jacques Jaccard and Harry Harvey. SP: W.B. Pearson and Jacques Jaccard. S: W.B. Pearson.

Beth Johnson is one of a party of English people in the African jungle country during World War I. The plot concerns efforts of the Central Powers to stir up a holy war among the natives through Mohammedan influence. Beth meets with numerous jungle adventures, and when she is captured by natives her friends take up the pursuit.

Marie Walcamp (Beth Johnson), Roy Hanford (Buck

***Top:* Kathleen O'Connor in *The Lion Man* (1919); *left:* Marie Walcamp in *The Lion's Claws* (1918); *bottom:* William Desmond (*raised hand*), Kermit Maynard (*behind Desmond*), Tom Santschi (*at bar*), Joe Bonomo (*raised arm*), and Buzz Barton (*in front of girl, black hat*) in *The Lone Defender* (1930)**

Masterson), Neal Hart (Captain Harris), Frank Lanning (Musa), Thomas Lingham (Captain Johnson), Alfred Allen (Colonel Leighton), Gertrude Astor (Lady Mary Leighton), Edwin August (Roger Hammond), Rex De Roselli (Rej Hari), Harry Von Meter (Captain Bogart), Leonard Clapham [Tom London] (Reglis), Sam Polo (Uula), Nigel De Brulier, Charles Brinley, Sam Appel.

1. A Woman's Honor. 2. Beasts of the Jungle. 3. Net of Terror. 4. A Woman's Scream. 5. The Secret Document. 6. The Dungeon of Terror. 7. Quicksand. 8. Into the Harem. 9. The Human Pendulum. 10. Escape Through the Flames. 11. Caught in the Coils. 12. The Spies' Cave. 13. In Disguise. 14. Hell Let Loose. 15. Bridge of the Beast. 16. The Jungle Pool. 17. The Well of Horror. 18. The Doom of Rej Hari.

380. The Lone Defender

(Mascot, 1930) Serial, 12 chapters, two reels each. D: Richard Thorpe. SP: William Presley Burt, Harry Fraser, and Ben Cohen. P: Nat Levine. Also released in feature form.

A special investigator for the Department of Justice, with the help of a German Shepherd dog whose master has been murdered, runs down The Cactus Kid and restores a mine to the daughter of the murdered man who discovered and developed it.

Rin-Tin-Tin (Rinty), Walter Miller (Ramon), June Marlowe (Dolores Valdez), Buzz Barton (Buzz), Josef Swickard (Juan Valdez), Lee Shumway (Amos Halkey), Frank Lanning (Burke), Robert Kortman (Jenkins), Arthur Morrison (Limpy), Lafe McKee (Sheriff), Bob Irwin (Deputy Sheriff), Julia Beharano (Duenna), Victor Metzetti (Red), Bill McGowan (Henchman), William Desmond, Kermit Maynard, Joe Bonomo, Tom Santschi.

1. The Mystery of the Desert. 2. The Fugitive. 3. Jaws of Peril. 4. Trapped. 5. Circle of Death. 6. Surrounded by the Law. 7. The Ghost Speaks. 8. The Brink of Destruction. 9. The Avalanche. 10. Fury of the Desert. 11. Cornered. 12. Vindicated.

381. The Lone Ranger

(Republic, March 1938) Serial, 15 chapters, two reels each. D: William Witney, John English. SP: Barry Shipman, George Worthington Yates, Franklyn Adreon, Ronald Davidson, and Lois Eby. Based on the radio serial by Fran

Striker. Supervision: Robert Beche. Assoc. P: Sol C. Siegel. Photography: William Nobles. Music: Alberto Colombo. A 69-minute feature version, with added footage of Raymond Hatton and Dickie Jones, was released April 10, 1940.

One of the most popular and lavishly produced of Republic serials. Five lawmen fight lawlessness in the old west in the post-Civil War era. One of the five is the unidentified Lone Ranger who, with his Indian companion Tonto, leads the forces of justice to victory against outlaw Mark Smith who, in his assumed role of finance commissioner Jeffries, lusts to be dictator of all Texas. One by one the rangers are killed until only Allan King, The Lone Ranger, remains. But the final triumph is his and following the defeat of the outlaw gang he rides off into the distance with the faithful Tonto.

Lee Powell (Allan King/The Lone Ranger), Chief Thunder Cloud (Tonto), Lynn Roberts (Joan Blanchard), Herman Brix [Bruce Bennett] (Bert Rogers), Lane Chandler (Dick Forrest), Stanley Andrews (Jefferies), Hal Taliaferro [Wally Wales] (Bob Stuart), George Cleveland (George Blanchard), George Letz [George Montgomery] (Jim Clark), William Farnum (Father McKim), John Merton (Kester), Sammy McKim (Sammy), Billy Bletcher (Lone Ranger's Voice), Yakima Canutt (Double for The Lone Ranger when masked), Silver Chief [horse] (Silver), Tom London (Felton), Raphael Bennett (Black Taggert), Maston Williams (Joe Snead), Charles Thomas (Blake), Allan Cavan (Brennan), Reed Howes (Brown), Walter James (Joe Cannon), Francis Sayles (Carpetbagger), Murdock McQuarrie (Matt Clark), Jane Keckley (Mrs. Clark), Phillip Armenta (Dark Cloud), Ted Adams (Drake), Jack Kirk, Art Dillard, Millard McGowan, Frank Ellis (Gunmen), Jimmy Hollywood (Guard), Carl Stockdale (Haskins), Bud Osborne (Hobart), Fred Burns (Holt), Inez Cody (Indian Woman), Jack Rockwell (Regan), Edmund Cobb (Rance), Jack Perrin (Morgan), Duke Green (Jailer), Forbes Murray (Marcus Jeffries), Edna Lawrence (Marina), Charles King (Morely), Frank Leyva (Pedro), Charles Whitaker (Perkins), J.W. Cody (Running Elk), Iron Eyes Cody (White Feather), Carl Saxe (Sentry), George Magrill (Sentry), Lafe McKee, Hank Bell, Tex Cooper, Perry Pratt, Toy Cline (Ranchers), Vinegar Roan, Blackie Whiteford, Joe Yrigoyen, Bill Yrigoyen, Duke Taylor, Jack Ingram, Robert Kortman, Curley Dresden, George Plues (Troopers), OTHERS: Ray Elliott, Art Felix, Ferry Frank, John Goodwin, Jack Hendricks, Wesley Hooper, Bobby Thompson, John Slater, Chuck Jennings, Glen Johnson, Henry Isabell, Al Lorenzen, Ralph LeFever, Les Cooper, Ken Cooper, Post Parks, Al Delmar, Loren Riebe, Jack Casey, Bill Jones, Gunner Johnson, John Bristol, Elmer Napier, Shorty Woods, Ike Lewin.

1. Heigh-Yo Silver. 2. Thundering Earth. 3. The Pitfall. 4. Agents of Treachery. 5. The Steaming Cauldron. 6. Red Man's Courage. 7. Wheels of Disaster. 8. Fatal Treasure. 9. The Missing Spur. 10. Flaming Fury. 11. The Silver Bullet. 12. Escape. 13. The Fatal Plunge. 14. Messengers of Doom. 15. The Last of the Rangers.

Top: **Lee Powell, Hal Taliaferro [Wally Wales], Herman Brix [Bruce Bennett], George Letz [George Montgomery], Lane Chandler, Chief Thundercloud, and Lynn Roberts; *bottom:* Lee Powell in *The Lone Ranger* (1938)**

Top: Robert Livingston and Chief Thunder Cloud; **bottom:** Robert Livingston, Chief Thunder Cloud, and Duncan Renaldo in *The Lone Ranger Rides Again* (1939)

382. The Lone Ranger Rides Again

(Republic, January 1939) Serial, 15 chapters, two reels each. D: William Witney and John English. SP: Franklyn Adreon, Ronald Davidson, Sol Shor, and Barry Shipman. Assoc. P: Robert Beche. Photography: William Nobles, Edgar Lyons. Music: Alberto Colombo. Based on the radio serial *The Lone Ranger* by Fran Striker.

Craig Dolan, a powerful cattleman, makes desperate attempts to rid the San Ramon Valley of innocent settlers. The Lone Ranger, in his guise as Bill Andrews, newcomer to the valley, is hired by Jed Scott, leader of a wagontrain, to help defeat the Black Raiders, suspected of being in the employ of Dolan. Helping him are Jean Vasquez and Tonto. Ultimately the trio learn that a nephew of Dolan is responsible for the outlaw activity and are successful in stopping the Black Raiders' activity.

Robert Livingstone (The Lone Ranger/Bill Andrews), Chief Thunder Cloud (Tonto), Duncan Renaldo (Juan Vasquez), Jinx Falken (Sue Dolan), Ralph Dunn (Bart Dolan), J. Farrell MacDonald (Craig Dolan), William Gould (Jed Scott), Rex Lease (Evans), Ted Mapes (Merritt), Henry Otho (Pa Daniels), John Beach (Hardin), Carleton Young (Black), Al Taylor (Colt), Glenn Strange (Thorne), Eddie Parker (Hank), Stanley Blystone (Murdock), Charles Whitaker (Black), Silver Chief [horse] (Silver), Billy Bletcher (Lone Ranger's Voice), Bob Robinson (Blackie), Ralph LeFever (Bill), Monte Montague (Tucker), Lafe McKee, Augie Gomez, Charles Hutchison, Cactus Mack, Horace Carpenter (Townsmen), Ted Wells (Cass), Buddy Roosevelt (Slade), Frank Ellis (Joe Parker), Forrest Taylor (Miller), Wheeler Oakman (Manny), Lew Meehan (Lynch), Fred Burns (Long), Jack Kirk (Sam Lawson), Nelson McDowell (Johnny), Ernie Adams (Grover), Eddie Dean (Cooper), Duke Lee (Deputy), Bob McClung (Danny Daniels), Betty Roadman (Ma Daniels), Howard Chase (Martin Gibson), Herman Hack, Bill Yrigoyen, Wesley Hopper, Bud Wolfe, Joe Yrigoyen, Duke Taylor, Forrest Burns, George DeNormand (Possemen), Joe Perez (Diego Vasquez), George Burton (Ed Powers), Tommy Coats, Howard Hickey, Barry Hayes, Burt Dillard, Cecil Kellogg, Carl Sepulveda (Raiders), Buddy Messenger (Rance), Jerome Ward (Safe Heavy), Roger Williams (Sheriff), Jack Montgomery (Smith), Post Parks (Stage Driver), Art Dillard (Stage Guard), Griff Barnette (E.B. Tully), Charles Regan, Chick Hannon, Art Felix, David Sharpe, Fred Schaefer (Cave Heavies).

1. The Lone Ranger Returns. 2. Masked Victory. 3. The Black Raiders Strike. 4. The Cavern of Doom. 5. Agents of Deceit. 6. The Trap. 7. The Lone Ranger at Bay. 8. Ambush. 9. Wheels of Doom. 10. The Dangerous Captive. 11. Death Below. 13. Exposed. 14. Besieged. 15. Frontier Justice.

383. Lord John's Journal

(Universal–Gold Seal, December 1915) Series, 5 episodes; episode 1, four reels; others, three reels. D: Edward J. LeSaint. Scen: Harvey Gates. S: C.N. and A.M. Williamson and Robert Lusk. P: Robert Lusk.

Lord John, a detective storywriter, becomes involved in determining why each of two fiancés of Grace Callender is found dead in the same place and each with a number of keys in his hand.

William Garwood (Lord John Haselmore), Stella Razeto (Maida Odell), Albert MacQuarrie (Doctor Ramese), Carmen Phillips (Jenny), Master Holbrook (Nickie), Sam Polo (Paul Teano), Grace Benham (Grace Callender), Malcolm Blevins (Richard Wayne), Ogden Crane (Roger Odell), T.D. Crittenden (Carr Price), Walter Belasco (Antonio Tostini), Doc Crane (L.J. Calit), Laura Oakley (Head Sister), Gretchen Lederer, Margaret Mayburn, Juan De La Cruz, Eddie Polo.

1. Lord John in New York. 2. The Gray Sisterhood. 3. Three-Fingered Jenny. 4. The Eye of Horus. 5. The League of the Future.

384. The Lost City

(Warner Bros., 1920) Serial, 15 chapters, two reels each. D: E.A. Martin. S: Frederic Chapin. P: William N. Selig. Feature version: *The Jungle Princess* (1920), released on the States Right market by Celebrated Players Film Corp.

Life-threatening adventures in the interior of Africa lead to the discovery of a lost white race.

Stanley Morton, young millionaire, and his friend, Mike Donovan, ex-pugilist, go on an airplane trip to Africa in search of big game. They reach a village ruled by slave-trader Gagga. The latter's warriors return from a raid with prisoners, among whom is Princess Elyata, whose father is king of the interior city of Tirzah, inhabited by whites. She refuses Gagga's advances. Morton and Donovan are thrown into the lion pit by Gagga. Momba, an elephant who dances to the music of Donovan's mouth organ, rescues them.

They in turn rescue Elyata from the pit by means of a rope thrown from their airplane. They head for the jungle but are obliged to land for lack of gasoline. Gagga pursues them. They are recaptured but escape again. The pursuit continues hotly, while wild beasts and all the dangers of the jungle threaten them on every hand.

Juanita Hansen (Princess Elyata of Tarik), George Chesebro (Stanley Morton), Frank Clark (Michael Donovan), Hector Dion (Gagga), Irene Wallace, Al Ferguson, Marjorie Lake, Jake Abraham.

1. The Lost Princess. 2. The City of Hanging Gourds. 3. The Flaming Tower. 4. Jungle Death. 5. The Puma's Victim. 6. The Man Eater's Prey. 7. The Bride of Death. 8. A Tragedy in the Sky. 9. In the Palace of Black Walls. 10. The Tug of War. 11. In the Lion's Jaw. 12. The Jungle Fire. 13. The Cave of Eternal Fire. 14. The Eagle's Nest. 15. The Lost City.

385. The Lost City

(Sherman S. Krellberg, 1935) Serial, 12 chapters, two reels each. Feature Title: *City of Lost Men*. D: Harry Revier. SP:

Top: George Chesebro and Juanita Hansen in *The Lost City* (1920); bottom: William "Stage" Boyd in *The Lost City* (1935)

Perley Poore Sheehan, Eddie Graneman, and Leon D'Usseau. S: Zelma Corroll, George M. Merrick, and Robert Dillon. P: Sherman S. Krellberg. Photography: Ronald Price and Ed Linden. Special Effects: Norman Dawn. Music: Lee Zahler. Assist. D: William Nolte and Richard L'Estrange.

Engineer Bruce Gordon is sent to Africa to find the power source causing worldwide earthquakes. There he finds the Lost City, built on the site of the home of a vanquished race of white Africans and ruled over by a mad scientist named Dr. Zolok, who has transformed natives into giants. Zolok forces the captive Dr. Manyus to invent destructive devices by threatening the doctor's daughter, who is also a captive.

The independent serials of the 1930s had a charm all their own. One has to have been a kid at that time to fully appreciate them.

Kane Richmond (Bruce Gordon), William "Stage" Boyd (Zolok), Claudia Dell (Natcha), Josef Swickard (Dr. Manyus), George F. Hayes (Butterfield), Eddie Featherstone (Jerry Delaney), William Bletcher (Gorzo), Milburn Moranti (Andrews), Sam Baker (Hugo), Margot D'Use (Queen Rama), Jerry Frank (Appolyn), Ralph Lewis (Reynolds), William Millman (Colton), Gino Carrado (Ben Ali), Henry Hall (Officer), Curley Dresden (Arab), Everett Brown (Giant), Budd Buster.

1. Living Dead Men. 2. Tunnel of Death. 3. Dagger Rock. 4. Doomed. 5. Tiger Prey. 6. Human Beasts. 7. Spider Men. 8. Human Targets. 9. Jungle Vengeance. 10. The Lion Pit. 11. The Death Ray. 12. The Mad Scientist.

386. Lost City of the Jungle

(Universal, May 1946) Serial, 13 chapters, two reels each. D: Ray Taylor and Lewis D. Collins. SP: Joseph F. Poland, Paul Huston, and Tom Gibson.

Meteorium 245, a defense against the atomic bomb, is sought by a power-mad Englishman, but thwarting his plans to rule the world is a United Peace Foundation investigator, a scientist's daughter, and a Pendrang native. The search for the rare substance takes all the principals to the lost city of the jungle, where the two leading villains wind up with the chest containing the 245, only to be blown to smithereens when the substance explodes during their getaway in a plane.

Russell Hayden (Rod Stanton), Jane Adams (Marjorie Elmore), Lionel Atwill (Sir Eric Hazarias), Keye Luke (Tai Shan), Helen Bennett (Indra), Ted Hecht (Doc Harris), John Eldredge (Dr. Elmore), John Miljan (Caffrom), John Gallaudet (Grebb), Ralph Lewis (Kurtz), John Mylong (Malborn), Dick Curtis (Henchman), George Lynn (Henchman), George Sorel, Arthur Space, Frances Chung, Gene Stutenroth [Gene Roth], Clarence Lung, Frank Lackteen, Wheaton Chambers, Sam Flint, Maurice Hugo.

1. Himalaya Horror. 2. The Death Flood. 3. Wave Length for Doom. 4. The Pit of Pendrang. 5. Fiery Danger. 6. Death's Shining Face. 7. Speedboat Missing. 8. Fire Jet Torture. 9. Zalabar Death Watch. 10. Booby Trap Rendezvous. 11. Pendrang Guillotine. 12. Jungle Smash-Up. 13. Atomic Vengeance.

387 The Lost Express

(Signal Film Corp., September 17, 1917) Serial, 15 chapters, two reels each. D: J.P. McGowan. S: Frederick B. Bennett. SP: J.P. McGowan.

This serial is about a disappearing train carrying a valuable formula for granulated gasoline. Miss Holmes has faced death in every conceivable form in her film career. In this film she drives cars off docks, jumps off bridges and buildings and participates in wrecks and explosions with utmost calm and without the luxury of a stuntdouble. In filming one of the most sensational chapters, she had to board an ore car on the top of a grade and fight a ruffian while the car ran away. The car got loose from the emergency brakes and actually did run away. That tearing crash at the end of the route was real. Helen escaped with her life by one of her innumerable miracles.

Helen Holmes (Helen Thurston), Leo Maloney (Pitts), Thomas G. Lingham (The Baron), F.O. Whitehead (Valquez), William Brunton (Charles Bonner), Edward Hearn (Francis Murphy), John McKinnon (General Thurston), Will M. Chapman.

1. The Lost Express. 2. The Destroyed Document. 3. The Wreck at the Crossing. 4. The Oil Well Conspiracy.

***Left:* Dick Curtis (*with gun*) and Jane Adams in *Lost City of the Jungle* (1946); *right:* Helen Holmes in *The Lost Express* (1917)**

Left: **Clyde Beatty and Cecelia Parker;** ***right:*** **Clyde Beatty, Wheeler Oakman, and Lew Meehan in** ***The Lost Jungle*** **(1934)**

5. In Deep Waters. 6. High Voltage. 7. The Race with the Limited. 8. The Mountain King. 9. The Looters. 10. The Secret of the Mine. 11. A Fight for a Million. 12. Law is Law (or, Daring Death). 13. Disowned (or, The Escape). 14. Trapped (or, Unmasked). 15. The Found Express (or, Return of the Lost Express).

388. The Lost Jungle

(Mascot, June 13, 1934) Serial, 12 chapters; Chapter 1, three reels; others, two reels. D: Armand Schaefer and David Howard. SP: Barney Sarecky, David Howard, Armand Schaefer, and Wyndham Gittens. S: Sherman Lowe and Al Martin. P: Nat Levine. Photography: Alvin Wyckoff and William Nobles. Music: Hal Chasnoff. Supervising Editor: Wyndham Gittens. A 106-minute feature version was also released.

Clyde Beatty journeys by dirigible to an uncharted island in the tropic seas in search of his sweetheart and a party of lost explorers. Crashing on the island during a storm, Beatty and a few others survive and Beatty finds his fiancée and her father. The group then sets out to find Professor Livingston, leader of the exploring expedition. They overcome white gold hunters, hostile natives, and fierce jungle beasts to achieve their goal.

Clyde Beatty (Himself), Cecilia Parker (Ruth Robinson), Syd Saylor (Larry Henderson), Warner Richmond (Sharkey), Wheeler Oakman (Kirby), Maston Williams (Thompson), J. Crauford Kent (Explorer), Lloyd Whitlock (Howard, Dirigible Pilot), Lloyd Ingraham (Bannister), Edward Le Saint (Captain Robinson), Lew Meehan (Flynn), Max Wagner (Slade), Wes Warner (Jackman), Jack Carlyle (The Cook), Jim Corey (Steve), Lionel Backus (Sandy), Ernie Adams (Pete), Harry Holman (Maitland), Mickey Rooney (Mickey), George F. Hayes (Dirigible Passenger), Wally Wales (Sandy), Charles [Slim] Whitaker (Al), Frank Lanning (Man of the Temple), Charlie Williams (Reporter), The Hagenback-Wallace Circus Animals.

1. Noah's Ark Island. 2. Nature in the Raw. 3. Hypnotic Eye. 4. Pit of Crocodiles. 5. Gorilla Warfare. 6. Battle of Beasts. 7. Tiger's Prey. 8. Lion's Brood. 9. Eyes of the Jungle. 10. Human Hyenas. 11. The Gorilla. 12. Take Them Back Alive.

389. The Lost Planet

(Columbia, May 1953) Serial, 15 chapters, two reels each. D: Spencer G. Bennet. SP: George H. Plympton and Arthur Hoerl. P: Sam Katzman. Assist. D: Charles S. Gould. Photography: William Whitley. Music: Mischa Bakaleinikoff.

A group of Americans experience all sorts of fantastic adventures, as they shuttle back and forth between Earth and the planet Ergro, battling an Ergroan electronics wizard who intends to conquer the universe. The scientific gadgets included the Prysmic Catapult, the Cosmic Cannon, the Degravitizer, the Axial Propeller, the De-Thermo Ray, the Thermic Disintegrator, and other bizarre mechanical creations. Columbia realized

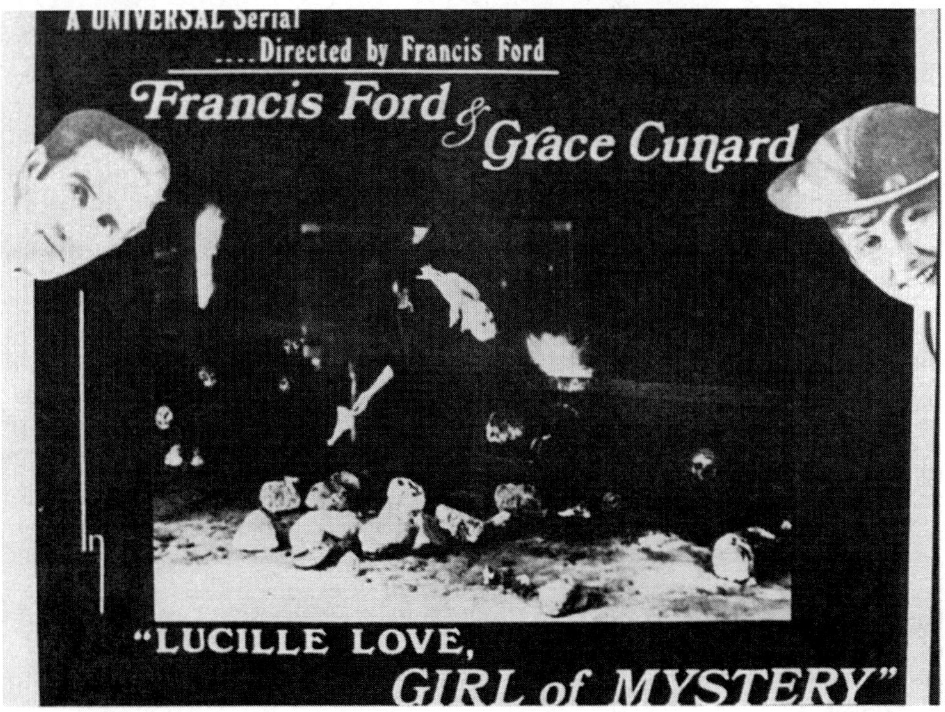

***Top:* Judd Holdren, Vivian Mason, and Ted Thorpe in *The Lost Planet* (1953); *bottom:* Francis Ford and Grace Cunard in *Lucille Love, Girl of Mystery* (1914)**

that the market for serials was falling off rapidly and that they were primarily fodder for children. Consequently, the chapterplays were made cheaply and the stories were created to appeal to children.

Judd Holdren (Rex Barrow), Vivian Mason (Ella Dorn), Ted Thorpe (Tim Johnson), Forrest Taylor (Professor Dorn), Michael Fox (Dr. Ernst Grood), Gene Roth (Reckov), Karl Davis (Karlo), Leonard Penn (Ken Wolper), John Cason (Hopper), Nick Stuart (Parl), Joseph Mell (Lah), Jack George (Jarva), Frederick Berest (Alden), I. Stanford Jolley (Robot #9), Pierre Watkin (Ned Hilton).

1. The Mystery of the Guided Missile. 2. Trapped by the Axial Propeller. 3. Blasted by the Thermic Disintegrator. 4. The Mind Control Machine. 5. The Atomic Plane. 6. Disaster in the Stratosphere. 7. Snared by the Prysamic Catapult. 8. Astray in Space. 9. The Hypnotic Ray Machine. 10. To Free the Planet People. 11. Dr. Grood Defies Gravity. 12. Trapped in a Cosmic Jet. 13. The Invisible Enemy. 14. In the Grip of the De-Thermo Ray. 15. Sentenced to Space.

390. The Lost Special

(Universal, December 1932) Serial, 12 chapters, two reels each. D: Henry McRae. S: Arthur Conan Doyle. SP: Ella O'Neill, George Plympton, Basil Dickey, and George Morgan.

Two college athletes and two young ladies solve the disappearance of The Golden Special, a train carrying gold from the Golconda Mines.

Frank Albertson (Tom Hood), Cecelia Parker (Betty Moore), Caryl Lincoln (Kate Bland), Ernie Nevers (Bob Collins), Francis Ford (Botter Hood), Frank Glendon (Sam Slater), Tom London (Dink), Al Ferguson (Gavin), Edmund Cobb (Spike), George Magrill (Lefty), Joe Bonomo (Joe), Harold Nelson (Professor Wilson), Jack Clifford (Doran), Reb Russell (Henchman).

1. The Lost Special. 2. Racing Death. 3. The Red Lantern. 4. Devouring Flames. 5. The Lightning Strikes. 6. The House of Mystery. 7. The Tank Room Terror. 8. The Fatal Race. 9. Into the Depths. 10. The Jaws of Death. 11. The Flaming Forest. 12. Retribution.

391. Lucille Love, Girl of Mystery

(Universal, April 14, 1914) Serial, 15 chapters, two reels each. D: Francis Ford. Scen: Grace Cunard and Francis Ford. S: James Keeley. Supervision: Otis Turner.

Hugo is filled with hatred for Sumpter Love, a principal witness against him in his ouster from West Point, who marries the girl Hugo loves. He becomes a spy and, years later, manages to steal defense plans entrusted to Love, pinning the blame on Lieutenant Gibson, an aide to Love and the sweetheart of Lucille, Love's daughter.

The story jumps about the globe as Lucille matches wits and physical endurance with Hugo as she tries to recover the secret plans and clear her fiancé's name. Jungle adventure, the wild West, underground kingdoms—they are all here in what was actually an expansion of a two-reel western. The film established Cunard and Ford as serial stars.

Grace Cunard (Lucille Love), Francis Ford (Loubeque/Hugo), Harry Schumm (Lieutenant Gibson), Ernest Shields (Thompson), E.M. Keller (Sumpter Love), Eddie Roland (Government Aviator), Wilbur Higby, Burton Law, Jean Hathaway, Billy White, Harry Ratenbury, John [Jack] Ford, Eddie Boland.

392. Lure of the Circus

(Universal, November 18, 1918) Serial, 18 chapters, two reels each. D: J.P. McGowan. S: William Wing. Scen: Hope Loring.

A thin plot line stretched over eighteen chapters as a showcase for the athletic Polo, who faced danger in a circus setting week after week.

Eddie Polo (Eddie Somers), Eileen Sedgwick (Alicia Page), Harry Carter (Edward Lawrence), Molly Malone (Nan Harden), Noble Johnson (Silent Andy), Frederick Starr (Steve Harden), Duke R. Lee (Richard Van Norman), Charles Hill Mailes (Malcolm Somers), James Gordon (Guy Brock), Andrew Waldrom (Dynamite Dan), Fred Montague (Howard Mason), Sidney Deane (Reynolds), Josie Sedgwick.

1. The Big Tent. 2. The Giant's Leap. 3. Beaten Back. 4. The Message on the Cuff. 5. The Lip Reader. 6. The Aerial Disaster. 7. The Charge of the Elephant. 8. The Human Ladder. 9. The Flying Loop. 10. A Shot for Life. 11. The Dagger. 12. A Strange Escape. 13. A Plunge for Life. 14. Flames. 15. The Stolen Record. 16. The Knockout. 17. A Race with Time. 18. The Last Trick.

393. The Lurking Peril

(Wistaria/Arrow, December 1919) Serial, 15 chapters, two reels each. D: George Morgan and Burton King. SP: Lloyd Lonergan and George Larkin. S: Lloyd Lonergan.

During a financial crunch, Donald Britt has sold the rights to his brain after his death to a fiendish professor who just can't wait to begin dissecting the brain, considered by the professor to be most unusual. Secretly he tries over and over to do away with Donald, often imperiling the young man's girlfriend as well.

George Larkin (Donald Britt), Anne Luther (Phyllis Charlton), William Betchel (Dr. Bates), Ruth Dwyer (Betty Bates), John Nicholson (Kersey), Peggy Shanor, Robert Coleson.

1. The $25,000 Contract. 2. At the Edge of the Cliff. 3. The Aviator's Victim. 4. A Bolt from Heaven. 5. The Man Trap in the Woods. 6. A Duel of Wits. 7. A Satanic Plot. 8. Helpless in a Madhouse. 9. The Hiding Place in the Slums. 10. The Den in Chinatown. 11. At a Maniac's Mercy. 12. Six Inches of Steel. 13. Trapped by Telegraph. 14. The Dynamite Ship. 15. The Last Plot of Bates.

394. Lyman H. Howe's Hodge Podge

(Lyman H. Howe Film Co., 1922–23) Series, 110 Episodes, one reel each. P/D: Lyman H. Howe. Supervision: Robert Gillaum. Narrative: James F. Clemenger.

This long forgotten series was a predecessor of Fitzpatrick Traveltalk films of the 1930s. So far as the author knows these films no longer physically exist. It's a shame that some of these segments could not have been preserved for later generations to see.

1. King Winter. 2. Sea Elephants. 3. The Garden of Geysers. 4. Hot Shots. 5. Mrs. Hippo. 6. Fishing from Taron. 7. Speed Demons. 8. Shooting the Earth. 9. A Flivver Elopement. 10. The Cat and the Fiddle. 11. Dipping in the Deep. 12. Why the Glove Trotter Trots. 13. Speedville. 14. Bottom of the Sea. 15. Liquid Lava. 16. A Sailor's Life. 17. A Movie Pioneer. 18. Jumping Jacks. 19. Realm of Sport. 20. A Tiny Tour of the U.S.A. 21. Snap Shots of the Universe. 22. A Jumble in the Jungle. 23. Frozen Water. 24. Hazardous Hunting. 25. A Crazy Quilt of Travel. 26. Whirligigs. 27. Earth's Oddities. 28. Hi-Flyers. 29. Topsy-Turvy Travel. 30. Lots of Knots. 31. Movie Morsels. 32. The Village School. 33. Earth's Other Half. 34. Mexican Melody. 35. Travel Treasures. 36. Pictorial Proverbs. 37. The Story Teller. 38. Knickknacks of Knowledge. 39. Magical Movies. 40. A Mythical Monster. 41. Mother Goose's Movies. 42. A Criss-Cross Cruise. 43. A Congress of Celebrities. 44. Neptune's Domain. 45. From A to Z Thru Filmdom. 46. Peeking at the Planets. 47. Chips off the Old Block. 48. The Alligator's Paradise. 49. A Merry-Go-Round of Travel. 50 Figures of Fancy. 51. A Key Hole Cruise. 52. A Movie Medley. 53. A Cluster of Kings. 54. The Wise Old Owl. 55. Climbing Into Cloudland. 56. A Bird of Flight. 57. A Scenic Treasure Chest. 58. Tales of a Traveler. 59. Capers of a Camera. 60. Bubbles of Geography. 61. Delving Into the Dictionary. 62. Here and There in Travel-Land. 63. Models in Mud. 64. A Whirl of Activity. 65. Recollections of a Rover. 66. Star Shots. 67. How to Please the Public. 68. Nicknames. 69. The Wandering Toy. 70. Pictorial Tidbits. 71. Conquering the Colorado. 72. The Peep Show. 73. On the Move. 74. Glorious Adventures. 75. A Patchwork of Pictures. 76. Shifting Scenes. 77. Question Marks. 78. A Dominion of Diversity. 79. A Moving Movie Show. 80. On the Streets. 81. Studio Stunts. 82. The Museum of Art. 83. A Flying Trip. 84. Over the Air. 85. A Medley of Rivers. 86. Speed Up. 87. Tidbits. 88. Jungle Giants. 89. Moneymakers of Manhattan. 90. Vagabond Melodies. 91. Highlights of Travel. 92. The Wonder Trail. 93. The Veldt. 94. All Around the Town. 95. The Prowlers. 96. Fury of the Storm. 97. Bubble Blowers. 98. Women's Work. 99. Little Thrills. 100. Traffic. 101. The Wonder City. 102. Down on the Farm. 103. Across America in Ten Minutes. 104. The Animal Fair. 105. Skipping About the Universe. 106. Women of Many Lands. 107. Out of the Ordinary. 108. Sawdust Sidelights. 109. Any Way to Get There. 110. Capers in Clay.

Lyman H. Howe's Famous Ride on a Runaway Train was released May 26, 1929 with Music and Sound Effects by Educational Studios.

395. Maciste

Maciste has been one of Italy's longest serving heroes, having originated in the mid-teens. Presented here are the silent Maciste films starring Bartolomeo Pagano, who played the part for thirteen years.

Maciste (Italy—Itala Film 1915). D: Giovanni Pastrone. Bartolomeo Pagano, Ada Marangoni, Felice Minotti. *Maciste Alpino* (Italy—Itala Film, 1916). D: Giovanni Pastrone, Romano Luigi Borgnetto, Luigi Maggi, Bartolomeo Pagano. *Maciste Atleta* (Italy—Itala Film, 1917). D: Vincenzo Denizot. Bartolomeo Pagano, Italia Almirante Manzini, Vincenzo Denizot. *Maciste Poliziotto* (Italy—Itala Film, 1917). Bartolomeo Pagano. *Maciste Medium* (Italy—Itala Film, 1917). Bartolomeo Pagano. [At least one other Maciste film was produced in 1917, starring Pagano and directed by Umberto Mozzato, but the title is undetermined]. *Maciste Sonambulo* (Italy—Itala Film, 1918). Bartolomeo Pagano. *Maciste I°* (Italy—Itala Film, 1919). D: Carlo

Campogalliani. Bartolomeo Pagano, Letizia Quaranta, Felice Minotti. *La Rivincita di Maciste* (Italy—Itala Film, 1919). D: Carlo Campogalliani. Bartolomeo Pagano, Letizia Quaranta, Felicio Minotti, Carlo Campogalliani, Erminia Zago. *La Trilogia di Maciste* (Italy, 1919) Series, 3 episodes. D: Carlo Campogalliani. Bartolomeo Pagano, Letizia Quaranta, Carlo Campogalliani, Gabriel Moreau, Felice Minotti. (1. Maciste Contro La Morte. 2. Il Viaggio Di Maciste. 3. Il Testamento Di Maciste.) *Maciste Innamorato* (Italy, 1919). D: R.L. Borgnetto. Bartolomeo Pagano, Letizia Quaranta, Linda Moglia. *Maciste in Vacanza* (Italy, 1920). D: R.L. Borgnetto. Bartolomeo Pagano, Henriette Bonard. *Maciste Salvato dalle Acque* (Italy, 1920). D: R.L. Borgnetto. Bartolomeo Pagano, Henriette Bonard, Mario Marat, Mario Woller Bruni, Emilio Vardannes. *Man soll es nicht für möglich halten oder ou Maciste und die Javanerin* (Germany—Jakob Karol–Film GmbH, 1922). D: Uwe Jens Krafft. SP: Robert Liebmann and Georg Jacoby. Bartolomeo Pagano, Carola Toelle, Paul Otto, Arnold Korff, Manja Tzatschewa, Arnold Marle, K. Rehberg, Karl Platen, Georg Baselt. *Maciste und die Tochter des Silberkönigs* (Germany—Jakob Karol–Film GmbH, 1922). D: Luigi Romano [Romano Luigi Borgnetto]. SP: Vanloo-Schmidt. Bartolomeo Pagano, Ludwig Hartau, Elena Makowska, Hans Junkermann, Otto Treptow, Heinrich Peer, Gerhard Ritterband, Kurt Lilien. *Maciste und der Sträfling Nr. 51* (Germany—Jakob Karol–Film GmbH, 1922). Bartolomeo Pagano, Karl Biebracks, Elsa Muller. *Maciste und die chinesische Truhe* (Germany—Jakob Karol–Film GmbH, 1923). D: Carl Boese. SP: Richard Hutter. Bartolomeo Pagano, Rudolf Lettinger, Grete Hollmann, Edwin H. Knopf, Elsie Fuller, Toni Wittels, Karl Falkenberg, Ferdinand Martini, Jakob Tiedtke, Gerhard Ritterband, Li Chun Di, Sybill Morel, Nien Tso Ling. *Maciste e il Nipote d'America* (Pittaluga-Ferti, 1924). D: Eleuterio Rodolfi. Bartolomeo Pagano, Pauline Polaire, Diomira Jacobini, Mercedes Brignone, Oreste Bilancia, Eleuterio Rodolfi. *Maciste Imperatore* (Pittaluga-Ferti, 1924). D: Guido Brignone. Bartolomeo Pagano, Elena Sangro, Lola Romanos, Gero Zambuto Andrea Miano, Felice Minotti, Domenico Gambino. *Maciste Contro lo Sceicco* (Pittaluga-Ferti, 1925). D: Mario Camerini. Bartolomeo Pagano, Cecyl Tryan, Rita D'Harcourt, Lido Manetti, Armando Pouget, Oreste Grandi, Franz Sala, Alex Bernard, Felice Minotti, Mario Saio, Michele Mikailoff, E.M. Costa. *Il Gigante delle Dolomiti* (Pittaluga-Ferti, 1926). D: Guido Brignone. Bartolomeo Pagano, Dolly Grey, Elena Lunda, Luigi Serventi, Andrea Habay, Felice Minotti. *Maciste nella Gabbia dei Leoni* (Pittaluga-Ferti, 1926). D: Guido Brignone. Bartolomeo Pagano, Elena Sangro, Alberto Collo, Franz Sala, Felice Minotti. *Maciste all'Inferno* (Pittaluga-Ferti, 1926). D: Guido Brignone. Bartolomeo Pagano, Pauline Polaire, Elena Sangro, Luzia Zanussi, Andrea Miano, Felice Minotti, Franz Sala. *Il Vetturale del Moncenisio* (Pittaluga, 1927). D: Baldassare Negroni. Bartolomeo Pagano, Rina de Liguoro, Alex Bernard, U. Cassinelli, Celio Bucchi, Giuseppe Brignone, Andrea Miano, Felice Minnotti. *Gli Ultimi Zar* (Pittaluga, 1928). D: Baldassare Negroni. Bartolomeo Pagano, Elena Lunda, Franz Sala, Sandro Rufini, Alberto Pasquali, Andrea Miano. *Guiditta e Oloferne* (Pittaluga, 1928). D: Baldassare Negroni. Bartolomeo Pagano, Jia Russkaja, Franz Sala, Giorgio Curti, C. Tedeschi, A. Bani, Lorelay, Felice Minotti.

396. La Maison du Mystère

(France—Films Albatros, 1922) Serial, 10 chapters. D: Alexandre Valkoff. S: Jules Mary. SP: A. Volkoff. Camera: Nicolas Toporkov. English Feature Title: *The House of Mystery*.

Ivan Mosjoukine, Charles Vanel, Helene Darly, Nicolas Koline, Benedict, Francine Mussey, Simone Genevois, W. De Siry [Strijewsky], Sylvia Grey, Barkewitch.

Portuguese: 1. O amigo desleal. 2. O segredo da lagöa. 3. Ódio e ambição. 4. A sentenca implacvel. 5. A ponte viva. 6. A voz do sangue. 7. Caprichos da sorte. 8. Luta sem tréguas. 9. A angústia do criminoso. 10. O amor triunfa.

William Duncan and Edith Johnson in *Man of Might* (1919)

397. Man of Might

(Vitagraph, January 1919) Serial, 15 chapters, two reels each. D: William Duncan. Scen: C. Graham Baker. S: Albert E. Smith and Cyrus Townsend Brady.

The only key to the location of a buried treasure is a chart flag cut up and divided years before among six adventurers. Pieced together, they are a treasure key—cut up they are useless. Dick and Polly have one piece and Scarface a second. He kills Polly's father, gets her flag and starts after the treasure. Other holders join Dick and Polly and they pursue Scarface to the Gulf of Mexico, battling bandits and hostile Aztecs.

Perhaps the plot sounds like standard serial fare, but it was served up in a far more realistic and palatable fashion in 1919 than was the case with serials filmed in the forties and fifties. And audiences were not as sophisticated then either. Filming took place in lower Mexico, southern California, the Arizona desert and as far north as San Francisco.

William Duncan (Dick Van Brunt), Edith Johnson (Polly Ransome), Joe Ryan (Scarface Bender), Walter Rodgers (George Tell), Del Harris (Joseph Tebbins), Otto Lederer (Juan Diaz), Frank Tokonaga (Chu Chen Ling), Willie Calles (Tomas, the Indian Chief), George Kuwa.

1. The Riven Flag 2. The Leap Through Space. 3. The Creeping Death. 4. The Gripping Hand. 5. The Human Shield. 6. The Height of Torment. 7. Into the Trap. 8. The One Chance. 9. The Crashing Horror. 10. Double Crossed. 11. The Ship of Dread. 12. The Volcano's Prey. 13. The Flood of Despair. 14. The Living Catapult. 15. The Rescue.

398. The Man Who Disappeared

(Edison, April 1915) Serial, 10 chapters, one reel each. D: Charles Brabin. Scen: Charles H. France. S: Richard Washburn Child.

John Perriton is in love with Mary Wales, whose brother is a rascal. To protect Mary from knowing that Nelson Wales has forged her name on a check, Perriton loans Nelson money to make restitution. Nelson later tries to steal Mary's jewels and murders the butler. In trying to protect Mary, John is framed by Nelson for the murder. The story unfolds around John's attempts to clear himself and regain the love of Mary.

Marc MacDermott (John Perriton), Barry O'Moore (Nelson Wales), Miriam Nesbitt (Mary Wales), Marjorie Ellison (Jennie), Harry Eytinge (Lipman, a Lawyer), Charles Ogle (Miens), T. Tamamoto (Den Keeper).

1. The Black Mask. 2. The Hunted Animal. 3. Double Cross. 4. The Light on the Wall. 5. With His Hands. 6. The Gap. 7. Face to Face. 8. A Matter of Minutes. 9. The Living Dead. 10. By the Aid of the Film.

399. Man with the Steel Whip

(Republic, July 19, 1954) Serial, 12 chapters, two reels each. D: Franklyn Adreon. SP: Ronald Davidson. Assoc. P: Franklyn Adreon. Music: R. Dale Butts. Special Effects: Howard and Theodore Lydecker.

A young rancher and a school marm conceive the idea of creating a legendary figure, El Látigo, to gain the confidence of superstitious reservation Indians, who believe the masked figure in a Spanish costume is the spirit of a former benefactor. With the support of the Indians, El Látigo is able to wage a battle against a saloon owner who uses renegade Indians and outlaws to cause friction between settlers and Indians so that he can acquire a portion of the reservation on which gold has been found. It was an old plot dusted off once more for the juvenile trade.

Richard Simmons (Jerry Randall/El Látigo), Barbara Bestar (Nancy Cooper), Dale Van Sickel (Crane), Mauritz Hugo (Barnett), Lane Bradford (Tosco), Toy Barcroft (Sheriff), Pat Hogan (Chief), Edmund Cobb (Lee), I. Stanford Jolley (Sloan), Tom Steele (Gage/Tom), Charles Stevens (Blackjack Sam), Harry Harvey (Jim Kirkwood), Stuart Randall (Harris), Guy Teague (Price), Alan Wells (Quivar), Art Dillard (Heavy), Chuck Hayward (Heavy), Tex Terry (Townsman), Walt LaRue (Townsman), Herman Hack (Townsman), Herman Hack (Townsman), Tom Monroe (Road Worker), Bob Clark (Mac), Charles Sullivan (Mike), Robert Henry (Orco), Chris Mitchell (Sam), Gregg Barton (Slanton), George Eldredge (Clem Stokes).

1. The Spirit Rider. 2. Savage Fury. 3. Mask of El Látigo. 4. The Murder Cave. 5. The Stone Guillotine. 6. Flame and Battle. 7. Double Ambush. 8. The Blazing Barrier. 9. The Silent Informer. 10. Window of Death. 11. The Fatal Masquerado. 12. Redskin Raiders.

Richard Simmons in *Man with the Steel Whip* (1954)

400. The Man Without a Face

(Pathé, January 15, 1927) Serial, 10 chapters, two reels each. D: Spencer G. Bennet. Scen: Joseph Anthony Roach. S: C.W. and Alice M. Williamson.

A mystery figure called both The Man Without a Face and The Master tries to keep two sisters from returning to the U.S. from China to claim an inheritance. A bank emissary aids them.

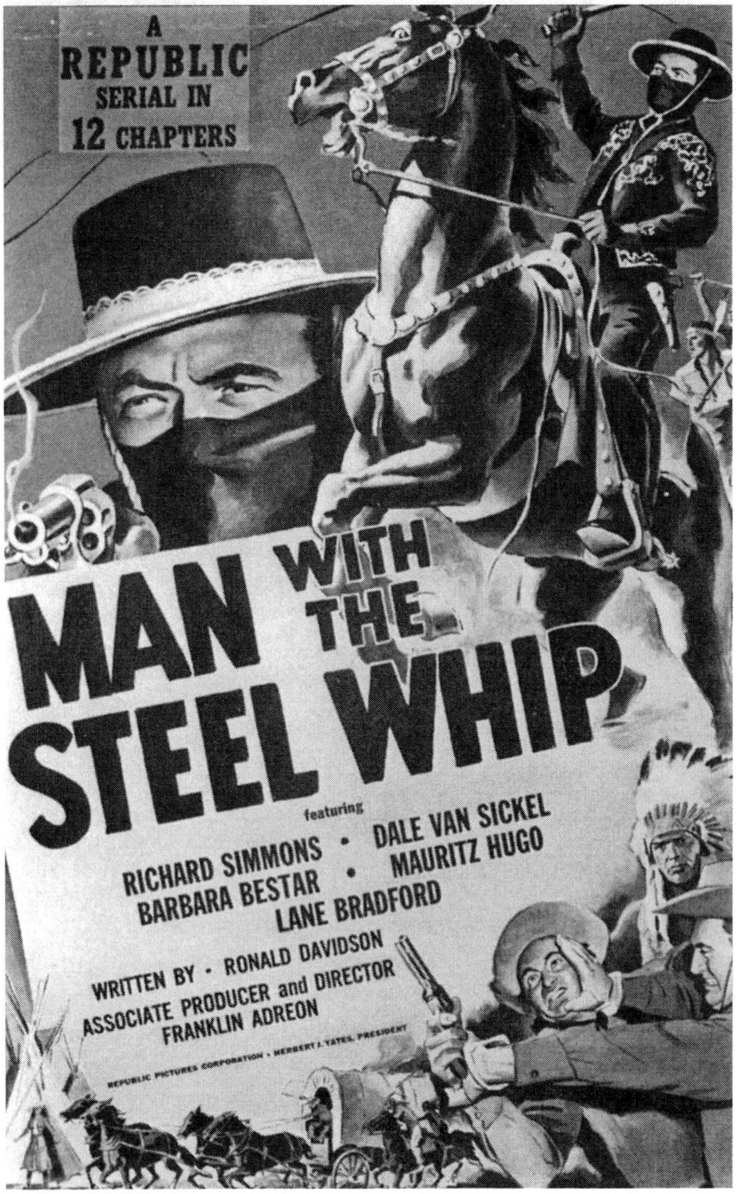

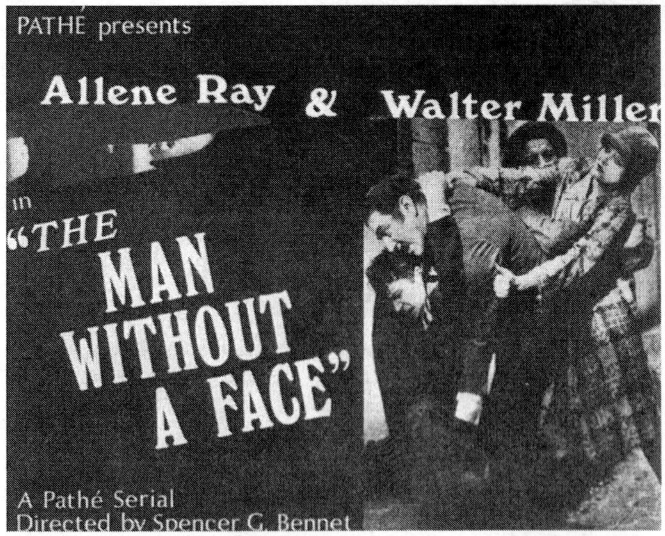

***Left:* Richard Simmons in *Man with the Steel Whip* (1954); *top:* Allene Ray and Walter Miller in *The Man Without a Face* (1928) *bottom:* Alfred Blutecher in *Manden Med De 9 Fingre* (1915)**

Allene Ray, Walter Miller (James Brisbane), E.H. Calvert, Sojin, Jeanette Loff, Gladden James, Kathleen Chambers, Richard R. Neill, Toshiye Schioka, Richard C. Travers.

1. A Perilous Mission. 2. The Barrage. 3. The Death Shell. 4. The Abduction. 5. The Mark of Crime. 6. The Road of Peril. 7. The Master Strikes. 8. The Crime Craft. 9. The Mysterious Visitor. 10. Unmasked.

401. Manden Med de 9 Fingre (English Title: The Man with the Missing Finger)

(Denmark—Nordisk Films, 1915–1916) Serial, 5 chapters. D: Anders W. Sandberg. SP: Hans Holten. Camera: Ejnar Olsen (Chapter 1, 2); Kaj Storm-Petersen (Chapter 3,4,5).

Aage Hertel (John Smith), Alfred Blutecher (Sylvester Jackson [Chapter 1, 2]), Birger von Gotta Schonberg (George Warren), Arne Weel (William Morne), Henry Seemann (Sylvester Jackson [Chapter 3,4,5]), Erik Holberg (Mr. Gaber), Peter Nielsen (Mr. Wendla), Robert Schmidt (Mr. Mylon), Asgar Meier (Mia Chanton), Frederik Jacobsen (Mr. Penton), Hugo Bruun (Harry Lawson), Rantz Skondrup, Johannes Ring.

1. The Murder in the Villa Falcon (released September 27, 1915) three reels. 2. The Midnight Express (released October 4, 1915) three reels. 3. Den falske Ingeniør (released October 16, 1916) three reels. 4. The Lonely House (released October 23, 1916) three reels. 5. The House by the Railway (released January 15, 1917) three reels.

402. Mandrake, the Magician

(Columbia, May 1939) Serial, 12 chapters, two reels each. D: Sam Nelson and Norman Deming. SP: Joseph F. Poland, Basil Dickey, and Ned Dandy. P: Jack Fier. Photography: Ben Kline. Music: Lee Zahler. Based on King Features newspaper character created by Lee Falk and Phil Davis.

Mandrake battles The Wasp for control of the radium energy machine invented by Professor Houston for medical treatment purposes. The Wasp knows it can be used as a lethal weapon of destruction. Learning that Mandrake is returning from Tibet with the formula for a platonite steel alloy needed to perfect the device, The Wasp orders his men to kidnap Houston and his prototype model. Thus begins a long struggle between Mandrake and his friends on one side and The Wasp and his criminal band on the other.

Warren Hull (Mandrake), Doris Weston (Betty), Al Kikume (Lothar), Rex Downing (Tommy), Edward Earle (Andre), Forbes Murray (Houston), Kenneth MacDonald (Webster), Don Beddoe (Raymond), Dick Curtis (Dorgan), John Tyrell (Dirk), Ernie Adams (Brown), George Chesebro (Baker), George Turner (Hall).

1. Shadow on the Wall. 2. Trap of The Wasp. 3. City of Terror. 4. The Secret Passage. 5. The Devil's Playmate. 6. The Fatal Crash. 7. Gamble for Life. 8. Across the Deadline. 9. Terror Rides the Rails. 10. The Unseen Monster. 11. At the Stroke of Eight. 12. The Reward of Treachery.

403. Mandrin

(France—Pathé-Consortium–Cinéma, 1924) Serial, 8 chapters. D: Henri Fescourt. Assist. D: Rene Barberis. S/SP: Arthur Bernede.

Romuald Joube (Louis Mandrin), Johanna Sutter (Tiennot), Hugues De Bagratide (Pistolet), Louis Monfils (Malicet), Jacqueline Blanc (Nicole Malicet), Mme. Ahnar (Mme. Malicet), Jeanne Helbling (La Pompadour), Jean Peyrière (Louis XV), Leclerc (Marquis d'Argenson), Gilbert Dalleu (Colonel de la Morliere), Andrée Valois (Martine), Rahna Kaliva (La Camargo), Paul Guide (Bouret d'Etigny), Emile Saint-Ober (Mi-Careme), Georges Bernier (Carnaval), Bardes (Voltaire).

Portuguese: 1. O revoltado. 2. O agente Pistolet. 3. O estranho prestidigitador. 4. [Unknown.] 5. [Unknown.] 6. O indulto do rei. 7. [Unknown.] 8. [Unknown.]

404. Manhunt of Mystery Island

(Republic, January 1945) Serial, 15 chapters, two reels each. D: Spencer Bennet, Yakima Canutt, and Wallace A. Grissell. SP: Albert DeMond, Basil Dickey, Jesse Duffy, Alan James, Grant Nelson, and Joseph Poland. Assoc. P: Ronald Davidson. Photography: Bud Thackery. Music: Richard Cherwin. Special Effects: Howard and Theodore Lydecker. Feature Title: *Captain Mephisto and the Transformation Machine*.

While on an expedition in search of new radium fields, Dr. Forrest, inventor of the Radiatomic Power Transmitter, disappears. His daughter asks criminologist Lance Reardon to help her find her father. Their search takes them to Mystery Island, owned by four men. One is secretly holding Dr. Forrest prisoner. By using a transformation chair the villain can become the exact counterpart of Captain Mephisto, original owner of the island some 200 years before. As Mephisto he tries every

Top: **Warren Hull and Doris Weston;** ***bottom:*** **Warren Hull, Don Beddoe, and Rex Downing in** ***Mandrake, the Magician*** **(1939)**

tactic possible to force the secret of the Radiatomic machine from Dr. Forrest and to kill Claire and Lance, but in the end he is killed himself, falling to his greedy schemes.

Linda Stirling (Claire Forrest), Roy Barcroft (Captain Mephisto/Higgins), Richard Bailey (Lance Reardon), Kenneth Duncan (Sidney Brand), Forrest Taylor (William Forrest), Forbes Murray (Henry Hargraves), Jack Ingram (Edward Armstrong), Harry Strang (Fred Braley), Edward Cassidy (Paul Melton), Frank Alten (John Raymond), Lane Chandler (Reed), Russ Vincent (Ruga), Si Jenks (Joe Benson), Duke Green (Clark), Dale Van Sickel (Barker/Lewis/Frazier/Sardon), Tom Steele (Lyons), Fred Graham (Blake), Eddie Parker (Captain Fallon), Duke Taylor (Hill).

1. Secret Weapon. 2. Satan's Web. 3. The Murder Machine. 4. The Lethal Chamber. 5. Mephisto's Mantrap. 6. Ocean Tomb. 7. The Death Drop. 8. Bombs Away. 9. The Fatal Flood. 10. The Sable Shroud. 11. Satan's Shadow. 12. Cauldron of Cremation. 13. Bridge to Eternity. 14. Power Dive to Doom. 15. Fatal Transformation.

405. Der Mann Ohne Namen

(Germany—Union Film der Ufa, 1921) Serial, 6 chapters. D: Georg Jacoby. SP: Robert Liebmann and Georg Jacoby. Based on de Ewald Gerhard Seeliger's "Peter Voss, der Millionendieb."

Harry Liedtke (Peter Voss), Georg Alexander (Detektiv Bobby Dodd), Mady Christians (Gert Lissen), Jacob Tiedtke (Vater Lissen), Paul Otto (Voss Sen), Edith Meller, Lori Leux, Manja Tzatschewa, Erich Kaiser-Titz, Karl Harbacher, Lovis Brody, Ferdinand v. Alten. Gustav Botz, Hubert V. Meyerinck. Henry Bender, Blandine Ebinger, Albert Paulig, Bruno Lopinski, Paul Morgan.

German: 1. Der Millionendieb. 2. Der Kaiser der Sahara. 3. Gilbe Bestien. 4. Die goldene Flut. 5. Der Mann mit den eisernen Nerven. 6. Der Sprung uber den Schatten. *Portuguese:* 1. O roubo dos milhãoes. 2. Por mares e por terras. 3. De um mundo ao outro. 4. A caminho da África. 5. Ladrão contra ladrão. 6. Na neve e ao frio.

406. The Mansion of Mystery

(Pizor/Capital, December 15, 1927) Serial, 10 chapters, two reels each. P/D: Robert J. Horner.

No information on the plot of this film, which went unnoticed by film reviewers and mainstream theaters alike. Its short circulation life was played out in backstreet and rural theaters. Film was never copyrighted nor, apparently, reviewed in the trade papers.

Barrymore's real name, under which he was sometimes billed, was Boris Bullock. Probably his greatest claim to any recognition at all was a string of poverty row westerns in which he was billed as Kit Carson.

Fred Church had been a minor western star and Jack Richardson played in countless films as a supporting player.

William Barrymore, Teddy Reaves, Fred Church, Kalla Pasha, Margaret Earl, Jack H. Richardson, Earl Gunn.

407. Mark of the Frog

(Pathé, March 25, 1928) Serial, 10 chapters, two reels each. D: Arch B. Heath. S: Edgar Wallace—*The Fellowship of the Frog*.

The Frog and his hirelings terrorize New York City until the hero is able to unmask the arch villain and put a stop to the crime wave. The story develops out of $1,000,000 in loot entrusted to one crook by another 20 years before. The first crook had to make his getaway in a hurry, but said he would be back after his share of the loot. In the meantime the holder of the money has gathered about him a band of criminals and tramps, all branded on the arm with the mark of the frog.

Donald Reed, Margaret Morris, George Harcourt, Gus De Well, Frank Lackteen, Tony Hughes, Frank B. Miller, Helen Greene, Ed Roseman, Sidney Paston, Morgan Jones, William Willis.

1. The Gas Attack. 2. Decoyed. 3. The Jail Delivery. 4. Triple Vengeance. 5. The Enemy Within. 6. Cross Fire. 7. Framed. 8. A Life at Stake. 9. A Race with Death. 10. Paying the Penalty.

408. Mascamor

(France—Cinématographes Phocea, 1918) Serial, 14 chapters. Distributor: E.L. Aubert. D/S/Scen: Pierre Marodon. Re-released in 1920 as feature *The Death Mask.*

This serial with a strong, compelling title is one of those melodramatic films which are without a doubt great favorites with the more youthful and less intelligent attendees of the movies. The story is a conglomeration of would-be melodramatic incidents which are entirely without originality and which also lack anything like cohesion.

The only thing to commend *Mascamor* is its harmlessness and freedom from suggestion. There are several love affairs, but sex never enters into the story. In this case villainy does not pursue womanhood; it is after something intangible and unexplained, although references are certainly made to the heroine's wealth and to some mysterious island in the Pacific in which villainy, masked and sinister, takes an unhealthy interest.

The production is of the gaudy, ornate type. The acting is on a par with the story, being for the main part crude and distinctly unconvincing.

Marthe Lenclud (May Stephenson), Pierre Marodon (Le peintre Jean), Susanne Roumestan (Claire De Precy), Mme. Rebell (Mme. De Precy), De Villette (M. De Precy), Benito Perojo (Marquis Francis Montoriel), Jose Davert (Le valet de Jean), Gino Talamo (Paul Ferrizini), Dartagnan (Baron Ferry), Bader (Robert Sturley).

Portuguese: 1. Três acontecimentos misteriosos. 2. Lançado as feras. 3. A carta postal. 4. O cheque de um milhão. 5. A caixa misteriosa. 6. A máscara mobil. 7. O antropofago. 8. Traição. 9. A mulher misteriosa. 10. As duas irmas. 11. A canção da morte. 12. A nota do violoncelo. 13. O destino. 14. Boomerang.

409. The Masked Marvel

(Republic, March 6, 1943) Serial, 12 chapters, two reels each. D: Spencer Bennet. SP: Royal Cole, Ronald Davidson, Basil Dickey, Jesse Duffy, Grant Nelson, George H. Plympton, and Joseph Poland. Assoc. P: W.J. O'Sullivan. Photography: Reggie Lanning. Music: Mort Glickman. Special Effects: Howard Lydecker. Feature Title: *Sakima and the Masked Marvel.*

The Masked Marvel, crimefighter, is employed by an insurance company to expose and apprehend Japanese agent Sakima, who is sabotaging war industries. The Masked Marvel's identity is unknown, but Alice, daughter of the murdered executive who sought his help, knows that The Masked Marvel is one of four investigators. Crane, the other top insurance executive, is secretly in league with Sakima.

Taking a cue from the popular *The Lone Ranger* (1939), the identity of The Masked Marvel is kept from the audience until the final chapter.

William Forrest (Martin Crane), Louise Currie (Alice Hamilton), Johnny Arthur (Mura Sakima), David Bacon (Bob Barton/The Masked Marvel), Tom Steele (The Masked Marvel [in mask]), Rod Bacon (Jim Arnold), Richard Clarke (Frank Jeffers), Anthony Warde (Killer Mace), Gayne Whitman (The Masked Marvel's Voice), Bill Healy (Terry Morton), Kenneth Harlan (Plant Guard), Nora Lane (Secretary), Duke Green (Karl/Kaler/Spike), Eddie Parker (Meggs), Bill Cody (Gorton), Carey Loftin (Grail), Dale Van Sickel (Bleek/Blunt/Kline), George J. Lewis (Philip Morton), Howard Hickman (Warren Hamilton), Thomas Louden (Mathews), Wendell Niles (Newscaster), Lester Dorr (Reporter), George Pembroke (Air Raid Warden), Stanley Price (Barnes), John Daheim (Bartender), Eddie Phillips (Bert), Ken Terrell (Foreman/Heavy), Allen Pomeroy (Chef), Crane Whitley (Curtiss), Forbes Murray (Doctor), Brooks Benedict (Photographer), Sam Flint (Police Sergeant), Sam Ash (Reporter), Robert Wilkie, Pat O'Shea, Jack O'Shea, George Suzanne (Heavies), Joe Yrigoyen (Gyp), Fred Graham (Hart/Pete), Roy Barcroft (Kern), Herbert Rawlinson (Kettering), Edward Van Sloan (A.M. MacRae), Harry Woods (Parsons), Nolan Leary (Gas Station Attendant), Lee Roberts (Guard), Lynton Brent (Guard), Sam Bernard (Parker), Harold Kruger (J.D. Stone), Tom London (Trucker), Bud Geary (Trucker), Frank O'-Connor (Watchman), Ernie Adams (Wilson), Betty Miles, Charles Hutchison, Preston Peterson, Thom Metzetti.

1. The Masked Crusader. 2. Death Takes the Helm. 3. Dive to Doom. 4. Suspense at Midnight. 5. Murder Meter. 6. Exit to Eternity. 7. Doorway to Destruction. 8. Destined to Die. 9. Danger Express. 10. Suicide Sacrifice. 11. The Fatal Mistake. 12. The Man Behind the Mask.

410. The Masked Menace

(Pathé, October 12, 1927) Serial, 10 chapters, two reels each. D: Arch B. Heath. SP: Paul Fairfax Fuller. S: Clarence Budington Kelland—"Still Face."

Young Dodd helps Grandma Newton and her ward, Faith, in their fight against a rival mill. A man known as "Still Face," who lives in the neighborhood, and who indulges in occult practices, falls in love with Faith, and even succeeds in making her like him. But when he captures both Faith and Dodd she is disillusioned. This mysterious man proves to be the murderer of Faith's father.

This is a rather routine cliffhanger based on the *Saturday Evening Post* story, but with evidence of originality and freshness in the situations, incidents, and other big points of the plot.

Larry Kent (Keats Dodd), Jean Arthur (Faith), Tom Holding (Carl Phillips), Laura Alberta (Grandma Newton), John F. Hamilton (The Half-Wit), William Norton Bailey, Bus De Well, Agnes De Pome, Tom MacLarnie, William Cavanagh, Sydney Paxton, Neill Bridges, Tully Nash, Edward Roseman.

1. Against Odds. 2. An Unknown Assassin. 3. The Enemy Strikes. 4. A Half-Wit's Fury. 5. An Attack at Midnight. 6. Checkmate. 7. By Hook or Crook. 8. Still Face Shows His Hand. 9. The Last Stand. 10. The Menace Unmasked.

411. The Masked Rider

(Arrow, May 1919) Serial, 15 chapters, two reels each. D: Aubrey C. Kennedy. S: Aubrey C. Kennedy. P: William Steiner.

Harry Myers (Harry Burrell), Ruth Stonehouse (Ruth Chadwick), Paul Panzer (Pancho), Edna M. Holland (Juanita), Marie Treador (Ma Chadwick), Blanche Gillespie (Blanche), Robert Tober (Santas), Jack Chapman (Captain Jack), Boris Karloff (A Badman), George Murdock, George Cravey.

1. The Hole in the Wall. 2. In the Hands of Pancho. 3. The Capture of Juanita. 4. The Kiss of Hate. 5. The Death Trap. 6. Pancho Plans Revenge. 7. The Fight on the Dam. 8. The Conspirators Foiled. 9. The Exchange of Prisoners. 10. Harry's Perilous Escape. 11. To the Rescue. 12. The Impostor. 13. Coals of Fire. 14. In the Desert's Grip. 15. Retribution.

412. The Master Key

(Universal, November 28, 1914) Serial, 15 chapters; Chapter 1, three reels; others, two reels. D: Robert Leonard. Scen: Calder Johnson. S: John Fleming Wilson. Supervision: Otis Turner.

Larry Kent in *The Masked Menace* (1927)

Top: **Robert Leonard and Ella Hall in *The Master Key* (1914); *bottom:* Harry Houdini in *The Master Mystery* (1919)**

Considered as one of Universal's finest serials, this story concerns a rich lode of ore that can only be found by following directions hidden in an oriental vase lying at the bottom of the ocean in a sunken ship. However, the location of the sunken ship is scratched on a key to the chest held by Gallon, who attempts to murder his partner to claim the gold for himself. Years later Gallon dies, leaving a daughter, Ruth, and a mediocre mine, "The Master Key." John Dore becomes Ruth's guardian and sweetheart and on her behalf battles Wilkerson, Gallon's old partner, for the key and its secret.

Robert Leonard (John Dore), Ella Hall (Ruth Gallon), Harry Carter (Harry Wilkerson), Jean Hathaway (Jean Darnell), Alfred Hickman (Charles Everett), Wilbur Higby (Tom Gallon), Charles E. Manly (Tom Kane), Jack Holt (Donald Faversham), Jim Corey (Wah Sing), Cleo Madison, Alan Forest, Mack V. Wright, Rupert Julian, Edward A. Mills, Robert Chandler, Marc Robbins.

1. Gold Madness. 2. A Shipwreck and Wrecked Hopes. 3. The Ghost Appears. 4. Over the Divide. 5. The Lost Vein. 6. Wilkerson Strikes. 7. The Battle in the Dark. 8. The Struggle on the Roof. 9. Arrested for Murder. 10. The Fight for the Mine. 11. The Secret of the Chest. 12. The Quest for the Idol. 13. A Queer Alliance. 14. The God Takes Toll. 15. Fate Unlocks the Doors.

413. The Master Key

(Universal, April 18, 1945) Serial, 13 chapters, two reels each. D: Ray Taylor and Lewis D. Collins. SP: Joseph O'Donnell, George H. Plympton, and Ande Lamb. S: Jack Natteford and Dwight Babcock.

A professor develops an Orotron machine that will extract gold from the ocean. Naturally, Nazi agents want it. The unidentified Master Key directs the foreign agents in attempts to steal and utilize the machine, while FBI agent Tom Brant, detective Jack Ryan, and reporter Janet Lowe doggedly pursue the saboteurs.

Milburn Stone (Tom Brant), Jan Wiley (Janet Lowe), Dennis Moore (Jack Ryan), Sarah Padden (Aggie), Russell Hicks (Chief O'Brien), Addison Richards (Garret Donohue), Byron Foulger (Prof. Elwood Henderson), Maris Wrixon (Dorothy Newton), Alfred LaRue (Migsy), George Lynn (Herman), Ken Terrell (Stuntman).

1. Trapped by Flames. 2. Death Turns the Wheel. 3. Ticket to Disaster. 4. Drawbridge Danger. 5. Runaway Car. 6. Shot Down. 7. Death on the Dial. 8. Bullet Serenade. 9. On Stage for Murder. 10. Fatal Masquerade. 11. Crash Curve. 12. Lightning Underground. 13. The Last Key.

414. The Master Mystery

(Octagon Films, March 1920) Serial, 15 chapters; Chapter 1, three reels; others, two reels. D: Burton King and E. Douglas Bingham. S/SP: Arthur B. Reeve and Charles A. Logue. P: B.A. Rolfe.

Quentin Locke, a secret service agent, opposes a ruthless business magnate who heads up International Patents, Inc., an organization out to suppress all competition and progress itself. Quentin soon finds himself fighting a metal monster called Q, the Automaton, which could withstand bullets and other offensive weapons. Unknown to Quentin, the metal monster was inhabited by a human. Throughout the serial the "Emissaries of the Automaton" tried their best to kill Quentin but without success.

Finally Quentin is able to penetrate the monster with an explosive bullet. Other opponents included "Deluxe Dora" and the "Madagascar Strangler."

The serial was a disappointing one; Houdini's magic on screen failed to click with audiences. The film made little, if any, money. Houdini went on to make several features, which likewise were poorly received.

Harry Houdini (Quentin Locke), Marguerite Marsh (Eva), Ruth Stonehouse (DeLuxe Dora), Floyd Buckley (Q, the Automaton), William Pike, Charles Graham, Edna Britton.

1. Living Death. 2. The Iron Terror. 3. The Water Peril.

4. The Test. 5. The Chemist's Shop. 6. The Mad Genius. 7. Barbed Wire. 8. The Challenge. 9. The Madagascan Madness. 10. The Binding Ring. 11. The Net. 12. The Death Noose. 13. The Flash of Death. 14. The Tangled Web. 15. Bound at Last (or) The Unmasking of the Automaton.

415. Masters of Venus

(England—1959) Serial, 8 chapters.

When two kids stow away on a manned spacecraft bound for Venus, they get into all sorts of exciting scrapes. To top it off, the kids and crew discover a lost civilization.

Ferdy Mayne.

416. Mathias Sandorf

(France—Union-Eclair, 1921) Serial, 9 chapters (?). D: Henri Fescourt. Assist. D: Jean-Louis Bouquet. Story: Jules Verne. SP: Henri Fescourt. Producer: Louis Nalpas (Nice).

This serial was condensed into a feature by Pathé and released in the U.S. as *The Isle of Zorda*.

Romuald Joubé (Mathias Sandorf), Yvette Andreyor (Sava Toronthal), Jean Toulout (Silas Toronthal), Paul Vermoyal (Sarcany), Gaston Modot (Carpéna), Armand Tallier (Pierre Bathory), Armand Dutertre (Birik), Henri Maillard (Ferrato), Gabrielle Ristori (Maria Ferrato), Mario Nasthasio (Zirone), Benevenuto-Nardo (Pescade), Milo-Poggi (Matifou), Nazzio (Ladislas Zathmar), Darnay (Etienne Bathory), Djemil Anik (Nasmir), Germaine Pelisse (Mme. Toronthal), Mme. De La Croix (Mme. Bathory).

417. Mefisto

(Spain—Studio Film, 1917) Serial, 12 chapters. D: José Maria Codina. Photography: Solá Mestres and Alfredo Fontanals.

Lola Paris, Baltasar Banquells, Blanca Valoris, Ramón Quadreny, Julián De La Cantera, Maria Alvarez De Burgos, Carmen Rodriguez, José Balaguer, Silvia Mariategui, Laura Bové, la "Tanguerita," Leander Cinca, Señora Fratti, Manolim, Menina Candidita Solá, Menina Banquells, Menina Margarita Espinosa.

Portuguese: 1. Nas ruinas do Castelo Mout. 2. Chegou a hora. 3. O pacto secreto. 4. A pantera vermelha. 5. [Unknown.] 6. [Unknown.] 7. Em poder do inimigo. 8. No posto do tormento. 9. [Unknown.] 10. [Unknown.] 11. A prisão da Marqueza. 12. O triunfo justiceiro.

418. Melting Millions

(Pathé, April 10, 1927) Serial, 10 chapters. D: Spencer G. Bennet. S: Joseph Anthony Roach.

A girl is adopted as a baby by a bandit. Years later, aided by a hero enamored of her and opposed by a band of wealthy criminals, she attempts to gain possession of a fortune that is rightfully hers. In addition to the hero, a mysterious stranger comes to her aid at the most climatic moments.

Allene Ray (Judy Winslow), Walter Miller (Lieutenant Palmer), E.H. Calvert, William Norton Bailey, Eugenia Gilbert, Frank Lackteen, John J. Richardson, George Kuwa, Albert Roccardi, Bob Burns, John Cossar, Ernie Adams, Richard C. Travers, Ann Gladman, William Van Dyke.

1. A Shot in the Dark. 2. Perilous Waters. 3. The Fatal Attack. 4. The Heiress of Craghaven. 5. The Hidden Harbor. 6. A Strange Voyage. 7. The Mysterious Prisoner. 8. The Impostor. 9. The Spy. 10. Exposed.

419. Die Memoiren des Satans

(Germany—Luna Film GmbH, 1917) Serial, 4 chapters. S: Robert Heymann, SP: Robert Heymann.

Friedrich Küehne (Satan), Ernst Hoffmann, Kurt Brenkendorf, Victor Senger, Ilse Oeser, Max Köhler, Cläre Bauer, Georg Anders, Grete Weixler, John Rappeport, Käthe Dorsch.

1. Dr. Mors. 2. Fanatiker des Lebens. 3. Der Fluchbeladen. 4. Der Sturz der Menschheit.

420. Memoiren eines Kammerdieners

(Germany—Esna-Film GmbH, 1921) Series, 2 episodes. D: Arthur Teuber. Scen: Arthur Teuber. S: Eugene Sue. Camera: Willy Grosstuck.

The reason for including this two episode series is because it stars Evi Eva, one of Germany's most popular actresses of the time.

Evi Eva, Ernst Hofmann, Tatjana Irran, Jutta, Jol, Antonie Jaeckel, Marian Lama, Max Wogritsch, G. Konarski, Erwin Fichtner, Fred Immler, Felix Hecht, Paul Ludwig, Willi Kaiser-Heyl, Frau Seeberg, Peggy Permont, Edmund Lowe, Syme Delmar, Karl Schall, Herr Arnoldi, Käthe Richter.

1. Martin, der Findling. 2. Basquines Vergeltung.

421. La Mendiante de Saint-Sulpice

(France, 1923) Serial, 10 chapters. D: Charles Burguet. SP: Charles Burguet. S: Based on novel by Xavier De Montepin.

Gaby Morlay, Charles Vanel, Andree Lionel, Suzanne Revonne, Maxine Desjardins, Gaston Modot, Camile Bardou, Maurice Schutz, Albert Bras, Berthe Jalabert, Andre Darel.

422. Mephisto

(France—Les Films Osso, 1930) Serial, chapters (?). D: Henri Debain and Rene Navarre. SP: Arthur Bernede.

René Navarre was France's first serial star, having played the lead in *Fantômas* (1914). Subsequently he starred in ten more silent serials, making him the country's foremost serial performer. As star of *Mephisto* he had the distinction of headlining France's last serial and its only sound one.

René Navarre (Prof. Bergmann), Jean Gabin (Jacques Miral), Alexandre Mihalesco (Nostradamus), Lucien Callamand, Jacques Maury, France Dhelia, Janine Ronceroy, Gil Lamb, Milly Mathis.

423. The Midnight Man

(Universal, August 1919) Serial, 18 chapters, two reels each. D: James W. Horne. Scen: Harvey Gates. S: James W. Horne and Frank Howard Clarke.

Top: **James J. Corbett in** ***The Midnight Man*** **(1919);** ***bottom: The Million Dollar Mystery*** **(1914)**

Despite the heavyweight champion of the world having the leading role, *The Midnight Man* was less than spectacular. It was more melodrama than an action epic, and Corbett was a much better boxer than he was an actor.

James J. Corbett (Bob Gilmore), Kathleen O'Connor (Nell), Joseph W. Girard (Morgan), Frank Jonasson (John Gilmore), Joseph Singleton (Arnold), Orral Humphrey (Ramah), Georgia Woodthorpe (Martha), William Sauter (Hargreaves), Noble Johnson (Spike), Sam Polo, Montgomery Carlyle, Ann Forrest.

1. Cast Adrift. 2. Deadly Enemies. 3. Ten Thousand Dollars Reward. 4. At Bay. 5. Unmasked. 6. The Elevator Mystery. 7. The Electric Foe. 8. Shadow of Fear. 9. The Society Hold-Up. 10. The Blazing Torch. 11. The Death Ride. 12. The Tunnel of Terror. 13. A Fight to the Finish. 14. The Jaws of Death. 15. The Wheel of Terror. 16. Hurled from the Heights. 17. The Cave of Destruction. 18. A Wild Finish.

424. Mike and Ike

(Universal, 1927–1929) Series, 26 episodes, two reels each. D: Francis Corby, Gus Meins, Roland Asher, Samuel Newfield. Based on the "Mike and Ike" cartoons by Rube Goldberg.

Future Western badman Charles King started his career as a comedian. He teams with Charles Dorety in the first eight entries in this series. Beginning with the ninth film, Joe Young and Ned LaSalle took over the roles. When known, the director's name appears in parentheses.

Charles King, Charles Dorety, Joe Young, Ned LaSalle, Thelma Daniels, Ethlyne Clair.

1. Dancing Fools (Francis Corby). 2. All for Uncle (Francis Corby). 3. Oh Mabel! (Francis Corby). 4. There's a Will (Francis Corby). 5. Dates for Two (Francis Corby). 6. What A Party (Francis Corby). 7. No Blondes Allowed (Francis Corby). 8. Taking the Count (Francis Corby). 9. Just the Type (Gus Meins). 10. Women Chasers (Francis Corby). 11. Cash Customers. 12. Whose Life? (Francis Corby). 13. Broke Out (Roland Asher). 14. Just Wait (Gus Meins). 15. Shooting the Bull (Gus Meins). 16. Husbands Won't Tell (Francis Corby). 17. And Morning Came. 18. Fish Stories. 19. Hold Your Horses. 20. Take Your Pick. 21. She's a Pippin'. 22. Finishing School (Gus Meins). 23. Early to Wed. 24. Good Skates. 25. This Way Please (Samuel Newfield). 26. Chaperones (Samuel Newfield).

425. The Million Dollar Mystery

(Thanhouser, July 1914) Serial, 23 chapters, two reels each. D: Howell Hansell [Jay Cainns directed the 23rd chapter]. S: Harold McGrath. Scen: Lloyd Lonergan. Re-released in 1918 as a six-reel feature by Randolph Film Corporation.

The story employs the well-proved formula of a pretty,

persecuted heroine with enemies more powerful than friends—at least until the climax—and embellished with a thrill or more for each chapter.

Crooks attempt to steal $1 million belonging to Hargreave and are aided by Countess Olga, who pretends friendship with Hargreave's daughter, Florence. Jim Norton, a newspaper reporter, in love with Florence, is instrumental in keeping the thieves, headed by Braine, from obtaining the money or harming Florence.

An extremely popular serial, it grossed almost $1.5 million on an investment of $125,000. This serial is given credit for starting the craze for masked conspirators.

Florence La Badie (Florence Hargreave), Marguerite Snow (Countess Olga), James Cruze (Jim Norton), Frank Farrington (Braine), Sidney Bracey (Hargreave), Irving Cummings (Russian Secret Agent), Alfred Norton (Stanley Hargreave), Lila Chester (Susan), Creighton Hale, Mitchell Lewis, Donald Gallagher, Fairbanks Twins, Claire Krall, William A. Sullivan, Baby Julie Cruze, Albert Froome, Nick Wood, Carey Hastings, Arthur Bauer, Eugene Moore.

1. The Airship in the Night. 2. The False Friend. 3. A Leap in the Dark. 4. The Top Floor Flat. 5. The Battle at the Bottom of the Sea. 6. The Coaching Party of the Countess. 7. The Doom of the Auto Bandits. 8. The Wiles of a Woman. 9. The Leap from an Ocean Liner. 10. Unknown. 11. In the Path of the Fast Express. 12. The Elusive Treasure Box. 13. The Secret Agent from Russia. 14. Tracked by the Secret Service. 15. The Borrowed Hydroplane. 16. Drawn into the Quicksand. 17. A Battle of Wits. 18. Trapped by Flames. 19. The Underground River. 20. The Secret Warning. 21. The Documents Out of the Treasure Box. 22. The Waterloo of the Conspirators. 23. The Mystery Solved.

426. The Miracle Rider

(Mascot, May 4, 1935) Serial, 15 chapters; Chapter 1, five reels; others, two reels. D: Armand Schaefer and B. Reeves Eason. S: Barney Sarecky, Wellyn Totman, Gerald and Maurice Geraghty. SP: John Rathmell. Photography: Ernest Miller and William Nobles. P: Nat Levine.

Texas Ranger captain Tom Morgan and Ruth, daughter of a murdered chieftain, battle to save the Ravenhead Indians from being driven off their land by Zaroff and his minions. Zaroff is secretly mining Indian ore, which he needs to produce the world's deadliest explosive, "X-94."

This was Mascot's only 15 chapter serial (with an extremely long first chapter) and Tom Mix's last film. It was Mascot's most popular serial, proving that Mix still had a magic name, and justifying the $10,000 a week salary he received while making the film. He had taken the job to obtain money to keep his ailing circus on the road.

Tom Mix (Tom Morgan), Joan Gale (Ruth), Charles Middleton (Zaroff), Jason Robards, Sr. (Carlton), Robert Kortman (Longboat), Edward Earle (Adams), Edward Hearn (Janes), Tom London (Sewell), Niles Welch (Metzger), Edmund Cobb (Vining), Ernie Adams (Stelter), Max Wagner (Morley), Charles King (Hatton), George Chesebro (Crossman), Jack Rockwell (Rogers), Stanley Price (Chapman), George Barton (Mort), Wally Wales (Texas Ranger), Buffalo Bill, Jr. (Daniel Boone), Dick Curtis (Outlaw), Frank Ellis (Outlaw), Dick Alexander (Outlaw), Hank Bell (Outlaw), Slim Whitaker (Outlaw), Earl Dwyer (Buffalo Bill), Robert Frazer (Black Wing), Lafe McKee (Colonel), Tony, Jr. [Horse] (Tony), Cliff Lyons (Mix's Double), Fred Burns (Doctor), Forrest Taylor) (Outlaw), Art Ardigan (Indian), Black Hawk (Chief Two Hawks), Chief Standing Bear (Chief Long Elk), Pat O'Malley (Sam Morgan).

1. The Vanishing Indian. 2. The Firebird Strikes. 3. The Flying Knife. 4. A Race with Death. 5. Double-Barreled Doom. 6. Thundering Hoofs. 7. The Dragnet. 8. Guerrilla Warfare. 9. The Silver Band. 10. Signal Fires. 11. A Traitor Dies. 12. Danger Rides with Death. 13. The Secret of X-94. 14. Between Two Fires. 15. Justice Rides the Plains.

427. Miracles of the Jungle

(Warner Bros., July 16, 1921) Serial, 15 chapters, two reels each. D: E.A. Martin and James Conway. S: E.A. Martin. P: William N. Selig.

Two Secret Service men in Africa to arrest a suspected

Top: **Edward Hearn, Tom Mix, and Ernie Adams in *The Miracle Rider* (1935); *bottom:* Ben Hagerty, Wilbur Higby, and Irene Wallace in *Miracles of the Jungle* (1921)**

murderer are at first harassed by his two daughters but later aid them in their escape from a villain. They clear the suspect with the help of a giant native and a mystic.

Ben Hagerty (Bob Hathaway), Wilbur Higby (Tom Cortland), Al Ferguson (Brian, the Red Fox), Frederic Peters (Zeda, the Zulu), John George (See'er of All), Genevieve Berte (Marian Madson), Irene Wallace (Helen Madson).

1. The City of Lions. 2. The Passage of Death. 3. The Jungle Attack. 4. The Leopard's Revenge. 5. The Storm in the Desert. 6. To the Rescue. 7. The Leopard's Lair. 8. Doomed to Death. 9. In the Hands of the Apes. 10. Midst Raging Tigers. 11. Twelve Against One. 12. Cheating Death. 13. The Heart of an Elephant. 14. The Lions' Leap. 15. All's Well that Ends Well.

428. Les Misérables

(France—Pathé-Consortium–Cinéma, 1925) Serial, 4 chapters. D: Henri Fescourt. Scen: Henri Fescourt. S: Victor Hugo. Assist. D: Rene Barberis. Producer: Louis Nalpas.

Gabriel Gabrio (Jean Valjean), Sandra Milovanoff (Fantine et Cosette), Jean Toulout (Javert), Paul Jorge (Mgr. Myriel), Nivette Saillard (Eponine), Renée Carl (La Thénardier), Jeanne-Marie Laurent (Mme. Magloire), Mme. De Castillo (Soeur Simplice), Clara Darcey-Roche (Mlle. Baptistine), Andrée Rolance (Cosette enfant), Francois Rozet (Marius), Georges Saillard (Thenardier), Paul Guide (Enjolras), Henri Maillard (Luc-Esprit Gillenormand), Charles Badiole (Gavroche), Dartegnan (Pontmercy), Victor Duyen (Fauchelevent), Marcelle Barry (Mme. Victurnien), Emilien Richaud (Bamatabois), Mlle. Darcy (Azelma).

1. Fantine. 2. Fantine et Cosette. 3. Marius. 4. Jean Valjean.

429. The Mishaps of Musty Suffer

(Essanay, April 1, 1916) Series, 30 episodes, one reel each.

Series 1: Harry Watson Jr. (Musty Suffer), H.H. McCullum (George Bickel), Dan Crimmins (Alma Hanlon), Della Connor (Cissy Fitzgerald), Rose Gore (William Thomas), Maxfield Moree. 1. Cruel and Unusual. 2. Keep Moving! 3. Hold Fast! 4. Going Up. 5. Look Out Below. 6. The Lightning Bell-Hop. 7. Bells and Belles. 8. Just Imagination. 9. Out of Order. 10. Coming Cown. *Series 2:* Harry Watson Jr. (Musty Suffer), Della Connor, Maxfield Moree, H.H. McCullum, Dan Crimmins. 1. Blow Your Horn. 2. Showing Some Speed. 3. While You Wait. 4. Local Showers. 5. A Pirate Bold. 6. Outs and Ends. 7. Strictly Private. 8. Active Service. 9. Partly Cloudy. 10. Fore and Aft. *Series 3:* Harry Watson Jr. (Musty Suffer), Maxfield Moree, Dan Crimmins, Della Connor. 1. The Fried Egg Hero. 2. The Soda Jerker. 3. Wet and Dry. 4. Truly Rural. 5. The Ladder of Fame. 6. Pure and Simple. 7. Spliced and Iced. 8. Starlight Sleep. 9. Musty B. Young. 10. Musty's Vacation.

Kenneth MacDonald, Ray Corrigan (as the ape), and Robert Lowery in *The Monster and the Ape* (1945)

430. Mr. Jack Series

(Vitagraph, March–May, 1916) Series, 11 episodes, one reel each. D: C. Jay Williams. Scen: Rudolph Block (1), Paul West (2), William B. Courtney (1), Bruno Lessing (4), Fred H. James (1), Ross D. Whytock (2).

A short comedy series starring the popular Frank Daniels.

[Numbers in parentheses indicates the number of episodes the player appeared in.] Frank Daniels (Mr. Jack) (11), Kate Price (2), Rose Tapley (5), William Cameron (1), Ida Williams (10), Betty Howe (3), Nellie Anderson (1), Garry McGarry (1), Mrs. Pillsbury (1), George Stevens (2), Mrs. C. Jay Williams (2), Eulalie Jensen (1), Logan Paul (1), Edward Elkas (1), William Gilson (1), Edward Boulden (1), Marguerite Forrest (2), J.P. Tucker (1), Arthur Cozine (1), Dave Burton (1), Belle Bruce (1), Edwina Robbins (1).

1. Mr. Jack, a Doctor by Proxy. 2. Mr. Jack a Hallroom Hero. 3. Mr. Jack Ducks the Alimony. 4. Mr. Jack Wins a Double-Cross. 5. Mr. Jack Trifles. 6. Mr. Jack Ducks the Alimony. 7. Mr. Jack Goes Into Business. 8. Mr. Jack Hires a Stenographer. 9. Mr. Jack Inspects Paris. 10. Mr. Jack's Artistic Sense. 11. Mr. Jack, the Has Magnet.

431. Los Misterios de Barcelona

(Spain—Hispano Films, 1915) Serial, 8 chapters. D: Alberto Marro. SP: Antonio Altadill. Remake of *The Exploits of Elaine*.

Clara Wilson, Joaquin Carrasco, Juan Argelagues, Jose Balaguer, Maria Reigada, Jose Durany, Pierre Smith, Isolina Fretti, Emilia De La Mata, Angelita Blanco, Juan Durany, Jose Marti, Manuel Arbo Del Val, Alicia Ventura, Francisco Carrasco.

1. Los deportados. 2. El barco contrabandista. 3. La herencia de los seis millones. 4–8 [Unknown.]

432. The Monster and the Ape

(Columbia, April 1945) Serial, 15 chapters, two reels each. D: Howard Bretherton. SP: Sherman Lowe and Royal K. Cole. Assist. D: Leonard J. Shapiro. P: Rudolph C. Flothow. Photography: L.W. O'Connell. Music: Lee Zahler.

An evil professor tries to steal the Metalogen, a robot, and the Metalogen metal from which it is made. He employs a trained gorilla to make things difficult for the Metalogen inventor, his daughter, and Ken Morgan, who represents the company for whom the Metalogen is intended.

Robert Lowery (Ken Morgan), George Macready (Ernest), Ralph Morgan (Professor Arnold), Carole Mathews (Babs Arnold), Willie Best (Flash), Jack Ingram (Nordik), Anthony Warde (Flint), Ted Mapes (Butler), Eddie Parker (Blake), Stanley Price (Mead), Kenneth MacDonald (Inspector Hamilton), Charles King (Policeman), Lee Shumway (Hardy), Bud Osborne (Guard at Zoo), Kit Guard (Guard at Zoo), Ray Corrigan (The Gorilla), John Elliott, Forbes Murray, George Eldredge.

1. The Mechanical Terror. 2. The Edge of Doom. 3. Flames of Fate. 4. The Fatal Search. 5. Rocks of Doom. 6. A Friend in Disguise. 7. A Scream in the Night. 8. Death in the Dark. 9. The Secret Tunnel. 10. Forty Thousand Volts. 11. The Mad Professor. 12. Shadows of Destiny. 13. The Gorilla at Large. 14. His Last Flight. 15. Justice Triumphs.

433. The Moon Riders

(Universal, April 1, 1920) Serial, 18 chapters, two reels each. D: Reeves Eason and Albert Russell. S: Albert Russell, George Hively, Theodore Wharton, William Piggott, and Karl Coolidge. SP: George Hively, Albert Russell, and Theodore Wharton.

This film, more than any other, established Art Accord as a leading movie cowboy. It was one of the most popular cliffhangers turned out by any studio in the silent era. With leading lady Mildred Moore, Art scampered through 18 galvanic chapters, chasing a treasure owned by a lost tribe of mysterious Indians. Naturally, there were bad guys who also wanted the treasure. But somehow Art stayed alive and finally got both the girl and the gold after two reels of spine-tingling adventures each week. (Art broke his leg during filming, holding up production several weeks.)

Art Acord (Buck Ravelle), Mildred Moore (Anne Baldwin), Charles Newton (Anne's Father), George Field (Egbert), Tote DuCrow (Warpee), Beatrice Dominquez (Rose), Albert MacQuarrie (Gant).

1. Over the Precipice. 2. Masked Marauders. 3. Red Rage of Jealousy. 4. Vultures of the Hills. 5. Death Trap. 6. Caves of Mystery. 7. The Menacing Monster. 8. At the Rope's End. 9. The Triple Menace. 10. The Moon Rider's Bride. 11. Death's Door. 12. Pit of Fire. 13. House of Doom. 14. Unmasked. 15. His Hour of Torture. 16. The Flaming Peril. 17. Rushing Waters. 18. Clearing Skies.

434. Mutt and Jeff

(U.S.A., 1911–1919) Series.

Very little information could be found on this series, as it was not copyrighted. An incomplete listing of episode titles follows. Each episode told a complete story.

Mutt and Jeff (1911). Mutt and Jeff and the Black Hand (1912). Mutt and Jeff and the Lady Stenographer (1912). Mutt and Jeff in the Theatrical Business (1917). Mutt and Jeff in Ireland (1919). Mutt and Jeff in London (1919). Mutt and Jeff in Paris (1919). Mutt and Jeff in Rome (1919). Mutt and Jeff in Spain (1919). Mutt and Jeff in Switzerland (1919). Mutt and Jeff in the Frozen North (1919). Mutt and Jeff in the Movies (1919).

435. Mutt and Jeff Cartoon Series

(U.S.A., 1915–1928) Over 500 films were made. (1915–1920 made by Mutt and Jeff Film Exchange; 1917–? Budd Fisher Films Corp.; 1925–1927 Associated Animators; 1927–1928 Short Films Syndicate)

Hock Shop (1916). Chamber of Horrors (1916). Interpreter (1916). Two for Five (1916). Promoters (1916). Harps and Haloes (1917). Hospital (1918). Dog Pound (1918). Cramps (1918). Wall Street (1918). Inventors (1918). Brave Toreador (1919). Bowling Alley (1920). Cold Turkey (1923). Around the World in 24 Hours (1924). Where Am I? (1925). Bombs and Boobs (1926). At Sea (1926). Cowboys (1926). Westward Whoa (1926). Tropical Island (1926). Missing Link (1926). Stretch in Time (1927).

436. Mylord l'Arsouille

(France—Société des Cinéromans, 1925) Serial, 3 chapters. D: Rene Le Prince. SP: Paul Dambry. Photography: Rene Gaveau.

Aime Simon-Girard, Maria Dalbaicin, Simone Vaudry, Anna Lefeuvrier, Jeanne-Marie Laurent, Jacques Guilhene, Albert Decoeur, Michael Floresco, Claude Merelle, Carlos Avril, Jean-Paul De Baere, Pierre Labry, Louis Blanche.

1. Nina. 2. La machine infernale. 3. Redemption.

437. Le Mystère de la Tour Eiffel

(France—Etablissements L. Aubert, 1927) Serial, 6 chapters. P: Film d'Art (Vandal et Delae). D: Julien Duvivier. Assist. D: A. Berthomieu. SP: Alfred Machard. Photography: R. Guichard and A. Thirard.

Tramel, Regine Bouet, Gaston Jacquet, Andrée Reynis, Jean Diener, Jimmy Gaillard, Viguier, Roger Piquard, Pierre Hot, Mme. Valentine, Mme. Darska.

Art Acord and Mildred Moore in *The Moon Riders* (1920)

438. Les Mystères de Paris

(France—Cinématographes Phocea, 1922) Serial, 8 chapters. D: Charles Burguet. SP: Eugene Sue. SP: Charles Burguet and André Paul Antoine.

Huguette Duflos (Fleur-de-Marie), Georges Lannes (Le Prince Rodolphe), Andrée Lionel (Sarah MacGrégor), Camille Bardou (Le Chourineur), Suzanne Bianchetti (Marquise d'Harville), Paul Vermoyal (Le Notaire Ferrand), Gilbert Dalleu (Le Maître d'école), Bérangère (La Chouette), Gaston Modot (Martial), Yvonne Sergyl (Louise Morel), Paul Guidé (Marquis d'Harville), Pierre Fresnay (François Germain), Madeleine Guitty (La Goualeuse), Berthe Jalabert (Mme. Séraphin), Charles Lamy (M. Pipelet), Mme. S. Suhamel (Mme. Pipelet), Desdemona Mazza (Cecile), Simone Vaudry (Claire Dubreuil), Pierrette Caillol (Rigolette), Mme. Berendt (La Louve), Marie-Rouvier (Mme. Georges), Sidèle Mundo (Mme. Georges), Ernest Maupain (Walter Murph), René Blancard (Bras-Rouge), Martin (Tortillard), Pillot (Tom Seyton), C. Liten (Morel), Regine Dumien (Fleur-de-Marie, enfant), Maxime Desjardins, Paul Bernard.

1. [Unknown.] 2. La ferme de Bouqueval. 3. [Unknown.] 4. Le ménage Pipelet. 5. Les suites d'un bal a l'ambassade. 6. Misère. 7. Le martyre de Louise Morel. 8. L' étude de Maître Ferrand.

439. The Mysteries of Fu Manchu

(England—Stoll Productions, 1923) Series, 15 episodes, two reels each. D: A.E. Colby. Based on characters created by Sax Rohmer.

Harry Agar Lyons (Fu Manchu), Fred Paul (Sir Neyland Smith), Joan Clarkson (Karamaneh), Humberston Wright (Dr. Petrie), Frank Wilson (Inspector Weymouth), H. Cundall, Pat Royale, Stacey Gaunt, Fred Raynham, D. Bland, Laurie Leslie, Robert English, Booth Conway, Charles Vane, Lewis Waller, Wyngold Lawrence.

1. Aaron's Rod. 2. The Call of Siva. 3. The Clue of the Pigtail. 4. The Cry of the Night Hawk. 5. The Fiery Hand. 6. The Fungi Cellars. 7. The Knocking on the Door. 8. The Man with the Limp. 9. The Miracle. 10. The Queen of Hearts. 11. The Sacred Order. 12. The Scented Envelope. 13. The Shrine of the Seven Lamps. 14. The Silver Buddha. 15. The West Case.

440. The Mysteries of Myra

(International Film Service/Pathé, April 24, 1916) Serial, 15 chapters; Chapter 1, three reels; others, two reels. D: Theodore and Leo Wharton. S: Hereward Carrington and Charles W. Goddard. SP: Charles W. Goddard.

The secret Black Order, a cult of powerful magicians who live in an underground city, is involved in thought transference, witchcraft, levitation, and general mysticism and skullduggery. Myra becomes a target of the group because of incriminating evidence which she has. During an experiment with sending out her astral body, an elemental spirit enters her body, leaving her astral self to drift through the netherworlds. The order captures a woman vampire and puts her to work on Myra's trail, along with a huge bulking "Thought Monster." But her fiancé, Dr. Payson Alden, an occult scientist, is able to protect her with a little magic of his own. This film is considered unique and perhaps the ultimate in horror fantasy serials of the silent era.

Jean Sothern (Myra Maynard), Howard Estabrook (Dr. Payson Alden), Allen Murname (Art Varney), M.W. Rale (The High Master), Bessie Wharton (Mrs. Maynard), Le Roy Baker.

1. The Road to Yesterday. 2. Poisoned Flower. 3. The Mystic Mirrors. 4. The Wheel of Spirit. 5. The Fumes of Fear. 6. The Hypnotic Clue. 7. The Mystery Mind. 8. The Neither. 9. The Invisible Destroyer. 10. Levitation. 11. The Fire-Elemental. 12. Elixir of Youth. 13. Witchcraft. 14. Suspended Animation. 15. The Thought Monster.

Jean Sothern and Howard Estabrook in *The Mysteries of Myra* (1916)

441. The Mysterious Airman

(Weiss Brothers Artclass, June 1, 1928) Serial, 10 chapters, two reels each. D: Harry Revier. SP: Arthur B. Reeve.

The Baker Airways, of which Jack Baker is president, have secured supremacy in civil aviation. They sustain severe loss, however, owing to the planes being destroyed by a gang of air pirates, headed by a mysterious Pilot X. Jack Baker, aided by his fiancée, Shirley Joyce, sets to work to outwit the gang, and the task provides a series of thrilling air adventures.

Walter Miller (Jack Baker), Eugenia Gilbert (Shirley Joyce), Robert Walker (William Craft), Eugene Burr (Albert Orren), Dorothy Talcott (Fawn Nesbitt), James A. Fitzgerald (Barney Madden), C.H. Allen

(James Joyce), Ray Childs (Henry Knight), Hugh Blair (Detective Mullens), Arthur Morrison (Perkins), Hamilton Morse (Mardos Kartoff).

1. The Winged Avenger. 2. The Sky Writer. 3. The Girl Who Flew Alone. 4. The Smoke Screen. 5. The Air Raid. 6. The Vampire Pilot. 7. The Faker Pilot. 8. The Air Raft. 9. The Hidden Hanger. 10. Mystery Pilot X.

442. Mysterious Doctor Satan

(Republic, December 1940) Serial, 15 chapters, two reels each. D: William Witney and John English. SP: Franklyn Adreon, Ronald Davidson, Norman S. Hall, Joseph Poland, and Sol Shor. Assoc. P: Hiram S. Brown, Jr. Music: Cy Feuer. Feature Title: *Dr. Satan's Robot.*

Dr. Satan needs a remote control device developed by Professor Scott before he can activate the mechanical man he has invented and use it for criminal purposes. Whenever Satan attempts to steal the remote control device, however, he is thwarted by the Copperhead, unaware that the man behind the copper mask is young Bob Wayne. Finally Dr. Satan kidnaps and forces Professor Scott to install the device in his mechanical man. But before he can do much harm with it Copperhead foils him and brings about Satan's death at the hands of his own creation.

Eduardo Ciannelli (Dr. Satan), Robert Wilcox (Bob Wayne/Copperhead), Ella Neal (Lois Scott), William Newill (Speed Martin), C. Montague Shaw (Thomas Scott), Jack Mulhall (Rand), Dorothy Herbert (Alice Brent), Charles Trowbridge (Governor Bronson), Edwin Stanley (Bevans), Walter McGrail (Stoner), Lynton Brent (Scarlett), Edward Cassidy (Barton), Eddie Parker (Chuck), Eddie Dew (Gas Station Attendant), Jack O'Shea (Heavy), Kenneth Harlan (Lathrop), Virginia Carroll (Nurse), Wally West (Palmer), Charles Hutchison (Proprietor), Yakima Canutt (Sailor), Bud Wolfe (Sailor), Duke Taylor (Watkins), Davison Clark (Wagner), Hal Price (Smith), Alan Gregg (Red), Patrick Kelly (Plant Heavy), Frank Ellis (Plant Heavy), Robert Wayne (Perry), Frank Brownlee (Panamint Pete), Floyd Criswell (Officer), George Allen (Spike), Bud Geary (Hallett), Martin Lamont (Steve), Tom Steele (Truck Heavy), Bill Wilkus (Truck Heavy), Al Seymour (Jake), Ernest Sarracino (Mike), Jerry Jerome (Green), John Bagni (Gray), Ted Stanhope (Glover), Bert LeBaron (Fallon), Paul Marion (Corbay), Archie Twitchell (Ross), Ken Terrell (Corwin), Al Taylor (Joe), Jimmy Fawcett (Al), William Stahl (Brock), Frank Conklin (Burns), James Bush (Co-Pilot), Harry Strang (Davis), Duke Green (Duke), Tristram Coffin (Wells), Bill Yrigoyen, David Sharpe, Lloyd Whitlock, Cy Slocum, Sam Garrett, Bob Rogers, Fred Schaefer, Helen Thurston.

1. Return of the Copperhead. 2. Thirteen Steps. 3. Undersea Tomb. 4. The Human Bomb. 5. Doctor Satan's Man of Steel. 6. Double Cross. 7. The Monster Strikes. 8. Highway of Death. 9. Double Jeopardy. 10. Bridge of Peril. 11. Death Closes In. 12. Crack-Up. 13. Disguised. 14. The Flaming Coffin. 15. Doctor Satan Strikes.

Top: **Walter Miller and Eugenia Golbert in *The Mysterious Airman* (1928);** ***bottom:*** **Eduardo Cianelli and Ella Neal in *Mysterious Doctor Satan* (1940)**

443. Mysterious Island

(Columbia, September 1951) Serial, 15 chapters, two reels each. D: Spencer G. Bennet. SP: Lewis Clay, Royal K. Cole, George H. Plympton. S: Jules Verne—"The Isle of Mystery." P: Sam Katzman. Assist. D: R.M. Andrews. Photography: Fayte Browne. Music: Mischa Bakaleinikoff.

Several Yankee prisoners escape a Confederate prison via balloon and days later find themselves marooned on a desert island. Here they encounter a spaceship carrying two men and a girl from Mercury. The Mercurians are seeking a mysterious and rare metal to be used in making an explosive capable of destroying the earth. The Yanks also encounter hostile natives, pirates, and Captain Nemo, who aids them because of his desire to stop Mercurian Rura. There were few dull moments as various plot twists were unveiled. However, the cost-cutting was obvious as Sam Katzman strived to bring the film in under budget.

Richard Crane (Captain Harding), Marshall Reed (Jack Pencroft), Karen Randle (Rulu), Ralph Hodges (Bert Brown), Gene Roth (Captain Shard), Hugh Prosser (Gideon Spillett), Terry Frost (Ayrton), Leonard Penn (Captain Nemo), Rusty Wescoatt (Moley), Bernard Hamilton (Neb), Frank Ellis, Zon Murray, Top [dog].

1. Lost in Space. 2. Sinister Savages. 3. Savage Justice. 4. Wild Man at Large. 5. Trail of the Mystery Man. 6. The Pirates Attack. 7. Menace of the Mercurians. 8. Between Two Fires. 9. Shrine of the Silver Bird. 10. Fighting Fury. 11. Desperate Chance. 12. Mystery of the Mien. 13. Jungle Downfall. 14. Men from Tomorrow. 15. The Last of Mysterious Island.

444. The Mysterious Mr. M

(Universal, July 23, 1946) Serial, 13 chapters, two reels each. D: Lewis D. Collins and Vernon Keays. SP: Joseph Poland, Paul Huston, and Barry Shipman. Assist. P: Joseph O'Donnell. Exec. P: Morgan B. Cox. Assist. D: Willard Sheldon, Charles M. Bennett, and Gordon Dobbs.

Two investigators seek to solve the case of the disappearance of a submarine inventor kidnapped by a gang headed by mysterious Mr. M.

Richard Martin (Kirby Walsh), Pamela Blake (Shirley Clinton), Dennis Moore (Grant Farrell), Jane Randolph (Marina Lamont), Danny Morton (Derek Mamont), Virginia Brissac (Grandma Waldron), Edmund MacDonald (Anthony Waldron), Byron Foulger (Wetherby), Joseph Crehan (Captain Blair), Jack Ingram (William Schrack), Joseph Hayworth (Donninger), William Brooks [William Ching] (Jim Farrell), John Hamilton (Doctor Kitredge), Keith Richards (FBI Agent Rutledge), Harry Strang (Bill Brewster), Jamesson Shade (Doctor Madison), George Eldridge (Thomas Elliott), Walden Boyle (Skinner), Donald Kerr (Turnkey), Don McGill (Evans), Emmett Vogan (Brophy), Robert Barron (Brock), George Magrill (Taxicab Driver), Bob Thom (Dowling), Jack Gargan (Gateman), Leo Kaye (Martin), Jack Lorenz (Bus Driver), Beatrice Roberts (Doctor Walker), Helen Deverell (Nurse), Eddie Parker (Mechanic and Double for Martin), Mauritz Hugo (Archer), Howard Negley (FBI Agent Castleton), Bruce Donovan (Steve), Cyril Delevanti (Jackson Parker), Anthony Warde (Martin Brandon), Daral Hudson (Sergeant Ed Winthrop), Perc Launders (Policeman), Casey MacGregor (Policeman), Jack Rockwell (Oil Field Guard), Frank Cody (Smith) Buck Harrington (Ticket Seller), Warren Jackson (Rogan), Doug Carter (Barren), Alfred Wagstaff (Dorgin), Billy Vernon (Sailor), Patricia Alphin (Miss Buckley), Dave Sharpe (Double for Dennis Moore), Franklin Parker (Carson).

1. When Clocks Chime Death. 2. Danger Downward. 3. Flood of Flames. 4. The Double Trap. 5. Highway Execution. 6. Heavier Than Water. 7. Stranger Coliseum. 8. When Friend Kills Friend. 9. Parachute Peril. 10. The Human Time-Bomb. 11. The Key to Murder. 12. High-Lien Smash-Up. 13. The Real Mr. M.

Richard Crane, Karen Randle, and Marshall Reed in *Mysterious Island* (1951)

445. The Mysterious Pearl

(Photoplay Serial/Berwilla, November 29, 1921) Serial, 15 chapters, two reels each. D: Ben Wilson and Duke Worne. SP: J. Grubb Alexander and Harvey Gates. P: Ben Wilson.

This serial has a most complicated plot. Victor Durand, a French scientist, has worked for years to perfect a method of making genuine pearls. He is obsessed with the idea to the exclusion of his young wife, Charlotte. Durand's method requires real pearls and human blood. Paul Kozloff, his laboratory assistant, aids him by stealing a pearl necklace. Later he learns that Durand's experiment has been successful and demands a half share in the secret on the threat of exposing Durand to the police. They fight. Durand's wife enters just in time to prevent Durand's killing of Kozloff.

Kozloff, vindictive and unforgiving, informs police that Durand is the thief. Durand and his wife flee the city. The pursuit leads across the continent and finally into the Algerian mountains, where Durand dies in a rock slide. A guide saves Charlotte. However, she becomes insane from the grief and tragedy, but gives birth to a daughter, Ariel.

Kozloff shows up and takes the baby and steals the secret formula. Ariel grows to young womanhood under the belief that Kozloff is her father. He has taught her to steal the pearls he needs to make genuine pearls. She becomes known as "The Pearl." Time passes. Ariel falls in love with Scott Mallory of Scotland Yard. The story takes a lot of twists and turns but in the end Ariel and Scott are married. She has been exonerated after her supposed dead father shows up in court and admits he killed the men who killed his wife and that he returned all the pearls taken by Ariel while she was under the spell of Kozloff so that she would not be a thief in fact. He kills Kozloff in the courtroom and then commits suicide.

Ben Wilson (Scott Mallory), Neva Gerber (Ariel/"The Pearl"/Charlotte Durand), Joseph W. Girard (Paul Kozloff), William Carroll (Victor Durand), Ashton Dearholt (Topper Lacey), Charles King, Duke Worne, Charles B. Mason.

1. The Pearl Web. 2. The Brass Spectre. 3. The Hand in the Fog. 4. Four Black Pennies. 5. Through the Door. 6. The Bride of Hate. 7. The Getaway. 8. Broken Fetters. 9. Leering Faces. 10. The Graven Image. 11. The Phantom Husband. 12. The Door Between. 13. The Living Death. 14. The Sting of the Lash. 15. The Pearl.

446. The Mysterious Pilot

(Columbia, November 1937) Serial, 15 chapters; Chapter 1, three reels; others, two reels. D: Spencer Gordon Rosener and George M. Merrick. S: William Byron Mowery—*The Silver Hawk*. P: Jack Fier and Louis Weiss. Photography: Edward Linden, Herman Schoop. Music: Abe Meyer.

Jim Dorn, an aerial mapper for the Royal Canadian Air Force, finds himself unexpectedly involved in an intricate web of murder, mystery, and intrigue when he aids Jean McNain, following a train accident in Title Pass. Jean is escaping from business tycoon Snowden Carter, who cased the wreck and murdered a man aboard the train, and from the police who believe her guilty of the murder.

Frank Hawks (Jim Dorn), Dorothy Sebastian (Jean McNain), Rex Lease (Kansas), Guy Bates Post (Bergelot), Kenneth Harlan (Snowden), Yakima Canutt (Luke), Frank Lackteen (Yoroslaf), Robert Terry (Casper), George Rosener (Fritz), Clara Kimball Young (Martha), Harry Harvey (Soft Shoe), Tom London (Kilgour), Ted Adams (Carlson), Earl Douglas (Jerry), Robert Walker (Boyer), Roger Williams (McCarthy), Esther Ralston (Vivian McNain), Dave O'Brien.

1. The Howl of the Wolf. 2. The Web Tangles. 3. Enemies in the Air. 4. In the Hands of the Law. 5. The Crack-Up. 6. The Dark Hour. 7. Wings of Destiny. 8. Battle in the Sky. 9. The Great Flight. 10. Whirlpool of Death. 11. The Haunted Mill. 12. The Lost Trail. 13. The Net Tightens. 14. Vengeance Rides the Airways. 15. Retribution.

447. The Mystery Box

(Davis Distributing/Vital Exchanges, June 6, 1926) Serial, 10 chapters, two reels each. D/S: Alvin J. Neitz. P: Ben Wilson.

A mysterious box is entrusted to Dolly Hampton with instructions to guard it with her life. Aided by her cowboy fiancé, who is eluding a posse on a false murder charge, the two manage to hang onto the box in spite of repeated attempts by outlaws and unknown parties to steal it. At the climatic moment the contents are revealed.

Ben Wilson (Jack Harvey), Neva Gerber (Dolly Hampton), Lafe McKee (Judd Hampton), Robert Walker (George Mason), Charles Brinley (Dan Collins), Alfred Hollingworth (Seth Dobbins), Jack Henderson ("Nose Paint" Wheeler), Yakima Canutt (Whipping Boss).

1. The Fatal Box. 2. A Tragic Legacy. 3. Daring Danger. 4. A Leap for Life. 5. Defying Fate. 6. Trapped by Outlaws. 7. Pendulum of Death. 8. The Miracle Rider. 9. Vengeance of the Mystery Box. 10. Vindicated.

448. The Mystery Mind

(Supreme, November 1920) Serial, 15 chapters, two reels each. D: William Davis, Fred Sittenham. S/SP? Arthur B. Reeve and John W. Grey.

Hypnotism and psychic forces play a significant role in this film. A scientific expedition is outfitted to investigate certain native drugs and vegetable poisons used by the natives along the upper reaches of the Orinoco, where reports credit the inhabitants with being head hunters, ruled by a native priest, Evil Eye. Doctor William Sutton, a famous toxicologist, inventor of surgical instruments and a psychologist, is placed in charge of the expedition. There are secret gold deposits on the Orinoco, venerated by the head hunters as the "gold of the gods" and most jealously guarded. Evil Eye and another priest, Carno, are the sole custodians of the secret location of the Eldorado. Intrigue and murder follow as members of the expedition follow their own desires.

J. Robert Pauline (Dr. Robert Dupont), Peggy Shanor (Vera Collins), Paul Panzer (Dr. Sutton), Ed Rogers (Carl Canfield), Violet MacMillian (Violet Bronson), De Sacia Saville.

1. The Hypnotic Clue. 2. The Fires of Fury. 3. The War of Wills. 4. The Fumes of Fear. 5. Thought Waves. 6. A Halo of Help. 7. The Nether World. 8. The Mystery Mind. 9. Dual Personality. 10. Hounds of Hate. 11. The Sleepwalker. 12. The Temple of the Occult. 13. The Blinding Ray. 14. The Water Cure. 15. The Gold of the Gods.

449. Mystery Mountain

(Mascot, December 3, 1934) Serial, 12 chapters, Chapter 1, three reels, others two reels. D: B. Reeves Eason and Otto Brower. SP: Bennett Cohen and Armand Schaefer. S: Sherman Lowe, Barney Sarecky, and B. Reeves Eason. P: Nat Levine. Supervisors: Victor Zobel and Armand Schaefer. Photography: Ernest Miller and William Nobles. Music: Lee Zahler and Abe Meyer.

A railroad tunnel is to be constructed through Iron Mountain. Only The Rattler knows that the mountain contains a rich gold vein. Ken Williams and his horse Tarzan thwart his plans.

Mystery Mountain was Mascot's top-grosser until surpassed by Tom Mix's *The Miracle Rider*. This was the first of two serials that Maynard was to make for Mascot. However, he was replaced by Gene Autry in *The Phantom Rider*.

Ken Maynard (Ken Williams), Tarzan [a horse] (Himself), Verna Hillie (Jane Corwin), Edward Earle (Frank Blayden), Lynton Brent (Matthews), Syd Saylor (Breezy Baker), Lafe McKee (Jim Corwin), Carmencita Johnson (Little Jane Corwin), Al Bridge (Tom Henderson), Edward Hearn (Lake),

Robert Hortman (Hank), Gene Autry (Thomas), Smiley Brunette (Guard), Wally Wales (Member Corwin Transportation Company), Jack Rockwell (Member Corwin Transportation Company), William Gould (Member Corwin Transportation Company), Philo McCullough (Chase), Steve Clark (Railroad Man), Lew Meehan (Red), Tom London (Morgan), George Chesebro (Anderson), Hooper Atchley (Dr. Edwards), Cliff Lyons (Maynard's Double), Art Mix (Henchman), Dick Dickinson (Henchman), Al Haskell (Henchman), Pascale Perry (Henchman), Edmund Cobb (The Rattler in disguise [otherwise not seen in the cast]), Jack Kirk, Curley Dresden.

1. The Rattler. 2. The Man Nobody Knows. 3. The Eye that Never Sleeps. 4. The Human Target. 5. Phantom Outlaws. 6. The Perfect Crime. 7. Tarzan the Cunning. 8. The Enemy's Stronghold. 9. The Fatal Warning. 10. The Secret of the Mountain. 11. Behind the Mask. 12. The Judgment of Tarzan.

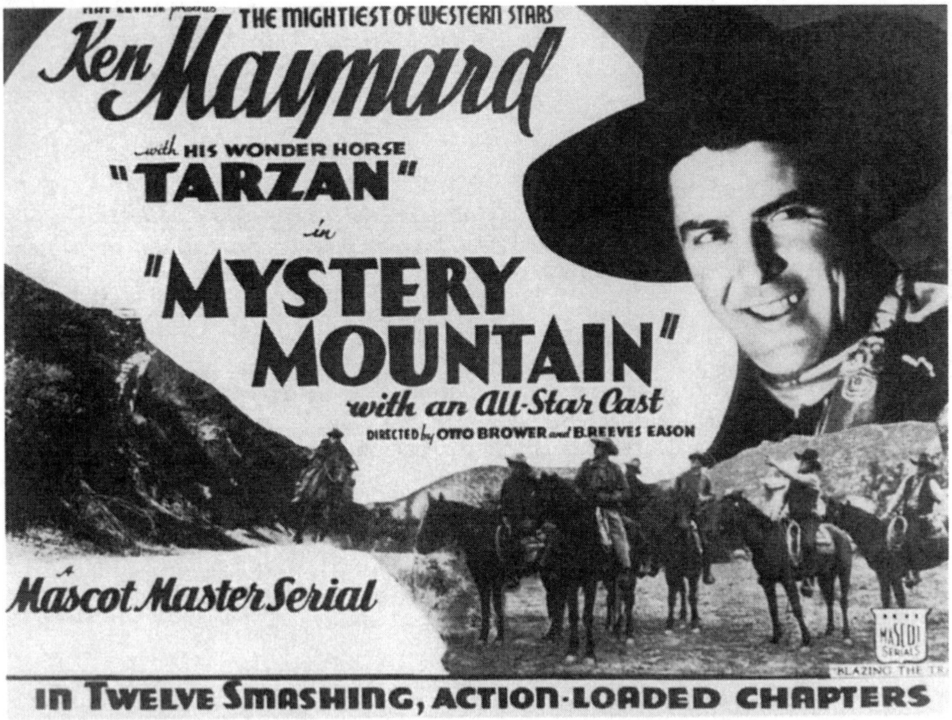

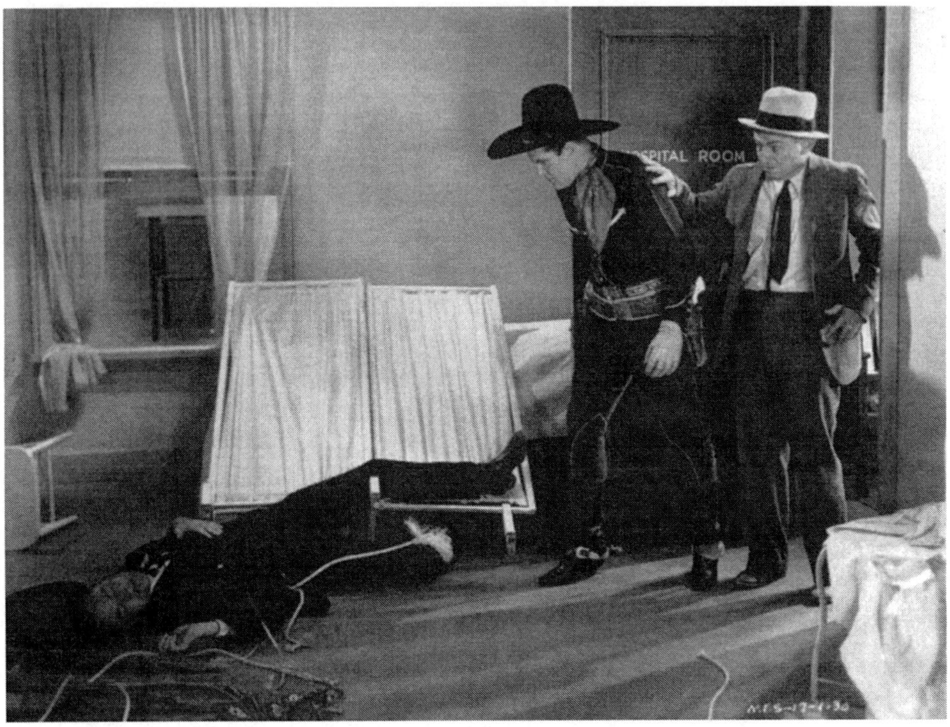

Top: **Ken Maynard;** ***bottom:*** **Ken Maynard and Syd Saylor in** ***Mystery Mountain*** **(1934)**

450. Mystery of the Double Cross

(Astra Film Corp./Pathé, March 18, 1917) Serial, 15 chapters, two reels each. D: William Parke. S: Jacques Futrelle. SP: Gilson Willets.

The story revolves around the efforts of Peter Hale, a wealthy young man returning to the United States on a transatlantic steamer to identify a beautiful young girl whose presence aboard the ship is mysterious. During a panic caused by the sighting of a submarine, her dress is torn at the shoulder and he catches a brief look at an unusual mark of a double cross on her arm. At the office of his father's lawyer, Peter learns that in order to inherit the Hale fortune, he must find and marry The Girl of the Double Cross, who is described as being perfect in mind and body and trained to be his wife. Failing to do so, the will assigns the Hale fortune to whoever does win her.

As Hale and the lawyer discuss the will, the door slowly opens and he catches another fleeting glimpse of the girl on the steamer. Barging through the door in hot pursuit, he finds her gone and his way barred by a mysterious masked stranger holding a gun and warning him not to follow. How Hale meets Phillipa Brewster, when he is certain she is the one he seeks, how she denies his premise, how he doubts her and seeks to prove that she is really The Girl of the Double Cross, despite her willing engagement to villainous Bridgey Bentley makes a fast-moving torrent of action and thrills revolving around one of the best serial characters ever devised—The Masked Stranger.

Mollie King (Phillipa Brewster), Leon Bary (Peter Hale), Ralph Stuart (Bridgey Bentley), Gladden James (Dick Annersley), Theodore Friebus (Jack Dunn), Robert Brewster (Herbert Brewster), Harry Fraser, Helene Chadwick, Clarine Seymour.

1. The Lady in Number 7. 2. The Masked Stranger. 3. An Hour to Live. 4. Kidnapped. 5. The Life Current. 6. The

Dead Come Back. 7. Into Thin Air. 8. The Stranger Disposes. 9. When Jail Birds Fly. 10. The Hole-in-the-Wall. 11. Love's Sacrifice. 12. The Riddle of the Cross. 13. The Face of the Stranger. 14. The Hidden Brand. 15. Mystery of the Double Cross.

451. Mystery of the River Boat

(Universal, October 1944) Serial, 13 chapters, two reels each. D: Ray Taylor and Lewis D. Collins. SP: Maurice Tombragel. S: Ande Lamb.

Oil-rich swampland in the bayou country inspires both greed and murder as the disinherited son of the Duval family tries to gain control of the land. Steve Langtry, returning home from college, is framed for a murder and jumps ship to escape. Police later believe in his innocence and solicit his help in rounding up the real criminals.

Robert Lowery (Steve Langtry), Eddie Quillan (Jug Jenks), Marion Martin (Celeste Eltree), Marjorie Clements (Jenny Perrin), Lyle Talbot (Rudolph Teller), Arthur Hohl (Clayton/Paul Duval), Oscar O'Shea (Captain Perrin), Manton Moreland (Napoleon), Ian Wolfe (Herman Einreich), Jay Novello (Pierre), Francis McDonald (Batiste), Anthony Warde.

1. The Tragic Crash. 2. The Phantom Killer. 3. The Flaming Inferno. 4. The Brink of Doom. 5. The Highway to Peril. 6. The Fatal Plunge. 7. The Toll of the Storm. 8. The Break in the Levee. 9. Trapped in the Quicksands. 10. Flaming Havoc. 11. Electrocuted. 12. Risking Death. 13. The Boomerang.

Top: **Robert Lowery, Francis McDonald, and Marjory Clements in *Mystery of the River Boat* (1944); *bottom:* Rex Lease and Kathlyn McGuire in *Mystery Pilot (1926)***

452. The Mystery of 13

(Burston, August 1919) Serial, 15 chapters, two reels each. D: Francis Ford. Scen: John B. Clymer. S: Elsie Van Name. P: Louis Burston.

A sinister cult of 13 hooded figures oppose the hero and heroine in the pursuit of a lost treasure.

Francis Ford (Phil Kelly/Jim Kelly), Rosemary Theby (Marian Green), Pete Gerald (Hugo Madiz), Mark Fenton (John Green), Ruth Maurice (Mary Hardon), Doris Dare (Rose), Nigel De Brulier (Raoul Ferrar), Elsie Van Name (Edith), Valeria Olivo (Ralph), Phil Ford (Butts), Jack Sackville, Jack Lowton.

1. Bitter Bondage. 2. Lights Out. 3. The Submarine Gardens. 4. The Lone Rider. 5. Blown to Atoms. 6. Single Handed. 7. Fire and Water. 8. Pirate Loot. 9. The Phantom House. 10. The Raid. 11. Bare Handed. 12. The Death Ride. 13. Brother Against Brother. 14. The Man Hunt. 15. The 13th Card.

453. Mystery Pilot

(Rayart, May 1926) Serial, 10 chapters, two reels each. D: Harry Moody. P: Sovereign Feature Productions.

A jewel case is desired by several parties, one of which is the Mystery Pilot. The case is in the hands of Colonel Mark Finlay, whose daughter, June, makes the acquaintance of Bob Jones, a young sailor. After innumerable adventures, the secret of the jewel case is disclosed and a treasure is divided.

Rex Lease (Bob Jones), Kathryn McGuire (June Finlay), Jack McReedy (Colonel Mark Finlay), Max Asher (George Smith), Barney Furey (Harry Jacobs/The Mystery Pilot), Ray Childs (Bull Joyce), J.W. Wylie (Slim), Fred Kelsey (Skipper Larsen).

1. Wings of Death. 2. Flying Fists. 3–10. [Unknown.]

454. The Mystery Rider

(Universal, November 25, 1928) Serial, 19 chapters, two reels each. D: Jack Nelson. S: George Morgan.

Norman Wentworth finds a method for producing rubber from the sap of the mesquite plant. He is killed by The Claw, a man with a deformed, clawlike hand, but not before confiding the secret formula to his daughter Grace. Her fiancé, Winthrop Lane, is secretly The Mystery Rider, who fights to protect her from The Claw and his gang.

William Desmond (Winthrop Lane/The Mystery Rider), Derelys Perdue (Grace Wentworth), Tom London (David Manning/The Claw), Bud Osborne (Bull Leonard), Walter Shumway (Norman Wentworth), Red Bassett (The Sheriff), Syd Saylor, Ben Corbett, John Bubanks, Slim Lucas, Gus Wadlow, Jack Shannon, Bud McClure.

1. The Clutching Claw. 2. Trapped. 3. The Stampede. 4. Hands Up. 5. Buried Alive. 6. The Fatal Shot. 7. Hurled Through Space. 8. Unmasked. 9. Doomed. 10. The End of the Trail.

455. The Mystery Ship

(Universal, December 1, 1917) Serial, 18 chapters, two reels each. D: Harry Harvey and Francis Ford. S: William Parker and Elaine Pearson. SP: Milton Moore.

Betty Lee searches for hidden treasure on an island after the man she thinks is her dying father gives her a map of its location. Her fiancé steals the map and tries to kill her. Betty and Miles' relationship gets off to a rocky start when he tries to sink her boat but ends with them as lovers. A mysterious individual comes to their rescue at climatic moments, using an armor-plated ship and other scientific equipment including an electric spray gun that paralyzes anyone caught in its sparks and a laser-like energy ray. The mystery figure turns out to be her father.

Neva Gerber (Betty Lee), Ben Wilson (Miles Gaston), Duke Worne (Betty's Fiancé), Nigel De Brulier (Betty's Father), Neal Hart, Harry Archer, Elsie Jane Wilson, Phil Ford, Elsie Van Name, Kingsley Benedict, Malcolm Blevins.

1. The Crescent Scar. 2. The Grip of Hate. 3. Adrift. 4. The Secret of the Tomb. 5. The Fire God. 6. Treachery. 7. One Minute to Leave. 8. Hidden Hands. 9. The Black Masks. 10. The Rescue. 11. The Line of Death. 12. The Rain of Fire. 13. The Underground House. 14. The Masked Riders. 15. The House of Trickery. 16. The Forced Marriage. 17. The Deadly Torpedo. 18. The Flight in Mid-Air.

456. Mystery Squadron

(Mascot, December 22, 1933) Serial, 12 chapters; Chapter 1, three reels; others, two reels. D: Colbert Clark and David Howard. SP: Barney Sarecky, Colbert Clark, David Howard, and Wyndham Gittens. S: Sherman Lowe and Al Martin. P: Nat Levine.

A mystery squadron, led by an unidentified leader calling himself The Black Ace, repeatedly attacks a huge dam construction project that threatens a secret gold mine. Two stunt pilots, Fred Cromwell and Bill Cook, are hired by Stephen Gray, owner of the construction firm, to protect the dam site. Hank Davis, foreman of the project and a friend of the two pilots, is revealed as The Black Ace and plunges to his death in the final chapter after an air fight with his erstwhile buddies.

Bob Steele (Fred Cromwell), Lucile Browne (Dorothy Gray), Guinn [Big Boy] Williams (Bill Cook), Jack Mulhall

Left: **Guinn [Big Boy] Williams, Jack Mulhall, and Bob Steele;** ***right:*** **Bob Steele and Lucile Browne in** ***Mystery Squadron*** **(1933)**

(Davis), J. Carrol Naish (Collins), Jack Mower (Carter), Robert Frazer (Dr. Flint), Purnell Pratt (Johnson), Lafe McKee (Stephen Gray), Robert Kortman (Bracken), Jack Perrin (Roberts), Kernan Cripps (Tom), Edward Hearn (The Sheriff), Edward Peil, Sr. (Pat Hermon), Wally Wales, Lew Meehan.

1. The Black Ace. 2. The Fatal Warning. 3. The Black Ace Strikes. 4. Man of Steel. 5. The Death Swoop. 6. Doomed! 7. Enemy Signals. 8. Canyon of Calamity. 9. Secret of the Mine. 10. Clipped Wings. 11. The Beast at Bay. 12. The Ace of Aces.

457. The Mystery Trooper

(Wonder Pictures/Syndicate, 1931) Serial, 10 chapters, two reels each. D: Stuart Paton. SP: Karl Krusada. S: Flora Douglas. P: Harry S. Webb and F.E. [Flora] Douglas. Photography: William Nobles and Edward Kull. Assist. D: Armand Schaefer and Raymond Hines.

Lost gold in Canada is sought by both good and evil forces. Jack Logan, who has inherited half of a map to the gold, comes to Canada followed by henchmen of outlaw Jean Gregg, who also seeks it. Logan joins forces with orphans Helen and Billy and the Indian, Red Eagle, who has some knowledge of the lost gold. The group is constantly protected by an unknown uniformed man calling himself The Mystery Trooper.

Although criticized by some historians as being one of the worst sound serials, one should remember that it was one of the first sound serials. It has its moments. And unsophisticated audiences of The Great Depression found it entertaining.

Robert Frazer (Jack Logan), Buzz Barton (Billy), Blanche Mehaffey (Helen), Al Ferguson (Jean Gregg), Charles King (Al or Mack [?]), William von Bracken (Red Eagle), White Cloud [a horse] (Himself), William Bertram.

1. The Trap of Terror. 2. Paths of Peril. 3. Fighting Fate. 4. The Cave of Horror. 5. The House of Hate. 6. The Day of Doom. 7. The Death Trail. 8. The Killer Dogs. 9. The Ghost City. 10. The Lost Treasure.

See also the re-issue title *Trail of the Royal Mounted.*

458. Nan of the North

(Arrow, March 1922) Serial, 15 chapters, two reels each. D: Duke Worne. S/SP: Karl Coolidge. P: Ben Wilson.

A Canadian mountie aids a maiden-in-distress and tries to keep a villain and a villainess from obtaining Titano, a powerful substance containing unlimited energy from a fallen meteorite. Nan stumbles upon the frozen corpse of a scientist and learns about Titano from a report found on his body. Unfortunately, a copy of the report has fallen into the hands of a Yukon gang of thieves who are determined to obtain the substance.

Ann Little (Nan), Leonard Clapham [Tom London] (Dick Driscoll), Joseph W. Girard (Yukon Hays), Hal Wilson (Gaspar Le Sage), Howard Crampton (Igloo), J. Morris Foster (Bruce Vane), Edith Stayart (Celeste).

1. Missile from Mars. 2. Fountain of Fury. 3. Brink of Despair. 4. In Cruel Clutches. 5. On Terror's Trail. 6. The Cards of Chance. 7. Into the Depths. 8. Burning Sands. 9. Power of Titano. 10. A Bolt from the sky. 11. The Ride for a Life. 12. Adrift. 13. Facing Death at Sea. 14. The Volcano. 15. Consequences.

459. Nattens Datter

(Denmark—Filmfabriken Danmark, 1915) Series, 2 episodes, three reels each. D: Kai Van Der AA Kuhle. SP: Kai Van Der AA Kuhle. Photography: Hans Folkmann.

Emilie Sannom (Nattens Datter, Daughter of the Night), Alfred Sjöholm (Tom Murray), Peter S. Andersen (Mac Irwing), Anna Müller (Lily Murray/Ritza/Zingra), Alfred Arnbak (Leo Barry), Peter S. Andersen (William Robinson), Jon Iversen (Tom Ralph), Helga Pauso (Lady Roas), Valdemar Möller.

1. På Liv og Død. 2. Redselens Hule. *Released in Brazil in 4 Episodes:* 1. Nas trevas. 2. Odio entre mulheres. 3. Para a vida e para a morte. 4. O antro do terror.

460. Neal of the Navy

(Balboa/Pathé, September 2, 1915) Serial, 14 chapters, two reels each. D: William M. Harvey and William Bertram. Scen: Douglas Bronston and Hamilton Osborne. S: Albert Payson Terhune.

The old story of a lost treasure, a map showing its location, opposing factions out to grab it, and the hero who sees that justice prevails.

William Courtleigh, Jr. (Neal Hardin), Lillian Lorraine (Annette Illington), William Conklin (Thomas Illington), Edward Brady (Hernandez), Henry Stanley (Ponto), Richard Johnson (Joe Welcher), Charles Dudley, Helen Lackaye, Bruce Smith, Lucy Blake.

1. The Survivors. 2. The Yellow Packet. 3. The Failure. 4. The Tattered Parchment. 5. A Message from the Past. 6. The Cavern of Death. 7. The Gun Runners. 8. The Yellow Peril. 9. The Rolling Terror. 10. The Sun Worshipers. 11. The Dreadful Pit. 12. The Worm Turns. 13. White Gods. 14. The Final Goal.

461. The Neglected Wife

(Balboa/Pathé, May 13, 1917) Serial, 15 chapters, two reels each. D: William Bertram. SP: Joseph Dunn and Will M. Ritchey. S: Mabel Herbert Hurne.

A love triangle leads to complications, with the heroine cast in the "other woman" role. The serial did little to further

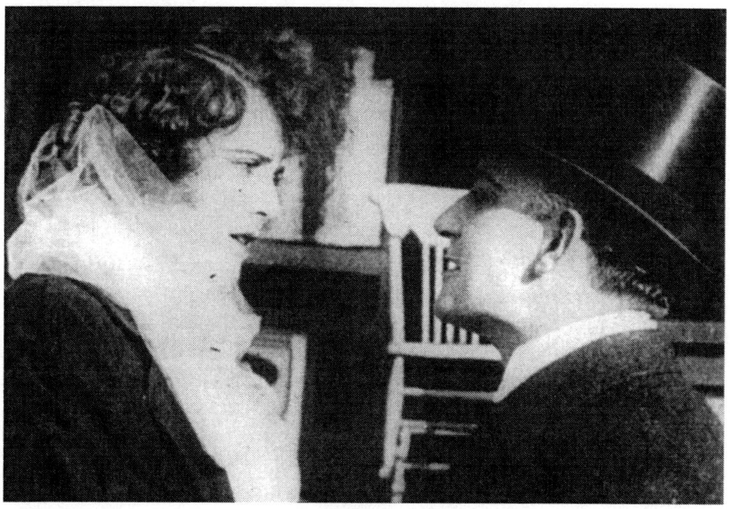

Ruth Roland in *The Neglected Wife* (1917)

Ruth's career. Its dearth of action and story were more typical of a society drama than of a serial thriller.

Ruth Roland (Margaret Warner), Roland Bottomley (Horace Kennedy), Corinne Grant (Mary Kennedy), Neil C. Hardin (Edgar Doyle), Philo McCullough (Frank Norwood), Mollie McConnell.

1. The Woman Alone. 2. The Weakening. 3. In the Crucible. 4. Beyond Recall. 5. Under Suspicion. 6. On the Precipice. 7. The Message on the Mirror. 8. A Relentless Fate. 9. Deepening Degradation. 10. A Veiled Intrigue. 11. A Reckless Indiscretion. 12. Embittered Love. 13. Revolting Pride. 14. Desperation. 15. A Sacrifice Supreme.

462. The New Adventures of J. Rufus Wallingford

(Wharton/Pathé, 1915-1916) Series, 14 episodes, two reels each. D: Theodore Wharton. S: George Randolph Chester. P: Leopold and Theodore Wharton.

J. Rufus Wallingford and Blackie Daw are con men extraordinares. Through the pleadings of Violet and Fanny Warden, whose father was ruined by the Falls clique, they make an attack on the Falls millions.

Burr McIntosh (J. Rufus Wallingford), Max Figman (Blackie Daw), Lolita Robertson (Violet Warden), Oliver Hardy, Malcolm Head, Lawrence Wood, Eddie O'Connor, Harry Marshall.

1. The Bungalow Bungle. 2. Three Rings and a Goat. 3. A Rheumatic Joint. 4. The Master Stoke. 5. The Lilac Splash. 6. A Trap for Trapp. 7. The Bang Sun Engine. 8. A Transaction in Summer Boarders. 9. Detective Blackie. 10. Apples and Eggbeaters. 11. A Stony Deal. 12. Buying a Bank with Bunk. 13. The Missing Heir. 14. Lord Southpaugh.

463. The New Adventures of Tarzan

(Burroughs—Tarzan/Dearholt–Stout–Cohen, 1935) Serial, 12 chapters. D: Edward Kull and W.F. McGaugh. SP: Charles F. Royal. Adaptation: Charles F. Royal and Edwin H. Blum. S: Edgar Rice Burroughs. Photography: Edward Kull and Earnest F. Smith. Assist. D: Wilbur McGaugh. P: Ashton Dearholt Expedition Pictures. Filmed on location in Guatemala and the Selig Zoo in Los Angeles; released in 1938 as a 72-minute feature *Tarzan and the Green Goddess*, comprising Chapters 3–12 plus some new material at the beginning. A 75-minute (later cut to 61 minutes) feature was released concurrently with the serial and using the serial title, made up of Chapter 1 plus a little more footage. The first chapter was five reels in length, with the remaining chapters being the standard two reels. Don Costello was stricken ill during production and his role was completed by Ashton Dearholt.

Tarzan travels to Guatemala in search of his friend, D'Arnot, a French explorer captured by the half-human inhabitants of an ancient Mayan ruin. He is followed by the Martling Expedition seeking the Green Goddess, a sacred monolith containing a fortune in gems as well as the secret of a powerful explosive. A group of rebel revolutionaries also want the explosive formula, as does the Guatemalan Secret Service.

In this film Tarzan is portrayed as an educated man, just as Burroughs wrote him. No "Me Tarzan, You Jane" dialogue.

Herman Brix [Bruce Bennett] (Tarzan), Ula Holt (Ula Vale), Frank Baker (Major Martling), Dale Walsh (Alice Martling), Harry Ernest (Gordon Hamilton), don Costello (Ragland), Ashton Dearholt (Ragland), Lewis Sargent (George), Merrill McCormick (Bouchart), Jack Mower (Blade), Jiggs [a chimp] (Nkima), Earl Dwire (Renegade), Mrs. Gentry (Queen Maya).

1. The New Adventures of Tarzan. 2. Crossed Trails. 3. The Devil's Noose. 4. River Perils. 5. Unseen Hands. 6. Fatal Fangs. 7. Flaming Waters. 8. Angry Gods. 9. Doom's Brink. 10. Secret Signals. 11. Death's Fireworks. 12. Operator No. 17.

464. The New Adventures of Terrance O'Rourke

(Universal, December 4, 1915) Series, 3 episodes, two reels each. P: Otis Turner. SP: Walter Woods and McGrew Willis. S: Louis Joseph Vance. D: Jacques Jaccard and J. Warren Kerrigan.

The adventures of a herioc and manly Irishman in Egypt and India who is caught up in many dangerous situations because of his love of the beautiful Beatrix. Though not a true serial, it maintains serial-like suspense. Kerrigan endows the character with all the herioc and manly qualities for which he is noted. In the first episode Terrance has a very exciting time in Turkey. A band of villains plan to lead a massacre against the English and they want the fearless Irishman to head the charge. He refuses, so the conspirators assign Princess Constantine to convince him. But instead she falls in love with him and aids him in his escape from the villainous band.

J. Warren Kerrigan (Terrance O'Rourke), Lois Wilson (Beatrix), Harry Carter (Duke Victor), Maude George (Princess Karen), Raymond Nye (Prince Aziz), Bertram Grassby (Chambret), Carmen Phillips (Princess Constantine), George Pextolat (Prince Vladislav), Roy Gallagher (Danny) William Holland (Danny [in third episode]), Eddie Polo (Eddie), Jay Morley (Captain De Bresas), Frederick Church.

1. Palace of Dust. 2. When a Queen Loved O'Rourke. 3. The Road to Paradise.

465. The New Exploits of Elaine

(Star Company/Pathé, April 5, 1915) Serial, 10 chapters, two reels each. D: George B. Seitz. Scen: Charles W. Goddard, George B. Seitz, and Bertram Millhauser. S: Arthur B. Reeve. P: Leopold and Theodore Wharton. Photography: Joseph Dubray.

Elaine is in love with Craig Kennedy, whose new torpedo is to be adopted by the U.S. government. Wu Fang, the ruthless oriental gangster, makes arrangements to steal one of the existing models. An admixture of thrills and melodramatic incidents abound, along with a little romance, as Elaine outthinks and outmoves Wu Fang to preserve this country's secrets.

Pearl White (Elaine Dodge), Creighton Hale (Walter Jameson), Arnold Daly (Craig Kennedy), Edwin Arden (Wu Fang), M.W. Rale (Long Sin), Bessie W. Wharton (Aunt Josephine), Gazelle March (Innocent Inez), Ah Ling Foo (Chinese Heavy).

1. The Serpent Sign. 2. The Cryptic Ring. 3. The Watching Eye. 4. The Vengeance of Wu Fang. 5. The Saving Circles. 6. Spontaneous Combustion. 7. The Ear in the Wall. 8. The Opium Smugglers. 9. The Tell-Tale Heart. 10. Shadows of War.

466. Nick Winter et ses Aventures

(France, 1921) Serial, 10 chapters. D: Nick Winter. Scen: Nick Winter.

Nick Winter.

1. Les oiseaux de nuit. 2. L'introuvable. 3. Un heritage difficile. 4. La villa mystérieuse. 5. La mort qui riôde. 6. L'étau se desserre. 7. Le drame de l'Alhambra. 8. L'audacieuse filature. 9. La malle vivante. 10. A la Jean-Bart.

467. Nirvana

(Germany—Esha Films/Progress Films, 1920) Series, 6 episodes. D: Fritz Bernhard. SP: Helmuth Ortmann. Photography: Joe Rive.

Evi Eva was at the height of her popularity when she starred in this series.

Evi Eva, Heinrich Schroth, Preben Riest, Bernhard Goetzke, Erich Kaiser-Titz, Anna Von Palen, Ludwig Rex, Wladimir Agajeff.

1. Das Haus des Schreckens. 2. Der Überfall auf die Telegraphenstation. 3. Der Ruf über das Meer. 4. Die brennende Stadt. 5. Der unterirdische Tempel. 6. Die Sühne.

468. Northwest Mounted Police

(Universal, September 1929-August 1930) Series, 13 episodes, two reels each. D: Josef Serigard.

A cattle thief imprisons the hero's girl and makes her tell the mountie that she is the cattle thief's sister, but the mountie does not fall for it, as he knows the girl has no brother. The mountie waits until the villain tries to make a getaway with the girl. The mountie gallops after him on his trusty steed and saves the girl and the honor of the NWMP.

Very little is known of Carson except that he was German and spoke English with a very heavy accent. With the advent of talkies he folded his tent and returned to Germany.

Ted Carson.

1. The Red Rider (9-21-29). 2. Man of Daring (10-19-29). 3. Border Wolf (11-16-29). 4. Red Coat's Code (12-14-29). 5. Trial of the Pack (1-11-30). 6. Badge of Bravery (2-8-30). 7. Crimson Courage (3-8-30). 8. Law in the Saddle (4-5-30). 9. Crooked Trails (5-3-30). 10. Wolf's Fangs (5-31-30). 11. Red Coat's Romance (6-28-30). 12. The Man Hunter (7-26-30). 13. The Lightning Rider (8-23-30).

469. La Nouvelle Aurore

(France—Eclair–Cinéromans, 1919) Serial, 15 chapters. D: Edouard-Emile Violet. S: Gaston Leroux—"Chri-Bibi."

René Navarre, José Davert, Rachel Devirys, Manuel Caméré, Suzanne Linker, Charles Casella, Marc Fabronis, Maurice de Canonge, Manzoni, Gorbio, Jacqueline Arly, Henriquez de L'Opera, Lise Musette, Frederic Mariotti.

Porteguese: 1. Palas nas galés. 2. A evasão. 3. Para a luz. 4. O combate do dia e da noite. 5. A lua de mel. 6. O julgamento de Palas. 7. Os pesadelos de Palas. 8. O herói e o bandido. 9. Os véus desfazem-se. 10. A vingança de Gorbio. 11. Duas dôres. 12. O valvário. 13. Gisèle. 14. O "Tullia." 15. Fatalidade.

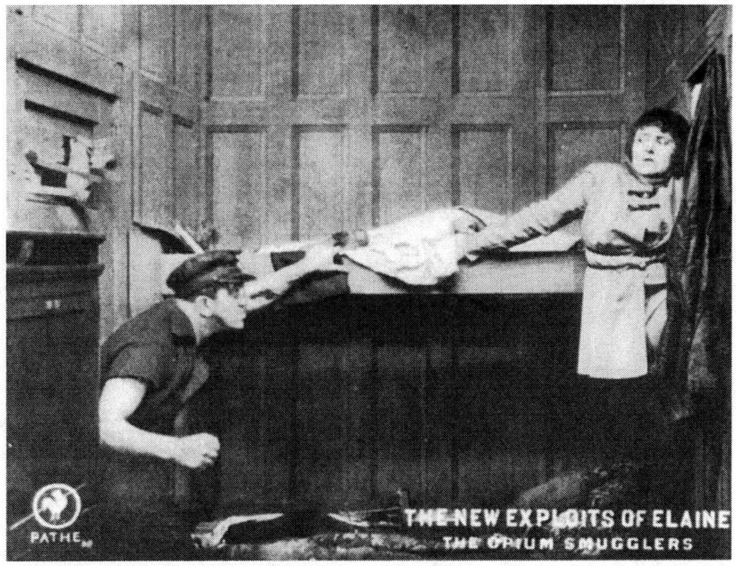

Pearl White in *The New Exploits of Elaine* (1915)

470. La Nouvelle Mission de Judex (English Title: *The Further Exploits of Judex*)

(France—Gaumont, 1917) Serial, 12 chapters. S: Arthur Bernede and Louis Feuillade. Scen: Arthur Bernede and Louis Feuillade. Photography: Klausse and A. Glattli. D: Louis Feuillade.

René Cresté (Judex), Marcel Lévesque (Cocantin), Yvette Andreyor (Jacqueline), Edouard Mathé (Roger de Trémeuse), Louis Leubas (Favraux), Gaston Michel (Kerjean), Emile Keppens (Milton), André Brunelle (Dr. Howey), Juana Borguèse (Baronèsse d'Apremont), Georgette de Nery (Primerose), Cyprian Giles (Gaby Belles Mirettes), Olinda Mano (Le petit Jean).

French: 1. Le mystère d'une nuit d'été 2. L'adieu au bonheur. 3. L'ensorcelée. 4. La chambre aux embûches. 5. La forêt hantée. 6. Une lueur dans les ténèbres. 7. La main morte. 8. Les captives. 9. Les papiers du docteur Howey. 10. Les deux destinées. 11. Le crime involontaire. 12. Châtiment. *Portuguese:* 1. O mistério de uma noite de verão. 2. Adeus, felicidade. 3. A enfeitiçado. 4. A casa das ciladas. 5. A mata tenebrosa. 6. Uma luz nas trevas. 7. A mão do esqueleto. 8. As duas prisioneiras. 9. Os papeis do dr. Howey. 10. Os dois destinos. 11. Um crime involuntário. 12. A expiação. *English:* 1. The Disappearing Documents—The Descent of the Secret—A Summer Night's Mystery. 2. Goodbye to Happiness. 3. Hypnotized—The Bewitched Woman. 4. The Tap Room—The Room of a Thousand Traps. 5. The Haunted Forest. 6. A Light in the Darkness. 7. The Dead Hand. 8. The Captives. 9. Doctor Howey's Papers. 10. The Two Destinies. 11. An Involuntary Crime. 12. Punishment.

471. Officer 444

(Davis Distributing/Goodwill, May 15, 1926) Serial, 10 chapters, two reels each. D/SP: Francis Ford. Serial was supposed to be released by Vital Exchanges, which went broke.

One of the crudest examples of the silent serial produced in the 1920s. Produced by an independent company, the picture was filmed in a hurry and was the final serial to feature the team of Ben Wilson and Neva Gerber. The story line focuses on Frog, a criminal villain who wants a secret formula in order to rule the world. Officer 444 is the hero who sets out to stop the Frog's evil doings. The heroine, Gloria Grey, falls into the hands of the Frog, naturally, before the serial concludes. The Frog's hideout is discovered and the crime network is ended.

Poorly staged scenes, a poor script, and unbelievable fight scenes caused viewers to laugh instead of take the scene seriously, as intended. The complete serial has survived and now may be viewed for comparison with other serials of the silent era or just for laughs.

Neva Gerber (Gloria Grey), Ben Wilson (Officer 444), Ruth Royce (the Vulture), Al Ferguson (Doctor Blackely), Lafe McKee (Capt. Jerry Dugan), Jack Mower (Michael Casey), Arthur Beckel (James Harverly), Harry McDonald (Snooky), Frank Baker (Dago Frank), Phil Ford, Francis Ford.

1. Flying Squadron. 2. Human Rats. 3. Trapped. 4. Gassed. 5. Missing. 6. The Radio Ray. 7. Death's Shadow. 8. Jaws of Doom. 9. Underground Trap. 10. Justice.

***Top: Officer 444* (1926); *bottom: The $1,000,000 Reward* (1930)**

472. On Guard

(Pathé, January 30, 1927) Serial, 10 chapters, two reels each. D: Arch B. Heath. SP: Paul Fairfax Fuller. S: Robert F. Glassburn.

Foreign agents attempt to hire the hero to help them gain certain valuable information about the U.S. Army. Instead the hero joins forces with a patriotic girl and together, aided at times by a mystery figure, they foil the spies' plans.

Cullen Landis (Bob Adams), Muriel Kingston (Betty Lee), Louise Du Pre (Catherine Nevens), Walter P. Lewis (James Stagg), Tom Blake (Sergeant-Major Murphy), Charles Marten (Colonel King), Edward Burns (Jackson), Jack Bardette, Gus De We, Tom Poland, Bob Semels, George Kelley.

1. Enemies Within. 2. Deception. 3. Silent Evidence. 4. The Sinister Warning. 5. False Orders. 6. Stolen Papers. 7. Hidden Watchers. 8. The Counterplot. 9. The Air Battle. 10. Foiled.

473. The $1,000,000 Reward

(Grossman Pictures, January 1920) Serial, 15 chapters; Chapter 1, three reels; others, two reels. D: George A. Lessey. S: Arthur B. Reeve and John W. Grey. Scen: Saul E. Harrison (?). P: Harry Grossman.

Story starts with the brewing of a conspiracy of double strength, as the victim of both plots is Betty Thorndyke, daughter of a diamond mine owner in South Africa. Betty has been carefully and secretly reared in California, and a reward is suddenly offered to find her by the stockholders of the mine, who are anxious that the property be divided. One of the stockholders wishes her dead so that he might benefit financially.

A band of crooks read of the offer and decide to win it, preferably by foul means.

Joining forces with the stockholder, William Russell, they set about trying to kill Betty. Morgan Spencer comes to the aid of Betty at every turn. At the end, the villains are disposed of and Betty gets her inheritance plus a proposal from Spencer.

Lillian Walker (Betty Thorndyke), Coit Albertson (Morgan Spencer), Charles Middleton (William Russell), George A. Lessey (James Bradley), Joseph Marba (Kenwah), Leora Spellman (Valarie Kernan), Bernard Randall (Kip Van Hoan), William Pike (James Forsythe), Ray Allen (Hannah Craven), George Connors, Louise Hotelling.

1. The Diamond Robbery. 2. The Escape. 3. The Rescue. 4. Elixir of Death. 5. A Dynamite Plot. 6-12. [Unknown.] 13. In the Shadow of Death. 14. [Unknown.] 15. [Unknown.]

474. The Oregon Trail

(Universal, March 12, 1923) Serial, 18 chapters; Chapter 1, three reels; others, two reels. D: Edward Laemmle. Scen: Anthony Coldeway, Douglas Bronston, and Jefferson Moffitt. S: Robert Dillon.

Opening with a three-reel episode, made necessary by the number of facts which must be "planted," the serial starts off as a worthy specimen of the historical chapter plays being put out by Universal. Among the historical material introduced is the decision by Washington and Jefferson to purchase the Louisiana territory, Napoleon selling it, Eli Whitney at work on the cotton gin, Lewis and Clark starting on their famous expedition and Oregon Indians seeking the White Man's Bible at St. Louis.

The story revolves about an independent trapper fighting an unscrupulous syndicate in the vast Oregon territory. The story is built around the overland expedition of Dr. Marcus Whitman.

Art Acord (Jean Brulet), Louise Lorraine (Rosita Velasquez), Ruth Royce (Narcisso Prentiss), Duke R. Lee (Dr. Marcus Whitman), Jim Corey (Rene Coulier), Burton C. Law (Reverend Henry Spaulding), Grace E. McLean (Mrs. Spaulding), Dick Cater (Dr. William Gray), Sidney De Gray (Hernandez Velasquez), William H. Rhyno, Walter Bytell, Frederic Peters.

1. Westward Ho! 2. White Treachery. 3. Across the Continent. 4. Message of Death. 5. Wagon of Doom. 6. Secret Foes. 7. A Man of God. 8. Seeds of Civilization. 9. Justice. 10. The New Era. 11. A Game of Nations. 12. To Save an Empire. 13. Trail of Death. 14. On to Washington. 15. Sante Fe. 16. Fate of a Nation. 17. For High Stakes. 18. Victory.

475. The Oregon Trail

(Universal, May 1939) Serial, 15 chapters, two reels each. D: Ford Beebe and Saul A. Goodkind. SP: Edmund Kelso, George Plympton, Basil Dickey, and W.W. Watson. P: Henry MacRae.

Emigrants traveling to the Oregon Territory are being attacked by Sam Morgan's gang to protect his syndicate's control of the territory's fabulous fur supply. Jeff Scott and Deadwood Hawkins, special government agents assigned to investigate the trouble, join the wagon train of John Mason.

Top: **Johnny Mack Brown and Louise Stanley;** ***bottom:*** **Johnny Mack Brown in** ***The Oregon Trail*** **(1939)**

Johnny Mack Brown (Jeff Scott), Louise Stanley (Margaret Mason), Fuzzy Knight ("Deadwood" Hawkins), Bill Cody, Jr. (Jimmie Clark), Forrest Taylor (Daggett), James Blaine (Sam Morgan), Jack C. Smith ("Bull" Bragg), Edward LeSaint (John Mason), Charles Stevens (Breed), Jim Torney (Idaho Ike), Roy Barcroft (Colonel Custer), Charles King (Dirk), Colin Kenny (Slade), Karl Hackett (Dan Clark), Warner Richmond (General Sherman), Kenneth Harlan (General Terry), Horace Murphy, Helen Gibson, Tex Young, Frank LaRue, Frank Ellis, Iron Eyes Cody, George Plues, Richard Alexander, Cactus Mack, Tom Smith, Lafe McKee, Chick Hannon, Jim Thorpe.

1. The Renegade's Revenge. 2. The Flaming Forest. 3. The Brink of Disaster. 4. Thundering Doom. 5. Stampede. 6. Indian Vengeance. 7. Trail of Treachery. 8. Redskin's Revenge. 9. The Avalanche of Doom. 10. The Plunge of Peril. 11. Trapped in the Flames. 12. The Baited Trap. 13. Crashing Timbers. 14. Death in the Night. 15. The End of the Trail.

476. Oriental Souls

(France—Gaumont, 1919) Serial, 3 chapters.

This film is listed in the United States Catalog of Copyright Entries, *Motion Pictures, 1912–1939*, as a serial and gives the three chapter titles. There is no other information. The author has been unable to find credits for the serial.

1. The Debt. 2. The Expiation. 3. The Tragedy at Moonlight.

Lon Chaney, Jr., and Helen Parish in *Overland Mail* (1942)

477. L'Orphelin de Paris

(France—Gaumont, 1924) Serial, chapters (?). D: Louis Feuillade. Scen: Louis Feuillade.

Réne Poyen (Felix Perrin), Fernand Herrmann (Le detective Claudin), Alice Tissot (Palmyre), Bouboule (Josette), Amedée Charpentier (L'oncle Constant), Emile Andre (M. Ducoudray), Nina Orlove, Lucien Desplanques, Mme. Frederik Fabre, Madeleine Crousse.

478. L'Orphelin du Cirque

(France, 1926) Serial, chapters (?). D: Georges Lannes. Scen: Georges Lannes.

Andre Nox, Tramel, Charles Vanel, Berthe Jalabert, Suzy Vernon, Yvette Langlais, San German, Moriss, Chocolat, Volbert, Redelsperger.

479. L'Orpheline

(France—Gaumont, 1921) Serial, 12 chapters. D: Louis Feuillade. Scen: Louis Feuillade.

Sandra Milowanoff (Jeannette), Georges Biscot (Némorin), Mlle. Greyjane (La comtesse Nadia), Blanche Montel (Dolorès), Jane Rollette (Phrasie, la bonne du café), Garaudet (L'abbé Moral), Rene Clair (Pierre Moral), Fernand Hermann (Comte de Réalmont), Amedée Charpentier (Le père Boulot), Emile Andre (Le père Sorbier), Edouard Mathe (Estebau), Robert Florey, Jeanne Marie Laurent, Violette Jyl, Alice Tissot, Mlle. Kithnou.

French: 1. Les malheurs de Némorin. 2. Orpheline. 3. Le complot. 4. L'intruse. 5. Délivrance. 6. Le traquenard. 7. A l'ombre de clocher. 8. La conquete d' un héritage. 9. Soirs de Paris. 10. Chagrin d'amour. 11. Le revenant. 12. Vers le bonheur. *Portuguese:* 1. As desventuras de Nemorin. 2. O testamento de Nádia. 3. A tramoia. 4. A intrusa. 5. O salvamento. 6. A cilada. 7. A sombra do campánario. 8. A conquista de uma heranca. 9. Noites de amor. 10. Penas de amor. 11. O ressuscitado. 12. A caminho da felicidade.

480. Overland Mail

(Universal, September 27, 1942) Serial, 15 chapters, two reels each. D: ford Beebe and John Rawlins. S: Johnston McCulley. SP: Paul Huston. P: Henry MacRae.

Jim Lane, Sierra Pete, and Buckskin Billy Burke investigate attacks on the Overlander Company, which has a contract to carry the U.S. mail. They soon learn that the attacks are led by white men disguised as Indians working for a rival company which wants the mail delivery franchise.

Lon Chaney, Jr. (Jim Lane), Don Terry (Buckskin Billy Burke), Noah Beery, Jr. (Sierra Pete), Helen Parrish (Barbara Gilbert), Bob Baker (Young Bill Cody), Noah Beery, Sr. (Frank Chadwick), Tom Chatterton (Tom Gilbert), Charles Stevens (Puma), Robert Barron (Charles Carson), Harry Cording (Sam Gregg), William Desmond (banker), Marguerite De La Mothe (Rose), Ben Taggart (Lamont), Jack Rockwell (Slade), Roy Harris [Riley Hill] (Mack), Carleton Young (Lem), Ethan Laidlaw (Jake), Jack Clifford (Sheriff Tyler), Chief Thunder Cloud (Chief Many Moons), Chief Many Treaties (Black Cloud), Forrest Taylor, Curley Dresden, Tom Steele, Henry Hall, William Gould, Edmund Cobb.

1. A Race with Disaster. 2. Flaming Havoc. 3. The Menacing Herd. 4. The Bridge of Disaster. 5. Hurled to the Depths. 6. Death at the Stake. 7. The Path of Peril. 8. Imprisoned in Flames. 9. Hidden Danger. 10. Blazing Wagons. 11. The Trail of Terror. 12. In the Claws of the Cougar. 13. The Frenzied Mob. 14. The Toll of Treachery. 15. The Mail Goes Through.

481. Overland with Kit Carson

(Columbia, July 21, 1939) Serial, 15 chapters; Chapter 1, three reels; others, two reels. D: Sam Nelson and Norman Deming. SP: Joseph F. Poland, Morgan B. Cox, Ned Dandy. P: Jack Fier. Photography: Benjamin Kline, George Meehan. Sound: Lambert Day, Wes Moreland. Music: Lee Zahler. Assist. D: Wilber McGaugh and Milton Carter. Reissued by Columbia in 1951.

Bill Elliott (Kit Carson), Iris Meredith (Carmelita Gonzales), Trevor Bardette (Arthur Mitchell/Pegleg), Richard Fiske (Lt. David Brent), Bobby Clack (Andy Gardner), LeRoy Mason (John Baxter), James Craig (Tennessee), Kenneth MacDonald (Winchester), Francis Savles (Dr. Parker), Olin Francis (Pierre), Dick Curtis (Drake), Dick Botiller (Natchez), Hal Taliaferro [Wally Wales] (Jim Stuart), Flo Campbell (Ma Stuart), John Tyrrell (Capt. Gilbert), Irene Herndon (Juanita), Ernie Adams (Thor), Stanley Brown (Higgins), Art Mix (Bill), Jack Rockwell (Red), Edward J. LeSaint (Vice President), Martin Garralaga (Colonel Martino), Iron Eyes Cody (Indian Brave), Carl Stockdale (Stevens), Eddie Foster (Bart), Lee Prather (White Eagle), Joe Garcia (Wilson), Hank Bell (Fitzpatrick).

1. Doomed Men. 2. Condemned to Die. 3. Fight for Life. 4. The Ride of Terror. 5. The Path of Doom. 6. Rendezvous with Death. 7. The Killer Stallion. 8. The Devil's Nest. 9. Blazing Peril. 10. The Black Raiders. 11. Foiled. 12. The Warning. 13. Terror in the Night. 14. Crumbling Walls. 15. Unmasked.

482. The Pacemakers

(R-C Pictures, March–July, 1925) Series, 12 episodes, two reels each. D: Wesley Ruggles. S: H.C. Witwer. Scen: James Gruen, Beatrice Van, Paul Gangelin.

A comedy series.

Alberta Vaughn, George O'Hara, Stanley Taylor, Kit Guard.

1. Welcome Granger. 2. He Who Gets Rapped. 3. Merton of the Goofies. 4. The Great Decide. 5. The Fast Male. 6. The Covered Flagon. 7. Madam Sans Gin. 8. Three Bases East. 9. The Merry Kiddo. 10. What Price Gloria? 11. Don Coo-Coo. 12. Miss Me Again.

Top: **Bill Elliott, Iris Meredith, and Richard Fiske in *Overland with Kit Carson*; *bottom:* Ray Corrigan, Hoot Gibson, Sammy McKim (*boy*), and Hal Taliaferro [Wally Wales] in *The Painted Stallion* (1937)**

483. The Painted Stallion

(Republic, June 5, 1937) Serial, 12 chapters; Chapter 1, three reels; others, two reels. D: William Witney, Alan James, Ray Taylor. SP: Barry Shipman and Winston Miller. Based on ideas by Hal G. Evarts. Assoc. P: J. Laurence Wickland. Photography: William Nobles and Edgar Lyons. Music: Raoul Kraushaar.

Clark Stuart, on his way to Santa Fe to negotiate a treaty between the U.S. and the New Mexico governor, joins a wagon train ramrodded by Walter Jamison. Also in the expedition are Jim Bowie and a Young Kit Carson. Later David Crockett becomes an ally. Alfredo Dupray, in control of the Santa Fe territory pending arrival of the new governor, plans to sabotage the treaty and substitute one of his own men for Stuart. He tries everything to stop the wagon train.

A mysterious Indian girl rider on a painted stallion appears frequently to warn the Americans of impending danger by shooting a whistling arrow.

Ray Corrigan (Clark Stuart), Hoot Gibson (Walter Jamison), Hal Taliaferro (Jim Bowie), Jack Perrin (Davy Crockett), Duncan Renaldo (Zamorro), LeRoy Mason (Alfredo Dupray), Sammy McKim (Kit Carson), Julia Thayer (The Rider), Yakima Canutt (Tom), Ed Platt (Oscar), Lou Fulton (Elmer), Maston Williams (Macklin), Charles King (Bull Smith), Duke Taylor (Bill), Loren Riebe (Pedro), George DeNormand (Oldham), Gordon DeMain (Governor), Vinegar Roan (Pete), Lafe McKee (Boat Officer), Frank Leyva (Captain of the Guard), Gregg Star Whitespear (Topek), Lee White (Peters), Paul Lopez (Secretary), Joe Yrigoyen (Rancher), Monte Montague (Tanner), Horace Carpenter (Old Timer), Edward Peil, Sr. (Marshal), Henry Hale (Juan), Don Orlando (Jose), Frankie Marvin (Clerk), Curley Dresden (Harris), John Big Tree (Indian Chief), Pascale Perry (Joe), Ralph Bucko, Roy Bucko, Leo Dupree, Babe DeFreest, Jose Dominquez, Augie Gomez, Al Haskell, Jack Padjan.

1. Trail to Empire. 2. The Rider of the Stallion. 3. The Death Leap. 4. Avalanche. 5. Valley of Death. 6. Thundering Wheels. 7. Trail Treachery. 8. The Whistling Arrow. 9. The Fatal Message. 10. Ambush. 11. Tunnel of Terror. 12. Human Targets.

484. Panopta

(Denmark—Palladium, 1918–1919) Series, 4 episodes. D: Kai Van Der Aa Kuhle. SP: Lily Van Der Aa Kuhle. Photography: Hans Folkmann. S: Zolva Bebe.

Emilie Sannon (Panopta), Victor Montell (Williams), Valdemar Moller, Jon Iversen, Robert Schyberg, William Jensen, Hertha Rindom, Aage Hyllested, Emmandel Gregers.

1. I Kvinderovernes Klor (Rel: 1-16-18-five reels). 2. Raedselshuset paa Soens Bund (Rel: 2-14-18–five reels). 3. Panopta III (Rel: 5-5-19-three reels). 4. Da Taarnklokken styrtede ned (Rel: 5-12-19-three reels).

485. Panther Girl of the Kongo

(Republic, February 1955) Serial, 12 chapters, two reels each. D: Franklyn Adreon. SP: Ronald Davidson. Assoc. P: Franklyn Adreon. Photography: Bud Thackery. Music: R. Dale Butts. Special Effects: Howard and Theodore Lydecker. Feature title: *The Claw Monsters*.

A doctor who has discovered a jungle diamond mine develops a hormone compound which causes ordinary crayfish to become monsters. He and his henchmen use the creatures to scare the natives away from the area of the mine. When Jean Evans, known as The Panther Girl, and big-game hunter Larry Sanders arrive in the area, Jean accidentally photographs the Claw Monsters, as the natives call them. Dr. Morgan realizes he can't afford to have the photos published, for it would bring on an investigation. Thus, Jean and Larry become targets for murder, but then outmaneuver their adversaries to win the victory.

Phyllis Coates (Jean Evans/Panther Girl), Myron Healey (Larry Sanders), Arthur Space (Dr. Morgan), John Daheim (Cass), Mike Ragan (Rand), Morris Buchanan (Tembu), Fred Graham (Nick Burgas), Roy Glenn, Sr. (Danka), Archie Savage (Ituri), Ramsay Hill (Commissioner Stanton), Naaman Brown (Orto), Dan Ferniel (Ebu), James Logan (Harris), Gene Stutenroth (Bartender), Charles Sullivan (Davis), Steve Calvert (Gorilla), Keith McConnell (Kent), Daniel Elam (Native), Wesley Gale (Native), DeForest Covan (Koango), Don Carlos (Semba), Alan Reynolds (Stanley), Marin Wilkins (Zemba), Walter Smith (Naganto), Tom Steele (Double for Healey).

1. The Clay Monster. 2. Jungle Ambush. 3. The Killer Beast. 4. Sands of Doom. 5. Test of Terror. 6. High Peril. 7. Timber Trap. 8. Crater of Flame. 9. River of Death. 10. Blasted Evidence. 11. Double Danger. 12. House of Doom.

486. Les Paris de L'Amour

(France—Etablissements L. Aubert, 1921) Serial, 13 chapters. D: Paul Garbagni. S: Marcel Allain.

Paul Amiot, Fernand Mailly, Helene Lutger, Claire Premore, Lisa Hestia, Maurice De Canonge, G. Cazalis, Albert Mayer.

Portuguese: 1. O pacto infame. 2. O réptil. 3. Amor e intrigas. 4. O verdadeiro conde. 5. [Unknown.] 6. [Unknown.] 7. Os primeiros revezes. 8. Paixão fatal. 9. Olho por olho. 10. Imprecação terrível. 11. Proezas do Guitão. 12. Transfusão de sangue. 13. Delícias do amor.

487. Paris Mystérieux

(France—Parisienne Films, 1920) Serial, 10 chapters. D: Louis Paglieri. SP: Georges Spitzmuller.

Georges Gauthier (Príncipe Jorge), Mlle. Seigneur (Fleury), Mlle. Marie Heil (Daria), Mme. Brindeau (Rainha Isabel), Phillip Damorès (Stog), Serre (Duque Miguel), Volbert (Nonô), Charland (Arsênio), Mlle. Desvignez (Louise), Dartagnan (Bankor).

Portuguese: 1. O homem das trevas. 2. A abandonada. 3. Na pele de outro. 4. A vingança da rainha Isabel. 5. Sentença de morte. 6. Um fato imprevisto. 7. Fatalidade. 8. Descerra-se o véu. 9. O juramento de Daria. 10. Paris libertade.

488. Parisette

(France—Gaumont, 1922) Serial, 12 chapters. D: Louis Feuillade. Scen: Louis Feuillade.

Sandra Milowanoff (Parisette), Georges Biscot (Cogolin), Fernand Hermann (Le banquier Stephan), Edouard Mathé (Pedro Alvarez), René Clair (Jean Vernier), Amedée Charpentier (Le père Lapusse), Jane Rollette (Mélanie Parent), Mlle. Greyjane (Mme. Stephan), Pierre de Canolle (Joseph), Derigal (Marquis de Costabella), Arnaud (Candido).

French: 1. Manoëla. 2. Le secret de Madame Stefan. 3. L'affaire de Neuilly. 4. L'enquete. 5. La piste. 6. Grand-père. 7. Le faux révérend. 8. Family-House. 9. L'impasse. 10. Le triomphe de Cogolin. 11. La fortune de Joaquim. 12. Le secret de Costabella. *Portuguese:* 1–8. [Unknown.] 9. Novas compleições. 10. A inocência triunfa. 11. O segredo da fortuna. 12. A náu "Mãe de Deus."

489. Patria

(International Film Service/Pathé, January 14, 1917) Serial, 15 chapters; Chapter 1, three reels; others, two reels. D: Theodore and Leo Wharton and Jacques Jaccard. SP: J.B. Clymer, Louis Joseph Vance, and Charles W. Goddard. S: Louis Joseph Vance, *The Last of the Fighting Channings*.

A controversial war preparedness serial pitting Patria Channing, owner of a large munitions factory, against agents of the Japanese and Mexican governments. Patria is the heir to a trust fund of $100 million in gold intended to aid the U.S. in the event of peril arising through its unpreparedness for war. Aided by Captain Donald Parr, secret service agent, she combats Baron Huroki, chief of the Japanese secret service, and Señor Juan de Lima of Mexico, who together are plotting the overthrow of the U.S. and the acquisition of the huge fortune.

The picture pulled no punches. It was explicitly stated that the invaders were Japanese and had invaded the U.S. from Mexico. President Wilson was so displeased at the film that he ordered Pathé to cut out all the names, flags, etc. that identified the invaders.

Irene Castle (Patria Channing), Milton Sills (Captain Donald Parr), Warner Oland (Baron Huroki), Dorothy Green (Fannie Blair), Georgia Majeroni (Juan de Lima), Wallace Beery (Pancho Villa), Marie Walcamp (Bess Morgan), Allan Murnane (Rodney Wrenn), Floyd Buckley, Nigel Barre, Charles Brinley, Jack Holt, George Lessey, M.W. Rale, Le Roy L. Baker, Rudolph Valentino. Dick Stewart.

1. Last of the Fighting Channings. 2. The Treasure. 3. Winged Millions. 4. Double Crossed. 5. The Island God Forgot. 6. Alias Nemesis. 7. Red Dawn. 8. Red Night. 9. Cat's Paw and Scapegoat. 10. War in the Dooryard. 11. Sunset Falls. 12. Peace on the Border. 13. Wings of Death. 14. Border Peril. 15. For the Flag.

490. Pearl of the Army

(Astra Film Corp./Pathé, December 3, 1916) Serial, 15 chapters, two reels each. D: Edward Jose. S: G.M. McConnell. Scen: George B. Seitz. Later recut into 10 chapters and re-released under same title but not by Pathé.

The Silent Menace tries to steal Panama Canal defense secrets, but the patriotic Pearl thwarts him at every turn and becomes a heroine to her country. From the beginning a romance between Pearl and Captain Payne existed. It should be remembered that the early serials were made primarily for adult audiences. Romance played a part, and this one was no exception.

Pearl White (Pearl Dare), Ralph Kellard (Captain Ralph Payne), Marie Wayne (Bertha Bonn), Theodore Friebus (Major Brent), W.T. Carleton (Colonel Dare), Floyd Buckley, Joe Cuny.

1. The Traitor. 2. Found Guilty. 3. The Silent Menace. 4. War Clouds. 5. Somewhere in Grenada. 6. Major Brent's Perfidy. 7. For the Stars and Stripes. 8. International Diplomacy. 9. The Monroe Doctrine. 10. The Silent Army. 11. A Million Volunteers. 12. The Foreign Alliance. 13. Modern Buccaneers. 14. The Flag Despoiler. 15. The Colonel's Orderly.

491. Pearl White Crystal Comedies

(Crystal, 1912–1914) Series, 135 episodes, one reel each. D: Phillips Smalley (primary), Joseph A. Golden (Secondary).

In the minds of the thousands of people familiar with her name, Pearl White is invariably linked with *The Perils of Pauline* (1914) and serials. Hardly anyone knows that she was quite a comedienne before she became the first serial queen and, without doubles, raced across rooftops, leaped from trains, tumbled down stairways, disappeared through trap doors, swarmed up fire escapes, endured the hazards of the mill saw, scuffled with a dozen ruffians, survived explosions, fires, onrushing flood waters, and numerous other indignities.

She put as much effort into her comedies as she did her serials and, to be expected, she was successful. People liked her. Crystal liked her. She left the comedy field voluntarily to become a serial star and receive higher wages.

Films 123–135 were advertised and believed to have been released but the release dates cannot be found.

Pearl White (Herself), Chester Barnett, Claude Belmont.

1. The Girl in the Next Room (10-6-12). 2. Her Dressmaker's Bills (10-13-12). 3. Bella's Beaus (10-20-12). 4. A Pair of Fools (10-26-12). 5. Oh, Such a Night (11-3-12). 6. The Gypsy Flirt (11-10-12). 7. The Chorus Girl (11-16-12). 8. Locked Out (12-1-12). 9. A Tangled Marriage (12-8-12). 10. The Mind Cure (12-15-12). 11. His Wife's Stratagem (12-22-12). 12. Her Visitor (12-29-12). 13. Her Kid Sister

Pearl White in *Pearl of the Army* (1916)

(1-5-13). 14. Heroic Herald (1-12-13). 15. A Dip Into Society (1-19-13). 16. Pearl's Admirers (1-26-13). 17. With Her Rival's Help (2-2-13). 18. Accident Insurance (2-9-13). 19. Strictly Business (2-16-13). 20. That Other Girl (2-23-13). 21. A Night in Town (3-2-13). 22. Who is the Goat (3-8-13). 23. Knights and Ladies (3-9-13). 24. Lovers Three (3-23-13). 25. The Drummer's Note Book (3-30-13). 26. Our Parents-in-Law (4-5-13). 27. Pearl as a Clairvoyant (4-6-13). 28. The Veiled Lady (4-13-13). 29. Two Lunatics (4-20-13). 30. Forgetful Flossie (4-27-13). 31. His Awful Daughter (5-3-13). 32. When Love is Young (5-3-13). 33. Pearl as a Detective (5-4-13). 34. Homlock Shermes (5-18-13). 35. Toodleums (5-25-13). 36. Where Charity Begins (5-24-13). 37. Mary's Romance (6-3-13). 38. The New Typist (6-8-13). 39. A Call from Home (6-17-13). 40. Will Power (6-22-13). 41. Who is in the Box? (6-28-13). 42. Muchly Engaged (6-28-13). 43. An Hour of Terror (6-28-13). 44. True Chivalry (7-5-13). 45. The Girl Reporter (7-6-13). 46. Pearl's Dilemma (7-13-13). 47. College Chums (7-19-13). 48. The Hall Room Girls (7-20-13). 49. The Broken Spell (7-22-13). 50. The Paper Doll (7-29-13). 51. Starving for Love (8-2-13). 52. What Papa Got (8-3-13). 53. A Child's Influence (8-5-13). 54. Oh! You Scotch Lassie (8-10-13). 55. Pearl and the Tramp (8-17-13). 56. Caught in the Act (8-19-13). 57. A Greater Influence (8-19-13). 58. His Aunt Emma (8-23-13). 59. That Crying Baby (8-23-13). 60. Much Ado About Nothing (9-2-13). 61. The Hand of Providence (9-6-13). 62. Lost in the Night (9-7-13). 63. Pleasing Her Husband (9-9-13). 64. A News Item (9-16-13). 65. Misplaced Love (9-21-13). 66. Pearl and the Poet (9-23-13). 67. His Lost Gamble (9-28-13). 68. Dress Reform (10-7-13). 69. The Woman and the Law (10-12-13). 70. Pearl's Mistake (10-14-13). 71. Willie's Great Scheme (10-18-13). 72. Hearts Entangled (10-19-13). 73. A Hidden Love (10-25-13). 74. Robert's Lesson (10-26-13). 75. The Rich Uncle (10-28-13). 76. The Fatal Plunge (11-2-13). 77. Girls Will Be Boys (11-4-13). 78. Out of the Grove (11-8-13). 79. When Duty Calls (11-9-13). 80. Pals (11-9-13). 81. Daisy Wins the Day (11-9-13). 82. At the Burglar's Command (11-11-13). 83. Oh! You Pearl (11-11-13). 84. Her Secretaries (11-15-13). 85. Out of the Grave (11-16-13). 86. The Cabaret Singer (11-23-13). 87. Hubby's New Coat (11-24-13). 88. The Convict's Daughter (11-30-13). 89. A Woman's Revenge (12-7-13). 90. Pearl's Hero (12-9-13). 91. First Love (12-14-13). 92. The Soubrette (12-16-13). 93. The Heart of an Artist (12-21-13). 94. The Lifted Veil (12-27-13). 95. Lure of the Stage (12-28-13). 96. The Kitchen Mechanic (12-30-13). 97. Shadowed (1-6-14). 98. The Ring (1-11-14). 99. It May Come to This (1-13-14). 100. A Father's Devotion (1-18-14). 101. The Shadow of Crime (1-25-4). 102. Oh! You Puppy (1-7-14). 103. A Grateful Outcast (2-1-14). 104. What Didn't Happen to Mary (2-3-14). 105. For a Woman (2-8-14). 106. Getting Reuben Back (2-10-14). 107. McSweeney's Masterpiece (2-14-14). 108. A Sure Cure (2-15-14). 109. Lizzie and the Iceman (3-8-14). 110. Going Some (3-31-14). 111. The Lady Doctor (4-5-14). 112. Get Out and Get Under (4-7-14). 113. A Telephone Engagement (5-5-14). 114. The Mashers (5-16-14). 115. The Dancing Craze (5-19-14). 116. Easy Money (6-2-14). 117. The Girl in Pants (6-27-14). 118. Her New Hat (6-30-14). 119. What Pearl's Pearls Did (7-14-14). 120. Willie's Disguise (8-11-14). 121. East Lynn in Bugville (9-22-14). 121. Some Collectors (10-13-14). 122. Oh! You Mummy (11-17-14). 123. Pearl and the Burglars. 124. Pearl's Adventure. 125. Pearl's Romance. 126. The Bunc That Failed. 127. Cops is Business. 128. The Maniac's Desire. 130. A Lady in Distress. 131. The Book Agents. 132. The Tell Tale Blotter. 133. Out of the Past. 134. When Love Was Young. 135. Who's the Goat.

Kay Aldridge in *Perils of Nyoka* (1942)

492. Perils of Nyoka

(Republic, June 22, 1942) Serial, 15 chapters, two reels each. D: William Witney. SP: Ronald Davidson, Norman S. Hall, William Lively, Joseph Poland, and Joseph O'Donnell. Assoc. P: W.J. O'Sullivan. Photography: Reggie Lanning. Music: Mort Glickman. Special Effects: Howard Lydecker. Feature title: *Nyoka and the Lost Secrets of Hippocrates.*

Nyoka, a white girl ruling a tribe of Bedouins, and at the same time searching for her lost father, joins forces with an expedition of archaeologists seeking the long lost tablets of Hippocrates, a treasure, and a Greek formula for curing cancer. They are opposed by Princess Vultura, leader of a bank of renegade Arabs. Reminiscent of the silent serials of Pearl White, Ruth Roland, and Juanita Hansen, this action-crammed serial is considered one of the best ever made by Republic.

Kay Aldridge (Nyoka Gordon), Clayton Moore (Larry Grayson), William Benedict (Red Davis), Lorna Gray [Adrian Booth]

(Vultura), Charles Middleton (Cassib), Tristram Coffin (Benito Torrini), George J. Lewis (Batan), Forbes Murray (Douglas Campbell), Robert Strange (Henry Gordon), John Davidson (Lhoba), George Pembroke (John Spencer), Georges Renavent (Maghreb), Ken Terrell (Ahmed), John Bagni (Ben Ali), Kenne Duncan (Abou), Arvon Dale (Bedouin), Ace [dog] (Fang), Art Dupuis (Hassan), Pedro Regas (Ibrahim), Tom Steele (Riffi), Emil Van Horn (The Gorilla Satan), Robert Barron (Sidi), Forrest Taylor (Translator), Al Kikume (Nuri), Herbert Rawlinson (Reynolds), Bud Wolfe (Tuareg Leader), Leonard Hampton (Yussuf), John Daheim (Arab), Iron Eyes Cody (Arab), Duke Taylor (Arab), Joe Garcia (Guard), Ken Terrell (Guard), Loren Riebe (Guard), Loren Riebe (Guard), Henry Wills (Guard), Yakima Canutt, George Plues, Cy Slocum, David Sharpe, Harry Smith, Tom Steele, George Suzanne, Duke Taylor, Dirk Thane, Jack O'Shea, Carey Loftin, Duke Green, Jerry Frank, John Daheim, Art Dillard (Tuaregs).

1. Desert Intrigue. 2. Death's Chariot. 3. Devil's Crucible. 4. Ascending Doom. 5. Fatal Second. 6. Human Sacrifice. 7. Monster's Clutch. 8. Tuareg Vengeance. 9. Burned Alive. 10. Treacherous Trail. 11. Unknown Peril. 12. Underground Tornado. 13. Thundering Death. 14. Blazing Barrier. 15. Satan's Fury.

Top: **Clayton Moore and Kay Aldridge in *Perils of Nyoka* (1942); *bottom:* Pearl White in *The Perils of Pauline* (1914)**

493. Perils of Our Girl Reporters

(Niagara Film Co./Mutual, December 28, 1916) Series, 15 episodes, two reels each. D: George W. Terwilliger. S: Edith Sessions Tupper.

These are varied stories, each complete in itself, in which girl reporters scoop the male competition and aid authorities in bringing to justice those who have stepped beyond the boundaries of the law.

Zena Keefe (Jessie Forsythe), Helen Green (Jessie Forsythe) [Helen was cast as the heroine but was replaced after the 3rd episode], Mildred E. Bailey, Earl Metcalfe, Mabel Montgomery, Ethel Sinclair, William Turner, Louis Huntington, Julia R. Hurley, George Arvine, George Richard, Felix Hainey, Anthony W. Matthews.

1. The Jade Necklace. 2. The Black Door. 3. Ace High. 4. The White Trail. 5. Many a Slip. 6. The Long Lane. 7. Smite of Conscience. 8. Birds of Prey. 9. Misjudged. 10. Taking Chances. 11. The Meeting. 12. Outwitted. 13. The Schemers. 14. The Counterfeiters. 15. Kidnapped.

494. The Perils of Pauline

(Pathé, March 31, 1914) Serial, 20 chapters, two reels each. D: Louis Gasnier and Donald McKenzie. Scen: George B. Seitz. S: Charles Goddard. P: Leopold and Theodore Wharton.

With the release of *The Perils of Pauline* the motion picture serial came into its own. A whole new genre was fashioned on the success of this crudely made chapter play and its phenomenally popular star, formerly a little-known comedienne with Crystal Studio. She captivated the world with her performances in the hair-raising scenes written for her.

Pearl Fay White earned screen immortality in the Pathé Studio, based in New Jersey, where, without benefit of doubles, she raced across rooftops to escape the clutches of the hooded terror, leaped from speeding trains, tumbled down stairways, disappeared through trapdoors, and swarmed up fire escapes. And it was there that she endured the desperate hazards of the mill saw, the onrushing flood waters, the leaps from the bridges, fires, explosions, and the jutting rocks of the Palisades. She could scuffle with a dozen ruffians without so much as mussing the blonde wig that hid her auburn hair and became her trademark. She was a woman uniquely fitted to fill the needs of millions of people living humdrum lives for escapist entertainment and vicarious thrills.

White's serial escapades and uninhibited personal life fulfilled the dreams of both the sweatshop working girls and the small town belles who wished for balls and marcelled Charles Dana Gibson boyfriends. She is one of the few silent picture stars to achieve a permanent place in American folklore.

In this most famous of all serials, Pauline is menaced by Koerner, who is after her inheritance. She is loved and protected by boyfriend Harry Marvin. Although Pauline's perils centered around the "villain-wants-inheritance" theme, the serial was a set of unrelated stories with equally dissimilar locations and casts of supporting players. No cliffhanger endings. Thus it more aptly should be classified as a series; however, it is here ranked as a serial because it is that in the minds of most movie fans. Each chapter is largely self-contained. Despite its crudeness and sloppy construction, it has remained the most famous of all movie serials.

Pearl White (Pauline), Crane Wilbur (Harry Marvin), Paul Panzer (Koerner/Raymond Owen), Edward Jose (Sanford Marvin), Francis Carlyle (Hicks), Clifford Bruce (The Gypsy Leader), Donald Mackenzie (Blinky Bill), Jack Standing (Ensign Summers), Eleanor Woodruff (Lucille), LeRoy Baker, Louise Dupre, Oscar Neu, Sam Ryan, Louis Gasnier, Joe Cuny, Charles Revada, Frank Redman, Sr., Floyd Buckley.

Apparently Pathé did not title the chapters. Subsequently, however, chapter titles were written and issued with the chapters by several different distributors. For example, Chapter 1 has been titled both "The Breath of Dead Centuries" and "Through Air and Fire," and Chapter 2 has been titled "The Will" as well as "Goddess of the Far West." Other titles used with various chapters are Pauline Takes the First Trick, Owen Wins the First Game, The Pirate and Pauline, The Treasure Hunters, A Flirty Buccaneer, The Courteous Reception, Baskinell's Quarry, Kaboff's Wild Horse, From Cloud to Cliff, Old Grigsby House Pays Penance, Double Cross Ranch, The Great White Queen, The Death Stone, Sophie McCallan's Wedding, Palmer Comes Back, A Hot Young Comet, Owen Offers a Reward, Owen Makes a Reputation, The Guest of Honor, Submarine B-2, A Paper Chase, The Mummy's Last Warning.

495. Perils of Pauline

(Universal, January 1934) Serial, 12 chapters, two reels each. D: Ray Taylor. SP: Ella O'Neill, Basil Dickey, George Plympton, and Jack Foley. S: Ella O'Neill and Charles W. Goddard.

The secret formula for a deadly gas is engraved on an ivory disc somewhere in Indochina. Both Dr. Hargrave, an American scientist, and Dr. Bashan and his gang search for it. Hargrave's daughter, Pauline, and a friend, Robert Ward, learn of Bashan's fiendish designs and struggle to protect Hargraves and the secret from him.

Evelyn Knapp (Pauline Hargrave), Robert Allen [aka Hugh Enfield and Craig Reynolds] (Robert Ward), James Durkin (Professor Hargrave), John Davidson (Dr. Bashan), Sonny Ray (Willie Dodge), Frank Lackteen (Fang), Pat O'Malley (Aviator), William Desmond (Professor Thompson), Adolph Muller (Captain), Josef Swickard (Foreign Consul), William Worthington (American Consul).

1. The Guns of Doom. 2. The Typhoon of Terror. 3. The Leopard Leaps. 4. Trapped by the Enemy. 5. The Flaming Tomb. 6. Pursued by Savages. 7. Tracked by the Enemy. 8. Dangerous Depths. 9. The Mummy Walks. 10. The Night Attack. 11. Into the Flames. 12. Confu's Sacred Secret.

Evalyn Knapp in *Perils of Pauline* (1934)

496. Perils of the Jungle

(Weiss Brothers Artclass, July 1927) 10 chapters, two reels each. D: Jack Nelson. S: H.P. Crist.

Intrigue, double cross, and animal jeopardy in the heart of the African jungle prevail as a father and daughter seek a treasure, the whereabouts of which is known only to the father. A companion seeks to steal the treasure once it is found. When the old man becomes ill, he entrusts a map of the location to Rod Bedford, a young man the party has met in Africa and whom the old man trusts. Rod proves trustworthy and is able to thwart the villain, "Brute" Hanley, reach treasure, and protect the girl, Phyllis.

The producer apparently decided on thrills at any cost, and this is where the picture errs. In some instances story structure, plausibility, and restraint suffer occasionally so that action can take the stage. Wild animals there are galore, threatening the principals at every alternate moment. The whole ferocious gamut of the jungle is paraded, from owls to crocodiles. Charging lions are as frequent as fights and rescues, of which there are many.

In 1945 a feature entitled *The White Gorilla* was composed mainly of stock footage from this serial. Eugenia Gilbert (Phyllis Manley), Frank Merrill (Rod Bedford), Albert J. Smith ("Brute" Hanley), Harry Belmore (Manley), Bobby Nelson (Kimko), Milburn Moranti (Marks), Will Herman (Moto), Walter Macy (Stephens), Frank Huttee (Renee).

1. Jungle Trails. 2. The Jungle King. 3. The Elephant's Revenge. 4. At the Lion's Mercy. 5. The Sting of Death. 6. The Trail of Blood. 7. The Feast of Vengeance. 8. The Leopard's Trap. 9. The Gorilla's Bride. 10. The Tiger's Den.

497. Perils of the Royal Mounted

(Columbia, May 24, 1942) Serial, 15 chapters, two reels each. D: James W. Horne. SP: Basil Dickey, Scott Littleton, Louis Heifetz, and James A. Duffy. P: Larry Darmour. Assist. D: Carl Hiecks. Photography: James S. Brown, Jr. Music: Lee Zahler.

The royal Mounties take on renegade white men and rebellious Indians who are attacking settlers in the Canadian wilds. Leading the renegades is Mort Ransome, and he does his best to defeat Mounties MacLane and Blake. Ransome conspires with medicine man Black Bear to agitate the normally friendly Indians. The Mounties survive numerous attempts to kill them. Dynamite explosions, Indian attacks, forest fires, leaps from burning bridges, and shootouts are all taken in stride as the Mounties get their man in the end. Both Black Bear and Ransome are killed and the rest of the gang rounded up.

Nell O'Day (Diana), Robert Stevens [Kellard] (Sergeant MacLane), Herbert Rawlinson (Winton), Kenneth MacDonald (Mort Ransome), John Elliott (Mountie Blake), Nick Thompson (Black Bear), Art Miles (Flying Cloud), Richard Fiske (Brady), Richard Vallin (Little Wolf), Forrest Taylor (Hinsdale), Kermit Maynard (Collins), George Chesebro (Gaspard), Jack Ingram (Baptiste), Iron Eyes Cody (Indian), Charles King (Outlaw), Al Ferguson (Outlaw), I. Stanford Jolley, Tom London.

1. The Totem Talks. 2. The Night Raiders. 3. The Water God's Revenge. 4. Beware, the Vigilantes. 5. The Masked Mountie. 6. Underwater Gold. 7. Bridge to the Sky. 8. Lost in the Mine. 9. Into the Trap. 10. Betrayed by Law. 11. Blazing Beacon. 12. The Mountie's Last Chance. 13. Painted White Man. 14. Burned at the Stake. 15. The Mountie Gets His Man.

498. Perils of the Secret Service

(Universal IMP, 1917) Series, 9 episodes, two reels each, except No. 8, which is three reels. D: George Bronson Howard (7), Jack Wells (1). Scen: George Bronson Howard (7), Luther Reed (1). P: Jack Wells, Kingsley Benedict. Founded on the Yorke Norrey stories.

A short-lived series of adventure stories.

Kingsley Benedict, Jay Belasco, M.K. Wilson, Violet Schram, Seymour Hastings, Harry Mann, Muriel Parker, Vola Smith, Malcolm Blevins, Clyde Benson, Clare Du Brey, L.C. Shumway, Jean Hersholt, Francis Marion, Frank Whitson, Roberta Wilson, C.G. Briden, Harry Archer, Francis McDonald, Elsie Jane Wilson, Arthur Hoyt, Bertram Grassby, Warda Lamont, Fred Harrington, Willard Wayne, Muriel Parker, Mignon

Nell O'Day and I. Stanford Jolley in *Perils of the Royal Mounted* (1942)

Anderson, Al MacQuarrie, Baron von Ritzau, Frank Lanning, Frank Tokonaga, Harry Schumm, Betty Schade.

1. The Last Cigarette. 2. The Clash of Steel. 3. Dreaded Tube. 4. Crimson Blade. 5. Man in the Trunk. 6. The Signet Ring. 7. International Spy. 8. The Master Spy. 9. The Mysterious Iron Ring.

499. Perils of the Wild

(Universal, August 27, 1925) Serial, 15 chapters, two reels each. D: Francis Ford. SP: Isadore Bernstein, William Lord Wright. S: Johann David Wyss—*Swiss Family Robinson*.

After a fight in a "Pub" in Liverpool, in the process of getting a crew together, the Swiss Family Robinson set sail for Australia with a cargo of flint-locks and gunpowder and, unknowingly with a pirate crew. There is also another passenger, Emily Montrose, who develops as the heroine. As the ship nears the pirates' base, the ship is seized by the crew. A heavy sea and storm follow and the pirates thinking the ship doomed abandon it and row their boat to a tropical island, their headquarters. The Swiss Family, later on, land on the other side of the island thinking it uninhabited except for the well-mannered animals. The Swiss Family set up a tent and prepare to adjust themselves to their new home. The adventures that follow are many.

Joe Bonomo (Frederick Robinson), Margaret Quimby (Emily Montrose), Jack Mower (Sir Charles Leicester), Alfred Allen (Captain William Robinson), Eva Gordon (Frau Mitilla Robinson), Jack Murphy (Jack Robinson), Howard Enstedt (Ernest Robinson), Francis Irwin (Francis Robinson), William Dyer (Black John), Albert Prisco (Tonie), Fannie Warren (Bonita), John Wallace (Pirate), James Welsh (Pirate), Phil Ford (Pirate), Sammy Gervon (Pirate), Boris Karloff.

1. The Hurricane. 2. The Lion's Fangs. 3. The Flaming Jungle. 4. The Treasure Cave. 5. Saved by the Sun. 6. The Jungle Trail. 7. Pirate Peril. 8. Winds of Fate. 9. Rock of Revenge. 10. The Rescue. 11. The Stolen Wedding. 12. Marooned. 13. Prisoners of the Sea. 14. The Leopard's Lair. 15. In the Nick of Time.

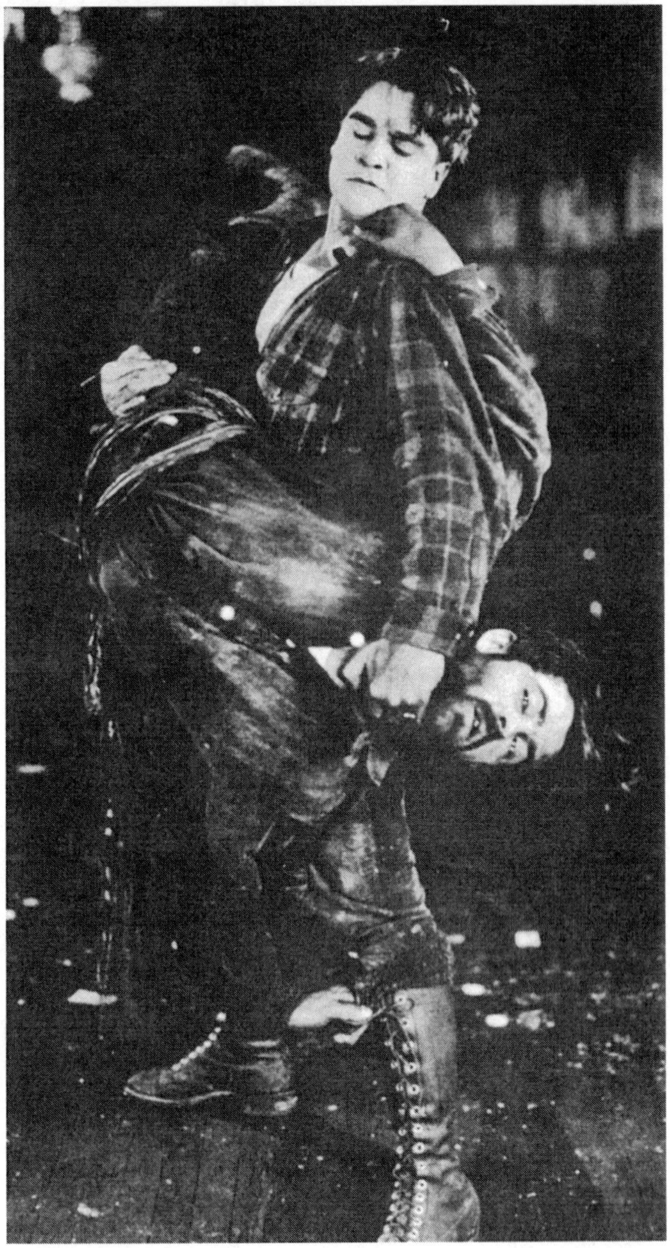

***Top left:* Joe Bonomo and Margaret Quimby in *Perils of the Wild* (1925); *bottom left; Perils of the Wilderness* (1956); *right:* William Desmond in *Perils of the Yukon* (1922)**

500. Perils of the Wilderness

(Columbia, January 6, 1956) Serial, 15 chapters, two reels each. D: Spencer G. Bennet. SP: George H. Plympton. P: Sam Katzman. Assist. D: Willard Sheldon. Photography: Ira H. Morgan. Music: Mischa Bakaleinikoff.

A deputy marshal from Montana, a Royal Canadian Mountie, and a female Canadian Secret Service agent prove too much for an outlaw czar in the great Canadian northwest, and his gang of cutthroats is smashed.

Dennis Moore (Laramie), Richard Emory (Sergeant Gray), Eve Anderson [Evelyn Finley] (Donna Blane), Kenneth MacDonald (Bart Randall), Rick Vallin (Little Bear), John Elliott (Homer Lynch), Don C. Harvey (Kruger), Terry Frost (Baptiste), Al Ferguson (Mike), Bud Osborne (Jake), Rex Lease (Sergeant Jim Rodney), Pierce Lyden (Amby), John Mitchum (Brent), Lee Roberts (Constable Scott), Stanley Price (Cragg), Kermit Maynard (Constable Walker), Ed Coch (Durk), John Hart, Robert Bice, Wally West, I. Stanford Jolley, Dan White, Jack Ingram, Frank Lackteen.

1. The Voice from the Sky. 2. The Mystery Plane. 3. The Mine of Menace. 4. Ambush for a Mountie. 5. Laramie's Desperate Chance. 6. Trapped in the Flaming Forest. 7. Out of the Trap. 8. Laramie Rides Alone. 9. Menace of the Medicine Man. 10. Midnight Marauders. 11. The Falls of Fate. 12. Rescue from the Rapids. 13. Little Bear Pays a Debt. 14. The Mystery Plane Flies Again. 15. Laramie Gets His Man.

501. Perils of the Yukon

(Universal, July 24, 1922) Serial, 15 chapters, two reels each. D: Perry Vekroff, Jay Marchant, and J.P. McGowan. S/SP: George Morgan and George Plympton.

A love triangle is set in early-day Alaska, with the daughter of a wealthy Russian trader loved by both hero Jack Merrill,

Sr. and villain Petroff, who tries to do away with Merrill. The Russian does not succeed in destroying the hero but does keep him in captivity long enough to mislead the girl. After a lapse of many years, the betrayed girl's daughter appears and becomes the object of Jack Merrill, Jr.'s affections.

William Desmond (Jack Merrill, Sr./Jack Merrill, Jr.), Laura La Plante (Olga), Fred Stanton (Ivon Petroff), Joe McDermott (Hogan), George A. Williams (Scott McPherson), Mack V. Wright (Lew Scully), Fred Kohler (Captain Whipple), Princess Neela (Neewah), Chief Harris (Numa), Joseph Girard, Ruth Royce, Clark Comstock.

1. Fangs of Jealousy. 2. Doomed. 3. Tricked by Fate. 4. Master and Man. 5. Terrors of the North. 6. Menace of Death. 7. Trapped by Fire. 8. Hurled into Space. 9. The Gold Rush. 10. Valley of Death. 11. A Race for Life. 12. The Path of Doom. 13. Martial Law. 14. Trail of Vengeance. 15. The Final Reckoning.

502. The Perils of Thunder Mountain

(Vitagraph, May 1919) Serial, 15 chapters, two reels each. D: Robert N. Bradbury and W.J. Bauman. S: Albert E. Smith and Cyrus Townsend Brady. Scen: Graham Baker.

An old man's will provides that his two nephews are to work his mine on shares, with allowances for his adopted daughter and two servants, the remainder of the gold to go to charity.

Morgan, a murderous crook, is openly disgusted at the charity clause in the will and suggests to Davis that they work the mine entirely for their own benefit and fight, play, or draw for the girl. Davis insists that the will be carried out explicitly.

Morgan sees a bright ray of hope in the clause of the will providing that "in case of the death of one administrator, the other succeeds to the double duty of trust and guardianship, with double the revenue for himself."

Antonio Moreno (John Davis), Carol Holloway (Ethel Carr), Kate Price, Jack Waltemeyer, George Stanley, A.D. Ragnier, Tote Du Crow, Charles Rich.

1. The Spear of Malice. 2. The Bridge Trap. 3. Teeth of Steel. 4. Cave of Terror. 5. The Cliff of Treachery. 6. The Tree of Torture. 7. The Lightning Lure. 8. The Iron Clutch. 9. Prisoner of the Deep. 10. The Flaming Sacrifice. 11. In the Ocean's Grip. 12. The Rushing Horror. 13. The River of Dread. 14. The Hut of Disaster. 15. Fate's Verdict.

503. The Phantom

(Columbia, December 24, 1943) Serial, 15 chapters, two reels each. D: B. Reeves Eason. SP: Morgan B. Cox, Victor McLeod, Sherman Lowe, and Leslie J. Swabacker. P: Rudolph C. Flothow. Assist. D: Richard Monroe. Photography: James S. Brown, Jr. Music: Lee Zahler. Based on the King Features newspaper cartoon created by Lee Falk and Ray Moore. Released in feature form in England.

Geoffrey Prescott becomes The Phantom when his father is killed, carrying on a tradition handed down from father to son for 400 years. The Phantom is dedicated to the extinction of piracy and crime in the jungle. The natives think of him as one person, ageless, immortal, a living jungle spirit. A renegade who is planning to build a secret airfield and use it to carve a private empire for himself, as well as to find a legendary lost city called Zolos, comes to the jungle. Also seeking the lost city

Top: **William Desmond in *Perils of the Yukon* (1922); *bottom;* Tom Tyler and Jeanne Bates in *The Phantom* (1943)**

is a scientific expedition that includes Diana Palmer, fiancée of Geoffrey. The forces of good and evil clash and The Phantom, known as "The Ghost Who Walks," must live up to his trust.

Tom Tyler (Geoffrey Prescott/The Phantom), Jeanne Bates (Diana Palmer), Kenneth MacDonald (Dr. Bremmer), Frank Shannon (Professor Davidson), Ace, the Wonder Dog (Himself), Guy Kingsford (Byron Andrews), Joe Devlin (Singapore Smith), Ernie Adams (Rusty), John S. Bagni (Moku), Edmund Cobb, George Chesebro.

1. The Sign of the Skull. 2. The Man Who Never Dies. 3. A Traitor's Code. 4. The Seat of Judgment. 5. The Ghost Who Walks. 6. Jungle Whispers. 7. The Mystery Well. 8. In Quest of the Keys. 9. The Fire Princess. 10. The Chamber of Death. 11. The Emerald Key. 12. The Fangs of the Beast. 13. The Road to Zolos. 14. The Lost City. 15. Peace in the Jungle.

504. The Phantom Creeps

(Universal, July 27, 1939) Serial, 12 chapters, two reels each. D: Ford Beebe and Saul A. Goodkind. S: Willis Cooper. SP: George H. Plympton, Basil Dickey, Mildred Barish. Released in feature form in England.

Dr. Alan Zorka has invented a devisualizer belt which renders him invisible, a robot eight feet tall, and a chemical that can put a whole army into suspended animation. The accidental death of his wife makes him bitter and he decides to become world dictator. Captain Bob West of Military Intelligence is assigned to see that Zorka does not turn his inventions over to a foreign power or use them against the U.S.

Bela Lugosi (Dr. Alex Zorka), Robert Kent (Captain Bob West), Dorothy Arnold (Jean Drew), Regis Toomey (Jim Daley), Edward Van Sloan (Chief Davis), Eddie Acuff (Mac), Lee J. Cobb (Construction Foreman), Charles King (Buck), Dora Clement (Mrs. Ann Zorka), Roy Barcroft (Parker), Forrest Taylor (Black), Karl Hackett (Brown), Robert Blair (Smith), Jerry Frank (Jones), Hugh Huntley (Perkins), Edward Wolf, Monte Vandergrift, Frank Mayo, James Farley, Reed Howes, George Magrill.

1. The Menacing Power. 2. Death Stalks the Highways. 3. Crashing Towers. 4. Invisible Terror. 5. Thundering Rails. 5. The Iron Monster. 7. The Menacing Mist. 8. Trapped in the Flames. 9. Speeding Doom. 10. Phantom Footprints. 11. The Blast. 12. To Destroy the World.

505. Phantom Empire

(Mascot, February 23, 1935) Serial, 12 chapters; Chapter 1, three reels; others, two reels. D: Otto Brower and B. Reeves Eason. S: Wallace MacDonald, Gerald Geraghty, and Hy Freedman. SP: John Rathmell and Armand Schaefer. Production Supervisor: Armand Schaefer. P: Nat Levine. Photography: Ernest Miller and William Nobles. Music: Lee Zahler. Special Effects: Howard and Theodore Lydecker. Two feature versions were edited from this serial: *Men with Steel Faces* and *Radio Ranch*. Released in United Kingdom as *Couldn't Possibly Happen*.

Gene Autry is part owner of Radio Ranch, from which he broadcasts a popular radio show designed to bring guests flocking to the dude ranch. Several scientists show up, secretly searching for a rich uranium deposit on the ranch and the possible existence of Murania, a fabled underground kingdom. They attempt to eliminate Autry, to stop his broadcasts, and bring about the closing of the ranch. Queen Tika and her prime minister Argo of Murania also want Radio Ranch closed because of the threat to Murania. Gene finds his way into the subterranean kingdom, there to do battle with the Muranians and to experience the wizardry of an advanced civilization before it is destroyed by an awesome death ray. The scientists above ground are subdued and Radio Ranch is saved.

This futuristic fancy filled with robots, television sets, death rays, and flame guns was exceedingly popular, thoroughly captivating rural audiences of the 1930s. Universal was thus encouraged to make *Flash Gordon* (1936) and Republic *Undersea Kingdom* a short time later.

Gene Autry (Gene Autry), Frankie Darro (Frankie Baxter), Betsy King Ross (Betsy Baxter), Dorothy Christie (Queen Tika), Wheeler Oakman (Argo), Charles K. French (Mal), Warner Richmond (Rab), Frank Glendon (Professor Beetson), Smiley Burnette (Oscar), William Moore (Pete), Edward Peil, Sr. (Dr. Cooper), Jack Carlyle (Saunders), Frankie Marvin (Frankie), Wally Wales [Hal Taliaferro] (Muranian), Buffalo Bill, Jr. [Jay Wilsey] (Muranian), Fred Burns (Muranian), Stanley Blystone (Muranian), Frank Ellis (Thunder Rider), Slim Whitaker (Thunder Rider), Wally West, Bob Burns, Bob Card, Bruce Mitchell, George Magrill, Champion (horse), Henry Hall, Peter Potter.

1. The Singing Cowboy. 2. The Thunder Riders. 3. The Lightning Chamber. 4. Phantom Broadcast. 5. Beneath the Earth. 6. Disaster from the Skies. 7. From Death to Life. 8. Jaws of Jeopardy. 9. Prisoners of the Ray. 10. The Rebellion. 11. A Queen in Chains. 12. The End of Murania.

Gene Autry, Dorothy Christy, and Wheeler Oakman in *Phantom Empire* (1935)

506. The Phantom Foe

(Pathé, October 11, 1920) Serial, 15 chapters, two reels each. P: George B. Seitz. D: Bertram Millhauser. S: George B. Seitz. SP: Frank Leon Smith.

Janet Dale, her father, and her aunt disappear and a peculiarly clad individual known as The Phantom is seen but never apprehended. His next move is always preceded by the flash of a giant foot. Flashback is used as the heroine tells the experiences of her youth in the far north and the events leading up to The Phantom's nefarious activity.

The title applies to a mysterious character, not one who dissolves before our eyes in usual serial fashion, but one with the power of bringing about a most mysterious disappearance.

Warner Oland (Uncle Lew Selkirk), Juanita Hansen (Janet Dale), Wallace McCutcheon (Steve Roycroft), William Norton Bailey (Bob Royal), Nina Casavant (Esther, Janet's Cousin), Thomas Goodwin (Jeremiah Dale), Harry Semels (The Phantom Foe), Joe Cuny (Andre Renoir), Tom Goodwin.

1. Doom. 2. Disappearance of Janet Dale. 3. Trail of the Wolf. 4. The Open Window. 5. The Tower Room. 6. The Crystal Ball. 7. Gun Fire. 8. The Man Trap. 9. The Mystic Summons. 10. The Foe Unmarked. 11. Through Prison Walls. 12. Behind the Veil. 13. Attack at the Inn. 14. Confession. 15. Retribution.

507. The Phantom Fortune

(Universal, March 19, 1923) Serial, 12 chapters, two reels each. D: Robert F. Hill. S/SP: Anthony W. Coldeway and George Hively.

The action centers around business and the philosophy of the "go-getter." The hero is an irresponsible young artist whose father is the head of a rubber manufacturing company that the big rubber interests are forcing to the wall in an attempt to secure the patents for a new process of manufacturing solid rubber tires. When the father dies, the son, Larry, takes up management of the company and is almost persuaded by Owens, the plant manager who is in league with the conspirators, to sell out and salvage what he can. However, he is inspired by the "It can be done" philosophy of his attractive secretary, Mary, and sets about to overcome all obstacles and put the business back on its feet.

William Desmond (Larry Barclay), Esther Ralston (Mary Rogers), Lewis Sargent (Speck O'Dawn), Harry De Vere (Graham Alexander), George Webb (Alexander Owens), Cathleen Calhoun (Nadine Hamilton), Albert Hart (The Flame), Dick Sutherland (The Ox), George Nichols, Jack Henderson, Pat Harmon, Tony West, Alfred Hollingsworth, Lawrence Hughes. J. Buckley Russell.

1. It Can be Done! 2. Never Say Die. 3. Work & Win. 4. Opportunity. 5. Against Big Odds. 6. Dangerous Waters. 7. The Plunge of Doom. 8. Diamond Cut Diamond. 9. The Last Hope. 10. A Million at Stake. 11. The Speed King. 12. Success.

William Desmond and Esther Ralston in *The Phantom Fortune* (1923)

508. The Phantom of the Air

(Universal, July 25, 1933) Serial, 12 chapters, two reels each. D: Ray Taylor. SP: Basil Dickey and George Plympton. S: Ella O'Neill.

A brilliant scientist, with a beautiful daughter, invents an astounding antigravity device. Seeking to revolutionize aviation, he employs a rugged pilot from the Border Air Patrol, who romances the daughter, fights off villains attempting to steal the invention, and executes plenty of spectacular air thrills.

Tom Tyler (Bob Raymond), Gloria Shea (Mary Edmunds), Leroy Mason (Mort Crome), Hugh Enfield (Blade) [Enfield was known as Robert Allen when he had the male lead in Universal's *Perils of Pauline;* later he became Craig Reynolds], William Desmond (Mr. Edmunds), Sidney Bracey (James Munson), Walter Brennan ("Skid"), Jennie Cramer (Marie), Cecil Kellog (Joe), Tom London (Patrol Radioman), Edmund Cobb (Smuggler), Wheeler Oakman (Smuggler), Bud Osborne (Smuggler).

1. The Great Air Meet. 2. The Secret of the Desert. 3. The Avenging Phantom. 4. The Battle in the Clouds. 5. Terror of the Heights. 6. A Wild Ride. 7. The Jaws of Death. 8. Aflame in the Sky. 9. The Attack. 10. The Runaway Plane. 11. In the Enemy's Hand. 12. Safe Landing.

509. The Phantom of the West

(Mascot, January 1, 1931) Serial, 10 chapters, two reels each. D: Ross Lederman. P: Nat Levine. S: Ford Beebe. Camera: Ben Kline. Music: Lee Zahler. Also released as a feature film.

Tom Tyler and Gloria Shea in *The Phantom of the Air* (1933)

Jim Lester aligns himself with Mona Cortez to try to prove her father is innocent of murdering Jim's father. Seven men in town know the identity of the murderer, but the Phantom and his League of the Lawless kill those who are about to talk. Jim himself is framed and becomes a murder suspect.

Tom Tyler (Jim Lester), Dorothy Gulliver (Mona Cortez), William Desmond (Martin Blain), Tom Santschi (Bud Landers), Tom Dugan (Oscar), Philo McCullough (Royce Macklin), Joe Bonomo (Keno), Kermit Maynard (Peter Drake), Frank Lanning (Francisco Cortez), Frank Hagney (Sheriff Ryan), Dick Dickinson (Stewart), Hallee Sullivan (Ruby Blain), Al Taylor (Deputy), Ernie Adams.

1. The Ghost Riders. 2. The Stairway of Doom. 3. The Horror in the Dark. 4. The Battle of the Strong. 5. The League of the Lawless. 6. The Canyon of Calamity. 7. The Price of Silence. 8. The House of Hate. 9. The Fatal Secret. 10. Rogues Roundup.

510. Phantom Police

(Rayart, March 1926) Serial, 10 chapters, two reels each. D: Robert Dillon.

The story deals with the dangerous work of the police in New York. Jack Wright, an officer on the force, is told to keep a lookout for Tracy Downs, suspected as the originator of a diamond robbery in Paris. Downs fled to Africa, and is now due to arrive home. Two chimpanzees were also involved in the robbery, and their services are requisitioned on behalf of crime detection. The chimps are very significant participants in most of the crucial scenes of the film.

Herbert Rawlinson (Jack Wright), Gloria Joy (Gloria Benton), Eddie Featherstone (Frank Randall), Purnell Pratt (Tracy Downs), Dick Gordon ("London Jimmy" Farewell), Rosemary Cooper (Miriam Wesley), James G. Davis (Carstairs), Jack Fowler (Everett Benton), James Gordon (The Governor), S.G. Wilcox (Inspector Dumphy), Max and Moritz (The Chimpanzees).

511. The Phantom Rider

(Universal, July 6, 1936) Serial, 15 chapters, two reels each. D: Ray Taylor. S/SP: George Plympton, Basil Dickey, Ella O'Neill, and Henry McRae. Camera: Allen Thompson and John Hickson. P: Henry McRae. Theme Song: "Hidden Valley" sung by Cactus Mack and his Saddle Tramps.

Outlaws try to gain control over Hidden Valley Ranch and its surrounding acres, knowing that a railroad is going to buy a right-of-way through the property. They are also aware that there is a hidden gold mine on the land. A map showing the location of the mine passes back and forth between Buck Grant and his principal antagonist, Harvey Delaney. To thwart Delaney and his minions, and not give away his identity, Buck becomes The Phantom Rider and saves the ranch for Mary Grayson whose father has been killed. The Phantom Rider, dressed totally in white and riding a white horse, proved to be a formidable foe.

Buck Jones (Buck Grant/The Phantom Rider), Maria Shelton (Mary Grayson), Diana Gibson (Helen Moore), Harry Woods (Harvey Delaney), Frank LaRue (Judge Holmes), George Cooper (Spooky), Joey Ray (Steve), Eddie Gribbon (Sheriff Mark), Helen Shipman (Lizzie), James Mason (Dirk), Charles Lemoyne (Roscoe), Jim Corey (Gabe), Lee Shumway (Blackie), Clem Bevins (Hudson), Cecil Weston (Ma Hudson), Matt McHugh (Shorty), Jim Thorpe (Indian), Charles King (Keeler), Curtis McPeters (PeeWee), Charles K. French (Ezra Honer), Tom London (Lew), Slim Whitaker, Frank Ellis, Drew Stanfield, Art Mix, Bob Reeves, Buffalo Bill, Jr., Glenn Strange, Blackjack Ward (Heavies), Hank Bell (Stage Driver), Lafe McKee (Jeff Grayson), Priscilla Lawson (Saloon Girl), George Plues (Piano Player), Olin Francis (Passenger), Iron Eyes Cody (Indian), Paul Regas (Red Eagle), Bob Fite, "Hi Pockets" Busse, Bill Scott, Jimmy Carroll (Singers), Eva McKenzie (Ma Horner), Orrin Burke (Blake), George Ovey (Barfly), Cliff Lyons (Jones' Double), Silver [a horse] (Himself), Allen Holbrook, Bob Card, Horace Murphy.

1. Dynamite. 2. The Maddened Herd. 3. The Brink of Disaster. 4. The Phantom Rides. 5. Trapped by Outlaws. 6. Shot Down. 7. Stark Terror. 8. The Night Attack. 9. The Indian Raid. 10. Human Targets. 11. The Shaft of Doom. 12. Flaming Gold. 13. Crashed Timbers. 14. The Last Chance. 15. The Outlaws' Vengeance.

512. The Phantom Rider

(Republic, January 26, 1946) Serial, 12 chapters, two reels each. Feature title: *Ghost Riders of the West*. D: Spencer Bennet and Fred Brannon. SP: Albert DeMond, Basil Dickey, Jesse Duffy, Lynn Perkins, and Barney Sarecky. Assoc. P: Ronald Davidson. Photography: Bud Thackery.

Music: Richard Charwin. Special Effects: Howard and Theodore Lydecker.

Dr. James Sterling, secretly The Phantom Rider, strives to enact an Indian police referendum. Fred Carson, seemingly allied to the cause of establishing an Indian police force to extend limited law enforcement jurisdiction to the Big Tree Reservation, uses his official status as the local Indian agent for selfish goals and employs outlaws to serve him. The Phantom Rider and his Indian friend Blue Feather, with an able assist now and then from Nugget, an old prospector, and Doris Shannon, the school marm, overcome apparently insurmountable odds and the Indian police become a working reality. Justice is meted out to Carson and his incorrigible cronies.

Robert Kent (James Sterling/The Phantom Rider), Peggy Stewart (Doris Shannon, LeRoy Mason (Fred Carson), George J. Lewis (Blue Feather), Kenne Duncan (Ben Brady), Hal Taliaferro [Wally Wales] (Nugget), Chief Thunder Cloud (Yellow Knife), Tom London (Ceta), Roy Barcroft (Marshal), Monte Hale (Cass), John Hamilton (Williams), Hugh Prosser (Keeler), Jack Kirk (Turner), Rex Lease (Randall), Tommy Coats (Tim), Joe Yrigoyen (Blackie/Ambusher/Logan), Bill Yrigoyen (Indian Renegade/Lookout), Jack O'Shea (Ace), Cliff Lyons (Dick), Walt LaRue, Cliff Parkinson, Carl Sepulveda (Ambushers), George Carleton (Banker), Dale Van Sickel (Bart/Lyons/Mack/Pete), Tom Steele (Clay), George Chesebro (Dalton), Wayne Burson (Deputy), Cliff Lyons (Dick), Post Parks (Driver/Tom), Fred Graham (Harry), Bob Duncan (Indian Guard), Augie Gomez (Indian Heavy), Robert Wilke, John Roy (Indian Rebels), Cactus Mack (Joe), Eddie Parker (Martin), Ted Mapes (Riot Leader), Duke Taylor (Schwartz), Hal Price (Simpson), James Linn (Thompson), Bud Bailey (Trail Heavy), Tex Cooper, Henry Wills.

1. The Avenging Spirit. 2. Flaming Ambush. 3. Hoof of Doom. 4. Murder Masquerade. 5. Flying Fury. 6. Blazing Peril. 7. Gauntlet of Guns. 8. Behind the Mask. 9. The Captive Chief. 10. Beasts at Bay. 11. The Death House. 12. The Last Stand.

513. Phantomas

(Berlin—Greenbaum–Film GmbH, 1917-1919) Series, 10 or more episodes. S/SP: Numbers in parentheses following names indicate which of the episodes were written by the person. Richard Wilde (3), Herman Fellner (4, 7), O. Schubert-Stevens (6), Paul Rosenhayn (7, 8), Victor Alt (10), Carl Boese (10).

Numbers in parentheses following names indicate in which episodes the actor appeared: Erich Kaiser-Titz (Phantomas 1–6), Rolf Loer (Phantomas 7–10), Bruno Ziener (2), Reinhold Schunzel (2), Else Eckersberg (2), Ludwig Trautmann (3), Kitty Dewall (3), Max Ruhbeck (3)], Karl Falkenberg (3), Franz Ramharter (3), Hanni Weisse (4), Anna V. Palen (4), Blandine Ebinger (8), Hugo Werner-Kahle (8), Michael Reiner-Steiner (8), Paul Westermeier (10), Grete Hollmann (10).

1. Am Hochzeitsabend. 2. Das Nachtgespräch. 3. Der Erbe von Het-Steen. 4. Die Glocken der Katharinenkirche. 5. Ein schärfer Schuss. 6. Ein Tropfen Gift. 7. Das gestohlene Hotel. 8. Der Teilhaber. 9. Der gelbe Schatten. 10. Um Diamanten und Frauen.

514. Le Pied Qui Étreint

(France—Gaumont, 1916) Series, 4 episodes. D/SP: Jacques Feyder. P: Les Fils Halley.

Kitty Hott (Eliane), André Roanne (Clarin Justel), Mlle. Musidora (Irma Vep), Réne Poyen (Bout-de-Zan), Georges Biscot, Marcel Levesque, Edouard Mathé, Suzanne Delvé.

1. Le Micro Bafouilleur sans fil. 2. Le Rayon noir. 3. La Girouette Humaine. 4. L' Homme au foulard a pois.

515. Pioneer Kid Series

(Universal, 1929–1930) Series, 13 episodes, two reels each. D: Jack Nelson.

Bobby Nelson was a very young, good looking kid who could both ride and act. He was six or seven years old when this series was made. He continued on into the 1930s as a support player in mostly independent westerns. He was the son of director Jack Nelson, who directed all of the following thirteen episodes.

Episode Titles, Releasing Dates, Supporting Actors

1. Boy and the Bad Man (9-7-29), Edmund Cobb. 2. Waif of the Wilderness (9-5-29). 3. The Kid Comes Thru (11-2-29). 4. Orphan of the Wagon Trail (11-0-29), Edmund Cobb. 5. Dangerous Days (12-28-29), Edmund Cobb, Marjorie Boner, Walter Shumway. 6. The Last Stand (1-25-30). 7. The Post of Honor (2-22-30). 8. The Danger Claim (3-22-30). 9. Six Gun Justice (4-19-30). 10. Alias the Bandit (5-17-30). 11. The Battling Kid (6-14-30). 12. Son of Courage (7-12-30). 13. The Pony Express Kid (8-9-30), Edmund Cobb.

516. Pirate Gold

(Pathé, August 15, 1920) Serial, 10 chapters; Chapter 1, three reels; others, two reels. D: George B. Seitz. SP: Bertram Millhauser. S: Frank Leon Smith.

Dreamer Ivanhoe Tuttle is taken in by two con artists and buys what is supposed to be a worthless treasure map. However, one of the thugs inadvertently gives Ivanhoe the correct longitude and latitude location of a real buried treasure that they know about. Realizing their foolishness, they attempt to regain the map. A pretty girl, Gabrielle, that Ivanhoe meets on a train also becomes involved in the treasure-seeking adventure.

Marguerite Courtot (Gabrielle Hall), George B. Seitz (Ivanhoe [Hoey] Tuttle), Frank Redman (Austin Tuttle), William Burt (Tanner), Joe Cuny (Kaidy), Harry Stone (Constable Peabody), Harry Semels (Siebert), Matthew Betz (Harmon).

1. In Which Hoey Buys a Map. 2. Dynamite. 3. The Dead Man's Story. 4. Treasure at Last. 5. Drugged. 6. Kidnapped. 7. Under Suspicion. 8. Knifed. 9. The Double Cross. 10. Defeat and Victory.

517. Pirate of Panama

(Universal, July 8, 1929) Serial, 12 chapters, two reels each. D: Ray Taylor. SP: Arthur Henry Gooden. S: William MacLeod Raine. Camera: Frank Redman.

Hero and heroine struggle to obtain the map to a buried treasure, but the villain and his cutthroats are equally determined to possess it.

Jay Wilsey was better known as Buffalo Bill, Jr., star of many westerns for Lester F. Scott's Action Pictures. In the sound era he became a supporting player in westerns after a few starring roles.

Top: **Marguerite Courtot and George B. Seitz (*center*) in *Pirate Gold* (1920); *bottom:* Walter Miller and Lucille Lund in *Pirate Treasure* (1934)**

Jay Wilsey (Jack Sedgwick), Natalie Kingston (Evelyn Wallace), Al Ferguson (Boris Bothwell), George Ovey (Jimmie Welch), Mary Sutton (Aunt Berry), Otto Bibbler (Teager).

1. Pirate Gold. 2. Mutiny. 3. The Treasure Chest. 4. The Pirate's Secret. 5. Vengeance. 6. Trapped by the Tide. 7. The Shadow of Death. 8. The Menacing Swamp. 9. The Signal of Hope. 10. Two Lives for One. 11. The Price of Greed. 12. The Greatest Treasure.

518. Pirate Treasure

(Universal, April 1934) Serial, 12 chapters, two reels each. D: Ray Taylor. SP: Basil Dickey, Jack Nelson, and George Plympton. S: Ella O'Neill.

On a tropical island, treasure buried by a pirate ancestor of Dick Moreland is sought by Dick as well as by corrupt lawyer Stanley Brassett.

Richard Talmadge (Dick Moreland), Lucille Lund (Dorothy Craig), Walter Miller (Stanley Brassett), Pat O'Malley (John Craig), William Desmond (Captain Carson), William E. Thorne (Drake), Del Lawrence (Robert Moreland), Ethan Laidlaw (Curt), George De Normand (Jed), Al Ferguson (Tony), Beulah Hutton (Marge), Philo McCullough, Monte Montague, Edmund Cobb (Sailor).

1. Stolen Treasure. 2. The Death Plunge. 3. The Wheels of Fate. 4. The Sea Chase. 5. Into the Depths. 6. The Death Crash. 7. Chasing Doom. 8. Mutiny. 9. Hidden Gold. 10. The Fight for the Treasure. 11. The Fatal Plunge. 12. Captured.

519. Pirates of the High Seas

(Columbia, October 1950) Serial, 15 chapters. D: Spencer G. Bennet and Thomas Carr. SP: Joseph F. Poland, David Mathews, George H. Plympton, and Charles R. Condon. P: Sam Katzman. Assist D: R.M. Andrews. Photography: Ira H. Morgan. Music: Mischa Bakaleinikoff.

Responding to a call for help from an old buddy, Jeff Drake sails his ship *The Viking* to a Pacific island to investigate strange attacks on his friend's ship by a pirate cruiser that disappears after an attack as mysteriously as it appeared before one. In dealing with the phantom ship mystery Jeff also clashes with an escaped war criminal seeking lost diamonds on the island.

Buster Crabbe (Jeff Drake), Lois Hall (Carol Walsh), Tommy Farrell (Kelly Walsh), Gene Roth (Frederick Whitlock), Tristram Coffin (Castell), Neyle Marrow (Kalama), Stanley Price (Lamar), Hugh Prosser (Roper), Symonia Boniface (Lotus Lady), William Fawcett (Ben Wharton), Terry Frost (Carter), Lee Roberts (Barker), Rusty Wescoatt (Adams), Pierce Lyden (Durk), I. Stanford Jolley (Turner), Marshall Reed (Shark), Charles Quigley (Merkie), John Hart (Jenkins).

1. Mystery Mission. 2. Attacked by Pirates. 3. Dangerous Depths. 4. Blasted to Atoms. 5. The Missing Mate. 6. Secret of the Ivory Case. 7. Captured by Savages. 8. The Vanishing Music Box. 9. Booby Trap. 10. Savage Snare. 11. Sinister Cavern. 12. Blast from the Depths. 13. Cave In. 14. Secret of the Music Box. 15. Diamonds from the Sea.

520. Pirates of the Pines

(Sovereign Feature Prod./Goodart, September 1928) Serial, 10 chapters, two reels each. D: J.C. Cook. SP: J.C. Cook and Harry Moody. P: Charles U. Penfield.

John Markham owns a big tract of timber land, which is coveted by a rival. The latter sets in motion a conspiracy to ruin Markham.

George O'Hara (John Markham), Rita Roma, Jack Mower, Robert Middleton, Sumner Getchell, King Zany.

1. Death's Marathon. 2. The Swirling Waters. 3. The

Left: **Buster Crabbe and Rusty Westcott in** ***Pirates of the High Seas*** **(1950);** ***top right:*** **George O' Hara in** ***Pirates of the Pines*** **(1928);** ***bottom right:*** **Walter Miller and Allene Ray in** ***Play Ball (1925)***

Ice Flood. 4. Wages of Sin. 5. Danger Ahead. 6. Burning Barriers. 7. Hands of Fate. 8. Flaming Masts. 9. Through Space. 10. The Duel in Mid-Air.

521. Play Ball

(Pathé, July 19, 1925) Serial, 10 chapters, two reels each. D: Spencer G. Bennet. SP: Frank Leon Smith. S: John J. McGraw.

A rookie baseball player, the disowned son of a U.S. senator, and a millionaire's daughter are in love. The girl's father is under the influence of a villainous count bent on getting funds for a dissident faction in his native land, while the senator is investigating the business practices of the millionaire.

Allene Ray (Doris Sutton), Walter Miller (Jack Rollins), Harry Semels (Count Segundo), J. Barney Sherry (Thomas W. Sutton), Mary Milnor (Maybelle Pratt), Wally Oettel (Rutger Farnsworth), Franklyn Hanna (Senator Hornell), Ed Maurelli (The Counsel).

1. To the Rescue. 2. The Flaming Float. 3. Betrayed. 4. The Decoy Wire. 5. Face to Face. 6. The Showdown. 7. A Mission of Hate. 8. Double Peril. 9. Into Segundo's Hands. 10. A Home Plate Wedding.

522. Plunder

(Pathé, January 18, 1923) Serial, 15 chapters, two reels each. D: George B. Seitz. Scen: Bertram Millhauser and George B. Seitz. S: Herbert Crooker. P: George B. Seitz.

The story concerns an ancient treasure, worth untold millions, buried deep in the earth under the spot where a modern skyscraper now stands. Both Pearl and the villain, in their separate ways, become aware of this buried treasure and vie with each other for its possession. But there's a catch to it. The skyscraper must first be bought before the treasure can be dug for. Stock in the building is held by many people; and each chapter concerns the efforts of Pearl and the heavy to outmaneuver each other in their acquisition of an owner's shares.

Naturally, the heavy resorts to theft and murder, Pearl resorts to honest practice. The advantage seesaws this way and that until, in the final chapter, Pearl wins out.

Plunder, Pearl White's last serial, was a solid success. There seems to have been a mild vogue in the early 1920s for pictures with the "Frankenstein" motif. One of the highlights of this film was a mad doctor, sparking lab, and a 12-foot monster the doctor is bringing to life.

Pearl White (Pearl Travers), Warren Krech [Warren Williams]

Pearl White in *Plunder* (1923)

(Mr. Jones), Harry Semels (Jud Deering), Tom McIntyre, J. Elwood Pool, Wally Oettel, William Naly, Charles Revada.

1. The Bandaged Man. 2. Held by the Enemy. 3. The Hidden Thing. 4. Ruin. 5. To Beat a Knave. 6. Heights of Hazard. 7. Mocked from the Grave. 8. The Human Target. 9. Game Clear Through. 10. Against Time. 11. Spunk. 12. Under the Floor. 13. The Swamp of Lost Souls. 14. The Madman. 15. A King's Ransom.

523. La Pocharde

(France—Ermolieff Films, 1921) Serial, 12 chapters. D: Henri Etievant. Scen: Henri Etievant. S: Jules Mary.

Jacqueline Forzane (Charlotte Lamarche), Princesa Kotchankidze (Clotilde de Thiellay), Emilien Richaud (Jean Berthelin), Alexandre Volkoff (Hubert de Thiellay), Gaston Riefller (Guy Mathis), Louis Gouget (Doctor Marignan), Norville (Georges Lamarche), Mlle. Kaschouea (Claire), Tamar Oxynska (Marie), Fernand Mailly.

1. Les flammes mortelles. 2. L'enfant du crime. 3. La mère aux sept douleurs. 4. Un crime dans les ruines. 5. Une lueur dans les ténèbres. 6. Le plus grand des crimes. 7. Les cendres du bonheur. 8. Claire et Louise. 9. Le fils du médecin. 10. L'amour qui naît. 11. Le fantôme du passé. 12. Les châtiments.

524. Poker D'As

(France—Cinéromans, 1928) Serial, 8 (?) chapters. D: Henri Desfontaines. Scen: Arthur Bernede.

René Navarre, Suzanne Delmas, Simone Mareuil, Genica Missirio, Jeanne Brindeau, Georges Paulais, Jean Devalde, Jean Peyrière, Albert Mayer, Pierre de Canolle.

525. The Police Reporter

(Weiss Brothers Artclass, March 1, 1928) Serial, 10 chapters, two reels each. D: Jack Nelson. S: Arthur B. Reeve. Supervision: George M. Merrick.

A police reporter and his girlfriend are pitted against an arch fiend called The Phantom, as the underworld tries to circumvent the justice system in the big city.

Walter Miller, Eugenia Gilbert, William A. Lowery, Robert Belcher, Kenneth Duncan.

1. The Phantom. 2. Code of the Underworld. 3. The Secret Tube. 4. The Flaming Idol. 5. The Phantom's Trap. 6. The Girl Who Dared. 7. The Wharf Rats. 8. The Mystery Room. 9. In the Phantom's Den. 10. The Law Wins.

526. Il Ponte dei Sospiri

(Italy—Albertini Films, 1920) Serial, 8 chapters. D: Domenico Gaido. SP: Michel Zevaco—"Le Pont des Soupirs." Scen: Giovanni Bertinetti.

Luciano Albertini (Rolando Candiano), Antonietta Calderari (Imperia), Onorato Garaveo (Scalabrino), Carolina White (Leonora), Luigi Stinchi (Altieri), Armando Pouget (Foscari), Carlo Cattaneo (Aretino), Bonaventura Ibañez (Dandolo), Vittorio Pieri (Doge Candiano), Agostino Borgato (Bembo), Romilde Toschi (Bianca), Magda Chirotti (Juana), Giuliu Falcini (Sandrigo), Signora De Chiesa (Dogaressa Silvia), Italia Vitakiani, Vittorio Pieri, Rie Bruns.

French: 1. L'ombre du sarcophage. 2. Le guet-apens. 3. La fuite dans la tempête. 4. Le pacte de la grotte noire. 5. La fête chez Imperia. 6. Ce que paut la haine. 7. Le calvaire d'une mère. 8. Expiation. *Italian:* 1. La bocca del leone. 2. La potenza del male. 3. Il dio della vendetta. 4. Il trionfo dell'Amore.

527. La Porteuse de Pain

(France—Agence Générale Cinématographique, 1923) Serial, chapters (?). D: René Le Somptier. Scen: René Le Somptier. S: Xavier de Montepin.

Suzanne Despres, Gabriel Signoret, Genevieve Felix, Germaine Rouer, Henri Baudin, Jacques Guilhene, Rene Koval Kerly, Ernest Maupain, J. Faure, Pierre Almette.

528. The Power God

(Davis Distributing/Goodwell, January 1926) Serial, 15 chapters, two reels each. D: Ben Wilson and Francis Ford. S: Rex Taylor, Harry Haven. P: Ben Wilson. Original distribution was to be by Vital Exchanges, which went broke.

Professor Sturgis invents a power producing machine that uses no fuel. A powerful fuel syndicate wants to suppress the machine. Before his death, the professor entrusts to his daughter Aileen the one secret of assembly that must be known before the machine can be made operative. The syndicate pursues Aileen to get the secret, but is frustrated when she is injured and loses her memory. The professor's assistant, Jim Thorp, manages to save both Aileen and the secret before the syndicate can extract the information from her.

Ben Wilson (Jim Thorp), Neva Gerber (Aileen Sturgis), Lafe McKee (Professor Daniel Sturgis), Allan Garcia (Weston Dore), Ruth Royce (Carrie, Dore's Wife), William H. Turner

(Jarvis Humphries), Catherine Kent (Mrs. Thorp, Jim's Mother), Nelson McDowell (Dr. Clark), Grover Eagle Wing (A Mysterious Character), Francis Ford (A Detective), Mary Brooklyn, Mary Crane, John Battaglia.

1. The Ring of Fate. 2. Trapped. 3. The Living Dead. 4. Black Shadows. 5. The Death Chamber. 6. House of Peril. 7. Hands in the Dark. 8. 59th Second. 9. Perilous Waters. 10. Bridge of Doom. 11. Treachery. 12. The Storm's Lash. 13. The Purloined Papers. 14. The Flaming Menace. 15. Wages of Sin.

Ben Wilson and Neva Gerber in *The Power God* (1925)

529. The Price of Folly (aka *Who Wins?*)

(Pathé, January 1918) Series, 8 episodes, three reels each. S: Will M. Ritchie.

This series, released two years after filming in 1916, was what was salvaged from a series called *Who Wins?* that was permanently shelved by Balboa. The reason for Balboa's action is not known. Each episode of *The Price of Folly* is complete in itself and leaves the audience to judge the wisdom of a course of action taken in the episode.

Ruth Roland, Frank Mayo, Lafe McKee, Conrad K. Arnold, Bruce Smith, Jimsy Maye, Neil C. Hardin. (Roles varied with each episode.)

1. Phantom Fame. 2. Counterfeit Clues. 3. The Catspaw. 4. Unknown. 5. Unknown. 6. In Poverty's Power. 7. The Rebound. 8. The Shifting Sands.

530. El Protegido de Satan

(Spain—Studio Film 1918) Serial, 14 chapters. D: José Mariá Codina. SP: S. Ardeval.

Lola Paris, Baltasar, Banquells, Blanca Valoris, Carmen Rodriguez, María Alvarez De Burgos, Anita Stephenson, Julian De La Cantera, Ramón Quadreny, José Balaguer, Silvia Mariategui, Leander Cinca, Elisa Romero, Juan Oliva, Luis Zepet.

Porteguese: 1. O club dos trusts. 2. Os conjurados. 3. O anel fatal. 4. Nas ruínas da antiga abadia. 5. O suplício do tonel. 6. Em plena festa. 7. Nas garras de Satanaz. 8. Um lobo com pele de cordeiro. 9. Entre feras. 10. Agonia de morto. 11. De bandido a bandido. 12. A estinha. 13. Vingança secreta. 14. Rehabilitação.

531. The Purple Mask

(Universal, December 31, 1916) Serial, 16 chapters; Chapter 1, three reels; others, two reels. S: Francis Ford. Scen: Grace Cunard and Francis Ford.

Patricia Montez is a lady Robin Hood known as Queen of the Apaches. She is pursued by detective Phil Kelly, who secretly is head of a strange gang to whom he is known only as a hooded figure called The Sphinx. Patricia steals from the rich and turns the proceeds over to the poor, keeping only a small part as her commission. A purple mask left behind at the scene of her robbery becomes her trademark.

Grace Cunard (Patricia Montez/Queen of the Apaches), Francis Ford (Phil Kelly/The Sphinx), Joan Hathaway (Eleanor Van Nuys), Peter Gerald (Pete Bartlett), Jerry Ash (Bull Sanderson), John Duffy (Silk Donahur), John Featherstone (Stephen Dupont), Mario Bianchi (Jacques, Patricia's Butler), Joe Moore (John Elliott), Gertrude Short (Mary Maclean), Leonard Clapham [Tom London] (Robert Jackson), William White (The King), Phillip Ford (Joe Butts), Abe Mundon.

1. The Vanished Jewels. 2. Suspected. 3. The Capture. 4. Facing Death. 5. The Demon of the Sky. 6. The Silent Feud. 7. The Race for Freedom. 8. Secret Adventure. 9. A Strange Discovery. 11. Garden of Surprise. 12. The Vault of Mystery. 13. The Leap. 14. The Sky Monsters. 15. Floating Signal. 16. A Prisoner of Love.

532. The Purple Monster Strikes

(Republic, October 6, 1945) Serial, 15 chapters, two reels each. Feature title: *D-Day on Mars*. D: Spencer Bennet and Fred Brannon. SP: Royal Cole, Albert DeMond, Basil Dickey, Lynn Perkins, Joseph Poland, and Barney Sarecky. Assoc. P: Bud Thackery. Music: Richard Cherwin. Special Effects: Howard and Theodore Lydecker.

A martian, sent in advance of an invasion, lands on Earth and kills Dr. Layton, inventor of a spacecraft capable of round trip flights to Mars. The martian enters the doctor's body and assumes his physical characteristics. He reports to Craig Foster, legal counsel for the Scientific Foundation, and Sheila Layton, the doctor's daughter, that The Purple Monster has stolen the secrets of the spacecraft. He then proceeds to build the spacecraft in a hidden wing of the observatory. Craig and Ann

Reed Howes and Mary Kornman in *Queen of the Jungle* (1935)

anticipate The Purple Monster's needs for certain materials and thwart his attempts to get them. After a female accomplice from Mars is discovered transforming herself, Craig and Sheila become aware that Dr. Layton is really The Purple Monster, who is destroyed by an electro-annihilator when he attempts a getaway in a spacecraft.

Linda Stirling (Sheila Layton), Dennis Moore (Craig Foster), Roy Barcroft (The Purple Monster), James Craven (Cyrus Layton), Bud Geary (Hodge Garrett), Mary Moore (Marcia), John Davidson (Emperor of Mars), Joe Whitehead (Carl Stewart), Emmett Vogan (Saunders), George Carleton (Paul Meredith), Kenne Duncan (Charles Mitchell), Rosemonde James (Helen), Monte Hale (Harvey), Wheaton Chambers (Benjamin), Frederick Howard (Crandall), Anthony Warde (Tony), Ken Terrell (Andy Martin), Tom Steele (Mears/Benham/Fritz), Cliff Lyons (Clay), John Daheim (Barnes), Fred Graham (Baker/Curry/Logan), Robert Blair (Evans), Carey Loftin (Mack), Henry Wills (Osborne/Mason), Dale Van Sickel (Policeman), George Chesebro (Shaw), Robert Wilkie (Workman), Polly Burson (Stuntwoman), Babe Defreest (Stuntwoman).

1. The Man in the Meteor. 2. The Time Trap. 3. Flaming Avalanche. 4. The Lethal Pit. 5. Death on the Beam. 6. The Demon Killer. 7. The Evil Eye. 8. Descending Doom. 9. The Living Dead. 10. House of Horror. 11. Menace from Mars. 12. Perilous Plunge. 13. Fiery Shroud. 14. The Fatal Trail. 15. Take-Off to Destruction.

533. The Purple Riders

(Vitagraph, February 1921) Serial, 15 chapters, two reels each. D: William Bertram. Scen: William B. Courtney, Colder Johnstone, and Graham Baker. S: Albert E. Smith and Cleveland Moffett.

Sheriff Dick Ranger's sweetheart, Betty Marsh, is the particular victim of "Purple Rider" bandits and their leader, the mysterious Purple Shadow; thus, Dick has a double motive to run them down and land them behind bars. Betty's brother has been accused of murdering their father, and Dick is committed to proving his innocence. The guilty party, the dead man's partner, is secretly The Purple Shadow. The sheriff finally unravels the mystery of The Purple Riders and captures Myers—The Purple Shadow.

Joe Ryan (Sheriff Dick Ranger), Elinor Field (Betty Marsh), Joseph Rickson (Rudolph Myers/The Purple Shadow), Maude Emory (Red Feather), Ernest Shields (Gerald Marsh), Walter Rodgers (Stephen Marsh), Charles Dudley (Doc Dreamer), Vincente Howard.

1. Love or Duty. 2. The Pool's Prey. 3. The Decoy. 4. The Fiery Trail. 5. The Fatal Pursuit. 6. Double Destruction. 7. Red Feather's Secret. 8. The Camouflage Trap. 9. The Betrayal. 10. The Fire Curtain. 11. The Stolen Millions. 12. The Infernal Machine. 13. A Devil Fish Foe. 14. The Frame-Up. 15. Buried Alive.

534. Quand on Aime

(France—1920) Serial, 10 chapters. D: Henry Houry. S: Pierre Decourcelle.

Julia Bruns, Arnold Daly, Renee Fagan, Paul Guide, Henri Bosc, Marthe Soleges, Berthe Jalabert, Avelot, Alexandre Colas.

535. Queen of the Jungle

(Screen Attractions, 1935) Serial, 12 chapters, two reels each. D: Robert Hill. S: J. Griffin Jay. Assist. D: Glen Cook. Music: Hal Chasnoff. Photography: William Hyer. Supervision: Herman A. Wohl. Built around footage from the silent *Jungle Goddess*, 1922. Also released as a six-reel feature.

David Worth returns to Africa to search for his childhood playmate, Joan Lawrence, who was lost years before when, on an expedition to Africa with their parents, the balloon she was playing in got loose and drifted over the jungle. When it was shot down by natives, Joan became a white priestess to the superstitious blacks and grew up as their queen. Once reunited with David they attempt to escape from the jungle and the natives who wish to hold her. A shipload of wild animal trappers, a band of Arabs, a masked rider, and a leopard woman wander in and out of the confused plot. There also is a sacred radium mine. Anyone missing the 1922 serial can see much of it here.

Reed Howes (David Worth), Mary Kornman (Joan Lawrence/Queen of Mu), George Chesebro (Ken Roberts), Lafe McKee (Kali), Eddie Foster (Rocco), Marilyn Spinner (Joan Lawrence as a girl), Dickie Jones (David Worth as a boy), William Walsh (John Lawrence), Robert Borman (Captain Blake), Barney Furey (Abdullah).

***Left:* Walter Miller and Ethlyne Clair in *Queen of the Northwoods* (1929); *right:* George Wallace and Aline Towne in *Radar Men from the Moon* (1952)**

1. Lost in the Clouds. 2. Radium Rays. 3. The Hand of Death. 4. The Native's Revenge. 5. Black Magic. 6. The Death Vine. 7. The Leopard Leaps. 8. The Doom Ship. 9. Death Rides the Waves. 10. The Temple of Mu. 11. Fangs in the Dark. 12. The Pit of the Lions.

536. Queen of the Northwoods

(Pathé, May 21, 1929) Serial, 10 chapters, two reels each. D: Spencer G. Bennet and Thomas L. Storey. SP: George Arthur Gray.

A mysterious villain, calling himself the Wolf-Devil and wielding a strange power over wolf packs, terrorized the Northwest. He dresses as a wolf, complete with an all-concealing wolf's headpiece to disguise his real identity. The Royal Mounted Police are called in to investigate.

Walter Miller (Inspector Steele), Ethlyne Claire (Miss Moreau), Tom London (Garvin/The Wolf-Devil), Frank Lackteen (Jacques De Brun), Edward Cecil (Fergus), George Magrill (Sergeant Bolt), Nelson McDowell ("Flapjack"), Jean Diamond (Moon River Lady), Arthur Taylor, Fred Burns, Arthur Dewey.

1. The Wolf-Devil's Challenge. 2. A Bottomless Grave. 3. Devil Worshipers. 4. Wings of Death. 5. The Wolf Devil Strikes. 6. The Leap of Death. 7. The Flaming Peril. 8. Brand of the Beast. 9. Trapped by the Fiend. 10. The Den of Evil.

537. Racing Blood

(Larry Darmour Prod./F.B.O., 1928) Series, 12 episodes, two reels each. D: Ralph Cedar, Albert Herman. S: H.C. Witwer. Scen: E.V. Durling, Charles Diltz, H.A. Woodmansee.

A comedy series.

Alberta Vaughn, Al Cooke.

1. Jessie's James. 2. The Wages of Synthetic. 3. You Just Know She Dares 'Em. 4. The Arabian Fights. 5. Ruth is Stranger Than Fiction. 6. The Sweet Buy and Buy. 7. Watch Your Pep. 8. Mild But She Satisfied. 9. That Wild Irish Pose. 10. The Six Best Fellows. 11. The Naughty Forties. 12. Broadway Ladies.

538. Radar Men from the Moon

(Republic, February 1952) Serial, 12 chapters, two reels each. D: Fred C. Brannon. SP: Ronald Davidson. Assoc. P: Franklyn Adreon. Photography: John MacBurnie. Music: Stanley Wilson. Special Effects: Howard and Theodore Lydecker. Feature Title: *Retik, the Moon Menace*.

Retik, leader of a race of moon men, attempts to soften Earth's defenses to prepare for an invasion. When the Earth experiences a series of mysterious explosions, Commando Cody and his aide are called on to investigate. Finding that an unknown element is being used in the ray guns of the enemy, Cody determines that it comes from the moon. He goes to the moon via rocket ship and in addition to the atomic substance he finds Retik and his vast laboratory, becomes a prisoner, and escapes. Cody and his friends are subjected to repeated attacks, but in a final encounter blast Retik's rocket ship to bits.

Shortly after completion of *Radar Men from the Moon*, a series of half-hour shows titled *Commando Cody—Marshal of the Universe* began on TV.

George Wallace (Commando Cody), Aline Towne (Joan Gilbert), Roy Barcroft (Retik), William Bakewell (Ted Richards), Clayton Moore (Graber), Peter Brocco (Krog), Bob Stevenson (Daly), Don Walters (Henderson), Tom Steele (Zerg), Dale Van Sickel (Alon), Wilson Wood (Hank), Noel Cravat (Robal), Baynes Barron (Nasor), Paul McGurie (Bream), Ted Thorpe (Bartender), Dick Cogan (Jones), Joe Bailey, Guy Teague, Dick Rich (Policemen), Tony Merrill (Sam), John Marshall (Smith), Arthur Walsh (Motorcycle Officer), Jack O'Shea (Doyle), Carey Loftin (Citizen), Harry Hollins (Brad), Paul Palmer (Bill), Stephen Gregory (Benson), Billy Dix (Duke), William Marke (Guard), Claude Dunkin (Kern), Sam Sabby (Moon Scout), Ken Terrell.

***Left:* George Wallace in *Radar Men from the Moon* (1952); *above:* John Merton and Eve Whitney in *Radar Patrol vs. Spy King* (1950)**

1. Moon Rocket. 2. Molten Terror. 3. Bridge of Death. 4. Flight to Destruction. 5. Murder Car. 6. Hills of Death. 7. Human Targets. 8. The Enemy Planet. 9. Battle in the Stratosphere. 10. Mass Execution. 11. Planned Pursuit. 12. Take-Off to Eternity.

539. Radar Patrol vs. Spy King

(Republic, January 1950) Serial, 12 chapters, two reels each.

D: Fred C. Brannon. SP: Royal Cole, William Lively, Sol Shor. Assoc. P: Franklyn Adreon. Photography: Ellis W. Carter. Music: Stanley Wilson. Special Effects: Howard and Theodore Lydecker.

Government attempts to build a radar network around the United States are being sabotaged by the organization headed by John Baroda, an espionage agent of unknown nationality. Aiding him is a female accomplice, Nitra.

The saboteurs kidnap Joan Hughes, a radar scientist in charge of the installation of the radar system at Keystone Station, the particular target of Baroda and his Gang. Radar Defense Bureau operator Chris Calvert is able to rescue Joan and thwart the activities of the saboteurs until they are finally put out of commission for good.

Kirk Alyn (Chris Calvert), Jean Dean (Joan Hughes), Anthony Warde (Ricco Morgan), George J. Lewis (Manuel Agura), Eve Whitney (Nitra), John Merton (John Baroda/The Spy King), Tristram Coffin (Franklyn Lord), John Crawford (Sands), Harold Goodwin (Miller), Dale Van Sickel (Lentz/Thomas), Tom Steele (Gorman/Ames), Eddie Parker (Dutch/Bender/Herb/White/Malloy/Nash), Forbes Murray (Committeeman), Frank O'Connor (Committeeman), Stephen Gregory (Hugh), Bert LeBaron (Nick), Bud Wolfe (Kraft), John Daheim (Jackson/Hanley), Charles Flynn (Finney), David Sharpe (Cliff), Carey Loftin (Heavy), Arvon Dale (Trooper), Frank Dae (John Clark), Art Dillard, Helen Thurston, Louis Volding, Joe Hooker.

1. The Fatal Fog. 2. Perilous Trail. 3. Rolling Fury. 4. Flight of the Spy King. 5. Trapped Underground. 6. Wheels of Disaster. 7. Electrocution. 8. Death Rings the Phone. 9. Tomb of Terror. 10. Death Dive. 11. Desperate Mission. 12. Day of Reckoning.

540. The Radio Detective

(Universal, April 25, 1926) Serial, 10 chapters, two reels each. D: William Crinley and William Craft. SP: Karl Krusada. S: Arthur B. Reeve.

Detective Craig Kennedy and a group of boy scouts help inventor/scout leader Easton Evans protect his "Evansite" discovery, that promises to make a big impact on the radio industry, from a crooked syndicate that wants it.

Jack Daugherty (Easton Evans), Margaret Quimby (Ruth Adams), John T. Prince (Craig Kennedy), Wallace Baldwin (Hank Hawkins), Howard Enstedt (Ken Adams), Jack Mower (Professor Ronald Varis), Florence Allen (Rae Varis), Sammy Gervon, George "Buck" Connors, George Williams, Monte Montague.

1. The Kick-Off. 2. The Radio Riddle. 3. The Radio Wizard. 4. Boy Scout Loyalty. 5. The Radio Secret. 6. Fighting for Love. 7. The Tenderfoot Scout. 8. The Truth Teller. 9. The Fire Fiend. 10. Radio Romance.

541. The Radio King

(Universal, October 30, 1922) Serial, 10 chapters, two reels each. D: Robert F. Hill. Scen/S: Robert Dillon.

A group of foreign agents, headed by an electrical wizard named Marnee, wish to steal certain radio inventions of a radio expert in the U.S. and to overthrow the government. Brad Lane's job is to see that both the secrets and the radio expert are protected. The conflict is fought with the aid of numerous electronic gadgets, including remote-controlled doors which in the end trap the villain and his gang.

Roy Stewart (Bradley Lane), Louise Lorraine (Ruth Leyden), Sidney Bracey (Marnee), Al Smith (Renally), Clark Comstock (John Leyden), Ernest Butterworth, Jr. (Jim Lawton), Fontaine La Rue (Doria), Slim Whittaker (The Mystery Man), Lee Meehan, Marion Faducha, Helen Brannean, Joseph North, D.J. Mitsoras, Laddie Earle, Charles Force.

1. A Cry for Help. 2. The Secret of the Air. 3. A Battle of Wits. 4. Warned by Radio. 5. Ship of Doom. 6. S.O.S. 7. Saved by Wireless. 8. The Master Wave. 9. The Trail of Vengeance. 10. Saved by Science.

542. Radio Patrol

(Universal, August 1937) Serial, 12 chapters, two reels each. D: Ford Beebe and Cliff Smith. SP: Wyndham Gittens, Norman S. Hall, and Ray Trampe. P: Barney Sarecky and Ben Koenig. Based on the newspaper feature of the same name by Eddie Sullivan and Charles Schmidt.

An ordinary radio patrol cop undertakes to protect a young boy and the secret formula for flexible bulletproof steel that has been left him by his father, who was killed by gangsters seeking the formula.

Grant Withers (Pat O'Hara), Catherine [Kay] Hughes (Molly Selkirk), Mickey Rentschier (Pinky Adams), Adrian Morris (Sam), Max Hoffman, Jr. (Selkirk), Frank Lackteen (Thata), Leonard Lord (Franklin), Monte Montague (Pollard), Dick Botellier (Zutta), Silver Wolf (Irish), C. Montague Shaw (Wellington), Wheeler Oakman (Stevens), Jack Mulhall (Desk Sergeant), Harry Davenport (Adams), William Royle (Inspector Clark), Richard Cramer (Radioman), Florence Wright (Nurse), Tom London (Heavy), Tom Steele, Eddie Parker, Frank Sully.

1. A Million Dollar Murder. 2. The Hypnotic Eye. 3. Flaming Death. 4. The Human Clue. 5. The Flash of Doom. 6. The House of Terror. 7. Claws of Steel. 8. The Perfect Crime. 9. Plaything of Disaster. 10. A Bargain with Death. 11. The Hidden Menace. 12. They Get Their Man.

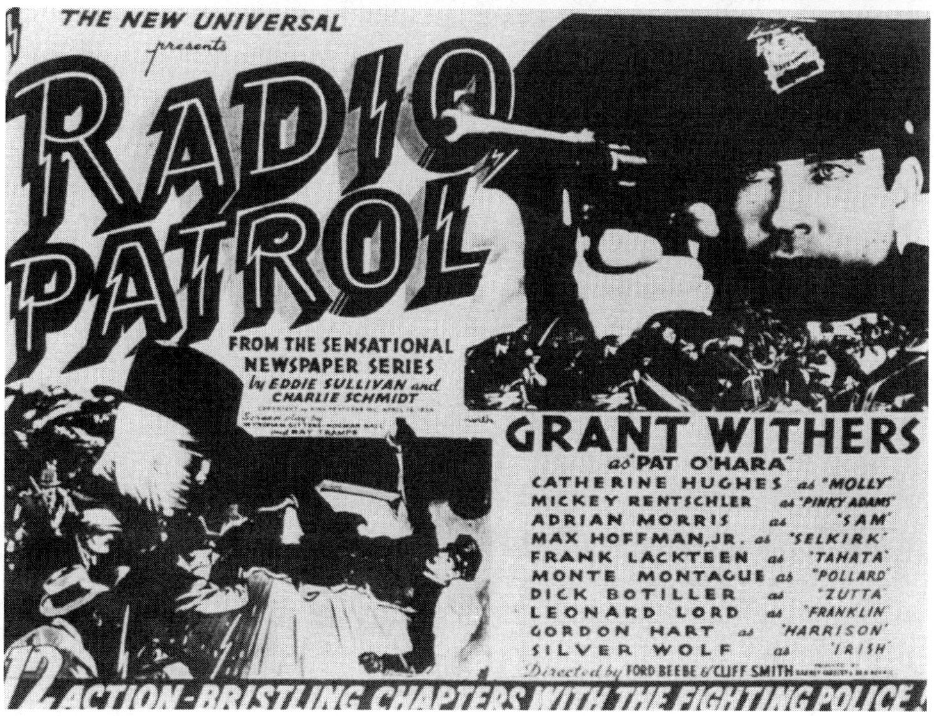

543. Raiders of Ghost City

(Universal, July 25, 1944) Serial, 13 chapters, two reels each. D: Ray Taylor and

Top right: **Louise Lorraine in *The Radio King* (1922); *bottom right:* Grant Withers in *Radio Patrol* (1937)**

Lewis Collins. SP: Luci Ward and Morgan Cox. P: Morgan Cox and Ray Taylor.

In the closing months of the Civil War a gang of outlaws pretending to be Confederates raid gold shipments coming from Oro Grande, California and destined for Union headquarters in Washington, D.C. Captain Steve Clark, a Union Secret Service agent, is determined to round up the gang. Steve and his friend Idaho discover that the raiders are not Confederates but outlaws with headquarters at Morel's saloon. Morel, in addition to being the gang leader, has ties with Prussian spies.

When Steve and his brother lead a raid on the saloon, his brother is killed. Pretty Cathy Haines, a Wells Fargo agent, is endangered. The raiders' second victim is Confederate captain Clay Randolph, who has accidentally discovered that Morel is conferring with the Prussian spies. Beginning with a lead given him by the dying Clay, Steve is able to round up the raiders and spies. Cathy gives up her Wells Fargo job to marry Steve and Idaho gets the job she vacates.

Dennis Moore (Captain Steve Clark), Wanda McKay (Cathy Haines), Lionel Atwill (Alex Morel), Joe Sawyer (Idaho Jones), Regis Toomey (Captain Clay Randolph), Virginia Christine (Trina Dessard), Eddy Waller (Doc Blair), Emmett Vogan (Carl Lawton), Addison Richards (Colonel Sewell), Charles Wagenheim (Abel Rackerby), Jack Rockwell, Edmund Cobb, Jack Ingram, Ernie Adams, George Eldredge, Gene Garrick, Chief Thunder Cloud, Herman Hack, Chick Hannon, Danny Morton, Richard Hunter, Rex Lease.

1. Murder by Accident. 2. Flaming Treachery. 3. Death Rides Double. 4. Ghost City Terror. 5. The Fatal Lariat. 6. Water Rising. 7. Bullet Avalanche. 8. Death Laughs Last. 9. Cold Steel. 10. Showdown. 11. The Trail to Torture. 12. Calling All Buckboards. 13. Golden Vengeance.

Top: **Lionel Atwill, Jack Ingram, and Dennis Moore in *Raiders of Ghost City* (1944); *bottom:* Ken Maynard in *The Range Fighter* (1926)**

544. The Railroad Raiders

(Signal Films/Mutual, April 9, 1917) Serial, 15 chapters, two reels each. D: J. McGowan. SP: Ford Beebe and others.

Helen Holmes assists her father, David Holmes, station agent at Deer's Head for the K. & W. Railroad. David is sentenced to prison when a dishonest agent steals $17,000 by having a look-alike for Holmes accept the money when it is delivered to the station. Wallace Burke, employed by the railroad's claim department, pitches in to help Helen clear her father and to round up the dregs of the West.

Helen Holmes (Helen Holmes), Leo Maloney (Wallace Burke), William Brunton (Roy Wilson), Will Chapman (David Holmes), Thomas Lingham (Morton Webb), William Buhler (Homer Frost), Paul C. Hurst, F.L. Hemphill, William Behrens, J.P. McGowan, Marvin Martin.

1. Circumstantial Evidence. 2. A Double Steal. 3. Inside Treachery. 4. A Race for a Fortune. 5. A Woman's Wit. 6. The Overland Disaster. 7. Mistaken Identity. 8. A Knotted Cord. 9. A Leap for Life. 10. A Watery Grave. 12. A Desperate Deed. 12. A Fight for a Franchise. 13. The Road Wrecker. 14. The Trap. 15. Mystery of the Counterfeit Tickets.

545. The Range Fighter

(Davis Distributing Corp., 1926) Serial, 10 chapters, two reels each. D: Clifford S. Elfelt, Paul Hurst, and Forrest Sheldon. S: Frank Howard Clark, Jay Inman Kane, and George Hively. SP: George Hively and Frank Howard Clark. P: Clifford S. Elfelt.

This serial was assembled from segments of the features *$10,000 Reward*, *Fighting Courage*, *The Demon Rider*, *The Haunted Ranch*, and *The Grey Vulture* to capitalize on the popularity of Ken Maynard and get some mileage out of his earlier films. Although the author's source information indicates 1926 as the year of release, it is possible that the serial was not released until somewhat later, since it is known to have had a talking prologue, music score, and sound effects. However, the film could have been recalled and these elements added after its initial release. It would be interesting to see how a serial was constructed using footage from five different features.

Terry Baldwin is left a huge ranch and power site by his uncle, Anse Baldwin, while the old man cut off his grandson with $1. The will provides, however, that Terry must clear his uncle of the charge of having murdered his partner and neighbor, Stephen Kellard. He must also clear the claim to the title of the power site, which has been jumped by the power interests, and turn over half of that property to the heirs of Stephen Kellard. Terry is opposed by a gang operating from the ranch and by Ralph Kellard, weakling son of Stephen. Ralph's sister, Judith, at first loathes Terry as the nephew of a murderer, but ultimately falls in love with him.

Ken Maynard (Terry Baldwin), Dorothy Devore (Judith Kellard), George Nichols, J.P. McGowan, Sheldon Lewis, Joseph Swickard, Buck Black, Billy Franey, Billy Gills, Charles Whitaker, Frank Ellis, Dick Sutherland, Hank Bell, Tarzan [a horse]. Although these actors appeared in the five features from which the serial was constructed, it does not follow that all of them appear in the serial.

1. Dynamite. [Other titles unknown.]

546. Range Rider

(Malobee/Pathé, 1922–1923) Series, 26 episodes, two reels each. D: Leo Maloney. S/SP: Leo Maloney, Ford Beebe,

Leo Maloney, Josephine Hill (22 films), Pauline Curley (4 films).

1. Come and Get Me (8-9-22). 2. Deputized (8-9-22). 3. The Bar-Cross War (9-27-22). 4. The Drifter (9-27-22). 5. His Own Law (10-4-22). 6. One Jump Ahead (12-1-22). 7. His Enemy's Friend (12-1-22). 8. Border Law (12-14-22). 9. Here's Your Men (12-14-22). 10. Under Suspicion (12-14-22). 11. Rough Going (12-16-22). 12. Partners Three (2-17-23). 13. Smoked Out (2-17-23). 14. The Extra Seven (2-17-23). 15. When Fighting's Necessary (2-23-23). 16. Doubled Cinched (2-23-23). 17. Lost, Strayed, or Stolen (2-23-23). 18. 100% Nerve (2-23-23). 19. Wings of the Storm (4-27-23). 20. The Unsuspecting Stranger (4-27-23). 21. Hyde and Zeke (4-27-3). 22. Tom, Dick, and Harry (6-6-23). 23. Steel-Shod Evidence (6-7-23). 24. Yellow Gold and Men (7-19-23). 25. Warned in Advance (7-19-23). 25. In Wrong Wright (8-7-23).

547. Rapax

(France, 1922) Serial, chapters (?). D: Paul Garbagni. Scen: Jean Faber.

Cazalis, Lise Hestia, Paul Amiot, Simone Genevois, Violette Jyl, Albert Mayer, Madeleine Erickson, Dartagnan.

548. Ray Whitely and His Bar-6 Cowboys

(RKO-Radio, 1937–1942) Series, 16 episodes. P: Bert Gilroy. D: Charles Roberts, Lou Brock, Jean Yarbrough, Harry D'Arcy.

These musical shorts were well received at a time when a comedy or cartoon usually accompanied the main feature and serial. Whitely was also playing sidekick to George O'Brien and later Tim Holt during the time these shorts were made. Comedy and music characterized the short, simple stories centered around Whitely's screen persona and singing voice. He would have been a natural for a series of his own but RKO failed to see the potential.

[Number in parentheses indicates how many appearances actor made, if known.] Ray Whitely, Ken Card, Willie Phelps, Norman Phelps, Earl Phelps, Virginia Vale (8) Kay Whitely (2), Lloyd Ingraham (5), Glenn Strange (3), Lee "Lasses" White (3), Curley Hoag (5), Jack Rice (2), Frankie Marvin (3), Cactus Mack (3), Emmett Lynn (2), Harry Harvey (2), Spade Cooley (2), Jane Kegley (2), Bob McKenzie (2), Hank Worden (2), Sandy Hall (2), Isabel Lamar, Ed Coke, Elvira Rios, Jay Novello, Jimmy Wakely, Jane Patten, Ester Belle, Ethan Laidlaw, Marie Mominieci, Robert Kent, Jane Walsh, Georgia Simmons, Pauline Haddon, Dick Elliott, Mary Parker, Tom Chatterton, Victor Wong, Jean Joyce, Chester Conklin, Kathryn Adams, Bob Burns, Mariska Aldrich.

1. Rhythm Wranglers (12-17-37, 19 min.). 2. A Buckaroo Broadcast (4-22-38, 18 min.). 3. Ranch House Romeo (4-7-39, 17 min.). 4. Sagebrush Serenade (6-6-39, 19 min.). 5. Cupid Rides the Range (9-8-39, 18 min.). Bandits and Ballads (12-15-39, 17 min.). 7. Molly Cures a Cowboy (3-22-40, 19 min.). 8. Corralling a School Marm (6-14-40, 20 min.). 9. Bar Buckaroos (11-8-40, 16 min.). 10. Prairie Spooners (1-31-41, 17 min.). 11. Redskins and Redheads (4-25-41, 17 min.). 12. The Musical Bandit (7-18-41, 17 min.). 13. California or Bust (11-11-41, 17 min.). 14. Keep Shooting (1-30-42, 17 min.). 15. Cactus Capers (4-23-42, 17 min.). 16. Range Rhythm (7-17-42, 17 min.).

549. Record Breakers

(Standard Cinema Corp., 1929–'30) Series, 13 episodes, two reels each. D: Albert Herman, Ralph Cedar, Lewis R. Foster, Phil Whitman. S/Scen: E.V. Durling, Hal Davitt, John Gray. P: Larry Darmour.

A comedy series.

Alberta Vaughn, Al Cooke.

1. As You Like It. 2. Meet the Quince. 3. Love's Labor Found. 4. They Shall Not Pass Out. 5. The Captain of His Roll. 6. The Sleeping Cutie. 7. Lost and Foundered. 8. Old Vamps for New. 9. The Setting Son. 10. The Dear Slayer. 11. Cash and Marry. 12. Land of the Sky Blue Daughters. 13. Eventually, But Not Now.

550. The Red Ace

(Universal, October 22, 1917) Serial, 16 chapters, two reels each. D/SP: Jacques Jaccard.

The film was set in the wilds of Canada and the thrills were as wild as the setting. Dr. Hirtzman, head of the foreign secret service, is seeking to help the enemies of the U.S. by keeping the supply of platinum from Lost Hope Mine in Canada

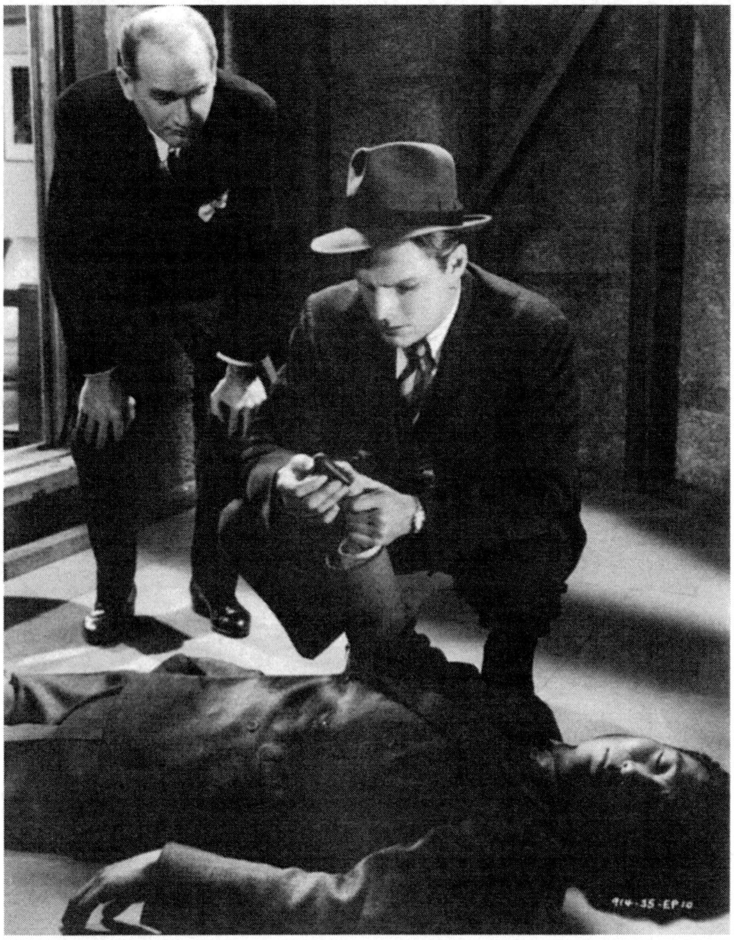

Top: **Buster Crabbe, Phillip Ahn, and William Ruhl in *Red Barry* (1938); *bottom:* Ruth Roland in *The Red Circle* (1915)**

from reaching the government. When Federal officers mistakenly believe the Dixon family, owners of the mine, to be guilty of collaboration with the enemy, Virginia Dixon struggles to clear the family name, discover the location of buried platinum which her brother hid before being killed, and to bring to justice the masked menace, The Terror. The overall construction of this serial made it superior to *Liberty*, and Miss Walcamp's popularity with the fans climbed.

Marie Walcamp (Virginia Dixon), Larry Peyton (Sergeant Winthrop), L.M. Wells (Fouchard), Bobby Mack (Messenger to Bodyguard), Charles Brinley (Steele Heffern), Harry Archer (Doctor Hirtzman), Noble Johnson (Little Bear), Yvette Mitchell (Red Fawn), Nellie Allen (Bertha Schriver), Marian Shelby.

1. Silent Terror. 2. Lure of the Unattainable. 3. A Leap for Liberty. 4. The Undercurrent. 5. In Mid-Air. 6. Fighting Blood. 7. The Lion's Claws. 8. Lair of the Beast. 9. A Voice from the Dead (or) Voice from the Past. 10. Hearts of Steel. 11. The Burning Span. 12. Overboard. 13. New Enemies. 14. The Fugitives. 15. Hell's Riders. 16. Virginia's Triumph.

551. Red Barry

(Universal, October 1938) Serial, 13 chapters, two reels each. D: Ford Beebe and Alan James. SP: Norman Hall and Ray Trampe. Based on King Features comic strip.

Two million dollars in bonds intended to buy fighter planes for an oriental nation, are stolen, and different factions strive to get them, with detective Red Barry and newspaperwoman Mississippi caught in the crossfire. Red's job is to recover the bonds and round up espionage agents and assorted other criminals. This he does, but only after the stolen bonds have changed hands several times.

Buster Crabbe (Red Barry), Frances Robinson (Mississippi), Wade Boteler (Inspector Scott), Edna Sedgwick (Natacha), Philip Ahn (Hong Kong Cholly), Frank Lackteen (Quong Lee), Cyril Delevanti (Wing Fu), Hugh Huntley (Valentine Vane), William Gould (Commissioner), William Ruhl (Mannix), Wheeler Oakman (Weaver), Stanley Price (Petrov), Earle Douglas (Igor), Charles Stevens (Captain Moy), Eric Wilton (Tubis), Tom Steele (Henchman), Lane Chandler, James Sheridan, Hugh Prosser, Gladden James, Edward Hearn, Dick Purcell.

1. Millions for Defense. 2. The Curtain Falls. 3. The Decoy. 4. High Stakes. 5. Desperate Chances. 6. The Human Target. 7. Midnight Tragedy. 8. The Devil's Disguise. 9. Between Two Fires. 10. The False Trail. 11. Heavy Odds. 12. The Enemy Within. 13. Mission of Mercy.

552. The Red Circle

(Balboa Feature Film Company/Pathé, December 16, 1915) Serial, 14 chapters, two reels each. D: Sherwood MacDonald. Scen: Will M. Ritchey and H.M. Horkeimer.

June Travis, as she assumes herself to be, is cursed with a family taint that causes her to commit acts against which her better self revolts. A crimson circle on the back of her hand is a sign of the curse. Detective Lamar, through a chance encounter with Ruth, sees the circle and believes her to be involved in a robbery. Jim sets about chasing down the curse.

A number of years before Mrs. Travis gave birth to a son while at about the same time Mrs. Borden gave birth to a daughter. When outlaws attacked the town both Mr. Travis and Mrs. Borden were killed. Jim Borden left town taking the Travis boy by mistake. June was then raised by Mrs. Travis who thought June to be her daughter. The film was kind of bizarre but audiences of 1916 relished it. Ruth was a sort of lady Jekyll and Hyde. But detective Lamar loved her and solved the riddle of the red circle curse.

Ruth Roland (June Travis), Frank Mayo (Dr. Max Lamar), Gordon Sackville (Chief of Police), Daniel Gilfether (Circle Jim Barden), Edward Peters (Son of Circle), Makato Inokuchi (the Butler), Corene Grant (Mary, June's Nurse), Mollie McConnell (Mrs. Travis), Lillian West (Alma LaSalle), Myrtle Reeves, Philo McCullough, Frank Erlinger, Andrew Arbuckle.

1. Nevermore. 2. Pity the Poor. 3. Twenty Years Ago. 4. In Strange Attire. 5. Weapons of War. 6. False Colors. 7. Third Degree (or) Two Captives. 8. Peace at Any Price. 9. Dodging the Law. 10. Excess Baggage. 11. Seeds of Suspicion. 12. Like a Rat in a Trap. 13. Branded as a Thief. 14. Judgment Day.

553. The Red Glove

(Universal, March 17, 1919) Serial, 18 chapters, two reels each. D: J.P. McGowan. Scen: Hope Loring. S: Douglas Grant (Pseudonym of Isabel Egenton Ostrander)—"The Fifth Ace."

A gang known as The Vultures terrorizes a section of the West and particularly threatens The Blue Chip, owned by Billie, with all parties seeking the riches of The Pool of Lost Souls. The bandits wear masks and headpieces of eagles' wings, and are under direction of Starr Wiley, agent of a certain oil company, and his confederate. A mystery concerning the heroine's birth is not explained until the conclusion of the story.

Trueman Van Dyke replaced Pat O'Malley as leading man in either Chapter 7 or 8.

Marie Walcamp (Billie), Pat O'Malley (Kern Thodes), Trueman Van Dyke (Kern Thodes), Thomas Lingham (Starr Wiley), Leon De La Mothe (The Vulture), Alfred Allen (Gentleman Geoff), Evelyn Selbie (Tiajuana), William Dyer, Andrew Waldon, Edgar Allen, Leon Kent.

1. The Pool of Lost Souls. 2. The Claws of the Vulture. 3. The Vulture's Vengeance. 4. The Passing of Gentleman Geoff. 5. At the Mercy of a Monster. 6. The Flames of Death. 7. A Desperate Chance. 8. Facing Death. 9. A Leap for Life. 10. Out of Death's Shadow. 11. In the Depths of the Sea. 12. In Death's Grip. 13. Trapped. 14. The Lost Millions. 15. The Mystery Message. 16. In Deadly Peril. 17. The Rope of Death. 18. Run to Earth.

554. The Red Rider

(Universal, July 16, 1934) Serial, 15 chapters, two reels each. D: Louis Friedlander [Lew Landers]. SP: George Plympton, Vin Moore, Ella O'Neill, and George Morgan. S: W.C. Tuttle—*The Redhead from Sun Dog*. P: Henry McRae.

Red Davidson attempts to clear his friend Silent Slade of murder charges after first relinquishing his job as sheriff because of allowing Slade to escape. Going to work on a ranch near the Mexican border, Red finds his old pal, the man he suspects is the real killer, and a beautiful girl.

Buck Jones (Red Davidson), Grant Withers (Silent Slade), Marion Shilling (Marie Maxwell), Walter Miller (Jim Breen), Richard Cramer (Joe Portos), Margaret LaMarr (Joan McKee), Silver [horse] (Himself), Edmund Cobb (Johnny Snow), Charles French (Robert Maxwell), J.P. McGowan (Scotty McKee), William Desmond (Sheriff), Mert Lavarre [John Merton] (Banty), Frank Rice (Harp), Jim Thorpe (Bill Abel), Monte Montague (Al Abel), Denny Meadows [Dennis Moore] (Cowboy), Jim Corey (Berg), Bud Osborne (Kelsey), Al Ferguson (Madden), Artie Ortego (Indian), Chester Gan (Cook), Tom Ricketts (Judge), Lee Beggs (Soapy), Charles Brinley (Gambler), Bud Kendricks (Townsman), Harry Royer (Soapy's Friend), Charles McMurphy (Shooting Victim), Frank Hagney (Saloon Tough), Jack Shannon (Ranch Hand), Chet Ryan (Wrangler), Cliff Lyons (Jones' Double), Tom Steele (Stuntman), Eddie Woehler, Jr. (Little Boy), King Baggott (Rancher), Art Mix (Henchman), Jack O'Shea (Henchman), Frank Ellis (Henchman), Rose Plummer, Bud Kendricks, Harry Royer, Hank Bell, Fred Burns, J. Frank Glendon, Jim Toney, William Steele.

1. Sentenced to Die. 2. A Leap for Life. 3. The Night Attack. 4. Treacherous Attack. 5. Trapped. 6. The Brink of Death. 7. The Fatal Plunge. 8. The Stampede. 9. The Posse Rider. 10. The Avenging Trail. 11. The Lost Diamonds. 12. Double Trouble. 13. The Night Raiders. 14. In the Enemy's Hideout. 15. Brought to Justice.

555. Reine-Lumiere

(France, 1921) Serial, chapters (?). D: René Navarre. Scen: René Navarre.

René Navarre.

556. The Return of Chandu

(Principal, October 1, 1934) Serial, 12 chapters, two reels each. D: Ray Taylor. P: Sol Lesser. SP: Barry Berringer. Adapted from the radio drama written by Harry A. Earnshaw, Vera M. Oldham, and R.R. Morgan. Story Supervision: Harry Hickson. Supervision: Frank Melford. Music: Abe Meyer. There were two features made from this serial: *The Return of Chandu* (using Chapters 1–4), 65 min., 1934: *Chandu of the Magic Island* (using Chapters 6–12), 60 min., 1934.

The Black Magic cult of Ubasti is determined to capture and sacrifice Nadji, Princess of Egypt, to the cult's god as a prelude to their rise to power on the magic island of Lemuria. Vindhyan rules over the cult and maintains a secret temple in the Los Angeles area from which he directs his nefarious activities until Nadji is kidnapped and taken to Lemuria. The cult believes that its demigoddess Ossanna may be restored to life and again rule the continent of Lemuria, now submerged in the waters of the Pacific, with the death of Nadji. Chandu is friend and protector of Nadji and all his great powers are summoned to protect her, his sister, niece, and nephew from the Black Magic cult. He is aided by the forces of White Magic and the power of Tyba, the White Magician.

This serial was made at Pathé Studios and exteriors used

***Top:* Bella Lugosi; *bottom:* Bella Lugosi and Maria Alba in *The Return of Chandu* (1934)**

the Skull Island village set from *King Kong* and the Port Dekang set from *The Son of Kong*. In *Chandu the Magician* (Fox, 1932), Edmund Lowe starred in the title role and Bela Lugosi co-starred as the arch villain "Baron Roxor." Cyril Armbruster, who was in charge of dialogue during production and who also appears in the serial, was the producer of the *Chandu* radio adventures.

Bela Lugosi (Frank Chandler [Chandu]), Maria Alba (Princess Nadji), Clara Kimball Young (Dorothy Regent), Lucien Prival (Vindhyan [High Priest of Ubasti]), Phyllis Ludwig (Betty Regent), Dean Benton (Bob Regent), Bryant Washburn (Prince Andre), Peggy Montgomert (Judy), Cyril Armbruster (Sutra [An Accomplice]), Elias Lazaroff (Bara [An Accomplice]), Dick Botiller (Morta [An Accomplice]), Frazer Acosta (Nito [The Butler]), Murdock McQuarrie (Voice of Ubasti), Jack Clark (Vitras [High Priest of Ubasti]), Josef Swickard (Tyba [The White Magician]), Harry Ealker (Tagora), Charles Meecham (Mr. James), Isobel LeMail (Mrs. James), Wilfred Lucas (Captain Wilson), Don Brodie (Reporter), Edward Peil (Airline Agent), Henry Hall (Curator), Beatrice Roberts (Lady), Iron Eyes Cody (Con Man), Elias Schaeffer (Old Man), Merrill McCormack (Sacrificial Aide), Cyril Armbruster (The Voice), Frank Lanning (False Constable), John Ince (Party Guest).

1. The Chosen Victim. 2. House on the Hill. 3. On the High Seas. 4. The Evil Eye. 5. The Invisible Circle. 6. Chandu's False Step. 7. The Mysterious Island. 8. The Edge of the Pit. 9. The Invisible Terror. 10. The Crushing Rock. 11. The Uplifted Knife. 12. The Knife Descends.

557. The Return of Cyclone Smith

(Universal, 1921) Series, 6 episodes. D: Jacques Jaccard. S/SP: George Morgan, Robert Dillon, and Anthony W. Coldeway. P: Jacques Jaccard and Jay Marchant.

A continuation of the series filmed in 1919.

Eddie Polo (Cyclone Smith), Kathleen Myers, Joseph Hazelton, Charles Brimley, Valeria Olivo.

1. Cyclone Smith's Vow (11-4-21). 2. A Battle Against Odds (11-4-21). 3. Square Deal Cyclone (11-28-21). 4. The Yellow Streak (12-5-21). 5. The Heritage of Hate (12-12-21). 6. A Race for a Rancho (12-19-21).

558. Return of the Riddle Rider

(Universal, March 28, 1927) Serial, 10 chapters, two reels each. D: Robert Hill and Jay Marchant. S/SP: Arthur B. Reeve and Fred J. McConnell.

Once again Randolph Parker, western newspaperman, dons his disguise to combat the lawless element that is attempting to take over the territory. The gang is led by a mystery figure who gives instructions to his minions by telephone, but The Riddle Rider soon puts a stop to his calls once and for all.

William Desmond (Randolph Parker), Lola Todd (Madge McCormack), Scotty Mattraw (Willie), Norbett Myles (James Archer), Tom London (Buck White), Grace Cunard (Vilda Dixon), Howard Davis (Hank Wilson), Lewis Dayton (James Thornley), Henry Barrows (Senator McCormack).

1. The Riddle Rider Rides Again. 2. A Day of Terror. 3. Not a Chance. 4. The Hold-Up. 5. The River of Flame. 6. The Trap. 7. The Crooked Deal. 8. The Rock Slide. 9. The Silencer. 10. Vengeance.

559. The Riddle Rider

(Universal, November 24, 1924) Serial, 15 chapters, two reels each. D: William Craft. SP/S: William Wing, Arthur H. Gooden, and George Pyper.

Randolph Parker is a crusading newspaperman in the western oil fields who dons the disguise of The Riddle Rider to dispense justice when the law breaks down. He takes particular delight in protecting Nan Madden, a beautiful young heiress whose ranch is threatened.

William Desmond (Randolph Parker/The Riddle Rider), Eileen Sedgwick (Nan Madden), Helen Holmes (Julie Dean), Claude Payton (Victor Raymond), William H. Gould (Jack

Archer), Hughie Mack (Willie), Ben Corbett (Monte Blade), Albert J. Smith, Margaret Royce, Yakima Canutt, Art Ortego.

1. The Canyon Torrent. 2. Crashing. 3. In the Path of Death. 4. Plunged Into the Depths. 5. Race for a Fortune. 6. Sinister Shadows. 7. The Swindle. 8. The Frame-Up. 9. False Faces. 10. At the Brink of Death. 11. Thundering Steeds. 12. Trapped. 13. The Valley of Fate. 14. The Deadline. 15. The Final Reckoning.

560. Riders of Death Valley

(Universal, July 1, 1941) Serial, 15 chapters, two reels each. D: Ray Taylor and ford Beebe. S: Oliver Drake. SP: Sherman Lowe, Basil Dickey, George Plympton, and Jack Connell. P: Henry MacRae. Photography: Jerome Ash and William Sickner. Music: Charles Previn. Song "Ride Along" by Milt Rosen and Everett Carter. Background Music: Mendelssohn's "Fingal's Cave Overture."

The Riders of Death Valley, a vigilante group, seek to protect miners against outlaws led by Wolf Reade, who hopes to take over all the mines in the Panamint District. Under the leadership of Jim Benton and Tombstone, the Riders drive the outlaws from the valley and secure for Mary Morgan the Lost Aztec Mine left her by an old prospector uncle. Advertised as a million dollar super serial, much of the money went to pay for the unusually strong cast.

Dick Foran (Jim Benton), Buck Jones (Tombstone), Leo Carrillo (Pancho), Charles Bickford (Wolf Reade), Lon Chaney, Jr. (Butch), Noah Beery, Jr. (Smokey), Guinn [Big Boy] Williams (Borax Bill), Jeanne Kelly [Jean Brooks] (Mary Morgan), James Blaine (Joseph Kirby), Monte Blue (Rance Davis), Glenn Strange (Tex), Roy Barcroft (Dirk), Ethan Laidlaw (Rusty), Dick Alexander (Pete), Jack Rockwell (Trigger), Frank Austin (Chuckawalla), Charles Thomas (Rimrock), William Hall (Gordon), James Guilfoyle (Judge Knox), Ernie Adams (Cactus), Edmund Cobb (Salty), William Pagan (Marshal), Jack Clifford (Lafe Hogan), Richard Travis (Joe Miller), Jack Perrin (Guard), Ivar McFadden (Bragg), Jerome Harte (Richards), Ruth Rickaby (Kate), Bud Osborne (Stage Driver), Charles [Slim] Whitaker (Ira Jackson), Don Rowan (Blake), Frank Brownlee (Slim), Art Miles (Evergreene), Ed Payson (Buck Hansen), James Farley (Graham), Alonzo Price (Wilson), Ted Adams (Hank), Dick Rush (Bartender), Ken Nolan (Cashier), Jay Michael (Cashier), Gil Perkins (Fighter), Duke York (Double), Silver [horse] (Himself).

1. Death Marks the Trail. 2. Menacing Herd. 3. Plunge of Peril. 4. Flaming Fury. 5. Avalanche of Doom. 6. Blood and Gold. 7. Death Rides the Storm. 8. Descending Doom. 9. Death Holds the Reins. 10. Devouring Flames. 11. Fatal Blast. 12. Thundering Doom. 13. The Bridge of Disaster. 14. A Fight to the Death. 15. The Harvest of Hate.

561. Riders of the Plains

(Arrow, September 15, 1924) Serial, 15 chapters, chapter one, three reels; others two reels. D: Jacques Jaccard. S: Karl Coolidge and Jacques Jaccard.

William Desmond in *The Return of the Riddle Rider* (1927)

Jack Perrin, Marilyn Mills, Ruth Royce, Charles Brinley, Kingsley Benedict, Running Elk, Robert Miles, Rhody Hathaway, Clark Comstock, Boris Karloff, Starlight [horse].

1. Red Shadows. 2. Dangerous Hazards. 3. A Living Death. 4. Flames of Fury. 5. Morgan's Raid. 6. Out of the Past. 7. A Fighting Gamble. 8. A Prisoner of War. 9. Pawns of Destiny. 10. Riding for Life. 11. In Death's Shadow. 12. Flaming Vengeance. 13. Thundering Hoofs. 4. Red Talons. 15. The Reckoning.

562. Riding with Buffalo Bill

(Columbia, November 11, 1954) Serial, 15 chapters, three reels each. D: Spencer G. Bennet. SP: George H. Plympton. P: Sam Katzman. Assist. D: Leonard Katzman. Photography: Ira H. Morgan. Music: Mischa Bakaleinikoff. Special Effects: Jack Erickson.

Bill Cody comes to the aid of a rancher under attack by outlaws and becomes embroiled in a fight to defeat the outlaw kingpin, who is trying to keep the railroad out of the territory.

Marshall Reed (Bill Cody), Rick Vallin (Reb Morgan), Joanne Rio (Maria Perez), Shirley Whitney (Ruth Morgan), Jack Ingram (Ace), William Fawcett (Rocky Ford), Gregg Barton (Bart), Ed Coch (Jose Perez), Steve Ritch (Elko), Pierce Lyden (Darr), Michael Fox (King Carney), Lee Roberts (Zeke), John Truex (Luke), Zon Murray, Al Cantor, Al Ferguson, Terry Frost, Ray Jones.

1. The Ridin' Terror from St. Joe. 2. Law of the Six Gun. 3. Raiders from Ghost Town. 4. Cody to the Rescue. 5. Midnight Marauders. 6. Under the Avalanche. 7. Night Attack. 8. Trapped in the Powder Shack. 9. Into an Outlaw Trap. 10. Blast to Oblivion. 11. The Depths of the Earth. 12. The Ridin' Terror. 13. Trapped in the Apache Mine. 14. Railroad Wreckers. 15. Law Comes to the West.

Marshall Reed in *Riding with Buffalo Bill* (1954)

563. Road O'Strife

(Lubin, April 3, 1915) Serial, 15 chapters, one reel each. D: John Ince and Howell Hansell. S/SP: Emmett Campbell Hall.

Alene, a ward of professor Gershorn, has lived a sheltered life. When she decides to see what the world outside his mansion is like, she meets Robert Dane, who resists taking advantage of her innocence and returns her home. There, she finds the professor dead and sees a mysterious ringed hand clutching the curtain. She runs screaming to Dane and strives to convince him and others that she is not mad when no sign of the murder can be found.

Crane Wilbur, Mary Charleson, Jack Standing, John Ince, Rosetta Brice, Charles Brandt, George Soule Spencer, Peter Lang, William H. Turner, Ferdinand Tidmarsh, Francis Joyner, Clarence Jay Elmer, Howard Mitchell, Abner Gray, Flora Lea, Josephine Longworth, Jack MacDonald, Gilbert Ely, Florence Hackett, Douglas Sibole, James Burns, George Trimble, Herbert Fortier, Frankie Mann, Percy Winter, Bernard Siegel, Frank Smiley, Walter Law, James Cassady, John Smiley, George Clark, William Cahil, Jack Delson, James Daly.

1. The House of Secrets. 2. The Face of Fear. 3. The Silver Cup. 4. The Ring of Death. 5. No Other Way. 6. The Strength of Love. 7. Into the Night. 8. In the Wolf's Den. 9. The Iron Hand of the Law. 10. The Unsparing Sword. 11. The Valley of the Shadow. 12. The Sacrifice. 13. The Man Who Did Not Die. 14. A Story of the Past. 15. The Coming of the Kingdom.

564. Roar of the Iron Horse

(Columbia, May 31, 1951) Serial, 15 chapters, two reels each. D: Spencer G. Bennet and Thomas Carr. SP: George H. Plympton, Sherman L. Lowe, and Royal K. Cole. P: Sam Katzman. Assist. D: R.M. Andrews. Photography: Fayte Browne. Music: Mischa Bakaleinikoff.

Work on the transcontinental railroad is being sabotaged by Karl Ulrick, also known as The Baron. An investigator, Jim Grant, is called in from Washington. He finds that Ulrick is controlling the Indians by bribing the tribal medicine man and that Ulrick secures Indian lands by using an Old Spanish land grant. A long struggle ensues between railroaders and The Baron's gang of outlaws and Indians.

Jock O'Mahoney (Jim Grant), Virginia Herrick (Carol Lane), William Fawcett (Rocky), Hal Landon (Tom Lane), Jack Ingram (Homer Lathrop), George Eldredge (Karl Ulrick/The Baron), Mickey Simpson (Cal), Myron Healey (Ace), Dick Curtis (Campo), Bud Osborne (Ezra), Rusty Wescoatt (Scully), Frank Ellis (Bat), Pierce Lyden (Erv), Hugh Prosser (Lefty), Rick Vallin (White Eagle).

1. Indian Attack. 2. Captured by Redskins. 3. Trapped by Outlaws. 4. In the Baron's Stronghold 5. A Ride for Life. 6. White Indians. 7. Fumes of Fate. 8. Midnight Marauders. 9. Raid on the Pay Train. 10. Trapped on a Trestle. 11. Redskins' Revenge. 12. Plunge of Peril. 13. The Law Takes Over. 14. When Killers Meet. 15. The End of the Trail.

565. The Roaring West

(Universal, June 26, 1935) Serial, 15 chapters, two reels each. D: Ray Taylor. S: Edward Earl Repp. SP: George Plympton, Nate Gatzert, Ella O'Neill, Basil Dickey, Robert Rothafel. P: Henry McRae. Photography: William Sicknew and Richard Fryer.

Montana Larkin and his pal Jinglebob ride into new territory to join an impending land rush. They possess a map giving the location of land on which there is a valuable mineral deposit and which they expect to secure in the land rush. Foiling them is Gillespie, foreman of Jim Parker's ranch, who beats them to the supposed location. Gillespie's attempted bribery to acquire Mary, Parker's daughter, fails and he is discharged. He begins a reign of terror when it is discovered that he filed on the wrong location and that Montana has filed on the real deposit. Montana is sworn in as a deputy sheriff and capture both Gillespie and his gang and Mary's heart.

Buck Jones (Montana Larkin), Muriel Evans (Mary Parker), Walter Miller (Gil Gillespie), Frank McGlynn, Sr. (Jinglebob Morgan), Harlan Knight (Clem Morgan), William Desmond (Jim Parker), Tom London (Butch), Charles King

Left: **Buck Jones, Frank McGlunn, Sr., and Silver;** ***above:*** **Buck Jones, Walter Miller, Charles King, and Charles Whitaker in** ***The Roaring West*** **(1935)**

(Tex), Charles Whitaker (Hank), Eole Galli (Ann Hardy), Pat O'Brien (Steve), Tiny Skelton (Happy), William Thorne (Marco Brett), Dick Rush (Sheriff), Harry Tenbrook (Limpy), George Ovey (Shorty), Buffalo Bill, Jr. (Slim), Lafe McKee (Stagecoach Passenger), Hank Bell (Stagecoach driver), Horace Carpenter (Land Agent), Jack Rockwell (Sheriff), Fred Stantley (Singer), Cliff Lyons (Jones' Double), Cecil Kellogg, Edmund Cobb, Fred Humes, John Bose, Bob Card, Bud McClure, Bobby Dunn, Silver [a horse], Buck Bucko, Roy Bucko.

1. The Land Rush. 2. Torrent of Terror. 3. Flaming Peril. 4. Stampede of Death. 5. Danger in the Dark. 6. Death Rides the Plain. 7. Hurled to the Depths. 8. Ravaging Flames. 9. Death Holds the Reins. 10. The Fatal Blast. 11. The Baited Trap. 12. The Mystery Shot. 13. Flaming Torrents. 14. Thundering Fury. 15. The Conquering Cowpunchers.

566. Robinson Crusoe of Clipper Island

(Republic, February 1936) Serial, 14 chapters; Chapter 1, three reels; others, two reels. D: Mack V. Wright, Ray Taylor. S/SP: Morgan Cox, Barry Shipman, and Maurice Geraghty. Supervision: J. Laurence Wickland. Assoc. P: Sol C. Siegel. P: Nat Levine. Photography: William Nobles. Music: Harry Grey. Feature Title: *Robinson Crusoe of Mystery Island.*

Mala is assigned by management of a corporation to investigate the burning of fuel storage tanks on Clipper Island and the sabotaging of the airship *San Francisco* over the island on its maiden voyage to Australia. A mysterious spy group headed by the unidentified "H.K." has caused both the fire and sabotage. They do not want a refueling station on the island because of a secret fortress and submarine base located there. Princess Melani and two animal friends, Rex, a horse, and Buck, a dog, aid Mala in besting the saboteurs and their native allies.

Ray Mala (Mala), Rex [a horse] (Himself), Buck [a dog] (Himself), Mamo Clark (Melani), Herbert Rawlinson (Grant Jackson), William Newill (Hank McGlaurie), John Ward (Anthony Tupper), John Dilson (E.G. Ellsworth), Selmer Jackson (Canfield/"H.K."), John Picorri (Porotu), George Chesebro (Draker), Robert Kortman (Wilson), George Cleveland (Goebel), Lloyd Whitlock (Lamar), Tiny Roebuck (Eppa), Tracy Lane (Larkin), Herbert Weber (Stevens), Edmund Cobb (Crosby/Harris), Edward Cassidy (Joe Davis), Bud Osborne (Ellie), Buddy Roosevelt (Wireless Operator), Anthony Pawley (Clark), Allen Connor (Tim Taylor/Agent), Evan Thomas (Agent), Allen Caven (Captain), Ralph McCullough (Chemist), David Horsley (Co-Pilot), Henry Sylvester (Fairchild), Jack Mack (Fosdick), Harry Strang (Grover), Oscar Hendrian (Guard), Val Duran (Half Caste), Lorene Riebe (Johnson), Allan Henry Hall (Mercer), Roscoe Gerall (Price), Don Brodie (Radioman), Frank Ellis (Rontree), Jerry Jerome (Wallace), Francis Walker (Spy), Frazer Acosta (Teekor), F. Herrick Herrick (Tollar), Loni Ornellas, Clarence Morrow, Jimmy Fawcett.

1. The Mysterious Island. 2. Flaming Danger. 3. Fathoms Below. 4. Into the Enemies' Camp. 5. Danger in the Air. 6. The God of the Volcano. 7. Trail's End. 8. The Jaws of the Beast. 9. The Case of the Winds. 10. Wings of Fury. 11. Agents of Disaster. 12. The Sea Trap. 13. Mutiny. 14. Thunder Mountain.

567. Le Roi de la Pedale

(France—Gaumont, 1925) Serial, chapters (?). D: Maurice Champreux. S/Scen.: Paul Cartoux, Henri Decoin.

Georges Biscot, Blanche Montel, Bouboule, Jean Murat, Jeanne-Maiie Laurent, Charpentier, Emile Vervet, Georgette Lhéry.

568. The Romance of Elaine

(Wharton Prod. Co./Pathé, June 14, 1915) Serial, 12 chapters, two reels each. D: George B. Seitz, Joseph A. Golden, and Louis Gasnier. Scen: Charles W. Goddard, George B. Seitz, and Bertram Millhauser. S: Arthur B. Reeve. P: Leopold and Theodore Wharton. Camera: Joseph Dubray.

The plans of Marcus Del Mar, alias Doctor X, a foreign agent engaged in mining America's harbors and land bridges, include stealing the torpedo designs left by the assumed Craig Kennedy. These plans, however, are sorely interfered with by Elaine Dodge and Walter Jameson. Whenever Del Mar is about to overcome Elaine, a mystery figure constantly on Del Mar's trail rescues her.

The film concentrates exclusively on the invention of incredible plot situations. Little attention is given to direction, editing, or lighting. But its technical ineptitudes seemed not to matter. Pearl White's name was sufficient to make the film a financial success.

Pearl White (Elaine Dodge), Creighton Hale (Walter Jameson), Arnold Daly (Craig Kennedy), Lionel Barrymore (Marcus Del Mar/Doctor X), Bessie E. Wharton (Aunt Josephine), George B. Seitz.

1. The Lost Torpedo. 2. The Gray Friar. 3. The Vanishing Man. 4. The Submarine Harbor. 5. The Conspirators. 6. The Wireless Detective. 7. The Death Cloud. 8. The Search Light Gun. 9. The Life Chain. 10. The Flash. 11. The Disappearing Helmet. 12. The Triumph of Elaine.

Top: **Mala and Mamo Clark in *Robinson Crusoe of Clipper Island* (1936); *bottom*: Pearl White in *The Romance of Elaine* (1915)**

569. Rouletabille Chez Les Bohemiens

(France—Pathé-Consortium–Cinéma, 1922) Serial, 10 chapters. D: Henri Fescourt. Assist. D: Rene Barberis. Art Director: Louis Nalpas. S: Gaston Leroux. SP: Henri Fescourt.

Gabriel De Gravonne (Rouletabille), Joë Hamman (Hubert de Lauriac), Romuald Joube (Andréa), Edith Jehanne (Odette de Lavardens), Jean Dehelly (Jean de Santierne), Suzanne Talba (Calliste), Camille Steyaert (La vieille Zina), Louis Monfils (Le Juge d'Instruction), Ayra-Ben-Thar (La danseuse aux boas), Willy Jr. (Un petit garçon).

1. Le livre des ancêtres. 2. L'arrestation. 3. L' instruction. 4. La poursuite. 5. La page déchirée. 6. L'enlèvement. 7. [Unknown.] 8. Le signe. 9. Les noces. 10. Le châtiment.

570. The Royal Mounted Rides Again

(Universal, October 1945) Serial, 13 chapters, two reels each. D: Ray Taylor and Lewis D. Collins. SP: Joseph O'Donnell, Tom Gibson Harold C. Wire. P: Morgan Cox.

Two Canadian Mounties are assigned to investigate the murder of a mine operator by an outlaw gang attempting to gain possession of rich gold mines. A number of other killings occur before the operator of the Yukon Palace is discovered to be the leader of the outlaws.

George Dolenz (Corporal Frenchy), Bill Kennedy (Wayne Decker), Duan Kennedy (June Bailey), Paul E. Burns (Bucket), Milburn Stone (Taggart), Robert Armstrong (Price), Danny Morton (Dancer), Addison Richards (Jackson Decker), Tom Fadden (Lode MacKenzie), Joseph Hawarth (Bunker), Helen Bennett (Madame Mysterioso), Joseph Crehan (Sergeant Nelson), Selmer

Jackson (Superintendent MacDonald), Daral Hudson (Ladue), George Lloyd (Kent), George Eldredge (Grail), Rondo Hatton (Bull), William Haade (Archer), Dick Alexander (Outlaw), Lane Chandler (Outlaw), Guy Wilkerson (Townsman).

1. Canaska Gold. 2. The Avalanche Trap. 3. River of Fire. 4. Skyline Target. 5. Murder Toboggan. 6. Ore Car Accident. 7. Buckboard Runaway. 8. Thundering Water. 9. Dead Men for Decoys. 10. Derringer Death. 11. Night Trail Danger. 12. Twenty Dollar Doublecross. 13. Flaming Showdown.

571. Runaway June

(Reliance, January 13, 1915) Serial, 15 chapters, two reels each. D: Oscar Eagle. Scen: Marc Edward Jones. S: George Randolph Chester and Lillian Chester.

A foolish bride is unable to face a minor domestic crisis and runs away, getting into a lot more trouble than she ever thought about having at home.

A mediocre serial at best, *Runaway June* was a success because of a nationwide publicity campaign and a unique contest that allowed theater patrons to participate. Fifty-five winners were treated royally for a week at the Panama-Pacific Exposition in San Francisco and the San Diego Exposition. There was also a song composed to advertise the serial. Thus, the serial did turn a profit.

Norma Phillips (June Warner), J.W. Johnston (Ned Warner), Myra Brooks (Aunt Debby), Winifred Burke (Inis Blethering), Evelyn Dumo (Marie, the Maid), Arthur Donaldson (Gilbert Blyer), Elizabeth Drew (Mrs. Villard), Margaret Loveridge (Tommy Thomas), Ricca Allen (Hononia Blyer), Charles Mason (Charles Cunningham), Ezra Walck (Edwards), Grace Edy (Anna), George Marlo (Bobby Blethering).

1. The Runaway Bride. 2. The Man in the Black Van Dyke. 3. Discharged. 4. The New Governess. 5. A Woman in Trouble. 6. The Siege of the House of O'Keefe. 7. The Tormentors. 8. Her Enemies. 9. Kidnapped. 10. Trapped on the Liner. 11. In the Clutch of the River Thieves. 12. The Spirit of the Marsh. 13. Trapped. 14. In the Grip of Poverty. 15. At Last, My Love.

572. Rustlers of Red Dog

(Universal, January 21, 1935) Serial, 12 chapters, two reels each. D; Louis Friedlander (Lew Landers). S: Nathanial Eddy. SP: George Plympton, Basil Dickey, Ella O'Neill, Nate Gatzert, and Vim Moore.

Three pals, Jack, Deacon, and Laramie, undertake to protect a wagon train carrying a huge amount of gold in one of the wagons. Bandits are determined to steal the gold. Renegade Indians likewise cause the trio much trouble. Jack is persuaded to accept the job as town marshal of Nugget and is able to kill Rocky, leader of the gang, in a shootout during an attempted looting of the town.

Johnny Mack Brown (Jack Woods), Joyce Compton (Mary Lee), Walter Miller (Deacon), Raymond Hatton (Laramie), Harry Woods (Rocky), Frederic Mackaye (Snakey), Charles K. French (Tom Lee), Lafe McKee (Bob Lee), William Desmond (Ira Dale), J.P. McGowan (Captain Trent), Edmund Cobb (Buck), Bud Osborne (Jake), Monte Montague (Kruger), Jim Thorpe, Chief Thunderbird, Ann D'Arcy, Fritzi Burnette, Grace Cunard, Virginia Ainsworth, Iron Eyes Cody, Wally Wales [Hal Taliaferro], Cliff Lyons, Slim Whitaker, Chief Many Treaties, Art Mix, Jim Corey, Bob Card, Bill McCall, Jerry Frank, Al Ferguson, Hank Bell, Henry B. Carpenter, Eddie Bugard, Buddy Wacker, Bernadet Sebastian, Jack Rockwell, George Magrill, Frank McCarroll, John Ince, Charles Murphy, Ted Billings, Artie Ortego, Harry Harvey, Harry Tenbrook, B.J. Wilson, Nelson McDowell.

1. Hostile Redskins. 2. Flaming Arrows. 3. Thundering Hoofs. 4 Attack at Dawn. 5. Buried Alive. 6. Flames of Vengeance. 7. Into the Depths. 8. Paths of Peril. 9. The Snake Strike. 10. Riding Wild. 11. The Rustlers Clash. 12. Law and Order.

573. Ruth of the Range

(Ruth Roland Serials/Pathé, October 14, 1923) Serial, 15 chapters; Chapter 1, three reels; others, two reels. D: Ernest C. Warde, W.S. Van Dyke, Frank Leon Smith. SP: Frank Leon Smith, Gilson Willets. P: M.C. Levee.

This was a mediocre effort revolving about Ruth's attempts to free her father from a group that wished to steal his formula for making "Fuelite," a substitute for coal. Ruth was temperamental at this stage of her career. She tried unsuccessfully to get her leading man, Bruce Gordon, fired. Ernest Warde was not filming much action, leaning to close-ups of Ruth instead. Pathé replaced him with W.S. Van Dyke, but Van Dyke soon quit to take another job. Gilson Willets, the scenarist, died during production leaving no notes as to how the serial should end. Frank Leon Smith took over, created his own riddle around existing footage and characters, and finished the serial as director.

Roland decided she needed a vacation and took off with the last two chapters yet to shoot. Her stuntman, Bob Rose, put on a wig and doubled for her in order to wrap up filming. Pathé moguls were frustrated and angry, but Ruth was too valuable a star to let her go.

Ruth Roland (Ruth Remington), Bruce Gordon (Bruce Burton), Ernest C. Warde (Robert Remington), Andrée Peyre (Judith), Lorimer Johnson (Peter Van Dyke), Pat Harmon (Jim Stain), Harry De Vere (J. Hamilton Camp), V. Omar Whitehead (Captain X), Bob Rose (Roland's Double).

1. The Last Shot. 2 The Seething Pit. 3. The Danger Trail. 4. The Terror Trail. 5. The Temple Dungeon. 6. The Pitfall. 7. The Fatal Count. 8. The Dynamite Plot. 9. The Lava Crusher. 10. Circumstantial Evidence. 11. The Desert of Death. 12. The Vial Test. 13. The Molten Menace. 14. The First Freight. 15. Promises Fulfilled.

574. Ruth of the Rockies

(Pathé, August 29, 1920) Serial, 15 chapters, two reels each. D: George Marshall. S: Johnston McCulley—"Broadway Bab" SP: Frances Guihan.

A Broadway waitress flees westward after finding a trunk full of diamonds unclaimed by a thief. Al Hoxie, unbilled, did stunting for Ruth and other cast members, although Ruth usually used Bob Rose as her double for dangerous sequences. It was all strictly business to Ruth. She saw no need to take a chance if there was no money in it.

Ruth Roland (Bab Murphy), Herbert Heyes (Justin Garret), Thomas Lingham (Edward Dugan), Jack Rollens (Sam Wilkes), Fred Burns (Burton), William Gilliss (Pendleton Pete), Gilbert [Pee Wee] Holmes (Shorty), Al Hoxie (Double for

Roland), Harry Maynard, Norma Bichole, Madeline Fairchild, Captain S.J. Bingham.

1. The Mysterious Trunk. 2. The Inner Circle. 3. The Tower of Danger. 4. Between Two Fires. 5. Double Crossed. 6. The Eagle's Nest. 7. Troubled Waters. 8. Danger Trails. 9. The Perilous Path. 10. Outlawed. 11. The Fatal Diamond. 12. The Secret Order. 13. The Surprise Attack. 14. The Secret of Regina Island. 15. The Hidden Treasure.

***Top:* Ruth Roland and Herbert Heyes; *bottom:* Ruth Roland in *Ruth of the Rockies* (1920)**

575. The Santa Fe Trail

(Arrow Film Corp., July 15, 1923) Serial, 15 chapters, two reels each. D: Ashton Dearholt and Robert Dillon. S: Ben Wilson. SP: Robert Dillon. Supervision: Ben Wilson. P: Neva Gerber.

This was another historical serial based on actual characters and incidents. Opposing the hero and heroine is a desperate gambler who, together with his henchmen, leads them into hazardous situations. The hero and heroine are exposed both to the attacks of the villains and to the perils of early frontier life. A huge cache of gold, to which there is a map, serves as the object of struggle. There is a considerable amount of historical reality in the background, together with two-fister fighting, fast riding, and some corking Indian stuff.

There are, to be sure, a few historical lapses and anachronisms, but serial audiences are not likely to worry about these, since there is excitement, action, danger and romance in abundance.

Jack Perrin (Kit Carson), Neva Gerber, James Welch, Elias Bullock, Wilbur McGaugh, Clark B. Coffey, Jose De La Cruz, Maria Laredo.

1. Mystery of the Trail. 2. Kit Carson's Daring Ruse. 3. Wagon of Doom. 4. The Half-Breed's Treachery. 5. The Gauntlet of Death. 6. Ride for Life. 7. Chasm of Fate. 8. Pueblo of Death. 9. The Red Menace. 10. A Duel of Wits. 11. Buried Alive. 12. Cavern of Doom. 13. Scorching Sands. 14. Mission Bells. 15. End of the Trail.

576. The Scarlet Arrow

(Universal, June 4, 1928) Serial, 10 chapters, two reels each. D: Ray Taylor. Scen: Arthur Henry Gooden. S: Frank Howard Clark.

Pat Casey, entrusted with a secret government mission, is having a few drinks in the Northern Lights Saloon at the trading post when he sees Fay Varden, the hostess of the joint, and is captivated by her charms. His unwelcome advances cause a brawl which is quelled by Bob North, Captain of the North West Mounted Police.

Rodney Masterson, manager of the North Western Fur Company's local branch, is secret owner of the saloon. With his cohort Brodsky, he is planning to dispose of some of his company's furs. They are also trying to find part of a torn map which will show the way to the gold mine of Masterson's former friend, whose daughter Kathleen has been his ward since the mysterious death of her father some years before.

Bob North visits Masterson's store trying to trace the fur thieves and meets Kathleen. While talking with Masterson, he intercepts a message which arrives on an arrow. Masterson, realizing that North is dangerous in his plans, promises Kathleen as the reward if Brodsky will do away with him. Baptiste, the trapper, overhears this conversation and tells Kathleen, whom he devotedly loves, to come to him if ever she needs help.

Later Kathleen is speculating on the meaning of a piece of torn map she found in an old trunk. She is interrupted by Masterson who demands the map. She escapes and flees to Baptiste for aid, asking him to get Captain Bob. While waiting she is caught in a terrible forest fire, and is only saved from death when Bob rescues her.

Thus, Chapter 1 gets this thriller off to a rousing start.

Francis X. Bushman, Jr. (Bob North), Hazel Keener (Kathleen MacGregor), Edmund Cobb (Pierre Baptiste), Al Ferguson ("Wolf" Brodsky), Aileen Goodwin (Fay Varden), Henry Herbert (Rodney Masterson), Clark Comstock (The Hermit), Monte Montague.

1. Flames of Courage. 2. Thundering Death. 3. Desperate Men. 4. Wild Bullets. 5. The Cave of Hazard. 6. Plunge of Peril. 7. Fires of Vengeance. 8. Call of the Northland. 9. Guardians of the North. 10. Held by the Law.

Jack Perrin and Neva Gerber in *The Santa Fe Trail* (1923)

577. The Scarlet Brand

(New-Cal Film Corp., December 7, 1927) Serial, 10 chapters, two reels each. D: Neal Hart. SP: Arthur Henry Gooden. P: William Steiner.

Jim Fraser, owner of the Circle Dot Ranch, has been shot by a rustling gang with whom Bart Jackson, his foreman, is secretly in league. Neal Haley, a stranger from the West, learns the story and tries to assist Mary Fraser, and a series of struggles and exciting incidents take place. Haley eventually wins and establishes Mary's claim.

Neal Hart (Neal Haley), William Quinn (Bart Jackson), Lucille Irwin (Mary Fraser), Carmen LaRoux (Rita Valdez), Henry Britt (Jim Fraser), William Callen (Joe), Tom Wortham (Slim).

1. Wheels of Death. 2. Thundering Hoofs. 3. Waters of Doom. 4. The Battle in the Clouds. 5. Fatal Bullets. 6. Millions at Stake. 7. Desert Fury. 8. Pledge of Hate. 9. The Devil's Stampede. 10. The End of the Trail.

578. The Scarlet Horseman

(Universal, January 22, 1946) Serial, 13 chapters, two reels each. D: Ray Taylor and Lewis D. Collins. SP: Joseph O'Donnell, Patricia Harper, and Tom Gibson. P: Morgan Cox.

An undercover Texas agent, sent to quell an Indian uprising, assumes the identity of The Scarlet Horseman, the legendary champion of the Comanches whose leadership they respect and follow. In this disguise he is able to combat the mysterious traitor known as Matosca, who is kidnapping wives and daughters of Texas senators in an attempt to force the senators to support the partition of Texas and to give the Comanches the right to vote, thus assuring the villains control of the territory occupied by the Indians. Gun smuggler Zero Quick and Comanche renegade leader Loma ally themselves with Matosca. In a final showdown Carla Marquette, daughter of a discredited state senator, is revealed to be Matosca.

Peter Cookson (Kirk Norris), Paul Guilfoyle (Jim Bannion/The Scarlet Horseman), Victoria Horne (Loma), Virginia Christine (Carla Marquette/Matosca), Janet Shaw (Elise Halliday), Danny Morton (Ballou), Harold Goodwin (Idaho), Edward M. Howard (Zero Quick), Jack Ingram (Tragg), Edmund Cobb (Kyle), Helen Bennett (Mrs. Halliday), Cy Kendall (Amigo Manana), Guy Wilkerson (Panhandle), Al Woods (Senator Halliday), Fred Coby (Tioga), Ralph Lewis (Pecos), Frank Lackteen (Kahona), Jack Rockwell (Saunders), Rex Lease (Tom Leach), Marshall Reed (Dan), Mauritz Hugo (Senator Barnes), Ernie Adams, Budd Buster, Pierce Lyden, Hal Taliaferro, Ellen Corby, William Desmond.

1. Scarlet for a Champion. 2. Dry Grass Danger. 3. Railroad Rescue. 4. Staked Plains Stampede. 5. Death Shifts Passengers. 6. Stop that Stage. 7. Blunderbuss Broadside. 8. Scarlet Doublecross. 9. Doom Beyond the Door. 10. The Edge of Danger. 11. Comanche Avalanche. 12. Staked Plains Massacre. 13. Scarlet Showdown.

579. The Scarlet Runner

(Vitagraph, October 2, 1916) Series, 12 episodes. D: Wally Van and P.S. Earle. Scen: George H. Plympton. S: C.H. and A.M. Williamson. P: Wally Van and P.S. Earle.

The series derives its name from the high-powered automobile purchased by Christopher Race. It is a means of earning his living when deprived by his rich uncle of his allowance, of which apparently he had made poor use. Following his purchase of the car he enters the service of a king traveling in disguise and helps to defeat a plot through which a friend is about to meet his death. Other adventures follow, each a separate and unrelated story.

Each episode has a different cast except for the continuing role of Earle Williams.

***Top:* Earle Williams in *The Greater Vitagraph* (1926); *bottom:* Jack Daugherty in *The Scarlet Streak* (1926)**

Earle Williams (Christopher Race), Marguerite Blake (Lady Ivy), L. Rogers Lytton (Baron Von Hess), Charles Kent (James Race), Dorothy Kelly (Miss Collingwood), Leila Blow (Mrs. Collingwood), Donald Hall (Sir Gordon Race), Lillian Tucker (Mrs. Dauray), William Dunn (Fitzgerald), Kalman Matus (Prince Mirco), John Costello (Ambassador Rudovico), Ethel Corcoran (Volda Rudovico), Zena Keefe (Sidney Chester/ Dorothy Herbert), Helen Pilsbury (The Mother), Walter McGrail (Morley Chester), Raymond Walburn (John Brown), Betty Howe (The Girl), Nellie Anderson (Landlady), Arthur Robinson (Ean Van Courtlandt), Billie Billings (Miss Warren),Thomas R. Mills (Tom Astley), Julia Swayne Gordon (Mme. Du Gueselin), Arthur Lehrman (Raoul), Don Cameron (Maurice Naylor), Gypsy O'Brien (Violet Hardcastle), Herbert Stanley (Fergus O'Neill), John Robertson (Paul Western), Grace Valentine (Grace Norwood), Richard Wangerman (Grace Norwood's Uncle), Edith Storey (Dorothy Herbert), Jean Stuart, Alex Kyle, Josephine Earle, Harold Forshay, Garry McGarry, Templar Saxe, Gordon Gray, Adolphe Menjou, Wally Van, Hattie De Laro, William Green, Anna Brody, Edward Elkas, Emanuel Turner.

1. The Car and His Majesty. 2. The Nurenberg Watch. 3. The Masked Ball. 4. The Hidden Prince. 5. The Jacobean House. 6. The Mysterious Motor Car. 7. The Red Whiskered Man. 8. The Glove and the Ring. 9. The Gold Cigarette Case. 10. The Lost Girl. 11. The Missing Chapter. 12. The Car and the Girl.

580. The Scarlet Streak

(Universal, December 20, 1925) Serial, 10 chapters, two reels each. D: Henry McRae. S: Leigh Jacobson—"Dangers of the Deep."

Professor Crawford has invented a doomsday machine called the "Scarlet Ray." Foreign agents bent on stealing it kidnap Mary, the professor's daughter. Bob Evans, a newspaper reporter, volunteers help to get her back. The tide turns one way, then the other, but in the end the machine is destroyed, the criminals are captured, and romance flourishes.

Jack Daugherty (Bob Evans), Lola Todd (Mary Crawford), John Elliott (Richard Crawford), Albert J. Smith (Count "K"), Al Prisco (Monk), Virginia Ainsworth (Leontine), Monte Montague (Butler).

1. The Face in the Crowd. 2. Masks and Men. 3. The Rope of Hazard. 4. The Death Ray. 5. The Lost Story. 6. The Plunge of Peril. 7. The Race of Terror. 8. The Cable of Courage. 9. The Dive of Death. 10. Universal Peace.

581. Scotty of the Scouts

(Rayart, September, 1926) Serial, 10 chapters, two reels each. D: Duke Worne.

The bone of contention here seems to be a valuable historic document stolen from the national museum. Scotty takes charge and pursues the quarry with a ruthlessness remarkable for one of his years, and he is undaunted by being blown up in a motor boat, a drop from sky to sea in a wrecked airplane, or a single-handed fight with several grown men. Now and again Scotty's scout friends rally to his aid. Finally, the document is recovered and the villains brought to justice.

Ben Alexander (Scotty Smith), Paddy O'Flynn (Tom Gallagher), Mary Jane Irving (Mary Andrews), Ben Hall (Charles Tennyson), Frank Baker (Millard Wilson), Albert J. Smith (Eric Jandrau), Edna May Cooper (Effie Middleton), Sam Lufkin (Jenkins).

(Titles were translated from the Portuguese titles).
1. Straight as the Justice. 2. In the Claws of Death. 3. The Death Diving. 4. Scouts' Bravery. 5. The Road of Danger. 6. Treacherous Waters. 7. In the Hands of Destiny. 8. Quicksand. 9. The Race of Death. 10. Scouts' Justice.

582. Scouts to the Rescue

(Universal, January [?] 1939) Serial, 12 chapters, two reels each. D: Ray Taylor and Alan James. SP: Wyndham Gittens, George Plympton, Basil Dickey, and Joseph Poland. S: Irving Crump.

Scouts become involved in the search for counterfeiters when they rescue a G-man from a plane crash in the wilds and find a large sum of counterfeit money. As things turn out, the father of one scout is implicated in the counterfeiting and is arrested by the G-man, only to escape. The scouts attempt to prove the man innocent, but in the process are imperiled by a gang of marauding Indians.

Jackie Cooper (Bruce Scott), Vondell Darr (Mary Scanlon), Edwin Stanley (Pat Scanlon), William Ruhl (Hal Marvin), Bill Cody, Jr. (Skeets Scanlon), David Durand (Rip Dawson), Ralph Dunn (Pug O'Toole), Jason Robards, Sr. (Doc), Frank Coghlan, Jr. (Ken), Ivan Miller (Turk Mortenson), Victor Adams (Hurst), Sidney Miller (Hermie), Dick Botiller (Leeka).

1. Death Rides the Air. 2. Avalanche of Doom. 3. Trapped by the Indians. 4. River of Doom. 5. Descending Doom. 6. Ghost Town Menace. 7. Destroyed by Dynamite. 8. Thundering Hoofs! 9. The Fire God Strikes. 10. The Battle at Ghost Town. 11. Hurtling Through Space. 12. The Boy Scouts' Triumph.

583. The Screaming Shadow

(Hallmark, February 1920) Serial, 15 chapters, two reels each. D: Duke Worne and Ben Wilson. S: J. Grubb Alexander and Harvey Gates. P: Frank G. Hall.

A scientist learns how to prolong human life through substitution of monkey glands and maintains an army of half-ape creatures who steal bodies to provide the glands to keep him young. John Rand is engaged in similar experiments to determine if monkey glands bring about longevity. The theory of this monkey gland process and its effect is brought out in a series of bizarre dramatic episodes. Press agents had a field day in what must have been the most sure-fire ad campaign ever run. "See this picture and learn how to live forever."

Ben Wilson (John Rand), Neva Gerber (Mary Landers), Frances Terry (Nadia), Howard Crampton (J.W. Russell), Joseph Girard (Baron Velska), William Dyer, William Carroll, Fred Gamble, P. Porter, Claire Mille, Joseph Manning.

1. A Cry in the Dark. 2. The Virgin of Death. 3. The Fang of the Beast. 4. The Black Seven. 5. The Vapor of Death. 6. The Hidden Menace. 7. Into the Depths. 8. The White Terror. 9. The Sleeping Death. 10. The Prey of Mong. 11. Liquid Fire. 12. Cold Steel. 13. The Fourth Symbol. 14. Entombed Alive. 15. Unmasked.

584. The Sea Hound

(Columbia, September 1947) Serial, 15 chapters, two reels each. D: Walter B. Eason and Mack Wright. SP: George H. Plympton, Lewis Clay, and Arthur Hoerl. Based on the radio program and comic magazine feature. P: Sam Katzman. Photography: Ira H. Morgan. Music: Mischa Bakaleinikoff.

Captain Silver and his crew, along with newly acquired friends, oppose a ruthless sea robber known as The Admiral, who poses as a trader and rubber planter but who is really after

Top: **Francis X. Bushman, Jr. in *The Scarlet Streak* (1926); *bottom:* Jackie Cooper and David Durand in *Scouts to the Rescue* (1939)**

Spanish gold that originally went down with a galleon. Ann Whitney's father is the key to the location of the gold, which has been removed from the sunken vessel, but he is captive of first The Admiral, then the island natives. Captain Silver is able to reunite father and daughter, obtain the treasure, and dispose of the would-be pirates.

Buster Crabbe (Captain Silver), James Lloyd (Tex), Pamela Blake (Ann Whitney), Ralph Hodges (Jerry), Spencer Chan (Kukai), Robert Barron (The Admiral), Hugh Prosser (Stanley Rand), Rick Vallin (Manila Pete), Jack Ingram (Murdock), Milton Kibbee (John Whitney), Al Baffert (Lon), Stanley Blystone (Black Mike), Robert Duncan (Sloan), Pierce Lyden (Vardman), Rusty Wescoatt (Singapore Manson), Emmett Lynn (Van Wart), William Fawcett (Andre), Delmar Costello (Malaya Jim), Tony Balbuena (Naylah).

1. Captain Silver Sails Again. 2. Spanish Gold. 3. The

Mystery of the Map. 4. Menaced by Ryaka. 5. Captain Silver's Strategy. 6. The Sea Hound at Bay. 7. In the Admiral's Lair. 8. Rand's Treachery. 9. On the Water Front. 10. On the Treasure Trail. 11. Sea Hound Attacked. 12. Dangerous Waters. 13. The Panther's Prey. 14. The Fatal Doublecross. 15. Captain Silver's Last Stand.

585. Sea Raiders

(Universal, 1941) Serial, 12 chapters, two reels each. D: Ford Beebe and John Rawlins. AP: Henry McRae. SP: Clarence Upson Young and Paul Huston.

"Sea Raiders" were foreign agents trying to steal a new type of torpedo boat. Billy and Toby are stowaways on a freighter that Elliott Carlton and Carl Tonjes, leaders of the Sea Raiders, have ordered blown up. The boys are rescued by their courageous pals. Together they find the Sea Raiders' island hideout and set out to investigate the saboteurs' underground arsenal on the seacoast. The chief of the band ruthlessly detonates the explosives stored in the arsenal.

Imprisoned by the explosion of the underground arsenal, Billy and Toby are rescued by Brack Warren, harbor police officer. Brack and Billy don the uniforms of captured Sea Raiders and board a yacht that serves as headquarters for the Raiders. They set off a secret bomb device which destroys Tonjes and his henchmen.

Billy Halop (Billy Adams), Huntz Hall (Toby Nelson), Gabriel Dell (Bilge), Benard Punsley (Butch), Hally Chester (Swab), Joe Recht (Lug), William Hall (Brack Warren), John McGuire (Tom Adams), Mary Field (Aggie Nelson), Edward Keane (Elliott Carlton), Marcia Ralston (Leah Carlton), Reed Hadley (Carl Tonjes), Stanley Blystone (Captain Olaf Nelson), Richard Alexander (Jenkins), Ernie Adams (Zeke), Jack Clifford (Anderson), Richard Bond (Krans), Morgan Wallace (Captain Lester), Eddie Dunn (Captain Meredith), Forrest Taylor (Nazi Scientist).

1. The Raider Strikes. 2. Flaming Torture. 3. The Tragic Crash. 4. The Raider Strikes Again. 5. Flames of Fury. 6. Blasted from the Air. 7. Victims of the Storm. 8. Dragged to Their Doom. 9. Battling the Sea Beast. 10. Periled by a Panther. 11. Entombed in the Tunnel. 12. Paying the Penalty.

586. Secret Agent X-9

(Universal, February 11, 1937) Serial, 12 chapters, two reels each. D: Ford Beebe and Cliff Smith. SP: Wyndham Gittens, Norman S. Hall, Ray Trampe, and Leslie Charteris. Character created by Dashiell Hammett. Assoc. P: Henry McRae.

Secret Agent X-9 is assigned to recover the crown jewels of Belgravia, and is ably assisted by Shara Graustark. A notorious jewel thief proves to be Blackstone, a well-known criminal, and the mastermind behind the jewel robberies.

Top left: **Milt Kibbe, Pamela Blake and Buster Crabbe in *The Sea Hound* (1947); *bottom left:* Scott Kolk in *Secret Agent X-9* (1937)**

Scott Kolk [Scott Colton] (Secret Agent X-9), Jean Rogers (Shara Graustark), Henry Hunter (Tommy Dawson), David Oliver (Pidge), Larry Blake (Wheeler), Monte Blue (Baron Michael Karsten), Henry Brandon (Blackstone), Lon Chaney, Jr. (Maroni), Max Hoffman, Jr. (Marker), Bentley Hewlett (Scarlett), George Shelley (Packard), Robert Dalton (Thurston), Leonard Lord (Ransom), Robert Kortman (Trader Delaney), Edward Piel, Sr. (The Fence), Lynn Gilbert (Rose), Jack Cheatham, Eddy Waller.

1. Modern Pirates. 2. The Ray that Blinds. 3. The Man of Many Faces. 4. The Listening Shadow. 5. False Fire. 6. The Dragnet. 7. Sealed Lips. 8. Exhibit A. 9. The Masquerader. 10. The Forced Lie. 11. The Enemy Camp. 12. Crime Does Not Pay.

587. Secret Agent X-9

(Universal, August 1945) Serial, 13 chapters, two reels each. D: Ray Taylor and Lewis D. Collins. SP: Joseph O'Donnell and Patricia Harper. S: Joseph O'Donnell and Harold C. Wire.

U.S. Secret Agent X-9, along with agents from Austria and China, battle the Japanese Black Dragon Intelligence Service headed by Japan's top female spy, Nabura. The Japanese wish to steal a secret formula for synthetic fuel and are operating from a base on Shadow Island, off the coast of China.

Lloyd Bridges (Secret Agent X-9), Keye Luke (Ah Fong), Jan Wiley (Lynn Moore), Victoria Horne (Nabura), Samuel S. Hinds (Solo), Cy Kendall (Lucky Number), Jack Overman (Marker), George Lynn (Bach), Clarence Lung (Takahari), Benson Fong (Hakahima), Arno Frey (Kapitan Graf), Gene Stutenroth (Yogel), Ann Codee (Mama Pierre), Edward M. Howard (Drag Dorgan), Edmund Cobb (Bartender), I. Stanford Jolley (Trent), John Merton (Parker), Jack Clifford (Pete), Budd Buster (Mace), Jack Rockwell (Henchman), Roger Cole (Henchman), Sayre Dearing (Henchman), Ferdinand Munier (Papa Pierre), Mauritz Hugo (Garr), Dick Scott (Miley), Bob Chinn, Angel Cruz, Albert Law (Japanese Sailors), George Chesebro (Test Man), Jack Cheatham (Constable), Carey Harrison (Constable), James Leong (Japanese Pilot), Rogue Esperitu (Japanese Pilot), Ted Hecht (Doctor Harold), Beal Wong (Korakaga), George Chung (Radio Operator), Leon Lontoc (Tichi), Paul Fung (Kanato), Joseph Kim (Saki), George Eldredge (Browder), Carey Loftin (Charlie), Tony Ellis (James), Hunan Elliott (Radio Operator), Nick Warwick (Haney), Henry Wadsworth (Roberts), Charles Miller (Blanchard), George Reynolds (Wiley), Luke Chan (Japanese Announcer), Charles Sullivan (Port Guard), Perc Launders (Messenger), John Roy (Lou), Eddie Hart (Sailor), Lee Fung (Sailor), Ed Luke (Sailor), Stanley Price (Duke),

1. Torpedo Rendezvous. 2. Ringed by Fire. 3. Death Curve. 4. Floodlight Murder. 5. Doom Downgrade. 6. Strafed by a Zero. 7. High Pressure Deadline. 8. The Dropping Floor. 9. The Danger Point. 10. Japanese Burial. 11. Fireworks for Deadmen. 12. Big Gun Fusillade. 13. Zero Minutes.

588. The Secret Code

(Columbia, September, 1942) Serial, 15 chapters, two reels each. D: Spencer G. Bennet. SP: Basil Dickey, Leighton Brill, Robert Beche. P: Larry Darmour. Assist. D: Carl Hiecke. Photography: James S. Brown, Jr. Music: Lee Zahler. Released in feature form in England.

Police Lieutenant Dan Barton arranges to have himself thrown off the force in disgrace as first step in his effort to smash an enemy spy ring led by Thyssen. Thyssen has just learned from Feldon, newly arrived from Berlin with a secret spy code, that the U.S. government has a top-secret formula for manufacturing synthetic rubber. When he assaults a government official while trying to "steal" the formula, Barton is captured by Thyssen and Feldon. He learns their plans for stealing the formula and then escapes to his rooms, where his girlfriend, reporter Jean Ashley is waiting. Dressed in a "Black Commando" suit—a black-hooded, tight fitting outfit—Barton goes forth to prevent the saboteurs from stealing the secret formula. The Black Commando braved a usual assortment of serial perils: an exploding building, a plunging airplane, bolts of dancing electricity, etc.

Paul Kelly (Dan Barton, Police Lieutenant), Anne Nagel (Jean Ashley, Reporter), Clancy Cooper (Pat Flanigan), Trevor Bardette (Jensen), Robert O. Davis (Thyssen), Gregory Gay (Feldon), Louis Donath (Metzgar), Eddie Parker (Berck), Beal Wong (Quito), Jacqueline Dalya (Linda), Alex Callam (Hogan), Eddie Woods (Kurt), Lester Dorr (Stahl), Franklyn Farnum (?).

1. Enemy Passport. 2. The Shadow of the Swastika. 3. Nerve Gas. 4. The Sea Spy Strikes. 5. Wireless Warning. 6. Flaming Oil. 7. Submarine Signal. 8. The Missing Key. 9. The Radio Bomb. 10. Blind Bombardment. 11. Ears of the Enemy. 12. Scourge of the Orient. 13. Pawn of the Spy Ring. 14. Dead Men of the Deep. 15. The Secret Code Smashed.

589. The Secret Four

(Universal, December 19, 1921) Serial, 15 chapters, two reels each. D: Albert Russell and Perry Vekroff. Scen: Anthony W. Coldeway. S: Anthony W. Coldeway.

No information on the story line. This was Polo's last Universal serial. There had been some changes in executive personnel which were not to Eddie's liking. He left to form his own Star Serial Company.

Eddie Polo in *The Secret Four* (1921)

Eddie Polo, Kathleen Myers, Doris Dean, Hal Wilson, William Welsh, Thelma Daniels.

1. Behind the Mask. 2. The House of Intrigue. 3. Across the Chasm. 4. The Dive of Despair. 5. Black Waters. 6. The Highway of Fate. 7. The Creeping Doom. 8. The Flaming Forrest. 9. The Fight in the Dark. 10. The Burning Pit. 11. The Stampede of Death. 12. Floods of Fury. 13. The Man Trap. 14. The Hour of 12. 15. Black Gold.

590. The Secret Kingdom

(Vitagraph, January 1, 1917) Serial, 15 chapters; Chapter 1, three reels; others, two reels. D: Theodore Marston and Charles J. Brabin. Scen: Basil Dickey. S: Louis J. Vance.

Top: **Lamar Johnson and Hylda Hollis in *The Secret of the Submarine* (1916); *bottom:* Don Terry, and William Desmond in *The Secret of Treasure Island* (1938)**

Crown Prince Phillip of Alonia is whisked away to America as a baby to prevent his murder. Prime Minister Simond had caused the assassination of both the boy's parents and taken over the throne. Two decades later the crown prince, having grown up as Phil Barr of the U.S.A., saves the life of Julia, daughter of Prince Simond. The prince, learning the identity of Phil, sends Madame Savatz to kill him but fails. Phil eventually establishes his birthright and wins the throne and Julia, with Prince Simond and Madame Savatz getting their just deserts. The Graustarkian film's location alternated between the mythical kingdom and the American West.

Charles Richman (Phil Barr/King Phillip), Dorothy Kelly (Princess Julia), Arline Pretty (Madame Savatz), William Dunn (Juan), Joseph Kilgour (Prime Minister Simond), De Jalma West (Count Ramon), Ned Finley, Charles Wellesley, Robert Whitworth.

1. Land of the Intrigue. 2. Royalty at Red Wing. 3. Sealed Packet. 4. Honorable Mr. Oxenham. 5. Carriage Call #101. 6. Human Flotsam. 7. Ghost Ship. 8. Rum Bay. 9. Swamp Adder. 10. A Goat Without Horns. 11. The White Witch. 12. The Shark's Nest. 13. The Tragic Masque. 14. The Portrait of a King. 15. The Tocsin.

591. The Secret of the Submarine

(American, March 1916) Serial, 15 chapters. D: George L. Sargent. Scen: C.C. Hoadley and William Parker. S: Russell E. Smith.

Dr. Ralph Burke, a scientist and inventor, perfects an apparatus enabling submarine craft to remain under water indefinitely without relying wholly upon compressed air stored in the boat. Lieutenant Jarvis Hope, U.S.N. is dispatched to witness a practical demonstration of the invention. Arriving in the city where Dr. Burke lives, Lieutenant Hope meets an old acquaintance, Hook Barnacle, whose life he once save. Hook had his right hand bitten off by a shark and an iron hook being substituted gained for him the odd sobriquet. Hood escorts the lieutenant to the Burke home and relates to Cleo, the doctor's daughter, how his life had been saved by the young naval officer. Cleo and Hope become mutually interested.

Dr. Burke is killed and various individuals and governments attempt to gain the secret of the doctor's invention. Lieutenant Hope, with the help of Cleo, with whom he has fallen in love, strives to get the secret for the U.S. Navy.

Juanita Hansen (Cleo Burke), Thomas Chatterton (Lieutenant Jarvis Hope), George Clancy (Hook Barnacle), Lamar Johnstone (Gerald Morton), George Webb (Mahlin), Hylda Hollis (Olga Ivanoff), William Tedmarsh (Satsuma), Harry Edmundson (Sextus), Hugh Bennett (Dr. Ralph Burke), Joseph Beaudry (Calvin Montgomery), Perry Banks, Leona Hutton, George Gebhart.

592. The Secret of Treasure Island

(Columbia, March 1938) Serial, 15 chapters, two reels each. D: Elmer

Clifton. SP: George Rosener, Elmer Clifton, and George Merrick. S: L. Ron Hubbard. Assist. D: Adrian Weiss. Assoc. P: Louis Weiss. P: Jack Fier. Photography: Edward Linden, Herman Schopp. Music: Abe Meyer. Special Effects: Ken Peach, Earl Bunn.

Carter Collins, The Shark, takes possession of an island reputed to contain hidden pirate treasure. Fortifying the island, he systematically seeks the gold and the remaining portion of the original location map. Reporter Larry Kent and his girl friend Toni Morrell decide to investigate the island and search for the gold.

Don Terry (Larry Kent), Gwen Gaze (Toni Morrell), Grant Withers (Grindley), Hobart Bosworth (Doctor X), William Farnum (Westmore), Walter Miller (Carter Collins/The Shark), George Rosener (Captain Cuttle), Dave O'Brien (Jameson), Yakima Canutt (Dreer), Warner Richmond (Captain Faxton), William Royle (Paul Thorndyke), Sandra Karina (Zanya), Joe Caits (Saltwater Jerry/Mole Man), Colin Campbell (Hawkins), Patrick J. Kelly (Professor), Frank Lackteen (Pedro), Edward Cassidy (Dolphin Captain), Josef Swickard (Ship's Doctor), Harry Harvey, Reed Howes, Louis Caits (Cortez Heavies), Clara Kimball Young (Cortez Woman), Blackie Whiteford (Mainland Henchman), Joe Girard (Newspaperman), Harry Burns (Pirate).

1. The Isle of Fear. 2. The Ghost Talks. 3. The Phantom Duel. 4. Buried Alive. 5. The Girl Who Vanished. 6. Trapped by the Flood. 7. The Cannon Roars. 8. The Circle of Death. 9. The Pirate's Revenge. 10. The Crash. 11. Dynamite. 12. The Bridge of Doom. 13. The Mad Flight. 14. The Jaws of Destruction. 15. Justice.

593. Secret Service in Darkest Africa

(Republic, August 1943) Serial, 15 chapters, two reels each. Feature title: *The Baron's African War*. Re-released in 1954 as serial titled *Man Hunt in the African Jungle*. D: Spencer Bennet. SP: Roy Cole, Basil Dickey, Jesse Duffy, Ronald Davidson, Joseph O'Donnell, and Joseph Poland. Assoc. P: W.J. O'Sullivan. Photography: William Bradford. Music: Mort Glickman. Special Effects: Howard Lydecker.

Nazi agents try to gain the support of African Arabs by deceiving them about the Dagger of Solomon and a forged scroll purported to be written by an ancient leader revered by the Arabs. Rex Bennett, an undercover agent, makes off with the symbols before the Nazis can use them. A running battle for possession of the supposedly valuable tokens ensues, with the Nazis enjoying some advantage through the undetected substitution of one of their own men for the Arab leader Sultan Abou Ben Ali, whom they have kidnapped. However, Rex is aided by French officer Pierre LaSalle and United Nations agent Janet Blake, and the tide is ultimately turned in their favor. The Nazi spy operation in North Africa is completely shattered.

Rod Cameron (Rex Bennett), Joan Marsh (Janet Blake), Duncan Renaldo (Pierre LaSalle), Lionel Royce (Sultan Abou Ben Ali/Baron Von Rommier), Kurt Kreuger (Ernst Muller), Frederic Brunn (Wolfe), Sigfrid Tor (Luger), Georges Renavent (Armand), Kurt Katch (Kurt Hauptmann), Ralf Harolde (Riverboat Captain), William Vaughn (Boschart), Reed Howes (American Officer) (Carey Loftin (Arab/Workman), George DeNormand (Elmir), Eddie Parker (Karl Koche/Café Heavy), Joe Yrigoyen (Arab/Wallah/Heavy), Buddy Roosevelt (Sniper), John Davidson (Sheik), Jack O'Shea (Marga), George J. Lewis (Kaba), Duke Green (Karl/Rama), Norman Nesbitt (Radio Announcer), Ken Terrell (Ahmed Ali), Frank Alten (Schloss), Emily LaRue (Zara), William Yetter (Commandant), Hans Von Morhart (Sub First Officer), Erwin Goldi (Colonel Von Raeder), John Royce (German Officer), John Bleifer (Kasar), Augie Gomez (M-23), Frederic Worlock (James Langley), Paul Marion (Abdul), Eddie Phillips (Bisra), Bud Geary (Blacksmith), Tom Steele (Heavy), John Daheim (Heavy), Harry Semels (Digger), Leonard Hampton (Digger), George Sorel (Doctor), Walter Fenner (Fedallah), Jacques Lory (Fireman), Ed Agresti (French Soldier), Jack Chefe (French Soldier), Charles LaTorre (Sufi), Nino Bellini (Supply Officer), George Magrill.

1. North African Intrigue. 2. The Charred Witness. 3. Double Death. 4. The Open Grave. 5. Cloaked in Flame. 6. Dial of Doom. 7. Murder Dungeon. 8. Funeral Arrangements Completed. 9. Invisible Menace. 10. Racing Peril. 11. Lightning Terror. 12. Ceremonial Execution. 13. Fatal Leap. 14. Victim of Villainy. 15. Nazi Treachery Unmasked.

594. Secret Service Saunders

(Rayart, May 1, 1925) Serial, 15 chapters, two reels each. D: Duke Worne. Scen: Robert Dillon. P: Ashton Dearholt [Richard Holt]

This independent serial turned out to be an embarrassment for all concerned. It was that bad. What the story is about is not known, although it obviously involved the Secret Service. It turned out to be Ann Little's last screen appearance.

Richard Holt (Richard Saunders), Ann Little (Ann Walters), Helen Broneau (Celeste Treavors), Clark Goffy, Frank Baker, Pierre Coudre, Ellis Houston.

1. The Plunge of Doom. 2. The Brink of Eternity. 3. Race of Death. 4. The Path of Peril. 5. Thundering Hoofs. 6. River of Dread. 7. Curse of Gold. 8. Tunnel of Horror. 9. Doomed. 10. Heritage of Hate. 11. The Brink of Despair. 12. Blasted Hopes. 13. Flames of Vengeance. 14. Destruction Bound. 15. The Final Reckoning.

595. La Secta de los Misteriosos

(Spain—Hispano Films) Serial, 3 chapters. D: Alberto Marro.

José Durany, Joaquin Carrasco, Helena Bernis, Francisco Aguilló, Emilia De La Mata, Alicia Ventura, Francisco Carrasco.

Spanish: 1. Los misteriosos. 2. La leyenda mora. 3. Los tesoros de la sultana. *Portugeuse:* 1. Os misteriosos. 2. A tortura das lanças de aço. 3. A lenda moura. 4. O mouro degolado. 5. O tesouro do sultão. 6. A corrente misteriosa.

596. Le Sept de Trefle

(France, 1918) Serial, 12 chapters. D: Rene Navarre.

René Navarre, Gina Manes, Henry Bose, Jacqueline Arly.

597. The Sequel to the Diamond from the Sky

(American/Mutual, November 27, 1916) Serial, 4 chapters, two reels each. D: Edward Sloman. Scen: Terry Ramsaye. Film also released as an eight-reel feature.

A continuation of *The Diamond from the Sky* (1915). Esther and Arthur are accidentally killed in a train wreck, leaving an orphaned baby son and the diamond, which is quickly stolen.

William Russell (Arthur), Rhea Mitchell (Esther Stanley),

Charlotte Burton, William Tedmarsh, Orral Humphrey, Vivian Marston, Blair Stanley, Ward McAllister, Dodo Newton.

1. Fate and Death. 2. Under Oath. 3. Sealed Lips. 4. The Climax.

598. The Seven Deadly Sins

(McClure/Triangle, 1917) Series, 7 episodes, 1–6 five reels; 7, seven reels.

This series is an exception to the author's intention not to cover feature films. Each film is a separate drama but each represents one of the seven deadly sins, and each has the characters of Adam and Eve represented in some capacity within the story. All of the films were based on stories from *The Ladies World* magazine. Entire series re-issued in 1918 in two-reel installments.

Envy. D: Richard Ridgeley. Released: January 20, 1917. Anna Murdock (Betty Howard), Shirley Mason (Eve Leslie), George Le Guere (Adam Moore), Lumsden Hare (Stanton Skinner).

Pride. D: Richard Ridgeley. Released: February 5, 1917. Shirley Mason (Eve Leslie), George Le Guere (Adam Moore), Helen Strickland (Miss Nelson Blanchard), Guido Colucci (Le Comte de Frais).

Passion. D: Richard Ridgeley. Released: February 26, 1917. Shirley Mason (Eve Leslie), George Le Guere (Adam Moore), Mabel Strickland (Aunt Annie), Clifford Bruce (Leonidas).

Greed. D: Theodore Marston. Released: February 12, 1917. Shirley Mason (Eve Leslie), George Le Guere (Adam Moore), Nance O'Neil (Alma), Alfred Hickman (Jimmie Hobson).

Wrath. D: Theodore Marston. Released: March 5, 1917. Shirley Mason (Ever Leslie), George Le Guere (Adam Moore), H.B. Warner (Feodor/The Grand Duke), Edith Hallar (Evelyn Burnham).

Sloth. D: Theodore Marston. Released: February 19, 1917. Shirley Mason (Eve Leslie), George Le Guere (Adam Moore), Charlotte Walker (Margaret Brent/Molly Pitcher/Sally Wells), Jack Meredith (Ingles).

The Seventh Sin (Selfishness). Shirley Mason (Eve Leslie), George Le Guere (Adam Moore), Ann Murdock (Betty Howard), H.B. Warner (Feodor/ The Grand Duke).

Victor Jory in *The Shadow* (1940)

599. The Seven Pearls

(Astra Film Corp./Pathé, September 16, 1917) Serial, 15 chapters, one reel each. D: Burton L. King (first 5 chapters), Donald McKenzie (last 10 chapters). S: Charles W. Goddard. SP: George B. Seitz.

Ilma Bay and her boyfriend Harry Drake must recover pearls taken by Harry from a necklace belonging to a Turkish Sultan, or Ilma must become a member of the Sultan's harem. Ilma's father is held captive pending Ilma's return at the end of six months. Perry Mason wants the pearls for himself and hampers efforts of Ilma and Harry to find them.

Mollie King (Ilma Bay), Creighton Hale (Harry Drake), Leon Bary (Perry Mason), John J. Dunn (Grady), Henry G. Sell (Handsome Jack), Floyd Buckley, Walter P. Lewis.

1. The Sultan's Necklace. 2. The Bowstring. 3. The Air Peril. 4. Amid the Clouds. 5. Between Fire and Water. 6. The Abandoned Mine. 7. The False Pearl. 8. The Man Trap. 9. The Message on the Wire. 10. The Hold-Up. 11. Gems of Jeopardy. 12. Buried Alive. 13. Over the Falls. 14. The Tower of Death. 15. The Seventh Pearl.

600. Sexton Blake

(England—British Filmcraft, 1928) Series, episodes undetermined. D: George A. Cooper, Leslie Eveleigh, George L. Banfield (different segments).

Langshorne Burton (Sexton Blake), Mickey Brontford, Mrs. Fred Emney, Fred Raynham, Leslie Perrin, Gabrielle Morton, Ronald Curtin, Roy Travers, Thelma Murray, Roy Raymond, Frank Atherly, Adeline Coffin, Marjorie Hume.

1. Blake, the Lawbreaker. 2. The Clue of the Second Goblet. 3. The Great Office Mystery. 4. Mystery of the Silent Death. 5. Sexton Blake, Gambler. 6. Silken Threads.

The silent era saw many films about British detective Sexton Blake. Several were feature-length but most were shorts. Sexton Blake movies continued to be made well into the sound era. C. Douglas Carlile starred as Sexton Blake in four of the following films (probably one-reelers) made in England by London Cinematograph/Gaumont:

1. Sexton Blake (1909). D/Scen: C. Douglas Carlile. 2. The Council of Three (1909). D/Scen: S. Wormald. 3. The Jewel Thieves Run to Earth (1919). 4. Lady Candale's Diamonds (1919). D/Scen: S. Workald. 5. The Kaiser's Spies (1914). D: Charles Raymond; Sexton Blake, ? 6. Britain's Secret Treaty (1914). D: Charles Raymond; Sexton Blake, ?

601. The Shadow

(Columbia, 1940) Serial, 15 chapters, two reels each. D: James W. Horne. SP: Joseph Poland, Ned Dandy, and Joseph O'Donnell. Adapted from the Shadow radio program on the Mutual Network. Based upon stories appearing in *Shadow Magazine*. P: Larry Darmour. Photography: James S. Brown, Jr. Music: Lee Zahler. Assist. D: Carl Hiecke. Sound: Tom Lambert.

A well-organized criminal group, headed by an unidentified criminal known as The Black Tiger, menaces the economic life of the city. Industrial leaders prevail upon criminologist Lamont Cranston, secretly The Shadow, to combat this menace. The handling of Maxwell Grant's invisible hero was poor and the serial was disappointing, although Jory was an excellent choice for the hero.

Victor Jory (The Shadow/Lamont Cranston/Lin Chang), Veda Ann Borg (Margot Lane), Robert Moore (Harry Vincent), Robert Fiske (Turner), J. Paul Jones (Stanford Marshall), Jack Ingram (Flint), Charles Hamilton (Roberts), Edward Piel, Sr. (Inspector Cardona), Frank LaRue (Commissioner Ralph Weston), Charles King (Russell), Eddie Featherstone (Williams), Lewis Sargent, Dick Botellier, Griff Barnett, Kit Guard, Philip Ahn, Charles K. French. Marin Sais, Franklyn Farnum, Frank Hagney, Jack Perrin, Lloyd Ingraham, Constantine Romanoff, Charles Sullivan, George DeNormand, Joe Caits.

1. Doomed City. 2. The Shadow Attacks. 3. The Shadow's Peril. 4. In the Tiger's Lair. 5. Danger Above. 6. The Shadow's Trap. 7. Where Horror Waits. 8. The Shadow Rides the Rails. 9. The Devil in White. 10. The Underground Trap. 11. Chinatown at Dark. 12. Murder by Remote Control. 13. Wheels of Death. 14. The Sealed Room. 15. The Shadow's Net Closes.

602. Shadow of Chinatown

(Victory, October 10, 1936) Serial, 15 chapters, two reels each. United Kingdom Title: *The Yellow Phantom*. Released as a 65-minute feature. D: Robert (Bob) Hill. SP: Isadore Bernstein and Basil Dickey. S: Rock Hawkey. Supervision: Sam Katzman. Special Dialogue: William Buchanan. Camera: Bill Hyer. Film Editor: Charles Henkel. Sound: Hans Weerin.

Sonya Rokoff, a Eurasian, is the West Coast representative of a European importing company. She is instructed by her superiors to close San Francisco's Chinatown to tourists because Chinese competition has become too great. She enlists the help of Victor Poten, also a Eurasian, but, unknown to her, he is a crazed scientist who hates not only Orientals but all people. He is so antihuman that his own accomplices, Sonya and Grogan, try to stop his devilish activities.

Assigned by her newspaper to investigate the strange happenings in Chinatown is reporter Joan Whiting. She enlists the help of novelist Martin Andrews.

The serial is an exciting one even though background music was at a minimum, the sets poor, and the dialogue laughable at times. However, the principal players do a fine job and even Charles King has a better than usual role.

Bela Lugosi (Victor Poten), Herman Brix [Bruce Bennett] (Martin Andrews), Joan Barclay (Joan Whiting), Lauana Walters (Sonya Rokoff), Maurice Liu (Willy Fu), Charles King (Grogan), William Buchanan (Healy), Forrest Taylor (Captain Walters), James B. Leong (Wong), Henry F. Tung (Dr. Wu), Paul Fung (Tom Chu), George Chan (Old Luee), Moy Ming (Wong's Brother), Jack Cowell (White Chink), Roger Williams (Harrison), John Elliott (Ship's Captain), Lester Door, Henry Hall.

1. The Arms of the God. 2. The Crushing Wall. 3. 13 Ferguson Alley. 4. Death on the Wire. 5. The Sinister Ray. 6. The Sword Thrower. 7. The Noose. 8. Midnight. 9. The Last Warning. 10. The Bomb. 11. Thundering Doom. 12. Invisible Gas. 13. The Brink of Disaster. 14. The Fatal Trap. 15. The Avenging Powers.

603. Shadow of the Eagle

(Mascot, February 1, 1932) Serial, 12 chapters, two reels each. D: Ford Beebe, Colbert Clark, and Wyndham Gittens. P: Nat Levine. Camera: Ben Kline and Victor Scheurich. Music: Lee Zahler. Stunt Supervisor: Yakima Canutt.

Skywriting messages from a pilot called The Eagle threaten an aircraft company. Nathan Gregory, now a carnival owner, becomes suspect. Craig McCoy, stunt pilot, is in love with Gregory's daughter and struggles to prove his potential father-in-law's innocence and recover plans for an invention that The Eagle has stolen from Gregory. Craig himself becomes a suspect before The Eagle is unmasked to reveal a member of the board of directors of the aircraft firm.

John Wayne (Craig McCoy), Dorothy Gulliver (Jean Gregory), Walter Miller (Danby), Kenneth Harlen (Ward), Edward Hearn (Nathan B. Gregory), Richard Tucker (Major Evans), Lloyd Whitlock (Green), Edmund Burns (Clark), Pat O'Malley (Ames), Little Billy (The Midget), Ivan Linow (Strong Man), James Bradbury, Jr. (Ventriloquist), Ernie Adams (Pat

John Wayne and Walter Miller in *Shadow of the Eagle* (1932)

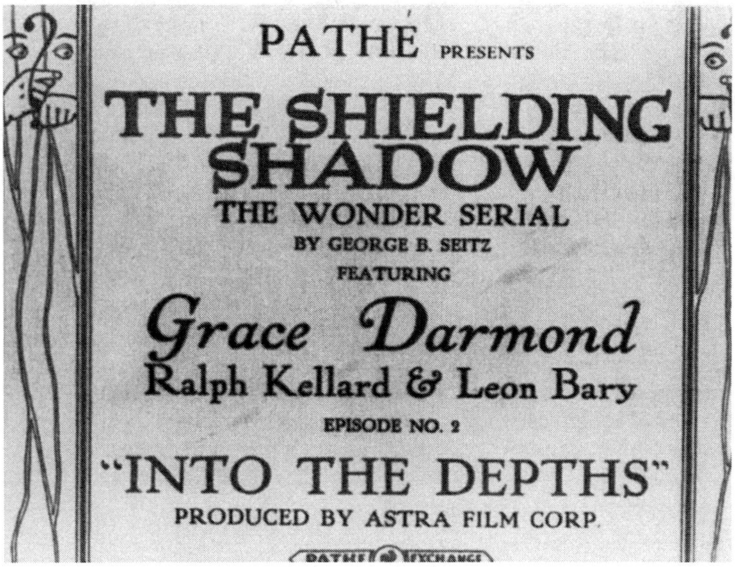

***The Shielding Shadow* (1916)**

Kelly), Roy D' Arcy (Gardner), Bud Osborne (Tim Moore), Yakima Canutt (Boyle), Billy West (The Clown), Monte Montague (Officer Callahan).

1. The Carnival Mystery. 2. Pinholes. 3. The Eagle Strikes. 4. A Man of a Million Voices. 5. The Telephone Cipher. 6. Code of the Carnival. 7. Eagle or Vulture? 8. On the Spot. 9. When Thieves Fall Out. 10. The Man Who Knows. 11. The Eagle's Wings. 12. The Shadow Unmasked.

604. Sherlock Holmes

(Franco-British/Eclair Company, 1912) Series, 8 episodes, two reels each. USA Release: Union Features/Universal. With the exception of *The Musgrave Ritual*, which was released in the USA in January 1913, all were released here in November 1912. D: Georges Treville. S: Sir Arthur Conan Doyle.

Georges Treville (Sherlock Holmes), M. Moyes (Doctor Watson).

The Speckled Band (1700 ft.) 28 min. The Reigate Squires (1800 ft.) 30 min. The Beryl Coronet (2300 ft.) 38 min. The Adventures of the Copper Beeches (1700 ft.) 28 min. The Mystery of Boscomb Vale (1700 ft.) 28 min. (cut to one-reel for U.S.A. release). The Stolen Papers (1400 ft.) 23 min. (from story "The Naval Treaty"). Silver Blaze (1300 ft.) 22 min. The Musgrave Ritual (1390 ft.) 21½ min.

605. The Shielding Shadow

(Astra Film Corp./Pathé, October 1, 1916) Serial, 15 chapters, two reels each. D: Louis Gasnier and Donald McKenzie. SP: George B. Seitz. S: Randall Parrish.

A box of mysterious pellets maintains the invisibility of the hero. When thieves steal the box, the hero attempts recovery.

Grace Darmond (Leontine), Ralph Kellard (Jerry Carson), Leon Barry (Sebastian Navarro), Madeline Traverse (Bianca), Lionel Brahm (The Bouncer), Frankie Mann (The Cabaret Singer), Leslie King ("One Lump Louie"), Hallan Mostyn, Madeline Francine.

1. The Treasure Trove. 2. Into the Depths. 3. The Mystic Defender. 4. The Earthquake. 5. Through Bolted Doors. 6. The Disappearing Shadow. 7. The Awakening. 8. The Haunting Hand. 9. The Incorrigible Captive. 10. The Vanishing Mantle. 11. The Great Sacrifice. 12. The Stolen Shadow. 13. The Hidden Menace. 14. Absolute Black. 15. The Final Chapter.

606. Shorty Hamilton (Series 1)

(Broncho, 1914–1915) Series, 18 episodes, two reels each. D: Francis Ford directed at least four and Thomas Ince one. Others remain a question mark, as the films were not copyrighted. No information on Series 2 available.

A run-of-the-mill comedy series that helped pay the rent at Broncho. Shorty Hamilton did his best, what with budget and time restrictions.

Shorty Hamilton (Shorty). Appearing in one or more episodes: Charles Ray, Enid Markey, Scott Sidney, Hershall Mayall, Fannie Midgley, Ben Wilson.

1. Shorty's Sacrifice (March 1914). 2. Shorty Escapes Matrimony (April 1914). 3. Shorty's Strategy (May 1914). 4. Shorty's Trip to Mexico (June 1914). 5. Shorty Gets in Trouble (June 1914). 6. [No information.] 7. Shorty Turns Judge (July 1914). 8. Shorty and the Aridville Terror (July 1914). 9. Shorty and the Fortune Teller (August 1914). 10. Shorty and Sherlock Holmes (October 1914). 11. Shorty Falls Into a Title (November 1914). 12. Shorty's Adventures in the City (February 1915). 13. Shorty's Secret (February 1915). 14. Shorty Among the Cannibals (April 1915). 15. Shorty Turns Actor (April 1915). 16. Shorty's Troubled Sleep (May 1915). 17. Shorty Inherits a Harem (August 1915). 18. Shorty's Ranch (September 1915).

607. The Sign of the Wolf

(Metropolitan, 1931) Serial, 10 chapters, two reels each. D: Forrest Sheldon and Harry S. Webb. S/SP: Betty Burbridge and Karl Krusada. P: Harry S. Wegg. Assist. D: Mel De Lay. Camera: William Nobles and Herbert Kilpatrick. Reissued in 1932 as a feature called *The Lone Trail* with Bennett Conan credited for the story/screenplay instead of Karl Krusada.

Two radioactive chains capable of transforming sand into precious jewels are stolen by explorer John Farnum in the Himalayas. In escaping through the jungle, he takes a little dog considered sacred by the natives. Years later Farnum, his daughter Ruth, and the dog King are in the American West, where ranchers Tom and Bud come to their aid when crooks attempt to steal the chains.

Rex Lease (Tom), Virginia Brown Faire (Ruth Farnum), Joe Bonomo (Bud), Jack Mower (Butch), Al Ferguson (Winslow), Josephine Hill (Pearl), Robert Walker (Joe), Edmund Cobb (Chief Kuba), Harry Todd (John Farnum), Jack Perrin (Jack), King [a dog] (Himself), Billy O'Brien.

1. Drums of Doom. 2. The Dog of Destiny. 3. The Wolf's Fangs. 4. The Fatal Shot. 5. The Well of Terror. 6. The Wolf Dogs. 7. Trapped. 8. The Secret Mark. 9. Tongues of Flame. 10. The Lost Secret.

608. El Signo de la Tribu

(Spain—Condal Films, 1915) Serial, 3 chapters. D: José Maria Codina. SP: C.A. Parrada and S. Parrada.

Vina De Velásquez (Azucena), Carmen Villasán (Dora), Gerardo Pena (Louis de Robles), Emilio Armengol (Conde de Armengol), José Reiguera (Zancudo), Hector Quintanilla (Garabito), Mas Galiano, Pablo Prou De Vendrell, Bastida, Mantúa, Moreno, Misericordia Ginestá, Danzarina Corma.

1. Las dos huérfanas. 2. El calvario de la virtud. 3. Crimen y expiación.

609. Der Silberkönig

(Germany—Delta Film GmbH, 1921) Serial, 4 chapters. D: Erik Lund. S: Arthur Schettere, Lothar Mendes.

Bruno Kastner, Eva Speyer, Leopoldine Konstantin, Hanni Reinwald, Leopold Von Ledebur, Paul Biensfeldt, Hermann Picha, Nien-Sön-Ling, Franz Schönfeld, Karl Platen, Georg Baselt, Josef Commer, Leonhard Haskel, Fritz Schulz, Gustav Botz, Wilhelm Diegelmann, Georg John, Friedel Fredy.

1. Der 13. Marz. 2. Der Mann der Tat. 3. Claim 36. 4. Rochesterstreet 29.

Rex Lease, Dorothy Gulliver, Al Ferguson (*standing at side of car*), and Joe Bonomo (*in rumble seat*) in *Sign of the Wolf* (1931)

610. The Silent Avenger (working title *For Love and Honor*)

(Vitagraph, April 20, 1920) Serial, 15 chapters; Chapter 1, three reels; others, two reels. D: William Duncan. S: Albert E. Smith, Cleveland Moffett. SP: C. Graham Baker, William B. Courtney.

No information on the story.

William Duncan (Phil Read), Edith Johnson (Helen Durham), Jack Richardson (Irving Somers), Virginia Nightingale (Francine), Ernest Shields (Jack Durham), William S. Smith (John Durham).

1. The Escape. 2. Fighting Back. 3. Within the Noose. 4. Tearing Through. 5. Blotted Out. 6. The Hidden Blow. 7. Dynamite Doom. 8. The Crusher. 9. Into the Jaws. 10. Blades of Horror. 11. Shot into Space. 12. Facing Eternity. 13. A Human Pendulum. 14. The Lakes of Fire. 15. The Final Trump.

611. The Silent Flyer

(Universal, January 3, 1927) Serial, 10 chapters, two reels each. D: William Craft. S: George Morgan. P: Nat Levine and Sam Bischoff. Original title: *The Sky Skidder*. Produced at California Studios but released through Universal.

A wild beast, half wolf, half dog, is attached to the hero, who rescues him from a trap. Efforts to obtain possession of a secret invention, a noiseless airplane engine, by the agent of a foreign power are thwarted by the secret service agent who, in addition to the wolf-dog, is aided by the daughter of the inventor of the engine.

Silver Streak [a dog] (Himself), Malcolm MacGregor (Lloyd Darrell), Louise Lorraine (Helen Corliss), George Williams (John Corliss), Albert J. Smith (Jack Hutchins), Anders Randolph (Benjamin Darrell), Edith Yorke (Mrs. Darrell), Arthur Morrison, Robert Walker, Dorothy Talcott, Thur Fairfax, Hughie Mack.

1. The Jaws of Death. 2. Dynamited. 3. Waters of Death. 4. The Treacherous Trail. 5. Plunge of Peril. 6. Fight of Honor. 7. Under Arrest. 8. Flames of Terror. 9. Hurled Through Space. 10. Love and Glory.

612. The Silent Mystery

(Burston/Silent Mystery Corp., November 1918) Serial, 15 chapters, two reels each. D: Francis Ford. S/Scen: Elsie Van Name. P: Louis Burston.

A jewel of great value is stolen in Egypt from a mummy by Mrs. Graham. The Priestess Kah follows Mrs. Graham and her daughter Betty back to the States determined to regain the gem. Strange things begin to happen to all who are associated with the "Eye of the World," as the gem is called.

Followers of Ford films will not be surprised at the gimmicks he uses: a pair of unattached hands that strangle various people, an undersea city run by a gang of crooks who plan to take over the world, and a huge ten-foot "soul-less creature" who kills the inevitable mad scientist who created him and who is now involved in the other derring-do. And of course Phil Kelly and his girlfriend, Betty Graham, fight the minions of the priestess throughout the fifteen chapters.

Francis Ford (Phil Kelly), Mae Gaston (Betty Graham), Rosemary Theby (Priestess Kah), Jerry Ash (Von Berg), Phil Ford (Chick), Elsie Van Name (Mrs. John Graham), Valeria Olivo, Hap H. Ward, Pete Gerald.

Portuguese: 1. A vinganca do Egito. 2. O juge do pavor. 3. O embuste. 4. Os antros da iniquidade [Dens of

Iniquity]. 5. O olho do mundo. 6. A magia de uma noite egípcia. 7. Os criminosos do deserto. 8. Garras e dentes. 9. Monstro ou homem. 10. A perseguicão dos espectros. 11. Sombras amarelas o. 12. Torturas do inferno. 13. Apanhados. 14. O revólver misterioso. 15. Línguas de fogo.

613. Sky Raiders

(Universal, March 1941) Serial, 12 chapters, two reels each. D: Ford Beebe and Ray Taylor. SP: Clarence Upson Young and Paul Huston. S: Eliot Gibbons. Assoc. P: Henry McRae.

Famed aviator Bob Dayton becomes the target of enemy agents who want plans for a new type of fighter plane and a bombsight that his company has developed. Dayton hires Tim Bryant, member of the Air Youth of America to do experimental work for him. Felix Lynx, agent for a foreign government, is kept informed of the Sky Raiders' plane by a spy in Dayton's office. Co-owner of Sky Raiders, Inc., is Ed Carey, who does his bit to defeat Lynx.

Donald Woods (Captain Bob Dayton), Billy Halop (Tim Bryant), Robert Armstrong (Lieutenant Ed Carey), Kathryn Adams (Mary Blake), Edward Ciannelli (Felix Lynx), Reed Hadley (Gaddens), Jacqueline Dalya (Innis Clair), Jean Fenwick (The Countess Irene), Irving Mitchell (Hinchfield), Edgar Edwards (Teal), John Holland (Hess), Roy Gordon (Major General Fletcher), Alex Callam (Captain Long), Bill Cody, Jr. (Jack Hurd), Roy Barcroft (Heavy), Dave O'Brien (Double for Woods).

1. Wings of Disaster. 2. Death Rides the Storm. 3. The Toll of Treachery. 4. Battle in the Clouds. 5. The Fatal Blast. 6. Stark Terror. 7. Flaming Doom. 8. The Plunge of Peril. 9. Torturing Trials. 10. Flash of Fate. 11. Terror of the Storm. 12. Winning Warriors.

614. The Sky Ranger

(Pathé, May 1, 1921) Serial, 15 chapters; Chapter 1, three reels; others, two reels. D: George B. Seitz. SP: Frank Leon Smith. P: George B. Seitz.

The serial opens with a young man's dream and then plunges into fast snappy action that is decidedly humorous, resembling a clean-cut farce comedy. The early scenes where George Rockwell is told by a fortune teller that he will marry a blonde, and his repeated attempts to become acquainted with her are pleasant ones. The film soon plunges into the plot which is based on the existence of a powerful light which has been invented by the girl's father, and which conspirators are seeking to secure.

The weird aspect of the story is introduced through the person of a mysterious character who appears in an airplane and becomes one of the conspirators. His airplane is equipped with a silent motor and achieves incredible speed. He has formerly been a stage magician and he uses his hypnotic powers at will. He is assisted by his niece, an attractive girl of more human temperament, who seeks to circumvent some of his more villainous designs.

George B. Seitz (George Oliver Rockwell), June Caprice (June Elliott), Harry Semels (Dr. Santro), Frank Redman (Professor Elliott), Joe Cuny (Murdock), Peggy Shanor (Tharen), Charles Revada (Bean), Spencer G. Bennet (Sergeant Doyle), Thomas Goodwin (The Butler).

1. Out of the Clouds. 2. The Sinister Signal. 3. In Hostile Hands. 4. Desert Law. 5. Mid-Air. 6. The Crystal Prism. 7. Danger's Doorway. 8. Dropped from the Clouds. 9. The House on the Roof. 10. Trapped. 11. The Seething Pool. 12. The Whirling Menace. 13. At the Last Minute. 14. Liquid Fire. 15. The Last Raid.

615. Smashing Barriers

(Vitagraph, September 1919) Serial, 15 chapters, two reels each. D: William Duncan. Scen: Graham Baker and R. Cecil Smith. S: Albert E. Smith and Cyrus T. Brady. Released by Vitagraph as a six-reel feature in 1923.

The hero goes out west, gets a job in a logging camp, falls in love with the owner's daughter, and is able to keep a gang from taking ownership of the camp.

William Duncan (Dan Stevens), Edith Johnson (Helen Cole), Walter Rodgers (Slicker Williams), William McCall (Henry Marlin), George Stanley (John Stevens), Fred Darnton (Benjamin Cole), Slim Cole ("Long Tom" Brown), Joe Ryan ("Wirenail" Hedges), Vincent Howard, Dorothea Wolbert.

1. The Test of Courage. 2. The Plunge of Death. 3. Tree-Hut of Torture. 4. The Deed of a Devil. 5. The Living Grave. 6. Downward to Doom. 7. The Fatal Flight. 8. The Murder Car. 9. The Dynamite Tree. 10. Overpowered. 11. The Den of Devilry. 12. Explosive Bullets. 13. Dead Fall. 14. Trapped Like Rats. 15. The Final Barrier.

616. Smith Series

(Pathé, 1926–1928) Series, 23 episodes, two reels each. P: Mack Sennett. D: Eddie Cline, Gil Pratt, Harry Edwards, Alf Goulding, Phil Whitman.

A comedy series revolving around the frustrations of a not-so-typical family. The series was a popular one. Ruth Hiatt was pretty, McKee had a unique comedy talent, and the child Mary Ann Jackson touched the heartstrings of audiences.

Ruth Hiatt, Raymond McKee, Mary Ann Jackson.

1. Smith's Baby (5-?-26). 2. Smith's Vacation (5-?-26). 3. Smith's Landlord (9-19-26). 4. Smith's Visitor (10-17-26). 5. Smith's Uncle (11-14-26). 6. Smith's Picnic (12-12-26). 7. Smith's Pets (1-9-27). 8. Smith's Customer (2-6-27). 9. Smith's New Home (3-6-27). 10. Smith's Surprise (4-3-27). 11. Smith's Kindergarten (5-1-27). 12. Smith's Pony (5-?-27). 13. Smith's Fishing Trip (5-29-27). 14. Smith's Cousin (6-?-27). 15. Smith's Cook (7-?-27). 16. Smith's Modiste Shop (7-?-27). 17. Smith's Candy Shop (8-21-27). 18. Smith's Army Life (2-?-28). 19. Smith's Holiday (2-?-28). 20. Smith's Farm Days (2-?-28). 21. Smith's Restaurant (7-?-28). 22. Smith's Catalina Rowboat Race (10-?-28). 23. Smith Baby's Birthday (1-?-29).

617. Snakeville Comedies

(Essanay, 1914–1915) Series, 21 episodes, one reel each. D: Roy Clements (Broncho Billy Anderson directing a few).

Snakeville was a mythical village which provided the setting for many of the Essanay comedies. The popular Alkali Ike series was set in Snakeville. The Snakeville comedies, serving up fine rural humor, were clean, and entertaining.

Victor Potel (Slippery Slim), Margaret Joslin (Sophie

Clutts), William Todd (Mustang Pete), Fred Church (Coyote Simpson/Rawhyde Bill), David Kirkland (Doc Killem), Marguerite Clayton, Broncho Billy Anderson, Augustus Carney, Ernest Van Pelt, Ben Turpin, Lloyd Bacon, Bell Mitchell, Robert McKenzie, Carey Turpin.

1. Snakeville and the Corset Demonstrator. 2. A Snakeville Courtship. 3. A Snakeville Epidemic. 4. A Snakeville Romance. 5. Snakeville's Beauty Parlor. 6. Snakeville's Blind Pig. 7. Snakeville's Champion. 8. Snakeville's Eugenic Marriage. 9. Snakeville's Fire Brigade. 10. Snakeville's Hen Medic. 11. Snakeville's Home Guard. 12. Snakeville's Most Popular Lady. 13. Snakeville's New Doctor. 14. Snakeville's New Sheriff. 15. Snakeville's New Waitress. 16. Snakeville's Peacemaker. 17. Snakeville's Reform Wave. 18. Snakeville's Rising Sons. 19. Snakeville's Twins. 20. Snakeville's Weak Woman. 21. The Snakeville Volunteer.

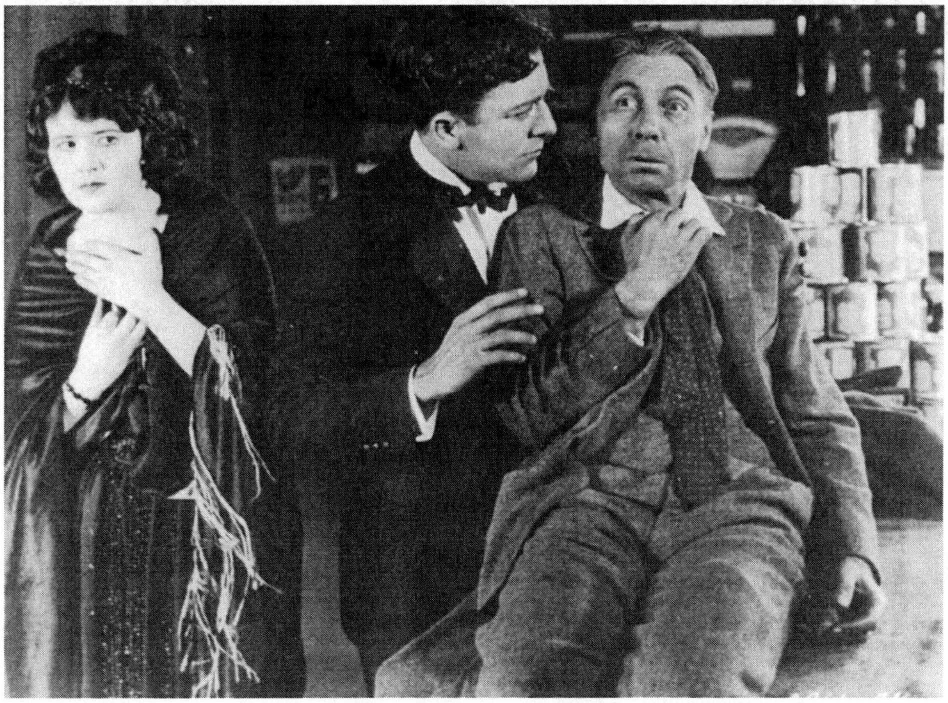

Margaret Livingston and Jack Mulhall in *The Social Buccaneer* (1923)

618. Snowed In

(Pathé, July 4, 1926) Serial, 10 chapters, two reels each. D: Spencer G. Bennet. SP: Frank Leon Smith.

Shirley Kane is out to prove her brother innocent of complicity in a series of mail robberies in the High Sierras and is assisted by forest ranger David Sheridan, who is more than happy to assist such a delectable morsel. Opposing them is a gang headed by a mysterious villain called Redfield, who dresses in a black commando suit and mask and periodically emerged from Room 28 of an abandoned hotel to carry out his unlawful activities. To say the hotel was abandoned is not quite accurate, since the principals scampered through it continuously. As customary with serials, the arch villain's identity was not revealed until the final chapter.

Always fetching, Allene seemed even more so this time around, even though she had no opportunity to wear beautiful clothes. Tightly constructed and expertly executed, *Snowed In* showed Pathé's superiority as a serial maker and what could be accomplished on a limited budget by dedicated people.

Allene Ray (Shirley Kane), Walter Miller (David Sheridan), Frank Austin (J.B. Swinnerton), Leonard Clapham [Tom London] (U.S. Marshal Thayer), Harrison Martell (Dr. Byrd), Charles West (Harron), J.F. McCullough (Howard Kane), Wally Oettel, John Webb Dillon, Natalie Warfield, Ben Walker, Bert Apling, George Magrill, Albert Kingsley.

1. Storm Warnings. 2. The Storm Starts. 3. The Coming of Redfield. 4. Redfield Strikes. 5. Buried. 6. The Enemy's Stronghold. 7. The Trap. 8. Thieves' Honor. 9. Daybreak. 10. The End of Redfield.

619. The Social Buccaneer

(Universal, January 8, 1923) Serial, 10 chapters, two reels each. D: Robert F. Hill. Scen: Anthony Coldeway. S: Frederic S. Isham.

A foreign princess whose throne is threatened must raise money to prevent undesirables from taking over the country. Young Jack Norton, who enjoys considerable social position in New York, befriends the princess and helps her save her throne. Working mostly undercover, to the outside world Norton is merely a New York playboy without much backbone or serious thought, a front that serves him in good stead as he pursues his objective of saving the princess and her throne.

Republic used the same idea with its *Zorro* and *Eagle* characters, as did Columbia with the *Batman* and *Superman* characters. Other studios, too, have used the same story gimmick.

Jack Mulhall (Jack Norton), Margaret Livingston (Princess Elise), William Welsh (Raymond Norton), Harry T. De Vere (Harvey Vail), Wade Boteler (Madison Ames), Percy Challenger (Steele), Lucille Ricksen (Lucille Vail), Robert Anderson (Terry Malone), George Connors (Phillip Dupre), Leonard Clapham [Tom London] (Louis Lenoir), Sidney Bracey (Bentley Craven), Tote Ducrow, Fontaine LaRue, W.T. Horne.

1. Missing Millions. 2. Secret Alley. 3. Tell-Tale Coin. 4. Spider's Web. 5. Black Shadows. 6. Into the Depths. 7. A Kingdom at Stake. 8. Treason. 9. The Coronation. 10. Justice Triumphant.

620. The Social Pirates

(Kalem, March, 1916) Series, 15 episodes, two reels each. D: James W. Horn.

Mona and Mary work as a team in exposing social injustices and bringing criminals to justice in a series of unrelated episodes.

Marin Sais (Mona), Ollie Kirby (Mary), True Boardman, Frank Jonasson, Paul C. Hurst, Jess Arnold, Tom Lingham, Edward Clisbee, Jess Whitney, Priscilla Dean, Robert E. Bradbury, E. Forrest Taylor, Robert Dell, Barney Furey, Ruth Snyder.

1. The Little Monte Carlo. 2. The Corsican Sisters.

3. The Parasite. 4. A War of Wits. 5. The Millionaire Plunger. 6. The Master Swindlers. 7. A Rogue's Nemesis. 8. Sauce for the Gander. 9. The Missing Millionaire. 10. Unmasking a Rascal. 11. The Fangs of the Tatler. 12. The Disappearance of Helen Mintern. 13. In the Service of the State. 14. The Music Swindlers. 15. Black Magic.

621. Son of Geronimo

(Columbia, November 6, 1952) Serial, 15 chapters, two reels each. D: Spencer G. Bennet. SP: George H. Plympton, Royal K. Cole, and Arthur Hoerl. P: Sam Katzman. Assist. D: Charles S. Gould. Photography: William Whitley. Music: Mischa Bakaleinikoff.

Indians under the leadership of Porico, self-styled son of Geronimo, are on the warpath against white settlers, whom Jim Scott and wagon train boss Tulsa are seeking to protect. Helping them are Frank Baker and his sister Ann.

Unscrupulous whites led by Ace Devlin and Rance Rankin join the Indians and manipulate them to the outlaws' advantage. When Scott is finally able to communicate with Porico, he convinces him that he has been duped and that the whites want peace. Together they defeat the outlaws and Porico personally kills Rankin.

Clay [Clayton] Moore (Jim Scott), Rodd Redwing (Porico), Tommy Farrell (Frank Baker), Eileen Rowe (Ann Baker), Bud Osborne (Tulsa), Marshall Reed (Ranch Rankin), John Crawford (Ace Devlin), Zon Murray (Bat), Rick Vallin (Eddie), Lyle Talbot (Colonel Foster), Chief Yowlachie (Geronimo), Wally West (Hardy), Frank Matts (Zeke), Sandy Sanders (Cliff), Bob Cason (Smoky), Frank Ellis, Anthony Dante, Al Cantor.

1. War of Vengeance. 2. Running the Gauntlet. 3. Stampede. 4. Apache Allies. 5. Indian Ambush. 6. Trapped by Fire. 7. A Sinister Scheme. 8. Prisoners of Porico. 9. On the Warpath. 10. The Fight at Crystal Springs. 11. A Midnight Marauder. 12. Trapped in a Flaming Tepee. 13. Jim Scott Tempts Fate. 14. A Trap for Geronimo. 15 Peace Treaty.

622. The Son of Tarzan

(National, May 1920–February 1921) Serial, 15 chapters; Chapter 1, three reels; others, two reels. Each chapter released as completed. D: Harry Revier. Assist. D: Arthur J. Flavin. SP: Roy Sommerville. Based on novel by Edgar Rice Burroughs. P: David P. Howells. Casting D: Jean Temple. Song: "Tarzan, My Jungle King," written and composed by Norman Stuckey and Osborne Tedman.

There was quite a bit of shuffling before the final cast was selected. At first Jack Hoxie was to play the lead, but he backed out. Lucille Rubey, wife of National's president, was to portray the feminine lead but director Revier did not want her for the part. With the backing of the producer and casting directress he got her replaced by Kathleen May. For whatever reason, May relinquished the role to Manilla Martan. Kamuela C. Searle got the lead role after Hoxie relinquished it.

Tarzan's son, Jack, is kidnapped by Tarzan's enemy, Ivan Paulovitch, and taken to Africa. There Jack manages to escape into the African jungle with the help of Akut, the ape. There he encounters Meriem, who is being held captive by a band of Arabs. Again with the help of Akut, Jack frees her. Jack (now called Korak) and Meriem grow to adulthood in the jungle and love blossoms between them. They are eventually reunited with Tarzan and Jane, who show up at their African estate.

Meriem, an heiress, is sought by evil Sheik Amor Ben Khatour, as well as by Paulovitch, for the purpose of holding her for ransom. Tarzan and Korak fight to protect her.

Both: **Clayton Moore and Bud Osborne in *Son of Geronimo* (1952)**

During the filming of the final chapter Kamuela C. Searle was actually killed by Tantor, the elephant, in a freak accident. The chapter was finished using a double.

Kamuela C. Searle (Korak, Son of Tarzan), P. Dempsey Tabler (Lord Greystoke/Tarzan), Manilla Martan (Meriem [as a young lady]), Karla Schram (Lady Greystoke/Jane), Gordon Griffith (Jack [Tarzan's son as a boy]), Mae Giraci (Meriem [as a child]), Eugene Burr (Ivan Paulovitch), Frank Morrell (Sheik Amor Ben Khatour) [Not to be confused with Frank Merrill, who was doubling for Elmo Lincoln at another studio], Ray Thompson (Malbihn), Tantor, the elephant (Himself), Akut, the ape (Himself), De Sacia Saville, Frank Earle.

1. Call of the Jungle. 2. Out of the Lion's Jaws. 3. The Girl of the Jungle. 4. The Sheik's Revenge. 5. The Pirate's Prey. 6. The Killer Mate. 7. The Quest of the Killer. 8. Coming of Tarzan. 9. The Kiss of the Beast. 10. Tarzan Takes the Trail. 11. Ashes of Love. 12. Meriem's Ride in the Night. 13. Double Crossed. 14. Blazing Hearts. 15. An Amazing Denouement.

623. Son of the Guardsman

(Columbia, October 24, 1946) Serial, 15 chapters, two reels each. D: Derwin Abrahams. SP: George H. Plympton, Harry Fraser, Royal Cole, and Lewis Clay. P: Sam Katzman. Assist. D: Mike Eason and Leonard Shapiro. Assoc. P: Mel DeLay. Photography: Ira H. Morgan. Music: Lee Zahler.

Dave Trent opposes his uncle Sir Edgar Bullard, a rubber baron in medieval England. Part of the prize in their struggle is Louise Markham, whose honor Trent defends. Fighting alongside Trent is an outlawed group organized to oppose evil doers. The group supports young Roger Mowbry, really Prince Richard, heir to a throne being misused by a wicked regent. Trent and his group are victorious and Richard is crowned king.

Robert Shaw (David Trent), Duan Kennedy (Louise Markham), Robert [Buzz] Henry (Roger Mowbry), Jim Diehl (Allan Hawk), Hugh Prosser (Red Robert), Leonard Penn (Mark Crowell), Wheeler Oakman (Lord Markham), Charles King (Sir Edgar Bullard), John Merton (Lord Hampton), Ray Bennett (Duncan), I. Stanford Jolley (Sir William Pryor), Belle Mitchell (Dame Duncan), Frank Ellis (Morgan), Al Ferguson (Lynn).

1. Outlaws of Sherwood Forest. 2. Perils of the Forest. 3. Blazing Barrier. 4. The Siege of Bullard Hall. 5. A Dagger in the Dark. 6. A Flight for Freedom. 7. Trial by Torture. 8. Mark Crowell's Treachery. 9. Crushed to Earth. 10. A Throne at Stake. 11. Double Danger. 12. The Secret of the Treasure. 13. Into the Depths. 14. The Lost Heritage. 15. Free Men Triumph.

Robert [Buzz] Henry and Robert Shaw in *Son of the Guardsman* (1946)

624. Son of Zorro

(Republic, January 18, 1947) Serial, 13 chapters, two reels each. D: Spencer Bennet and Fred C. Brannon. SP: Franklyn Adreon, Basil Dickey, Jesse Duffy, and Sol Shor. Assoc. P: Ronald Davidson. Photography: Bud Thackery. Music: Mort Glickman. Special Effects: Howard and Theodore Lydecker.

A discharged cavalry officer assumes the role of the masked Zorro, an ancestor of his, when he finds crooked politicians are running the territory around his home town and taking advantage of the populace. He manages to thwart the schemes of the crooks and to expose the ringleaders.

George Turner (Jeffrey Stewart/Zorro), Peggy Stewart (Kate Wells), Roy Barcroft (Boyd), Edward Cassidy (Moody), Ernie Adams (Hyde), Stanley Price (Pancho), Edmund Cobb (Stockton), Charles King (Dow), Newton House (Haynes), Eddie Parker (Melton), Jack Kirk (Charlie Grimes/Blake), Wheaton Chambers (Caleb Baldwin), Bud Wolfe (Hart/Haskill), Tex Terry (Cowboy), Ken Terrell (George Thomas), Fred Graham (Quirt), Si Jenks (Fred), Jack O'Shea (Hood), Tom Steele (Spike/Leach), Dale Van Sickel (Ted/Kaw/Forney/Dale/Murray), Mike Frankovich (Auctioneer), Pierce Lyden (Lem Carter), Rocky Shahan (Clark), Ted Adams (Cody), Gil Perkins (Dole), Tom London (Mark Daniels), Joe Phillips (Sniper/Deputy), Post Parks (Driver), Cactus Mack (Green), Art Dillard (Deputy), George Bell (Deputy), Frank O'Connor (Jailer), Howard Mitchell (Louis Wells), Ted Mapes (Larkin), Al Ferguson (Raider), Herman Hack (Raider), Tommy Ryan (Messenger), Carl Sepulveda (Milt), George Chesebro (Tom), John Daheim (Van), Doc Adams, Roy Bucko, Ralph Bucko, Pascale Perry, Silver Harr, Frank Ellis, Tommy Coats, Joe Balch.

1. Outlaw Country. 2. The Deadly Millstone. 3. Fugitive from Injustice. 4. Buried Alive. 5. Water Trap. 6. Valley of Death. 7. The Fatal Records. 8. Third Degree. 9. Shoot to Kill. 10. Den of the Beast. 11. The Devil's Trap. 12. Blazing Walls. 13. Checkmate.

Bela Lugosi in *S O S Coast Guard* (1937)

625. S O S Coast Guard

(Republic, September 1937) Serial, 12 chapters, two reels each. D: William Witney and Alan James. SP: Barry Shipman, Franklyn Adreon. S: Morgan Cox and Ronald Davidson. Assoc. P: Sol C. Siegel. Photography: William Nobles. Music: Raoul Kraushaar. Also released as a feature film.

Boroff, an unscrupulous international fiend, has developed a disintegrating gas which he intends to sell to a foreign power as a war weapon. He must secure certain basic ingredients before any sizable amount of the gas can be manufactured. Coast guardsman Terry Kent and newspaper woman Jean Norman strive hard to thwart the villain's objective. With the aid of Jean's brother, a chemist, a counter-gas is developed. In a showdown with the Coast Guard Boroff's own gas becomes his own downfall.

Ralph Byrd (Terry Kent), Bela Lugosi (Boroff), Maxine Doyle (Jean Norman), Richard Alexander (Thorg), Herbert Rawlinson (Commander Boyle), Lee Ford (Snapper McGee), John Picorri (G.A. Rackerby), George Chesebro (L.H. Degado), Ranny Weeks (Weis), Joe Mach (Adamic Captain), Lawrence Grant (Rabinisi), Thomas Carr (Jim Kent), Carleton Young (Dodds), Allen Connor (Dick Norman), Robert Walker (Black), Herbert Weber (Belden), Dick Sheldon (Attendant), Gene Marvey (Blake), Jack Clifford (Carter), Lee Frederick (Citizen), Tom Ung (Charlie), Roy Barcroft (Goebel), Jack Daley (Captain), King Mojave (Driver), Alexander Leftwick (Froman), Eddie Phillips, Reed Sheffield, Frank Wayne, Warren Jackson, Dick Scott (Boat Heavies), Joseph Girard (Green), Lester Dorr (Intern), Buddy Roosevelt (Scott), Rex Lease (Orderly), Curley Dresden, Henry Morris, Vinegar Roan, James Millican (Dock Heavies), Frankie Marvin (Sniper), Jack Ingram (Seaman), Frank Ellis (Kelp Worker), Edward Cassidy (Johnson), Jack Roberts (Jones), Earl Bunn, Kit Guard (Kelp Heavies), Henry Hale (Krohn), Duke Taylor (Loader), Audrey Gaye (Supervisor), Robert Dudley (Stationmaster), Roger Williams (Sloan), Frank Fanning, Frank Meredith, John Gustin (Policemen), Billie Van Every (Operator), Harry Stang (Manager), Charles McMurphy (Mate), Edwin Mordant (Meade), Michael Morgan (Moore), Floyd Criswell (Motorcycle Heavy), Dan Wolheim (Slarson), Forrest Dillon, Duke York (Sea Heavies), Jerry Frank (Sam), Henry Otho (Sailor), Pat Mitchell (Radioman), Alan Gregg (Payne), Loren Riebe (Pete), Richard Beach, Teddy Mangean, Yakima Canutt, Robert Wilkie, Baldy Cook, Jack Long, Jerry Larkin, Leon Davidson, Clarke Jennings, Bobbie Koshay, Norwood Edwards.

1. Disaster at Sea. 2. Barrage of Death. 3. The Gas Chamber. 4. The Fatal Shaft. 5. The Mystery Ship. 6. Deadly Cargo. 7. Undersea Terror. 8. The Crash. 9. Wolves at Bay. 10. The Acid Trail. 11. The Sea Battle. 12. The Deadly Circle.

626. Speed

(Pathé, October 22, 1922) Serial, 15 chapters, two reels each. D: George B. Seitz. Scen: Bertram Millhauser. S: Charles Hutchison.

Speed Stansbury pursues a man to South America who can prove him innocent of murder and bank robbery, but the man is part of the mob controlled by a master criminal who wants Speed convicted in the hopes of acquiring the fortune to which Speed is heir. Following Speed into the tropics is Lucy Durant, the girl he loves.

It was all downhill for Hutchison following *Speed*. He made one more serial, which he produced himself, but he lost a good deal of his money on the venture. He ended his career in the Thirties and Forties playing bit parts. His ego did not endear him to co-workers and when he lost his athletic prowess, through age and living the fast life, serial fans lost interest in him.

Charles Hutchison (Speed Stansbury), Lucy Fox (Lucy Durant), John Webb Dillon (Edwin Stansbury), Harry Semels (Jim Sprague), Cecile Bonnel (Vera Harper), Winifred Verina (Mrs. Sprague), Joe Cuny (Hagerty), Tom Goodwin (J.J. Stansbury), Charles Reveda (Pious Pedro), Henry R. Gray.

1. The Gateway. 2. Nerve. 3. Pious Pedro. 4. The Quagmire. 5. Fighting Mad. 6. Panic. 7. Jaws of Danger. 8. Caught. 9. Hit or Miss. 10. Buried Alive. 11. Into the Crusher. 12. Trimmed. 13. Risky Business. 14. The Peril Rider. 15. Found Guilty.

627. Spell of the Circus

(Universal, January 12, 1931) Serial, 10 chapters, two reels each. D: Robert F. Hill. S/Continuity: Ian McClosky Heath.

Butte Morgan hopes to gain control of a circus by marrying the owner's daughter, Maria. She, however, prefers Jack Grant, headliner of the wild west concert. Love prevails in spite of the villain's attempts to kidnap and force Maria into marriage and his sabotage of the circus.

Francis X. Bushman, Jr. (Jack Grant), Alberta Vaughn (Maria Wallace), Tom London (Butte Morgan), Walter Shumway (George Wallace), Charles Murphy (Hank Harris), Monte Montague (Totto), Bobby Nelson (Bobby).

1. A Menacing Monster. 2. The Phantom Shadow. 3. Racing with Death. 4. A Scream of Terror. 5. A Leap for Life. 6. A Fatal Wedding. 7. A Villain Unmasked. 8. The Baited Trap. 9. The Terror Tent. 10. The Call of the Circus.

628. The Spider Net

(Tenneck/Goodwill, 1926) Serial, unknown number of chapters. P: Hans Tirsler.

No information available on the plot of this film. It was never copyrighted, and few historians are aware that it was ever made. It was not an original film but was composed of footage taken from various films in the series of two-reelers that starred Eileen Sedgwick and the dog Lightning. The film had very little distribution on the state-right market. Miss Sedgwick, when contacted by the author, was unaware that such a serial had been constructed from her two-reelers. Few, if any, biographical books on Gary Cooper mention this short serial.

Eileen Sedgwick, Lightning [a dog], Robert Walker, Tom London, Harry Semels, Frank Lackteen, Wilbur McGaugh, William A. Lowery, Hal Water, Gary Cooper.

629. The Spider Returns

(Columbia, May 1941) Serial, 15 chapters, two reels each. D: James W. Horne. SP: Jesse A. Duffy and George H. Plympton. S: Morgan B. Cox, Lawrence E. Taylor, John Cutting, and Harry Fraser. P: Larry Darmour. Photography: James S. Brown, Jr. Music: Lee Zahler. Released in England in feature form. Based on "The Spider" magazine stories authored first by Reginald Thomas (Maitland Scott); later *Popular Publications* began using a house name, "Grant Stockworth," as the author of the Spider Stories.

When a gang of saboteurs, led by The Gargoyle, a mysterious and powerful foreign agent, threatens national defense projects, socialite Richard Wentworth, alias The Spider and Blinky McQuade, returns to war with the underworld. *The Spider Returns* is a less serious serial than *The Spider's Web.* James Horne was noted for some rather hilarious scenes in his serials, but he seems to have outdone himself here. If not taken

Top: **Corbet Harris as The Gargoyle;** *bottom:* **Keene Duncan, Alden Chase, Dave O'Brien, Warren Hull and Mary Ainslee in** ***The Spider Returns*** **(1941)**

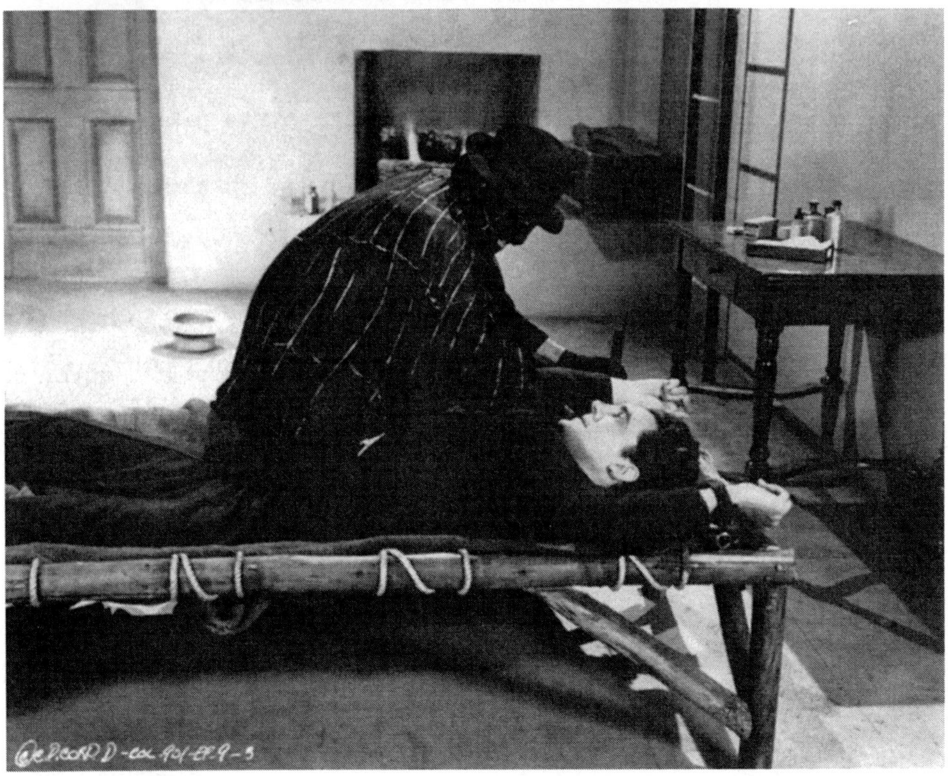

***Top:* Iris Meredith; *bottom:* Richard Fiske and Warren Hull (the Spider) in *The Spider's Web* (1938)**

seriously (as the actors obviously did not do), it is a fun serial to watch.

Warren Hull (Richard Wentworth/The Spider/Blinky McQuade), Mary Ainslee (Nita Van Sloan), Dave O'Brien (Jackson), Joe Girard (Commissioner Kirk), Kenneth Duncan (Ram Singh), Corbet Harris (McLeod/The Gargoyle), Bryant Washburn (Westfall), Charles Miller (Van Sloan), Anthony Warde (Trigger), Harry Harvey (Stephen), Alden Chase (Jenkins), Charles Hamilton, George Larkin, Dale Van Sickel, Jack Mulhall, Jack Perrin, Lane Chandler.

1. The Stolen Plans. 2. The Fatal Time-Bomb. 3. The Secret Meeting. 4. The Smoke Dream. 5. The Gargoyle's Trail. 6. The X-Ray Eye. 7. The Radio Boomerang. 8. The Mysterious Message. 9. The Cup of Doom. 10. The X-Ray Belt. 11. Lips Sealed by Murder. 12. A Money Bomb. 13. Almost a Confession. 14. Suspicious Telegrams. 15. The Payoff.

630. The Spider's Web

(Columbia, October 1938) Serial, 15 chapters, two reels each. D: Ray Taylor and James W. Horne. SP: Robert E. Kent, Basil Dickey, George Plympton, and Martie Ramson. Based upon "The Spider" magazine stories. Photography: Allen G. Siegler. P: Jack Fier. Exec. P: Irving Briskin. Music: Morris Stoloff. Released in feature form in England.

Criminologist Richard Wentworth is secretly The Spider, arch enemy of the underworld, as well as Blinky McQuade, a shady underworld character. In the latter disguise he is able to learn many things about underworld activity. A criminal organization headed by The Octopus attempts to demoralize the nation's communication and utilities. The Spider goes into action with his faithful confidantes to foil and unmask The Octopus and put a stop to his nefarious activities.

Warren Hull (Richard Wentworth/Blinky McQuade/The Spider), Iris Meredith (Nita Van Sloan), Richard Fiske (Jackson), Kenneth Duncan (Ram Singh), Forbes Murray (Commissioner Kirk), Donald Douglas (Jenkins), Charles Wilson (Chase), Marc Lawrence (Steve), John Tyrrell (Grafton), Beatrice Curtis (Kate), Paul Whitney (Grey), Edward Earle (Adams), Eddie Foster (Lefty), Frank Bruno (Monk), Gordon Hart (Mason), Bentley Hewlett (Crane), Lee Prather (Morris), Eddie Fetherston (Tom), John Roy (Chemist), Gloria Blondell (Chase's Secretary), Beatrice Blinn (Stenographer), Gene Anderson, Jr. (Johnnie), Stanley Mack (Nick), Chet Lynn (Florist), Lester Dorr (Martin), Bob Perry (Tim), Dick Stanley (Steve's Heavy), Joe Palma (Steve's Heavy), Bud Geary (Steve's Heavy), Roger Williams (Steve's Heavy Driver), King Mojave (Mike), Al Herman (Malean), Harry Depp (Oswald), Edward Peil, Sr. (Jones), Duke York (Heavy), Lane Chandler (Trigger), Tom London (Cop), Edmund Cobb (Police Announcer), Rose Plummer (Woman), Dick

York (Heavy), Johnny Sinclair (Writer), Edward J. LeSaint (Doctor), Richard Terry (Intern), Joe Sully (Heavy), Frank Mills (Heavy), Al Klein (Saber), Harry Strang (Heavy), Dan Wolheim (Barkeep), Kit Guard (Heavy), Harry Tenbrook (Workman), Ann Schaefer (Woman), Bill Patton (Whitey Heavy), Oscar G. Hendrian (Whitey Heavy), Dick Durrell (Dennis), Lee Shumway (Sergeant), Gene Stone (Cashman), Eddie Hearn (Desk Sergeant), Steve Clark (Mask), Earl Bunn (Mask), Harry Myers (Detective), Francis Walker (Farmer), Al Ferguson (Mechanic), William Whitney (Cop), James Carlisle (Fire Captain), Harry Semels (Heavy), Dick Dickinson (Man), Malcolm McTaggart (Elevator Boy), Lew Meehan (Burke), Nestor Paive (Red), Sid D'Albrook (Spike), Tony Merlo (Chauffeur), Jack Hennessy (Chauffeur), William Worthington (Cantlon), Roy Brent (Ted), Harry Hollingsworth (Inspector), Jack Gardner (Reporter), Ernie Adams (Beggar), Brooks Benedict (Steve Driver), Herman Cripps (Mulvaney).

1. Night of Terror. 2. Death Below. 3. High Voltage. 4. Surrender or Die. 5. Shoot to Kill. 6. Sealed Lips. 7. Shadows of the Night. 8. While the City Sleeps. 9. Doomed. 10. Flaming Danger. 11. The Road to Peril. 12. The Spider Falls. 13. The Man Hunt. 14. The Double Cross. 15. The Octopus Unmasked.

631. Die Spinnen (aka *Die Abenteuer des Kay Hoog*; aka *The Spiders*)

Germany—Decla–Bioscop, 1919) Serial, 2 chapters. D: Fritz Lang. SP: Fritz Lang. P: Erich Pommer. Camera: Emil Schuemann (1st chap.); Karl Freund (2nd chap.).

Das Geheimnis der Sphinx and *Um Asiens Kaiserkrone* were written to be filmed as Chapters 3 and 4, but were never filmed. However, the two chapters making up *Die Spinnen* were very popular. It was a shame Chapters 3 and 4 were not filmed. Nevertheless, the two chapters filmed formed a coherent whole. An American adventurer, Kay Hoog, battles it out with Lio-Sha and her gang of Spiders led by Four-Finger John. The object of the battles is possession of a fabulous diamond able to bestow mastery of the world upon its possessor. The two chapters are feature length (80 and 97 minutes respectively). All kinds of scientific wizardry was used and the battle between good and evil moved about the world, with the hero saving several damsels in distress.

Carl De Vogt (Kay Hoog), Ressel Orla (Lio Sha), Lil Dagover (Priestess to the Sun King), Edgar Pauly (Four-Finger John), Paul Morgan (Scientific Expert), Georg John (Dr. Telphas), Rudolf Lettinger (Terry Landon, the King of Diamonds), Meinhardt Maur, Harry Frank, Thea Zander, Reiner-Steiner, Friedrich Küehne, Paul Biensfeldt.

1. Der Goldene See. 2. Das Brillanten Schiff.

632. Spy Smasher

(Republic, March 1942) Serial, 12 chapters, two reels each. D: William Witney. SP: Ronald Davidson, Norman S. Hall, Joseph Poland, William Lively, and Joseph O'Donnel. Assoc. P: W.J. O'Sullivan. Photography: Reggie Lanning. Music: Mort Glickman. Special Effects: Howard Lydecker. Based on characters appearing in *Whiz Comics* and *Spy Smasher* magazines. Feature Title: *Spy Smasher Returns* (1966).

Spy Smasher and his twin brother pursue a German agent called The Mask who is operating in the U.S. They thwart The Mask's attempts to set up a counterfeiting operation and to steal a new bombsight and a weapon capable of melting engines in flight. However, the brother is killed when he takes Spy Smasher's place in an attempt to rescue Eve Corby. Spy Smasher kills The Mask and other Nazi agents when he runs a motorboat at full speed into the side of a submarine, jumping to safety before the crash. *Spy Smasher* was one of the better serials of the 1940s.

Kane Richmond (Spy Smasher/Alan Armstrong/Jack Armstrong), Marguerite Chapman (Ever Corby), Sam Flint (Admiral

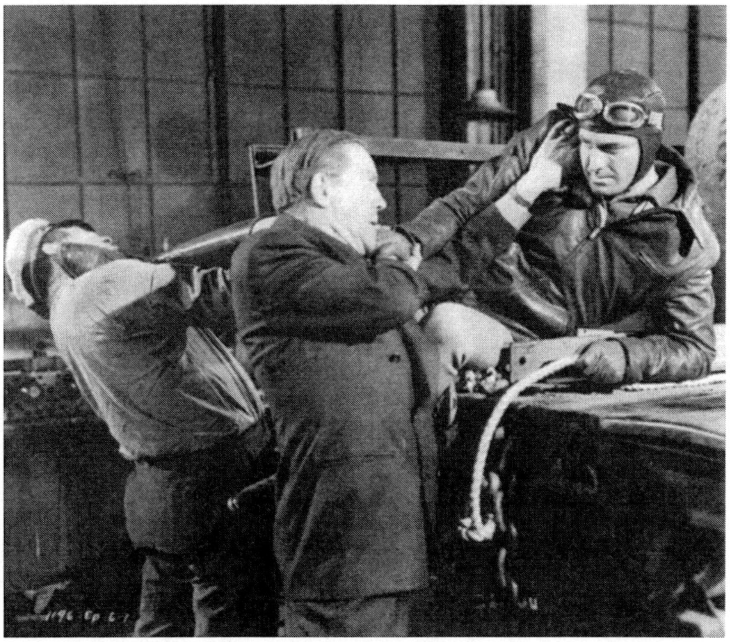

Left: **Kane Richmond and Marguerite Chapman;** ***right:*** **Kane Richmond and Tom London in** ***Spy Smasher*** **(1942)**

Corby), Hans Schumm (The Mask), Tristram Coffin (Drake), Franco Corsaro (Pierre Durand), Hans Von Morhart (Capt. Gerhardt), Georges Renavent (Governor LeConte), Robert O. Davis (Colonel Von Kahr), Henry Zynda (Ritter Lazar), Paul Bryar (Lawlor), Tom London (Crane), Richard Bond (Hayes), Crane Whitely (Dr. Hauser), John James (Steve), Yakima Canutt (Armored Car Driver), Max Waizman (Auto Clerk), Howard Hughes (Barn Heavy 1), Charley Phillips (Barn Heavy 2), Martin Faust (Blacksmith), Tome Steele, Eddie Jauregui, John Daheim, Bob Jamison, Walter Low (Brick Heavies), Jerry Jerome (Burns), Buddy Roosevelt (Commandant), Jack Arnold (Camera Clerk), Martin Garralaga (Captain), Carleton Young (Taylor/Power Clerk), Robert Wilke (Chief Operative), Bud Wolfe (Craig/Policeman), William Forrest (Gerald Douglas), Nick Vehr (Dungeon Guard), Duke Taylor (Fritz/Storm Trooper), Sid Troy (Gold Heavy), Ray Parson (Livingston), Jimmy Fawcett (Lewis/Policeman), Lee Phelps (Guard), Lowden Adams (Headwaiter), George Sherwood (Jailer), Ken Terrell (Jerry/Policeman/Storm Trooper), Louis Tomei (Joe), Carey Loftin (Launch Heavy), Leonard St. Leo (Lieutenant), Duke Green (Lumber Heavy), Charles Regan (Café Manager), Bert LeBaron (Mechanic), Bill Wilkus (Pipe Heavy 1), Loren Riebe (Pipe Heavy 2), Dudley Dickerson (Train Porter), Cy Slocum (Private), John Peters (Sub Quartermaster), Arvon Dale (Thornton), Roy Brent, Ray Hanson, Ray Jones (Soldiers), Tommy Coats (Squad Leader), Hugh Prosser (Squadron Leader), Frank Alten (Storm Trooper Captain), George J. Lewis (Stuart), Robert Stevenson (Torpedo Chief), Gil Perkins (Valve Sailor), Pat Moran (Waiter), John Buckley (Walker), Dave Sharpe (Warehouse Sniper/Double for Richmond), Jack O'Shea, James Dale.

1. America Beware. 2. Human Target. 3. Iron Coffin. 4. Stratosphere Invaders. 5. Descending Doom. 6. The Invisible Witness. 7. Secret Weapon. 8. Sea Raiders. 9. Highway Racketeers. 10. 2700° Fahrenheit. 11. Hero's Death. 12. V…

633. Stanley in Africa

(Centaur Pictures, 1915) Series, 7 episodes, two reels each. P: David Horsley. D: Frank Montgomery.

Thrilling adventures in darkest Africa as Stanley and party seek out Doctor Livingston. Each episode complete in itself with a continuing cast.

Roy Watson (Henry M. Stanley), Herr Batty (Captain Batty), Edward Roberts (Jack Wilson), Charles Gay (Andrea), Mona Darkfeather (Ada), Maria Manley (Nina), Anna DeLisle (Old Hag), Charles Wheelock, A. Van Werp, Court Tietze, Captain Jack Bonavita and his Bostic Animals.

1. Stanley's Close Call. 2. Stanley's Search for the Hidden City. 3. The White King of the Zaras. 4. Stanley at Starvation Camp. 5. Stanley and the Slave Traders. 6. Stanley and the Voodoo Worshippers. 7. Stanley in Darkest Africa.

634. The Steel Trail

(Universal, August 27, 1923) Serial, 15 chapters, two reels each. D: William Duncan. S/Scen: George Plympton, Karl Coolidge, and Paul M. Bryan.

John Armstrong, at the head of a wealthy combine of ranchers, is building a railroad through the San Marcos Valley. Secret but powerful interests oppose the enterprise. A famous engineer is called in to finish the work within thirty days so that the Armstrong group will not be deprived of their franchise. Adventures and mishaps accompany the battle of wits and skill waged between the engineer and his hidden foes. The romantic element is supplied in the love affair between the engineer and Armstrong's daughter. That's the plot in brief—rather stereotyped in structure but possessing suspense and romance for all that.

William Duncan (Bruce Boyd), Edith Johnson (Judith Armstrong), Harry Carter (Mark Zabel), Ralph McCullough (Frank Norton), Harry Woods (Morris Blake), John Cossar (Colonel John Armstrong), Albert J. Smith (Ralph Dayton), Janet Ford (Helen Dayton), Mabel Randall (Anna), Catherine Calhoun (Olga).

1. Intrigue. 2. Dynamite. 3. Wildfire. 4. Blown from the Cliff. 5. Headed On. 6. Crushed. 7. The Gold Rush. 8. Judith's Peril. 9. The Dam Bursts. 10. The Trap. 11. The Fight on the Cliff. 12. The Tottering Bridge. 13. Between Two Fires. 14. Burning Fumes. 15. Ten Seconds to Go.

635. Le Stigmate

(France—Etablissements Gaumont, 1925) Serial, 6 chapters. D: Louis Feuillade and Maurice Champreux. S: Louie Feuillade. SP: Louis Feuillade.

Jane Murat (Lewis Johnson), Nina Orlove (Irene), Francine Mussey (Manon), Joe Hamman (L'inspecteur Coursan), Bouboule (Genevieve), J.P. Stock (Nordier), Amedée Charpentier (La Comble), Selric (Gidard), E. De Romero (Mahoud Khan), Germaine Chambert (Mme. Delestang), Georgette Lhery (Liliane), Mme. Fabre (Maman Routiolle), Janine Blanleuil (Gaby).

1. Le mort vivant. 2. Les deux mères. 3. L'evasion. 4. Nocturnes. 5. La mère prodigue. 6. La main.

636. Stingaree

(Kalem, November 24, 1915) Series, 12 episodes. D: James W. Horne. Scen: James W. Horne. S: E.W. Hornung. P: James W. Horne.

Wealthy Irving Randolph is falsely denounced as a deliberate murderer by his greedy young brother when Randolph, during a rifle shooting contest, accidentally kills a man with whom he has had an altercation. Fleeing to Australia, Randolph becomes known as the bandit Stingaree and is aided in his Robin Hood–like adventures by his friend Howie and his sweetheart Ethel.

True Boardman (Irving Randolph/Stingaree), Marin Sais (Ethel Porter), Paul C. Hurst (Howie), Thomas Lingham (Guy Kentish/Professor Lucius Brady/Carmichael), Frank Jonasson (Inspector Kilbride/Vanheimert/Governor/Bishop Methuen), William Brunton (Robert Randolph), James W. Horne (Oswald), Ollie Kirby (Mrs. Green), Edward Clisbee (Sergeant Cameron/Chaplain/John Trent/Trooper Bowen), Joseph Barber (Inspector), Hoot Gibson, Jack Lott, Janet Rambeau.

1. An Enemy of Mankind. 2. A Voice in the Wilderness. 3. The Black Hole of Glenrenald. 4. To the Vile Dust. 5. A Bushranger at Bay. 6. The Taking of Stingaree. 7. The Honor of the Road. 8. The Purification of Mulfers. 9. The Duel in the Desert. 10. The Villain Worshipper. 11. The Moth and the Star. 12. The Darkest Hour.

637. The Strange Case of Mary Page.

(Essanay, January 24, 1916) Serial, 15 chapters, two reels each. D: J. Charles Haydon. S: Frederick Lewis. SP: Frederick Lewis and H.H. Sheldon.

David Pollock, a theatrical magnate, is murdered and Mary Page, on whom he had forced his attentions, is accused. Phil Langdon, her suitor, stands by her. The story is told in flashback—a rather novel idea at the time.

Henry B. Walthall (Phil Langdon, Attorney), Edna Mayo (Mary Page), Sydney Ainsworth (David Pollock), Harry Dunkinson (E.H. Daniels, Show Manager), John Cossar (Prosecuting Attorney), Frank Dayton (Dan Page), Frankie Raymond (Mrs. Page), John Thorne (Jim Cunningham), Arthur Bates (Young Gambler), Edmund Cobb, Frank Hamilton, Frances Benedict, William Chester, Miss Valli, Tom Cummerford, Jessie Jones, Honus Smith, Ernest Cossart.

1. The Tragedy World. 2. The Trail. 3. The Web. 4. The Mark. 5. The Alienist. 6. The Depths. 7. A Confession. 8. The Perjury. 9. The Accusing Eye. 10. The Clue. 11. The Raid. 12. The Slums. 13. Dawning Hope. 14. Recrimination. 15. The Verdict.

638. Strings of Steel

(Universal, June 28, 1926) Serial, 10 chapters, two reels each. D: Henry McRae. SP: Phillip Dutton Horn and Oscar Lund.

Ned Brown, a young engineer in the employ of the Excelsior Telephone Company a rival of the Bell Company, designs a new transmitting device. Jim Hogan, an underworld political power is ambitious to control the telephone interests, and with the help of Ned's superior, Peter Allen, tries to undermine the company. Gloria Norton, Ned's girlfriend and central operator of the Excelsior Company, helps save Ned's design when Allen attempts to steal it. Later Ned is employed by the Bell Company to conduct tests on their own version of a transmitter which they count on to revolutionize telephone communication. Hogan and Allen and their gang attempts to stop Ned's work.

William Desmond (Ned Brown), Eileen Sedgwick (Gloria Van Norton), Albert J. Smith (Peter Allen), Arthur Morrison (Jim Hogan), George Ovey (Willie Gray), Grace Cunard (Bowery Belle), Alphonse Martel (Alexander Graham Bell), Taylor N. Duncan (Theodore N. Vail), Blanche Fisher, Dorothy Gulliver.

1. The Voice on the Wire. 2. The First Central. 3. Fighting for Love. 4. The Power of Might. 5. Kings of the Wire. 6. Voice of the Continent. 7. Telephone Poles. 8. War of the Wire. 9. When Lightning Strikes. 10. Love and Victory.

639. Stuart Webbs

(Berlin—May-Film, 1914-1914 [Films 1 & 2]), (Berlin—Stuart Webbs Film Co., Reicher U. Reicher, 1917–1919 [Films 4–14]), (Stuart Webbs Film Company, 1920 [Films 15–19]), (Stuart Webbs Film Company,

Top: Stingaree **(1915);** ***bottom:*** **Henry B. Walthall and Edna Mayo in** ***The Strange Case of Mary Page*** **(1916)**

William Desmond and Eileen Sedgwick in *Strings of Steel* (1926)

München, 1921–1924 [Films 20–22]), (Münchener Lichtspielkunst AG [Emelka], München, 1924–1925 [Films 23–28]), (Berlin—DLS Deutsches Lichtspiel–Syndikat AG, 1929 [Film 29]), (Berlin—Omnia–Film GmbH, 1929 [Film 30]) Series, 30 episodes. D: Joe May (Films 1–3), Dr. Johannes Guter (6–11), Max Obal (14, 17–25, 27–28), Franz Seitz (26), Rudolf Meinert (29–30).

(Numbers in parentheses indicate the film the actor was in.) Ernst Reicher (Stuart Webbs [1–28]), Ralph Cancy (Stuart Webbs [29]), Karl Ludwig Diehl (Stuart Webbs [30]), Lupu Pick (3), Werner Krauss (3), Eva Cron (4), Hans Gleissner (4), Paul Braun (4), Ria V. Jankowska (5), Franz Verdier (5), Hans Rauer (5), Marija Leiko (6), Erwin Botz (6), Frieda Richard (6, 8), Sigmund Aschenbach (6), Herr Helfer (6), Carmen Torre (7), Thea Sandten (7), Carl Auen (7), Andress von Horn (7), Ralf Lindau-Schulz (7), Esther Carena (8), Aruth Wartan (8, 22), Ernst Lakowsky (8), Lina Salten (8), Willi Kaiser-Heyl (10), Stella Harf (16), Grete Reinwald (19), Wolfgang von Schwind (22), Hermann Pfanz (23), Alexandra Sorina (23, 24), Rolf Munz [Jack Mylong-Munz] (23), Claire Kronburger (23), Fritz Greiner (23), Arnold Marle (24), Magda Simon (24), Ernst Bosser (24), Klara Kronburger (24, 26), Jack Mylong-Munz (24, 26), Ruth Weyher (25), Gertrud de Lalsky (25), Adolf Wohlbruck (25), Georg Vogelsand (25), Hermann Nesseltrager (25), Imogen Robertson (26), Maria Minzenti (26), Otto Wernicke (26), Karl Falkenberg (26), Ferdinand Martini (26, 27, 28), Manfred Kompel (26, 27, 28), Margarete Schlegel (27), Friedl Haerlin (27), George Henrich (27), Helena Mokowska (27, 28), Josef Berger (27), Siegfried Raabe (27), Hilde Horst (28), Klara Ney (28), Otto Kronburger (28), Betty Bird (29), Suzy Vernon (29), Gaston Modot (29), Livio Pavanelli (29), Paul Horbiger (29), Fred Doderlein (29), Ferdinand Hart (29), Arnold Korff (29), Jean Murst (30), Marcella Albani (30), Charles Willy Kayser (20), Hans Schickler (20), Betty Astor (30), Gerturde Berliner (30), Borwin Walth (30), Gerhard Dammann (30), Oscar Homolka (30).

1. Die Geheinsvolle Villa. 2. Das Panzergewölbe. 3. Die Pagode. 4. Das treibende Floss. 5. Der Todesstern. 6. Die Diamantenstiftung. 7. Ein rätselhafter Blick. 8. Die Geisterjagd. 9. Der Eisenbahnmarder. 10. Der Teufelswälzer. 11. Der Stier von salanda. 12. Der Stellvertreter. 13. Die Launen des Glückes. 14. Die Bruder von St. Parasitus. 15. Der Meister. 16. Der Sprung ins Dunkle. 17. Die weisse Rose. 18. George Bully. 19. Das Rattenloch. 20. Der grosse Chef. 21. Die graue Elster. 22. Im letzten Augenblick. 23. Die Perlen des Dr. Talmadge. 24. Die Malayische Dschonke. 25. Der Fluch der bösen Tat. 26. Das Parfum der Mrs. Worrington. 27. Der Schuss im Pavillon. 28. Das Geheimnis einer Stunde. 29. Das grüne Monokel. 30. Masken.

640. Stunt Cowboy Series

(Universal, 1927–29) Series, 25 episodes, two reels each. D: Bruce Mitchell (Episodes 1–13), Walter Fabian (Episodes 14–25).

Little is known of Bob Curwood. Curwood was just a screen name. He was born in Romania on March 17, 1900. He was a onetime Naval cadet with a previous career in European circuses before going into films. He was a little man standing 5' 8½" and weighing 145 pounds. An accent probably ruled out his making any sound westerns.

Bob Curwood.

Episode Titles, Releasing Dates, Supporting Actors

1. The Scrappin Fool (9-17-27), Violet Bird. 2. A Dangerous Double (10-15-27), Shirley O'Hara. 3. The Battling Buckaroo (11-12-27), William A. Steele. 4. Riding Wild (12-10-27). 5. Boss of the Rancho (1-9-28). 6. The Brand of Courage (2-4-28), Peggy Montgomery. 7. The Looters (3-3-28). 8. The Payroll Roundup. (3-31-28). 9. Hidden Money (4-28-28). 10. Framed (5-26-28). 11. The Valiant Rider (6-23-28). 12. The Gold Claim (7-21-28). 13. The Getaway (8-18-28). 14. Speed and Spurs (9-8-28), Alma Rayford, George Chesebro, Tom Froman, George Chandler. 15. A Romeo of the Range (10-6-28), Lilian Gilmore, Howard Davies, Frank Baker, Helen Broneau. 16. The Secret Outlaw (11-10-28), Della Peterson, George Chesebro, Kenneth Duncan. 17. The Death's Head (12-8-28). 18 The Range of Fear (9-1-29), Derelys Perdue, George Chesebro, William McCall. 19. The Range Wolf (2-9-29). 20. Kidnapped (3-16-29). 21. Days of Daring (4-13-29). 22. Cowboy Pluck (5-18-29), Lotus Thompson, Frank M. Clark, Ted Oliver, Bay Johnstone. 23. Playing False (6-15-29). 24. Ridin' Leather (7-20-29), Lotus Thompson *or* Regina Doyle, Bud Osborne, William McCall. 25. The Lone Rider (8-10-29), Lotus Thompson *or* Regina Doyle, Robert Kortman, George Chandler.

641. Sunken Silver

(Pathé, May 10, 1925) Serial, 10 chapters, two reels each. D: George B. Seitz. Scen: Frank Leon Smity. S: Albert Payson Terhune—"Black Caesar's Clan."

Descendants of the original pirates, a Secret Service agent, a beautiful girl, and modern-day crooks all seek a $15 million treasure sent to the bottom of the sea off the Florida coast by pirates in the early 1800s.

There is no wordy introduction to start the action. The foreword simply states that when the United States completed negotiations for the Louisiana Purchase in 1804, practically all the money, fifteen million in silver dollars, was prepared for shipment to France. The ship bearing this treasure was lured to a watery grave on the Florida Coast by Black Caesar, the notorious pirate—and the resting place of this sunken silver is guarded by descendants of the pirates' cohorts, known as "conchs." Others are after the treasure, so is the United States Government.

Under the direction of George Seitz, who is to serials what Mack Sennett is to comedies, the picture rates as a hum-dinger. Much footage was actually shot in the Florida Everglades.

Allene Ray (Claire Standish), Walter Miller (Gavin Brice), Frank Lackteen (Rodney Hade), Albert Roccardi ("Conch" Leader), Jean Brunette (Bobby Burns), Gordon Bennet (Doug), Charlie Fang (Sato), Ivan Linow (Rako), Frank Wunderlee (Milo Standish).

1. Watched. 2. On Secret Service. 3. The Hidden Way. 4. Fangs. 5. Sea Tigers. 6. In Double Peril. 7. Face to Face. 8. The Shadow on the Stairs. 9. The Secret Panel. 10. The End of the Trail.

642. Superman

(Columbia, July 1948) Serial, 15 chapters, two reels each. D: Spencer G. Bennet and Thomas Carr. P: Sam Katzman. Assist. D: R.M. Andrews. Photography: Ira H. Morgan. Music: Mischa Bakaleinikoff. SP: Arthur Hoerl, Lewis Clay, and Royal Cole. Adaptation: George H. Plympton and Joseph F. Poland. Based on the Superman character appearing in *Superman* and *Action Comics*.

Superman, alias Clark Kent, is rocketed to Earth from Krypton before that planet explodes. He is found by an old couple who raise him as their own son. He becomes a newspaper reporter on *The Daily Planet* of Metropolis, keeping his identity a secret but appearing as Superman whenever he is needed to fight crime or to aid in emergencies where his super powers can save lives and lessen misery. He finds an able antagonist in The Spider Lady, who is after a reducer ray which she plans to use to subjugate governments.

Kirk Alyn (Clark Kent/Superman), Noel Neill (Lois Lane), Tommy Bond (Jimmy Olson), Pierre Watkin (Perry White), Carol Forman (The Spider Lady), George Meeker (Driller), Jack Ingram (Anton), Terry Frost (Brock), Charles Quigley (Dr. Hackett), Herbert Rawlinson (Dr. Graham), Forrest Taylor (Professor Leeds), Stephen Carr (Morgan), Charles King (Conrad), Rusty Wescoatt (Elton), Nelson Leigh (Jor El), Luana Walters (Lara), Robert Barron (Rozan), Edward Cassidy (Eben Kent), Virginia Carroll (Mrs. Kent), Alan Dinehart III (Clark Kent as a boy), Ralph Hodges (Clark Kent as a teenager), Jack George (Track Walker), Gene Roth (Train Conductor), Peggy Wynn (Flo, the Operator), Frank Ellis (Mine Security Guard), Rube Scharfer (Grady), Stanley Price (Crandall), Paul Stader (Irwin), Reed Howes (Jackson), Leonard Penn (Ward).

1. Superman Comes to Earth. 2. Depths of the Earth. 3. The Reducer Ray. 4. Man of Steel. 5. A Job for Superman. 6. Superman in Danger. 7. Into the Electrical Furnace. 8. Superman to the Rescue. 9. Irresistible Force. 10. Between Two Fires. 11. Superman's Dilemma. 12. Blast in the Depths. 13. Hurled to Destruction. 14. Superman at Bay. 15. The Payoff.

643. Surcouf

(France—Société des Cinéromans, 1925) Serial, 8 chapters. D: Louitz-Morat. Scen: Arthur Bernede.

Jean Angelo (Surcouf), Jacqueline Blanc, Maria Dalbaicin, Daniel Mendaille, Louis Monfils, Pierre Hot, Johanna Sutter, Thomy Bourdelle, Henri Keppens, Marthe Blanchard, Antonin Artaud, Beaulieu, Ghasne, Frederic Mariotti.

Portugeuse: 1. A mocidade de Surcouf. 2. Os pontões ingleses. 3. Trágicos esponsais. 4. Alma de herói. 5. A perseguição. 6. Mensageiro oficial. 7. Mordedura de serpenta. 8. A resposta de Bonaparte.

644. Sweedie

(Essanay, 1914–1915) Series, 24 (Minimum) episodes, one reel each. P/D: Wallace Beery produced, directed, or co-directed a number of these shorts. Scen: Louella Parsons scripted many of the comedy shorts.

Kirk Alyn in *Superman* (1948)

Wallace Beery (Sweedie, the Swedish Housemaid), Ben Turpin (as principal support), Betty Brown, Leo White.

1. Sweedie the Swatter. 2. Sweedie and the Lord. 3. Topsy-Turvy Sweedie. 4. Sweedie and the Double Exposure. 5. Sweedie Springs a Surprise. 6. Sweedie's Skate. 7. Sweedie's Clean-Up. 8. The Fickleness of Sweedie. 9. Sweedie Learns to Swim. 10. Sweedie and the Trouble Maker. 11. Countess Sweedie. 12. Sweedie at the Fair. 13. Sweedie and the Hypnotist. 14. Sweedie Collects for Charity. 15. Sweedie and the Sultan's Present. 16. Sweedie's Suicide. 17. Sweedie and Her Dog. 18. Sweedie Goes to College. 19. Sweedie's Hopeless Love. 20. Sweedie Learns to Ride. 21. Sweedie in Vaudeville. 22. Sweedie's Hero. 23. Sweedie's Finish. 24. Sweedie and the Janitor [Universal; story and direction by Beery].

645. Tailspin Tommy

(Universal, October 29, 1934) Serial, 12 chapters; Chapter 1, three reels; others, two reels. D: Louis Friedlander [Lew Landers]. SP: Norman S. Hall, Vin Moore, Basil Dickey, and Ella O'Neill. Based on the cartoon strip by Hal Forrest.

Two gangsters try every means possible to gain control of Three Point Airlines, but are foiled by Tailspin Tommy and his friends.

Maurice Murphy (Tailspin Tommy), Noah Beery, Jr. ("Skeeter" Mulligan), Patricia Farr (Betty Lou Barnes), Walter Miller (Bruce Hoty), Grant Withers (Milt Howe), John Davidson (Wade "Tiger" Taggart), Edmund Cobb (Speed Walton), Al Ferguson (Curly), Belle Daube (Mrs. Tompkins), Lee Beggs (Deacon Grimes), Charles A. Browne (Paul Smith), Denny Meadows [Dennis Moore] (Herb Slack), Monte Montague (Cliff), Jack Leonard (Al), Chester Gann (Flapjack), Ritz Rozelle (Mary Dale), Walter Fabian (Bevan), Lew Kelly (Vic Morton), Bryant Washburn (Director Grant), Ethan Laidlaw (Bart Dink), Charles Murphy (Pug Nelson), Bud Osborne (Grease Rowley), King Baggot (Inspector), William Desmond (Sloane), John Ince (Eric Peabody), Lynton Brent (Jack Bradley), William Worthington (Doctor), Ann Darling (Nurse), Walter Brennan (Intern), Slim Whitaker, Gertrude Astor, Jim Corey, Harold Goodwin, Beulah Hutton, Frank Brownlee.

1. Death Flies the Mail. 2. The Mail Goes Through. 3. Sky Bandits. 4. The Copper Room. 5. The Night Flight. 6. The Baited Trap. 7. Tommy to the Rescue. 8. The Thrill of Death. 9. The Earth Gods Roar. 10. Death at the Controls. 11. Rushing Waters. 12. Littleville's Big Day.

Jean Rogers and Clark Williams in *Tailspin Tommy in the Great Air Mystery* (1935)

646. Tailspin Tommy in the Great Air Mystery

(Universal, October 1935) Serial, 12 chapters, two reels each. D: Ray Taylor. SP: Ray Cannon, Ella O'Neill, Basil Dickey, Robert Herschon, and George Plympton. Based on the comic strip by Hal Forrest. Assoc. P: Henry McRae.

Horace Raymore, a villainous American, and Manuel Casmetta of the Central American island of Nazil, attempt to seize control of valuable oil lands, operating from a sophisticated jungle fortress equipped with modern weapons and fighting planes. Tailspin Tommy, his pal Skeeter, and girlfriend Betty Lou are hired to survey the oil properties and blaze a pipeline from the air. Although in constant peril, the trio are aided in time of crisis by a masked pilot in the "Eagle Plane," which appears out of an artificial cloud at vital moments, then disappears into another smoke screen.

Clark Williams (Tailspin Tommy Tompkins), Jean Rogers (Betty Lou Barnes), Noah Beery, Jr. (Skeeter Mulligan), Bryant Washburn (Ned Curtis), Helen Brown (Mrs. Tompkins), Delphine Drew (Inez Alvarado), Pablo Alvarez (Don Alvarado), Matthew Betz (Horace Raymore), Herbert Heywood (Manuel), James Burtis (Bill McGuire), Pat O'Brien (Milt Howie/The Eagle Pilot), William Desmond, Paul Ellis, Charles A. Browne.

1. Wreck of the Dirigible. 2. Roaring Fire God. 3. Hurled from the Skies. 4. Bolt from the Blue. 5. The Torrent. 6. Crash in the Clouds. 7. Flying Death. 8. Crossed and Double-Crossed. 9. Wings of Disaster. 10. Doomed in a Dungeon. 11. Desperate Chances. 12. The Last Stand.

647. Tales of the Old West

(Universal, 1923) Series, 7 episodes (?). D: Duke Worne.

Roy Stewart.

Episode Titles, Releasing Dates, Supporting Actors

1. God's Law (3-17-23), Gertrude Olmstead, James Welch, Leonard Clapham (Tom London). 2. The Guilty Hand (4-7-23), Gertrude Olmstead, Leonard Clapham (Tom London). 3. Hard to Beat (4-25-23). 4. A Fight for a Mine (5-18-23). 5. Better Than Gold (6-2-23), Gertrude Olmstead. 6. Forced to Fight. 7. The Showdown.

648. Der Tanz auf dem Vulkan

(Germany—Central–Film–Vertrieg [Eichberg-Film], 1920) 2 episodes. D: Richard Eichberg. SP: Arthur Teuber. Photography: Joe Rive.

This two episode film is unimportant except that Bela Lugosi is in the cast. The film is hardly a serial or a series and certainly is not a memorable film. Serial buffs will want to add it to their list of Lugosi films.

Lee Parry, Violette Napierska, Robert Scholz, Bela Lugosi, Gustav Birkholz, Felix, Hecht, Kurt Fuss.

1. Sybil Young. 2. Der Tod des Grossfursten.

649. Tao

(France—Société des Cineromans, 1923) Serial, 10 chapters. D: Gaston Ravel. Scen: Gaston Ravel and Tony Lekain. S: Arnould Galopin. Art D: Louis Nalpas.

Mary Harald, Andrée Brabant, Joe Hamman, Aicha, Gaston Nores, Paul Hubert, Tony Lekain, Andre Deed.

1. O segrado do Bonzo. 2. Uma intriga engenhosa. 3. Sob a mascara. 4. Historia de um roubo. 5. Situacao complicada. 6. Atribulacoes de Catavento. 7. De Paris a Dakar. 8. Amores e rancores. 9. O casamento de Raimunda. 10. Nas Trevas do templo.

Buster Crabbe in *Tarzan the Fearless* (1933)

650. Tarzan the Fearless

(Principal, August 11, 1933) Serial, 15 chapters, two reels each. D: Robert F. Hill. SP: Basil Dickey, George Plympton, and Walter Anthony. Supervision: William Lora Wright. P: Sol Lesser. Camera: Harry Newman and Joe Brotherton. Based on characters created by Edgar Rice Burroughs. Film also released in a condensed 85-minute feature version.

Tarzan aids Mary Brooks and Bob Hall in the search for Mary's father, who is a prisoner of the people of Zor, god of the Emerald Fingers. Mary's guide Jeff wants Mary and secretly seeks a lost treasure, aided by Nick in his endeavors. The followers of Zor further complicate the situation by trying to kill everyone. However, Tarzan triumphs and, though he speaks no English, wins Mary as his mate.

Buster Crabbe (Tarzan) [Lesser attempted to borrow Weissmuller from MGM for this serial but couldn't; hence the casting of Crabbe], Jacqueline Wells (Mary Brooks) [a.k.a. Diane Duval and Julie Bishop], E. Alyn Warren (Doctor Brooks), Edward Woods (Bob Hall), Philo McCullough (Jeff Herbert), Matthew Betz (Nick Muran), Frank Lackteen (Abdul), Mischa Auer (High Priest Eltar), Carlotta Monti (Priestess of Zor), Symonia Boniface (Arab Woman), Darby Jones (Head Barrier), Al Kikuma (Warrior), George DeNormand (Guard).

1. The Dive of Death. 2. The Storm God Strikes. 3. Thundering Death. 4. The Pit of Peril. 5. Blood Money. 6. Voodoo Vengeance. 7. Caught by Cannibals. 8. The Creeping Terror. 9. Eyes of Evil. 10. The Death Plunge. 11. Harvest of Hate. 12. Jungle Justice.

651. Tarzan the Mighty

(Universal, August 12, 1928) Serial, 15 chapters, two reels each. D: Jack Nelson and Ray Taylor. Scen: Ian McClosky. S: Edgar Rice Burroughs—*Jungle Tales of Tarzan*.

Deep in the jungle is a village inhabited by the descendants of pirates. Black John, a beachcomber, has worked on the superstitions of these primitive people until he dominates them completely. He conducts a ceremony with incantations to set the evil spirits against Tarzan and his apes, who have raided their cattle.

Mary and Bob, sister and brother castaways, are living among the tribe. Black John, despite Mary's protest, determines to make her his bride. Before he can do so, however, she is seen by Tarzan taking a bath in a forest pool. He is fascinated by this strange and beautiful creature. Suddenly he is horrified to see a swarm of crocodiles sliding into the pool from the opposite shore. His battle-cry acquaints Mary with her desperate situation. She swims frantically for the bank pursued by a monster crocodile. Death seems inevitable when Tarzan dives from a tree and tackles the beast with his bare hands. Thereafter Tarzan fights to keep Black John from forcing marriage on Mary and to free her brother held captive by the villain, who also plans to pass himself off as Lord Greystoke and take what rightfully belongs to Tarzan.

Frank Merrill (Tarzan), Natalie Kingston (Mary Trevor), Bobby Nelson (Bobby Trevor), Al Ferguson (Black John), Lorimer Johnson (Lord Greystoke), Tantor [the elephant] (Himself). [Frank Merrill was a replacement for Joe Bonomo, who had broken his leg in the early stages of production. Merrill proved to be a much better Tarzan than Bonomo had been.]

1. The Terror of Tarzan. 2. The Love Cry. 3. The Call of the Jungle. 4. The Lion's Leap. 5. Flames of Hate. 6. The Fiery Pit. 7. The Leopard's Lair. 8. The Jungle Traitor. 9. Lost in the Jungle. 10. Jaws of Death. 11. A Thief in the Night. 12. The Enemy of Tarzan. 13. Perilous Paths. 14. Facing Death. 15. The Reckoning.

652. Tarzan the Tiger

(Universal, December 9, 1929) Serial, 15 chapters, two reels each. D: Henry McRae. SP: Ian McClosky Heath. S:

Edgar Rice Burroughs—"Tarzan and the Jewels of Opar." Released in both silent and semi-sound versions. The sound version had a crude musical score, sound effects, and a few lip-synchronized lines on a record. It was this film that initiated the famous Tarzan yell.

Werper, posing as a friendly scientist, sells Jane into slavery after Tarzan's estate is raided by Arabs. In a fight, Tarzan received a blow on the head which leaves him confused for much of the film, but he finally regains his senses, rescues Jane, bests the villain, and saves the jewels of Opar.

This was Frank Merrill's second and last appearance as Tarzan. A third serial, "Tarzan the Terrible," was announced for him but was not made. Lillian Worth had also played Queen La in *The Adventures of Tarzan* (Numa, 1921).

Frank Merrill (Tarzan [Earl of Greystoke]), Natalie Kingston (Jane), Lillian Worth (Queen La of Opar), Al Ferguson (Werper), Sheldon Lewis (Achmet Zek), Frank Lanning (Mohammed Bey).

1. Call of the Jungle. 2. The Road to Opar. 3. The Altar of the Flaming God. 4. The Vengeance of La. 5. Condemned to Death. 6. Tantor, the Terror. 7. In Deadly Peril. 8. Loop of Death. 9. Flight of Werper. 10. Prisoner of the Apes. 11. The Jaws of Death. 12. The Jewels of Opar. 13. A Human Sacrifice. 14. Tarzan's Rage. 15. Tarzan's Triumph.

653. The Telephone Girl

(R-C/F.B.O., 1924) Series, 12 episodes, two reels each. D: Malcolm St. Clair, Percy Pembroke. Scen: Darryl Francis Zanuck, George Marion, Jr. From the *Cosmopolitan* magazine stories by H.C. Witwer.

Vaughn's portrayal of the quick-thinking, slick, slangy, sophisticated telephone operator assured success of the series. She had a sparkling personality and was quite adept at comedy. Audiences could identify with her misfortunes for they were the kind that the ordinary person might have.

The stories deal with the love affairs of a telephone operator who works in a New York hotel, where her baby stare and intriguing ways cause plenty of agitation to masculine hearts. Each episode has a complete little story of its own but all the episodes are somewhat related.

Alberta Vaughn (Gladys Murgatroyd), Gertruce Short, Charles King, Arthur Rankin, Douglas Gerrard, Al Cooke, Kit Guard, Jim Moore.

1. Julius Sees Her. 2. When Knighthood was in Tower. 3. Money to Burns. 4. Sherlock's Home. 5. King Leary. 6. William Tells. 7. For the Love of Mike. 8. The Square Sex. 9. Bee's Knees. 10. Love and Learn. 11. Faster Foster. 12. Hello and Good-Bye.

654. Tempest Cody—Spur and Saddle

(Universal, August 20–October 16, 1919) Series, 9 episodes. D: Jacques Jaccard (4), George Holt (4), Henry McRae (1). SP: George Hively (7), Anthony Coldeway (1), Wycliffe A. Hill (1).

Marie Walcamp, Episode 1: Robert Anderson, Charles Brinley, Ben Corbett, Leonard Trainer, Slim Paggette, Archie Ricks, Eugenie Forde, A. MacPherson. Episode 2: Robert Anderson, Charles Brinley. Episode 3: Robert Anderson, Charles Brinley, Ben Corbett, Gabe Price. Episode 4: unknown. Episode 5: Carl Miller, Jack Walters, Betty Srack. Episode 6: unknown. Episode 7: Carl Miller, Arizona Brady. Episode 8: Frank Braidwood, Bert Sprotte, Madge Hunt, John Linge. Episode 9: Beulah Booker, Frank Braidwood, Harry Schumm.

1. Tempest Cody Hits the Trail (8-20-19). 2. Tempest Cody Flirts with Death (8-3-19). 3. Tempest Cody Rides Wild (9-9-19). 4. Tempest Cody's Man Hunt (9-19-19). 5. Tempest Cody Plays Detective (9-30-19). 6. Tempest Cody Gets Her Man (9-30-19). 7. Tempest Cody Turns the Tables (10-?-19). 8. Tempest Cody Bucks the Trust (10-11-19). 9. Tempest Cody, Kidnapper (10-16-19).

Allene Ray and Jack Mower in *Ten Scars Make a Man* (1924)

655. Ten Scars Make a Man

(Pathé, October 12, 1924) Serial, 10 chapters, two reels each. D: William Parke. S: Phillips Barry. P: C.W. Patton.

Rita and Jean are attending a boarding school in the East. Jack proposes to Jean but is told he must acquire ten scars before he could marry her. Exactly why is not made clear. However, his first scar comes quickly as he attempts to rescue Jean from the clutches of the fencing master and is blackjacked from behind.

Both girls are threatened with expulsion from school unless they pay the villain a lot of money. Out West their father owns a large ranch but has mysteriously disappeared. Back at home Rita manifests a personal problem. She labors under the belief that she is the descendant of a flirtatious Spanish countess and that she has inherited the same power of attraction for men. She carries on a series of love affairs, and it is up to Jean to see that she is not taken advantage of.

Jack tackles and solves all of the problems the girls are having, exposes the villain, and wins the hand of Jean. Most of the story takes place in the West; thus, it should be classified as a western.

Allene Ray (Jean Morell), Jack Mower (Jack O'Day), Rose Burdick (Rita Morell), Frank Whitson (Henry O'Day), Larry Steers (Edgar Venable), Leon De La Mothe (Luther Candle), Harry Woods (Buck Simpson), Frank Lanning (Aztinca), Lillian Gale (Maria), Scott McKee.

1. Two Girls and a Man. 2. Cowboy Chivalry. 3. Westward Bound. 4. The Cattle Raid. 5. Through the Hills. 6. Midnight Marauders. 7. Unmasked. 8. Liquid Gold. 9. The Valley of the Legend. 10. The End of the Quest.

656. Tenderfoot Thriller

(Universal, 1928–29) Series, 12 episodes, two reels each. D: Walter Fabian.

Few movie patrons of the 1930s and 1940s had any inclination that the semicomic character they saw in many movies was at one time a Western star; yet at one time he made a series of comedy westerns for Universal that were popular enough for the company to extend production for a total of twelve films.

George Chandler.

Episode Titles, Releasing Dates, Director (in italics), Supporting Actors

1. A Tenderfoot Hero (9-29-28), *Walter Fabian;* Gloria Gray, Wilbur Mack, William Malan. 2. Saps and Saddles (10-27-28), *Walter Fabian;* Regina Doyle, Tom Forman, Kenneth Duncan. 3. A Clean Sweep (12-1-28), *Walter Fabian;* Regina Doyle, Nelson McDowell, Al Ferguson, William McCall. 4. A Fighting Tenderfoot (12-24-28), *Walter Fabian;* Dorothy Dix, Otto Bibber, Bud Osborne. 5. A Daring Dude (2-2-29), *Walter Fabian;* Regina Doyle. 6. Two-Gun Morgan (3-2-29), *Walter Fabian;* Kathryn Crawford, Bill Patton, Otto Bibber, William McCall, Syd Saylor. 7. Riding for Love (4-6-29), *Walter Fabian;* Kathryn Crawford, Walter Shumway. 8. Red Romance (5-4-29), *Walter Fabian;* Regina Doyle, Wilbur Mack, Buck Connors, Syd Saylor. 9. The Thrill Hunter (6-8-29), *Walter Fabian;* Lotus Thompson, Wilbur Mack, Buck Connors, Robert Kortman. 10. A Close Call (7-6-29), *Walter Fabian;* Elinor Flynn, Bill Patton, William McCall. 11. The Go Get 'Em Kid (8-3-29), *Walter Fabian;* Elinor Flynn, Bud Osborne, Buck Connors. 12. A Tenderfoot Terror (8-31-29), *Walter Fabian.*

Chandler was one of the founders and past president of Screen Actors Guild.

Allene Ray in *The Terrible People* (1928)

657. The Terrible People

(Pathé, August 5, 1928) Serial, 10 chapters, two reels each. D: Spencer G. Bennet. SP: George Arthur Gray. S: Edgar Wallace.

A famous forger finally commits a murder and is executed, but before he dies he threatens the detective and the judge, etc., with drastic vengeance at the hands of the "Terrible People." Two cloaked villains stalk through this thriller.

Left: **Joyce Bryant, Forrest Taylor, and Jack Ingram;** ***right:*** **Joyce Bryant in** ***Terry and the Pirates*** **(1940)**

Allene Ray (Nora Sanders), Walter Miller (Arnold Long), Larry Steers (Jack Crayley), Allan Craven (Joshua Monkford), Alice McCormack (Alice Cravel), Wilfred North (Godley Long), Fred Vroom (Clayton Shelton), Thomas Holding (Sonny Cravel), Gilbert Clayton (Krill), William Bletcher (Proody), Mary Foy, Joy Auburn.

1. The Penalty. 2. Disaster. 3. The Claws of Death. 4. Hidden Enemies. 5. The Disastrous Rescue. 6. The House of Peril. 7. In the Enemy's Hands. 8. The Dread Professor. 9. The Death Trap. 10. The Capture.

658. The Terror of the Range

(Pathé, February 2, 1919) Serial, 7 chapters, two reels each. D: Stuart Paton. S: W.A.S. Douglas—"The Wolf-Faced Man." SP: Lucian Hubbard. P: Diando Film Corporation.

A United States government agent clashes with a mysterious bandit wearing a wolf's head whenever he leads his marauders down a blood thirsty trail of murder and looting.

The shortest serial ever released by Pathé.

Betty Compson (Thelma Grant), George Larkin (John Hardwick), H.P. Carpenter (James Grant), Fred M. Malatesta (Black John), Ora Carew (Vampire), True Boardman (Broncho Haryigan), Walter McNamera, Alice Saunders, Billy Quinn.

1. Prowlers of the Night. 2. The Hidden Chart. 3. The Chase of Fear. 4. The Midnight Raid. 5. A Threat from the Past. 6. Tangled Tales. 7. Run to Earth.

659. The Terror Trail

(Universal, July 1921) Serial, 18 chapters, two reels each. D: Edward Kull. S/Scen: Edward Kull, John W. Grey, and George H. Plympton.

Eileen Sedgwick (Vera Vernan/Elaine Emerson), George Larkin (Bruce Barnes), Theodore Brown (Bertram Russell), Albert J. Smith (Hunch Henderson), Barney Furey (Holmes), Pierre M. Courdec.

1. The Mystery Girl. 2. False Clues. 3. The Mine of Menace. 4. The Door of Doom. 5. The Bridge of Disaster. 6. The Ship of Surprise. 7. The Palace of Fear. 8. The Peril of the Palace. 9. The Desert of Despair. 10. Sands of Fate. 11. The Menace of the Sea. 12. The Isle of Eternity. 13. The Forest of Fear. 14. The Lure of the Jungle. 15. The Jaws of Death. 16. The Storm of Despair. 17. The Arm of the Law. 18. The Final Reckoning.

660. Terry and the Pirates

(Columbia, 1940) Serial, 15 chapters, two reels each. D: James W. Horne. SP: Mark Layton, George Morgan, Joseph Levering. Based upon the cartoon strip characters created by Milton Caniff. P: Larry Darmour. Photography: James S. Brown, Jr. Music: Lee Zahler.

Terry's father disappears in the Asian jungle while seeking the secrets of a lost civilization. His expedition has been captured by the jungle pirates of Fang, local warlord who seeks a legendary treasure said to be hidden beneath the lost civilization's Temple of Mara. Terry and his friends battle Fang, his henchman Stanton, and Fang's Tiger Men.

William Tracy (Terry Lee), Granville Owens (Pat Ryan), Joyce Bryant (Normandie Drake), Allen Jung (Connie), Victor De Camp (Big Stoop), Sheila Darcy (Dragon Lady), Dick Curtis (Fang), J. Paul Jones (Doctor Lee), Forrest Taylor (Allen Drake), Jack Ingram (Stanton), Steve Clemento (Gori), Kit Guard, Charles King, Eddie Fetherstone, Constantine Romanoff.

1. Into the Great Unknown. 2. The Fang Strikes. 3. The Mountain of Death. 4. The Dragon Queen Threatens. 5. At the Mercy of a Mob. 6. The Scroll of Wealth. 7. Angry Waters. 8. The Tomb of Peril. 9. Jungle Hurricane. 10. Too Many Enemies. 11. Walls of Doom. 12. No Escape. 13. The Fatal Mistake. 14. Pyre of Death. 15. The Secret of the Temple.

661. Terry of the Times

(Universal, July 17, 1930) Serial, 10 chapters, two reels each. D: Henry McRae. S: Hal Hodes. Released in both silent and sound versions.

A criminal band known as the Mystic Mendicants attempts to keep Terry from inheriting the *Times* by preventing him from fulfilling provisions of his father's will to marry by a certain date. A treacherous, and as it turns out, fake brother of publisher Robert McCoy, Terry's uncle, disguises himself as Macy, the paper's publisher, and attempts to block Terry's marriage and his interference with the Mendicants' criminal operations.

Reed Howes (Terry), Lotus Thompson (Eileen Parks), Sheldon Lewis (Macy), John Oscar (Rastus), William Hayes (Patch Dugan), Mary Grant (Moll), Norman Tomson (Blind Man), Kingsley Benedict (Hunchback), Taylor Holmes.

1. The Mystic Mendicants. 2. The Fatal 30! 3. Death's Highway. 4. Eyes of Evil. 5. Prowlers of the Night. 6. The Stolen Bride. 7. A Doorway of Death. 8. A Trail of Trickery. 9. Caught in the Net. 10. A Race for Love.

662. El Testamento de Diego Rocafort

(Spain—Hispano Films, 1916) Serial, 6 chapters. D: Alberto Marro.

Joaquim Carrasco, Maria Reigada, José Durany, Francisco Carrasco.

1. El secuestro. 2. Los enmasca rados. 3. El duelo. 4. Los monederos falsos. 5. Los espansales. 6. El Montserrat.

663. Tex Granger

(Columbia, April 1, 1948) Serial, 15 chapters, two reels each. Based on the "Tex Granger" stories in *Calling All Boys* and *Tex Granger* comics. D: Derwin Abrahams. SP: Arthur Hoerl, Lewis Clay, Harry Fraser, and Royal Cole. P: Sam Katzman. Assist. D: Mike Eason. Photography: Ira H. Morgan. Music: Mischa Bakaleinikoff.

Tex Granger purchases a western newspaper in Three Buttes, where Dancer Carson, through his loan office, is operating outside the law. The marshal is actually an outlaw, and another badman, operating more-or-less independently of the marshal or Carson, and is determined to enrich himself in whatever way he can. Tex, on occasion, dons a mask to become a mysterious fighter for good and ultimately is able to subdue the criminal element.

Top: **Reed Howes (*standing, lighter suit*), Lotus Thompson, and Sheldon Lewis (*on floor*) in *Terry of the Times* (1930); *bottom:* I. Stanford Jolley, William Fawcett (*center*), and Robert Kellard in *Tex Granger* (1948)**

Robert Kellard [Robert Stevens] (Tex Granger), Peggy Stewart (Helen Kent), Buzz Henry (Tim), Duke, the Wonder Dog (Himself), Smith Ballew (Blaze Talbot), Jack Ingram (Reno), I. Stanford Jolley (Dancer Carson), Terry Frost (Adams), Jim Diehl (Conroy), Britt Wood (Sandy), Bill Brauer (Joe Hall), Stanley Blystone, John Hart, Eddie Parker, Edmund Cobb, Al Ferguson, Charles Whitaker, Charles King.

1. Tex Finds Trouble. 2. Rider of Mystery Mesa. 3. Dead or Alive. 4. Dangerous Trails. 5. Renegade Pass. 6. A Crooked Deal. 7. The Rider Unmasked. 8. Mystery of

the Silver Ghost. 9. The Rider Trapped. 10. Midnight Ambush. 11. Renegade Roundup. 12. Carson's Last Draw. 13. Blaze Takes Over. 14. Riding Wild. 15. The Rider Meets Blaze.

664. Tex Williams Western Shorts

(Universal, 1947–50) Series, 18 episodes, two reels each. D/P: Will Cowan.

A series of unrelated western stories featuring the music of Tex Williams and his band. The series format is similar to that of the RKO series starring Ray Whitley and his Six-Bar Cowboys.

Tex Williams, Deuce Spriggins, Smokey Rogers, Patricia Alphin, Judy Clark, Jimmie Dodd, Lina Romay, Cactus Soldin, Stanley Andrews, William Haade, Barbara Payton, Joe Granby, Lane Bradford, Donna Martell, Myron Healey, William Cassidy, Forrest Taylor, George Lloyd, Monte Montague, Harry Calkin, Terry Frost, George Eldredge, Judd Holdren, Leslie Kimmell, Jim Hayward, William Tannen, Kenneth MacDonald, Bob Wilkie, Jess Fargo, Shirley Allard, Jack Ingram, Fred Kohler, Jr., Edmund Cobb, Bob Anderson, James Linn, Patricia Hall, Tris Coffin, Leslie Banning, Marshall Reed, Franklin Parker, Steve Clark, Chuck Hayward, Ray Jones, Robert O'Neill, Ann Pearce, Felipe Turich, Harry Lauter, Holly Bane, Harry Vijar, James Linn, Ethan Laidlaw.

1. Tex Williams and His Western Caravan (8-27-47, 25 min.). 2. Western Whoopee (6-23-48, 15 min.). 3. Six-Gun Music (1-6-49, 25 min.). 4. Cheyenne Cowboy (2-10-49, 25 min.). 5. West of Laramie (3-24-49, 23 min.). 6. Silver Butte (7-28-49, 27 min.). 7. The Girl from Gunsight (9-15-49, 24 min.). 8. The Pecos Pistol (10-27-49, 26 min.). 9. Coyote Canyon (11-17-49, 24 min.). 10. South of Santa Fe (12-22-49). 11. Gold Strike (3-30-50, 24 min.). 12. Prairie Pirates (5-5-50, 23 min.). 13. Cactus Caravan (7-6-50, 26 min.). 14. The Fargo Phantom (7-9-50, 25 min.). 15. Ready to Ride (10-5-50, 25 min.). 16. Rustler's Ransom (1950, 25 min.). 17. Western Courage (1950, 25 min.). 18. Ready to Ride (10-5-50, 25 min.).

665. The Texas Ranger

(Universal, 1927–28) Series, 13 episodes, two reels each.

1. The Fighting Texan (9-10-27) D: Josef Sevigard; S/Sp: George W. Pyper; Fred Gilman, Lillian Gilmore, Walter Shumway, L.A. Poff, John Hall. 2. On Special Duty (10-8-27) D: Walter Fabian; S: Brandt Wiley; SP: William Lester; Fred Gilman, Gloria Gray, Cuyler Supplee, Buck Connors. 3. The Law Rider (11-5-27) D: Walter Fabian; S/SP: George W. Pyper; Fred Gilman. 4. The Smiling Wolf (12-5-27) D: Walter Fabian; S: Carol Holloway; Fred Gilman. 5. The Lone Ranger (12-31-27) D: Walter Fabian; S/SP: Arthur Henry Gooden; Fred Gilman, Peggy O'Day, Ted Oliver. 6. Wolves of the Range (1-28-28) D: Walter Fabian; S/SP: George W. Pyper; Fred Gilman, Peggy Montgomery. 7. An Unexpected Hero (2-25-28) D: Walter Fabian; S/SP: George Morgan; Fred Gilman, Marjorie King. 8. Battling Justice (3-24-28) D: Walter Fabian; S/SP: George W. Pyper; Fred Gilman. 9. Gauge of Battle (4-21-28) D: Walter Fabian; S/SP: Basil Dickey; Fred Gilman. 10. Fighting Destiny (5-19-28) D: Walter Fabian; S: Meta Sterns; SP: Basil Dickey; Fred Gilman. 11. The Ambuscade (5-22-28) D: Josef Levigard; S/SP: Basil Dickey; Fred Gilman. 12. The Card of Destiny (7-14-28) D: Walter Fabian; S/SP: Basil Dickey; Fred Gilman. 13. The Ranger Patrol (8-11-28) D: Walter Fabian; S/SP: Basil Dickey; Fred Gilman, Slim Whitaker.

666. The Third Eye

(Pathé, May 23, 1920) Serial, 15 chapters, two reels each. D: James W. Horne. S: H.H. Van Loan. Scen: William Parker.

A pretty movie star becomes the victim of a murderous gang, the head of which has fallen in love with her, and also has marked her as a useful addition to the gang. In his scheme to revenge himself on her for refusing to obey him, he feigns death when she shoots him with a studio revolver, and later it is found that the moving picture camera has recorded the event, leaving the hand that turned the crank a mystery. A struggle then begins between the young woman, aided by her sweetheart, and the leader of the gang for possession of the film.

The young woman is lured to the gang's headquarters, and is later commissioned to kill a man she will find in a certain room at a masked ball. The man proves to be her sweetheart. She breaks the dagger with which she is to stab him and places the stub in his clothing with the appearance that the deed has been done. She then goes to regain the film which she has been promised for the carrying out of the deed. However, before she has it in her possession the gang leader's would-be sweetheart phones him that he has been duped.

Thus begins a fifteen chapter struggle for the film.

Eileen Percy, Warner Oland, Jack Mower, Olga Grey, Mark Strong.

1. The Poisoned Dagger. 2. The Pendulum of Death. 3. In Destruction's Path. 4. Daggers of Death. 5. The Black Hand Bag. 6. The Death Spark. 7. The Crook's Ranch. 8. Trails of Danger. 9. The Race for Life. 10. The House of Terrors. 11. The Long Arm of Vengeance. 12. Man Against Man. 13. Blind Trails of Justice. 14. At Bay. 15. Triumph of Justice.

667. Three-Fingered Kate

(British & Colonial Kinematograph Company, 1909–1912) Series. D: H.O. Martinek. S: Harold Brett (1912 entries).

Episode Titles and Casts • *The Exploits of Three-Fingered Kate* (1909); Ivy Martinek (Kate), Alice Moseley (Mary), Charles Calvert (Daniel "Sheerluck" Finch). • *Three-Fingered Kate—Her Second Victim, the Art Dealer* (1909); Ivy Martinek (Kate), Alice Moseley (Mary), Charles Calvert ("Sheerluck" Finch). • *Three-Fingered Kate—Her Victim, the Banker* (1910; Ivy Martinek (Kate), Alice Moseley (Mary), Edward Durrant (Rickshaw). • *Three-Fingered Kate—The Episode of the Sacred Elephants* (1910); Ivy Martinek (Kate), Alice Moseley (Mary), Charles Calvert ("Sheerluck" Finch), Edward Durrant (Rickshaw). • *Three-Fingered Kate—The Wedding Presents* (1912); Ivy Martinek (Kate), Alice Moseley (Mary), Charles Calvert ("Sheerluck" Finch), Fred Paul (Sir Douglas Carrington), Olympia Sumner (Evadne Carrington), Jack Stokes (Chalmers), W. Gladstone Haley (Tarvin), Bessie Booker (Friend). • *Three-Fingered Kate—The Case of the Chemical Fumes* (1912); Ivy Martinek (Kate), Alice Moseley (Mary), Charles Calvert ("Sheerluck" Finch), Edward Durrant (Baron Rochid), Harold Brett

(Carrick Carthew). • *Three-Fingered Kate—The Pseudo-Quartette* (1912); Ivy Martinek (Kate), Alice Moseley (Mary), Charles Calvert ("Sheerluck" Finch), W. Gladstone (Snookey), Edward Durrant (Lord Malcolm).

668. The Three Musketeers

(Mascot, April 22, 1933) Serial, 12 chapters; Chapter 1, three reels; others, two reels. D: Armand Schaefer and Colbert Clark. SP: Norman Hall, Colbert Clark, Ben Cohn, and Wyndham Gittens. S: Based loosely on the story by Alexander Dumas. P: Nat Levine. Photography: Ernest Miller and Tom Galligan. Music: Lee Zahler. Dialogue: Ella Arnold. Released in 1948 by Favorite Films as 70-minute feature *Desert Command*.

Three legionnaires, Clancy, Renard, and Schmidt, are rescued from desert rebels by Tom Wayne, an American aviator. The four become involved in thwarting the attempts of the mysterious leader of a desert tribal cult that is attempting to wipe out the Foreign Legion.

Jack Mulhall (Clancy), Raymond Hatton (Renard), Francis X. Bushman, Jr. (Schmidt), John Wayne (Tom Wayne), Ruth Hall (Elaine Corday), Creighton Chaney [Lon Jr.] (Armand Corday), Hooper Atchley (El Kadur), Gordon DeMain (Colonel Duval), Robert Frazer (Major Booth), Noah Beery, Jr. (Stubbs), Al Ferguson (Ali), Edward Peil, Sr. (Ratkin/El Shaitan), William Desmond (Captain Boncour), George Magrill (El Maghreb), Robert Warwick (Colonel Brent), Emile Chautard (General Pelletier), Rodney Hildebrandt (Demoyne), Merrill McCormick (Heavy), Ken Cooper (Arab), Wilfred Lucas, Yakima Canutt.

1. Fiery Circle. 2. One for All and All for One. 3. The Master Key. 4. Pirates of the Desert. 5. Rebels' Rifles. 6. Death's Marathon. 7. Naked Steel. 8. The Master Strikes. 9. The Fatal Cave. 10. Trapped. 11. The Measure of a Man. 12. The Glory of Comrades.

669. Thunderbolt Jack

(Arrow Film Corp., 1921) Serial, 15 chapters, two reels each. D: Francis Ford or Murdock MacQuarrie (?). S: Joe Brandt. Supervision: Ben Wilson.

Bill Halliday and his wife, Martha, have a section of land which they mortgage to send their son Jack to college. Bull Flint is the big man of a small town near the Halliday ranch. He is supposedly a wealthy rancher but in reality is the head of a gang of rustlers whose depredations have terrorized the entire region. He is assisted by his young brother and by Manuel, a half-breed who is his lieutenant and who does most of his dirty work. Oil is discovered on the Halliday ranch and Bull plots to secure it. He tricks Halliday into signing what Halliday believes is a second mortgage but in reality is a deed to the ranch.

Bess Morgan is the daughter of a rancher who has come West for his health. He has a valuable homestead which Flint desires because of its water rights. Bess is

Top: **John Wayne and Ruth Hall in *The Three Musketeers* (1933);** ***bottom:*** **Jack Hoxie and Marin Sais in *Thunderbolt Jack* (1920)**

a particularly well-built, good-looking woman, fond of outdoor life, an excellent shot and horsewoman. Both Flint and his brother try to force their attentions on her.

Jack learns what is going on back home and returns determined to get his folks' ranch back. He quickly makes the acquaintance of Bess and together they fight Flint and his gang at every turn.

Jack Hoxie (Jack Halliday), Marin Sais (Bess Morgan), Chris Frank ("Bull" Flint), Al Hoxie (Bud), Steve Clemento (Manuel Garcia), Edith Stayart (The White Queen).

Top: **Jack Hoxie in *Thunderbolt Jack* (1920);** ***bottom:*** **Linda Stirling, Duncan Renaldo, and Allan Lane in *The Tiger Woman* (1944)**

1. The Thunderbolt Strikes. 2. Eight to One. 3. Held for Hostage. 4. The Vanishing Man. 5–8. [Unknown.] 9. Dungeon (or Jaws) of Death. 10–12. [Unknown.] 13. The Death Pyre. 14. [Unknown.] 15. [Unknown.]

670. The Tiger Band

(Holmes Productions/Warner Bros., 1919) Serial, 15 chapters, two reels each. Tentative Title: "The Danger Trail." D: Gilbert P. Hamilton. Released on the independent market.

No information on the plot of this serial.

Helen Holmes (Helen Warren), Jack Mower (Jim Stone), Dwight Crittendon (Jackson Warren), Omar Whitehead (Wong), William Brunton (Jose Galvez), Bert Hadley ("The Villain"), Tukio Aoyama.

1. Chang the Mighty. 2. The Brand of Hate. 3. The Stolen Engine. 4. In the Power of Chang. 5. The Great Leap. 6. The Mysterious Friend. 7. At Close Quarters. 8. A Race with Death. 9. A Perilous Escape. 10. Trapped. 11. The Death Hazard. 13. The Flaming Peril. 14. The Masked Man's Treachery. 15. The Masked Man's Claws [aka Masked Man Pays].

671. The Tiger Woman

(Republic, May 1944) Serial, 12 chapters, two reels each. D: Spencer Bennet, Wallace Grissell. SP: Royal Cole, Ronald Davidson, Basil Dickey, Jesse Duffy, Grant Nelson, and Joseph Poland. Assoc. P: W.J. O'Sullivan. Photography: Bud Thackery. Music: Joseph Dubin. Special Effects: Theodore Lydecker. Reissued in 1951 as *Perils of the Darkest Jungle*. Feature Title: *Jungle Gold*.

Unscrupulous agents of a rival oil company attempt to delay the development of a new oil field by the Inter-Ocean Oil Company, which must bring in the field within a specified time or lose its lease. Allen Saunders, trouble shooter for Inter-Ocean is sent to the jungle oil field to investigate. When the enemy attempts to kill him, The Tiger Woman intervenes. She is the white queen of a jungle tribe, having been brought up in the jungle after being lost as a child in a plane crash. The villains suspect that she is Rita Arnold, heiress to a large fortune. In addition to smashing the oil project, they try to secure proof of the Tiger Woman's identity, intending to kill her and substitute another girl in her place.

Linda Stirling (The Tiger Woman/Rita Arnold), Allan Lane (Allen Saunders), Duncan Renaldo (Jose Delgado), George J. Lewis (Morgan), LeRoy Mason (Fletcher Walton), Crane Whitley (Tom Dagget), Robert Frazer (Ramgah), Rico de Montez (Tegula), Stanley Price (Mac), Nolan Leary (Scott), Kenne Duncan (Gentry), Marshall Reed (Foster), Fred Graham (Joe/Steve/Hardin/Goff), Tom Steele (Lance/Largo/Karl), Charles Hayes (Bartender), Duke Green (Flint/Grat/Heavy), Frank Marlowe

(Burt), George Renavent (Commandant), Tom London (Dumont), Rex Lease (Mart), Al Ferguson (Lou/Heavy), Eddie Parker (Cherkin/Trooper/Guard), Roy Darmour (Officer), Bert LeBaron (Pete), Paul Gustine (Pilot), Robert Wilkie, Walt LaRue, Bud Geary, John Daheim (Heavies), Dale Van Sickel (Krants/Frank), Ken Terrell (Bolton/Dixon), Carey Loftin (Slim), Cliff Lyons (Trooper/Rand), Bud Wolfe (Tony), Herman Hack (Wilson), Joe Molina, Harry Smith, Catherine McLeod, Augie Gomez, Babe DeFreest.

1. Temple of Terror. 2. Doorway to Death. 3. Cathedral of Carnage. 4. Echo of Eternity. 5. Two Shall Die. 6. Dungeon of the Doomed. 7. Mile a Minute Murder. 8. Passage to Peril. 9. Cruise to Cremation. 10. Target for Murder. 11. The House of Horror. 12. Triumph Over Treachery.

672. The Tiger's Shadow

(Pathé, December 23, 1928) Serial, 10 chapters, two reels each. D: Spencer G. Bennet. Continuity: George Gray. S: George Gray.

"The Tiger," the terror of crooks, repeatedly interrupts the criminal activities in the home of Amos Crain, a wealthy invalid adventurer, in which Crain's pretty ward and Tony Kent are involved. The Tiger attempts to prevent the theft of a fortune hidden in a grandfather's clock. Eventually the crooks are arrested and the Tiger unmasked. He is none other than Amos himself.

Gladys McConnell (Jane Barstow), Hugh Allan (Larry Trent), Frank Lackteen (Doctor Sandro), Edward Cecil (Slayton), Harry Semmels (Hawks), Broderick O'Farrell (Amos Crain), Henry Hebert (Andre Blane), Paul Weigel (Martin Meeker), F.F. Guenste (Briggs, the Butler), John Webb Dillon (Ladd, the Gardener), Floyd Ames (Marks), Bruce Gordon (Bennie), Jean Porter (Flora), Richard Cramer (Rough House Rowan), George Kern (Boss Collins), Blackie Whiteford (McCord).

1. The Storm Breaks. 2. The Tiger's Mark. 3. The Secret Mission. 4. The Danger Trail. 5. The Gas Chamber. 6. Behind the Clock. 7. The Tiger's Claw. 8. Prisoners in the Sky. 9. A Desperate Chance. 10. The Sky Clears.

673. The Tiger's Trail

(Astra Film Corp./Pathé, April 20, 1919) Serial, 15 chapters, two reels each. D: Robert Ellis and Paul C. Hurst. SP: Arthur B. Reeve and Charles A. Logue. S: Gilson Willets.

Hindu tiger worshippers and western cutthroats attempt to cheat Belle Boyd out of rich mines that rightfully belong to her as a result of a pact between her father and two other men.

Ruth Roland (Belle Boyd), George Larkin (Jack Randall), Mark Strong (Jim Gordon/Randolph Gordon), Harry G. Moody (Tiger Face), George Field (Salonga), Fred L. Kohler (Bull Shotwell), Easter Walters (Hilda, the Spy), Bud Osborne (Henchman), Chet Ryan (Juvenile), Mlle. Dion (Dancehall Queen).

1. The Tiger Worshippers. 2. The Glowing Eyes. 3. The Human Chain. 4. Danger Signals. 5. The Tiger Trap. 6. The Secret Assassin. 7. Flaming Waters. 8. Danger Ahead. 9. Racing Torrent. 10. Bringing in the Law. 11. In the Breakers. 12. The Two Amazons. 13. The False Idol. 14. The Mountain Hermit. 15. The Tiger Face.

Hugh Allen and Gladys McConnell in *The Tiger's Shadow* (1928)

674. Tih-Minh

(France—Gaumont, 1919) Serial, 12 chapters. D/SP: Louis Feuillade. [U.S.A. Title: *In the Clutches of the Hindoo*]. [Revived at the New York Film Festival in 1980].

Mary Harald (Tih-Minh), Rene Cresté (Jacques d'Athys), Georges Biscot (Placide), Edouard Mathé (Sir Francis Grey), Louis Leubas (L'asiatique Kistna), Gaston Michel (Dr. Gilson), Marquet (Dr. Clauzel), Emile André (Dr. Davesnes), Georgette Farboni (Marquise Dolorès), Jane Rollette (Rosetta), Mlle. Lugane (Jane d'Athys), Mme. De La Croix (Mme. d'Athys).

1. Le philtre d'oubli. 2. Dramas dans la nuit. 3. Les mysteres de la Villa Circé. 4. L'homme dans la malle. 5. Chez les fous. 6. Oiseaux de nuit. 7. L'evocation. 8. Sous le voile. 9. La branche du salut. 10. Mercredi. 11. Le document. 12. Justice.

675. Tim Tyler's Luck

(Universal, November 1937) Serial, 12 chapters, two reels each. D: Ford Beebe and Wyndham Gittens. SP: Wyndham Gittens, Norman S. Hall, and Ray Trampe. Based on the newspaper strip of the same name by Lyman Young.

Tim Tyler takes a ship to Africa to look for his father who is somewhere in gorilla country. Aboard the same ship is Lora Graham, seeking Spider Webb, the criminal who had committed a diamond robbery for which her brother has been framed. In his quest to find a fabulous treasure of ivory, Spider Webb kills Tim's father and takes over his armored jungle cruiser. Tim and Lora team up with Sergeant Gates to bring the criminal to justice in the gorilla-infested jungle country.

Frank [Frankie] M. Thomas, Jr. (Tim Tyler), Frances Robinson (Lora Lacey [Graham]), Norman Willis (Spider Webb), Jack Mulhall (Sergeant Gates), Al Shean (Professor Tyler), Earle Douglas (Lazarre), Anthony Warde (Garry Drake), Alan Gregg (Trader Brent), Everett Brown (James Conway), Kenneth Harlan (Captain Clark), William Benedict (Spud), Eddie Parker, Stanley Blystone, Pat O'Brien, Frank Mayo, Bill McClain, Al Bridge, Ethan Laidlaw, Philo McCullough, Edwin J. Brady, Tom Steele.

Frankie Thomas, Jack Mulhall (*center*), and Kenneth Harlan in *Tim Tyler's Luck* (1937)

1. Jungle Pirates. 2. Dead Man's Pass. 3. Into the Lion's Den. 4. The Ivory Trail. 5. Trapped in the Quicksands. 6. The Jaws of the Jungle. 7. The King of the Gorillas. 8. The Spider Caught. 9. The Gates of Doom. 10. A Race for Fortune. 11. No Man's Land. 12. The Kimberley Diamonds.

676. The Timber Queen

(Ruth Roland Serials/Pathé, July 16, 1922) Serial, 15 chapters, two reels each. D: Fred Jackson. SP: Bertram Millhauser. S: Val Cleveland. P: Hal Roach.

Ruth locks horns and wits with a timber trust for possession of a large tract of timber she has inherited. There was a lot of toppling timber in it, hard riding, gunfights, explosions, hand to hand encounters, the hero inevitably unfairly outnumbered but triumphant, and the usual western stunt stuff built around galloping horses, careening buckboards, and thundering trains.

Each chapter leaves Ruth in such a dangerous predicament that even the skeptic will be interested in knowing how she escaped, only to see her get into another. But each chapter leaves the curiosity at the boiling point.

Ruth Roland (Ruth Reading), Bruce Gordon (Don Mackay), Val Paul (James Cluxton), Leo Willis (Bull Joyce), Frank Lackteen (Vance), Bull Montana, Al Ferguson, Otto Freez, Chris Linton.

1. The Log Jam. 2. The Flaming Forest. 3. Guilty as Charged. 4. Go Get Your Man. 5. The Yukon Trail. 6. The Hidden Pearl. 7. Mutiny. 8. The Smuggler's Cave. 9. Horned Fury. 10. Human Vultures. 11. The Runaway Engine. 12. The Abyss. 13. The Stolen Wedding. 14. One Day to Go. 15. The Silver Lining.

677. Timber Tales (Lumberjack)

(Universal, 1922–23) Series, 8 episodes, two reels each. D: Duke Worne.

Trepidation reigned supreme as lethargy and serenity were shuttled to the sidelines in a demonstration of Universal's short film know-how. In this unusually rollicking and rigorous series, Stewart agitatedly, and sometimes ferociously, set about to quell the bestial qualities of his fellow man. Although he sometimes tried pacification, his rampagious tendencies usually detonated before many minutes of the two-reelers had slipped by. Audiences could count on blusterous action in a Stewart oater, often realistic and unsubdued in its intensity.

Roy Stewart.

Episode Titles, Releasing Dates, Supporting Actors 1. Giants of the Open (9-30-22), Andree Tourneur, Albert J. Smith, Buck Connors. 2. Blue Blood and Red (10-21-22). 3. Rustlers of the Redwoods (11-17-22), Andrée Tourneur. 4. Timberland Treacher (12-2-22), Esther Ralston, Albert J. Smith, Jim Corey. 5. King of the Forest (12-23-22). 6. The Doomed Sentinel (1-13-23). 7. Hearts of Oak (2-2-23), Vera Reynolds, Albert J. Smith, Joseph W. Girard. 8. Knights of the Timber (2-24-23), Carol Holloway.

678. Timothy Dobbs, That's Me

(Universal, August–October, 1916) Series, 10 episodes, two reels each. D/P: Wallace Beery. Scen: Bess Meredyth and R.A. Dillon.

Combination of comedy and action. Each episode entirely independent of the others.

Carter DeHaven (Timothy Dobbs), Ruth Clifford (Dollie), Robert Milash (Jeff/Jenkins), Dan Duffy (Tom), Viola Smith (Mary), Gilbert Hammond (The Emperor), Ruby Cox (The Leading Lady), C. Norman Hammond (Roman Hero), Marcia Moore (Polly), Mina Cunard, Helen Leslie, L.M. Wells, Margaret Whistler, George Hernandez, Ivor McFadden, C. Casey, Marcia Moore.

1. The Soda Jerk. 2. A Thousand a Week. 3. He Became a Cop. 4. From the Rogue's Gallery. 5. Hired and Fired. 6. He Almost Lands an Angel. 7. A Hero by Proxy. 8. Borrowed Plumes. 9. Breaking Into Society. 10. Fame at Last.

679. Titi Ier, Roi des Gosses

(France—Société des Cinéromans, 1926) Serial, 3 chapters. D: René Leprince. S: Pierre Gilles Veber.

Jean Toulout, Roby Guichard, Yvette Langlais, Jeanne De Balzac, Simone Vaudry, Renée Heribel, André Marnay, Lucien Dalsage, Jean Peyrière, Tania Daleyme, Darcey-Roche, Andrée Standard.

1. Le couronnement de Titi. 2. Titi, chef de famille. 3. Titi détective.

680. I Topi Grigi (Gray Mice)

(Italy—Tiber Films, 1917) Serial, 8 chapters. D: Emilio Ghione. S: Pio Vanzi. SP: Emilio Ghione.

Emilio Ghione (Za-la-Mort), Kally Sambucini (Za-la-Vie), Albert-Francis Bertone (Grigione), H. Fiorin (Musoduro), Alfredo Martinelli (Leo), Signora B. Pasquali (La vecchia Camilla), Ida Carloni Talli, Giuseppe Carrera.

1. La busta nera. 2. La tortura. 3. Il covo. 4. La rete di corda. 5. La corsa al milione. 6. Aristocrazia canaglia. 7. 6000 voltas. 8. A mezza quaresima.

681. Le Tour de France de Deux Enfants

(France—Pathé-Consortium, 1924) Serial, 5 chaptes. D: Louis de Carbonnat. Scen: G. Bruno.

Gregoire Willy, Louis Legeay, Benedict, Derigal, Davesnes, Mme. Sapiani, Grandet.

682. Trader Tom of the China Seas

(Republic, January 1954) Serial, 12 chapters, two reels each. D: Franklyn Adreon. SP: Ronald Davidson. Assoc. P: Franklyn Adreon. Photography: Bud Thackery. Music: R. Dale Butts. Special Effects: Howard and Theodore Lydecker. Feature Title: *Target—Sea of China*.

When island trader Tom Rogers learns from his dying friend, James Dean, that a Nazi thug named Kurt Daley sabotaged his ship, he confers with Major Conroy, supposedly a retired military officer. Conroy tells him that he is unofficially spearheading an effort to track down gun smugglers and that foreign agents are supplying arms to natives and encouraging them to revolt against the United Nations Protectorate. Tom volunteers to help put down the subversive activity. Assisting him is United Nations employee Vivian Wells.

Harry Lauter (Tom Rogers), Aline Towne (Vivian Wells), Lyle Talbot (Barent), Robert Shayne (Conroy), Fred Graham (Kurt Daley), Victor Sen Yung (Wang), Richard Reeves (Rebel Chief), Ramsay Hill (British Colonel), Tom Steele (Gursan/Mike), Dale Van Sickel (Ambusher), John Crawford (Bill Gaines), Jan Arvan (Khan), Duane Thorsen (Hal), Ken Terrell (Mate), Robert Bice (Paine), Budd Buster (Trail Heavy), Bill Chandler (Soldier), George Selk (Ole), Charley Phillips (Baggage Clerk), Bert LeBaron (Fireman), Bill Hudson (James Dean), Richard Alexander (Gorth), Saul Gorss (Native), Steve Conte (Horseman), Charles Sullivan (Pilot), Rush Williams (Yank), Jerry Brown.

1. Sea Saboteurs. 2. Death Takes the Deck. 3. Five Fathoms Down. 4. On Target. 5. The Fire Ship. 6. Collision. 7. War in the Hills. 8. Native Execution. 9. Mass Attack. 10. Machine Murder. 11. Underwater Ambush. 12. Twisted Vengeance.

683. The Trail of the Octopus

(Hallmark, October 1919) Serial, 15 chapters; Chapter 6, five reels; others two reels. D: Duke Worne. S: J. Grubb Alexander.

The plot is a good one and the "chase" factor is ushered in from the desire of two groups to gain possession of every one of the daggers (that's right—daggers!) necessary to open a certain treasure vault. Carter Holmes, the master criminologist, and his pretty girlfriend oppose the Octopus and his gang. The chase becomes international as of the end of Chapter 6 when all of the characters wind up on a ship headed for China. Of course there is a disappearance now and then and evidences of crime and stealth and also many fights. But these are all extremely essential in a serial and impart the necessary melodramatic thrills.

This is not one of the greatest serials ever made, but for those audiences that like serials this one could be banked on to please and to keep them coming back for more.

Ben Wilson (Carter Holmes), Neva Gerber (Ruth Stanhope), Howard Crampton (Dr. Reid Stanhope), Marie Pavis (Madame Zora), William Carroll (Omar), William Dyer (Sandy McNab), Allan Garcia (Al Kasim).

1. The Devil's Trademark. 2. The Purple Dagger. 3. Face to Face. 4. The Hand of Want. 5. The Eye of Satan. 6. Behind the Mask. 7. The Dance of Death. 8. Satan's Soulmate. 9. The Chained Soul. 10. The Ape Man. 11. The Red Death. 12. The Poisoned Talon. 13. The Phantom Mandarin. 14. The House of Shadows. 15. The Yellow Octopus.

684. Trail of the Royal Mounted

(Guaranteed Pictures) Serial, 10 chapters, two reels each. D: Stuart Paton. SP: Karl Krusada. S: Flora Douglas. P: Harry S. Webb and F.E. (Flora) Douglas. Photography: William Nobles and Edward Kull. Assist. D: Armand Schaefer and Raymond Hines.

Harry Lauter and Aline Towne in *Trader Tom of the China Seas* (1954)

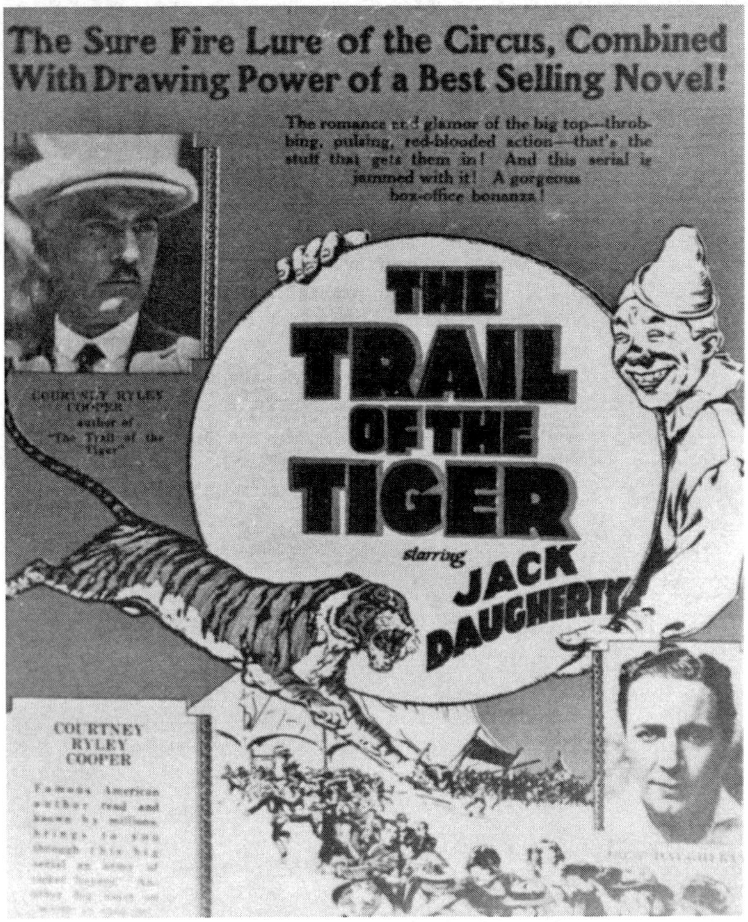

This serial is merely a re-issue of *The Mystery Trooper* but with different main and chapter titles. The new chapter titles follow.

1. Clutches of Death. 2. The Perilous Trail. 3. Shadows of Evil. 4. The Pit of Doom. 5. Escape from Danger. 6. The Devil's Warning. 7. Path of Faith. 8. Fangs of the Killer. 9. The Phantom Warning. 10. Fight to the Finish.

685. The Trail of the Tiger

(Universal, November 7, 1927) Serial, 10 chapters, two reels each. D: Henry McRae. Scen: Karl Krusada and Leigh Jacobson. S: Courtney Ryley Cooper.

Real circus atmosphere is definitely an asset. The circus shots are authentic, and a fine inside view of how the "big top" really functions is given. The hero is given an undercover job with the circus by his uncle who owns the show. It seems that the circus manager has been stealing a significant part of the receipts, and it is Jack's job to uncover the evidence. The manager has a ward with whom Jack falls in love as soon as he meets her. The suspense mounts with the introduction of the Mysterious Mountebanks, a secret organization of circus performers who have it in for the rascally circus manager.

Jack Daugherty (Jack Stewart), Frances Teague (Trixie Hemingway), Jack Mower ("Tiger" Jordan), John Webb Dillon (John Hemingway), Charles Murphy (Rube Murphy), William Platt (Babs, the Dwarf), Jack Richardson (Ned Calvert).

1. The Mystic Mountebanks. 2. The Trap of Terror. 3. The Shaggy Monster. 4. The Tiger Strikes. 5. Flaming Fury. 6. The Tiger's Lair. 7. The Hour of Fear. 8. The Flight of Terror. 9. Buried Alive. 10. The Reckoning.

Top: **Jack Daugherty in *The Trail of the Tiger* (1927);** ***bottom:*** **Stuart Holmes and Frankie Mann in *Trailed by Three* (1920)**

686. Trailed by Three

(Pathé, April 4, 1920) Serial, 15 chapters, two reels each. D: Perry N. Vekroff. Scen: Charles T. Dazey.

Jane Creighton is the daughter of a missionary on the South Sea island of Manoa, the natives of which have been enslaved by Rankin who has set himself up as ruler by reason of the fear he inspired in his black subjects. Anoto, the chief of the tribe, has collected a large number of very valuable pearls which his tribesmen have taken from the sea and with which he hopes to buy back from Rankin the freedom of his tribe.

Jane volunteers to go with Anoto to New York to sell the pearls. Their plans are overheard and Rankin orders his lieutenant, Roscoe Trent, to follow them and steal the pearls. In New York, Michael Casserly, posing as a friend of jeweler James Carewe, is also out to get the pearls. Thus begins 15 chapters of struggle for possession of the pearls. Jane is aided by young Tom Carewe who falls in love with her.

Frances Mann (Jane Creighton), Stuart Holmes (Michael Casserly), Wilfred Lytell (Tom Carewe), John Webb Dillon (Roscoe Trent), John P. Wade (James Carewe), William Welsh (Aboto), Ruby Hoffman, John Wheeler, May Tong, Ethel Key, Sam Kim.

1. The Mystery Pearls. 2. Trapped in Chinatown. 3. The Tyrant of the South Seas. 4. The Prison Ship. 5. Buried Alive. 6. Wanted for Burglary. 7. In the Pasha's House. 8. The Fifteenth Wife. 9. The Pasha's Revenge. 10. The Slave Market. 11. The Torture Trap. 12. The Burning Fuse. 13. The Door of Death. 14. The Hidden Crime. 15. The Reckoning.

687. Le Travail

(France—Les Films D'Art, 1919) Serial, 7 chapters. D: Henri Pouctal. S: Emile Zola. SP: Henri Pouctal.

Léon Mathot (Lucien Froment), Huguette Duflos (Josine), Raphaël Duflos (Delaveau), Claude Mérelle (Fernande Delaveau), Juliette Clarens (Suzanne Boigelin), Marc Gérard (Jourdan), Raymond Fabre (Bonaire), Camille Bert (Boigelin), Andrée Brabant, Andrée Lionel, Charpentier, Davesnes, Jacques Amiot, Gilbert Dalleu, Delaunay, Juliette Clarens, Simone Damaury, Jean Peyrière, Halma, Marcel Delaître, Jacques Robert, Monti, Henriette Gautier, Fabien Haziza, Olinda Mano, Simone Genevois, Maurice Forget, Dolly Fairlie.

1–3. Unknown. 4. Hino ao trabalho. 5. Justica. 6. O advento da democracia. 7. Ordem e progresso.

688. The Trey O'Hearts

(Universal–Gold Seal, August 4, 1914) Serial, 15 chapters; Chapter 1, three reels; others, two reels. D: Wilfred Lucas (Chapter 1–6) and Henry McRae (Chapter 7–15). Scen: Bess Meredyth. S: Louis Joseph Vance.

Judith, along with her hate-filled, crippled father, strives to kill hero Alan Law whose dead father is blamed for the affliction of the old man. Unlike her sister and father, Rose, Judith's twin sister, is a lovable person and in love with Alan. However, Judith eventually falls in love with Alan. When Rose is killed by a bolt of lightning that strikes the chapel where she and Alan have just been married, Judith, a repentant villainess, secretly takes her sister's place and Alan is never the wiser.

Like many early serials, this one was designed for adult entertainment, rather than for the front row kids who constituted the main audience for later serials of the cliff-hanger type.

Cleo Madison (Rose Trine/Judith Trine), George Larkin (Alan Law), Edward Sloman (Seneca Trine), Tom Walsh (Barcus), Roy Hanford (Marrophat), Charles Brinley, Doris Pawn, George Bacus.

1. Flower of the Flames. 2. White Water. 3. The Sea Venture. 4. Dead Reckoning. 5. The Sunset Tide. 6. The Crack O' Doom. 7. Stalemate. 8. The Mock Rose. 9. As the Crow Flies. 10. Steel Ribbons. 11. The Painted Hills. 12. The Mirage. 13. The Jaws of Death. 14. The First Law. 15. The Last Trump.

689. Il Triangolo Giallo

(Italy—Tiber Films, 1917) Serial, 4 chapters. D: Emilio Ghione. SP: Emilio Ghione.

Emilio Ghione, Kally Sambucine, Odette De Virgili, Ignazio Lupi, Matsumato, Emma Virgili.

1. Il cavalieri del triangolo. 2. L' acpua chi parla. 3. Il mattone insanguinato. 4. La rivincita di Za.

690. Les Trois Mousquetaires

(France—Pathé-Consortium, 1921) Serial, 12 chapters. D: Henri Diamant-Berger. Scen: Henri Diamant-Berger. S: Alexandre Dumas.

Aimé Simon-Girard (D'Artagnan), Henri Rollan (Athos), Charles Martinelli (Porthos), Pierre de Guingand (Aramis), Maxime Desjardins (De Treville), Pierrette Madd (Constance Bonacieux), Jean Joffre (Bonacieux), Claude Mérelle (Milady de Winter), Gaston Jacquet (De Winter), Charles Dullin (Padre Joseph), Paul Hubert (Felton), Armand Bernard (Planchet), Marcel Vallée (Mousqueton), Max Charlier (D'Artagnan Pai), Blanche Altem (Dona Estephania), Edouard De Max (Richelieu), Gaston Rieffler (Louis XIII), Henri Baudin (De Rochefort), Jeanne Desclos (Rainha Ana d'Austria), Mme. Joffre (Madre Superiora), Germaine Larbaudière (Duqueza de Chevreuse), Pré Fils (Grimaud), Stacquet (Bazin), Talmont (Giovanni), Harryso (Executor), Bureau (De Wardes), Mme. Vaudrey (Madame D'Artagnan), Andrew F. Brunelle, Albert Préjean.

Portuguese: 1. A estalagem de Meung. 2. Os mosqueteiros so rei. 3. A costureira da rainha. 4. As agulhas de ouro. 5. Pela honra da rainha. 6. O baile dos almotáceis. 7. O pavilhoa d'Etrées. 8. A estalagem do pombal vermelho. 9. O bastião de São Gervasio. 10. A torre de Portsmouth. 11. O convento de Bethune. 12. A cabana do Rio Lys.

691. Trooper 77

(Rayart, November 1926) Serial, 10 chapters, two reels each. D: Duke Worne. S: George W. Pyper. P: W. Ray Johnston.

A man is murdered in a roadhouse, and Phil Manning imagines that he is the criminal. His desire to escape leads him to join the State Constabulary, in which his brother Steve is an inspector. Steve, who is trying to solve the mystery, takes the field as "Trooper 77," and is crossed by Robert Kincaid, a suave villain who, besides planning the murder in question, has been involved in a plot that landed Mary Stanhop's father in jail.

Mary seeks to obtain the evidence from Kincaid that will free her father. She saves Steve after he has been knocked into a river. Subsequently the two live through a series of exciting adventures until the miscreants are finally run to earth.

Herbert Rawlinson (Steve Manning/Trooper 77), Hazel Deane (Mary Stanhop), Jimmy Aubrey (Mike Riordan), Duke Worne (Phil Manning), Ruth Royce (Claire Gorday), Thomas Lingham (Robert Kincaid).

692. The Two Sleuths

D: Mack Sennett.

This was a series of one-reel detective comedies. The first five were made for Biograph, the final five for Keystone.

Mack Sennett, Fred Mace.

Biograph: 1. $500,000 Reward (8-21-11). 2. Trailing the Counterfeiters (10-12-11). 3. Their First Divorce Case (11-2-11). 4. Caught with the Goods (12-25-11). 5. Their First Kidnapping Case (4-10-12). *Keystone:* 1. At it Again (11-4-12). 2. A Bear Escape (11-25-12). 3. The Stolen Purse (2-10-13). 4. The Sleuth's Last Stand (3-3-13). 5. The Sleuths at the Floral Parade (3-6-13). (Appearing in the last title were Mabel Normand and Ford Sterling.)

693. Ultus

(Great Britain, 1915–1917) Series, 8 (?) episodes. No information on this series other than the episode titles.

1. The Townsend Mystery. 2. The Ambassador's Diamond. 3. Ultus and the Secret of the Night. 4. The Traitor's Fate. 5. The Grey Lady. 6. Ultus and the Cabinet Minister's Overcoat. 7. The Three-Button Mystery. 8. The Man From the Dead.

694. Under the Crescent

(Universal–Gold Seal, May 29, 1915) Series, 6 episodes, two reels each. D: Burton King. Scen: Nell Shipman.

Adventures of an American actress in Old Egypt.

Ola Humphrey (the American Actress), William Dowlan (Stanley Clyde), Edward Sloman (Prince Ibrahim Tousson), Helen Wright (Princess Tousson), Carmen Phillips (Princess Uarda), William Quinn (Said Pasha), H.E. Canfield (Sir Godfrey), Orral Humphrey (Mehemit Ali), Edna Maison (Princess Zohna).

1. The Purple Iris. 2. The Cage of the Golden Bars. 3. In the Shadow of the Pyramids. 4. For the Honor of a Woman. 5. In the Name of the King. 6. The Crown of Death.

695. Undersea Kingdom

(Republic, June 1936) Serial, 12 chapters; Chapter 1, three reels; others, two reels. Feature title: *Sharrad of Atlantis*. D: B. Reeves Eason and Joseph Kane. SP: John Rathmell, Maurice Geraghty, and Oliver Drake. S: Tracy Knight and John Rathmell. Supervision: Barney Sarecky. Photography: William Nobles and Edgar Lyons. Music: Harry Grey. P: Nat Levine.

A series of earthquakes are believed to be originating from the bottom of the ocean where the continent of Atlantis was supposed to have vanished. Professor Norton has invented a counteracting ray that will stop an impending quake. He enlists the help of naval officer Crash Corrigan and the two, along with a newspaper woman, the professor's son, and two sailors descend to the ocean floor in a special submarine, where they are drawn into an inland sea of the dome-covered Atlantis. They find two factions in deadly combat—The White Robes and The Black Robes.

Unga Khan, leader of the Black Robes, has harnessed the atom and is directing a disintegrating machine at North America as part of a plan to take over the upper world. Crash and his friends ally themselves with The White Robes and bring about the downfall of Khan, though Atlantis itself perishes.

Ray Corrigan (Crash Corrigan), Lois Wilde (Diana Compton), Monte Blue (Unga Khan), William Farnum (Sharad), Boothe Howard (Ditmar), Lee Van Atta (Billy Norton), Raymond Hatton (Gasspom), C. Montague Shaw (Norton), Smiley Burnette (Briny Deep), Lon Chaney, Jr. (Hakur), Lane Chandler (Darius), Jack Mulhall (Andrews), Frankie Marvin (Salty), Malcolm McGregor (Zogg), Ralph Holmes (Martos), John Merton (Moloch), Ernie Smith (Gourck), John Bradford (Joe), Lloyd Whitlock (Clinton), Eddie Parker, Al Seymour, George DeNormand, Alan Curtis, Tom Steele, Wes Warner, Dan Rowan (Guardsmen), Bill Yrigoyen (Charioteer), Kenneth Lawton (Doctor), Everett Kibbons (Antony), Millard McGowan, William Stahl (Chamber Guards), Rube Schaeffer (Magna), David Horsley (Sentry), Jack Ingram, Tracy Lane.

1. Beneath the Ocean Floor. 2. Undersea City. 3. Arena of Death. 4. Revenge of the Volkites. 5. Prisoners of Atlantis. 6. The Juggernaut Strikes. 7. The Submarine Trap. 8. Into the Metal Tower. 9. Death in the Air. 10. Atlantis Destroyed. 11. Flaming Death. 12. Ascent to the Upperworld.

Ray Corrigan, Lon Chaney, Jr. (*at point of sword*), Monte Blue, and Montague Shaw in *Undersea Kingdom* (1936)

696. Universal Ike and Universal Ike Jr. Series

(Universal, 1914) Series, 23 episodes. D: Harry Edwards (directed some but not necessarily all).

Although Augustus Carney plays the role of Universal Ike in this comedy series, an unknown actor was hired to play the part of Universal Ike Jr. Carney was a veteran of vaudeville and was one of the most popular comedians during the period 1910–1914.

Augustus Carney (Universal Ike), Louise Glaum.

1. Universal Ike Gets a Coat (March). 2. Universal Ike Has One Foot in the Grave (March). 3. Universal Ike Makes a Monkey of Himself. 4. Universal Ike in the Battle of Little Tin Horn. 5. Universal Ike's Wooing (March). 6. Universal Ike Has His Ups and Downs (April). 7. Universal Ike and the School Belle (April). 8. Universal Ike Almost a Hero (May).

9. Universal Ike Gets a Line on His Wife (May). 10. Universal Ike in Pursuit of the Eats (May) (Helen Thatchers, Fred Hornby, and Harry Moodie also credited to this film). 11. Universal Ike Jr. and His Mother-in-Law (June). 12. Universal Ike Jr. in a Battle Royal (June). 13. Universal Ike Jr. in a Case of the Doctor (June). 14. Universal Ike Jr. is Kept from Being an Actor (June). 15. Universal Ike Jr. and the Vampire (July). 16. Universal Ike Jr. Bearly Won Her (July). 17. Universal Ike Jr. at the Dance of Little L.O. (August). 18. Universal Ike Jr. in Cupid's Victory (August). 19. Universal Ike Jr. in His City Elopement. 20. Universal Ike Jr. in the Dangers of a Great City (August). 21. Universal Ike Jr. on His Honeymoon (August). 22. Universal Ike Jr. Almost Gets Married (August). 23. Universal Ike Jr.'s Legacy.

697. The Valley of Vanishing Men

(Columbia, December 17, 1942) Serial, 15 chapters, two reels each. D: Spencer Gordon Bennet. SP: Harry Fraser, Lewis Clay, George Gray. P: Larry Darmour. Photography: James S. Brown, Jr. Music: Lee Zahler.

A cowpoke, Bill Tolliver, searches for his father, a prospector, in New Mexico and discovers that an outlaw has joined forces with an ousted European general to enslave Mexican patriots to work in a gold mine. Also planned for is a rebellion against Benito Juarez and the government of Mexico. In a final showdown Bill and American forces are joined by Mexican forces to defeat the outlaws.

Bill Elliott (Wild Bill Tolliver), Slim Summerville (Missouri Benson), Carmen Morales (Consuelo Romeros), Kenneth MacDonald (Jonathan Kincaid), Jack Ingram (Butler), George Chesebro (Taggert), John Shay (Mullins), Tom London (Slater), Arno Frey (Carl Engler), Julian Rivero (Jose), Roy Barcroft (Jed Lucas), Lane Chandler (Roberts), Ted Mapes (Elliott's Double), Ernie Adams (Bartender), Robert Fiske (Harvey Cole), Lane Bradford, Art Dillard, Frank Ellis (Henchmen), I. Stanford Jolley (Ed Torrence), Sherry Tansey, Rose Plummer, Roy Bucko (Townspeople), Michael Vallon (Marshal), Chief Thunder Cloud (Chief Tall Tree), Tex Palmer (Stage Driver), Forrest Taylor (Dr. Williams), Horace B. Carpenter (Raider's Cook), Iron Eyes Cody (Many Eyes), Kit Guard (Man in Saloon), Hank Bell (Prospector), Kenne Duncan (Logan), Karl Hackett (Prisoner), Thornton Edwards (Pablo).

1. Trouble in Canyon City. 2. The Mystery of the Ghost Town. 3. Danger Walks by Night. 4. Hillside Horror. 5. Guns in the Night. 6. The Bottomless Well. 7. The Man in the Gold Mask. 8. When the Devil Drives. 9. The Traitor's Shroud. 10. Death Strikes at Seven. 11. Satan in the Saddle. 12. The Mine of Missing Men. 13. Danger on Dome Rock. 14. The Door that Has no Key. 15. Empire's End.

698. The Vampire Son of Nostradamus (English Translation)

(Mexico, 1959) Television series, 12 episodes, 25 minutes each. D: Frederico Curiel.

This television series was edited into four dubbed theatrical features and issued to U.S. television by K. Gordon Murray. The evil vampire must contend with the efforts of professor Dwan to destroy him. Though Nostradamus emerged alive after apparently being dispatched by Dwan (much as the Frankenstein monster did) on several occasions, in the end he is killed by silver bullets fired by policemen.

German Robles (Nostradamus), Domingo Soler (Professor Dwan).

La Maldicion de Nostradamus. (TV: The Curse of Nostradamus), (Estudios America-1959). *Nostradamus el Destructor de Monstruos*. (TV: The Monster Demolisher), (Estudios America-1959). *Nostradamus el Genio de las Tinieblas*. (TV: The Genie of Darkness), (Estudios America-1959). *La Sangre de Nostradamus*. (TV: The Blood of Nostradamus), (Estudios America-1959).

699. Les Vampires

(France—Etablissements Gaumont, 1915–'16) Serial, 10 chapters. D: Louis Feuillade. S: George Meirs. SP: Georges Meirs and Louis Feuillade.

This was one of Feuillade's most popular serials. The Vampires were a gang of hooded killers. Overshadowing star Edouard Mathé was Irma Vep, the sexy actress, dressed in a tight-fitting black costume, who played Musidora, the "vampire girl." Both in *Fantômas* and *Les Vampires* the protagonists, emerging from the slums, were anything but romantic figures. Nevertheless, the movie-going public liked them. World War I was in progress and the time spent watching *Les Vampires* was an escape from reality, though the story was somewhat morbid.

Edouard Mathé (Philippe Guérande), Marcel Lévesque (Oscar Mazamette), Jean Aymè (Le grand Vampire), Irma Vep (Musidora, the "Vampire Girl"), Delphine Renot (Mme. Guerande, mère), Stacia Napierkowska (Marfa Koutiloff), Fernand Herrmann (Moréno, cambrioleur), Gaston Michel (Le valet Benjamin), Renée Carl (Andalouse du recit historique), Miss Edith (Comtesse de Kerlor), Louis Leubas (Satanas), Bréon (Secrétaire de Satanas), Moriss (Venenos), Louise Lagrange (Jane Brémontier, fiancée de Guérande), Jeanne-Marie Laurent (Mme. Brémontier), Poupette (Hortense), Bout-de-Zan, J.F. Martial, Mlle. Delvé, Mlle. Keppens. Mlle. Herlor, Suzanne Le Bret, Germaine Rouer, Maurice Schutz, Jacques-feyder.

1. La tête coupée. 2. La bague qui tue. 3. Le cryptogramme rouge. 4. Le spectre. 5. L' évasion du mort. 6. Les yeux qui fascinent. 7. Satanas. 8. Le maître de la foudre. 9. L' homme des poisons. 10. Les noces sanglantes.

In the U.S.A. the film was released in nine chapters of three reels each, with the serial title *The Vampires, The Arch Criminals of Paris*. 1. The Detective's Head. 2. The Red Notebook. 3. The Ghost. 4. The Dead Man's Escape. 5. The Eyes That Hold. 6. Satanas. 7. The Master of Thunder. 8. The Poison Man. 9. The Terrible Wedding.

700. The Vanishing Dagger

(Universal, June 7, 1920) Serial, 18 chapters, two reels each. Working Titles: "The 13th Hour" and "The Broken Idol." D: Ed Kull and Eddie Polo. Scen: Hope Loring and George W. Pyper. S: Hope Loring, Jacques Jaccard, and Milton Moore.

Polo filmed part of this serial in England and part of it on the Universal lot. It had quite an original plot revolving about the vanishing dagger, and one that kept twisting and turning with any number of unexpected surprises right up to the close. The plot moves at a good clip and the serial is a solid one fully

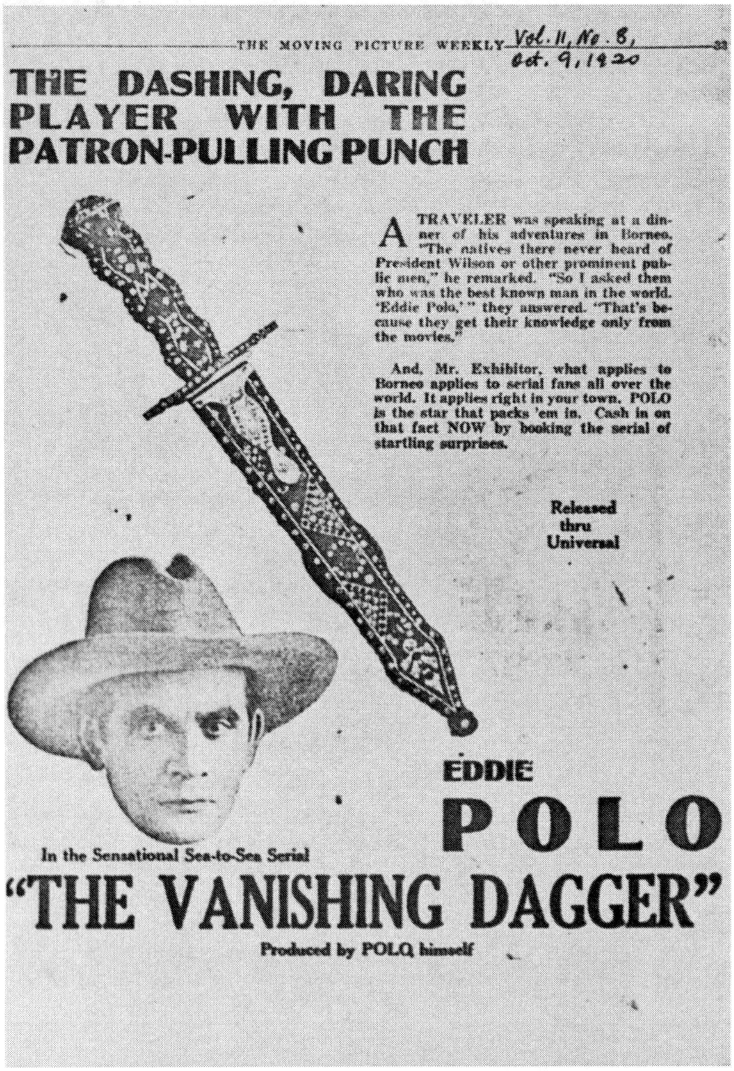

up to Universal standards. However, the cast and crew found working with and for Polo unpleasant. By this time his ego was soaring.

Eddie Polo (John Edward Grant), Thelma Percy (Elizabeth Latimer), G. Normand Hammond (Sir George Latimer), Laura Oakley (Lady Mary Latimer), Ray Ripley (Prince Narr), Karl Silvera (Prince Zan), Ruth Royce (Sonia, Narr's Favorite Wife), Thomas Lingham (King Claypool), Peggy O'Dare (Nell), Texas Watts (Len, Grant's Man), Arthur Jarvis (Sir Richard Upton), Leah Cross, Leslie T. Peacocke, J.P. McGowan.

1. The Scarlet Confession. 2. The Night of Terror. 3. In Death's Clutches. 4. On the Trail of the Dagger. 5. The End of the Rustlers. 6. A Terrible Calamity. 7. Plunged to His Doom. 8. In Unmerciful Hands. 9. Ferocious Foes. 10. When London Sleeps. 11. A Race to Scotland. 12. An Evil Plot. 13. Spears of Death. 14. Walls of Doom. 15. The Great Pendulum. 16. Beneath the Sea. 17. Beasts of the Jungle. 18. Silver Linings.

701. The Vanishing Legion

(Mascot, June 1, 1931) Serial, 12 chapters. D: B. Reeves Eason. S: Wyndham Gittens, Ford Beebe, and Helmer Bergman. P: Nat Levine. Photography: Benjamin Kline, Ernest Miller, and Jo J. Novak. Film also released in feature form.

Young Jimmy Williams is a friend of Rex, King of the Wild Horses. His father is falsely accused of murder and Jimmy and Rex help him escape both the law and The Vanishing Legion, an outlaw gang that wants him dead. Mysterious leader of The Vanishing Legion is The Voice, so named because his instructions to the gang come via telephone or wireless. Happy Hardigan becomes involved in helping Jimmy when The Vanishing Legion tries to stop Happy from delivering equipment to an oil company The Voice wants to buy out cheap.

Harry Carey (Happy Hardigan), Edwina Booth (Caroline Hall), Rex, King of Wild Horses (Himself), Frankie Darro

Top left: **Eddie Polo in *The Vanishing Dagger*; *bottom left:* Harry Carey and Robert Kortman; *right:* Harry Carey, Edwina Booth, Frankie Darro, and Lafe McKee in *The Vanishing Legion* (1931)**

(Jimmy Williams), Philo McCullough (Stevens), William Desmond (sheriff), Lafe McKee (Hornbeck), Robert Kortman (Larno), Edward Hearn (Jed Williams), Paul Weigal (Laribee), Olive Fuller Golden (Miss Lewis), Pete Morrison (Dopey), Frank Brownlee (Bishop), Tom Dugan (Board Member), Yakima Canutt (Rider of the Vanishing Legion), Dick Dickinson (Rider of the Vanishing Legion), Bob Walker (Allen), Al Taylor (Sheriff of Slocum), Dick Hatton (Dodger), Joe Bonomo (Stuffy), Boris Karloff (Voice of The Voice), Bill Wolff, Charlie Schaefer.

1. The Voice from the Void. 2. The Queen of the Night Riders. 3. The Invisible Enemy. 4. The Fatal Message. 5. The Trackless Trail. 6. The Radio Riddle. 7. The Crimson Clue. 8. The Doorway of Disaster. 9. When Time Stood Still. 10. Riding the Whirlwind. 11. The Capsule of Oblivion. 12. The Hoofs of Horror.

702. Vanishing Millions

(Sierra, January 1926) Serial, 15 chapters, two reels each. D: Alvin J. Neitz.

The greatest banking institution in San Francisco receives information from a deranged criminal that he is to rob their vaults that day. The president scoffs at the idea but, as a precaution, extra guards are stationed. The president and his daughter attend a reception at the house of Mrs. Douglas, known as "The Mysterious Lady in Black." News comes that the bank guards have been killed and the vaults robbed. Among the guests is Professor Telden, who secretly has a huge gorilla named Congo in captivity. Only Mrs. Douglas and Telden know it was Congo that committed the murders, under the guidance of the professor's uncanny willpower.

The daughter, Vivian, is in love with Dave Merrill, a young journalist, who is assigned by his editor to clean up the mystery of the "Vanishing Millions." The pair combine to solve the mystery and are involved in amazing adventures in which the professor and several other nefarious characters are working at cross purposes.

William Fairbanks (Dave Merrill), Vivian Rich (Vivian Telden), Alec B. Francis, Sheldon Lewis, Bull Montana, Edward Cecil, William Lowery, George Kotsonaro, Ethel Childers, Margaret Knights, J.P. Lockney.

(In Portuguese) 1. Uma noite de terror. 2. A Armadilha do Subterraneo. 3. O Balanco da Morte. 4. O Cavaleiro do Azul. 5. Unknown. 6. Unknown. 7. Hipnotizada. 8. A Corrida Pela Vida. 9. Unknown. 10. Unknown. 11. Desafiando o Perigo. 12. A Casa do Terror. 13–15. Unknown.

703. The Vanishing Rider

(Universal, January 16, 1928) Serial, 10 chapters, two reels each. D: Ray Taylor. SP: Val Cleveland. SP: George H. Plympton.

The Butch Bradley outlaw gang is thwarted at every turn by a mysterious masked man who steals the gold bullion from the gang that the gang itself had stolen. Desmond has a dual role playing both the masked rider and his twin brother Jim Davis. Both are secret service agents.

William Desmond (Jim Davis/The Vanishing Rider), Ethlyne Claire (Mary Allen), Nelson McDowell (Pop Smith), Bud Osborne (Butch Bradley), Boris Karloff (Villain).

1. The Road Agent. 2. Trapped. 3. A Fight for Life. 4. Brother Against Brother. 5. The Wings of Fury. 6. The False Message. 7. The Waters of Death. 8. The Bargain of Fear. 9. The Last Stand. 10. Vengeance.

704. The Vanishing Shadow

(Universal, July 1934) Serial, 12 chapters, two reels each. D: Louis Friedlander [Lew Landers]. SP: Het Manheim, Basil Dickey, and George Morgan. S: Ella O'Neill. Camera: Richard Fryer.

Stanley Stanfield, an electrical engineer, invents a vest-like apparatus which permits the wearer to vanish, leaving only a shadow. With the aid of Carl Van Dorn, himself a famed electrical wizard, he determines to bring about the fall of power-crazed, money-mad Wade Barnett and his cohort, Dorgan, who is responsible for the death of Stanfield's father. Gloria Grant, actually Barnett's daughter who has rejected her father's methods and adopted an alias, joins forces with Stanfield and Van Doran.

Onslow Stevens (Stanley Stanfield), Ada Ince (Gloria Grant), Walter Miller (Ward Barnett), James Durkin (Carl Van Dorn), William Desmond (MacDonald), Richard Cramer (Dorgan), Sidney Bracey (Denny), Edmund Cobb (Kent), Beulah Hutton, J. Frank Glendon, Monte Montague, Jack Richardson, Al Ferguson, Bud Osborne, Tom London, William L. Thorne.

1. Accused of Murder. 2. The Destroying Ray. 3. The Avalanche. 4. Trapped. 5. Hurled from the Sky. 6. Chain Lightning. 7. The Tragic Crash. 8. The Shadow of Death. 9. Blazing Bulkheads. 10. The Iron Death. 11. The Juggernaut. 12. Retribution.

705. Vanishing Trails

(Canyon, September 1920) Serial, 15 chapters, two reels each. D: Leon de la Mothe. P: William N. Selig. S: William E. Wing. SP: William E. Wing.

Cowpoke Silent Joe and crafty land baron Steve Durant square off as Durant strives to steal treasure belonging to a murdered man. Siding with justice, Durant's daughter gives aid and comfort to the strong, silent cowboy.

Franklyn Farnum (Silent Joe), Duke R. Lee (Steve Durant), Mary Anderson (Durant's Daughter, Lou), L.M. Wells (William Stillman), Harry Lonsdale (Grandon), Vester Pegg (Rankin), W.A. Orlamond (the Shadow), Pedro Leon (Bully Drake), Bud Osborne (Skip Brandt), Prince [dog] (Himself).

1. The Midnight Mystery. 2. Silent Joe's Death Warrant. 3. The Dreadful Scourge. 4. Vengeance. 5. Death Pursues. 6. The Brand of Hate. 7. Death Shadows. 8. The Daredevil. 9. A Livid Fate. 10. The Mansion of Mystery. 11. Rails of Destruction. 12. The Final Hour. 13. The Death Trap. 14. For Murder. 15. Unmasked.

706. The Vanishing West

(Mascot, October 15, 1928) Serial, 10 chapters, two reels each. D: Richard Thorpe. SP: Wyndham Gittens. P: Nat Levine. S: Karl Krusada and William Lester.

Jack Marvin is a fugitive from justice, though innocent of any crime. A villainous uncle of Jack's little boy Wally Lee tries to become the boy's guardian so he can gain possession of a mysterious fortune. However he was thwarted by Jack's

Top: **Jack Perrin (*checkered shirt*), Eileen Sedgwick (*blonde*), Helen Gibson, and Fred Church (*sheriff*) in *The Vanishing West* (1928); *bottom:* George B. Seitz and Marguerite Courtot in *Velvet Fingers* (1920)**

friends and Jack's name was cleared. The film was practically an all-star picture. Nine stars or former stars headed the cast.

Jack Perrin (Jack Marvin), Eileen Sedgwick (Betty Kincaid), Jack Daugherty (Jim Marvin), Yakima Canutt (Steve Marvin), Leo Maloney (Jack Trent), William Fairbanks (Long Collins), Mickey Bennett (Wally Lee), Helen Gibson (Mrs. Kincaid), Bob Burns (Robert Lee), Fred Clark, Harry Lorraine, Aaron Edwards, Tom Bay, Ed Waldron.

1. The Trail to Yesterday. 2. The Flaming Trap. 3. Thundering Hoofs. 4. The Balance of Fate. 5. The Chasm of Danger. 6. Roaring Wheels. 7. The Phantom Roper. 8. The Tunnel of Terror. 9. The Fatal Second. 10. The End of the Trail.

707. The Veiled Mystery

(Vitagraph, September 20, 1920) Serial, 15 chapters, two reels each. D: F.J. Grandon, Webster Cullison, and William J. Bowman. Scen: Graham Baker. S: Albert E. Smith and Cleveland Moffett. Adaptation: William B. Courtney.

Abe Sawyer is guardian of Ralph Moore's sweetheart, Ruth Sawyer. He wishes to do away with Moore in order to keep control of Ruth's fortune. Ethel Seymour is Ruth's devoted friend. Script writers led audiences to believe that The Veiled Mystery was a woman, but Abe Sawyer turned out to be the criminal.

Antonio Moreno (Ralph Moore), Pauline Curley (Ruth Sawyer), Henry A. Barrows (Abe Sawyer), Nenette de Courey (Ethel Seymour), Walter L. Rogers (Doctor Lyons), George Reed (Tom), W.S. Smith (Richard Seymour), George Cooper, Valeria Olivo, Frank Lackteen.

1. The Menace. 2. The Quicksand. 3. The Sea Demon. 4. Trapped in Mid-Air. 5. The Well of Despair. 6. The Fiery Furnace. 7. Human Targets. 8. The Span of Death. 9. A Slide for Life. 10. A Demon's Device. 11. The Smoke of Doom. 12. A Climax of Hate. 13. The Sinister Stroke. 14. The Veil's Secret. 15. The Accounting.

708. Velvet Fingers

(Pathé, December 5, 1920) Serial, 15 chapters, two reels each. D/S: Bertram Millhauser. P: George B. Seitz. SP: James Shelly Hamilton.

An Arsene Lupin serial with a Sherlock Holmes twist. The plot is woven around a smooth second-story man, a gentlemanly Raffles, whose object is to collect jewels and valuables at the expense of the owners and engage in a battle of wits with a criminologist.

George B. Seitz (Velvet Fingers), Marguerite Courtot (Lorna George), Harry Semels (Professor Robin), Lucille Lennox (Clara), Frank Redman (Pinky), Tommy Carr (Mickey), Joe Cuny (Needless Smith), Al Franklyn Thomas, Edward Elkas.

1. To Catch a Thief. 2. The Face Behind the Curtain. 3. The Hand from Behind the Door. 4. The Man in the Blue Spectacles. 5. The Deserted Pavilion. 6. Unmasked. 7. The House of 1000 Veils. 8. Aiming Straight. 9. The Broken Necklace. 10. Shots in the Dark. 11. The Other Woman. 12. Into Ambush. 13. The Hidden Room. 14. The Trap. 15. Out of the Web.

709. Vendémiaire

(France—Gaumont, 1919) Serial?, 2 chapters. D: Louis Feuillade.

The catalog of Copyright Entries: *Motion Pictures, 1912–1939* indicates that this is a serial, even though it shows the film as having two chapters—leastwise that were copyrighted. In George Geltzer's article on French silent features and serials in *Classic Images* No. 151, page 8, he writes that the film was released for showing in England on July 3, 1919 and does not identify it as a serial. The English title was *Beyond the Pale.*

René Cresté, Mary Harold, Edouard Mathé, Louis Leubas.

1. The Vineyard. 2. The Vintage Vat.

***The Ventures of Marguerite* (1915)**

710. Vengeance and the Woman

(Vitagraph, December 24, 1917) Serial, 15 chapters, two reels each. D: William Duncan. S: Albert E. Smith and Cyrus Townsend Brady. SP: Garfield Thompson and Edward J. Montague.

Black Jack and Red Johnson escape from jail swearing vengeance against Henry Blake, a wealthy mine owner who was the cause of their convictions. They first kidnap Blake's wife, then, when Blake rescues her, they try other means of satisfying their hatred. Blake also is taken prisoner, and the situations used in relating this portion of the serial are a succession of daredevil exploits. Each chapter is complete in itself; there are no cliffhanger endings.

William Duncan (Henry Blake), Carol Holloway (Bessie Blake), George Holt (Black Jack), Tex Allen (Red Johnson), Vincent Howard (Commanche Pete), Fred Burns (Jim Morgan), S.E. Jennings (Cal Hawkins), Walter Rodgers.

1. The Oath. 2. Loaded Dice. 3. The Unscaled. 4. The Signalling Cipher. 5. The Plunge of Destruction. 6. Lure of Hate. 7. Wolf Trap. 8. Mountain of Devastation. 9. Buried Alive. 10. The Leap for Life. 11. The Cavern of Terror. 12. The Desperate Chance. 13. Sands of Doom. 14. The Hand of Fate. 15. The Reckoning.

711. The Ventures of Marguerite

(Kalem, October 29, 1915) Series, 16 episodes, one reel each. D: Hamilton Smith, John E. Mackin, and Robert Ellis.

As heiress to a large fortune, Marguerite is able to satisfy her love for beautiful clothes and taste for adventure, while confronted by a multitude of schemers and gangsters bent on reducing her to poverty. These single-reel dramas were some of the strongest ever issued by Kalem. Each episode tells a complete story. Because the clothes worn by the dainty little star embodied the latest of Dame Fashion's dictums, *The Ventures of Marguerite* was closely followed and studied by feminine fans from New York to the tiniest hamlets in the country.

Marguerite Courtot (Marguerite), Richard Purdon (Bob Winters), E.T. Roseman, Paul Sherman, Bradley Barker, Edwin Brandt, William Sherwood, Julia Hurley, Phil Hardy, Helen Lindroth, Frank Holland, Robert Vaughn, Harry Edwards, F.B. Vernoy, Walter McEwen, Anna Reader, Otto Niemeyer, Freeman Barnes, H.A. Barrows, Stella Jenno, A. Lever, Eleanor Lewis, Lois Howell, R.A. Bennett, Joseph Sullivan, Roland Bottomley, Richard Forrest Cummings, Hassen Mussali, Joe Sullivan.

1. When Appearances Deceive. 2. The Rogue Syndicate. 3. The Kidnapped Heiress. 4. The Veiled Priestess. 5. A Society Schemer. 6. The Key to a Fortune. 7. The Ancient Coin. 8. The Secret Message. 9. The Oriental's Plot. 10. The Spy's Ruse. 11. The Crossed Clues. 12. The Tricksters. 13. The Sealskin Coat. 14. The Lurking Peril. 15. The Fate of America. 16. The Trail's End.

712. Veritas Vincit

(Germany—May–Film GmbH, 1919) Series, 3 episodes. D: Joe May. Scen: Ruth Goetz and Richard Hutter. S: Joe May and de Baron Zois.

Mia May, Johannes Riemann, Magnus Stifter, Emil Albes, Wilhelm Diegelmann, Ferry Sikla, Paul Biensfeldt, Georg John, Leopold Bauer, Lina Paulsen, Friedrich Küehne, Bernhard Goetzke, Adolf Klein, Olga Engl, Josef Klein, Max Laurence, Anders Wikmann, Hermann Picha, Emmy Wyda, Masria Forescu.

713. Vidoco

(France, 1923) Serial, chapters (?). D: Jean Kemm. Scen: Henriette Kemm.

René Navarre was one of France's best-known and most popular serial stars. However, the author must apologize for an inability to unearth more information on his serials.

René Navarre (Vidoco), Elmire Vautier, Rachel Devirys, Genica Missirio, Pocalas Plet.

714. The Vigilante

(Columbia, May 22, 1947) Serial, 15 chapters, two reels each. Based on *The Vigilante* adventure feature in *Action Comics*. D: Wallace Fox. SP: George H. Plympton, Lewis Clay, Arthur Hoerl. P: Sam Katzman. Assist. D: Mike Eason. Photography: Ira H. Morgan. Music: Mischa Bakaleinikoff.

The Vigilante, a government undercover agent, is really Greg Sanders, a western movie star. An assignment takes him to the ranch of wealthy George Pierce, secretly gang leader X-1, who is after a string of pearls called the "100 Tears of Blood." The pearls have been concealed in the hooves of five stallions belonging to Pierce's guests. Pierce stops at nothing in his efforts to acquire the cursed pearls, but The Vigilante is victorious and Pierce is killed in a final showdown. Prince Amil, one of the guests, destroys the pearls with acid to prevent the curse of the pearls from hurting others.

Ralph Byrd (Greg Sanders/The Vigilante), Ramsay Ames (Betty Winslow), Lyle Talbot (George Pierce), George Offerman, Jr. (Stuff), Robert Barron (Prince Amil), George Chesebro (Walt), Edmund Cobb (Miller), Frank Marlo (Rabin), Hugh Prosser (Captain Reilly), Jack Ingram (Silver), Eddie Parker (Doc), Bill Brauer (Thorne), Frank Ellis (Sadlow), Terry Frost (Lefty), Ted Mapes (Tex Collyer), John Fostine (Azar), Wally West (Scar), Ted Adams, Al Ferguson, Bud Osborne, Kermit Maynard.

1. The Vigilante Rides Again.
2. Mystery of the White Horses.
3. Double Peril. 4. Desperate Flight.
5. In the Gorilla's Cage. 6. Battling the Unknown. 7. Midnight Rendezvous.
8. Blasted to Eternity. 9. The Fatal Flood.
10. Danger Ahead. 11. X-1 Closes In.
12. Death Rides the Rails. 14. Closing In.
15. The Secret of the Skyroom.

Top: **Raymond Hatton, William Desmond, Robert Livingston, and Guinn [Big Boy] Williams; *bottom:* Robert Kortman, Fred Kohler, Sr. (*center*), and Robert Livingston in *The Vigilantes Are Coming* (1936)**

715. The Vigilantes Are Coming

(Republic, October 1936) Serial, 12 chapters; Chapter 1, three reels; others two reels. D: Mack V. Wright and Ray Taylor. SP: John Rathmell, Maurice Geraghty, Winston Miller. S: Maurice Geraghty and Leslie Swabacker. Supervision: J. Laurence Wickland. Photography: William Nobles, Edgar Lyons. Music: Harry Grey. P: Nat Levine.

The story is set in California in 1844. Don Loring's father and brother are killed by General Jason Burr when they discover he is secretly mining gold on their land, using kidnapped peons. Don adopts the black mask and cape of The Eagle to bring Burr's gang to account. He is assisted by a band of confidants he has organized. Posing as a simple-minded organist in the local mission, he is not suspected by Burr and the outlaws or Count Raspinoff and the Russian Cossacks who provide the gang with military muscle in return for gold.

Robert Livingston (Don Loring/The Eagle), Kay Hughes (Doris Colton), Guinn [Big Boy] Williams (Salvation), Raymond Hatton (Whipsaw), Fred Kohler (Jason

Burr), Robert Warwick (Ivan Raspinoff), William Farnum (Father Jose), Robert Kortman (Boris Petroff), John Merton (Rance Talbot), Lloyd Ingraham (John Colton), William Desmond (Anderson), Ray Corrigan (Captain Fremont), Yakima Canutt (Barsam), Tracy Lane (Clem Peters), Philip Armetta (Dark Feather), Bud Osborne (Harris), Bud Pope (Ivan), Steve Clemente (Pedro), Henry Hall (Loring), Stanley Blystone (Kramer), Joe Delacruz (Peon), Wally West, Al Taylor, Frankie Marvin, Fred Burns, Jack Ingram, Jack Kirk, Jack Kinney, Bob Jamison, Herman Hack, Wes Warner, Len Ward, Pascale Perry, Vinegar Roan, Lloyd Saunders, John Slater, Jerome Ward, Tommy Coates, Ken Cooper, Frank Ellis, Sam Garrett.

1. The Eagle Strikes. 2. Birth of the Vigilantes. 3. Condemned by Cossacks. 4. Unholy Gold. 5. Treachery Unmasked. 6. A Tyrant's Trickery. 7. Wings of Doom. 8. A Treaty with Treason. 9. Arrow's Flight. 10. Prison of Flame. 11. A Race with Death. 12. Fremont Takes Command.

716. Vindicta

(France—Gaumont, 1923) Serial, 5 chapters. D: Louis Feuillade. Scen: Louis Feuillade.

Georges Biscot, Ginette Maddie, Andrée Lionel, Lucien Dalsace, Fernand Herrmann, Michel Floresco, Lise Jaux, Derigal, Deneyrieux, Charpentier.

1. La terre qui tremble. 2. L'intrus. 3. L'emmuré. 4. Le mariage de Blanche Cesarin. 5. Soir nuptial.

717. Vingt Ans Après (English Title: *Twenty Years After*)

(France, 1922) Serial, chapters (?). A sequel to *Les Trois Mousquetaires*. D: Henri Diamant-Berger. S: Alexandre Dumas. Scen: Henri Diamant-Berger.

In this serial Jean Yonnel replaced Simon-Girard, who had played the part of D'Artagnan in *Les Trois Mousquetaires* (1921).

Jean Yonnel (D'Artagnan), Henri Rollan, Pierre de Guingand, Charles Martinelli, Marguerite Moreno, Jean Perier, Jane Pierly, Max Charlier, Jean Daragan, Simone Vaudry, Denise Legeay, Beatrice Bretty, Marthe Vinot, Armand Bernard, Edouard de Max, Pierrette Madd, Marcel Vallee, Harry Krimer, Paul Hubert, Albert Prejean, Raimond Aimos, Betove, Jacques Arnna.

718. The Voice from the Sky

(G. Y.B. Films, 1930) Serial, 10 chapters, two reels each. D/P: Ben Wilson. S: Robert Dillon. Photography: William Nobles. This was the first 100 percent sound serial, though the production was quite crude.

A mad inventor has the capability of suspending all energy in the earth's atmosphere and throwing his voice into the sky so that a whole city can hear it. He threatens to destroy everyone with his scientific weapons unless his demands are met. A young detective and his sweetheart thwart the scheme and unmask the villain.

Wally Wales [Hal Taliaferro] (Jack Deering), Jean Dolores [Neva Gerber] (Jean Lowell), Robert Walker (Edgar Bellim), J.P. Lockney (Geoffrey Mentor), Al Haskell (Patch Eye), Cliff Lyons (Humpy), John C. McCallum (The Man from Nowhere), Merle Ferris (Mrs. Deering).

1. Doomed. 2. The Cave of Horror. 3. The Man from Nowhere. 4. Danger Ahead. 5. Desperate Deeds. 6. Trail of Vengeance. 7. The Scarlet Scourge. 8. Trapped by Fate. 9. The Pit of Peril. 10. Hearts of Steel.

719. The Voice on the Wire

(Universal, March 18, 1917) Serial, 15 chapters, two reels each. D: Stuart Paton. Scen: J. Grubb Alexander. S: Eustace Hale Ball.

Laroux, a scientist, develops a theory which becomes known as The Living Death and, to put it to the test, mummifies the wife of a fellow scientist, Dr. Reynolds. Reynolds seeks revenge on Laroux and other members of the radical Black Seven. Detective John Shirley and his colleague Polly Marion seek to solve the mystery of Reynold's weird powers and of the crime wave he starts.

Ben Wilson (John Shirley), Neva Gerber (Polly Marion), Joseph W. Girard (Dr. Reynolds), Francis McDonald (Red Warren), Kingsley Benedict, Nigel De Bruiler, Howard Crampton, L.M. Wells, Frank MacQuarrie, Frank Tokonaga, Ernest Shields, Hoot Gibson.

1. The Oriental Death Punch. 2. The Mysterious Man in Black. 3. The Spider's Web. 4. The Next Victim. 5. The Spectral Hand. 6. The Death Warrant. 7. The Marked Room. 8. High Finance. 9. A Stern Chase. 10. The Guarded Heart. 11. The Thought Machine. 12. The Sign of the Thumb. 13. Twixt Death and Dawn. 14. The Light Dawn. 15. The Living Death.

720. Vultures of the Sea

(Mascot, August 1, 1928) Serial, 10 chapters, two reels each. D: Richard Thorpe. P: Nat Levine. S/SP: Wyndham Gittens, William Burt.

Vultures of the Sea is produced more along the lines of a feature picture with each of the chapters almost a story in itself. It is a sea tale having to do with the rough crew aboard a ship. There has been a murder committed because there is loot hidden aboard the ship. An innocent man is condemned to the gallows and he has but thirty days to live.

His son is satisfied of his innocence and he ships out aboard the ship to clear up the mystery. He falls in love with the girl owner of the ship, who has been left in charge of the cruel mate. Attempts are made to do away with the youth and the girl. They have some thrilling experiences, coming through them all safely, until the real murderer is discovered and the loot recovered.

The production is exceptional for a serial. There are many remarkable shots in the rigging of the ship and elsewhere. There is action with almost every foot of each chapter.

Johnnie Walker, Shirley Mason, Tom Santschi, Frank Hagney, Boris Karloff, John Carpenter, George Magrill, Joe Bennett, Arthur Dewey, Joseph Mack, John P. Lockney, Lafe McKee.

1. The Hell Ship. 2. Cast Adrift. 3. Driven to Port. 4. Scum of the Seas. 5. The Harbor of Danger. 6. The Stolen Ship. 7. At the Mercy of the Flames. 8. The Fight for Possession. 9. The Traitor. 10. The End of the Quest.

721. W.C. Tuttle Comedy Westerns

(Universal, 1925–27) Series, 25 episodes, two reels each. D: Vin Moore. S: W.C. Tuttle. SP: Robert McKenzie on most films.

Gilbert "Pee Wee" Holmes, Benny Corbett.

1. Just Cowboys (10-3-25). 2. Shootin' Wild (10-4-25). 3. Too Many Bucks (11-4-25). 4. Breakin' Loose (12-5-25). 5. The Hero of Piperock (1-16-26). 6. The Big Game (2-2-26). 7. One Wild Time (3-2-26), Fay Wray and Dorothy Gulliver in this film. 8. Fade-Away Foster (4-2-26), Janet Gaynor in this film. 9. Desperate Dan (4-22-26). 10. The Rescue (6-19-26). 11. Let Loose (7-17-26). 12. When East Meets West (8-21-26). 13. Piperock Goes Wild (9-25-26). 14. A Man's Size Pet (10-23-26). 15. Barely Reasonable (11-27-26). 16. Hen Punchers of Piperock (12-18-26). 17. Too Much Progress for Piperock (1-15-27). 18. Tied Up (2-12-27). 19. A Strange Inheritance (3-5-27). 20. When Oscar Went Wild (4-2-27). 21. The Pride of Piperock (4-23-27). 22. Flaming Snow (5-14-27). 24. The Piperock Blaze (6-11-27). 24. The Rest Cure (6-25-27). 25. Cows is Cows (7-9-27).

Jack Knapp replaced Holmes in *Flaming Snow. A Cinch for the Gander* not in copyright catalog but is believed to be part of this series.

722. Wally Wales Featurettes

(William M. Pizor, May–November, 1934) Series, 7 episodes, two reels each. P: William M. Pizor. D: Robert Emmett [Tansey]. SP: Al Lane and Robert Emmett. Photography: Brydon Baker. Editor; Arthur Cohen.

These seven two-reel Westerns were good little films, if you happened to be real dyed-in-the-wool shoot-em-up fans. The stories were not outstanding, but the players were. Casts were composed of former stars and players familiar to Western audiences. Wally Wales was a good lead and the horse Silver King, formerly the steed of Fred Thomson, was a real asset to the series.

Wally Wales, Silver King [horse], Franklyn Farnum, Yakima Canutt, Al Hoxie, Jim Sheridan [Sherry Tansey], Peggy Djarling, Fred Parker, Francis Walker, Fay McKenzie, Karla Cowan, Jack Kirk, Barney Beasley, Herman Hack, Ace Cain, Dorothy Crittin, Merla Bratton, Tex Miller.

1. Arizona Cyclone (May 1934, 19 min.). 2. Sundown Trail (June 1934, 18 min.). 3. Carrying the Mail (July 1934, 27 min.). 4. The Desert Man (August 1934, 19 min.). 5. Pals of the West (September 1934, 27 min.). 6. The Lone Rider (October 1934, 27 min.). 7. West of the Law (November 1934, 20 min.).

723. Way of a Man

(Pathé, January 20, 1924) Serial, 10 chapters, two reels each. D: George B. Seitz. SP: George B. Seitz. S: Emerson Hough. P: C.W. Patton. Also released in a nine-reel version.

Ellen Meriweather and John Cowles find both romance and excitement on a wagon train headed for the gold fields of California. However, a treacherous white renegade, Gordon Orme, incites Indians to attack the train. It is almost wiped out along the way but eventually it reaches the gold fields, Orme is defeated, and Ellen and John prepare to face life together.

The Pathé lustre was in evidence as George Sietz put his players through their paces. Allene was obviously more at home on a horse than her leading man, Harold Miller, though he was an adequate thrill maker.

Allene Ray (Ellen Meriweather), Harold Miller (John Cowles), Bud Osborne (Gordon Orme), Lillian Gale (Mandy McGovern), White Horse (Auberry), Kathryn Appleton (Grace Sheraton), Chet Ryan, Lillian Adrian, Florence Lee.

1. Into the Unknown. 2. Redskin and White. 3. In the Toils of the Torrent. 4. Lost in the Wild. 5. White Medicine. 6. The Firing Squad. 7. Gold! Gold! 8. The Fugitive. 9. California. 10. Trail's End.

724. What Happened to Mary?

(Edison, July 1912) Series, 12 episodes, one reel each. D: Walter Edwin, J. Searle Dawley, and others. Scen: Bannister Merwin, James Oppenheim, and Horace G. Plympton. Produced in collaboration with *The Ladies World* magazine.

Though not the serial prototype, this was the forerunner of all serials. Each one-reel episode was a complete entity in itself, revolving its immediate dramatic and melodramatic problems within the framework of a single episode and designed more for story and suspense situations than action. Its installment connections were loose and its episode endings lacked the localized holdover suspense later identified with serials.

The stories were first published in *The Ladies World* prior to their screening. Mary is a foundling raised by a storekeeper who has been promised $1,000 if he will marry her to one of the local young men. The story chronicles her experience in making a new life for herself after having run away from her foster father. In the end, despite rival claimants and the skullduggery of villain Billy Peart, Mary receives her fortune of $10,000.

Mary Fuller (Mary), Bliss Milford (Daisy), Marc MacDermott (Lieutenant Straker), Charles Ogle (Richard Craig, Mary's Uncle), Barry O'Moore (Henry, Craig's Son), Bigelow Cooper (Mr. Foster, the Lawyer), William Wadsworth (Billy Peart), Miriam Nesbitt (Spy), Harold Shaw (Reverend Cooper), Henry Eytinge (Secretary, Occidental Trust Co.), Walter Edwin (Manager of the Society Queen), Yale Banner (Mr. Cleare), James Smith (Stage Manager), Carey Lee (Leading Lady), Arthur Houseman (Comedian), Ben Wilson, May Abbey, Edna Flugrath.

1. The Escape from Bondage. 2. Alone in New York. 3. Mary in Stage Land. 4. The Affair at Raynor's. 5. A Letter to the Princess. 6. A Clue to her Parentage. 7. False to their Trust. 8. A Will and a Way. 9. A Way to the Underworld. 10. The High Tide of Misfortune. 11. A Race to New York. 12. Fortune Smiles.

725. The Whirlwind

(Allgood Pictures, November, 1919) Serial, 15 chapters, two reels each. D/SP: Joseph A. Golden.

Robert Darrell, nicknamed "The Whirlwind" because of his reckless daring in riding his motorcycle, makes the acquaintance of Helen Graydon in a thrilling and unusual manner. Helen's saddle horse is spooked by a passing automobile and runs away with her. Dashing through the woods, across a small river, the frightened horse carries his beautiful rider along the brink of a cliff. Robert follows and when he can he speeds alongside the horse and lifts Helen off the horse's back.

Robert quickly falls in love with Helen but is opposed by her fiancé, Neville Carnley, who is secretly the head of a band of ingenious and daring criminals. He is jealous of any man who is at all attentive to Helen and directs his gang to frame or kill Robert. Much of this activity is carried out by Carnley's

***Left:* Charles Hutchison in *The Whirlwind* (1920); *above:* Malcolm MacGregor and Viva Tattersall in *Whispering Shadows* (1933)**

chief lieutenant, known as "The Wolf." Helen soon learns that Carnley is a crook and aids Darrell as he fights to bring the gang to justice.

Charles Hutchison (Robert Darrell), Edith Thornton (Helen Graydon), Richard R. Neill (Neville Carnley), Ben Walker (Benson), Barbara Allen (Kate Delaro), Karl Dane (The Wolf), Edward Waters (Buckley), John Lamont (Scotty), Helen Griley (Mrs. Stockton), Paul Fisher (Mr. Stockton), Morton Thatcher (Baron de Langes), Earl Douglas (Blacky), Frank Hagney.

1. The Trap. 2. The Waters of Death. 3. The Hooded Terror (?). 4. The Drop to Death. 5. Over the Precipice. 6. On the Brink. 7. In Mid Air. 8. A Fight for Life. 9. Amid the Flames. 10. The Human Bridge. 11. In the Depths of the River. 12. Hanged by the Neck. 13. In the Lion's Cage. 14. A Life at Stake. 15. The Missing Bride.

726. The Whispering Shadow

(Mascot, January 15, 1933) Serial, 12 chapters, Chapter 1, three reels, others two reels. D: Albert Herman and Colbert Clark. P: Nat Levine. S/SP: Barney Sarecky, George Morgan, Norman S. Hall, Colbert Clark, and Wyndham Gittens. Camera: Ernest Miller and Edgar Lyons. Music: Abe Meyer. Also released as a six-reel feature.

Professor Strang, ostensibly the proprietor of the House of Mystery, a wax museum, is actually a foreign agent who has brought jewels to this country as security for a loan. They have been stolen and hidden in the Empire Trucking warehouse by an escaped convict. The Whispering Shadow seeks the jewels to finance his plot to conquer the world. Others also desire the gems. Each attack by The Whispering Shadow is preceded by neutralization of all radio equipment in the radio lab atop the warehouse.

Bela Lugosi (Professor Strang), Henry B. Walthall (President Bradley), Viva Tattersall (Vera Strang), Malcolm McGregor (Jack Foster), Robert Warwick (Detective Raymond), Ethel Clayton (Countess), Roy D'Arcy (Steinbeck), Karl Dane (Sparks), Lloyd Whitlock (Young), Robert Kortman (Slade), Lafe McKee (Jerome), George J. Lewis (Bud Foster), Jack Perrin (Williams), Max Wagner (Kruger), Kernan Cripps (Foreman), Eddie Parker (Driver), Gordon DeMain (Detective), George Magrill (Mitchell), Tom London (Dupoint), Lionel Bacus (Jarvis), Norman Feusier (Deane).

1. The Master Magician. 2. The Collapsing Room. 3. The All-Seeing Eye. 4. The Shadow Strikes. 5. Wanted for Murder. 6. The Man Who was Czar. 7. The Double Room. 8. The Red Circle. 9. The Fatal Secret. 10. The Death Warrant. 11. The Trap. 12. King of the World.

727. Whispering Smith Rides

(Universal, June 6, 1927) Serial, 10 chapters, two reels each. D: Ray Taylor. Scen: Arthur Henry Gooden. S: Frank Hamilton Spearman. Remade by Universal in 1931 as *The Lightning Express*.

Adventures of a western railroad detective in defending a young woman whose illegal guardian is trying to cheat her and to stop railroad construction.

Wallace MacDonald (Whispering Smith), Rose Blossom, J.P. McGowan, Clark Comstock, Henry Herbert, W.M. McCormick, Harry Todd, Willie Fung, Frank Ellis.

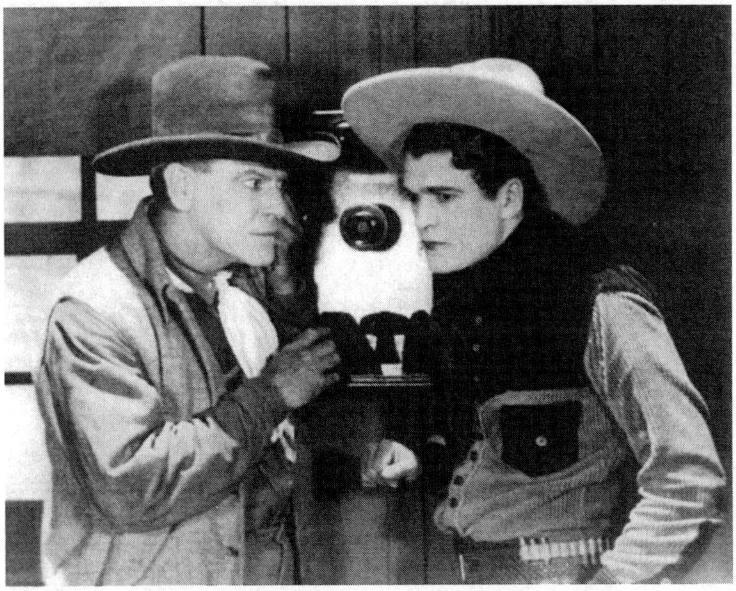

Top left: **Wallace MacDonald and J.P. McGowen;** ***bottom left:*** **Wallace MacDonald and Rose Blossom in** ***Whispering Smith Rides*** **(1927);** ***top right:*** **Ruth Roland in** ***White Eagle*** **(1922)**

1. Lawless Men. 2. Caught in the Crash. 3. Trapped. 4. The Ambush. 5. Railroad Gold. 6. The Interrupted Wedding. 7. A Coward of Conscience. 8. The Bandit's Bargain. 9. The Trail of Sacrifice. 10. A Call of the Heart.

728. White Eagle

(Ruth Roland Serials/Pathé, January 1, 1922) Serial, 15 chapters, two reels each. D: W.S. Van Dyke and Fred Jackman. S/SP: Val Cleveland. Supervised by Hal Roach. P: Ruth Roland.

Ruth Randolph learns that the trident tattooed on the palm of her left hand is an ill omen. Two Indians overpower her while she is motoring but she is rescued by Phil Stanton. Ruth is lured to the Golden Canyon by Jim Loomis, who is in league with Gray Wolf, chief of the Buffalo tribe, who wishes to secure possession of the Golden Pool, an inexhaustible supply of molten gold. This pool is to go to the tribe chosen by Ruth, who, it is proved by the trident, is their Princess White Eagle. She is imprisoned but rescued by a mysterious masked man dressed in white. He takes her to his home, which is carved out of solid rock.

But she escapes and finally seeks food and shelter at the home of Stone Ear, a deaf mute. Phil finds her and she decides to return to 'Frisco, but Loomis and his gang foil her again. As Ruth is about to enter Golden Canyon she is again halted by the White Rider, who warns her not to enter the canyon. She disobeys his orders, however, enters the Indians' camp and is proclaimed by them to be Princess White Eagle. Gray Wolf realizes that if Ruth dies in the near future his tribe may be granted the Golden Pool. The action picks up without a letdown until things are resolved in Chapter 15.

Ruth Roland (Ruth Randolph), Earl Metcalfe (Phil Stanton), Harry Girard (Jim Loomis), Virginia Ainsworth (Julia Wells), Otto Lederer (Gray Wolf), Bud Osborne (Standing Bear), Frank Lackteen (Crouching More), Gertrude Douglas (Moonlight), Louise Emmons (Stone Ear), Frank Valrose (Feather Foot), Chick Morrison (Bill Henley), The White Rider (?).

1. The Sign of the Trident. 2. The Red Men's Menace. 3. A Strange Message. 4. The Lost Trail. 5. The Clash of the Clans. 6. The Trap. 7. The Mysterious Voyage. 8. The Island of Terror. 9. The Flaming Arrow. 10. The Cave of

Peril. 11. Danger Rails. 12. Win or Lose. 13. Clash of the Clans. 14. The Pivoted Rock. 15. The Golden Pool.

729. White Eagle

(Columbia, January 31, 1941) Serial, 15 chapters, two reels each. D: James W. Horne. S: Fred Myton. Adapted from the 1932 *White Eagle* Feature. SP: Arch Heath, Morgan B. Cox, John Cutting, Lawrence Taylor. P: Larry Darmour. Photography: James S. Brown, Jr. Music: Lee Zahler.

White Eagle, a pony express rider, defends the innocence of his people against charges that they are responsible for atrocities actually committed by a gang headed by Bert Darnell and Gregory Cantro, who dress their men as Indians.

Buck Jones (White Eagle), Raymond Hatton (Grizzly), Dorothy Fay (Janet), James Craven (Bert Darnell), Jack Ingram (Gregory Cantro), Chief Yowlachie (Running Deer), Charles King (Brace), John Merton (Romino), Edmund Cobb (Dave), Roy Barcroft (Pendleton), Edward Hearn (Gardner), Al Ferguson (Butch), John Paul Jones (General Allen), Edward Cecil (Sprague), Silver [a horse] (Himself), Yakima Canutt, George Chesebro, George Larkin, Constantine Romanoff, Keene Duncan, Kit Guard, Harry Tenbrook, Jack Richardson, Charles Hamilton, Edward Peil, Sr., Eddie Featherstone, Hank Bell, Lloyd Whitlock, Dick Cramer, Jack O'Shea, Richard Ellis, Robert Elliott, Merrill McCormack, Steve Clark, Horace B. Carpenter, Bob Woodward, Chick Hannon, Bud Osborne.

1. Flaming Teepees. 2. The Jail Delivery. 3. The Dive Into Quicksand. 4. The Warning Death Knife. 5. Treachery at the Stockade. 6. The Gun-Cane Murder. 7. The Revealing Blotter. 8. Bird-Calls of Deliverance. 9. The Fake Telegram. 10. Mystic Dots and Dashes. 11. The Ear at the Window. 12. The Massacre Invitation. 13. The Framed-Up Showdown. 14. The Fake Army General. 15. Treachery Downed.

730. The White Horseman

(Universal, May 30, 1921) Serial, 18 chapters; Chapter 1, three reels; other, two reels. D: Albert Russell. S: Ford Beebe and Albert Russell. P: William Lord Wright.

Wayne Allen is willed what appears to be worthless land occupied by two squatter brothers. While out foraging they find an ancient bracelet inscribed with instructions of how to reach the base of a mountain where they discover a system of underground mines once to an Indian tribe thought extinct. The brothers also find a chest of blue opals.

Centuries before an unwarlike tribe, to escape marauding tribes, had built a city underground with sliding gates that looked like the face of the cliff. By day they worked their fields outside and at night returned to their hole in the wall and shut it behind them until the next morning. Two members of this tribe still live and they know the secret method of opening the door.

Wayne Allen gets involved along with a girl and her father and his twin brother, the latter a dirty heavy, of course. Allen was looked upon as a reincarnation of a white horseman who,

Top: **Buck Jones and Raymond Hatton in *White Eagle* (1941); *bottom:* Art Acord and Iva Forrester in *The White Horseman* (1921)**

centuries before, according to Indian legend had befriended the tribe and protected it against its enemies. Bad guys under the leadership of The Spider also want the mountain's treasures.

Art Acord (Wayne Allen), Duke R. Lee (John Ramsey/Richard Ramsey), Iva Forrester (Juanita), Hank Bell (The Spider), Beatrice Dominguez (Zona), Tote DuCrow (Cuevas), Marie Tropic (Onava).

1. Cave of Despair. 2. The Spider's Web. 3. The Mummy Man. 4. The Death Trap. 5. Trails of Treachery. 6. Furnace of Fear. 7. Brink of Eternity. 8. Pit of Evil. 9. The Opal Bracelet. 10. In the Enemy's Hands. 11. A Race with Death. 12. The Bridge of Fear. 13. The Hill of Horror. 14. A Jest of Fate. 15. A Conquest of Courage. 16. Fire of Fury. 17. The Wings of Destiny. 18. The Avenging Conscience.

731. Who Is Number 1?

(Paramount, October 29, 1917) Serial, 15 chapters, two reels each. D: William Bertram or Frank H. Crane (sources disagree). S: Anna Katherine Green.

The mysterious Number One is bent on destroying the Hale family, and Aimee Villon is just as determined to protect it out of love for Tommy Hale. The complicated revenge story takes quite a twist as it progresses, ending with the revelation that Aimee herself is Number One and bringing to light previously unknown relationships among the principal characters.

Kathleen Clifford (Aimee Villon), Cullen Landis (Tommy Hale), Gordon Sackville, Neil C. Hardin, Ruth Smith, Ethel Ritchie, Coreen Grant.

1. The Flaming Cross. 2. The Flying Fortress. 3. The Sea Crawler. 4. A Marine Miracle. 5. Halls of Hazard. 6. The Flight of the Fury. 7. Hearts in Torment. 8. Walls of Gas. 9. Struck Down. 10. Wire of Wrath. 11. The Rail Raiders. 12. The Show Down. 13. Cornered. 14. No Surrender. 15. The Round-Up.

732. Who Pays?

(Balboa/Pathé, March 1915) Series, 12 episodes, three reels each. D: Harry Harvey and H.M. Horkheimer (possibly others). Scen: William Ritchie.

Each episode is a complete drama in itself with no connection with any other story in the series. The episodes were unique in that each was three reels long. Though there were no cliff-hanging ending, each did end with a challenge to the audience: who was responsible for the misfortune of the principal characters? Different roles were played by the principals in each episode.

Ruth Roland, Henry King, Edwin J. Brady, Daniel Gilfether, Mollie McConnell, Charles Dudley, Gypsy Abbott, Frank H. Dietl, Margaret Landis.

1. The Pursuit of Pleasure. 2. The Price of Fame. 3. When Justice Sleeps. 4. The Love Liar. 5. Unto Herself Alone. 6. Houses of Glass. 7. Blue Blood and Yellow. 8. Today and Tomorrow. 9. For the Commonwealth. 10. The Pomp of Earth. 11. The Fruit of Folly. 12. Toil and Tyranny.

733. Who Will Marry Mary?

(Edison, July 26, 1913) Series, 6 episodes, one reel each. Produced in collaboration with *The Ladies World* magazine. D: Walter Edwin. Scen: Ida Damon.

Mary Cuyler unexpectedly inherits a great fortune and finds it a pleasant experience. But several romances of the heiress fizzle when she finds that the suitors are overly interested in her yearly income of $122,000 from the Silver Star Mine in California. However, she proposes to Captain Bradford when she finds that he has no interest in her money, as such, but has endangered himself and sacrificed his own material well-being out of love for her.

Mary Fuller (Mary Cuyler), Ben Wilson (Captain Justin Bradford), Richard Tucker (Duke Leonardo de Ferrara), Harry Beaumont, Miriam Nesbitt, Marc MacDermott, Harold Shaw, William Wadsworth, May Abbey.

1. A Proposal from the Duke. 2. A Proposal from the Spanish Don. 3. A Proposal from the Sculptor. 4. A Proposal from—Nobody. 5. A Proposal Deferred. 6. A Proposal from Mary.

734. Who's Guilty?

(Columbia, December 1945) Serial, 15 chapters, two reels each. D: Howard Bretherton and Wallace Grissell. SP:

Left: **Kathleen Clifford and Cullen Landis in *Who Is Number 1?* (1917); *above:* Mary Fuller in *Who Will Marry Mary?* (1913)**

Ande Lamb and George H. Plympton. P: Sam Katzman. Photography: Ira H. Morgan. Music: Lee Zahler. Released in feature form in England.

A detective tries to find out who is behind the attempts to murder various members of a wealthy family. Eventually he proves that a member thought dead is really alive and is the mystery Voice. The Voice and a brother attempt to murder everyone else in the family to gain the family fortune for themselves.

Robert Kent (Bob Stewart), Amelita Ward (Ruth Allen), Tim Ryan (Duke Ellis), Jayne Hazard (Rita Royale), Minerva Urecal (Mrs. Dill), Belle Mitchell (Sara Caldwell), Charles Middleton (Patton/Walter Calvert), Davison Clark (Henry Calvert), Sam Flint (Horace Black), Bruce Donovan (Curt Bennett), Jack Ingram (Sergeant Smith), Milton Kibbee (Morgan Calvert), Nacho Galindo (Pancho), Roberto Tafur (Jose), Wheeler Oakman (Smiley), Charles King (Burk), Anthony Warde (Edwards).

1. Avenging Visitor. 2. The Unknown Strikes. 3. Held for Murder. 4. A Killer at Bay. 5. Human Bait. 6. The Plunge of Doom. 7. A Date with Fate. 8. Invisible Hands. 9. Fate's Vengeance. 10. The Unknown Killer. 11. Riding to Oblivion. 12. The Tank of Terror. 13. White Terror. 14. A Cry in the Night. 15. The Guilty One.

735. Wild West

(Pathé, September 27, 1925) Serial, 10 chapters; Chapter 1, three reels; others, two reels. D: Robert F. Hill. SP: J.F. Natteford.

The story revolves around a stranded tent show and combines all the elements of the wild west and circus life. It was actually filmed on the 101 Ranch in Oklahoma.

Awaiting the opening of the Cherokee Strip to homesteaders are Doctor Powers, owner of a medicine show, Colonel Hardcastle and his wife, and the three Miller brothers. Hardcastle's wife leaves him and takes their daughter. Twenty years later Hardcastle is known as Tom Osborne and has a large ranch, managed by Jimmy Whitehawk, the half-breed son of Powers. The Miller brothers have put together their large ranch and the 101 Wild West Show. A boy adopted by one of the Miller brothers is in league with cattle rustlers.

Polly Breen is a circus performer that Whitehawk falls in love with. The relationships of the various principals are somewhat confusing, requiring that one keep up with the story on a weekly basis to avoid getting lost as to what is going on. The 101 Ranch Show becomes the primary set for the action.

Jack Mulhall (Jimmy Whitehawk), Helen Ferguson (Polly Breen), Ed Burns (Colonel Hardcastle/Tom Osborne), Eddie Phillips (Bob Miller), Fred Burns (Joe Miller), Larry Steers (Dr. Alonzo Powers), George Burton (Dan Norton), Milla Davenport (Chalky Withers), Virginia Warwick (Elsie Withers), Dan Dix (Pat Casey), Gus Saville, Buck Lucas, Nowatta Slim Richardson.

1. The Land Rush. 2. On the Show. 3. The Outlaw Elephant. 4. Ride 'Em Cowboy! 5. The Rustler's Stampede. 6. The Diamond Girl. 7. The Champion Cowboy. 8. Under the Buffalo. 9. Stolen Evidence. 10. The Law Decides.

736. Wild West Days

(Universal, May 20, 1937) Serial, 13 chapters, two reels each. D: Ford Beebe and Cliff Smith. SP: Wyndham Gittens, Norman S. Hall, and Ray Trampe. P: Ben Koenig and Henry McRae. S: W.R. Burnett—*Saint Johnson. Saint Johnson* was also the story basis for the three versions of *Law and Order*, 1932, 1940, and 1953.

Three saddle pals protect a young couple threatened by a gang whose leader is a crooked newspaper publisher who wants possession of their mine. Hostile Indians are allied with the crooks and the two lawless forces give the three adventurers a rough time of it.

Johnny Mack Brown (Kentucky Wade), Lynn Gilbert (Lucy Monroe), Robert Kortman (Trigger), George Shelley (Dude), Frank Yaconelli (Mike), Frank McGlynn, Jr. (Larry Monroe), Russell Simpson (Keeler), Francis McDonald (Purvis), Walter Miller (Doc Hardy), Chief Thunder Cloud (Red Hatchet), Al Bridge (Steve), Charles Stevens, Edward J. LeSaint, Bruce Mitchell, Frank Ellis, Bud Osborne, Jack Clifford, Hank Bell, Lafe McKee, Joe Girard, William Royle, Mike Morita, Robert McClung, Sidney Bracey, Iron Eyes Cody.

1. Death Rides the Range. 2. The Redskin's Revenge. 3. The Brink of Action. 4. The Indians are Coming. 5. The Leap for Life. 6. Death Stalks the Plains. 7. Six Gun Law. 8. The Gold Stampede. 9. Walls of Fire. 10. The Circle of Doom. 11. The Thundering Herd. 12. Rustlers and Redskins. 13. The Rustler's Roundup.

737. The Winking Idol

(Universal, February 21, 196) Serial, 10 chapters, two reels each. D: Francis Ford. Scen: Arthur Henry Gooden and George Morgan. S: Charles E. Van Loan.

The Winking Idol, a small statue, is the key to a gold cache hidden away by Indians years past. Though the Idol has brought misfortune to both their fathers, Dave Ledbetter and Jean Wilson try to find it. They also search for the man who many years before, in an attempt to get the gold, shot Dave's father and framed Jean's for the crime.

Helen Ferguson in *Wild West* (1925)

738. Winners of the West

(Universal, September 26, 1921) Serial, 18 chapters, two reels each. D: Ed Laemmle. S/Scen: Ford Beebe and Robert Dillon.

The picturesque background of the story is the period of 1849, when gold was discovered on Sutter's Creek and Captain John C. Freemont, with the help of Arthur Standish, started west over the pathless and perilous prairies to blaze a wagon route for civilization. Trying to "stay with a good thing," the script writers again had Art seeking a lost treasure and fighting for possession of the map indicating its whereabouts. Love and romance were on the same trail and by the time Art reaches the end of his journey, he has both gold and girl.

Art Acord (Arthur Standish), Burton C. Law (Captain John C. Freemont), Myrtle Lind (Elizabeth Edwards), Burt Wilson (Doctor Edwards), Percy Pembroke (Louis Blair), Jim Corey (Squire Blair).

1. Power of Gold. 2. Blazing Arrow. 3. Perils of the Plains. 4. The Flame of Hate. 5. The Fight for a Fortune. 6. Buried Alive. 7. Fires of Fury. 8. Pit of Doom. 9. Chasm of Peril. 10. Sands of Fear. 11. Poisoned Pool. 12. Duel in the Night. 13. Web of Fate. 14. Trail of Mystery. 15. Unmasked. 16. Hidden Gold. 17. Cave of Terror. 18. The End of the Trail.

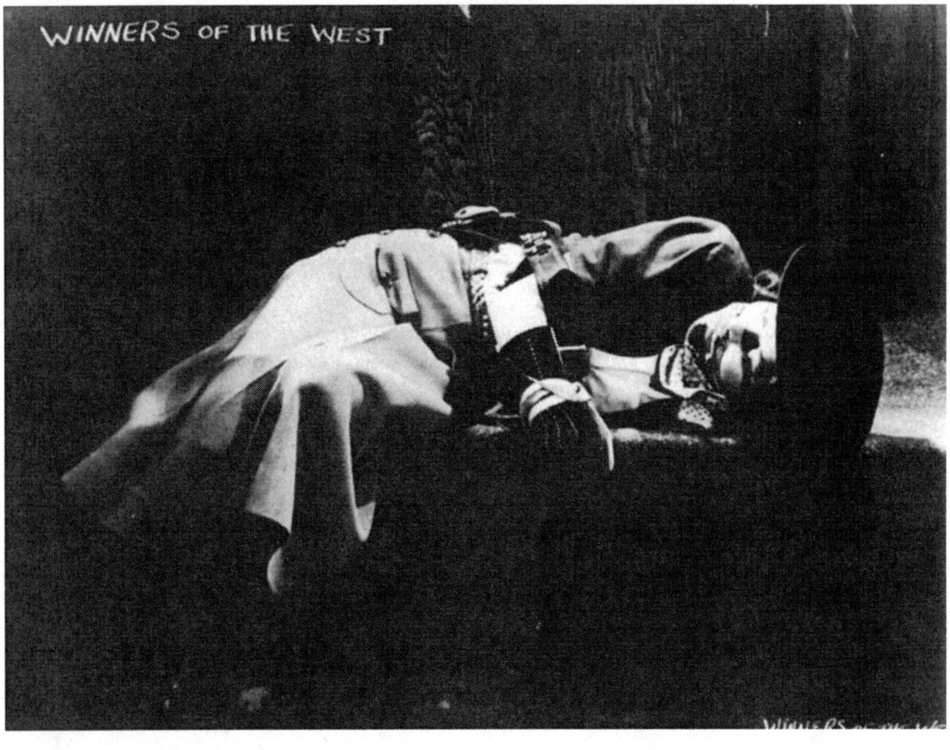

***Top:* Art Acord and Myrtle Lind; *bottom:* Myrtle Lind in *Winners of the West* (1921)**

William Desmond (Dave Ledbetter), Eileen Sedgwick (Jean Wilson), Jack Richardson (Crawford Lange), Grace Cunard (Thora Lange), Monavana (Komi), Herbert Sutch (Jim Wilson), Les Sailor [Syd Saylo], Dorothy Gulliver, Art Ortega, Helen Broneau, Vanna Carroll.

1. The Eye of Evil. 2. Buzzards' Roost. 3. Crashing Timbers. 4. Racing for Love. 5. The Vanishing Bride. 6. The Torrent of Terror. 7. Flames of Fear. 8. The Fight at the Falls. 9. In Danger of Dynamite. 10. The Lost Lode.

739. Winners of the West

(Universal, July 2, 1940) Serial, 13 chapters, two reels each. D: Ford Beebe and Ray Taylor. SP: George H. Plympton, Basil Dickey, and Charles R. Condon. P: Henry McRae. Camera: Jerome Ash, William Sickner, John Hickson. Song: "The Drinks Are on the House"—Everett Carter and Milton Raison, sung by Vyola Vonn.

Jeff Ramsay, assistant to John Hartford, President of the Hartford Transcontinental Railroad, is fighting to advance the line through Hell's Gate Pass. King Carter, self-styled ruler of the land beyond the pass, plans to block the railroad.

Carter hires Snakeye, a renegade halfbreed, to lead the Indians on raids against the construction camps. Claire Hartford is captured and held hostage until Jeff and Tex Houston come to her rescue.

Spurred on by Carter, the Indians rob wagon supply trains, drive surveyors off and burn down the telegraph station. Finally, in a battle at Black Hawk, Carter's gang is wiped out by Jeff and his friend, Jim Jackson. Carter is turned over to the law, and a peace treaty is signed with War Eagle. Jeff, and his bride, Claire, are happy as pioneers welcome the first transcontinental train.

Dick Foran (Jeff Ramsay), Anne Nagel (Claire Hartford), James Craig (Jim Jackson), Tom Fadden (Tex Houston), Charles Stevens (Snakeye), Trevor Bardette (Raven), Harry Woods (King Carter), Chief Yowlachie (Chief War Eagle), Edward Keane (John Hartford), William Desmond (Brine), Edmund Cobb (Maddox), Roy Barcroft (Logan), Chuck Morrison (Blade), Edgar Edwards (Tim), Jack Voglin (Cavalry Sergeant), Edward Cassidy (Marshal

Nick Bowers), Slim Whitaker (Lacey), Alan Bridge (Captain Jarvis), George Plues (worker), Vyola [Viola] Vonn (Rita), James Blaine (Senator Dodson), Evelyn Selbie (Squaw), Robert Long (Sergeant Brown), Hank Worden (Saloon Tramp), Henry Hall (Old Timer), James Farley (Greeley), Earl Douglas (Ed Craig), James [Jim] Pierce (Charlie Nelson), George Magrill (Henchman), Bud Osborne (Henchman), Paul Reed (Lieutenant Jones), Robert [Bob] Kortman (Goebel), Grace Cunard (Woman), Bill Hunter (Stark), Horace B. Carpenter (Saloon Patron), Charles Sherlock (Sergeant Blue), Harry Tenbrook (Rooney), Tom London (Webb), Iron Eyes Cody (Indian), Charles Brunner (Indian), Frank Ellis (Joe), Jim Corey (Worker), Fred Graham (Double for Woods), Eddie Parker (Double for Foran), Cliff Lyons (Double for Foran and Fadden), Ken Terrell (Double), Gene Alsace [Rocky Camron] (Soldier), Rose Plummer (Townswoman), Universal Jack, Bud McClure, Tex Palmer, Dick Rush (Townsmen).

1. Redskins Ride Again. 2. The Wreck at Red River Gorge. 3. The Bridge of Disaster. 4. Trapped by Redskins. 5. Death Stalks the Trail. 6. A Leap for Life. 7. Thundering Terror. 8. The Flaming Arsenal. 9. Sacrificed by Savages. 10. Under Crashing Timbers. 11. Bullets in the Dark. 12. The Battle at Blackhawk. 13. Barricades Blasted.

Frankie Darro and Rin-Tin-Tin, Jr. in *The Wolf Dog* (1933)

740. With Stanley in Africa

(Universal, January 23, 1922) Serial, 18 chapters, two reels each. D: William Craft and Ed Kull. Scen: George H. Plympton. S: George H. Plympton.

A young newspaper woman aids Stanley in his search for Doctor Livingston in the wilds of Africa, with hero and heroine caught up in an attempt to revive the African slave trade. An especially captivating serial for the time.

George Walsh (Stanley), Louise Lorraine, Charles Mason, William Welsh, Gordon Sackville, Jack Mower, Fred Kohler.

1. Jaws of the Jungles. 2. The Grip of the Slavers. 3. Paths of Peril. 4. Find Livingston. 5. The Flaming Spear. 6. Lost in the Jungle. 7. Trail of the Serpent. 8. Pool of Death. 9. Menace of the Jungle. 10. The Ordeal. 11. The Lion's Prey. 12. The Forest of Flame. 13. Buried Alive. 14. The Lair of Death. 15. The Good Samaritan. 16. The Slave's Secret. 17. The White Tribe. 18. Out of the Dark.

741. The Wolf Dog

(Mascot, September 30, 1933) Serial, 12 chapters, Chapter 1, three reels, others, two reels. D: Colbert Clark and Harry Frazer. SP: Al Martin, Colbert Clark, and Wyndham Gittens. S: Barney Sarecky and Sherman Lowe. P: Nat Levine. Assist. D: George Webster, Louis Germonprez, and Jean Yarbrough. Photography: Harry Neumann, William Nobles, and Tom Galligan. Production Supervisor: Victor Zobel.

Bob Whitlock invents an electric ray that can destroy ships at a distance of several miles. Norman Bryan, general manager of the Courtney Steamship Lines, plans to steal it. Bob becomes friends with a young boy, Frank, and his dog Pal. All three are involved in a desperate struggle to stay alive and protect the invention until it can be turned over to the government.

Rin-Tin-Tin, Jr. [A dog] (Pal), George J. Lewis (Bob Whitlock), Frankie Darro (Frank Courtney), Boots Mallory (Irene Courtney), Henry B. Walthall (Jim Courtney), Hale Hamilton (Norman Bryan), Fred Kohler (Stevens), Sarah Padden (Mrs. Stevens), Max Wagner (Dave Harmon), Niles Welch (Mason), Gordon DeMain (Murphy), Donald Reed (Swan), Stanley Blystone (Lang), Tom London (Brooks), George Magrill (Pete), Dickie Moore (The Kid), Carroll Nye (Radio Announcer), Harry S. Northrup (Captain Bethel), Lane Chandler (Pilot), Cornelius Keefe, Lafe McKee, Yakima Canutt, Lionel Backus, Lew Meehan, Leon Hoomes, Jack Kenney, Wes Wagner.

1. The Call of the Wilderness. 2. The Shadow of a Crime. 3. The Fugitive. 4. A Dead Man's Hand. 5. Wolf Pack Law. 6. The Gates of Mercy. 7. The Empty Room. 8. Avenging Fangs. 9. Wizard of the Wireless. 10. Accused! 11. The Broken Record. 12. Danger Lights.

742. Wolves of Kultur

(Western Photoplays/Pathé, October 13, 1918) Serial, 15 chapters; Chapter 1, three reels; others, two reels. D/SP: Joseph A. Golden.

An unnamed foreign power poses a serious threat to American security in the World War I era. The plot is replete with spies, sabotage, traitors, stolen inventions, and cliff-hanger endings.

Leah Baird, Charles Hutchison, Sheldon Lewis, Betty Howe, Mary Hull, Edmund Dalby, Austin Webb, William Cavanough.

Leah Baird in *Wolves of Kultur* (1918)

1. The Torture Trap. 2. The Iron Chair. 3. Trapping the Traitors. 4. The Ride to Death. 5. Through the Flames. 6. Trails of Treachery. 7. The Leap of Despair. 8. In the Hands of the Hun. 9. The Precipice of Death. 10. When Woman Wars. 11. Betwixt Heaven and Earth. 12. Tower of Tears. 13. The Huns' Hell Trap. 14. Code of Hate. 15. The Reward of Patriotism.

743. Wolves of the North

(Universal, September 21, 1924) Serial, 10 chapters, two reels each. D: William Duncan. Scen: Frank H. Clark. S: Katherene and Robert Pinkerton—"The Free Trader."

The film is all about fur piracy in the Hudson Bay area and conflict between small-time traders and fur syndicate. It was shot during the winter at McCall, a summer resort on the Salmon River in Idaho. Alan Gray, free trader, beats up Dan Martin and Pierre DuPree, fur pirates, who accuse him of poaching. Helen Mears' father, manager of the powerful North Company post, nearly loses his job because of the inroads made on the company's business by the Chester Post, Madge's free trading company.

Bob Hunter, manager of the Chester Post, is fired for drunkenness, and tries to abduct Madge, but is beaten up by Alan, who Madge appoints as Bob's successor. Though they are competitors, Alan saves Helen many times from fur thieves and in the end wins her for his bride.

William Duncan (Alan Gray), Edith Johnson (Helen Mears), Joseph W. Girard (John MacLoed), Clark Comstock (Grimwood Means), Esther Ralston (Madge Chester), Edward Cecil (Henry Allardyce), Harry Woods (Bob Hunter), Joe Dominguez (Jerry Snowbird), Frank Rice (Dan Martin), Robert Homans (Simon Blake), Joe Bonomo (Pierre DuPree), Leo White (Sir Percival Pembroke), Melvina Polo.

1. The Fur Pirates. 2. The Wolf Pack. 3. The Avalanche. 4. Passions of War. 5. The Blizzard. 6. Flames of Peril. 7. The Man Hunt. 8. The Trail of Gold. 9. A Trick of Fate. 10. The Stolen Map.

744. A Woman in Grey

(Serico Producing Corp., January 22, 1920) Serial, 15 chapters, two reels each. D: James Vincent. S: C.N. and A.M. Williamson. Scen: Walter Richard Hall. P: George H. Wiley.

The story centers around the Armory residence, scene of the murder of its old housekeeper, Mrs. Haynes. Her adopted daughter, Florence Haynes, was convicted of the crime and died in prison. Mary Edwards, a servant, disappeared after testifying against Florence. Now, Wilfred Armory buys the old place at a tax sale, believing that his late father had hidden a treasure there.

Armory's secretary, Tom Thurston, encounters Ruth Hope, a woman dressed in grey, when he goes to check the place out. A jeweled ornament covers her left wrist, where Mary Edwards had a scar. Armory arrives with his niece, Paula Wynne. They discover a message, written in code, in the family bible. Now, the mysterious J. Havilland Hunter appears. He knows the secret passageways in the old house.

All parties battle for the secret message and the Armory code which may decipher it. Hunter is after it with his thugs. The true story of the murder is eventually told, characters unmasked, and Ruth is revealed as the daughter of Wilfred Armory, believed to have died with his wife. The people involved were all connected to the Haynes murder.

Henry G. Sell and Arline Pretty filled the lead roles, with capable but unknown actors in the supporting roles. Miss Pretty was the real drawing card. A veteran screen actress (she began at Universal in 1913), Miss Pretty rose to stardom at Vitagraph in 1916–17, an ascent climaxed by her role in *The Secret Kingdom*, a Graustarkian serial whose locale alternated between the mythical kingdom and the American West. She had also been leading lady to Douglas Fairbanks, Sr. As a result, she was reasonably well known to screen fans.

Actually the house chosen to portray the Armory estate is as much a star as any of the human actors. Its sliding wall panels, mysterious staircases inside the walls and other trick devices brought into play by the story line lent themselves well to the eerie feeling sought by the writers, and certainly made access by the villain considerably easier. The end result is a most representative example of the silent serial at its best—when writers still had faith in its appeal and future, and audiences shared that faith at the boxoffice by their reappearance week after week to see how the heroine survived.

Arline Pretty (Ruth Hope), Henry G. Sell (Tom Thurston), Fred Jones (J. Havilland Hunter), James A. Heenan (Wilfred Armory), Margaret Fielding (Paula Wynne), Ann Brodie (Naomi Trail), Jane Mair (Grace Carleton), Jack Newton (Ralph Gordon),

J.W. Driscoll (Dr. Lepell), Jack Manning (Gangster), Walter Chapin (Gangster), Violet de Bicari, Adelaine Fitzgallen.

1. The House of Mystery. 2. The Dagger of Death. 3. The Trap of Steel. 4. The Strangle Knot. 5. The Chasm of Fear. 6. The Grip of Fate. 7. At the Mercy of Flames. 8. The Drop to Death. 9. Burning Strands. 10. House of Horrors. 11. Fight for Life. 12. Circumstantial Evidence. 13. The Secret Chamber. 14. Pages of the Past. 15. Exonerated.

745. A Woman in the Web

(Vitagraph, April 8, 1918) Serial, 15 chapters, two reels each. D: Paul C. Hurst and David Smith. S: Albert E. Smith and Cyrus Townsend Brady. SP: Albert E. Smith and Cyrus Townsend Brady.

Princess Olga Muratoft of Russia is aided by American Jack Lawford as she attempts to stay alive and gain freedom during the Russian Revolution.

Hedda Nova (Princess Olga Muratoft), J. Frank Glendon (Jack Lawford), Robert Bradbury (Baron Kovsky), Otto Lederer (Colonel Bormsk), Chet Bryan (Ivan, the Cossack), Hoot Gibson (Vassily, Ivan's Brother), Patricia Palmer (Countess Irsky), George Kuwa.

1. Caught in the Web. 2. The Open Switch. 3. The Speeding Doom. 4. The Clutch of Terror. 5. The Hand of Mystery. 6. Full Speed Ahead. 7. The Crater of Death. 8. The Plunge of Horror. 9. The Fire Trap. 10. Out of the Dungeon. 11. In the Desert's Grip. 12. Hurled to Destruction. 13. The Hidden Menace. 14. The Crash of Fate. 15. Out of the Web.

746. The Yellow Arm

(Pathé, June 19, 1921) Serial, 15 chapters, two reels each. D: Bertram Millhauser. SP: James Shelley Hamilton. P: George B. Seitz.

Chinese attempt to do away with Joel Bain, whose father had married a Chinese princess and taken her from China. They also try to take his children by force. Suzanne Valette and Jerry Engleson, seeking refuge from a storm in Joel Bain's home, are mistaken for members of his family and become involved in all the shenanigans. Doris and Jack Bain are kidnapped by three Chinese, emissaries of an old dynasty isolated somewhere in the Gobi Desert. The two children are collateral descendants of ancient Chinese royalty, and are needed by revolutionists to sit on the throne of China. The kidnapping, rescue, re-kidnapping, etc., of the two kids comprise the dangers and excitement of the story.

Juanita Hansen (Suzanne Valette), Warner Oland (Joel Bain), Marguerite Courtot (Doris Bain), Stephen Carr (Jack Bain), William N. Bailey (Jerry Engleson), Tom Keith (Alan Marsh), Al Franklyn Thomas.

1. House of Alarms. 2. Vengeance of the East. 3. A Strange Disappearance. 4. At Bay. 5. Danger Ahead. 6. A Nest of Knaves. 7. Into the Dead of Night. 8. Smuggled Aboard. 9. Kingdom of Deceit. 10. The Water Peril. 11. Pawns of Power. 12. Price of a Throne. 13. Behind the Curtain. 14. The False Goddess. 15. The Miracle.

747. The Yellow Cameo

(Pathé, June 3, 1928) Serial, 10 chapters, two reels each. D: Spencer G. Bennet. S/SP: George Arthur Gray.

Vincent Cottrell of San Sebastian has discovered from an old document the existence of a treasure buried somewhere on his ranch. The clue is engraved inside a yellow cameo ring he has given to his sister, Kay. Spraker, the ranch manager, has the information, and puts Vincent out of the way. He plots to get the cameo, and the story proceeds with various attempts on Kay Cottrell and her rescue on each occasion by a mysterious stranger and dog.

Allene Ray (Kay Cottrell), Edward Hearn (Terry Lawton), Cyclone [a dog] (Himself), Noble Johnson (Smoke Dawson), Tom London (Spraker), Harry Semels (Black Gavin), Frederick Dana (Sheriff), Walter Shumway (Deputy Sheriff), Maurice Klein, Ed Snyder, Frank Redman.

1. The Train Robbery. 2. The Mystery Man. 3. The Race for Life. 4. In the Path of Doom. 5. The Signal Tower. 6. The Tower of Death. 7. The Fangs of Fury. 8. The Devil's Cauldron. 9. The Underworld Peril. 10. The Lost Treasure.

748. The Yellow Menace

(Serial Film Co./Unity Sales, September 4, 1916) Serial, 16 chapters, two reels each. D: William Kennedy. Scen: Aubrey M. Kennedy and Louis Tracy. P: William Steiner.

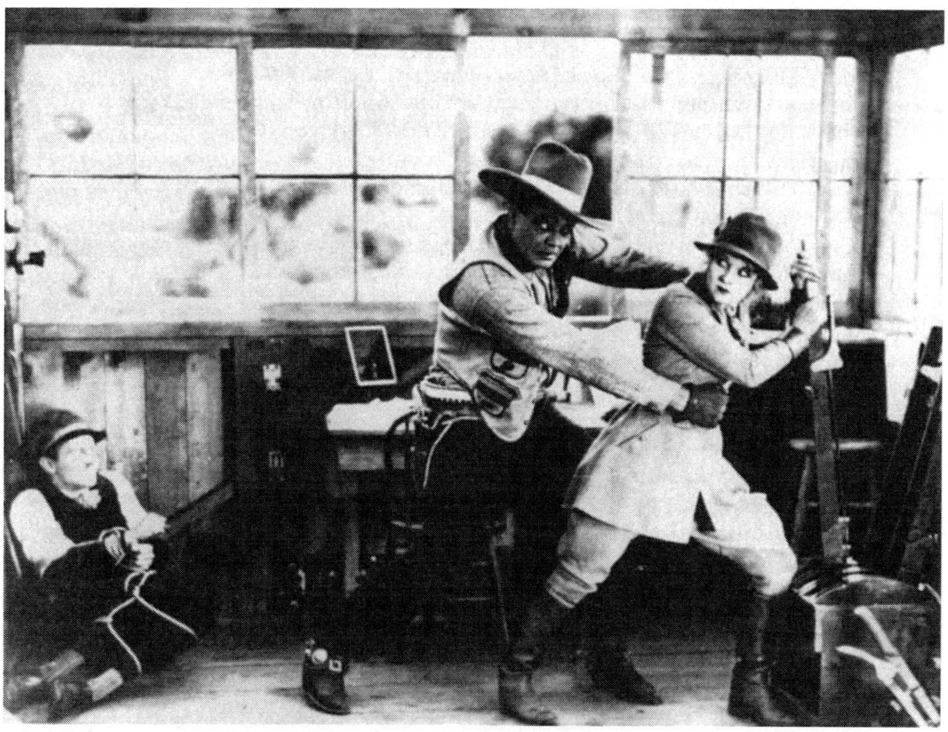

Allene Ray in *The Yellow Cameo* (1928)

Edwin Stevens in *The Yellow Menace* (1916)

Ali Singh is a fanatical Mongolian determined to destroy the United States. He and his followers stir up much trouble but are defeated when the Secret Service steps in. Frank Lackteen began his film career in this serial and went on to menace serial heroines and heroes for many years.

Edwin Stevens (Ali Singh), Florence Malone (Princess Nadice), Margaret Gale (Margaret Brown), Armand Cortes (Hong Kong Harry), Dave Wall (J.D. Bronson), Tina Marshall (Mary Manning), Eric Mayne (Errol Manning), J.A. Hall (Captain Kent), William McKay (Porcupine Patterson), Ray Gahres (Foo Jong), Mary T. Rose (Miss Mirell), Frank Lackteen (Chinese Heavy), Marie Treador, Emile La Croix.

1. Hidden Power. 2. The Mutilated Hand. 3. The Poisonous Tarantula. 4. Plot of a Demon. 5. The Haunted House. 6. The Torture Chamber. 7. Drops of Blood. 8. The Time-Clock Bomb. 9. The Crystal Globe. 10. A Message from the Sky. 11. The Half-Breed's Hatred. 12. Airplane Accident. 13. The Spy and the Submarine. 14. Interrupted Nuptials. 15. The Pay of Death. 16. The Final Strand.

749. Young Eagles

(Romance Productions; First Division, July 1, 1934) Serial, 12 chapters, two reels each. D: Spencer Gordon Bennet (Chapter 1), Vin Moore (Chapter 2, 3, 4), Eduard Laurier (Chapters 5–12). SP: Elizabeth Hayter. S: Harry O. Hoyt. P: George W. Stout. Production Manager: Ashton Dearholt. Photography: William C. Hyer, Edward Kull. Assist. D: William Billings. Technical D: Charles Clagg. Music: Alze Taconia.

A plane with two plucky boy scouts crashes in the wilds of a Central American jungle. The pilot, Angus McLean, suffers a broken leg and becomes separated from the boys. The boys almost exhaust their extensive survival training as they fight off jungle bandits, savage natives and wild animals in an effort to find McLean and reach a gold-laden lost temple.

Bobbie Cox (Bobby Ford), Jim Vance (Jim Adams), Carter Dixon (Angus McLean), Philo McCullough (Condylos), Frank Lackteen (Jose Pinardo), Johnson [a dog] (Himself).

1. The Crash. 2. Drums of Hate. 3. City of the Dead. 4. Bridge of Doom. 5. Treasure Trails. 6. Fangs of Flame. 7. Tropic Fury. 8. Wings of Terror. 9. The Lost Lagoon. 10. Jungle Outlaws. 11. Trapped. 12. Out of the Sky.

750. Zombies of the Stratosphere

(Republic, July 1952) Serial, 12 chapters, two reels each. D: Fred C. Brannon. SP: Ronald Davidson. Assoc. P: Franklyn Adreon. Photography: John MacBurnie. Music: Stanley Wilson. Special Effects: Howard and Theodore Lydecker. Feature Title: *Satan's Satellites*.

Martians intend to explode an H-bomb sufficiently powerful to send Earth spinning out into space so Mars can take Earth's place in a more desirable location with respect to the Sun. Larry Martin of Inter-Planetary Patrol fights to keep the Martians or their earthly stooges from getting necessary H-bomb ingredients.

Judd Holdren (Larry Martin), Aline Towne (Sue Davis), Wilson Wood (Bob Wilson), Stanley Waxman (Harding), John Crawford (Roth), Craig Kelly (Steele), Ray Boyle (Shane), Leonard Nimoy (Narab), Tom Steele (Truck Driver), Paul Gustine (Pilot), Jack Shea (Policeman), Henry Roland, George Magrill, Frank Alton (Heavies), Lane Bradford (Marex), Clifton Young (Ross), Norman Willis (Tarner), Davidson Clark, Floyd Criswell (Officers), Robert Strange (Kettler), Jack Mack (Gomez Operator), Dale Van Sickel (Telegrapher), Roy Engel (Lawson), Jack Harden (Kerr), Gayle Kellogg (Dick), Robert Garabedian (Elah), Ken Terrell, John Daheim, Paul Stader.

1. The Zombie Vanguard. 2. Battle of the Rockets. 3. Undersea Agents. 4. Contraband Cargo. 5. The Iron Executioner. 6. Murder Mine. 7. Death on the Waterfront. 8. Hostage of Murder. 9. The Human Torpedo. 10. Flying Gas Chamber. 11. Man vs. Monster. 12. Tomb of the Traitors.

751. Zorro Rides Again

(Republic, December 1937) Serial, 12 chapters; Chapter 1, three reels; others, two reels. D: William Witney and John English. SP: Barry Shipman, Franklyn Adreon, Morgan Cox, John Rathmell, and Ronald Davidson. Associate P: Sol C. Siegel. Photography: William Nobles. Music: Alberto Colombo. Released as a feature under the same title in 1959.

To the world James Vega is a spineless, rich wastrel, but as Zorro he comes to the aid of the California-Yucatan Railroad when it is threatened by a gang of outlaws ostensibly headed by El Lobo, but secretly masterminded by Marsden, supposedly an upstanding citizen.

John Carroll (James Vega/Zorro), Helen Christian (Joyce Andrews), Duncan Renaldo (Renaldo), Noah Beery, Sr. (Marsden), Yakima Canutt (Zorro in Disguise), Dick Alexander (Brad Dace/El Lobo), Reed Howes (Philip Andrews), Nigel de Brulier (Don Manual Vega), Robert Kortman (Trelliger), Jack Ingram (Carter), Roger Williams (Manning), Edmund Cobb (Larkin), Tom London (O'Shea), Mona Rico (Carmelita), Harry Strang (O'Brien), Jerry Frank (Duncan), George Mari (Boy), Paul Lopez (Captain of Rurales), Pair O'Dice (El Rey), Frank Leyva (Gonzales), Murdock McQuarrie (Jones), Chris-Pin Martin (Pedro), Ray Teal (Pete), Hector Sarno (Lerda), Joseph Swickard (Old Man), Al Taylor, Merril McCormick, Duke Taylor, Art Felix, Forest Burns, Loren Riebe, Jack Hendricks, Vinegar Roan (Raiders), Rosa Turich (Tia), Brooks Benedict (Starcroft), Frank Ellis, Frank McCarroll, Jack Kirk, Bob Jamison, Al Haskell, Frankie Marvin, Jason Robards.

1. Death from the Sky. 2. The Fatal Minute. 3. Juggernaut. 4. Unmasked. 5. Sky Pirates. 6. The Fatal Shot. 7. Burning Embers. 8. Plunge of Peril. 9. Tunnel of Terror. 10. Trapped. 11. Right of Way. 12. Retribution.

752. Zorro's Black Whip

(Republic, December 16, 1944) Serial, 12 chapters, two reels each. D: Spencer Bennet and Wallace Grissell. SP: Basil Dickey, Jesse Duffy, Grant Nelson, and Joseph Poland. Zorro character created by Johnston McCulley. Assoc. P: Ronald Davidson. Second Unit D: Yakima Canutt. Photography: Bud Thackery. Music: Richard Cherwin. Special Effects: Theodore Lydecker.

Top: **John Carroll (Zorro) and Dick Alexander in *Zorro Rides Again* (1937);** ***bottom:*** **Linda Stirling and George J. Lewis in *Zorro's Black Whip* (1944)**

Barbara Meredith takes over her murdered brother's newspaper and continues the fight against the lawless element of Crescent City. She also assumes her brother's secret identity as The Black Whip, a masked avenger who is an expert with cattle whip and gun. She is aided by Vic Gordon, government secret agent working with a federal commissioner. The commissioner is murdered by the outlaw gang headed by Hammond, ostensibly a respectable citizen.

Linda Stirling (Barbara Meredith/The Black Whip), George J. Lewis (Vic Gordon), Lucien Littlefield (Tenpoint Jackson), Francis McDonald (Hammond), Hal Taliaferro [Wally Wales] (Baxter), John Merton (Ed Harris), John Hamilton (Walsh), Tom Chatterton (Merchant), Tom London (James Bradley), Jack Kirk (Wetherby), Jay Kirby (Randolph Meredith), Si Jenks (Zeke Haydon), Stanley Price (Hedges), Tom Steele (Ed Hull/Ambusher/Citizen), Duke Green (Brown/Evans), Dale Van Sickel (Karl/Danley/Heavy), Carl Sepulveda, Augie Gomez, Marshall Reed (Citizens), Bill

Reed Hadley in *Zorro's Fighting Legion* (1939)

Yrigoyen (Burke), Cliff Lyons (Ambusher/Heavy), Ken Terrell (Mike), Roy Brent (Wagner), Carey Loftin (Dirk), Cliff Parkinson (Ed), Nolan Leary (Payne), Robert Wilkie (Bill Slocum), Forrest Taylor (Becker), Red Graham (Black), Roy Brent, Duke Taylor, Post Parks, Vinegar Roan (Heavies), Babe DeFreest (Double for Stirling).

1. The Masked Avenger. 2. Tomb of Terror. 3. Mob Murder. 4. Detour to Death. 5. Take Off that Mask. 6. Fatal Gold. 7. Wolf Pack. 8. The Invisible Victim. 9. Avalanche. 10. Fangs of Doom. 11. Flaming Juggernaut. 12. Trail of Tyranny.

753. Zorro's Fighting Legion

(Republic, December 16, 1939) Serial, 12 chapters; Chapter 1, three reels; others, two reels. D: William Witney, John English. SP: Ronald Davidson, Franklyn Adreon, Morgan Cox, Sol Shor, Barney Sarecky. Assoc. P: Hiram S. Brown, Jr. Photography: Reggie Lanning. Music: William Lava.

Don Diego, alias Zorro, organizes a fighting legion to protect gold shipments headed for Mexico's treasury. One of the mine officials in San Mendolita secretly conspires to steal much of the area's gold and assumes the role of Don del Oro, the armored god revered by the suspicious Indians, whom he uses to support his gang's activities. Zorro defeats the outlaws, and Don del Ora, alias Pablo, a mine magistrate, is killed by the Indians he has misused.

Reed Hadley (Don Diego Vega/Zorro), Sheila Darcy (Volita), William Corson (Ramon), Leander de Cordova (Felipe), C. Montague Shaw (Pablo/Don del Oro), Edmund Cobb (Gonzales), Charles King (Valdez), John Merton (Manuel), Budd Buster (Juan), Carleton Young (Benito Juarez), Guy D'Ennery (Don Francisco), Billy Bletcher (Voice of Don del Oro), Paul Marion (Kala), Joe Molina (Tarmac), Ken Terrell (Martin), Bud Geary (Dungeon Heavy), Cactus Mack (Cisco), Jack O'Shea, Jerome Ward, Millard McGowan (Cave Heavies), Curley Dresden (Tomas), Jim Pierce (Moreno), Helen Mitchel (Donna Maria), Al Taylor (Rico), Charles Murphy (Pepito), Jason Robards, Sr. (Cantina Owner), Bill Yrigoyen (Stage Driver), Yakima Canutt (Soldier/Double for Hadley), Reed Howes, Barry Hays, Joe McGuinn (Soldiers), Eddie Cherkose (Pedro), Max Marx (Presidio Guard), Gordon Clark (Miguel Torres), Jerry Frank (Throne Guard), Ernest Sarracino (Sebastian), Alan Gregg (Salvador), Ralph Faulkner (Rodriguez), George Plues (Garcia), Jack Moore (Fernando), Theodore Lorch (Carlos), Jack Carrington (Antonio Gomez), Carl Sepulveda (Orlando), Wylie Grant (Martinez), Martin Faust (Mabesa), Bob Wilbur (Hernandez), John Wallace (Jailer), Burt Dillard (Jaimo), Jimmy Fawcett (Jose), Victor Cox (Heavy), Augie Gomez (Indian), Buel Bryant (Renaldo), Norman Lane (Ricardo), Frank Ellis, Ted Mapes, Joe Yrigoyen, Henry Wills.

1. The Golden God. 2. The Flaming "Z." 3. Descending Doom. 4. The Bridge of Peril. 5. The Decoy. 6. Zorro to the Rescue. 7. The Fugitive. 8. Flowing Death. 9. The Golden Arrow. 10. Mystery Wagon. 11. Face to Face. 12. Unmasked.

754. Zudora (The Twenty Million Dollar Mystery)

(Thanhouser, November 21, 1914) Serial, 20 chapters, two reels each. D: Howell Hansell. Scen: Lloyd Lonergan and F.W. Doughty. S: Daniel Carson Goodman and Harold McGrath. Re-released in 1919 as a 10-chapter serial by Arrow Pictures under title *The Demon Shadow*.

In this sequel to *The Million Dollar Mystery* (1914), a cache of money is also the catharsis that sets off the rapidly moving events, as Zudora, the heroine, and her newspaper reporter boyfriend try to unravel the mystery and elude death at every turn.

In the first six chapters Cruze played a Hindu mystic. Later he became a mysterious hero, and thus the Hindu was disposed of permanently. With the tenth chapter the title was changed to *The Twenty Million Dollar Mystery*.

Marguerite Snow (Zudora), James Cruze (Hassam Ali/Jim Baird), Harry Benham (John Storm), Sidney Bracy (Tom Hunt, the Detective), Frank Farrington (Captain Radcliffe), Mary Elizabeth Forbes (Mme. Du Val), Jane Fairbanks (Mrs. Ramsey), Morgan Niblack (Mr. Brine), Helen Badgley.

1. The Mystic Message of the Spotted Collar. 2. The Mystery of the Sleeping House. 3. The Mystery of the Dutch Cheese Maker. 4. The Secret of the Haunted Hills. 5. The Case of the Perpetual Glare. 6. The Case of the McWinter Family. 7. The Mystery of the Lost Ships. 8. The Foiled Elopement or the Mystery of the Chang Case. 9. Kidnapped or The Mystery of the Missing Heiress. 10. The Gentlemen Crooks and the Lady. 11. A Message from the Heart. 12. A Bag of Diamonds. 13. The Secret of Dr. Munn's Sanatorium. 14. The Missing Million. 15. The Robbery of the Ruby Coronet. 16. The Battle of the Bridge. 17. The Island of Mystery. 18. The Cipher Code. 19. The Prisoner in the House. 20. The Richest Woman of the World.

SELECTED BIBLIOGRAPHY

"Actress [Lynne Roberts] Divorces Man Who Laughs at Films." *Los Angeles Mirror*, November 15, 1961.
"Actress [Lynne Roberts/Mary Hart] Ruled Not Wed Legally, Loses Alimony." *Los Angeles Times*, Friday, May 25, 1951, Part II, p. 3.
Adams, Les. "An Interview with 'Slingin' Sammy Baugh." *Those Enduring Matinee Idols*, Vol. 3, No. 26, 397-398.
_____. Editor-Publisher. *Yesterday's Saturdays*, Nos. 1–18, 1974–1982.
_____ and Rob Tucker. "Wild Bill Hickok," "Overland with Kit Carson," and "Valley of Vanishing Men." *Yesterday's Saturdays,* No. 18 (1982).
The Adventures of Captain Marvel. Cliffhanger Ending and Escape Pictorials. Chicago: Jack Mathis Advertising, n.d.
Ankerich, Michael G. "The Real Peggy Stewart: Behind the Cowgirl Image." *Classic Images*, No. 169 (July 1989), 8–10.
_____. "Talented Western Heroine [Jennifer Holt]." *Classic Images*, Nos. 178–179 (April–May 1990) (2 Parts).
"Anna Little of the Mustang Company." *Motion Picture Magazine (*March 1916), 112–113.
"Anne Gwynne Weds Lawyer." *Los Angeles Examiner* (Monday, December 31, 1945).
Barbour, Alan G., ed. *Cliffhanger: A Pictorial History of the Motion Picture Serial.* New York: A & W Publications, 1977.
_____. *Days of Thrills and Adventure.* New York: Macmillan Company, 1970, 168 pp.
_____. "Flash Gordon." *The Serial: Volume 1.* Kew Gardens, NY: Screen Facts, 1967, 167–175.
_____. *Great Serial Ads.* Kew Gardens, NY: Screen Facts Press, 1965.
_____ *High Roads to Adventure.* Kew Gardens, NY: Screen Facts Press, 1971.
_____. *Hit the Saddle.* Kew Gardens, NY: Screen Facts Press, 1969.
_____. *Movie Ads of the Past, No. 1: The B Western.* Kew Gardens, NY: Screen Facts Press, 1966.
_____. *Old Movies 1: The B Western.* Kew Gardens, NY: Screen Facts Press, 1969.
_____. *Old Movies 2: The Serial.* Kew Gardens, NY: Screen Facts Press, 1969.
_____. *Old Movies 3: The B Western.* Kew Gardens, NY: Screen Facts Press, 1970.
_____. *Old Movies 4: The Serial.* Kew Gardens, NY: Screen Facts Press, 1970.
_____. *Screen Ads Monthly*, 4 Vols. Kew Gardens, NY: Screen Facts Press, 1967–68.
_____. *Screen Nostalgia Illustrated*, Nos. 1–8. Kew Gardens, NY: Screen Facts Press, 1975.
_____. *The Serial*, 4 Vols. Kew Gardens, NY: Screen Facts Press, 1967–1971.
_____. *Serial Favorites.* Kew Gardens, NY: Screen Facts Press, 1971.
_____. *Serial Pictorial.* Nos. 1–8, Kew Gardens, NY: Screen Facts Press, n.d.
_____. *Serial Quarterly*, Nos. 1–7, Kew Gardens, NY: Screen Facts Press (January-March 1966–July-September 1967).
_____. *Serial Showcase.* Kew Gardens, NY: Screen Facts Press, 1968.
_____. *The Serials of Columbia* Kew Gardens, NY: Screen Facts Press, 1968.
_____. *The Serials of Republic.* Kew Gardens, NY: Screen Facts Press, 1965.
_____. *A Thousand and One Delights.* New York: Collier Books, 1971.
_____. *A Thousand Thrills.* Kew Gardens, NY: Screen Facts Press, 1971.
_____. *Thrill After Thrill.* Kew Gardens, NY: Screen Facts Press, 1971.
_____. *The Thrill of it All.* New York: Collier Books, 1971.
Bawden, J.E.A. "Why, If It Isn't Ann Rutherford!" *Filmography*, Vol. IV, No. 1 (3rd and 4th Quarters 1973), 12–21.
Baxter, John. *Stunt: The Story of the Great Movie Stunt Men.* Garden City, NY: Doubleday and Company, Inc., 1974.
Beaumont, Charles. "Don't Miss the Next Thrilling Chapter!" *Show Business Illustrated*, Vol. I (March 1962), 52–56, 78–80.
"Blackhawk." *Serial Quarterly*, Vol. 1, No. 4 (October–December 1966), 18–32.
Blair, Earl W., Jr. "Reminiscing with Henry Brandon." *Those Enduring Matinee Idols,* Vol. II (December 1972–January 1973), 291–292.
_____. "Republic Today!" *Film Collector's Registry*, No. 68 (September 1976), 11.
_____. "Rocketman Flies Again." *Film Collector's Registry*, No. 69 (October 1976), 11–13.
Bodeen, DeWitt. "Antonio Moreno." *Films in Review*, Vol. XVII, No. 6 (June-July 1767), 325–344.
_____. "Kathlyn Williams." *Films in Review*, Vol. XXXV (February 1984), 67–79.

_____. "Evelyn Brent." *Films in Review*, Vol. XXVII, No. 6 (June-July), 339–361.
Bonomo, Joe. *The Strongman.* New York: Bonomo Studios, 1968.
Bosch, Peter. "Unmasking the Masked Marvel." *Serial World*, No. 37 (Spring 1984), 11–12, 13–22.
Brady, Thomas. "Cowboy Versus Crooner." *Auckland* [New Zealand] *Star* (Saturday, November 8, 1941).
Braff, R.E. "An Index to the Films of Jack Perrin." *Classic Images*, No. 193, 18, 27, 30, C7–9.
Breeden, Ab. "Ab Breeden in Hollywood: Dorothy Gulliver." *Wrangler's Roost*, No. 69 (April 1984).
Brennen, Tom. "I Can't Forget Fred Thomson." *Classic Film Collector*, No. 30 (1971) 11.
Briggs, Colin. "Ann Rutherford." *Hollywood Studio Magazine*, Vol. 18, No. 6 (June–July 1985), 27–29.
Brock, Patrick. "Mae Clark [sic]." *Hollywood Studio Magazine*, Vol. 19, No. 2 (January–February 1986), 28–29.
Bruner, Frank V. "The Real Pearl White." *Motion Picture Magazine* (July 1919), 32–33, 102.
_____. "What Sort of a Fellow is Pearl White?" *Photoplay Journal* (February 1919).
"Buck Jones: Coconut Grove Night Club Fire Victim." *New York Times* (November 29, 1942), Page 1, Column 1; (November 30, 1942), Page 13, Column 2.
"Buck Jones Dies as He Lived; In Harness and Before Public." *Hollywood Reporter* (December 1, 1942).
"Buck Jones Is Dead of Injuries in Fire." *New York Times* (December 1, 1942).
"Buck Jones Last Rites Held at Hollywood." *Boxoffice* (December 12, 1942).
"Buck Jones Rides Again for Villains." *New York World Telegram* (April 7, 1937).
"Buck Jones, The King of the Cowboys." *Boys Cinema Annual* (Christmas, 1936).
Burgess, Beth. "The Lady of the Lions [Kathlyn Williams] Reconsiders." *Photoplay* (January 1917).
"Captain America." *Cliffhanger Ending and Escape Pictorials.* Northbrook, IL: Jack Mathis Advertising, n.d.
Carayannis, P.A. "Notes on 'New Adventures of Tarzan.'" *Classic Images*, Nos. 97–98 [Two Parts] (July-August 1983).
"Carmelita Geraghty." Obituary. *Variety Weekly* (Wednesday, July 13, 1966).
Carville, Virginia. "Death Went Dancing." *Redbook Magazine* (November 1952), 62–63.
Casali, Edgar. "Birth of the Serial and Its European Development." *Classic Film Collector*, No. 45 (Winter 1974), X–1, 13.
_____. "Francis [sic] Gifford: Waiting for the Morning." *Hollywood Studio Magazine*, Vol. XVI, No. 4 (March 1983), 31–32.
Chaney, Warren H. "Jim Bannon: His Story." *Western Film Collector*, Vol. III, No. 1 (Winter 1976), 50–85.
_____. "Who Was That Masked Man?" *Nostalgia News*, 5 pages (n.d.).
Chiti, Roberto, and Mario Quargnolo. *Bianco E Nero*. Anno XV, Numero 7 (Luglio 1954), 16–28.
Cline, William C. *In the Nick of Time.* (Jefferson, NC: McFarland & Co., Inc., 1984).
_____. "Miracles on a Daily Basis: Special Effects by Howard and Theodore Lydecker." *Cliffhanger*, No. 7, 25–28.
_____. "Remembrance of Serial Idols Past." *Those Enduring Matinee Idols*, Vol. 1, Chapter 10 (April–May 1971), 132–134.
_____. *Serials-ly Speaking*. Jefferson, NC: McFarland & Co., Inc., 1994.
Cocchi, John. "The Films of Allan Lane." *Screen Facts*, Vol. IV, No. 19 (1968), 50–58.
_____. "The Films of Roy Rogers and Gene Autry." *Screen Facts*, Vol. 1, No. 5 (1963), 47–61.
Collura, Joe. "The Endurance of Steele [Tom]." *Classic Images*, No. 150, 52–53, 61.
_____. "Evelyn Finley: Perils of the Wilderness and Much More." *Cliffhanger*, No. 12 (May 1990), 7–14.
_____. "George J. Lewis: Foregoing the Fame." *Cliffhanger*, No. 12, 19–25.
_____. "Keye Luke: Number One Son Was a Serial Sidekick Too." *Cliffhanger*, No. 13, 53–61.
_____. "Marion Shilling: A Serial Sweetheart." *Cliffhanger*, No. 20, 4–10.
_____. "Marion Shilling: Riding the Hollywood Trail." *Classic Images*, No. 129 (March 1986), 22–23, 58.
"Color Biography of Cecilia Parker." Fox Film Studio Publicity. 1931.
"Comics in Cinema." *Cinema*, Vol.V (1969).
Connor, Edward. "The First Eight Serials of Republic." *Screen Facts*, Vol. II, No. 7 (1964), 52–61.
_____. "The Genealogy of Zorro." *Films in Review* (August–September 1957), 330.
_____. "The Golden Age of Republic Serials." *Screen Facts*, Nos. 17 and 18 [Two Parts] (1968), 49–61; 20–35.
_____. "The Serial Lovers." *Films in Review*, Vol. 6 (August–September 1955), 330–332.
_____. "The Twelve Tarzans." *Films in Review* (October 1960), 452–463.
"Converging on Lucile Browne." *Those Enduring Matinee Idols*, Vol. 1, Chapter 4 (April–May 1970), 39–48.
Coons, Minard. "The Gunman From Bodie." [Jones, McCoy, Hatton.] *Film Collector's Registry*, Vol. 6, No.5 (May 1974), 12.
_____. "An Interview with Peggy Stewart." *Film Collector's Registry*, No. 57 (November 1975), 5–9.
_____ and Allan Easterling. "The Jolly Villain: An Interview with I. Stanford Jolly." *Film Collector's Registry*, No. 67 (September 1976), 3–6.
Copeland, Bobby J. "Cliffhanger/Cowgirl Challenge." *Cliffhanger*, No. 17, 25.
_____."On the Festival Trail with Peggy Stewart." *Favorite Westerns & Serial World*, No. 28, 33–35.
_____. "Remembering Nell O'Day." *Under Western Skies*, No. 36 (August 1989).
Coriell, Vernell. "Elmo, the Mighty." *Classic Film Collectors*, No. 20 (Spring 1968), 12–13.
Couto, Carlos de Paula. "Universal Serial Stars of the Silent Era." *Classic Film Collector*, No. 48 (Fall 1975), 24–28.
Crivello, Kirk. "Passing Parade/Veda Ann Borg." *Hollywood Studio Magazine* (February 1978).
Crossland, Howard. "Serials on British TV and a Look at 'King of the Rocketmen.'" *Serial World*, No. 34 (Spring 1983), 30–36.
"Culture Begins at 40 for Mae Clarke." *San Francisco Examiner* (September 3, 1964), 28.
"Daredevil Eddie Polo, Now 85, Plans Comeback." *Los Angeles Mirror* (March 3, 1961).
"Daredevil Wanted One Real Film." *Hollywood Citizen News* (June 15, 1961).
"Daredevils of the Red Circle." *Variety* (July 12, 1939).
"Daredevils of the Red Circle." *Cliffhanger Ending and Escape Pictorials.* Chicago: Jack Mathis Advertising, n.d.
"Daredevils of the West." *Cliffhanger Ending and Escape Pictorials.* Northbrook, IL: Jack Mathis Advertising, n.d.
Darst, Stephen. "Old Film Serial Director Decries Sex and Violence in Movies of Today." *St. Louis Review* (1975).
Davies, Wallace E. "Truth About Pearl White." *Films in Review* (November 1959), 537–548.

Davis, Henry B. "Films of Irene Rich." *Classic Images*, No. 157 (July 1988), 15.

_____. "The Films of Madge Bellamy." *Classic Images*, No. 176 (February 1990), 26–27, 30.

Davis, Jr., Henry R. "Clara Kimball Young Was the Kind of a Beautiful Woman Who Has Little Practical Sense." *Films in Review* (August–September 1961), 419–425.

Davy, Darl. "Davy on 16mm: William Elliott." *Film Fan Monthly*, No. 94 (April 1969), 17.

Daynard, Donald. "Bennet's Serials." *Films in Review*, Vol. XIV (October 1963).

_____. "The Lydeckers: Masters of Miniature Mayhem." *The New Captain George's Whizzbang*, No. 16 (n.d.), 2–8.

_____. "The Perils of Linda [Stirling]." *The New Captain George's Whizzbang*, No. 18 (n.d.), 8–14.

_____. "Roy Barcroft—Best of the Badmen." *The New Captain George's Whizzbang*, No. 7 (n.d.), 2–5.

Dellinger, Paul. "The Adventures of Captain Marvel." *Cliffhanger*, No. 2, 5–18.

_____. "The Adventures of Red Ryder." *Cliffhanger*, No. 11, 5–18.

_____. "Batman." *Cliffhanger*, No. 13, 41–50.

_____. "Blackhawk." *Cliffhanger*, No. 6, 5–23.

_____. "Ghost of Zorro." *Under Western Skies*, No. 28 (August 1984), 23–31.

_____. "Kay Aldridge's Next Chapter." *Cliffhanger*, No. 1 (Winter 1983), 23–33.

_____. "Marshall Reed, the Heroic Villain." *Under Western Skies*, No. 14 (May 1981), 33–42.

_____. "Mysterious Doctor Satan." *Cliffhanger*, No. 14, 5–16.

_____. "Return of Captain America." *Cliffhanger*, No. 7, 5–15.

_____. "Riders of Death Valley." *Under Western Skies*, No. 28 (August 1984), 58–74.

_____. "Rod Cameron: Super Serial Hero." *Cliffhanger*, No. 4, 3–18.

_____. "Secret Service in Darkest Africa." *Cliffhanger*, No. 17, 26–39.

_____. "Six-Gun Zorros." *Under Western Skies* (January 1981), 15–24.

_____. "The Spider Returns." *Cliffhanger*, No. 5, 5–18.

_____. "Spy Smasher." *Cliffhanger*, No. 7, 29–44.

_____. "The Superman Saga." *Cliffhanger*, No. 12, 27–44.

_____. "The Three Musketeers." *Cliffhanger*, No. 20, 11–26.

DeMarco, Mario A. *Buster Crabbe—King of the Serial Aces*. West Boylston, MA: DeMarco Publications,1984.

_____."Eddie Polo: The Daredevil of the Serials." *Cliffhanger*, No. 6, 25–29.

_____. "Eddie Polo, The Thrill Maker." *Movie Collector's World*, No. 311 (March 3, 1989), 38.

_____. "Girls of the Golden West." *Movie & Film Collector's World*, No. 190 (July 13, 1984), 25–26.

_____. *The Lone Rangers of Silver Screen & Television*. West Boylston, MA: DeMarco Publications, n.d.

_____. *The Photostory and the Dean of Cowboy Stars—Hoot Gibson*. West Boylston, MA: DeMarco Publications, n.d.

_____. *The Photostory of Battling Bob Steele*. West Boylston, MA: DeMarco Publications, n.d.

_____. *Photostory of the Screen's Greatest Cowboy: Tom Mix*. West Boylston, MA: DeMarco Publications, n.d.

_____. "Rin-Tin-Tin—Mascot's Great Canine Serial Ace." *Cliffhanger*, No. 23, 5–8.

_____. *Those Wonderful Movie Serial Heroes*. West Boylston, MA: DeMarco Publications, 1989.

_____. *Those Wonderful Movie Villains of the 'B' Western and Serials*. West Boylston, MA: DeMarco Publications, n.d.

_____. "Way Back When." *Westerns and Serials*, No. 35, 39.

DeRoos, Robert. "Hollywood's Mother Hen." [Helen Ferguson] *TV Guide*, No. 4 (1961), 28–30.

"Dick Tracy Returns." *Variety* (August 10, 1938).

"Dick Tracy Story (The)." *Screen Thrills Illustrated* (June 1962), 52–59.

Dino, Tom. "The Heroine of the Cliffs [Pearl White]." *Classic Film Collector*, No. 14 (Spring 1966), 13.

Downey, Ron and Linda, editors and publishers. *Cliffhanger*. Waynesville, NC: World of Yesterday Press.

Doyle, Billy. "Lost Players: Allene Ray." *Classic Images*, Vol. 5, No. 4 (1981), 25–32.

Drew, William M. "Esther Ralston." *American Classic Screen*, Vol. 5, No. 4 (1981), 25–32.

"Drums of Fu Manchu." *Variety* (February 21, 1940).

"Drums of Fu Manchu." *Cliffhanger Ending and Escape Pictorials*. Chicago: Jack Mathis Advertising, n.d.

Dumbrille, Erwin, and Gene Fernett. "Sam Katzman: Movie Pioneer." *Film Collectors Registry* (October 1973), 9–10.

_____. "Eddie Polo, The Thrill Maker." *Movie Collectors World*, No. 311 (March 3, 1989).

Edmonds, L.G. *Big U: Universal in the Silent Days*. Cranbury, NJ: A.S. Barnes and Company, 1977.

"Edna Murphy." *New York City American* (May 7, 1925).

Essoe, Gabe. *Tarzan of the Movies*. New York: Citadel Press, 1968.

Evans, Delight. "The Man Uncomfortable [Jack Holt]." *Photoplay Magazine* (November 1922), 30, 33, 95.

Everett, Eldon K. "Bertram Milhauser Remembers Pearl White." *Classic Images*, No. 55 (Summer 1977), 48–49.

_____. "Ford Beebe Recalls Helen Holmes and J.P. McGowan." *Classic Images*, No. 86 (August 1982), 34.

_____. "Ford Beebe Recalls Leo Maloney." *Classic Images*, No. 68 (March 1980), 12–13.

_____. "Ford Beebe Remembers Art Acord." *Classic Images*, No. 66, 48.

_____. "The Great Grace Cunard-Francis Ford Mystery." *Classic Film Collector*, No. 39 (Summer 1973), 22–25.

_____. "A Postscript to Pearl White." *Classic Film Collector*, No. 55 (Summer 1977), 48–19.

_____. "Ruth Roland, Queen of the Cliffhangers." *Classic Images*, No. 83 (1982), 25.

Everson, William K. "Serials with Sound." *Films in Review*, IV (June-July 1953), 271–276.

"Exhibs Seize on Serials to Woo Tots Away from Telesets." *Variety* (November 9, 1950).

Eyck, John Jen. "Speaking of Pearls." *Photoplay* (September 1917).

Eyles, Allen. *John Wayne and the Movies*. New York: A.S. Barnes & Co., 1976.

"Fading, Fading—One Man Rule; Yates' Republic Exit Latest Instance." *Variety* (July 8, 1959).

Fenin, George N., and William Everson. *The Western*. New York: Grossman Publishers, 1963. Revised Edition 1973.

Feret, Bill. "Lure of the Tropics [Frances Gifford]." *Hollywood Studio Magazine*, Vol. XVI, No. 4 (March 1984), 26–27.
_____. *Lure of the Tropics*. New York: Proteus Books, 1985.
Fernett, Gene. "An Interview with Theodore Lydecker." *Film Collector's Registry*, Vol. V (November 1973), 1, 6.
_____. "Jack English Looks Back." *Classic Film Collector*, No. 21 (Summer 1968), 52, 55.
_____. "Ken Maynard: In Real Life and in the World of Make Believe." *Under Western Skies*, No. 8 (October 1976), 17–32.
_____. "Nat Levine: The Serial King." *Views and Reviews*, Vol. 1 (Summer 1969), 22–31.
_____. *Next Time Drive Off the Cliff*. Cinememories Pub. Co., 1968.
_____. "Spencer Gordon Bennett [sic] Biography Off the Press." *Classic Film Collector*, No. 36 (Fall 1972), 63.
Fidler, Jimmie. "Jimmie Fidler's Hollywood [Buck Jones]." (Syndicated Column). *New York Post* (March 12, 1937).
"Fighting Devil Dogs." *Variety* (May 18, 1938).
Filho, Jose Simoes. "The Devil Horse." *Wild West Stars*, No. 20, 3–6.
_____. "The Serials: Clancy of the Mounted and Custer's Last Stand." *Wild West Stars*, No. 16 (August–September 1973), 3–7.
Filk, Robert. "Joan Woodbury: B-Movie Actress Who Lives the Part." *Collector's World*, No. 238. (May 16, 1986), 34.
"Film and TV Actress Helen Parrish Dies." *Hollywood Citizen-News* (February 23, 1959).
"Film Blonde [Claudia Dell]Weds Agent." *Los Angeles Times* (December 30, 1937).
Fitzgerald, Michael G. *Universal Pictures*. New Rochelle, NY: Arlington House Publishing Co., 1977.
"Flash Gordon's Trip to Mongo." *Variety* (February 16, 1938).
Fletcher, Adele Whitely. "Reconsidering Pearl." *Motion Picture Magazine* (February 1921), 28–29, 96.
"Flying G-Men." *Variety* (March 29, 1939).
Ford, Charles. "The French Serials 1913–1928." *Films in Review*.
"Franklyn Farnum, Silent Star, Dies." *The Citizens-News* (July 5, 1961).
"Franklyn Farnum the Fighting Grin." *Western Revue*, Vol. 3, No. 2 (June 1976).
"Freed, Doran [Ann] Given SAG Tribute Lunch." *Variety* (November 1, 1988).
"From Tarzan to Lion Man." *Screen Thrills Illustrated* (April 1963), 7–9.
Fulbright, Tom. "Jane Novak Recalls the Golden Era of the Silver Screen." *Hollywood Studio Magazine* (March 1972), 11–12.
Fuller, Mary. "My Summer Vacation." *Photoplay* (June 6, 1915), 111–114.
Furman, Bruce. "Trails End for a Legend [Ray Corrigan]." *Serial World*, No. 8 (Fall 1976).
Gassaway, Gordon. "Louise of the Lions [Louise Lorraine]." *Motion Picture Classic* (July 1922), 36–37, 79.
Gebhart, Myrtle. "The Gold Girl [Madge Bellamy]." *Motion Picture Magazine* (April 1922).
_____. "The Real Ruth Roland." *Picture Play* (December 1926).
Geltzer, George. "An Index to the Silent American Serial." New Theodore Huff Memorial Film Society. New York: August 1955.
_____. "40 Years of Cliffhanging." *Films in Review*, Vol. VIII (February 1957), 60–68.
_____. "Ruth Roland." *Films in Review*, Vol. XI, No. 9 (November 1960), 539–548.
"Gene Autry of Westerns Goes Over Big with Fans." *New York World-Telegram* (May 14, 1938).
Gibson, Helen. "In the Very Early Days." *Films in Review*, Vol. 19, No. 1 (January 1961), 28–34.
Gifford, Frances. "A Letter from Frances Gifford." *Hollywood Studio Magazine*, Vol. XVI (August 1983), 4.
Glut, Don. "Interview: Tom Steele." *The Town Crier* (n.d.), 2.
"G-Men vs. The Black Dragon." *Serial World*, No. 36. (Winter 1984), 3–7.
"G-Men vs. The Black Dragon." *Serial Quarterly*, Vol. 2, No. 1 (January–March 1967).
Goldbuck, Willis. "The Primitive [Ruth Roland]." *Motion Picture Magazine* (December 1921).
_____. "Still Waters [Molly Malone]." *Motion Picture Classic* (June 1921), 44–45.
"Good Excuse Wins [Claudia Dell]." *Los Angeles Examiner* (December 31, 1934).
Gordon, Richard. "Reflections of 'The Clutching Hand.'" *Classic Images*, No. 119, 60.
"Gordon of Ghost City." *Boys Cinema*, Nos. 735–745 (January 6, 1934-March 24, 1934) [12 Parts].
Grau, Robert. "Writing a Serial Story." *The Theatre of Science*, Chapter XI, pp. 233–246. New York: Broadway Book Company, 1914.
"Green Archer (The)." *Serial Quarterly*, Vol. 2. No. 1 [cover says "No. 5" (January–March 1967), 13 pp.
Hagner, John G. "Yak: Super Stuntman." *Classic Film Collector*, No. 128 (Summer 1967), 13.
Hall, Alice. "The Ninety-Nine Lives of Pearl White." *Pictures and Picturegoer* (February 1921).
_____. "Roughing It with Ruth Roland." *Pictures and Picturegoer* (June 1921).
Hall, John. "Big Boy [Williams]." *Wrangler's Roost*, No. 77, 6 pp.
_____. "Cheyenne Harry [Harry Carey]." *Wrangler's Roost*, No. 64, 3 pp.
_____. "Mr. Glenn [Bob Custer]." *Wrangler's Roost*, No. 78, 6 pp.
Hardy, Phil, Editor. *Science Fiction*. New York: William Morrow Co., 1984.
_____. *The Western*. New York: William Morrow Co., 1983.
Hare, William. "The Outspoken Don 'Red' Barry." *American Classic Screen* (July–August 1977), 33–34.
Harmon, Jim, and Donald F. Glut. *The Great Movie Serials: Their Sound and Fury*. Garden City, NY: Doubleday and Co., 1972.
Harrison, Louis Reeves. "What Happened to Mary?" *The Moving Picture World* (July 5, 1913), 26.
Harwood, John. "Tarzans and Janes." *Classic Film Collector*, Vol. II, p. 5.
"Haunted Harbor." *Serial Quarterly*, Vol. 1, No. 4 (October–December 1966), 1–17.
"'Hazards of Helen': Them Were the Days!" *Los Angeles Herald-Examiner* (Sunday, September 9, 1962), B-4.
"Helen Gibson 44th Year." *Variety* (July 31, 1959).
"Helen Holmes Dies at 58." *Los Angeles Examiner* (July 10, 1950).
"Heroine of Silent Screen [Madge Bellamy] Dies in California at 89." *Los Angeles Times* (January 25, 1990).
Hewetson, Alan. "Comics in Cinema." *Cinema*, Vol. . (1969).
"High Explosive Hero [Joe Bonomo]." *Screen Thrills Illustrated* (June 1962), 10–15.
"Hi-Ho Silver." *New York Post* (July 25, 1940).

"Hi-Yo Silver." *Variety* (April 17, 1940).
Hise, Jim Van. "The Fighting Devil Dogs." *Film Collectors Registry*, Vol. 6, No. 11 (November 1974), 7–9.
_____. "The Spider's Web." *Film Collectors Registry*, Vol. 7, No. 4 (April 1975), 9–11.
Hoaglin, Jess L. "All About Esther [Ralston]." *Hollywood Studio Magazine*, Vol. 7, No. 8 (December 1972), 22–23.
_____. "Down Memory Lane: Dorothy Gulliver." *Hollywood Studio Magazine*, Vol. 5, No. 9 (June 1982), 50.
_____. "Down Memory Lane: Irene Rich." *Hollywood Studio Magazine* (April 1982), 37.
_____. "Madge Bellamy." *Hollywood Reporter* (October 7, 1975).
_____. "Nell O'Day." *Classic Images*, No. 102, (January 1984), 9.
_____. "Where Are They Now [Cecilia Parker]?" *Hollywood Reporter* (April 13, 1975).
_____. *Wherever Is...* [Peggy Stewart]*?* Newell, Iowa: Biteline Pub. Co., 1983, 70.
Hoffman, Eric. "Adios Duncan [Renaldo]." *Serial World*, No. 23 (Summer 1980), 27–28.
_____. "Blackhawk." *Serial World*, No. 11 (Summer 1977), 4–12.
_____. "Daredevils of the Red Circle." *Serial World*, No. 35 (Summer 1983), 3–8, 17.
_____. "Saturday Matinee Spy Hunters of World War Two." *Serial World* (1974).
_____. "The Screen Avengers: The Comic Heroes of the Cliffhangers." *Mediascope*, No. 19 (May–June 1976), 4–19.
_____. "Spy Smasher." *Serial World*, No. 14 (Spring 1978), 6–19.
_____. "Undersea Kingdom." *Those Enduring Matinee Idols*, Vol. 1. (December 1970–January 1971), 90–93.
_____, and Bob Malcomson. "Dick Tracy's G-Men." *Those Enduring Matinee Idols*, Chapter 18, Vol. 2, No. 8 (August–September 1972), 250–255.
_____. "Drums of Fu Manchu." *Those Enduring Matinee Idols*, Vol. II (December 1972–January 1973), 284–290.
_____. "Hawk of the Wilderness." *Those Enduring Matinee Idols*, Chapter 15, Vol. 2, No. 5 (February–March 1972), 206–210.
"Hollywood Business Woman [Shirley Grey]." *New York Evening Post* (May 22, 1933).
"Hollywood Changes But John Wayne Goes On Forever." *The Daily (OK) Ardmorite* (Wednesday, September 27, 1978), 6–A.
"Hollywood Holts Are a Rare Threesome." *Richmond (VA) Times-Dispatch* (December 6, 1942).
Holt, Jennifer. "Celebrity Talk: Heroine in the Family." *Favorite Westerns/Serial World*, No. 25 (April 1987), 15–16.
"Holt of the Secret Service." *Serial Quarterly*, Vol. 2, No. 3 [No. 7 on cover], 41–60.
"Holt of the Secret Service." *Variety* (February 4, 1942).
"Holt—Who Goes There [Jack Holt]?" *Motion Picture Classic* (January 1919), 29, 66.
Horwitz, James. *They Went Thataway*. New York: E.P. Dutton & Co., 1976.
"Houseboy Admits Strangling Ex-Star [Rhea Mitchell]." *Los Angeles Times* (September 21, 1957).
Hoveyda, Fereydoun. "Grandeur et Decadence du Serial." *Cahiers du cinéma*, Nos. 58, 59, 60 (April, May, June 1956).
Howe, Herbert. "The Diplomat of Hollywood [Kathlyn Williams]." *Photoplay* (September 1924), 63.
_____. "His Last Fifty Cents [Jack Holt]." *Photoplay* (July 1926), 91, 133.
_____. "A Star in Search of Her Soul [Pearl White]." *Photoplay* (June 1923).
Humphrey, Hal. "TV Moms Too Good to Be True." *Los Angeles Mirror* (February 4, 1961).
Hurst, Richard M. "Cliffhangers." *Serial World*, No. 21 (Winter 1980), 5–8.
_____. "Comic/Serial Crossovers: A Cross-Fertilization Fraught with Danger." *Serial World*, No. 23 (Summer 1980), 16–17; No. 24 (Fall 1980), 4–5.
"I-deas: Spy Smasher Triumphs Again." *Edwardsville (IL) Intelligencer* (November 29, 1973).
"I [Esther Ralston] Wore Thousand-Dollar Dresses." *TV Guide* (August 18, 1962), 26–28.
Irvine, Clarke. "Helen Holmes." *Motion Picture World* (January 16, 1916).
"Jack Ingram: A Nice 'Bad' Man." *Western Film Collector*, Vol. 1, No. 3 (July 1973), 16–18, 30.
Jackson, Gregg, Jr. "Burn Em Up Barnes Is Back in S.W.: Interview with Jack Mulhall." *Serial World*, No. 4 (n.d.).
_____. "Serial World Interviews Rocketman Tris Coffin." *Serial World*, No. 10 (Spring 1977), 3–9.
_____. "Serial World Interviews Walter Reed." *Serial World*, No. 19 (Summer 1979), 19–22.
Jameux, Charles. "William Witney and John English." *Positif*, No. 88 (October 1967).
Jennings, John. "End of the Legend [Tom Mix]." *Tucson (AZ) Citizen* (October 11, 1990).
Jewell, James C. "Helen Holmes and the Hazards of Helen." *The World of Yesterday*, No. 25 (December 1979), 61.
Johaneson, Bland. "Good-by Boys, I'm Through [Pearl White]." *Photoplay* (April 1924).
John Wayne and the Great Cowboy Heroes. New York: Starlog Press, 1979, 31–32.
"John Wayne as the Last Hero." *Time* (August 8, 1969).
"John Wayne: Still Bigger Than Life." *Scouting*, Vol. 67, No. 3 (May–June 1979), 12–13.
Johnson, Julian. "The Girl on the Cover." *Photoplay* (April 1920).
Jordan, Joan. "Wanted: A Chance to Ride [Jack Holt]!" *Photoplay* (August 1921), 34.
Jordon, Don, and Edward Connor. "Judge Hardy and Family [Cecilia Parker]." *Films in Review*, Vol. XX, No. 1 (January 1974), 1–10.
"Jungle Girl." *Variety* (June 4, 1941).
"Jungle Queen." *Serial Quarterly*, Vol. 2, No. 3 [No. 7 on cover], 9–22.
"Jungle Queen." *Serial World*, No. 24 (Fall 1980), 6–7, 10.
"Jungle Raiders." *Serial Quarterly*, Vol. 2, No. 2 (April–June 1967), 14.
"Junior G-Men of the Air." *Serial Quarterly*, Vol. 1, No. 3 (July–September 1966), 11 pp.
"Junior G-Men of the Air." *Variety* (May 27, 1942).
Katchmer, George A. "Art Acord, the Holy Terror." *Classic Images*, No. 80 (February 1982), 32, 35, 55.
_____. "Daredevil George Larkin." *Classic Images*, No. 104 (February 1984), 45–47.
_____. "Forgotten Cowboys and Cowgirls [Allene Ray]." *Classic Images*, No. 181 (July 1990), 56–57.
_____. "Guinn 'Big Boy' Williams." *Classic Images*, No. 83 (May 1982), 30–31.
_____. "In Complete and Utter Admiration of Jack Hoxie." *Classic Images*. Part I: No. 85 (July 1982), 31–33; Part II: No. 86 (August 1982), 30–32.

_____. "Ken Maynard: Dr. Jekyll or Mr. Hyde?" *Classic Images*, No. 102 (December 1983), 49–51.
_____. "The Kids Loved Jack Perrin." *Classic Images*, No. 149 (November 1987), 13–15.
_____. "King of the Serials, Walter Miller." *Classic Images*, No. 116 (February 1985), 17–18, C8.
_____. "The Old But Young Harry Carey." *Classic Images*, No. 112 (October 1984), 16–20.
_____. "Remembering the Great Silents: Forgotten Cowboys and Cowgirls. Part III [Carol Holloway]." *Classic Images*, No. 174 (December 1989), 48.
_____. "Remembering the Great Silents: More Forgotten Cowboys and Cowgirls [Ethlyne Clair]." *Classic Images*, No. 172 (October 1989), C14, 52.
_____. "Ruth Mix: A Chip Off the Old Block." *Classic Images*, No. 100 (October 1983), 34–35.
_____. "The Screen Girl of Action, Ruth Roland." *Classic Images*, No. 123 (October 1985), 23–26.
_____. "The Smiling Cowboy, Franklyn Farnum." *Classic Images*, No. 97 (July 1983), 38–39.
"Kathlyn Williams." *Films in Review*, Vol. XXX (February 1984), 67–69.
Kelez, Steve. "Captain America." *Film Fan Monthly*, No. 61/62 (July–August 1966), 25–26.
"King of the Carnival." *Serial Quarterly*, No. 1 (January–March 1966), 8 pp.
"King of the Mounties." *Cliffhanger Ending and Escape Pictorials*. Northbrook, IL: Jack Mathis Advertising, n.d.
"King of the Rocketmen." *Serial World*, No. 34 (Spring 1983), 32–36.
"King of the Royal Mounted." *Serial Quarterly*, Vol. 1, No. 3 (July–September 1966), 8 pp.
"King of the Serials to Do 100th Film." *New York Herald Tribune* (October 31, 1952).
Kinnard, Roy. "Actress Phyllis Coates Interviewed." *Filmfax*, No. 13 (December 1988), 52–53.
_____. *Fifty Years of Serial Thrills*. Metuchen, NJ: Scarecrow Press, 1983.
Knight, Mac. "Ann Little and the 1980 Cinevent." *Classic Images* (August 1982), 11, 19.
Kohl, Len. "Buster Crabbe: The King of the Serials." *Movie Collector's World*, No. 205 (February 8, 1985).
Klumph, Inez, and Helen. *Screen Acting*, Chapter 36. New York: Falk Publishing Co., 1922, 202–207.
Krohn, Lewis G. "An Extensive List of U.S. Silent Serials." *The World of Yesterday*, Nos. 24 & 25 (1979).
_____. "Kay Aldridge, Republic Serial Queen." *Screen Thrills and the Nostalgia Monthly* (Premier Issue).
_____. "Thrills and Action on the Installment Plan." *Classic Images*, No. 130 (April 1986), 51–53.
Lahue, Kalton C. *Bound and Gagged: The Story of the Silent Serial*. New York: Castle Books, 1968.
_____. *Continued Next Week: A History of the Moving Picture Serial*. Norman: University of Oklahoma Press, 1964.
_____. "Continued Next Week—Louise Lorraine." *8mm Collector*, No. 13 (Fall–Winter, 1965), 5.
_____. *Ladies in Distress*. Cranbury, NJ: A.S. Barnes & Co., 1971.
_____. *Riders of the Range: The Sagebrush Heroes of the Sound Screen*. New York: Castle Books, 1973.
_____. *Winners of the West*. New York: A.S. Barnes & Co., 1970.
Lamberti, Mark E. "Jean Rogers." *Epic*, Vol. 1, No. 1 (September 1977), 51+.
_____. "Jean Rogers, Second Feature Lady." *Remember When*, No. 16 (1974).
Lamparksi, Richard. *Whatever Became of…* [Joyce Compton]*?* New York: Ace Books, 1970, 170–171..
_____. *Whatever Became of…?* New York: Ace Books, Vol. III, 206–207.
Langley, W.D. "William Witney." *Films in Review*, Vol. XXVII (June 1976), 381.
Laube, Chris. "Before the Serials Spoke." *Classic Images*, No. 69 (May 1980), 22.
Lauritzen, Einar, and Gunnar Lundquist. *American Film Index 1908–1915*. Stockholm: Film-Index 1976, 704 pp.
_____ *American Film Index 1916–1920*. Stockholm: Film-Index, 1983.
"A Legend Made a Movie Star [Wild Bill Elliott]." *Wild West Stars*, Vol. 3, No. 9, 3–12.
Leonard, John. *Wild Bill Elliott*. 1976, 95 pp.
Lewis, Patricia Ann. "Evelyn Finley First Stunt Woman." *Favorite Westerns/Serial World*, No. 25 (April 1987), 37.
Lilly, Tim. "Apprenticeship in Action: An Account of John Wayne's Participation in the Mascot Serials." *Cliffhanger*, No. 6, 37–43.
"Linda Stirling's Fond Memories of the Serials." *The New Captain George's Whizzbang*, No. 18 (n.d.), 15.
"A Little Lesson in Spanish [Marin Sais]." *Photoplay* (March 1907), 81.
"The Lone Ranger." *Variety* (February 9, 1938).
"The Lone Ranger Rides Again." *Serial Quarterly*, Vol. 1, No. 3 (July–September 1966), 19 pp.
"The Lone Ranger Rides Again." *Variety* (February 15, 1939).
"The Lone Ranger Story." *Screen Thrills Illustrated* (February 1965), 6–13.
"The Lost City." *Serial World*, Nos. 25–29 (1981–1982).
"Louise Lorraine." *Classic Images*, No. 75 (1981), 16.
Luchbiler, Don. "Hiss the Villain, Cheer Pearl [White]." *Classic Film Collector*, No. 26 (Winter 1970), EX4.
Lyden, Pierce. "Stunt Girl." *Classic Images*, No. 137 (November 1986), 61.
"Lynne Roberts." *Wild West Stars*, Vol. 1, No. 4, 8.
Lyons, Timothy J. "Hollywood and World War I, 1914–1918 [Brief references to the serials of the period]." *The Journal of Popular Film*, Vol. 1, No. 1 (Winter 1972), 15–30.
McCleary, Charles. "Chick Carter Detective." *Serial World*, No. 33 (Winter 1983), 17–19.
_____. "Dick Tracy." *Serial World*, No. 20 (Fall 1979), 14–22.
_____. "Government Agents vs. Phantom Empire." *Favorite Westerns & Serials Plus*, No. 19 (Fall 1984), 70–72.
_____. "How the Serials Rate." *Serial World* (n.d.), 6–7.
_____. "King of the Forest Rangers." *Serial World*, No. 23 (Summer 1980), 21–23.
_____. "The Sea Hound." *Serial World*, No. 32 (Fall 1982), 18–22.
McClelland, Doug. "The Perils of Frances Gifford." *Cliffhanger*, No. 2 (Spring 1983), 20–32.
McClure, Arthur F,. and Ken D. Jones. *Heroes, Heavies and Sagebrush*. New York: A.S. Barnes & Co., 1972, 351 pp.
McCord, Merrill T. *Perils of Kay Aldridge: Life of the Serial Queen*. Washington, DC: Alhambra Publishers, 1979.

McCrea, Joel. "Hoot Gibson: Even the Heroine Blackened His Eye." *Western Stars*, Vol. 1, No. 5 (Spring 1950), 75.
McElwee, John P. "John Wayne." *The Big Reel* (February 1988), 41–44.
Mackenzie, Donald. "Chapter from Unpublished Book on Pearl White." *Classic Film Collector*, No. 26 (Winter 1970), 6, 13.
"Madge Bellamy Edition." *Fox Folks* (September 1925).
"Madge Make-Believe." *Photoplay* (March 1921).
"Mainly About Madge [Bellamy]." *Picture and Picturegoer* (July 1926).
Malcomson, Bob. "Flash Gordon." *Those Enduring Matinee Idols*, Chapter 9, Vol. 1 (February–March 1971), 106–109; Chapter 10, Vol. 1 (April–May 1971), 126–129.
_____."The Green Hornet." *Those Enduring Matinee Idols*, Chapter 26, Vol. 3, No. 6. (n.d.), 381–384.
_____. "The Sound Serial." *Views and Reviews*, Vol. III (Summer 1971), 12–26.
_____. "Sound Serials of Yesteryear." *Yesteryear*, No. 1 (n.d.), 2–6.
_____. "Zorro's Fighting Legion." *Those Enduring Matinee Idols*, Chapter 19, Vol. 2, No. 9 (October–November 1972), 266–272.
_____, and Eric Hoffman. "King of the Royal Mounted." *Those Enduring Matinee Idols*, Vol. III (n.d.), 338–340.
"Mandrake the Magician." *Variety* (June 28, 1939).
Manski, Albert. "Silver Screen Memories: The Serials." *Classic Images*, No. 132 (June 1986), 55.
"Marguerite Courtot." *Motion Picture Magazine* (June 1915), 116.
Martin, Mike. "Leading Ladies in 'B' Westerns." *Classic Images*, No. 116 (February 1985), 25–29.
Martinez, Al. "Roy Rogers and Gene Autry: Two Old-Time Cowboy Stars Reflect a Heroic Age." *Los Angeles Times* (February 27, 1977), Sec. CC, Part II, 3, 5–6.
"The Masked Marvel." *Serial Quarterly*, No. 2 (April–June 1966), 13 pp.
Mathis, Jack. *Valley of the Cliffhangers*. Northbrook, IL: J. Mathis Advertising, n.d.
Melchois, L.G. "A Tribute to Kane Richmond, 'the Other Serial Hero.'" *Those Enduring Matinee Idols*, Chapter 29, Vol. 3, No. 9 (n.d.), 438–439.
"Men with Steel Faces." [Feature version of serial *Phantom Empire*.] *Variety* (May 8, 1940).
Michael, Earl. "The Serials of Republic." *Screen Facts*, Vol. 1 (1963), 52–64.
Midi-Minuit Fantastique, No. 7 (September 1963), 33–35.
Miller, Don. *"B" Movies*. New York: Curtis Books, 1973, 350 pp.
_____. *Hollywood Corral*. New York: Popular Library Publishers, 1976, 255 pp.
Miller, Lee O. *The Great Cowboy Stars of Movies and Television*. New Rochelle, NY: Arlington House Publishers, 1979, 384 pp.
"The Miracle Rider [Tom Mix]." *The Courier Express Special Edition*, DuBois, PA (October 1980), 8.
"The Miracle Rider [Tom Mix] in Hard Cover." *Serial World*, Nos. 26–28 (Spring–Summer–Fall 1981).
"Miss Ruth Roland." *Moving Picture World* (March 7, 1914).
Mitchell, George, and William K. Everson. "Tom Mix." *Films in Review* (October 1957), 387–397.
Mix, Olive Stokes, and Eric Heath. *The Fabulous Tom Mix*. Englewood Cliffs, NJ: Prentice-Hall, 1957.
Mix, Paul E. *The Life and Legend of Tom Mix*. Cranbury, NJ: A.S. Barnes & Co., 1972.
Montanye, Lillian. "The Lone Star Girl [Allene Ray]." *Motion Picture Classic* (April 1921), 26, 28.
Moore, Doug. "Pauline Moore: Girl of the Golden West." *American Classic Screen*, Vol. 4, No. 2 (Winter 1980), 37–39.
Moulton, Herbert. "Film Beauty [Evelyn Brent] Would Like to Play a Real Hag." *The Pre-View* (September 19, 1928).
Mullett, Mary B. "The Heroine of a Thousand Dangerous Stunts [Pearl White]." *American Magazine* (May 1918).
Murray, James. "Don Red Barry." *Wild West Stars*, Vol. 2, No. 7 (n.d.), 5–6.
"Mysterious Doctor Satan." *Cliffhanger Ending and Escape Pictorials*. Chicago: Jack Mathis Advertising. n.d.
"Mysterious Island." *Serial Quarterly*, Vol. 2, No. 2 (April–June 1967), 15 pp.
"Mysterious Pilot." *Variety* (January 26, 1938).
"The Mystery Trooper." *Those Enduring Matinee Idols*, Chapter 8, Vol. 1 (December 1970–January 1971), 103.
Nareau, Bob. "Frankie Darro, the Forgotten Little Cowboy." *Westerns and Serials*, No. 32 (n.d.), 26–28.
_____. *The Real Bob Steele and a Man Called "Brad."* Mesa, AZ: Dakine Co., 1991.
Naylor, Hazel Simpson. "All Over the Plot at Pathé." *Motion Picture Magazine* (May 1918), 45–48.
Neman, Daniel. "In Those Westerns She [Jennifer Holt] Was Queen of the Greek Chorus." *The Richmond (VA) News Leader* (Tuesday, July 25, 2989). 29.
"Nemesis of the Underworld [The Spider]." *Screen Thrills Illustrated* (May 1964), 7–11.
Nevins, Frances M., Jr. "Ballet of Violence: The Films of William Witney." *Films in Review*, Vol. XXV (November 1974).
"New Contract for Shirley Grey." *New York Herald Tribune* (February 22, 1933).
"A New Kalem Star [Ruth Roland]." *Moving Picture World* (December 5, 1914).
New York Times Film Reviews 1913–1931. New York: New York Times and Arno Press, 1970, Vol. 1 of 6 volumes, 787.
Nicholas, John A. *Riding Up to Glory: The Life of Tom Mix*. Dearborn, MI: E.J. Kneip and Associates, 1969.
Norris, M.G. (Bud). *The Tom Mix Book*. Waynesville, NC: World of Yesterday Press, 1989.
Nye, Doug. *Action Packed Cliffhangers*. South Carolina Educational Television, 1938.
Oakley, Vic. "Peggy Stewart." *Wrangler's Roost*, No. 55. (n.d.).
"Old Moments Difficult for Wayne." *The Daily Ardmorite (OK) Carousel* (Sunday, March 18, 1979).
Old Movies 4: The Serial. Vol. 1, No. 4 (Alan Barbour, Ed.).
Osborne, Robin. "Serial Spotlight: Man of Menace—Trevor Bardette." *Wrangler's Roost*, No. 46 (June 1976), 4 pp.
"Overland Mail." *Variety* (December 13, 1939).
"Overland with Kit Carson." *Serial Quarterly*, No. 1 (January–March, 1966), 5 pp.
"The Painted Stallion." *Those Enduring Matinee Idols*, Chapter 10, Vol. 1 (April–May, 1971), 121–123.
Parish, James R., and William T. Leonard. *Hollywood Players*. Carlstadt, NJ: Rainbow Books, 1977, 126–131.
Parish, James Robert, and Michael R. Pitts. "Adventures of Captain Marvel." *The Great Science Fiction Pictures*. Metuchen, NJ: Scarecrow Press, 1976, 3–4.

_____. "Brenda Starr, Reporter." *The Great Gangster Pictures*. Metuchen, NJ: Scarecrow Press, 1976, 56–57.
_____. "Custer's Last Stand." *The Great Western Pictures II*. Metuchen, NJ: Scarecrow Press, 1988, 83–85.
_____. "Daredevils of the Red Circle." *The Great Science Fiction Pictures*. Metuchen, NJ: Scarecrow Press, 1976, 81–83.
_____. "Dick Tracy's G-Men." *The Great Gangster Pictures*. Metuchen, NJ: Scarecrow Press, 1976, 111–112.
_____. "The Exploits of Elaine." *The Great Science Fiction Pictures*. Metuchen, NJ: Scarecrow Press, 1976, 116–117.
_____. "Federal Agents vs. Underworld, Inc." *The Great Gangster Pictures II*. Metuchen, NJ: Scarecrow Press, 1987, 142–143.
_____. "Hawk of the Hills." *The Great Western Pictures*. Metuchen, NJ: Scarecrow Press, 1976, 128–130.
_____. "Holt of the Secret Service." *The Great Gangster Pictures II*. Metuchen, NJ: Scarecrow Press, 1987, 200–201.
_____. "The Indians Are Coming." *The Great Western Pictures*. Metuchen, NJ: Scarecrow Press, 1976, 158–159.
_____. "The Lone Ranger." *The Great Western Pictures*. Metuchen, NJ: Scarecrow Press, 1976, 199–200.
_____. "Patria." *The Great Spy Pictures*. Metuchen, NJ: Scarecrow Press, 1974, 372–374.
_____. "The Riddle Rider." *The Great Western Pictures*. Metuchen, NJ: Scarecrow Press, 1976, 294–295.
_____. "Ruth of the Rockies." *The Great Western Pictures*. Metuchen, NJ: Scarecrow Press, 1976, 314.
_____. "Zorro's Fighting Legion." *The Great Western Pictures*. Metuchen, NJ: Scarecrow Press, 1976, 411–412.
Parkhurst, C.M. "George J. Lewis: The Face is Familiar." *Those Enduring Matinee Idols*, Chapter 19, Vol. 2, No. 9 (October–November, 1972), 273–275.
_____. "The Lone Ranger Rides Again." *Those Enduring Matinee Idols*, Vol. 2 (April–May, 1972), 218–221.
_____. "Men of Action: Tom Steele." *Those Enduring Matinee Idols*, Chapter 17, Vol. 2, No. 7 (June–July 1972), 244–245.
Parsons, Louella O. "Helen Holmes Dies at 58." *Los Angeles Examiner* (July 10, 1950).
"Pearl White." *Pictures and Picturegoer* (October 9, 1920).
"Pearl White." *Moving Picture World* (January 23, 1915).
"Pearl White Dead: Ex-Star of Movies." *New York Times* (August 5, 1938).
Peltret, Elizabeth. "When the Celluloid Clock Strikes Twelve [Carol Holloway]." *Motion Picture Magazine* (June 1919), 69–70.
"Perils of Thunder Mountain." *Serial Quarterly*, Vol. 1, No. 4 (October–December 1966), 33–56.
Perry, Cynthia. "Robert Livingston: Cowboy, Comic, and Crooner." *Under Western Skies*, No. 33 (n.d.), 30–31.
Peterson, Elizabeth. "The Serial Girl: Marie Walcamp." *Motion Picture Magazine* (September 1919), 82–83.
Pflening, Fred D. Jr. "Ken Maynard's Diamond 'K' Ranch Wild West, Circus, and Indian Congress." *The White Tops* (November–December 1959), 9–10.
_____. *Tim McCoy's Real Wild West and Rough Riders of the World*. Columbia, OH: Pfening & Snyder, 1955.
"The Phantom." *Screen Thrills Illustrated*, Vol. 2, No. 2 October 1963, 7–11.
"The Phantom Creeps." *Variety* (August 16, 1939).
"The Phantom Empire." *Wild West Stars*, Double Issue Nos. 24–25 (n.d.) 19–22.
"The Phantom Rider." *Boys Cinema*, 15 Chapters, Nos. 869–883 (August 8, 1936–November 14, 1936).
"The Phantom Rider." *Those Enduring Matinee Idols*, Chapter 8, Vol. 1 (December 1970–January 1971), 97.
Phillips, Anthony. "Art Acord—Western Real-Life Tragedian." *8mm Collector*, No. 14 (Spring 1966), 11.
Pilk, Robert. "Carol Forman Interview." *Cliffhanger*, No. 4, 51–55.
Pitts, Michael R. "Gilbert Roland, the Most Virile Actor in Movies." *Classic Film Collector*, No. 33 (Winter 1971), 56–57.
Pontes, Bob. "An Interview with Nell O'Day." *Favorite Westerns*, No. 12 (June 1983), 17–20.
_____. "An Interview with Joan Woodbury." *Favorite Westerns*, No. 8 (January 1983), 5, 18.
_____. "*Favorite Westerns* Interviews Ms. Lois January." *Favorite Westerns*, No. 9 (March 1983), 21–22.
"Popular Players [Kathy Williams]." *Moving Picture World* (August 23, 1913).
Powell, Craig. "We Ride the Range with Daredevil Bob Steele." *Wild West Stars*, Vol. 2, No. 6 (n.d.).
Powell, Larry. "Marion Shilling: Remembering Buck Jones." *Under Western Skies*, No. 33, 45.
Price, Bob. "Buck Jones." *Screen Thrills Illustrated*, Vol. 3, No. 1 (August 1964), 26–33.
_____. "King of the Jungleland." *Screen Thrills Illustrated* (September 1962), 20–25.
_____. "The Man Behind the Mask." *Screen Thrills Illustrated* (August 1964), 7–15.
_____. "Serial Queens." *Screen Thrills Illustrated* (January 1963), 12–18.
_____. "Shazam." *Screen Thrills Illustrated* (September 1962), 12–19.
_____. "Tom Tyler." *Screen Thrills Illustrated*, Vol. 2, No. 2 (October 1963), 34–39.
Ragan, David. *Who's Who in Hollywood 1900–1976*. New Rochelle, NY: Arlington House Publishers, 1976, 662.
Rainey, Buck. "Anne Gwynne: Her Wholesomeness and Charm Made Her a Favorite on the 'B' Market." *Under Western Skies*, No. 30 (1984), 41–47.
_____. "Art Acord, an Enigma." *Western Revue*, Vol. 2, No. 2 (Summer 1975), 1–13.
_____. "Ben Wilson: Revered Serial King and Neglected Western Star." *Under Western Skies*, No. 34 (May 1988), 25–41.
_____. "The Black Book." *Serial World*, No. 33 (Winter 1983), 23–24.
_____. "Blake of Scotland Yard." *Western and Serials Combined Issue*, FW # 31; SW #51 (1989), 18–19.
_____. "The Broken Coin." *Cliffhanger*, No. 2 (Spring 1983), 42–49; No. 3 (1984), 29–44; No. 9 (September 1988), 41–51.
_____. "Brothers Al and Jack Hoxie—Cinema Trailblazers." *Western Revue* (August, 1977), 20 pp.
_____. "Carol Forman Reminisces." *Serial World*, No. 37 (Spring 1984), 3–10.
_____. "Cinema Cowboys on the Sawdust Trail." *Classic Images*, No. 101 (November 1983, 12–15, 37; No. 102 (December 1983), 35–37; No. 103 (January 1984), 41–43, C–7; No. 104 (February 1984), 27–29.
_____. "Cleo Madison." *Classic Images*, No. 143 (May 1987), 17–20.
_____. "A Conversation with Linda Stirling, Sensuous Siren of the Serials." *Film Collector's Registry*, No. 71 (December 1976), 3–7.
_____. "Dave O'Brien." *Classic Images*. Part I: No. 186 (December 1990): Part II: No. 187 (January 1991).
_____. "Dick Foran." *Classic Images*, No. 190 (April 1991), 38–41, 49.
_____. "Duncan Renaldo, Everyone's Amigo." *The Nostalgia Monthly*, No. 8 (August 1978), 31–35.

_____. "Eileen Sedgwick." *Classic Images*, No. 129 (March 1986), 17–18.
_____. "Esther Ralston." *Classic Images*, Nos. 111 (September 1984), 23–24, and 112 (October 1984), 31.
_____. "Evelyn Finley." *Under Western Skies*, No. 18 (May 1982), 34–64.
_____. *The Fabulous Holts*. Nashville, TN: Film Collectors Press, 1976.
_____. "The Fast Express." *Serial World*, No. 34 (Spring 1983), 46–50.
_____. "The Film Career of Buster Crabbe." *Western Film Collector*, Vol. 2, No. 3 (July 1974), 2–17.
_____. "The Film Career of William Duncan." *Classic Film Collector*, No. 55 (Summer 1977), 24–26.
_____. "A Final Reckoning." *Cliffhanger*, No. 14. (n.d.).
_____. "The Fire Fighters." *Serial World*, No. 32 (Fall 1982), 11–12.
_____. "Fred Thomson, Great but Forgotten Hero." *Western Film Collector*, Vol. 1, No. 3 (July 1973), 4–15.
_____. "Gene Autry: A Cowboy Phenomenon." *Saddle Aces of the Cinema*. San Diego and New York: A.S. Barnes & Co., 1980, 241–259.
_____. "Hal Taliaferro: No Stranger to Horse Operas." *Western Revue* (Spring 1986), 3–7.
_____. "Harry Carey, the Beloved Scout Who Pioneered the Way." *Western Revue* (August 1977), 15 pp.
_____. "Harry Woods—Best of the Badmen." *Favorite Westerns & Serial World*, Issue 35 (n.d.), 40–43.
_____. "Herman Brix/Bruce Bennett." *Cliffhanger*, No. 10 (June 1989), 36–51.
_____. *Heroes of the Range*. Metuchen, NJ: Scarecrow Press, 1987; Waynesville, NC: World of Yesterday Press, 1987.
_____. "The Holts." *Views and Reviews* (Summer 1984), 11–18.
_____. "Hoot Gibson, Cowboy." *Films in Review*, Vol. XXIX, No. 8. (October 1978), 471–484.
_____. "'Hoss Opera' Stars 1900–1973." *Wild West Stars*, Vol. 4, No. 14, (n.d.) 2–13.
_____. "Kane Richmond." *Classic Images*, No. 158 (August 1988), 22, C7.
_____. "Kathlyn Williams: A Mature Woman of Graphic, Poignant Charm, Exuding Courage and Poise in Every Conceivable Peril." *Cliffhanger*, No. 5 (May 1985), 19–26.
_____. "Kermit Maynard." *Heroes of the Range: Yesterday's Saturday Matinee Movie Cowboys*. Waynesville, NC: World of Yesterday Press, 1987, 71–101.
_____. "Jack Mulhall: The Ever-Smiling Irishman with an Enviable Serial Career." *Cliffhanger*, No. 13 (1990), 5–40.
_____. "Jack Perrin, Hero of a Bygone Era." *The Big Reel* (January 1986), 33.
_____. "Jean Arthur." *Classic Images*, Nos. 105–106, (March–April, 1984), 17–19, 42–43.
_____. "Jean Rogers: Talent, Versatility, Wholesomeness, Beauty, and Irrefragable Sexuality Combined to Make Her the Queen of the Serial World in the Late Thirties." *Cliffhanger*, No. 4 (December 1984), 37–50.
_____. "John 'Dusty' King." *Classic Images*, No. 157 (July 1988), C17–C18.
_____. "Leo Maloney, Ranger Rider of the Roaring 20's." *Under Western Skies*, No. 28 (August 1984), 47–57.
_____. *The Life and Films of Buck Jones: The Sound Era*. Waynesville, NC: World of Yesterday Press, 1991, 388 pp.
_____. "The Lone Ranger Rides Again." *The Nostalgia Monthly*, No. 8 (August 1978), 31–35.
_____. "Lorna Gray/Adrian Booth, A Beautiful Brunette Whose Endowments Won a Host of Fans." *Classic Images*, No. 119 (May 1985), 44–45.
_____. "Neal Hart, America's Pa." *Wild West Stars*, No. 31 (n.d.), 2–10.
_____. "Neva Gerber." *Blazing West and Serial Classics*, No. 2 (1986), 4–5.
_____. "Pearl White." *Serial World*, No. 34 (Spring 1983) 42–45; No. 35 (Summer, 1983), 20.
_____. "The Pearl White Film List." *Serial World*, No. 36 (Winter 1984), 18.
_____. "Peggy Stewart: The Sweetheart of the Republic Lot in the Mid–1940's and a Special Favorite of Sagebrush Fans." *Classic Images*, No. 136 (October 1986), 3+.
_____. "Perils of the Wild." *Cliffhanger*, No. 12 (1989), 15+.
_____. "Phyllis Coates: She Was Hollywood's Last Try at a Serial Queen." *Classic Images*, No. 138 (December 1986), 33–34.
_____. "Ralph Byrd." *Classic Images*, No. 155 (May 1988), C31–C34.
_____. "The Ranger Fighter." *Serial World*, No. 33 (Winter 1983), 20–22.
_____. "Reminiscences of Buck Jones." *Remember When*, Nos. 18–19 (1975).
_____. "Reminiscences of Jack Holt." *Remember When*, No. 15 (1974), 4 pp.
_____. "Reminiscences of Tim McCoy." *Remember When*, No. 16 (1974), 9 pp.
_____. "Rex Lease: A Pleasant and Competent Performer Who Enhanced 15 Serials." *Cliffhanger*, No. 11 (1989), 19–50.
_____. "Rex, King of the Wild Horses." *Film Collector's Registry*, No. 61 (February 1976) 9–11.
_____. "The Roaring West." *Cliffhanger*, No. 12 (1989), 57–62.
_____. "Rod Cameron." *Screen Thrills*, Special Edition, Vol. 1, Nos. 11 and 12 (July 1979), 3 pages unnumbered.
_____. "Roy Stewart, a Page from the Past." *Classic Film Collector*, No. 56 (Fall 1977), 30–32, 35, 51, 56.
_____. "Ruth Roland." *Serial World*, Part I: No. 35 (Summer 1983), 21; Part II: No. 36 (Winter 1984), 20–21, Part III: *Serial Classics*, No. 1 (1984), 18.
_____. *Saddle Aces of the Cinema*. San Diego: A.S. Barnes & Co., 1980, 307 pp.
_____. *The Saga of Buck Jones*. Nashville: Western Film Collectors Press, 1975. 126 pp.
_____. "Sidekick Portrayals of Raymond Hatton." *Classic Images*, Nos. 163 (January 1989), 46–47, 49; 164 (February 1984), 47–48, 55; 165 (March 1984), 42, 44, 46–47.
_____. "Tarzan the Mighty." *Cliffhanger*, No. 12 (1990), 45–50.
_____. "Tarzan the Tiger." *Cliffhanger*, No. 12 (1990), 51–56.
_____. *Those Fabulous Serial Heroines*. Metuchen, NJ: Scarecrow Press, 1990; Waynesville, NC: World of Yesterday Press, 1990.
_____. "Tim McCoy, the Last Rough Rider." *Film Collector's Registry*, No. 77 (June 1977), 3–10.
_____. "Tom Mix, a Page from the Past." *The Nostalgia Monthly*, No. 4 (April 1978), 43–47.
_____. "Trailin' Art Acord—Another View." *Favorite Westerns* No. 12 (June 1983), 12–15.
_____. "A Tribute to Yakima Canutt." *The Big Reel*, No. 139 (December 1985), 67–69.

_____. "Virginia Brown Faire." *Classic Images*, No. 142 (April 1987), 13–16.
_____. "Yak." *Western Revue* (August 1977), 9 pages.
_____. "Zorro Rides Again .. Again .. and Again." *Western Film Collector*, Vol. III, No. 1 (Winter 1976), 2–24.
Rathmell, John. *Burn 'Em Up Barnes*. Akron, OH: Saalfield Publishing Co., 1935.
Ray, J.C. "In Defense of Columbia Serials and Director Horne." *Cliffhanger*, No. 16, 58–59.
"Red Barry." *Those Enduring Matinee Idols*, Chapter 16, Vol. 2, No. 6, 222–223.
"The Red Rider." *Boys Cinema*, Nos. 774–788 (October 13, 1934–January 29, 1935) [15 Episodes].
Reeve, Arthur B. *Romance of Elaine*. New York: Harper & Brothers, 1915. [Novelization].
Reid, Dixie. "Buster Crabbe." *Houston Chronicle*, Vol. 27 (July 1980).
Reinhart, Ted. "In Memory of Rod Cameron." *Favorite Westerns*, No. 17 (1984), 11–12.
_____. "Johnny Mack Brown and Nell O'Day." *Favorite Westerns*, No. 5, 18–21.
_____."Lee Powell…Things Didn't Work Out Right." *Screen Thrills*, No. 4.
_____. "Masked Rider of the Plains." *Classic Images*, No. 103 (January 1984), 51–52.
Remon, Cesar. "American Serial Actors Honored in Hollywood." *Westerns & Serials*, No. 39, 24.
Remont, Fritzi. "Marie [Walcamp]: The Mystic." *Motion Picture Classic* (January 1920), 48–49, 72.
"Republic Sets Budget for Features, Westerns, Serials." *New York Sun* (February 28, 1941).
"Republic Will Turn Out Escape Films, Says Yates." *New York World-Telegraph* (September 9, 1939).
"The Return of Captain America." *Screen Thrills Illustrated*, Vol. II (February 1964), 24.
"The Return of Chandu (The Magician)." *Screen World*, No. 21 (Winter 1980), 14–19.
"Revelations of Ruth Roland." *Pictures and Picturegoer* (January 1927).
"Reviews of 'Perils of Pauline.'" *Blackhawk Bulletin*, B–253 (July 1974), 64–66.
Reynolds, Roger. "When Pauline Had Her Perils." *8mm Collector*, No. 2 (September 1962). Reprinted from *Rochester Times-Union*.
Rhode, Eric. *Tower of Babel: Speculations on the Cinema*. New York: Chilton Books, 1966, 85–105.
Rhodes, Gary Don "Louise Currie." *Classic Images*, No. 156 (June 1988), C27, 55.
_____. "Watch for the Next Terror-Filled Episode, or The serials of Bela Lugosi." *The Big Reel*, No. 156 (May 15, 1987), 3.
Ricci, Mark, Boris Zmijewsky and Steve Zmijewsky. *The Films of John Wayne*. New York: Citadel Press, 1970, 288 pages.
"Riders of Death Valley." *Serial World*, No. 34 (Spring 1983), 10–22, 29–30.
Ringold, Gene. "Veda Ann Borg." *Films in Review*, Vol. XVI, No. 3 (March 1965), 180–190.
"Rites Set for 'Hazards of Helen' Star." *Los Angeles Daily News* (July 10, 1950).
"The Roaring West." *Boys Cinema*, Nos. 829–843 (November 1935–February 1936), 15 Episodes.
"The Roaring West." *Those Enduring Matinee Idols*, No. 7 (October–November 1970), 77.
Roberts, John. "Dead End Kids in Films and Serials." *Serial World*, No. 36 (Winter 1984), 10–12.
_____. "Dick Tracy." *Favorite Westerns & Serials Plus*, No. 20, p. 66.
_____. "Warren Hull and 'Mandrake the Magician.'" *Westerns & Serials*, FW #31, SW #51, 12.
Roberts, Stewart. "Tom Mix, the Tinsel Cowboy." *Westerner*, Vol. 4, No. 4 (July–August 1972), 12–23.
Roberts, William. "Cliffhangers." *Los Angeles Times* (November 20, 1946).
Robinson, David. "Judex." *Movie of the Silent Years*. London: Orbis, 1984, 86–87.
"Robinson Crusoe of Clipper Island." *Those Enduring Matinee Idols*, Chapter 9, Vol. 1 (February–March 1971), 110–112.
Roland, Ruth. "Personality in Dress." *Photoplay* (June 1915).
_____. "What a Home Means to Me." *Motion Picture Magazine* (November 1915).
Rollin, Betty. "The Return of the (Whoosh! There Goes One!) Superhero!" *Look* (March 22, 1966), 113–114.
Rosa, Joseph G. "Buck Jones, Bona Fide Hero." *True West* (July–August 1966), 20–21, 64.
Rothel, David. *Who Was That Masked Man? The Story of the Lone Ranger*. Cranbury, NJ: A.S. Barnes & Co., 1976.
_____. *Who Was That Masked Man? The Story of the Lone Ranger*. Revised Edition. Cranbury, NJ: A.S. Barnes & Co., 1981.
Round, Richard. "Maker of Melodrama: Louis Feuillade." *Film Comment* (November–December 1976). 8–11.
Rovin, Jeff. "Flash Gordon's Trip to Mars." *From Jules Verne to Star Trek*. New York and London: Drake Publishers, 1977, 47.
Rowlands, Dave. "Remember Dave Sharpe?" *Screen Thrills*, No. 4 (n.d.), 21.
_____. "Yakima Canutt." *Wild West Stars*, Vol. 2, No. 6 (n.d.), 12–13.
Rubin, Jay. "Jay Rubin Interviews Buster Crabbe." *Classic Film Collector*, No. 43 (Summer 1974), 9–10.
Rubin, Sam. "Kathlyn Williams." *Classic Film Collector*, XIV (Spring 1966), 9.
Russell, Bill. "Chief Thundercloud: Real 'Tonto' to Most Western Fans." *Western Revue* (Spring 1976), 25–27.
_____. "The Little Giant of Westerns." *Western Revue* (May 1978).
_____. "Jack Perrin: The Man in the Big Stetson." *Western Revue* (August 1977), 7 pages.
_____. "The Story of Republic's Classic Serial: The Lone Ranger." *Western Revue* (Spring 1976), 1–2.
_____. "Trailing 'Crash' Corrigan." *Western Revue*, No. 1 (Summer 1975), 14–21.
"Ruth Roland." *Motion Picture World* (July 11, 1914, and July 24, 1915).
"Ruth Roland Up-to-Date." *Pictures and Picturegoer* (October 27, 1917).
Rutherford, John H. "The Adventures of Sir Galahad." *Cliffhanger*, No. 3 (January 1984), 4–22.
_____. "The Crimson Ghost on Screen." *Cliffhanger*, No. 7 (n.d.), 45–50.
_____. "Undersea Kingdom." *Cliffhanger*, No. 5 (n.d.), 27–33.
"The Saga of Superman." *Screen Thrills Illustrated*, Vol. 1 (June 1962), 30–37; Vol. 2 (September 1962), 42–48; Vol. 3 (January 1963), 52–57.
St. Johns, Adele Rogers. "Just a Good Business Man [Ruth Roland]." *Photoplay* (August 1922).
St. Johns, Ivan. "A Chip Off the Old Block [Ruth Mix]." *Photoplay Magazine* (July 1925).
Sanford, Harry. "An Interview with William (Bill) Witney." *Those Enduring Matinee Idols* (February–March 1973), 309–311.
_____. "Joseph Kane: A Director's Story." *Views and Reviews*, Part I: Vol. V (September 1973), 31–38; Part II: Vol. V (December 1973), 17–25.

_____. "Men of Action." *Those Enduring Matinee Idols*, Vol. 2, No. 6 (n.d.), 224–225.
Scapperotti, Dan. "Bat-History 101." *Cinefantastique* (November 1989), 50.
_____. "Memories of Fu Manchu." *Starlog*, No. 114 (January 1987), 60–64.
Schaefer, Randall. "Ace Drummond." *Cliffhanger*, No. 20 (n.d.), 29–46.
_____. "Daughter of Don Q." *Cliffhanger*, No. 16 (n.d.), 45–57.
Schmid, Peter Gridley. "An Animal Chat with Kathlyn Williams." *Motion Picture Classic* (January 1917), 33–34, 36.
Schutz, Wayne. *The Motion Picture Serial: An Annotated Bibliography*. Metuchen, NJ: Scarecrow Press, 1992, 375 pages.
Scott, John L. "Adrian Booth [Lorna Gray], Western Star, Shoots for Helen Morgan Role." *Los Angeles Times* (May 1, 1945).
"The Sea Hound." *Serial Quarterly*, No. 4 (October–December 1966), 57–64.
Seale, Jim. "Ruth Roman: The Rise of a New Roman Empire." *Los Angeles Times Magazine* (January 1986), 19.
"The Secret Code." *Serial Quarterly*, Vol. 2, No. 1 (January–March 1967), 18 pages.
Seiverling, Richard F. *Tom Mix—Portrait of a Superstar*. Hershey, PA: Keystone Publishers, 1991, 320 pages.
"The Serial Girl—Marie Walcamp." *Motion Picture Magazine* (September 1919).
Serial Report, Chapter 20 (January–February 1997). [Profiles of Linda Stirling and Kane Richmond.]
"Serials." *Flashback*, Vol. 1 (April 1972), 44–49.
"Serials of Buck Jones." *Yesterday's Saturdays*, Vol. 1, No. 3 (September 1974), 42–47.
"Shadow of Chinatown." *Serial Quarterly*, No. 2 (April–June 1966, 17 pages.
"She [Phyllis Coates] Married the Boss." *Los Angeles Times* (August 28, 1955).
Sheridan, Oscar M. "Pearl [White] in Paris." *Pictures and Picturegoer* (November 1923).
Sherman, Sam. "Broadway to Bowery and Back: The Story of Huntz Hall." *Screen Thrills Illustrated*, No. 5 (July 1963), 41–45.
_____. "Buck Rogers." *Spacemen*, Vol. 6 (June 1963), 16–21.
_____. "Republic Studios: Hollywood Thrill Factory." *Screen Thrills Illustrated*, No. 1 (January 1963), 24–31.
_____. "Republic Studios: Hollywood Thrill Factory." *Screen Thrills Illustrated*, No. 2 (October 1963), 12–17.
Shipley, Glenn. "Allene Ray, Top Serial Star." *Classic Images*, No. 148 (October 1987), 43.
_____. "King of the Serial Directors: Spencer Gordon Bennet." *Views and Reviews* (Fall 1969).
Shirley, Glenn. "Art Acord." *True West*, Special Issue No. 212, Vol. 32, No. 8 (1985), 16–22.
_____. "Buck Jones." *True West*, Special Issue No. 212, Vol. 32, No. 8 (1985), 54–61.
_____. "Cowboy Strongman Tom Tyler." *Old West*, Vol. II, No. 2 (Winter 1974), 8–38.
_____. "Harry Carey." *True West*, Special Issue No. 212, Vol. 32, No. 8 (1985), 24–30.
_____. "The 'Reel' West of Buck Jones." *Westerner*, Vol. 3, No. 7 (October 1971), 14–19, 56,58.
Shirk, Adam Hull. "Ann Little and the Great Desire." *Motion Picture Classic* (January 1919), 36–37.
Shoenberger, Jim. "The Fighting Marines." *Those Enduring Matinee Idols*, Chapter 5, Vol. 1 (June–July 1970), 52–53; Chapter 6, Vol. 1 (August–September 1970), 64–65.
_____. "A Final Visit with Reed Hadley." *Film Collector's Registry*, Vol. VII (January 1975), 5, 9.
_____. "An Interview with I. Stanford Jolley." *Film Collector's Registry*, Vol. VI (March 1974), 1, 4.
_____. "Reminiscing with Linda Stirling." *Those Enduring Matinee Idols*, Chapter 13, Vol. 2, No. 3 (October–November 1971), 175–176.
_____. "Reminiscing with Reed Hadley." *Those Enduring Matinee Idols*, Chapter 25, Vol. 3, No. 5 (1974), 366–368.
"Silent Film Actress [Rhea Mitchell] Slain." *Los Angeles Examiner* (September 17, 1957).
Slide, Anthony. *The Big V: A History of the Vitagraph Company*. Metuchen, NJ: Scarecrow Press, 1976, 224 pages.
_____. *Early American Cinema*. International Film Guide Series. Cranbury, NJ: A.S. Barnes & Co., 1970.
_____. *The Idols of Silence: Stars of the Cinema Before the Talkies* (1976), 208 pages.
_____. "The Kalem Serial Queens." *The Silent Picture* (Winter 1968), 7–10.
_____. "Review of 'Perils of Pauline.'" *Selected Film Criticism: 1912–1920*. Metuchen, NJ: Scarecrow Press, 1982, 197–198.
Slobb, Kermit, and Nick Nicholls. "Resident Badman [Charles King]." *Classic Images*, No. 133 (July 1986), 16–18.
Smith, Agnes. "She [Marguerite Courtot] Hates Broadway." *Photoplay Magazine* (February 1920), 118–119.
Smith, Bertha H. "Nervy Movie Lady [Kathlyn Williams]." *Sunset* (June 1914).
Smith, Chester J. "Vultures of the Sea." *Motion Picture News* (December 1928).
Smith, Frank Leon. "The First American Serial." *Films in Review* (February 1958), 108–109.
_____. "The Man Who Made Serials." *Films in Review*, Vol. VII (October 1956), 375–383.
_____."Pearl White and Ruth Roland." Letter. *Films in Review* (December 1960).
Smith, Frederick. "A Pearl [White] in the Rough." *Motion Picture Classic* (January 1919), 16–19, 72.
Smith, Jeff. "Cliffhanger Classics—Chapterfilm Adventures from Decades Past: The Adventures of Captain Marvel." *Film Fax*, Vol. 9 (February–March 1988), 56–58.
Smith, Lewis. "Along Came Buck [Jones]." *Horse and Rider* (March 1973), 42–48.
"Son of Geronimo." *Serial Quarterly*, No. 2 (April–June 1966), 12 pages.
"S O S Coast Guard." *Variety* (April 22, 1942).
"S O S Coast Guard." *Those Enduring Matinee Idols*, Vol. 1, Chapter 10 (April–May 1971), 124–125.
Spater, Alan P. "Charles B. Middleton: The Screen's Most Awesome Villain Remembered." *Classic Images*, No. 104 (February 1984), C8; No. 105 (March 1984), 33–35; No. 106 (April 1984), 60–61; No. 126 (December 1985), C17–C18.
Spencer, Gary. "A Comedy Serial: The Iron Claw." *Westerns and Serials Combined Issue*, Favorite Westerns #26; Serial World #46 (n.d.), 22–23.
_____. "The Jesse James Serial Trilogy." *Favorite Westerns & Serials Plus*, No. 20 (n.d.), 31–33.
_____. "The Last Frontier." *Westerns and Serials*, No. 35 (n.d.), 66–67.
_____. "The Lightning Express." *Favorite Westerns & Serials*, No. 40 (n.d.), 18–19.
_____. "The Mystery Trooper." *Westerns and Serials*, No. 42 (n.d.), 56–63.
_____."The Perils of Pauline—The Sound Serial." *Westerns and Serials Combined Issue*, Favorite Westerns #28, Serial World #48 (n.d.), 40–46.

_____. "The Serial Appearances of Matthew Betz." *Westerns and Serials*, No. 40 (n.d.), 28–29.
_____. "Some Notes on Rex Lease." *Westerns and Serials Combined Issue*, Favorite Westerns #30, Serial World #50 (n.d.), 22–25.
"The Spider Returns." *Serial Quarterly*, Vol. 1, No. 3 (July–September 1966), 13 pages.
"The Spider's Web." *Variety* (January 11, 1939).
"Spy Smasher Tops Serial Poll." *Film Collector's Registry*, No. 61 (February 1976), 4.
Squire, Harry. "Ken Maynard, Immortal Cowboy Star." *Classic Film Collector*, No. 56 (Fall 1977), 53, 63.
Stainton, Walter R. "Pearl White in Ithaca." *Films in Review* (May 1951).
Stanaway, John. "The Battle of the Serial Studios: Universal vs. Republic, The Best of the Golden Age Serials, 1936–1946." *Serial Classics*, No. 1, Collector's Edition (n.d.), 4–10.
Stanke, Don. "Ruth Roman." *Film Fan Monthly*, No. 142 (April 1973), 11–24.
Stanley, John. "'Disc Man': Period Piece for Thrills and/or Laughs." *San Francisco Sunday Examiner Chronicle* (January 26, 1975).
Starling, Bart. "Jean Arthur." *Hollywood Studio Magazine*, Vol. 20, No. 9 (September 1987), 19–23.
Stedman, Raymond William. *The Serials: Suspense and Drama by Installment* (Norman: University of Oklahoma Press, 1971).
Steinbrunner, Chris, and Burt Goldblatt. "Flash Gordon." *Cinema of the Fantastic*. New York: Galahad Books, 1972, 125–150.
Steiner, Michael. "The Robot Report: The Clanking Cliffhangers." *Fantastic Films* (January 1980), 40–47.
Stephenson, Ron. "Concerning Serials and Trends." *Those Enduring Matinee Idols*, Vol. 3 (n.d.), 444–446.
Sterling, Ray. "Pearl White—Woman Wizard." *Photoplay World* (May 1919).
Stewart, Bill. "Chapter 13 [Obituary information on 26 serial performers]." *Those Enduring Matinee Idols*, Chapter 9, Vol. 1 (February–March 1971), 116–117.
Stirling, Linda. "Introduction." *Cliffhanger: A Pictorial History of the Motion Picture Serial*, by Alan G. Barbour. Secaucus, NJ: Citadel Press, 1977, v.
_____. "My Life as a Serial Queen." *Movie Digest* (May 1973), 44–49.
Stoginski, John. "Colonel Tim McCoy—Serially Speaking." *Those Enduring Matinee Idols*, Chapter. 28, Vol. 3, No. 8 (n.d.), 424–426.
_____. "A Man Named [Buck] Jones." *Those Enduring Matinee Idols*, Chapter 26, Vol. 3, No. 6 (n.d.).
Strickland, A.W., and Forrest J Ackerman. *A Reference Guide to American Science Fiction Films*. Bloomington, IN: TIS Publications, 1981. The volume covers the following serials: The Black Box (1915) 79–82. The House of Hate (1918) 150–152. The Hidden Hand (1917) 141–142. The New Exploits of Elaine (1915) 96–99. Nan of the North (1922) 220–221. The Screaming Shadow (1920) 209–211. The Fire Detective (1929) 334–335. The Flaming Disc (1920). The Exploits of Elaine (1914) 65–71. The Invisible Ray (1920) 205–207. The Jungle Goddess (1922) 233–236. Blake of Scotland Yard (1927) 318–320. The Branded Four (1920) 186–188. The Power God (1925) 305–307. The Radio Detective (1926) 312–314. The Radio King (1922) 238–241. The Master Mystery (1919) 162–167. Officer 444 (1926) 310–312. The Secret of the Submarine (1916) 129–132. The Ventures of Marguerite (1915) 107–109. The Carter Case (1919) 157–159. The Crimson Stain Mystery (1916) 112–117. The Diamond Master (1929) 332–334. The Diamond Queen (1921) 215–217.
Stringham, Jim. "Ace Drummond." *Those Enduring Matinee Idols*, Chapter 8, Vol. 1 (December 1970–January 1971), 96–97.
_____. "The Ace of Scotland Yard." *Serial World*, No. 22 (Spring 1980), 13.
_____. "Beasts of Paradise." *Westerns and Serials Combined Issue*, Favorite Westerns #29, Serial World #49 (n.d.), 34–38.
_____. "The Black Coin." *Those Enduring Matinee Idols*, Chapter 9, Vol. 1 (February–March 1971), 113.
_____. "Blake of Scotland Yard." *Film Fan Monthly*, No. 69 (March 1967), 11–12.
_____. "Blake of Scotland Yard." *Serial World*, No. 32 (Fall 1983), 23–26; No. 33 (Winter 1983), 4–9.
_____. "Captain Video." *Westerns and Serials*, No. 36 (n.d.), 20–25.
_____. "Custer's Last Stand." *Favorite Westerns & Serials Plus*, No. 20 (Winter 1985), 34–35; No. 21 (Spring 1985), 62–63; No. 22 (Summer 1985), 6–9; No. 24 (Winter 1986), 3–5.
_____. "Drums of Fu Manchu." *Serial World*, No. 28 (Fall 1981), 6–9, 12–15; No. 29 (Winter 1982), pages unknown.
_____. "Eddie Rickenbacker's Ace Drummond." *Serial World*, No. 8 (Fall 1976), 4–13.
_____. "Edgar Rice Burroughs' 'Jungle Girl.'" *Those Enduring Matinee Idols*, No. 25 (1973) 362–365; No. 26 (1974) 385–388.
_____. "A Fine Crop of Lemons." *Film Fan Monthly* (May 1967), 10–11.
_____. "The Four Independents." *Those Enduring Matinee Idols*, Chapter 7, Vol. 1 (October–November 1970), 74–77.
_____. "Gordon of Ghost City." *Favorite Westerns*, Nos. 5, 6, 7 (1982).
_____. "The Great Adventures of Wild Bill Hickok." *Serial World*, No. 9 (Winter 1977), 12–23.
_____. "Haunted Harbor." *Westerns & Serials*, Combined Issue, Favorite Westerns #31; Serial World #51 (n.d.), 36–39, 66.
_____. "Haunted Harbor Photo Story." *Westerns and Serials*, No. 32 (n.d.), 32–36.
_____. "Heroes of the West." *Favorite Westerns*, No. 2 (n.d.), unnumbered pages; No. 3 (n.d.), 24–27.
_____. "The Hurricane Express." *Those Enduring Matinee Idols*, Chapter 19, Vol. 2, No. 9 (October–November 1972), 276–278.
_____. "Jungle Girl." *Serial World*, No. 23 (Summer 1980), 4–11.
_____. "Jungle Goddess." *Western and Serial*, No. 34 (n.d.), 56–57.
_____. "The Last Frontier." *Film Fan Monthly*, No. 80 (February 1968), 13–14.
_____. "Mad Scientists and Magicians." *Film Fan Monthly*, No. 76 (October 1967), 13–15.
_____. "Mandrake the Magician Illustrated." *Westerns and Serials*, No. 32 (n.d.), 24–25.
_____. "The Phantom of the Air." *Serial World*, No. 30 (n.d.), 22–24.
_____. "Radio Patrol." *Serial World*, No. 12 (Fall 1977), 4–10.
_____. "Raiders of Ghost City." *Westerns and Serials*, Nos. 40, 41, 42 (n.d.).
_____. "The Secret of Treasure Island." *Those Enduring Matinee Idols*, Chapter 13, Vol. 2, No. 3 (October–November) 1971, 170–180.
_____. "The Shadow." *Those Enduring Matinee Idols*, Vol. 22 (April–May 1973), 320–321.
_____. "The Shadow: A Columbia Serial Filmbook." *Serial World*, No. 13 (Winter 1978), 3–9.
_____. "Spy Smasher." *Those Enduring Matinee Idols*, Chapter 29, Vol. 3, No. 9 (n.d.), 434–437.
_____. "Tailspin Tommy in the Great Air Mystery." *Those Enduring Matinee Idols*. [Issue unknown.]
_____. "Tarzan the Tiger." *Favorite Westerns,* No. 25 (n.d.), 7–11.

_____. "Terry and the Pirates." *Those Enduring Matinee Idols*, Vol. 25 (1973), 330–331.
_____. "The Tiger Woman." *Serial Classics*, No. 1 Collector's Edition (n.d.), 11–17.
Strumpt, Charles K. "Fearless Clyde Beatty." *Cliffhanger*, No. 2 (Spring 1985), 33–39.
Sulski, Jim. "The Girl Who Was Dale Arden." *Fantastic Films*, Vol. II, No. 2 (June 1979), 56–61.
_____. "The Man Who Was Flash Gordon: An Exclusive Interview with Larry 'Buster' Crabbe." *Fantastic Films*, No. 6 (February 1979), 54–57.
Summers, Murray. "Laura LaPlante in 'Her Reel Life.'" *Filmograph*, Vol. II, No. 3 (3rd Quarter 1971), 23–43.
Sunfield, Elmer. "Perils of Pauline [Moore]." *Hollywood Magazine* (June 1937), 50–53.
"Superman." *Screen Thrills Illustrated* (June 1962), 30–37; (September 1962), 42–48 (January 1963), 52–57.
"Superman vs. Captain Marvel: Their Only Battle Was in Court." *Variety* (July 8, 1987), 34.
Sutton, David. "A Post Interview with John Wayne: Image vs. Man." *The Saturday Evening Post* (March 1976), 55–57, 117, 120.
Swann, Thomas Burnett. "Serial Queens to Stellar Queens." *The Heroine or the Horse*. Cranbury, NJ: A.S. Barnes Co., 1972, 41–54.
Swilling, Herb. "Jean Carmen AKA Julia Thayer and the Countess." *Favorite Westerns* (November 1984), 9–10.
_____. "Remembering Nell O'Day." *Westerns and Serials*, No. 31 (July 1989), 24–25.
"Tarzan and the Green Goddess." *Variety* (June 1, 1938).
Taylor, Frank. "John Wayne—America's Shooting Star." *Hollywood Studio Magazine*, Vol. II, No. 12 (n.d.), 10–15.
"'TEMI' Talks with Larry 'Buster' Crabbe." *Those Enduring Matinee Idols*, No. 14 (December 1971–January 1972), 193–194.
Terry, Clifford. "The Lone Ranger Unmasked." *Chicago Tribune Magazine* (April 15, 1973), 27–29.
"Terry and the Pirates." *Serial Quarterly*, No. 2 (April–June 1966), 12 unnumbered pages.
"That Hardy Perennial, the Serial." *New York Times* (January 26, 1976), Section IX: 4.
Thayer, John E. "Proudly We Hail [Helen Holmes]." *Classic Film Collector*, No. 57 (Winter 1977), 8.
_____. "Star Sheen of 1916 [Juanita Hansen]." *Classic Film Collector*, No. 58 (Spring 1978), 8–9.
"Theatrical Cliffhanger Serials of Yesteryear Still Sell 'Far Out.'" *Variety* (February 12, 1964).
"The 13 Faces of Tarzan." *Screen Thrills Illustrated* (June 1962), 4–9.
Thomas, Anthony. "Tim McCoy." *Films in Review*, Vol. XIX, No. 4 (April 1968), 218–230.
Thomas, Bob. "Hollywood's General of the Armies." *True, the Man's Magazine* (July 1966), 47–48, 86–89.
Thomas, Ray G. "Here's to the Ladies: Louise Stanley." *Those Enduring Matinee Idols*, Chapter 25, Vol. 3, No. 5 (n.d.), 374–375.
Thorne, Bradley D. "The Green Hornet." *Modern Monsters*, No. 4 (October–November 1966), 72–77.
Thornton, Jimmy. "Prologue: The Green Hornet." *Those Enduring Matinee Idols*, Chapter 25, Vol. 3, No. 5 (n.d.), 370–373.
Tiggers, John III. "Captain Midnight." *Memory Lane*, Special Edition (September 1980), 50–53.
Tom Mason on Top. Big Little Book # 1102. Racine, WI: Whitman Publishing Co. 1935. [Novelization of "The Miracle Rider."]
"Tom Mix" Obituary. *The New York Times* (Sunday, October 13, 1940), 1.
"Tom Mix" Obituary. *The Philadelphia Inquirer* (Sunday, October 13, 1940), 1.
"Topics of the Times: Battle of the Serials." *New York Times*, Vol. 30 (July 1938), 12.
Toppman, Lawrence. "Thrill-a-Week Era Lives in Collection of Movie Serials." *Charlotte Observer* (January 10, 1981).
"Tracy's G–Men." *Variety* (August 23, 1939).
"Trader Tom of the China Seas." *Serial Quarterly*, No. 1 (January–March 1966), 10 unnumbered pages.
Tredinnick, William, Jr. "Collecting the Tarzan Films." *Movie & Film Collectors World*, Vol. 196 (October 1984), 12.
Trewin, J.C. "One Thing After Another: Being a Discourse on Serials." *Sight and Sound* (Autumn 1947), 106–107.
Trost, Mark. "Rating How the Serials Rate: A Rebuttal to Chuck McCleary's Highly Controversial Articles from Issues 4 and 5." *Serial World*, No. 6 (n.d.), 2–3.
Truart, T.S. "Byrd's Jutting Jaw Was Perfect for Republic's Tracy." *San Francisco Sunday Examiner & Chronicle* (February 6, 1977).
Tully, Jim. "Laura LaPlante." *Vanity Fair* (January 1928).
_____. "A Top Rider." *Photoplay* (January 1926).
Turner, George. "Making the Flash Gordon Serials." *American Cinematographer* (June 1983), 56–62.
_____, and Michael H. Price. *Forgotten Horrors: Early Chillers from Poverty Row*. New York: A.S. Barnes & Co., 1979. The volume includes coverage of the following serials: The Clutching Hand, Dick Tracy, The Fighting Marines, The Hurricane Express, King of the Kongo, King of the Wild, The Lightning Warrior, The Lost City, Phantom of the West, and Tarzan the Fearless.
Tuska, Jon. "From the 100 Finest Westerns: The Lightning Warrior." *Views and Reviews*, Vol. II (Spring 1971) 50.
_____. "The Golden Age of the Western Serial." *The Filming of the West*. New York: Doubleday & Co., 1976, 341–346.
_____. "In Retrospect: Ken Maynard." *Views and Reviews,* Vol. 1, No. 1 (Summer 1969), 6–21; Vol. 1, No. 2 (Fall 1969), 23–25; Vol. 1, No. 3 (Winter 1970), 23–42.
_____. "In Retrospect: Tim McCoy." *Views and Reviews*, Vol. 2, No. 1 (Summer 1970), 10–27; Vol. 2, No. 2 (Fall 1970), 12–30; Vol. 2, No. 3 (Winter 1971), pages unknown; Vol. 2, No. 4 (Spring 1971), 12–41.
_____. "An Interview with Spencer Gordon Bennet." *Those Enduring Matinee Idols*, Chapter 17, Vol. 2, No. 7 (June–July 1972), 240–241.
_____. "Overland with Kit Carson—A Cinematography." *Those Enduring Matinee Idols*, Vol. II (June–July 1971), 146–148; Vol II (August–September 1971), 163–165.
_____. "The Phantom Empire." *Views and Reviews*, Vol. 4, No. 2 (Winter 1972) 45–52; Vol. 4, No. 3 (Spring 1973), 278–30.
_____. "The Vanishing Legion." *Views and Reviews,* Vol. 3, No. 2 (Fall 1971), 16–33; Vol. 3, No. 3 (Winter 1972), 10–26; Vol. 3, No. 4 (Spring 1972), 22–39; Vol. 4, No. 2 (Fall 1972), 56-79; Vol. 4, No. 3 (Winter 1973), 34-52; Vol. 4, No. 4 (Spring 1973), 28–47; Vol. 4, No. 1 (Summer 1973), 64–68.
_____. *The Vanishing Legion: A History of Mascot Pictures, 1927–1935*. Jefferson, NC: McFarland & Co., Inc., 1982.
_____, Vicki Piekarski, and David Wilson. "Spencer Gordon Bennet." *Close–Up: The Hollywood Director*. Metuchen, NJ: Scarecrow Press, 1978, 94–135.
Uselton, Ron A. "The Wampas Baby Stars." *Films in Review*, Vol. XXI (February 1970), 73–97.
Van Buren, Walter C. "Serial Queens of the Silent Screen." *Memory Lane*, Vol. I, No. 7 (May 1980), 41–46.

Van Hise, James. "The Fighting Devil Dogs." *Film Collector's Registry*, Vol. 6, No. 11 (November 1974), 7–9.
_____. *Serial Adventures*. Las Vegas: Pioneer Books, 1990, 154 pages.
_____. *Serial Adventures Book: The Green Hornet*. Las Vegas: Pioneer Books, 1989. 100 pages.
_____. *Serial Adventures Book: The Phantom*. Las Vegas: Pioneer Books, 1989. 100 pages.
_____. *Serial Adventures Book: The Shadow*. Las Vegas: Pioneer Books, 1989. 100 pages.
_____. *The Serial Adventures of Blackhawk*. Las Vegas: Pioneer Books, 1989. 100 pages.
Variety Film Reviews. New York: Garland Publishing Co. 16 Volumes.
"Veda Ann Borg." *Films in Review*, Vol. XVI, No. 3 (March 1965), 188–190.
Vermilye, Jerry. "Jean Arthur." *Films in Review*, Vol. XVII, No. 6 (June–July 1966), 329–346.
Victorek, D. "Men of Action: Dave O'Brien." *Those Enduring Matinee Idols*, Chapter 18, Vol. 2, No. 8 (August–September 1972), 256–257.
"Video Tape Reviews: Tarzan the Tiger." *Classic Images*, Vol. 123 (October 1985), 57.
"The Vigilante." *Serial Quarterly*, Vol. 2, No. 3 [cover says No. 7] (n.d.), 24–40.
Virgines, George E. "Adios, Amigo [Jack Hoxie]." *Frontier Times*, Vol. 39, No. 5 (August–September 1965), 21, 60–61.
Vivian, Ronald. "The Phantom Empire." *Serial World*, No. 19 (Summer 1979), 4–14.
_____. "The Phantom Rider" *Serial World*, No. 19 (Summer 1979), 4–14.
_____. "Revisiting the Lost City." *Serial World*. Part I: Vol. 22 (Spring 1980), 22–25; Part II: Vol. 25 (Winter 1981), 7–8; Part III: Vol. 26 (Spring 1981), 18–19; Part IV: Vol. 27 (Summer 1981), 7–12; Part V: Vol. 28 (Fall 1981), 26–28; Part VI: Vol. 29 (Winter 1982), 12–13.
_____. "Roar of the Iron Horse." *Serial World*. Part I: No. 20 (Fall 1979), 24–25, 27. Part II: No. 21 (Winter 1980), 26–31.
Wade, Peter. "A Little of Everything—and Then Some More [Pearl White]." *Motion Picture Classic* (January 1917), 2 pages.
Walker, Earl. "The Adventures of Kathlyn." *8mm Collector*. Part I: Vol. 10 (Winter 1964), 6; Part II: Vol. 11 (Spring 1965), 24; Part III: Vol. 12 (Summer 1965), 10; Part IV: Vol. 13 (Fall–Winter 1966), 23+; Part V: Vol. 14 (Spring 1966), 9.
Walker, Marvin. "Buck Jones, Western Cowboy." *Buck Jones Western Stories*, Vol. 1, No. 1 (November 1936), 83–86.
"Wally Wales Has Ruth Mix, Daughter of Tom, for Lead." *The Brooklyn Daily Times* (July 19, 1931).
Walton, Jeff. "Dracula in the Cliffhangers." *Screen World*, Vol. 22 (Spring 1981), 3–5.
_____. "Serial Scrapbook." *Classic Images*, No. 202 (April 1991), 42.
Wannen, Rich. "Sound Serial Features: A First Review." *Classic Images*. Part I: No. 136 (October 1986), C16–C19; Part II: No. 137 (November 1986), C3–C8; Part III: No. 138 (December 1986), 14–17.
Ward, Jim. "The Buck Jones Story." *Wild West Stars*, Vol. 2, No. 5 (1970), 1–10.
_____. "Tom Mix Was Deputy Sheriff in East Tennessee." *Wild West Stars*, Vol. 2, No. 6 (1970), 11.
Weathers, Stormy. "The Kid [Bob Steele]." *Under Western Skies* (August 1984).
_____. "The Phantom." *Cliffhanger*, No. 4 (n.d.), 19–34.
Weaver, Tom. "The Crimson Ghost." *Serial World*. Part I: No. 24 (Fall 1980), 14–20; Part II: No. 25 (Winter 1981), 14–15, 18.
_____. "Phyllis Coates, Superman's Girl Friend." *Starlog*. Part I: No. 138 (January 1989), 49–52, 70; Part II: No. 139 (February 1989), 49–52, 57.
Weiner, Beth. "Ex–Actress [Eleanor Stewart] is Content with Role as Author, Grandmother." *Rancho Bernardo (CA) Journal* (March 7, 1985), A10.
Weiss, Ken. "Flash, Ming and Zarkoff, Should Have Been Played by Moe, Larry, and Curly?" *Film Collector's Marketplace* (April 1977), 16–17.
_____, and Ed Goodgold. *To Be Continued*. New York: Crown Publishers, 1972.
Weitzel, Edward. "When Juanita Hansen, New Pathé Star, First Met a Quintette of Lions." *The Moving Picture World* (January 24, 1920), 575.
Weltman, Manuel, and Raymond Lee. *Pearl White, the Peerless Fearless Girl*. San Diego: A.S. Barnes & Co., 1969.
"Western Hall of Fame: Tom London, 1882–1963." *Screen Thrills Illustrated*, No. 8 (May 1964), 34–35.
"What Happened to Mary?" *The Ladies World* (August 1912), unnumbered pages.
Wheatly, Reg. "Serial Spotlight—Clancy of the Mounted." *Wrangler's Roost*, No. 77 (n.d.), 2 unnumbered pages.
_____. "Serial Spotlight—The Last Frontier." *Wrangler's Roost*, No. 78.
_____. "Serial Spotlight—The Red Rider." *Wrangler's Roost*, No. 76 (September 1986).
White, Jack R. "Houdini and His Movies." *Classic Film Collector*, No. 29 (Winter 1970), 46–47.
White, Pearl. "The Fatal Ring." *Motion Picture World* (July 21, 1917), 423–424.
_____. "Putting It Over." *Motion Picture Magazine* (February 1917), 61–62.
"White Eagle." *Boys' Cinema*, No. 686 (February 4, 1933), 9–16, 26–27.
"Wife Says Actor Liked Boat Better Than Her [Dorothy Short and Dave O'Brien]." *Los Angeles Times* (July 11, 1953).
"William Desmond." *The Blue Book of the Screen*, edited by Ruth Wing. Gravure Publishing Co., 1923.
Williams, Nick. "A Tribute to Edmund Cobb." *Filmograph*, No. 1 (1970), 3–15.
_____. "Billy Bletcher: The Voice of the Lone Ranger." *Western Revue* (Spring 1976), 28.
_____. "Leo Maloney." *Western Film Collector*, Vol. 1, Nos. 4 & 5 (November 1973), 16–21, 42.
_____, and John Stoginski. "Peg of Our Hearts." *Western Film Collector*, Vol. 1, No. 6 (January 1974), 10–19, 35.
Williams, Whitney. "A Cowboy Actor Who Was the Real McCoy." *Los Angeles Times* (February 5, 1978).
Wilmott, Vaun. "Superman Ruined Me in Movies, Says Top–Notch Actor, First to Play Hero [Kirk Alyn]." *National Tattler* (June 2, 1974), 31.
Wilson, Bill. "The Hard-Boiled Gentleman [Jack Holt]." *Classic Images*, No. 73 (January 1981), 31.
_____ "Give Me Liberty." *Classic Images*, No. 127 (January 1986), C20.
Wilson, David. "Kicking Away Gravity: The Saga of Four Great Hollywood Stuntmen." *American Classic Screen*, Vol. 5, 26–29.
Wilson, John Fleming. *The Master Key*. New York: Grosset & Dunlap, 1914. Photoplay Edition with 25 illustrations.
"Winslow of the Navy." *Variety* (January 7, 1942).

Witney, William. *In a Door, Into a Fight, Out a Door, Into a Chase*. Jefferson, NC: McFarland & Company, 1995, 256 pp.
Wood, Thomas. "The Sad State of the Serial." *New York Times* (December 22, 1946), Sec. 2: X7.
Wright, Mack V. "Serial, Stunts, and Six Guns." *Screen Thrills Illustrated* (February 1964), 26–31.
Wyatt, Edgar M. *More Than a Cowboy: The Life and Films of Fred Thomson and Silver King*. Raleigh, NC: Wyatt Classics, 1988, 124–125.
York, Norman. "Buck Jones: King of the Cowboys; Admired by Millions." *Ozark Cinema Review* (1975), 12–14, 16.
Zinman, David. *Saturday Afternoon at the Bijou*. New Rochelle, NY: Arlington House Publishers, 1973, 19–41.

INDEX

All references are to entry numbers. Film titles are italicized.